The National Underwriter Company
a Division of ALM Media, LLC

2019 Cancellation & Nonrenewal
Hannah E. Smith, J.D.

Highlights of the 2019 Edition

Cancellation & Nonrenewal outlines how insurers can legally terminate insurance policies in the 50 states, District of Columbia, Guam, Puerto Rico, and the Virgin Islands. It covers both cancellation and nonrenewal of standard property & casualty insurance policies, as governed by the states. Some states defer to policy language, which are the standard forms by Insurance Services Office (ISO) and the National Council on Compensation Insurance (NCCI).

This publication includes information on all major lines of business within both commercial and personal lines, such as the following:

Commercial Lines of Business

- Agricultural Capital Assets (Output Policy)
- Businessowners
- Capital Assets Program
- Commercial Auto
- Commercial Crime
- Commercial General Liability
- Commercial Inland Marine
- Commercial Property
- Commercial Umbrella
- E-Commerce
- Equipment Breakdown
- Farm
- Financed Premiums
- Management Protection
- Medical Professional Liability
- Surplus Lines
- Workers' Compensation

Personal Lines of Business

- Dwelling fire
- Homeowners
- Personal Auto
- Personal Umbrella

Professionals will benefit from the *2019 Cancellation and Nonrenewal* as it features:

- An easy-to-use format providing comprehensive coverage of the subject matter
- Rules, regulations, and policies broken down by state, as well as cell phone restrictions; data breach notification laws; and fraud definition, reporting, and bureaus
- Fair claims processing information
- Agency cancellation notice requirements
- Several charts outlining line of business termination, policyholder notification, state insurance provisions for military personnel, cancellation by line of business, claim handling requirements, and more!

Additional information and charts can be found within the supplementary online version at www.fcands.com/CNR.

Cancellation & Nonrenewal comes to you from The National Underwriter Company and the editors of FC&S®, which is committed to keeping you up-to-date on the latest insurance coverage interpretations and analyses. It is the authoritative reference tool for agents and underwriters who need to know how a policy may be legally terminated by an insurer.

Related Titles Also Available:

- Licensing & Surplus Lines Law
- General Liability Insurance Coverage: Key Issues in Every State

For customer service questions or to place orders for any of our products, please call 1-800-543-0874 or email customerservice@nuco.com.

2019 Cancellation & Nonrenewal

For The 50 States, District of Columbia, Territories, and Possessions

Hannah E. Smith, J.D.

This publication is designed to provide accurate and authoritative information in regard to the subject matter covered. It is sold with the understanding that the publisher is not engaged in rendering legal, accounting, or other professional service. If legal advice or other expert assistance is required, the services of a competent professional person should be sought.— from a Declaration of Principles jointly adopted by a Committee of the American Bar Association and a Committee of Publishers and Associations.

International Standard Serial Number: 1087-545X

International Standard Book Number: 978-1-949506-17-4

Copyright 2019 by The National Underwriter Company

The National Underwriter Company
a division of ALM Media, LLC.
4157 Olympic Blvd., Suite 225
Erlanger, KY 41018
1-800-543-0874
www.nationalunderwriter.com

Printed in the United States of America

ABOUT THE NATIONAL UNDERWRITER COMPANY
A DIVISION OF ALM MEDIA, LLC

For over 110 years, The National Underwriter Company, *a division of ALM Media, LLC* has been the first in line with the targeted tax, insurance, and financial planning information you need to make critical business decisions. Boasting nearly a century of expert experience, our reputable Editors are dedicated to putting accurate and relevant information right at your fingertips. With *Tax Facts*, *Tools & Techniques*, *Field Guide*, *FC&S®*, *FC&S Legal* and other resources available in print, eBook, CD, and online, you can be assured that as the industry evolves National Underwriter will be at the forefront with the thorough and easy-to-use resources you rely on for success.

Update Service Notification

This National Underwriter Company publication is regularly updated to include coverage of developments and changes that affect the content. If you did not purchase this publication directly from The National Underwriter Company, *a division of ALM Media, LLC* and you want to receive these important updates sent on a 30-day review basis and billed separately, please contact us at (800) 543-0874. Or you can mail your request with your name, company, address, and the title of the book to:

The National Underwriter Company
a division of ALM Media, LLC
4157 Olympic Boulevard
Suite 225
Erlanger, KY 41018

If you purchased this publication from The National Underwriter Company, *a division of ALM Media, LLC*, directly, you have already been registered for the update service.

Contact Information

To order any National Underwriter Company title, please

- call 1-800-543-0874, 8-6 ET Monday–Thursday and 8 to 5 ET Friday
- online bookstore at www.nationalunderwriter.com, or
- mail to Orders Department, The National Underwriter Company, *a division of ALM Media, LLC*, 4157 Olympic Blvd., Ste. 225, Erlanger, KY 41018

ABOUT THE EDITORS

Editor

Hannah E. Smith, J.D. and **CPCU Candidate**, is an editor of the FC&S Bulletins®. She graduated from Salmon P. Chase College of Law and the University of Cincinnati with a BA in Psychology. Publications she has contributed to include the Personal Auto Policy Coverage Guide, 5th Edition, Commercial General Liability Coverage Guide 12th Edition, the Small Business Auto Coverage Guide, and the 2015, 2016 and 2017 Cancellation & Nonrenewal and Licensing & Surplus Lines books.

Legal Research Assistants

Logan B. Tucker is a second year student at at Salmon P. Chase College of Law.

Nathan J. Allen is a second year student at Salmon P. Chase College of Law.

Editorial Services

Connie L. Jump, Senior Manager, Editorial Operations.

Emily Brunner, Editorial Assistant.

TABLE OF CONTENTS

Introduction ix
Standard Policy Provisions xi

States—Alphabetical

Alabama 1
Alaska 12
Arizona 29
Arkansas 43
California 56
Colorado 76
Connecticut 91
Delaware 108
District of Columbia 132
Florida 151
Georgia 178
Guam 197
Hawaii 204
Idaho 221
Illinois 234
Indiana 264
Iowa 278
Kansas 293
Kentucky 304
Louisiana 325
Maine 343
Maryland 361
Massachusetts 382
Michigan 395
Minnesota 412
Mississippi 432
Missouri 439
Montana 454
Nebraska 470
Nevada 485
New Hampshire 505
New Jersey 515
New Mexico 537
New York 555

North Carolina	575
North Dakota	593
Ohio	616
Oklahoma	628
Oregon	641
Pennsylvania	658
Puerto Rico	677
Rhode Island	686
South Carolina	706
South Dakota	721
Tennessee	733
Texas	747
Utah	763
Vermont	777
Virgin Islands	787
Virginia	795
Washington	808
West Virginia	822
Wisconsin	833
Wyoming	847
Agency Cancellation Notice Requirements	www.fcands.com/CNR
Cancellation by Major Line of Business	www.fcands.com/CNR
Claims Handling Requirements Chart	www.fcands.com/CNR
Insurance Departments	www.fcands.com/CNR
Intercompany Transfer Chart	www.fcands.com/CNR
Line of Business Termination Withdrawal Requirements	www.fcands.com/CNR
Policyholder Notification Chart	www.fcands.com/CNR
State Provisions for Military Personnel	www.fcands.com/CNR

Complete information on the *2019 Cancellation and Nonrenewal* book is in the Introduction. The volume has been updated with current state legislation as of November 1, 2019. Additional information is located at http://www.fcands.com/CNR. This includes three charts, which are updated periodically throughout the year:

Intercompany Transfer Chart
Policyholder Notification Chart
Line of Business Terimination / Withdrawal Requirements

INTRODUCTION

This is the twenty-second edition of The National Underwriter Company's *Cancellation & Nonrenewal* annual. It is vitally important to agents and underwriters to know how a policy may be legally terminated by an insurer. They need to know if there is an underwriting period where the policy may be cancelled for any reason; the allowable reasons for midterm cancellation; and the allowable reasons for nonrenewal. They also need to know the type and number of days' notice required to be given to the insured.

This book provides answers in an easy-to-use format. The introduction outlines the standard reasons for termination as written into the standard policies from Insurance Services Office (ISO) and the National Commission on Compensation Insurance (NCCI). Although many might think that most of the differences are in personal lines coverage, most states place limitations on the termination of commercial lines coverage as well.

Then, on a state-by-state basis, any differences for that state are examined line-by-line. The differences are based on the amendatory endorsements filed by ISO. In some instances, a state's insurance code is unclear about termination of a particular line. It appears that in those cases, ISO has filed provisions it thinks will be acceptable to the regulator.

In other states, the provisions of the amendatory endorsement are actually more restrictive than the state's law. If an insurer has adopted that amendatory endorsement, then it must abide by the provisions of that endorsement, instead of the law.

Several states have made significant changes in their statutes, so while there is not a lot of "new" information, there are significant updates available.

The book includes Fraud Insurance Bureaus by State and lists contact information for each state's insurance fraud bureau if they have one. With cybersecurity becoming such an issue, the Status of Data Breach Notification Laws is important to carriers and there are requirements for those who have suffered a data breach to notify those whose data has been compromised.

It is critically important to insurance departments that claims are handled promptly and insureds and claimants are treated fairly; the Claims Handling Requirements chart provides important information in the handling of claims. Included is when a claim must be acknowledged, when correspondence must be responded to, time within which a claim must be paid or an explanation given as to why payment is delayed, and other pertinent information required by insurance departments.

As in previous editions, where available, the statutory references for each state's entries are included. Differences between amendatory endorsements and the state code are noted.

INTRODUCTION

If an insurer has adopted an amendatory endorsement that differs from the state code, it must abide by the terms of the endorsement unless the insured would suffer. For example, if an amendatory endorsement says that the reason for cancellation will be provided, but the code does not specify that requirement, the insurer still must show the reason. Another example: if the code enumerates certain allowable reasons for cancellation and the endorsement contains reasons not shown in the code, the insurer may only use the reasons listed in the code.

The editors of this book have reviewed state statutes, regulations, and insurance division web pages. As we have often done with the Cancellation and Nonrenewal book, we asked the various state insurance departments to review our files before we went to print. We find the assistance of the states to be very valuable as they help us provide the most accurate and up to date information available at the time of printing. We thank each and every state insurance department that assisted us in this endeavor. Not every state is able to review our material, however, and it is possible that statutes, regulations and procedures have been changed since this material has been reviewed. At times the statutes conflict with the information provided by the insurance department. While we strive to use the most current information, if you have questions please contact the appropriate department directly.

This book is designed to provide accurate and authoritative information (based on information from the states) in regard to the subject matter covered. It is offered with the understanding that the writer is not engaged in rendering legal, accounting, or other professional service. If legal advice or other expert assistance is required, the services of a competent professional should be sought.

Comments or suggestions about this book may be addressed to the editor at 800-543-0874, or via email: fcspublic@sbmedia.com. We welcome new ideas for content you may find useful.

STANDARD POLICY PROVISIONS

The following is the framework for each state's information. This framework reflects the information contained in the basic policies, as filed by ISO and NCCI, as well as the individual state statutes.

COMMERCIAL LINES

ISO's commercial lines policies are actually coverage parts. Each may be packaged with other coverage parts in any combination. Many of the coverage parts do not include cancellation or nonrenewal provisions. Instead, they rely on the Common Policy Conditions (IL 00 17). The Common Policy Conditions assumes that the ISO policy may be cancelled at any time for any reason. Because the policy may be cancelled at any time, the standard policy makes no provision for nonrenewal. ISO's programs are available in all states. In some, their standard provisions are preempted by state laws, which specify nonrenewal provisions and greatly restrict the right to cancel. We will detail these restrictions in each state section.

COMMON POLICY CONDITIONS – IL 00 17

1. **Cancellation Notice Requirements:**

    A. Restrictions on Cancellation – None.

    B. Cancellation Notice Requirements:

    1. Ten days for nonpayment; thirty days for any other reason.

    2. Reason for cancellation is not required on the notice.

    3. Proof of mailing.

2. **Nonrenewal:** There are no nonrenewal provisions in the Common Policy Conditions. When the state restricts the reasons for cancellation or specifies other periods of time for mailing or requires nonrenewal, these provisions are included in state amendatory endorsements.

LINE OF BUSINESS / APPLICABLE FORMS

A. Agricultural Capital Assets (Output Policy) / AG 00 01

In regards to mortgageholders, the standard cancellation provisions of ten days for nonpayment of premiums and thirty days for any other reason apply. The unmodified AG 00 01 also allows the insurer to elect not to renew with ten days notice to the mortgageholder before the expiration date of the policy.

STANDARD POLICY PROVISIONS

B. Businessowners / BP 00 03

In addition to the standard cancellation provisions of ten days for nonpayment and thirty days for any other reason, the unmodified BP 00 03 allows the insurer to cancel with a five day notice if any one of the following conditions exists at any building that is covered by the policy:

1. The building has been vacant or unoccupied sixty or more consecutive days. This does not apply to:

    a. Seasonal unoccupancy; or

    b. Buildings in the course of construction, renovation or addition.

    Buildings with sixty-five percent or more of the rental units or floor area vacant or unoccupied are considered unoccupied under this provision.

2. After damage by a Covered Cause of Loss, permanent repairs to the building:

    a. Have not started, and

    b. Have not been contracted for,

    within thirty days of initial payment of loss.

3. The building has:

    a. An outstanding order to vacate;

    b. An outstanding demolition order; or

    c. Been declared unsafe by governmental authority.

4. Fixed and salvageable items have been or are being removed from the building and are not being replaced. This does not apply to such removal that is necessary or incidental to any renovation or remodeling.

5. Failure to:

    a. Furnish necessary heat, water, sewer service or electricity for thirty consecutive days or more, except during a period of seasonal unoccupancy; or

STANDARD POLICY PROVISIONS

    b. Pay property taxes that are owing and have been outstanding for more than one year following the date due, except that this provision will not apply where you are in a bona fide dispute with the taxing authority regarding payment of such taxes.

Notice should be mailed or delivered to the last known mailing address of the first Named Insured. Any premium refund due shall be sent to the first Named Insured. If notice is mailed, proof of mailing will be considered sufficient proof of notice.

C. **Capital Assets Program / OP 00 01**

This policy contains the standard ten days notice for cancellation for nonpayment of premium, and thirty days notice for cancellation for any other reason.

D. **Commercial Auto / CA 00 01, CA 00 05, CA 00 10, CA 00 12, CA 00 20**

These policies contain no cancellation provisions. The Common Policy Conditions or other amendatory form must be included if written as a stand alone policy to explain the terms in which the policy will be cancelled.

E. **Commercial Crime / CR 00 20; CR 00 21; CR 00 22; CR 00 23; CR 00 24; CR 00 25; CR 00 26; CR 00 27; CR 00 28; CR 00 29; CR 00 40; CR 00 41**

Policy provisions allow the insurer to void coverage in the event of fraud by the insured as it relates to the insurance at any time. It is also void if the first named insured or any other insured, at any time, intentionally conceal or misrepresent a material fact concerning the insurance; the property covered under this insurance; the insured's interest in the property covered under the insurance; or a claim under the insurance.

F. **Commercial General Liability CG 00 01; CG 00 02**

The Common Policy Conditions apply to these coverage parts. However, these policies also include a Nonrenewal provision. These policies may be nonrenewed for any reason. A thirty day notice is required. Proof of mailing is sufficient proof. These provisions apply to all Commercial General Liability coverages except as follows:

1. Owners & Contractors Protective / CG 00 09

    a. Special Cancellation Notice Requirements:

    (1) Ten days for nonpayment; thirty days for any other reason.
    (2) Reason not required.
    (3) Proof of mailing.
    (4) All notices must be sent to the named insured and the contractor designated in the declarations.

STANDARD POLICY PROVISIONS

    b. Special Nonrenewal Notice Requirements:

        (1) Thirty days for any reason.
        (2) Reason is not required.
        (3) Proof of mailing is sufficient proof.

2. Railroad Protective / CG 00 35

    a. Special Cancellation Notice Requirements:

        (1) Sixty days for any reason is required.
        (2) Reason is not required.
        (3) Proof of mailing is sufficient proof.
        (4) All notices must be sent to the named insured and the contractor and any involved governmental authority designated in the declarations.

    b. Special Nonrenewal Notice Requirements:

        (1) Thirty days for any reason is required. This is not statutory.
        (2) Reason is not required.
        (3) Proof of mailing is sufficient proof.
        (4) All notices must be sent to the named insured and the contractor and any involved governmental authority designated in the declarations.

3. Underground Storage Tank / CG 00 42

    a. Special Cancellation Notice Requirements:

        (1) Ten days for nonpayment, fraud or material misrepresentation; sixty days for any other reason.
        (2) Reason is required.
        (3) Certified mail.
        (4) All notices must be sent to the named insured, the contractor, and any involved governmental authority or other contracting party shown in the declarations.

    b. Special Nonrenewal Notice Requirements

        (1) Sixty days.
        (2) Reason not required.
        (3) Certified mail.
        (4) All notices must be sent to the named insured, the contractor, and any involved governmental authority or other contracting party shown in the declarations.

STANDARD POLICY PROVISIONS

G. **Commercial Inland Marine / CM 00 01, CM 00 20, CM 00 21, CM 00 22, CM 00 26, CM 00 28, CM 00 29, CM 00 45, CM 00 52, CM 00 59, CM 00 66, CM 00 67**

These policies contain no cancellation provisions, so the Common Cancellation Provisions form must be attached. However, an additional form, CM 00 01 – Commercial Inland Marine Conditions, allows the insurer to void coverage in any case of fraud, intentional concealment or misrepresentation of a material fact, by the named insured or any other insured, at any time, concerning coverage; covered property; the named insured's interest in the covered property; or a claim under the coverage part.

H. **Commercial Property is applicable to Building and Personal Property Coverage, Builders' Risk Coverage and Time Element Coverage / CP 00 10, CP 00 17**

CP 00 90 – Conditions allows the insurer to void coverage in any case of fraud, intentional concealment or misrepresentation of a material fact, by the named insured or any other insured, at any time, concerning coverage; covered property; the named insured's interest in the covered property; or a claim under the coverage part.

I. **Commercial Umbrella / CU 00 01**

This policy contains no cancellation provisions. The Common Policy Conditions or other amendatory form must be included if written as a stand alone policy to explain the terms in which the policy will be cancelled.

J. **E-Commerce provides coverage for loss that the insured becomes legally obligated to pay as a result of its wrongful acts associated with the content posted to its Website. / EC 00 10**

    a. Special Cancellation Notice Requirements:

        (1) Ten days for nonpayment; thirty days for any other reason.

        (2) Reason not required.

        (3) Proof of mailing is sufficient proof of notice.

K. **Equipment Breakdown / EB 00 20**

Conditions allows the insurer to void coverage in any case of fraud, intentional concealment or misrepresentation of a material fact, by the named insured or any other insured, at any time, concerning coverage; covered property; the named insured's interest in the covered property; or a claim under the coverage part.

STANDARD POLICY PROVISIONS

L. **Farm / FB 00 01, FB 04 01, FP 00 12, FP 00 13, FP 00 14**

These policies contain no cancellation provisions. The Common Policy Conditions or other amendatory form must be included if written as a stand alone policy to explain the terms in which the policy will be cancelled.

M. **Management Protection / MP 00 01, MP 00 02, MP 00 03, MP 00 04, MP 00 05, MP 00 06, MP 00 07**

These policies contain no cancellation provisions. The Common Policy Conditions or other amendatory form must be included if written as a stand alone policy to explain the terms in which the policy will be cancelled.

N. **Medical Professional Liability / PR 00 01; PR 00 02; PR 00 03; PR 00 04; PR 00 05; PR 00 06; PR 00 07; PR 00 08; PR 00 09; PR 00 10; PR 00 11; PR 00 12; PR 00 13; PR 00 14**

These policies contain no cancellation provisions. However, they do contain a nonrenewal condition requiring a thirty day notice, with proof of mailing. The Common Policy Conditions or other amendatory form must be included if written as a stand alone policy to explain the terms in which the policy will be cancelled.

O. **Worker's Compensation / WC 00 00 00**

The standard NCCI worker's compensation policy allows the insurer to cancel the policy at any time for any reason. A ten day notice must be mailed to the insured. Proof of mailing is required. The reason for cancellation does not have to be shown. Many states require advance notification to the overseeing governmental authority before a cancellation can become effective. The standard policy does not include non-renewal provisions.

P. **Surplus Lines**

Some states apply their cancellation and nonrenewal statutes to surplus lines policies and some do not. Where available, each state's treatment indicates that state's position on cancellation of surplus lines policies.

Q. **Financed Premiums**

When an insured borrows money from a premium finance company to pay his premiums, he may become subject to different cancellation requirements if he fails to make payments to the premium finance company. In some states, the premium finance company may send notice of cancellation due to nonpayment.

STANDARD POLICY PROVISIONS

In other states, the premium finance agreement contains a power of attorney from the insured to the finance company. The finance company must first send a notice to the insured giving a certain number of days to "cure the delinquency." If the insured does not pay within that time period, then the finance company, using its power of attorney, may request that the insurer cancel the policy as of the date on its original notice to the insured. Any unearned premium is then returned to the finance company.

PERSONAL LINES

PERSONAL PROPERTY COVERAGES

In contrast to Commercial Lines, personal property policies include a number of restrictions on the insurer's right to cancel. Personal Lines introduces an Underwriting Period, also known as the "free look". The ISO policies allow the insurer sixty days to decide whether to accept the individual risk or not. During this time, the policy may be cancelled for any reason. Many states have adopted this as a standard rule, which may also be applicable to commercial lines. Upon completion of the Underwriting Period, the ISO policies contain severe restrictions on the insurer's right to cancel. These are limited to fraud or material misrepresentation, and substantial changes in the risk in addition to nonpayment. Not all states include these limitations. We will contrast the ISO policy provisions to the individual statutory requirements.

Personal Lines also include nonrenewal provisions. In the standard ISO policy, the insurer's right to not renew a piece of business is unrestricted.

Definition: In addition to refusal to issue based on an application, a declination also includes the following:

1. The offering of coverage in a company in the group of insurers that differs from the company requested on the application.

2. The offering of coverage terms that differ from those requested on the application.

3. The refusal of an agent or broker to submit a nonbinding application or written request for coverage.

Notice to the applicant: The insurer, agent, or broker who makes the declination must send a written notice advising the applicant of the specific reasons for the declination. If the reason for declination is not sent, the notice must advise the applicant that the reasons will be provided within twenty-one days of his or her request. The applicant's request must be received within ninety days of the date of the notice.

STANDARD POLICY PROVISIONS

If an insurer declines a submission, it must provide the agent or broker with a written explanation of the reason(s) for the declination. If the agent or broker cannot, then place the applicant in an admitted market (other than a residual market mechanism), the agent or broker must provide the applicant with a written explanation.

All agents, brokers, and direct-writing insurers must provide an application or other means of making a written request for insurance to all prospective applicants.

DWELLING FIRE; HOMEOWNERS & PERSONAL UMBRELLA

I. **CANCELLATION PROVISIONS**

   A. **Underwriting Period: Sixty days**

   B. **Restrictions on Cancellation:**

     1. During the underwriting period: there are no restrictions on cancellation.

     2. After the underwriting period: the policy may be cancelled only for the following reasons.

        a. Nonpayment.

        b. If there has been a material misrepresentation of fact which if known would have caused the insurer not to issue the policy.

        c. If the risk has changed substantially since the policy was issued.

   C. **Cancellation Notice Requirements:**

     1. During the underwriting period: Ten days for any reason.

     2. After the underwriting period: Ten days for nonpayment; thirty days for any other allowable reason.

     3. Reason is not required on the notice.

     4. Proof of mailing.

II. **NONRENEWAL PROVISIONS**

   A. **Restrictions on Nonrenewal: None.**

STANDARD POLICY PROVISIONS

   B. **Nonrenewal Notice Requirements:**

      1. Thirty days.

      2. Reason not required.

      3. Proof of mailing.

   C. **Other Cancellation/Nonrenewal Provisions:**

When this policy is written for a period of more than one year, the company may cancel for any reason at the anniversary by letting the insured know at least thirty days before the date cancellation takes effect.

LINE OF BUSINESS / FORMS

1. Dwelling / DP 00 01; DP 00 02; DP 00 03

Cancellation Notice Requirements:

1. During the underwriting period: Ten days for any reason.
2. After the underwriting period: Ten days for nonpayment; thirty days for material misrepresentation or substantial change in the risk.
3. Reason is not required on the notice.
4. Proof of mailing.

Nonrenewal Notice Requirements:

1. Thirty days.
2. Reason not required.
3. Proof of mailing.

2. Homeowners / HO 00 01; HO 00 02; HO 00 03; HO 00 04; HO 00 05; HO 00 06

Cancellation Notice Requirements:

1. During the underwriting period: Ten days for any reason.
2. After the underwriting period: Ten days for nonpayment; thirty days for material misrepresentation or substantial change in the risk.

STANDARD POLICY PROVISIONS

3. Reason is not required on the notice.

4. Proof of mailing.

Nonrenewal Notice Requirements:

1. Thirty days.

2. Reason not required.

3. Proof of mailing.

3. Personal Umbrella / DL 98 01

Cancellation Notice Requirements:

1. During the underwriting period: Ten days for any reason.

2. After the underwriting period: Thirty days.

3. Ten days for nonpayment anytime.

4. Reason is not required on the notice.

5. Proof of mailing.

Nonrenewal Notice Requirements:

1. Thirty days.

2. Reason not required.

3. Proof of mailing.

PERSONAL AUTO

Declinations

Personal Automobile PP 00 01

Definition: In addition to refusal to issue based on an application, a declination also includes the following:

1. The offering of coverage in a company in the group of insurers that differs from the company requested on the application.

STANDARD POLICY PROVISIONS

2. The offering of coverage terms or rates substantially less favorable than requested on the application.

3. The refusal of an agent or broker to submit a nonbinding application or written request for coverage.

Notice to the applicant: The insurer, agent, or broker who makes the declination must send a written notice advising the applicant of the specific reasons for the declination. If the reason for declination is not sent, the notice must advise the applicant that the reasons will be provided within twenty-one days of his or her request. The applicant's request must be received within ninety days of the date of the notice.

If an insurer declines a submission, it must provide the agent or broker with a written explanation of the reason(s) for the declination. If the agent or broker cannot, then place the applicant in an admitted market (other than a residual market mechanism), the agent or broker must provide the applicant with a written explanation.

All agents, brokers, and direct-writing insurers must provide an application or other means of making a written request for insurance to all prospective applicants.

Like the Homeowner and Dwelling programs, the standard ISO personal auto policy allows unrestricted cancellation during the underwriting period and greatly restricts the allowable reasons for midterm cancellations. Like the personal property policies, the insurer's right to nonrenew is unrestricted. As with the Personal Property policies, we will contrast the ISO policy provisions and endorsements with each state's cancellation and nonrenewal requirements.

I. CANCELLATION PROVISIONS

   A. **Underwriting Period:** Sixty days.

   B. **Restrictions on Cancellation:**

      1. During the underwriting period: there are no restrictions on cancellation.

      2. After the underwriting period: the policy may be cancelled only for the following reasons.

         a. For nonpayment of premium.
         b. If your driver's license or that of:
            (1) Any driver who lives with you.

STANDARD POLICY PROVISIONS

        (2) Any driver who customarily uses "your covered auto" has been suspended or revoked. This must have occurred:
        (i) During the policy period.
        (ii) Since the last anniversary of the original effective date if the policy period is other than one year.
    c. If the policy was obtained through material misrepresentation.

C. Cancellation Notice Requirements:

1. During the underwriting period: Ten days for any reason.

2. After the underwriting period: Ten days for nonpayment; twenty days for any other allowable reason.

3. Reason required on the notice.

4. Proof of mailing.

II. NONRENEWAL PROVISIONS

A. Restrictions on Nonrenewal: there are no restrictions on nonrenewal.

B. Nonrenewal Notice Requirements:

1. Twenty days.

2. Reason not required.

3. Proof of mailing.

C. Other Cancellation/Nonrenewal Provisions:

1. Less than six months, we will have the right not to renew or continue this policy every six months, beginning six months after its original effective date.

2. Six months or longer, but less than one year, we will have the right not to renew or continue this policy at the end of the policy period.

3. One year or longer, we will have the right not to renew or continue this policy at each anniversary of its original effective date.

STANDARD POLICY PROVISIONS

4. Automatic Termination occurs when the company offers to renew or continue and you or your representative do not accept, this policy will automatically terminate at the end of the current policy period. Failure to pay the required renewal or continuation premium when due shall means that the insured did not accept the company's offer of renewal.

5. If you obtain other insurance on "your covered auto", any similar insurance provided by this policy will terminate as to that auto on the effective date of the other insurance.

ALABAMA

For details on cancellation procedures for the standard policy, refer to the Standard Policy section.

On April 10, 2007, the Alabama Department of Insurance issued Regulation 136 [codified in AL ADC 482-1-136-.05] dealing with nonrenewal of a category or group of existing insureds based on the insurer's desire to reduce exposure to a potential catastrophic event, such as a hurricane. This regulation requires the insurer to send a written notice of coverage restriction or nonrenewal to the DOI no less than 150 days prior to the effective date of any proposed effective date. The notice shall include the types of policies, the type of restriction or restrictions, whether the policies in their entirety are being nonrenewed, the category or group of policyholders to be affected, the number of policyholders to be affected, and the names of the Alabama counties in which policyholders to be affected reside.

Insurers must provide written notice to the insured no less than 120 days prior to the effective date of coverage restriction or nonrenewal.

The notice requirements apply each time an insurer makes a decision to impose a coverage restriction and/or nonrenew coverage to a separate and/or additional category or group of existing insureds.

If current policy forms remain inconsistent with this regulation, legal counsel should be consulted.

COMMERCIAL LINES
AGRICULTURAL CAPITAL ASSETS
Alabama Code §2-31-6

Alabama makes no changes from the standard policy for most applications.

All commercial grain dealers, which includes grain elevators, storage facilities, transporters, or any referred to as a "grain broker" other than a farmer buying grain for feed or seed or feed and seed dealers, are required to maintain an insurance policy to cover all depositors of grain.

Every fire and extended coverage insurance policy so filed shall contain a provision that it may not be cancelled by the principal or insurance company, except on ninety days prior notice in writing, by certified mail, to the commissioner mailed on the same day to the principal. The cancellation shall not affect the liability accrued or which may accrue under such insurance policy before the expiration of the ninety days. The notice shall contain the termination date.

ALABAMA

The grain dealer shall immediately notify all depositors of grain when there is a notice of cancellation of his fire and extended coverage insurance policy, and further, the commissioner shall be responsible to assure notice of insurance cancellation is given to all depositors of grain within thirty days from date of notice from the principal or insurance company.

BUSINESSOWNERS

Alabama makes no changes from the standard policy.

COMMERCIAL AUTO

AL DOI Bulletin No. 2010-10

Insurers may not cancel or nonrenew a policy based solely on a claim arising from a catastrophe, natural disaster, acts of nature, or weather-related causes. Insurers may not do any of the following acts based solely on a claim arising from a catastrophe, natural disaster, acts of nature, or weather-related causes:

1. Apply a premium surcharge.

2. Offer to place the coverage in another rating tier if the action would result in a higher premium.

3. Offer to place the coverage through an affiliated insurer if the action would result in a higher premium.

An insurer's failure to abide by the above regulations results in a violation of the Trade Practices Law (Alabama Code §27-12-1 *et seq.*).

COMMERCIAL CRIME

Alabama makes no changes from the standard policy.

COMMERCIAL GENERAL LIABILITY

Alabama Code §35-8A-313

Alabama makes one change from the standard policy: If the policy covers a condominium, the insurer must send a thirty-day notice of cancellation or nonrenewal to the association, each unit owner, and each mortgagee or beneficiary under a deed of trust holding a certificate or memorandum of insurance.

ALABAMA

COMMERCIAL INLAND MARINE

Alabama Code §27-13-22

Alabama makes no changes from the standard policy.

COMMERCIAL PROPERTY

AL DOI Bulletin No. 2010-10; DOI Regulation 482-1-136

Insurers may not cancel or nonrenew a policy based solely on a claim arising from a catastrophe, natural disaster, acts of nature, or weather-related causes. Insurers may not do any of the following acts based solely on a claim arising from a catastrophe, natural disaster, acts of nature, or weather-related causes:

1. Apply a premium surcharge.

2. Offer to place the coverage in another rating tier if the action would result in a higher premium.

3. Offer to place the coverage with another insurer if the action would result in a higher premium.

An insurer's failure to abide by the above regulations results in a violation of the Trade Practices Law (Alabama Code §27-12-1 *et seq.*). See Bulletin No. 2010-10 for further information regarding rating rule updates and permitted acts involving fraud, concealment, misrepresentation, or removal of discounts in relation to catastrophes, natural disasters, acts of nature, or weather-related causes.

A 150-day written notice of cancellation is required to the commissioner and 120 days' notice to insureds when the insurer is:

1. Imposing a wind exclusion or hurricane deductible, or increasing an existing hurricane deductible, where the restriction applies to a category or group of existing insureds at renewal and is not a result of prior claims history.

2. Nonrenewing coverage to a category or group of existing insureds based upon the insurer's desire to reduce its exposure to a potential catastrophic event.

COMMERCIAL UMBRELLA

Alabama makes no changes from the standard policy.

ALABAMA

EQUIPMENT BREAKDOWN

Alabama makes no changes from the standard policy.

FARM

Alabama makes no changes from the standard policy.

PROFESSIONAL LIABILITY

Alabama makes no changes from the standard policy.

WORKERS COMPENSATION

Alabama makes no changes from the standard policy.

SURPLUS LINES

Surplus lines policies in Alabama are not subject to regulation for cancellation and nonrenewal.

FINANCED PREMIUMS

Alabama Code §27-40-11

If the premium finance agreement contains a power of attorney, the finance company may request, in the name of the insured, that the insurer cancel the policy due to nonpayment. The finance company must first give the insured ten days to pay. The premium service company shall also mail a notice of cancellation to the insured at his last address as set forth in its records, and such mailing shall constitute sufficient proof of delivery. After this notice has expired, if the insured fails to make payment, the premium service company may thereafter request, in the name of the insured, cancellation of such insurance contract by mailing to the insurer a notice of cancellation, and the insurance contract shall be cancelled as if such notice of cancellation had been submitted by the insured himself, but without requiring the return of the insurance contract.

All statutory, regulatory, and contractual restrictions providing that the insurance contract may not be cancelled unless notice is given to a governmental agency, mortagee, or other third party shall apply where cancellation is effected under the provisions of this section. The insurer shall give the prescribed notice on behalf of itself or the insured to any governmental agent, mortagee, or other third party on or before the second business day after the day it receives the notice of cancellation from the premium finance company and shall determine the effective date of cancellation taking into consideration the number of days' notice to complete the cancellation.

ALABAMA

PREMIUM INCREASES

In a letter to insurers dated August 30, 1985, titled "Unfair Trade Practices," the Alabama insurance commissioner established the requirement that insurers must provide a thirty-day notice to the commissioner before sending any notice to the insureds of any premium increase upon renewal. This provision has been codified in AL ADC 482-1-091-.30 for long term care policies and certificates. This provision has not been codified for other lines of insurance. In a bulletin dated June 8, 2016, titled "Bulletin No. 2016-04," the commissioner replaced the original unfair trade practices letter, but did not supersede AL ADC 482-1-136. The thirty-day notice requirement remains in place, but the circumstances have been expanded upon in Bulletin No. 2017-04, which revised and replaced Bulletin No. 2016-04 on June 22, 2017. Insurance companies are now required to give 30 days' notice to the insured for the following actions:

1. Any company initiated premium increase on personal lines policies, and a premium increase greater than 15% for commercial lines policies.

2. Non-renewal of coverage on any personal or commercial lines policies.

"Failure by companies to provide such notice will be considered by the Department to be an unfair trade practice". In addition, the commissioner reiterated the guidelines established by the NAIC in the June 1985 NAIC resolution. Contact the Alabama Department of Insurance or seek legal advice. (Bulletin No. 2017-04 available at: http://www.aldoi.gov/pdf/legal/2017-04%20-%20Cancellation%20or%20non-renewal%20of%20policies,%20premium%20increase%20notification.pdf).

PERSONAL LINES
DWELLING FIRE

AL DOI Bulletin No. 2010-10; DOI Regulation 482-1-136

Insurers may not cancel or nonrenew a policy based solely on a claim arising from a catastrophe, natural disaster, acts of nature, or weather-related causes. Insurers may not do any of the following acts based solely on a claim arising from a catastrophe, natural disaster, acts of nature, or weather-related causes on new or renewal policies:

1. Apply a premium surcharge.

2. Offer to place the coverage in another rating tier if the action would result in a higher premium.

3. Offer to place the coverage with another insurer if the action would result in a higher premium.

ALABAMA

An insurer's failure to abide by the above regulations results in a violation of the Trade Practices Law (Alabama Code §27-12-1 *et seq.*). See Bulletin No. 2010-10 for further information regarding rating rule updates and permitted acts involving fraud, concealment, misrepresentation, or removal of discounts in relation to catastrophes, natural disasters, acts of nature, or weather-related causes.

A 150-day notice of cancellation is required to the commissioner and 120 days' notice to insureds when the insurer is:

1. Imposing a wind exclusion or hurricane deductible, or increasing an existing hurricane deductible, where the restriction applies to a category or group of existing insureds at renewal and is not a result of prior claims history.

2. Nonrenewing coverage to a category or group of existing insureds based upon the insurer's desire to reduce its exposure to a potential catastrophic event.

HOMEOWNERS

AL DOI Bulletin No. 2010-10; DOI Regulation 482-1-136

Insurers may not cancel or nonrenew a policy based solely on a claim arising from a catastrophe, natural disaster, acts of nature, or weather-related causes. Insurers may not do any of the following acts based solely on a claim arising from a catastrophe, natural disaster, acts of nature, or weather-related causes for new or renewal policies:

1. Apply a premium surcharge.

2. Offer to place the coverage in another rating tier if the action would result in a higher premium.

3. Offer to place the coverage with another insurer if the action would result in a higher premium.

An insurer's failure to abide by the above regulations results in a violation of the Trade Practices Law (Alabama Code §27-12-1 *et seq.*). See Bulletin No. 2010-10 for further information regarding rating rule updates and permitted acts involving fraud, concealment, misrepresentation, or removal of discounts in relation to catastrophes, natural disasters, acts of nature, or weather-related causes.

A 150-day notice of cancellation is required to the commissioner and 120 days' notice to insureds when the insurer is:

1. Imposing a wind exclusion or hurricane deductible, or increasing an existing hurricane deductible, where the restriction applies to a category or group of existing insureds at renewal and is not a result of prior claims history.

ALABAMA

2. Nonrenewing coverage to a category or group of existing insureds based upon the insurer's desire to reduce its exposure to a potential catastrophic event.

PERSONAL AUTO

Alabama Code §27-23-20 to 27-23-28

Although ISO's amendatory endorsement (PP 01 87) does not indicate that Alabama law is any different than the basic policy, the code is quite different. This section shows what is permitted by state law. Contact the Alabama Department of Insurance or seek legal advice. These provisions do not apply to any policy that insures more than four automobiles.

Cancellation during the Underwriting Period

Length of Underwriting Period: Sixty days.

Length of Notice: Ten days for cancellation due to nonpayment of premium, twenty days for all other situations.

Reason for Cancellation: Not required on the notice, except when cancelling for nonpayment.

Proof Required: Proof of mailing.

Cancellation after the Underwriting Period

The policy may be cancelled **only** for the following reasons:

1. Nonpayment of premium.

2. The policy was obtained through a material misrepresentation.

3. Any insured violated any of the terms and conditions of the policy.

4. The named insured failed to disclose fully his motor vehicle accidents and moving traffic violations for the preceding thirty-six months if called for in the application.

5. The named insured failed to disclose in his written application or in response to inquiry by the broker, or insurer or its agent, information necessary for the acceptance or proper rating of the risk.

6. Any insured made a false or fraudulent claim or knowingly aided or abetted another in the presentation of such a claim.

7. Failure to maintain membership in any group or organization when such membership is a prerequisite to the purchase of such insurance.

ALABAMA

8. The named insured or any other operator who either resides in the same household or customarily operates an automobile insured under such policy:

    a. Has within the thirty-six months prior to the notice of cancellation had his driver's license under suspension or revocation.

    b. Is, or becomes, subject to epilepsy or heart attacks, and such individual does not produce a certificate from a physician testifying to his unqualified ability to operate a motor vehicle safely.

    c. Has an accident record, conviction record (criminal or traffic), physical, mental or other condition which is such that his operation of an automobile might endanger the public safety.

    d. Has within the thirty-six months prior to the notice of cancellation been addicted to the use of narcotics or other drugs.

    e. Uses alcoholic beverage to excess.

    f. Has been convicted or forfeited bail during the thirty-six months immediately preceding the notice of cancellation for:

        (1) Any felony.

        (2) Criminal negligence resulting in death, homicide or assault arising out of the operation of a motor vehicle.

        (3) Operating a motor vehicle while in an intoxicated condition or while under the influence of drugs.

        (4) Being intoxicated while in, or about, an automobile or while having custody of an automobile.

        (5) Leaving the scene of an accident without stopping to report.

        (6) Theft or unlawful taking of a motor vehicle.

        (7) Making false statements in an application for a driver's license.

        (8) Has been convicted of or forfeited bail for three or more violations, within the thirty-six months immediately preceding the notice of cancellation, of any law, ordinance or regulation limiting the speed of motor vehicle laws of any state, violation of which constitutes a misdemeanor, whether or not the violations were repetitions of the same offense or different offenses.

ALABAMA

9. The insured automobile is:

   a. so mechanically defective that its operation might endanger public safety;

   b. used in carrying passengers for hire or compensation; except the use of an automobile for a car pool shall not be considered use of an automobile for hire or compensation;

   c. used in the business of transportation of flammables or explosives;

   d. an authorized emergency vehicle;

   e. changed in shape or condition during the policy period so as to increase the risk substantially;

   f. subject to an inspection law and has not been inspected or, if inspected, has failed to qualify.

Length of Notice: Ten days for nonpayment of premium; twenty days for any other reason.

Reason for Cancellation: Not required.

Proof Required: Proof of mailing.

Nonrenewal

Length of Notice: Twenty days.

Reason for Nonrenewal: Not required.

Proof Required: Proof of mailing.

Other Cancellation/Nonrenewal Provisions

Insured must request the reason(s) for cancellation not less than fifteen days prior to the effective date of cancellation. The insurer must mail or deliver to the insured within five days the reason(s) for cancellation within five days after nonpayment of the premium. When the cancellation is for reasons other than nonpayment of premium, the insurer must notify the insured of the availability of the assigned risk plan.

Even though the Alabama amendatory endorsement (PP 01 87) does not indicate any changes to the standard cancellation provisions of the personal auto policy, insurers must follow the Alabama Code. The Alabama Code has no provisions for nonrenewal, so the provisions of

ALABAMA

the policy will apply, unless the insurer decides to nonrenew a category or group of insureds in order to reduce exposure to a potential catastrophic event. (See Alabama DOI Bulletin dated Jan. 3, 2007).

There shall be no liability on the part of and no cause of action of any nature shall arise against any insurer, its authorized representative, its agents, its employees, or any firm, person, or corporation furnishing to the insurer information as to reasons for cancellation for any statement made by any of them in any written notice of cancellation, for the providing of information pertaining thereto, or for statements made or evidence submitted at the hearings conducted in connection therewith.

An insurer shall not cancel or nonrenew an automobile insurance policy if based solely on a claim arising from a catastrophe, natural disaster, acts of nature, or weather-related causes. (See Alabama DOI Bulletin No. 2010-10).

AL DOI Bulletin No. 2010-10

Insurers may not cancel or nonrenew a policy based solely on a claim arising from a catastrophe, natural disaster, acts of nature, or weather-related causes. Insurers may not do any of the following acts based solely on a claim arising from a catastrophe, natural disaster, acts of nature, or weather-related causes for new or renewal policies:

1. Apply a premium surcharge.

2. Offer to place the coverage in another rating tier if the action would result in a higher premium.

3. Offer to place the coverage with another insurer if the action would result in a higher premium.

An insurer's failure to abide by the above regulations results in a violation of the Trade Practices Law (Alabama Code §27-12-1 et seq.). See Bulletin No. 2010-10 for further information regarding rating rule updates and permitted acts involving fraud, concealment, misrepresentation, or removal of discounts in relation to catastrophes, natural disasters, acts of nature, or weather-related causes.

An insurer shall neither: 1) apply a premium surcharge to an automobile insurance policy, nor 2) offer to place the coverage of an automobile insurance policy in another rating tier with the same insurer or place the coverage through an affiliated insurer if either such action would result in a higher premium if based solely on a claim arising from a catastrophe, natural disaster, acts of nature, or weather-related causes.

ALABAMA

PERSONAL UMBRELLA

Alabama makes no changes to the standard policy.

FRAUD

Ala. Code § 27-12A-1 to 42

Alabama has a comprehensive statutory scheme with the passage of Act No. 2012-429 (HB-323), to define insurance fraud, to authorize the department to oversee and investigate fraud, to provide confidentiality of information and files, to provide assessments on insurer, to establish the Insurance Fraud Unit, to provide certain immunity from civil liability for certain persons reporting and investigating suspected insurance fraud, to provide civil and criminal penalties, to authorize the commissioner of insurance to promulgate rules necessary to implement, and administer this act for the purpose to amend 10A-20-6.16 and 27-21A-23 Code of Alabama 1975.

Reporting insurance fraud is mandatory for insurance professionals in Alabama. Report at http://www.aldoi.gov/FraudUnit/ReportFraud.aspx or 1-800-654-0775. (Ala. Code § 27-12A-21).

Insurers must include a fraud warning in insurance paperwork that states the following:

> "Any person who knowingly presents a false or fraudulent claim for payment of a loss or benefit or who knowingly presents false information in an application for insurance is guilty of a crime and may be subject to restitution, fines, or confinement in prison, or any combination thereof." Ala. Code §27-12A-20.

FAIR CLAIMS PROCESSING

Alabama does not have a comprehensive statutory scheme outlining insurer duties and standards of operation when processing claims at this time.

ALASKA

For details on cancellation procedures for the standard policy, refer to the Standard Policy section. For details on state fraud provisions and fair claims processing procedures, refer to the end of this section.

COMMERCIAL LINES
AGRICULTURAL CAPITAL ASSETS; BOP; C. AUTO; CRIME; CGL (CGL; LIQUOR; MARKET SEGMENTS; OCP; POLLUTION; PRODUCTS; RR PROT); CIM; C. PROP.; C. UMB.; EQUIPMENT BREAKDOWN; FARM; PRO. LIAB.

Alaska Stat. §§21.36.220, 21.36.235, 21.36.240, 21.36.255 and 21.36.260

Length of Underwriting Period: N/A.

Length of Notice: Twenty days for nonpayment of premium or if insured does not provide underwriting information; ten days for either conviction of a crime that involves increasing an insured-against hazard or discovery of fraud in obtaining the policy or pursing a claim; sixty days for any other reason.

Reason for Cancellation: Required on the notice.

Proof Required: Certificate of mailing or electronic confirmation of receipt by intended recipient.

Nonrenewal

Length of Notice: Forty-five days.

Reason for Nonrenewal: Not required.

Proof Required: Certificate of mailing or electronic confirmation of receipt by the intended recipient.

Other Cancellation/Nonrenewal Provisions

1. Cancellation by the insurer requires a pro rata refund of the unearned premium. Cancellation by the insured is at pro rata less a maximum fee of 7.5 percent.

2. A forty-five day written notice is required in the event of a premium increase of more than 10 percent—for a reason other than an increase in coverage or exposure—or a material restriction or reduction in coverage that the insured did not request.

ALASKA

3. Under the OCP Coverage Part notice of cancellation or nonrenewal must also be sent to the listed contractor.

4. Under the Railroad Protective Coverage Part notice of cancellation or nonrenewal must also be sent to the listed contractor and any involved governmental authority.

COMMERCIAL GENERAL LIABILITY (UNDERGROUND STORAGE TANKS)

Alaska Stat. §§21.36.220, 21.36.235, 21.36.240 and 21.36.255

Cancellation during the Underwriting Period

Length of Underwriting Period: N/A.

Length of Notice: Twenty days for nonpayment of premium or failure to provide underwriting information; ten days for either conviction of a crime that involves increasing an insured-against hazard or discovery of fraud in obtaining a policy or in pursuing a claim; sixty days for any other reason.

Reason for Cancellation: Required on the notice.

Proof Required: Certificate of mailing or electronic confirmation of receipt by intended recipient.

Nonrenewal

Length of Notice: Sixty days.

Reason for Nonrenewal: Not required.

Proof Required: Certificate of mailing.

Other Cancellation/Nonrenewal Provisions

1. Cancellation by the insurer requires a pro rata refund of the unearned premium. Cancellation by the insured is at pro rata less a maximum fee of 7.5 percent.

2. A forty-five day written notice is required in the event of a premium increase of more than 10 percent—for a reason other than an increase in coverage or exposure—or a material restriction or reduction in coverage that the insured did not request.

3. The Alaska code calls for a forty-five day notice of nonrenewal for all commercial policies. If an insurer has adopted the ISO amendatory endorsement (CG 30 07), it must

ALASKA

give a sixty-day notice on underground storage tank (UST) policies. Also, although the code does not require mailing via certified mail, if the insurer has adopted the ISO's endorsement, it must send notices on UST policies via certified mail.

WORKERS COMPENSATION
Alaska Stat. §§21.36.220 and 21.36.240

The policy may be cancelled for any reason.

Length of Notice: Twenty days for nonpayment of premium or failure by the insured to provide the necessary underwriting information; ten days for reasons 1 and 2; sixty days for any other reason.

1. If the insured is convicted of a crime that increases the hazard.

2. Fraud or material misrepresentation in obtaining the insurance or in pursuing a claim under the policy.

Reason for Cancellation: Required on the notice.

Proof Required: Certificate of mailing or certified mailing receipt or electronic confirmation of receipt by intended recipient.

Nonrenewal

Length of Notice: Forty-five days.

Reason for Nonrenewal: Not required.

Proof Required: Certificate of mailing or certified mailing receipt.

Other Cancellation/Nonrenewal Provisions

1. All notices must also be sent to the Alaska Workers Compensation Board.

    Note: The above cancellation requirements are those contained on NCCI's Cancellation and Nonrenewal Endorsement, WC 54 06 02. That endorsement also refers the reader to code sections 21.36.220 and 21.36.240. The requirements laid out in the NCCI endorsement differ from those outlined in the Alaska Code. Insurers may want to seek legal advice or contact the Alaska Department of Insurance.

ALASKA

SURPLUS LINES

Alaska Stat. §21.34.110 and 3 Alaska Admin. Code §25.070

A nonadmitted insurer may not issue a notice of cancellation for nonpayment of premium and a contract of insurance placed by a surplus lines broker is not binding upon the insured and a premium charged is not due and payable until one of these requirements are satisfied:

1. The surplus lines broker has notified the insured in writing, that the insurer with whom the surplus lines broker places the insurance does not hold a certificate of authority issued by Alaska and is not subject to its supervision, and, in the event of the insolvency of the surplus lines insurer, losses will not be covered under the Alaska Insurance Guaranty Association Act. A copy of said notice shall be maintained by the surplus lines broker with the records of the contract, available for examination.

2. The producing broker has notified the insured and the surplus lines broker in writing that the insurer with whom the surplus lines is placed does not hold a certificate of authority issued by Alaska and is not subject to Alaska's supervision, and, in the event of the insolvency of the surplus lines insurer, losses will not be covered under the Alaska Insurance Guaranty Association Act. A copy of said notice shall be maintained by the producing broker and the surplus lines broker with the records of the contract, available for examination.

An eligible surplus lines insurer shall include in each policy an Alaska Policyholder Notice regarding nonrenewal and premium increase, in a format approved by the director. A licensed surplus lines broker shall ensure the required notice is part of each surplus lines policy. The latest format is in Bulletin B 08-06 https://www.commerce.alaska.gov/web/portals/11/pub/Bulletins/B08-06.pdf (3 Alaska Admin Code §25.050).

FINANCED PREMIUMS

Alaska Stat. §06.40.140

If the premium finance agreement contains a power of attorney, the finance company shall give not less than ten days' written notice to the borrower, by mailing by certified mail or documented by an affidavit of mailing, of the licensee's intent to cancel the insurance policy unless the default is cured within that ten-day period. A copy of the notice shall also be mailed by certified mail or documented by an affidavit of mailing to the insurance agent indicated on the premium finance agreement. The finance company must first give the insured ten days to pay. If the insured fails to make payment within that ten day period, then the finance company may, in the name of the insured, cancel the insurance policy by mailing by certified mail or documented by an affidavit of mailing to the insurer a notice of cancellation. The insurance policy

ALASKA

shall be cancelled as if the notice of cancellation had been submitted by the named insured. Return of the policy by the insured is not required. All statutory, regulatory, and contractual restrictions providing that the insurance policy may not be cancelled unless notice is given to a governmental agency, mortgagee, or other third-party shall apply. The insurer shall give the prescribed notice on behalf of itself or the borrower to any governmental agency, mortgagee, or other third-party on or before the fifth business day after the day it receives the notice of cancellation from the licensee and shall determine the effective date of cancellation taking into consideration the number of days' notice required to complete the cancellation.

PERSONAL LINES
DWELLING FIRE & HOMEOWNERS

Alaska Stat. §§21.36.210, 21.36.220, 21.36.235, 21.36.255

Cancellation during the Underwriting Period

Length of Underwriting Period: Sixty days.

Length of Notice: Ten days for reasons 2 and 3 below; twenty days for nonpayment of premium; thirty days for reasons 4 and 5, below.

Reason for Cancellation: Required on the notice, even though ISO's amendatory endorsements say nothing about the reason being shown.

Proof Required: Certificate of mailing or electronic confirmation of receipt by intended recipient.

Cancellation after the Underwriting Period

The policy may be cancelled **only** for the following reasons:

1. Nonpayment of premium, including nonpayment of additional premium, justified by a physical change in the insured property or a change in its occupancy or use.

2. Conviction of the named insured of a crime having as one of its necessary elements an act increasing an insured-against hazard.

3. Discovery of fraud or material misrepresentation made by the insured or a representative of the insured in obtaining the insurance or by the insured in pursuing a claim under the policy.

4. Discovery of a grossly negligent act or omission by the insured that substantially increases the insured-against hazards.

ALASKA

5. Physical changes in the insured property that results in the property becoming uninsurable.

6. Entire abandonment of the property that increases a hazard insured against; if a policy is cancelled under this paragraph, in addition to the notice required under AS 21.36.220, the insurer shall give notice of cancellation of the policy to lender on file with the insurer at the time of the cancellation; in this paragraph, "entire abandonment" means the property is no longer occupied by the insured as defined by the policy and does not have contents of substantial utility; however, property is not entirely abandoned if the insured or an agent for the insured demonstrates that the property is being reasonably maintained and monitored for a condition that might cause damage to the property.

Length of Notice: Ten days for reasons 2 and 3; twenty days for nonpayment of premium; thirty days for reasons 4 and 5.

Reason for Cancellation: Required on the notice, even though the amendatory endorsement says nothing about the reason being shown.

Proof Required: Certificate of mailing or electronic confirmation of receipt by intended recipient.

Nonrenewal

Length of Notice: Thirty days. Even though the Alaska Code calls only for a twenty day notice of nonrenewal, a thirty day notice must be given if an insurer is using the ISO policy. That policy calls for a thirty day notice and the Alaska Special Provisions endorsements (DP 01 54 and HO 01 54) make no change to the nonrenewal provision.

Reason for Nonrenewal: Not required.

Proof Required: Certificate of mailing.

Other Cancellation/Nonrenewal Provisions

Cancellation by the insurer requires a pro rata refund of the unearned premium. Cancellation by the insured is at pro rata less a maximum fee of 7.5 percent. If the policy is written for a period of more than one year, the insurer may cancel on the anniversary date with a thirty-day written notice. If an insurer is not using the ISO policy, Alaska Stat. §21.36.240 only requires a twenty-day written notice.

If the named insured is age seventy or older, any notice must also be sent to his or her designee. Any insured age seventy or older must receive an annual notice of his or her right to a designee.

ALASKA

A twenty-day written notice is required in the event of a premium increase of more than 10 percent—for a reason other than an increase in coverage or exposure—or a material restriction or reduction in coverage that the insured did not request.

PERSONAL AUTO

Alaska Stat. §§21.36.210, 21.36.220 and 21.36.235 through 21.36.260

Cancellation during the Underwriting Period

Length of Underwriting Period: Sixty days.

Length of Notice: Ten days after sixty day underwriting period when insured is convicted of a crime that has as one of its necessary elements an act increasing the insured against hazard or for fraud or material misrepresentation in obtaining the policy or pursuing a claim; twenty days for nonpayment of premium; thirty days for any other reason.

Reason for Cancellation: Required.

Proof Required: Certificate of mailing or electronic confirmation of receipt by the intended recipient.

Cancellation after the Underwriting Period

The policy may be cancelled **only** for the following reasons:

1. Nonpayment of premium.

2. Revocation or suspension of the driver's license of the named insured; or that of any driver who lives with the named insured or customarily uses the named insured's auto.

   Such revocation or suspension must have occurred during the policy period. If the policy is a renewal, the revocation or suspension must occur during the policy period or 180 days immediately preceding its effective date.

Length of Notice: Twenty days for nonpayment of premium. Statute allows for shorter notice periods. However insurers using unaltered ISO forms comply with the twenty-day notice requirement.

Reason for Cancellation: Required.

Proof Required: Certificate of mailing or electronic confirmation of receipt by the intended recipient.

ALASKA

Nonrenewal

Length of Notice: Twenty days.

Reason for Nonrenewal: Not required.

Proof Required: Certificate of mailing or electronic confirmation of receipt by the intended recipient.

Other Cancellation/Nonrenewal Provisions

If the named insured cancels the policy, the insurer retains a maximum cancellation fee of 7.5 percent of the unearned premium. However, there are certain conditions under which that fee is not kept. These include the following: after disposing of the car, the insured purchases another policy from the insurer within thirty days; the insured's auto is repossessed; the insured enters the armed forces; the insured's car was destroyed or stolen and the insured requests cancellation within thirty days; the policy is written for longer than one year and the cancellation is after the first year.

If the named insured is age seventy or older, any notice must also be sent to his or her designee. Any insured age seventy or older must receive an annual notice of his or her right to a designee.

A twenty-day written notice is required in the event of a premium increase of more than 10 percent—for a reason other than an increase in coverage or exposure—or a material restriction or reduction in coverage that the insured did not request. Note: Even though the requirement for this notice does not appear on the Alaska Amendatory Endorsement, it still must be sent.

If the policy is cancelled for other than nonpayment, the insured must be notified of possible eligibility for automobile insurance through the assigned risk or automobile insurance plan. The notification must be included in the notice of cancellation or nonrenewal.

PERSONAL UMBRELLA

Alaska Stat. §§21.36.210, 21.36.220, 21.36.255

Cancellation during the Underwriting Period

Length of Underwriting Period: Sixty days.

Length of Notice: Twenty days for nonpayment of premium; ten days for conviction of insured of a crime that has as one of its necessary elements an act that increases the insured against hazard or discovery of a fraud or material misrepresentation in obtaining the policy or pursuing a claim; thirty days for any other reason.

ALASKA

Reason for Cancellation: Required.

Proof Required: Certificate of mailing or electronic confirmation of receipt by intended recipient.

Cancellation after the Underwriting Period

The policy may be cancelled **only** for the following reasons:

1. Nonpayment of premium.

2. Conviction of the insured of a crime having as one of its necessary elements an act increasing an insured-against hazard.

3. Discovery of fraud or material misrepresentation made by the insured or a representative of the insured in obtaining the insurance or by the insured in pursuing a claim under the policy.

4. Discovery of a grossly negligent act or omission by the insured that substantially increases the insured-against hazards.

5. Physical changes in the insured property that causes the property to become uninsurable.

6. Entire abandonment of the property that increases a hazard insured against.

Length of Notice: Thirty days.

Reason for Cancellation: Required.

Proof Required: Certificate of mailing or electronic confirmation of receipt by intended recipient.

Nonrenewal

Length of Notice: Twenty days.

Reason for Cancellation: Not required.

Proof Required: Certificate of mailing or electronic confirmation of receipt by intended recipient.

ALASKA

Other Cancellation/Nonrenewal Provisions

If the insured is seventy years of age or older and has made a written request, the insurer must also notify a designee of a termination of coverage. Any insured age seventy or older must receive an annual notice of his or her right to a designee.

FRAUD

Alaska Stat. §§21.36.360 and 21.36.390

General Information and Definitions

A fraudulent insurance act is one that is committed by a person who, with intent to injure, defraud, or deceive:

1. Collects a sum as premium or charge for insurance if the insurance has not been provided or is not in due course going to be provided, subject to acceptance of the risk by the insurer.

2. Presents to an insurer a written or oral statement in support of a claim for payment or other benefit under an insurance policy knowing that the statement contains false, incomplete, or misleading information or omits information concerning a matter material to the claim.

3. Assists or conspires with another to prepare or make a written or oral statement that is presented to an insurer in support of a claim for a benefit under an insurance policy, knowing that the statement contains false, incomplete, or misleading information or omits information concerning a matter material to the claim.

4. Willfully collects as premium or charge for insurance a sum in excess of the premium or charge applicable to the insurance as specified in the policy by the insurer in accordance with the applicable classifications and rates approved by the director, or, in cases where classifications and rates are not subject to approval, the premiums collected are in excess of the premiums and charges applicable to the insurance as specified in the policy and fixed by the insurer.

5. Fails to make disposition of funds received or held or misappropriates funds received or held representing premiums or return premiums.

6. Fails to pay its tax liability when due.

7. Makes a written or oral statement in response to an insurer's inquiries related to another person's claim for payment or other benefit under an insurance policy,

ALASKA

knowing that the statement contains false, incomplete, or misleading information or omits information concerning a matter material to the claim.

8. A fraudulent insurance act is committed by a person forming or proposing to form an insurer, an insurance holding corporation, a stock corporation to finance an insurer or insurance production, a corporation to manage an insurer, a corporation to be attorney-in-fact for a reciprocal insurer, or a syndicate for any of these purposes that advertises, or solicits or receives funds, agreement, stock subscription, or membership on account unless the person has applied for and has received from the director a solicitation permit as required by AS 21.69.

9. A fraudulent insurance act is committed by a person who makes a false sworn statement that the person does not believe to be true as to matter material to an examination, investigation, or hearing of the division.

10. A fraudulent insurance act is committed by a person if:

    (1) as to a matter material to an examination, investigation, or hearing by the division, the person makes two or more sworn statements that are irreconcilably inconsistent to the degree that one of them is necessarily false; and

    (2) the person does not believe one of the statements to be true at the time the statement is made.

11. A fraudulent insurance act is committed by a person who with intent to deceive, knowingly exhibits a false account, document, or advertisement, relative to the affairs of an insurer, a corporation, or syndicate of the kind described in AS 21.69.060, formed or proposed to be formed.

12. A fraudulent insurance act is committed by a person who wrongfully removes or attempts to remove records from the place where they are required to be kept under AS 21.69.390(a) or who conceals or attempts to conceal records from the director.

13. A criminal insurance act is committed by a person doing business in this state or relative to a subject resident, located, or to be performed in this state who knowingly:

    (1) writes, places, or causes to be written or placed in this state or relative to a subject resident, located, or to be performed in this state a policy, duplicate policy, or contract of insurance of any kind or character, or general or floating policy upon persons or property resident, situated, or located in this state, from or through

ALASKA

a person not authorized to transact business under AS 21.27 or a risk retention group or purchasing group not registered under AS 21.96.090; or

(2) pays a commission or other form of remuneration to a person, firm, or organization for the writing or placing of insurance coverage in this state or relative to a subject resident, located, or to be performed in this state unless that person, firm, or organization is authorized under AS 21.27 to transact the kind or class of insurance written or placed, or, in the case of a risk retention group or purchasing group, is registered under AS 21.96.090.

14. A criminal insurance act is committed by a person in this state or relative to a subject resident, located, or to be performed in this state who acts as an insurance producer, managing general agent, third-party administrator, reinsurance intermediary broker, reinsurance intermediary manager, surplus lines broker, or independent adjuster without being licensed by the director as required under this title or as a risk retention group or purchasing group without being registered as required under AS 21.96.090. A criminal insurance act is committed by an insurance producer, managing general agent, third-party administrator, reinsurance intermediary broker, reinsurance intermediary manager, or surplus lines broker who solicits or takes application for, procures, or places for others any insurance for which the person is not licensed as required under AS 21.27 or for which the license of the person has been suspended or revoked. A criminal insurance act is committed by a person in this state or relative to a subject resident, located, or to be performed in this state who acts as or on behalf of a risk retention group or a purchasing group that is not registered under AS 21.96.090.

15. A criminal insurance act is committed by an insurance producer, managing general agent, third-party administrator, reinsurance intermediary broker, reinsurance intermediary manager, or surplus lines broker who knowingly compensates or offers to compensate in any manner a person other than an insurance producer, managing general agent, third-party administrator, reinsurance intermediary broker, reinsurance intermediary manager, or surplus lines broker licensed as required under this title in this or another jurisdiction, for procuring or in any manner helping to procure applications for or to place insurance in this state. A criminal insurance act is committed by a person in this state or relative to a subject resident, located, or to be performed in this state who acts as or on behalf of a risk retention group or a purchasing group that is not registered under AS 21.96.090. This subsection does not apply to the payment of compensation that is not contingent upon volume of business transacted in the form of salaries to the regular employees of the insurance producer, managing general agent, third-party administrator, reinsurance intermediary broker, reinsurance intermediary manager, or surplus lines broker.

16. A criminal insurance act is committed by a person who has placed insurance with an unauthorized insurer and refuses to obey an order by the director to produce for

ALASKA

examination all policies and other documents evidencing the insurance and the amount of premiums paid or agreed to be paid for the insurance.

17. A criminal insurance act is committed by a director of a domestic stock or mutual insurer who votes for or concurs in a declaration or payment of a dividend to stockholders or members other than as authorized under AS 21.69.490 - 21.69.500.

18. A criminal insurance act is committed by an agent, managing general agent, third-party administrator, reinsurance intermediary broker, reinsurance intermediary manager, or other representative of an insurer involved in the procuring or issuance of an insurance contract who intentionally fails to report to the insurer the exact amount of consideration charged as premium for the contract and to maintain records showing that information.

19. A fraudulent insurance act is committed by a person who, with intent to injure, defraud, or deceive, knowingly makes a false or fraudulent statement or representation in or with reference to an application for insurance.

20. A fraudulent insurance act is committed by a person who

    1. violates a provision of this title or a regulation issued under it;

    2. falsely makes, completes, or alters a certificate of insurance or other document relating to insurance;

    3. knowingly possesses a forged certificate of insurance or other document relating to insurance; or

    4. knowingly issues a forged certificate of insurance or other document relating to insurance.

Reporting Requirements

An insurer or licensee that has reason to believe that a fraudulent claim has been made against it must send the director a report disclosing information that the director may require.

An insurer or licensee that has reason to believe that an insurance producer with which it is doing business is involved in a defalcation, embezzlement or a violation of the provisions of AS §21.36.360, §21.36.030, or §21.36.050 shall immediately send the director a report disclosing the basis for that belief and any other information that the director may require.

ALASKA

A Uniform Fraud Report Form is available on the Alaska Division of Insurance Web site at https://www.commerce.alaska.gov/web/ins/Resources/Fraud.aspx.

Corroborating documentation may be requested, such as: the name, address, and telephone number of any suspects or witnesses; color copies of any photos or videos concerning the matter; and the name of the insurance company, if known.

Completed forms should be mailed to:

> Alaska Division of Insurance
> 550 W 7th Ave. Ste 1560
> Anchorage, AK 99501
> FAX: (907) 269-7910

Alternatively, persons with reason to believe that insurance fraud is being committed can speak to an investigator at 907-269-7900 or 1-800-467-8725.

Penalties and Statute of Limitations
AS §§21.36.360 and 21.36.910

Upon the institution of proceedings, if the director determines that a person violated the Alaska fraud provisions, the director will serve the person an order requiring that person to cease and desist from engaging in the act or practice.

In addition to a cease and desist order, the director may, after a hearing, order restitution, assess a penalty of not more than $2,500 for each violation or $25,000 for engaging in a general business practice in violation of the Alaska fraud provisions.

If the director determines after a hearing that the person charged knew or should have known that the person was in violation of the Alaska fraud provisions, in addition to the penalty described above, a suspension or revocation of the person's license and a penalty of not more than $25,000 for each violation or $250,000 for engaging in the general business practice in violation of this chapter may also be ordered by the director.

If a cease and desist order has been violated, the director may certify the relevant facts to the superior court for proceedings under AS 44.62.590. The superior court may order the violator to comply with the order, pay an additional penalty of not more than $1,000,000 for each violation, may revoke or suspend the violator's license, and may bar the violator from transacting the business of insurance in the future.

In determining the penalty imposed, the director will consider the amount of loss or harm caused by the violation and the amount of benefit derived by the person by reason of

ALASKA

the violation, the seriousness of the violation, the promptness and completeness of remedial action, whether the violation was a single act or a trade practice, and deterrence of the violator or others.

A fraudulent or criminal insurance act that is committed to obtain $10,000 or more is a class B felony; a defendant convicted of a class B felony may be sentenced to a definite term of imprisonment of not more than ten years.

A fraudulent or criminal insurance act that is committed to obtain $500 or more but less than $10,000 is a class C felony; a defendant convicted of a class C felony may be sentenced to a definite term of imprisonment of not more than five years.

A fraudulent or criminal insurance act that is committed to obtain less than $500 is a class A misdemeanor; a defendant convicted of a class A misdemeanor may be sentenced to a definite term of imprisonment of not more than one year.

FAIR CLAIMS PROCESSING

Alaska Stat. §21.36.125;

*3 Alaska Admin. Code §§26.010 through 26.300
(amended by 2015 AK REG TEXT 368106 (NS))*

Any person transacting a business of insurance who participates in the investigation, adjustment, negotiation, or settlement of a claim shall promptly undertake the investigation of a claim after notification of the claim is received, and shall complete the investigation within thirty working days, unless the investigation cannot reasonably be completed using due diligence.

Any person transacting a business of insurance who participates in the investigation, adjustment, negotiation, or settlement of a first-party or third party claim must:

1. Within ten working days after receipt of notification of a claim, give written acknowledgement to the claimant identifying the person handling the claim, including the person's name, address, telephone number, the firm name, and the file number; payment of the claim within ten working days after notification is satisfactory acknowledgement; provision of necessary claim forms, written instructions, and assistance as required in (3) of this subsection is satisfactory acknowledgement; notification of a claim to an agent constitutes notification to the principal.

2. Within fifteen working days after receipt, make an appropriate reply to all other communications from a claimant which reasonably indicates that a response is

expected; receipt of a communication by an agent constitutes receipt by the principal.

3. Upon receipt of notification of a claim, promptly provide necessary claim forms, instructions, and assistance so that the claimant is able to comply with legal, policy, or contract provisions and other reasonable requirements. (3 Alaska Admin. Code § 26.040).

Any person transacting a business of insurance who participates in the investigation, adjustment, negotiation, or settlement of a first-party claim:

1. Shall advise a first-party claimant in writing of the acceptance or denial of the claim within fifteen working days after receipt of a properly executed statement of claim, proof of loss, or other acceptable evidence of loss unless another time limit is specified in the insurance policy, insurance contract, or other coverage document; payment of the claim within this time limit constitutes written acceptance; a written denial of the claim must state the specific provisions, conditions, exclusions, and facts upon which the denial is based; if additional time is needed to determine whether the claim should be accepted or denied, written notification giving the reasons that more time is needed shall be given to the first-party claimant within the deadline.

    While the investigation remains incomplete, additional written notification shall be provided forty-five working days from the initial notification, and no more than every forty-five working days thereafter giving the reasons that additional time is necessary to complete the investigation; if there is a reasonable basis supported by specific information for suspecting that a first-party claimant has fraudulently caused or wrongfully contributed to the loss, and the basis is documented in the claim file, this reason need not be included in the written request for additional time to complete the investigation or the written denial; however, within a reasonable time for completion of the investigation and after receipt of a properly executed statement of claim, proof of loss, or other acceptable evidence of loss, the first-party claimant shall be advised in writing of the acceptance or denial of the claim.

2. Shall, within thirty working days after receipt of a properly executed statement of claim, proof of loss, or other acceptable evidence of loss, pay those portions of the claim not in dispute.

3. May not fail to settle first-party claims on the basis that responsibility for payment must be assumed by others, except as may be expressly provided by provisions of the insurance policy, insurance contract, or other coverage document. (3 Alaska Admin. Code § 26.070).

ALASKA

A person transacting a business of insurance who participates in the investigation, adjustment, negotiation, or settlement of a first-party or third-party property claim or motor vehicle claim shall:

1. Offer specific comparable replacement property or cash settlement.

2. Provide reasonable written explanation of the valuation.

3. Include the first party claimant's deductible if any.

Note: Insurer may not recommend that a third-party claimant make a claim under the claimant's own coverage in order to delay or avoid paying a claim where liability and damages are reasonably clear. (3 Alaska Admin. Code §26.080 and 3 Alaska Admin. Code §26.090).

ARIZONA

For details on cancellation procedures for the standard policy, refer to the Standard Policy section.

COMMERCIAL LINES
AGRICULTURAL CAPITAL ASSETS; BOP; CAPITAL ASSETS; C. AUTO; CRIME; CGL (all coverage parts); CIM; C. PROP.; C. UMB; EQUIPMENT BREAKDOWN; FARM; AND PROFESSIONAL LIABILITY

Arizona Revised Statutes §§20-1671 to 20-1677; ISO form CA 02 02 for commercial auto policies.

Cancellation during the Underwriting Period

Length of Underwriting Period: Fifty-nine days.

Length of Notice: Ten days for nonpayment of premium; forty-five days for any other reason.

Reason for Cancellation: Specific facts must be stated.

Proof Required: Proof of mailing (certified) or first class mail using intelligent mail barcode or another similar tracking method used or approved by the United States Postal Service.

Cancellation after the Underwriting Period

The policy may be cancelled **only** for the following reasons (reasons 2-8 must be stated in the policy):

1. Nonpayment of premium.

2. If the insured is convicted of a crime that increases the hazard insured against.

3. Fraud or material misrepresentation on the application, in continuing the policy, or in pursuit of a claim.

4. Substantial change in the risk assumed (if such change should not have been foreseen by the insurer or contemplated in the rate).

5. Substantial breach of contractual duties or conditions.

6. If the insurer loses its reinsurance for the risk.

ARIZONA

7. If the director of insurance determines that to continue on the policy would be a violation of the state's insurance laws or would jeopardize the insurer's solvency.

8. Acts or omissions by the insured that materially increase the hazard insured against.

Length of Notice: Ten days for nonpayment; forty-five days for any other allowable reason.

Reason for Cancellation: Specific facts must be stated.

Proof Required: Proof of mailing (certified) or first class mail using intelligent mail barcode or another similar tracking method used or approved by the United States Postal Service.

Nonrenewal

Length of Notice: Forty-five days.

Reason for Nonrenewal: Not required.

Proof Required: Proof of mailing (certified) or first class mail using intelligent mail barcode or another similar tracking method used or approved by the United States Postal Service.

Other Cancellation/Nonrenewal Provisions

1. The insurer does not have to send notice of nonrenewal under these conditions:

    a. The insurer or a company in the same insurance group offers to issue a renewal policy; or

    b. The insured obtains (or agrees in writing to obtain) coverage elsewhere.

2. If the insurer renews under any of the following conditions, a thirty-day advance notice is required:

    a. Premium increase.

    b. Deductible changed.

    c. Reduced limits.

    d. Substantial reduction in coverage.

    These notices must be sufficiently specific for the insured to make an informed decision and not just a vague notice that these things may change.

3. The notice of cancellation and any refund of unearned premium may be mailed separately, but both must be mailed within the same time frame as required for length of notice. If a premium has been financed, a refund of unearned premium shall be returned as provided in section 6-1416. (Arizona Revised Statutes §20-1674 as amended by 2017 Ariz. HB 2232).

   4. If the insurer does not provide such a thirty-day notice, the coverage provided to the named insured remains in effect until notice is given or until the effective date of replacement coverage obtained by the named insured, whichever occurs first.

   5. For the purposes of this section, notice shall be considered given if an insurer delivers new policy terms and conditions thirty days before the expiration date of the policy.

   6. Cancellation and nonrenewal notices may be delivered electrically, consistent with title 44, chapter 26, if both parties have agreed to this ahead of time. (A.R.S. §20-1676, A.R.S. §20-1674, A.R.S. §44-7005).

AGRICULTURAL CAPITAL ASSETS; FARM

Arizona Revised Statutes §§20-1651 to 20-1656.

(Applicable when the policy covers a one to four family dwelling that is used for residential purposes or when it covers personal property of a person residing in such a dwelling.)

Cancellation during the Underwriting Period

Length of Underwriting Period: Fifty-nine days.

Length of Notice: Ten days for nonpayment; thirty days for any other reason.

Reason for Cancellation: Not required.

Proof Required: Proof of mailing.

Cancellation after the Underwriting Period

The policy may be cancelled **only** for the following reasons:

   1. Nonpayment of premium.

   2. If the insured is convicted of a crime that increases the hazard insured against.

   3. Fraud or material misrepresentation on the application, in continuing the policy, or in pursuit of a claim.

ARIZONA

4. Grossly negligent acts or omissions by the insured that substantially increases any of the hazards insured against.

5. Substantial change in the risk assumed (if such change should not have been foreseen by the insurer or contemplated in the rate).

6. If the director of insurance determines that to continue on the policy would be a violation of the state's insurance laws or would jeopardize the insurer's solvency.

7. If the insured does not take reasonable steps to eliminate or reduce any conditions at the insured premises which contributed to a loss in the past or will increase the probability of future losses.

Length of Notice: Ten days for nonpayment; thirty days for any other allowable reason.

Reason for Cancellation: Required on the notice.

Proof Required: Proof of mailing.

Nonrenewal

Length of Notice: Thirty days.

Reason for Nonrenewal: Required on the notice. The amendatory endorsement says nothing about providing the reason, implying that the reason does not need to be shown. However, the statute clearly says that the reason for nonrenewal is required.

Proof Required: Proof of mailing.

Other Cancellation/Nonrenewal Provisions

If the insurer nonrenews based on the condition of the premises, the insured must be given thirty days to rectify that condition, after which time the policy will be renewed. If the insured does not take care of the matter within thirty days, he must be given another thirty days, subject to payment of the premium. Also, a thirty-day notice must be given if the insurer conditions renewal upon the reduction or elimination of coverages.

Even though the Arizona statute says that the above paragraph is the only condition that applies to nonrenewal of such policies, the ISO Cancellation and Nonrenewal endorsement (IL 02 58) is arranged in such a manner that it also applies the sixty-day notice requirement on CP and farm policies that cover residential properties, under the following circumstances:

ARIZONA

1. Premium increase.

2. Deductible changed.

3. Reduced limits.

4. Substantial reduction in coverage.

It is clear this provision applies when more than four dwellings are insured. It is unclear if this provision would apply to a policy covering one to four dwellings. Legal advice should be obtained in the event of any questions. Also, if these provisions do not apply to CP and farm policies covering residential properties, the amendatory endorsement needs to be clarified.

WORKERS COMPENSATION
Arizona Revised Statutes §23-961

A thirty-day notice must be mailed (with proof of mailing) to the insured and to the Industrial Commission of Arizona for cancellation. The Arizona statute also allows for nonrenewal with a thirty-day notice.

SURPLUS LINES
Arizona Revised Statutes §20-1671

Arizona cancellation and nonrenewal laws do not apply to surplus lines policies.

FINANCED PREMIUMS
Arizona Revised Statutes §6-1415

If the premium finance agreement contains a power of attorney enabling the licensee to cancel any insurance contract or contracts listed in the agreement, the insurance contract or contracts shall not be cancelled by the licensee unless the cancellation is in accordance with this section. The finance company must first give the insured ten days to pay. If the insured fails to make payment within that ten day period, then the finance company mails the notice of cancellation to the insurer and the cancellation is processed as of the finance company's original default date. Return of the policy by the insured is not required. If statutory, regulatory and contractual restrictions provide that the insurance contract may not be cancelled unless notice is given to a governmental agency, mortgagee or other third party, the insurer shall give the prescribed notice on behalf of itself or the insured to any governmental agency, mortgagee or other third party on or before the fifth business day after the day it receives the notice of

ARIZONA

cancellation from the finance company. The effective date of cancellation shall be as stated in the insurance policy.

PERSONAL LINES
DWELLING FIRE, HOMEOWNERS, UMBRELLA, CPL & IM

Arizona Revised Statutes §§20-1651 to 20-1656 and ISO Form DP 01 02 and HO 01 02

Cancellation during the Underwriting Period

Length of Underwriting Period: Fifty-nine days.

Length of Notice: Ten days for any reason.

Reason for Cancellation: Required on the notice.

Proof Required: Proof of mailing.

Cancellation after the Underwriting Period

The amendatory endorsements (DP 01 02 and HO 01 02) say that the policy may be cancelled **only** for the following reasons:

1. Nonpayment of premium.

2. Material misrepresentation of a fact that would have caused the insurer to not issue the policy.

3. Substantial change in the risk assumed (if such change should not have been foreseen by the insurer or contemplated in the rate).

4. If the insured does not take reasonable steps to eliminate or reduce any conditions at the insured premises that contributed to a loss in the past or will increase the probability of future losses.

Arizona law allows cancellation for grossly negligent acts or omissions by the insured that substantially increase any of the hazards insured against and a determination by the commissioner that continuation of the policy will place the insurer in violation of the state's insurance laws. However, insurers using the ISO forms should be guided by legal counsel since they are not included in the policy.

Length of Notice: Ten days for nonpayment; thirty days for any other reason.

ARIZONA

Reason for Cancellation: Required on the notice. The amendatory endorsement says nothing about providing the reason, implying that the reason does not need to be shown. However, the statute clearly says that the reason for cancellation is required.

Proof Required: Proof of mailing.

Nonrenewal

Length of Notice: Thirty days.

Reason for Nonrenewal: Required on the notice. The amendatory endorsement says nothing about providing the reason, implying that the reason does not need to be shown. However, the statute clearly says that the reason for nonrenewal is required.

Proof Required: Proof of mailing.

Other Cancellation/Nonrenewal Provisions

If the insurer nonrenews based on the condition of the premises, the insured must be given thirty days to rectify that condition, after which the policy will be renewed. If the insured does not take care of the matter in thirty days, he or she must be given another thirty days, subject to payment of the premium.

After thirty days, a binder may not be declined based on information from a consumer report.

Even though the Arizona Special Provision endorsements (DP 01 02 and HO 01 02) say nothing about it, statute requires a thirty-day notice requirement when the insurer reduces, limits or eliminates coverage.

Legal advice should be obtained in the event of any questions. Also, if these provisions do not apply to CP and Farm policies covering residential properties, the amendatory endorsement needs to be clarified.

PERSONAL AUTO

Arizona Revised Statutes §§20-1631 to 20-1632.01(amended by Chapter 383 Senate Bill 1293 effective August 6, 2018), 28-4009

Cancellation during the Underwriting Period

Length of Underwriting Period: Fifty-nine days.

Article 11 – Cancellation or Non-Renewal of Automobile Insurance. In this article (A.R.S. §20-1631), "motor vehicle" means a licensed, motor-driven vehicle, but does not mean: (A1) a

ARIZONA

private passenger or station wagon type vehicle used as a public or livery conveyance or rented to others; (A2) any other four-wheel motor vehicle of a load capacity of 1,500 pounds or less used in the business of transporting passengers for hire, property or equipment or using as a public or livery conveyance or rented to others; (A3) a vehicle with a load capacity more than 15,00 pounds; (A4) or a vehicle that otherwise qualifies but only when the vehicle is logged into a transportation network company's digital network. An insurer may refuse to renew if the named insured establishes a primary residence outside Arizona, (B) a motor vehicle used as a public or livery conveyance or rented to others does not include a motor vehicle used in the course of volunteer work for a tax-exempt organization

Length of Notice: Pursuant to subsection 20-1631(G), this article does not apply to any policy that has been in effect less than sixty days at the time notice of cancellation is mailed or delivered by the insurer unless the policy is a renewal, or to policies: insuring any motor vehicle other than a private passenger motor vehicle; insuring the motor vehicle hazards, such as garages, motor vehicle sales agencies, repair shops, service stations or public parking places; or providing insurance only on an excess basis.

Reason for Cancellation: Not required; insurer can cancel for any reason.

Proof Required: Certified mail or post office certificate.

Cancellation after the Underwriting Period

After a policy has been in effect for sixty days, or if the policy is a renewal, effective immediately, the company shall not exercise its right to cancel or fail to renew the insurance afforded under the policy except for the following reasons:

1. Nonpayment of premium.

2. The insurance was obtained through fraudulent misrepresentation.

3. Suspension or revocation (during the policy period) of the driver's license of the named insured or anyone who regularly uses the covered auto.

4. If the named insured or anyone who regularly uses the covered auto becomes permanently disabled either physically or mentally. However, such an individual may produce a certificate from a physician or a registered nurse practitioner testifying to that individual's ability to operate a motor vehicle.

5. If the named insured or anyone who regularly uses the covered auto is or has been convicted during the thirty-six months immediately preceding the effective date of the policy or during the policy period for:

a. Criminal negligence resulting in death, homicide, or assault, and arising out of the operation of a motor vehicle.

b. Operating a motor vehicle while intoxicated or under the influence of drugs.

c. Leaving the scene of the accident.

d. Making false statements in an application for a driver's license.

e. Reckless driving.

However, the named insured may agree to exclude such an individual.

6. The insurer is placed in rehabilitation or receivership by the Insurance Department or judicial order.

7. If the covered auto is used regularly and frequently for commercial purposes by the named insured or anyone else who customarily, regularly, and frequently uses it.

8. A ruling by the Director of Insurance that to continue the policy would place the insurer in violation of the laws of Arizona or jeopardize its solvency.

Length of Notice: A nonpayment cancellation is effective on the date the notice is mailed (typically, the eighth day after the due date). Arizona statute requires a minimum grace period of seven days for the payment of any premium except the first payment, during which grace period the policy shall continue in full force. The notice is mailed and becomes effective on the eighth day; ten days prior to the effective date for any other reason.

Reason for Cancellation: Required, must state nonpayment of premium.

Proof Required: Certified mail or post office certificate or first class mail using intelligent mail barcode or another similar tracking method used or approved by the United States Postal Service.

Nonrenewal

Length of Notice: Ten days prior to the effective date for nonpayment of premium; forty-five days for any other reduction or elimination of coverage.

Reason for Nonrenewal: Required on the notice. The insurer may only nonrenew for the reasons listed under "Cancellation After the Underwriting Period" above, or as described in "Other Cancellation/Nonrenewal Provisions", below.

ARIZONA

Proof Required: Certified mail or post office certificate or first class mail using intelligent mail barcode or another similar tracking method used or approved by the United States Postal Service.

Other Cancellation/Nonrenewal Provisions

If the insurer offers renewal and the insured does not pay the renewal premium when due (thus refusing the renewal offer), the insurer can cancel for nonpayment of premium. The insurer must allow the minimum seven day grace period, after the premium due date, for the payment of the premium. If payment has not been received by the end of the seven days, the company can issue a notice of cancellation and effectuate the cancellation on the eighth day. The notice must be sent via certified mail. If the insured obtains other coverage or notifies the insurer that he does not want to renew the policy, the insurer terminates the policy effective on the date requested by the insured, by sending a legal notice of termination.

An insurer shall not issue a motor vehicle insurance policy in Arizona unless the cancellation and renewal provisions of A.R.S. §20-1631 are included in the policy.

Failure to renew or nonrenew does not include the issuance and delivery of a new policy within the same insurer or an insurer under the same ownership or management as the original insurer. An insurer may transfer any of its policies to an affiliated insurer. No insurer shall transfer policyholders because of their location of residence, age, race, color, religion, sex, national origin or ancestry. Transfers by an insurer pursuant to this subsection shall not be construed to permit a new unrestricted sixty-day period for cancellation or nonrenewal.

A person who believes nonrenewal was unlawful may file a written objection with the director. (A.R.S. §20-1633).

Insurers are no longer required to cover drivers while using a private vehicle while logged into a transportation network company's digital network to provide transportation network services, unless expressly authorized by the terms of the policy.

FRAUD

Arizona Revised Statutes §§20-461, 20-463, 20-466

General Information and Definitions

It is a fraudulent practice and unlawful for a person to knowingly present an oral or written statement to or by an insurer, reinsurer, insurance producer or agent that contains untrue statements of material fact or that fails to state any material fact with respect to:

1. An application for the issuance or renewal of an insurance policy.

2. The rating of an insurance policy.

3. A claim for payment or benefit pursuant to an insurance policy.

4. Premiums paid on any insurance policy.

5. Payments made pursuant to the terms of any insurance policy.

6. An application for a certificate of authority.

7. The financial condition of an insurer, reinsurer or purported insurer.

8. The acquisition of an insurer or reinsurer or the concealing of any information concerning any fact material to the acquisition.

Reporting Requirements

Arizona law requires that any insurer who believes a claim is fraudulent is required to make a fraud referral to the Arizona Department of Insurance (ADOI) Fraud Unit in a form prescribed by the director of insurance.

An insurer that believes a fraudulent claim has been or is being made shall send to the director, on a form prescribed by the director, information relative to the claim including the identity of parties claiming loss or damage as a result of an accident and any other information the fraud unit may require. The director shall review the report and determine if further investigation is necessary, the director may conduct an independent investigation to determine if fraud, deceit or intentional misrepresentation in the submission of the claim exists. If the director is satisfied that fraud, deceit or intentional misrepresentation of any kind has been committed in the submission of a claim, the director may report the violations of the law to the reporting insurer, to the appropriate licensing agency and to the appropriate county attorney of the attorney general for prosecution.

A person or an officer, employee or agent of the person acting within the scope of employment or agency or that officer, employee or agent, who in good faith files a report or provides other information to the fraud unit pursuant to this section is not subject to civil or criminal liability for reporting that information to the fraud unit.

If an individual believes that a fraudulent claim has been made, that individual may file a report with the ADOI Fraud Unit with as many details as possible: the suspect's name, date of birth, Social Security number, insurance company, the type of claim the person is filing, etc. There is no mandatory format for individuals to use. The director shall keep the identity of an informant confidential, including any information that might identify the informant, unless the request for information is made by a law enforcement agency, the attorney general or a county attorney for purpose of a criminal investigation or prosecution.

ARIZONA

Insurance companies who believe a fraudulent claim is being made are required to send information relative to the claim and any other information the ADOI Fraud Unit may require using the prescribed form, available on the ADOI Fraud Unit web site at https://insurance.az.gov/reporting-insurance-fraud.

Reports are to be filed with the ADOI Fraud Unit by phone at (602) 364-2140, by fax at (602) 912-8419, or by mail to:

> ADOI – Fraud Unit
> 100 N. 15th Avenue, Suite 102
> Phoenix, AZ 85007

There are two methods of referring claims to the ADOI Fraud Unit:

1. Complete the Fraud Referral Form (available on the ADOI Fraud Unit web site) and mail it to the address shown above, or fax the form to (602) 912-8419.

2. Members of the National Insurance Crime Bureau (NICB) may have referrals submitted to them copied to the ADOI Fraud Unit. NICB offers insurers the option of sending a copy of their referrals to the appropriate State Department of Insurance. Simply indicate in the box provided that the referral should be copied to the ADOI Fraud Unit.

Penalties and Statute of Limitations

Insurance fraud is a crime—a class six felony that can mean time in jail, a maximum fine of $150,000 and possibly a civil penalty of $5,000 for each violation, plus restitution. The statute of limitations is seven years from the time the fraud is discovered. (Ariz. Rev. Stat. §§ 13-107; 13-801; 20-466.01 and 02).

Antifraud Procedures

Insurers are required to include substantially the following statement on their forms, in at least twelve-point type:

"For your protection, Arizona law requires the following statement to appear on this form. Any person who knowingly presents a false or fraudulent claim for payment or a loss is subject to criminal and civil penalties." (Ariz. Rev. Stat. Ann. § 20-466.03).

The ADOI Fraud Unit investigative process includes the following steps:

1. Upon receiving a referral from an insurance company or an individual, the ADOI Fraud Unit staff will first evaluate it to determine whether it merits a full investigation. If a referral is judged to warrant further examination, it is assigned to an investigator.

ARIZONA

2. Once a case is opened, the ADOI Fraud Unit will not comment on it, nor does it comment on any ongoing investigation.

3. Investigations recommended for criminal prosecution are referred to the Attorney General's Office or the County Attorney's Office.

4. All referrals, including those that are determined not to merit a full investigation, are entered into the Fraud Unit's database. Subsequent referrals may then be compared to the information in the database for similar claims or patterns.

FAIR CLAIMS PROCESSING

Arizona Revised Statutes §20-461 and Ariz. Admin. Code R20-6-801

In prescribing rules to implement A.R.S. §20-461, Arizona's unfair claim settlement practice section, the director shall follow, to the extent appropriate, the National Association of Insurance Commissioners (NAIC) Unfair Claims Settlement Practices Model Regulation.

Under the NAIC Unfair Claims Settlement Practices Model Regulation, the Standards for Prompt, Fair and Equitable Settlements Applicable to All Insurers are set forth as follows:

1. Within fifteen working days after receipt by the insurer of properly executed proofs of loss, the first party claimant shall be advised of the acceptance or denial of the claim by the insurer. No insurer shall deny a claim on the grounds of a specific policy provision, condition, or exclusion unless reference to such provision, condition, or exclusion is included in the denial. The denial must be given to the claimant in writing and the claim file of the insurer shall contain a copy of the denial.

2. If a claim is denied for reasons other than those described above and is made by any means other than writing, an appropriate notation shall be made in the claim file of the insurer.

3. If the insurer needs more time to determine whether a first party claim should be accepted or denied, it shall so notify the first party claimant within fifteen working days after receipt of the proofs of loss, giving the reason more time is needed. If the investigation remains incomplete, the insurer shall, forty-five days from the date of the initial notification and every forty-five days thereafter, send to such claimant a letter setting forth the reasons additional time is needed for investigation.

4. Insurers shall not fail to settle first party claims on the basis that responsibility for payment should be assumed by others except as may otherwise be provided by policy provisions.

ARIZONA

5. Insurers shall not continue negotiations for settlement of a claim directly with a claimant who is neither an attorney nor represented by an attorney until the claimant's rights may be affected by a statute of limitations or a policy or contract time limit, without giving the claimant written notice that the time limit may be expiring and may affect the claimant's rights. Such notice shall be given to first party claimants thirty days and to third party claimants sixty days before the date on which such time limit may expire.

6. No insurer shall make statements which indicate that the rights of a third party claimant may be impaired if a form or release is not completed within a given period of time unless the statement is given for the purpose of notifying the third party claimant of the provisions of a statute of limitations.

7. An insurer shall not attempt to settle a loss with a first party claimant on the basis of a cash settlement which is less than the amount the insurer would pay if repairs were made, other than in total loss situations, unless such amount is agreed to by the insured.

ARKANSAS

For details on cancellation procedures for the standard policy, refer to the Standard Policy section.

COMMERCIAL LINES
AGRICULTURAL CAPITAL ASSETS; BOP; CAPITAL ASSETS; C. AUTO; CRIME; CGL (all coverage parts); CIM; C. PROP.; C. UMB.; EQUIPMENT BREAKDOWN; FARM; FARM UMB; PROF. LIAB.

Arkansas Code §§23-63-109, 23-66-206, 23-79-307

Declinations

An insurer may not decline a submission or limit the amount of coverage offered to an applicant based upon the nonrenewal of the applicant's previous property or casualty policy. No insurer shall refuse to underwrite a risk and issue a new policy, or renew a policy, based solely on an insured's past occurrence or history of claims arising from natural causes.

Cancellation during the Underwriting Period

Length of Underwriting Period: Sixty days.

Length of Notice: Ten days for nonpayment; twenty days for any other reason.

Reason for Cancellation: Required on the notice.

Proof Required: Proof of mailing.

Cancellation after the Underwriting Period

The policy may be cancelled **only** for the following reasons:

1. Nonpayment of premium.

2. Fraud or material misrepresentation on the application, in the renewal process, or in making a claim.

3. Occurrence of a material change that substantially increases any hazard insured against.

4. Violation of any local fire, health, safety, building or construction regulation or ordinances with respect to any insured property or its occupancy that substantially increases any hazard insured against.

ARKANSAS

5. Nonpayment of membership dues required to issue or maintain the policy.

6. Material violation of a material provision of the policy.

Length of Notice: Ten days for nonpayment; twenty days for any other reason.

Reason for Cancellation: Required on the notice **only** for nonpayment.

Proof Required: Proof of mailing.

Nonrenewal

Length of Notice: Sixty days.

Reason for Nonrenewal: Not required.

Proof Required: Proof of mailing.

Other Cancellation/Nonrenewal Provisions

For policies issued for more than twelve months with express provisions allowing an annual adjustment of premium, insurers must give at least thirty days advanced notice in writing that the premium will be changed on the anniversary date.

No policy shall be cancelled or nonrenewed solely due to claims arising from natural causes.

If premiums will increase by twenty-five percent or more upon renewal, insurers must notify agents thirty days in advance and insureds ten days in advance.

WORKERS COMPENSATION

Arkansas Code §11-9-408

Arkansas requires a ten-day notice for nonpayment cancellation; thirty day notice for cancellation for any other reason. If the employer procures other insurance within the notice period, the effective date of the new policy is the cancellation date of the old policy. All notices must also be mailed to the Arkansas Workers Compensation Commission.

SURPLUS LINES

Arkansas Code §§23-66-205 and 23-66-206

Cancellation during the Underwriting Period

Length of Underwriting Period: Sixty days.

Length of Notice: Ten days for nonpayment; twenty days for any other reason.

ARKANSAS

Reason for Cancellation: Required on the notice only for nonpayment.

Proof Required: Proof of mailing.

Cancellation after the Underwriting Period

The policy may be cancelled **only** for the following reasons:

1. Nonpayment of premium.

2. Fraud or material misrepresentation on the application, in the renewal process, or in making a claim.

3. Occurrence of a material change that substantially increases any hazard insured against.

4. Violation of any local fire, health, safety, building or construction regulation or ordinances with respect to any insured property or its occupancy that substantially increases any hazard insured against.

5. Nonpayment of membership dues required to issue or maintain the policy.

6. Material violation of a material provision of the policy.

Length of Notice: Ten days for nonpayment; twenty days for any other reason.

Reason for Cancellation: Required on the notice for nonpayment.

Proof Required: Proof of mailing.

Nonrenewal

Length of Notice: Ten days for nonpayment; twenty days for any other reason.

Reason for Nonrenewal: Required on the notice for nonpayment.

Proof Required: Proof of mailing.

FINANCED PREMIUMS

Arkansas Code §23-89-301

The Arkansas Code equates nonpayment to a finance company with nonpayment of premium. Thus, ten days' notice for nonpayment of premium is required.

ARKANSAS

PERSONAL LINES
DWELLING FIRE & HOMEOWNERS

Arkansas Code §§23-66-206, 23-63-109 and 23-88-105

Declinations

An insurer may not decline a submission or limit the amount of coverage offered to an applicant based upon the nonrenewal of the applicant's previous property or casualty policy. No insurer shall refuse to underwrite a risk and issue a new policy, or renew a policy, based solely on an insured's past occurrence or history of claims arising from natural causes.

Cancellation during the Underwriting Period

Length of Underwriting Period: Sixty days.

Length of Notice: Ten days for nonpayment; twenty days for any other reason.

Reason for Cancellation: Required on the notice for nonpayment.

Proof Required: Proof of mailing.

Cancellation after the Underwriting Period

The policy may be cancelled **only** for the following reason:

1. Nonpayment of premium.

2. Fraud or material misrepresentation on the application, in the renewal process, or in making a claim.

3. Occurrence of a material change that substantially increases any hazard insured against.

4. Violation of any local fire, health, safety, building or construction regulation or ordinances with respect to any insured property or its occupancy that substantially increases any hazard insured against.

5. Nonpayment of membership dues required to issue or maintain the policy.

6. Material violation of a material provision of the policy.

Length of Notice: Ten days for nonpayment; twenty days for any other reason.

Reason for Cancellation: Required on the notice for nonpayment.

Proof Required: Proof of mailing.

ARKANSAS

Nonrenewal

Length of Notice: Thirty days.

Reason for Nonrenewal: Required on the notice.

Proof Required: Proof of mailing.

Other Cancellation/Nonrenewal Provisions

When written for a term of more than one year, the policy may be cancelled at the anniversary date with a twenty-day notice.

A notice of cancellation must be given to any lienholders listed on the policy.

PERSONAL AUTO

Arkansas Code §§23-89-301 through 23-89-308

Declinations

An insurer may not decline a submission or limit the amount of coverage offered to an applicant based upon the nonrenewal of the applicant's previous property or casualty policy. No insurer shall refuse to underwrite a risk and issue a new policy, or renew a policy, based solely on an insured's past occurrence or history of claims arising from natural causes.

Cancellation during the Underwriting Period

Length of Underwriting Period: Sixty days.

Length of Notice: Ten days for nonpayment; twenty days for any other reason.

Reason for Cancellation: Required on the notice. Although not indicated that the reason must be given in ISO's amendatory endorsement (PP 01 77), it is required by statute.

Proof Required: Proof of mailing.

Cancellation after the Underwriting Period

The policy may be cancelled **only** for the following reasons:

1. Nonpayment of premium.

ARKANSAS

2. The named insured or any driver of the insured vehicle is convicted of:

   a. Driving while intoxicated.

   b. Homicide or assault arising out of the use of a motor vehicle.

   c. Three separate convictions of speeding or reckless driving, or any combination of the two during the policy period, including the three months prior to the effective date of the policy.

3. Suspension or revocation of the driver's license or registration of:

   a. The named insured.

   b. Any driver who lives with the named insured or who customarily uses the insured auto.

      The suspension or revocation must occur during the policy period or, if the policy is a renewal, during the policy period or the 180 days immediately preceding the effective date.

4. Fraud or misrepresentation of a material fact, the knowledge of which would have caused the insurer to decline to issue the policy.

5. Nonpayment of membership dues when required, if membership in the association is necessary for the purchase of insurance.

   If the insurer has adopted the ISO amendatory endorsement, it may not use reason 2 or 5 to cancel a personal auto policy; reason 2 is excluded only in instances where alcohol or controlled substances were involved.

Length of Notice: Ten days for nonpayment of premium; twenty days for any other reason.

Reason for Cancellation: Required on the notice. Although not indicated that the reason must be given in ISO's amendatory endorsement (PP 01 77), it is required by statute.

Proof Required: Proof of mailing.

Nonrenewal

Length of Notice: Thirty days.

ARKANSAS

Reason for Nonrenewal: Required on the notice. Although not indicated that the reason must be given in ISO's amendatory endorsement (PP 01 77), it is required by statute.

Proof Required: Proof of mailing.

Other Cancellation/Nonrenewal Provisions

1. If the policy term is less than six months, the insurer may nonrenew every six months, beginning six months after the original effective date.

2. If the policy term is one year or longer, the insurer may nonrenew the policy at each anniversary of the original effective date.

3. Upon cancellation or nonrenewal, the insured must be notified of the availability of the assigned risk plan.

4. An auto policy may not be cancelled solely because of the administrative suspension or revocation of the insured's driver's license due to the influence or use of alcohol or a controlled substance as set forth in Arkansas Code §5-63-104. (Ark. Code Ann. § 27-22-106).

5. An insurer may not rescind the BI and PD coverages for fraud or misrepresentation if the insured is involved in an at-fault accident that injures a third party or damages someone else's property. (Ark. Code Ann. § 23-89-303).

6. An insurer may not decline a submission or limit the amount of coverage offered to an applicant based upon the nonrenewal of the applicant's previous property or casualty policy. (Trade Practices Act).

7. A notice of cancellation must be given to any lienholders listed on the policy. (Trade Practices Act).

8. If a policy term is longer than one year or does not have a fixed expiration date, the policy is considered as written for successive policy periods or terms of one year. The policy may be terminated at the expiration of any annual period upon giving twenty days notice of cancellation. This cancellation is not subject to the requirements set forth above. (Ark. Code Ann. § 23-89-301).

9. A named insured has the right to reject in writing all or any one or more of the coverages that every automobile liability insurance policy covering any private passenger motor vehicle issued or delivered in Arkansas should provide, including minimum medical and hospital benefits, income disability, and accidental death benefits. After a named insured

ARKANSAS

or applicant for insurance rejects all or any one or more of this coverage, the insurer or any of its affiliates are not required to notify any insured in any renewal, reinstatement, substitute, amended, or replacement policy as to the availability of such coverage. (Ark. Code Ann. § 23-89-203).

PERSONAL UMBRELLA

Arkansas Code §23-66-206

Cancellation during the Underwriting Period

Length of Underwriting Period: Sixty days.

Length of Notice: Ten days for nonpayment; twenty days for any other reason.

Reason for Cancellation: Required for nonpayment.

Proof Required: Proof of mailing.

Cancellation after the Underwriting Period

Length of Notice: Ten days for nonpayment; twenty days for any other reason.

Reason for Cancellation: Required for nonpayment.

Proof Required: Proof of mailing.

Nonrenewal

Length of Notice: Ten days for nonpayment; twenty days for any other reason.

Reason for Cancellation: Required for nonpayment.

Proof Required: Proof of mailing.

FRAUD

Arkansas Code §§23-66-501 to 23-66-513 and 23-100-101 to 23-100-107

General Information and Definition

A fraudulent insurance act is an act or omission committed by a person who knowingly and with intent to defraud, conceal, misrepresent or deceive commits any of the following:

1. Presents false information as part of, in support of, or concerning a fact material to one or more of the following:

ARKANSAS

   a. An application for the issuance or renewal of an insurance policy or reinsurance contract.

   b. The rating of an insurance policy or reinsurance contract.

   c. A claim for payment or benefit pursuant to an insurance policy or reinsurance contract.

   d. Premiums paid on an insurance policy or reinsurance contract.

   e. Payments made in accordance with the terms of an insurance policy or reinsurance contract.

   f. A document filed with the commissioner or the chief insurance regulatory officer of another jurisdiction.

   g. The financial condition of an insurer or reinsurer.

   h. Formation, acquisition, merger, reconsolidation, dissolution, or withdrawal from one or more lines of insurance or reinsurance in all of part of this state by an insurer or reinsurer.

   i. The issuance of written evidence of insurance.

   j. The reinstatement of an insurance policy.

2. Solicits or accepts insurance risks on behalf of an insurer by a person who knows or should know that the insurer is insolvent at the time of the transaction.

3. Removes, conceals, alters, or destroys the assets or records of an insurer.

4. Embezzles, abstracts, purloins, or converts moneys, funds, premiums, credits, or other property of an insurer.

5. Transacts the business of insurance in violation of laws requiring a license, certificate of authority, or other legal authority for the transaction of the business of insurance.

6. Attempts to commit, aids or abets the commission of, or conspires to commit the acts or omissions specified above and as follows.

7. Issues false, fake, or counterfeit insurance policies, certificates of insurance, insurance ID cards, policy declaration pages or policy covers, or insurance binders or other temporary contracts of insurance.

ARKANSAS

8. Possesses, or possesses with the intent to distribute, the aforementioned.

9. Possesses any device, software, or printing supplies used to manufacture the aforementioned.

10. Falsely holds himself, herself, or itself out as a representative of an insurance company or assists another in furtherance of that misrepresentation to receive a benefit under an insurance claim, contract, or policy.

Fraud Warning

Claim forms, proofs of loss, or any similar documents, however designated, seeking payment or benefit pursuant to an insurance policy, and applications for insurance (preferred), regardless of the form of transmission, shall contain the following statement or a substantially similar statement:

> "Any person who knowingly presents a false or fraudulent claim for payment of a loss or benefit or knowingly presents false information in an application for insurance is guilty of a crime and may be subject to fines and confinement in prison." (A.C.A. §23-66-503).

Reporting Requirement

A person engaged in the business of insurance having knowledge or reasonable belief that a fraudulent insurance act is being, will be, or has been committed must provide to the insurance commissioner the information required by, and in a manner prescribed by, the commissioner. Otherwise, any other person not engaged in the business of insurance having knowledge or reasonable belief that a fraudulent insurance act is being, will be, or has been committed may provide to the commissioner the information required by, and in a manner prescribed by, the commissioner, and is strongly encouraged to do so. Any person engaged in the business of insurance who knowingly fails to report shall be guilty of a Class A misdemeanor.

Upon the request of the commissioner or the commissioner's employees, examiners, investigators, agents, or representatives, a person engaged in the business of insurance must provide to the commissioner all information relevant pertaining to any investigation of a fraudulent act or related criminal violation. The refusal of any person to fully comply with the commissioner's request for information will be grounds for the suspension, revocation, denial, or nonrenewal of any license or authority held by the person to engage in insurance or other business subject to the commissioner's jurisdiction. Any proceeding for the suspension, revocation, denial, or nonrenewal of any license or authority shall be conducted pursuant to A.C.A. §23-63-213 and 23-64-512. (A.C.A. 23-66-505).

ARKANSAS

To report a suspected case of fraud to the Criminal Investigation Division (CID):

1. Mail or fax to the CID a copy of the Uniform Suspected Insurance Fraud Reporting Form to:

   State of Arkansas
   Insurance Fraud Investigation Division
   1200 West Third Street
   Little Rock, Arkansas 72201-1904
   Fax: (501) 371-2799

2. Complete the national NAIC Online Reporting Form available at https://eapps.naic.org/ofrs/.

   Contact the CID by phone at (866) 660-0888 or (501) 371-2790 or by email at Criminal.Investigations@arkansas.gov

Penalties and Statute of Limitation

A person who is found in violation of the insurance fraud provisions of the Arkansas Code Annotated, and is engaged in the business of insurance, is subject to suspension or revocation of license, civil penalties of up to $10,000 per violation, or both. Such person may also be made to make restitution to persons aggrieved by such violations. (ACA §23-66-512).

A person convicted of a violation of the insurance fraud provisions of the Arkansas Code Annotated by a court of competent jurisdiction, and is not engaged in the business of insurance, will be guilty of a Class D felony. Such person or persons will be ordered to pay restitution to person aggrieved by the violation in addition to a fine or imprisonment. A person convicted of this violation will be disqualified from engaging in the business of insurance. (ACA §23-66-512).

Antifraud Provisions

Insurers must have antifraud initiatives reasonably calculated to detect, prosecute, and prevent fraudulent insurance acts. Such initiatives may include, but are not limited to:

1. Fraud investigators, who may be insured employees or independent contractors.

2. An antifraud plan submitted to the insurance commissioner. Antifraud plans submitted to the commissioner will be privileged and confidential and will not be a public record and will not be subject to discovery or subpoena in a civil or criminal action.

ARKANSAS

Insurance companies that are licensed in the State of Arkansas are required to support the CID through an annual assessment. The antifraud assessment filing **must be** received on or before June 1 (or at alternate times that the commissioner prescribes) of each year or late penalties will be assessed in accordance with ACT 337 of 1997. (A.C.A. §23-100-101). Insurers must submit Anti-fraud Assessment Form, a copy of the Schedule T, and a payment made payable to the State Insurance Department Criminal Investigation Division Trust Fund.

Forms and payment should be submitted at: http://www.optins.org/# Insurers must file premium taxes, antifraud assessments, and financial regulation fees through Optins. Other methods of filing will no longer be accepted. This is not applicable to surplus lines insurers. See a complete list of due dates for different fees and taxes at the Optins link listed above. Fees are based on the amount of Arkansas premiums collected, with a maximum of $1,000. See the following bulletin for more details: Bulletin 12-2016 available at https://insurance.arkansas.gov/uploads/bulletins/12-2016.pdf. (23-100-104 as amended by 2017 Arkansas Laws Act 283 (S.B. 247)).

FAIR CLAIMS PROCESSING

Arkansas Administrative Code §§054.00.43-1 to 054.00.43-17

Every insurer, upon receiving notification of a claim shall, within fifteen working days, acknowledge the receipt of such notice unless payment is made within such period of time. If an acknowledgement is made by means other than in writing, an appropriate notation of such acknowledgement shall be made in the claim file of the insurer and dated. Notification given to an agent of an insurer shall be notification to the insurer. Insurers shall furnish forms for proof of loss within twenty calendar days after a loss has been reported, or thereafter waive proof of loss requirements. Insurers shall not require a claimant to calculate depreciated value of personal property on forms for proof of loss.

Every insurer shall complete investigation of a claim with forty-five calendar days after notification of claim, unless such investigation cannot reasonably be completed within such time. If an investigation cannot be completed with the forty-five day time period, insurers shall notify claimants that additional time is required and include with such notification the reasons therefore.

Within fifteen working days after receipt by the insurer, the first-party claimant shall be advised of the acceptance or denial of the claim by the insurer. No insurer shall deny a claim on the grounds of a specific policy provision, condition, or exclusion unless reference to such provision, condition, or exclusion is included in the denial. The denial must be given to the claimant in writing and the claim file of the insurer shall contain a copy of the denial.

ARKANSAS

If the insurer needs more time to determine whether a first-party claim should be accepted or denied, it shall so notify the first-party claimant in writing within fifteen working days after receipt of the proof of loss, stating the reasons more time is needed. If the investigation remains incomplete, the insurer shall, forty-five calendar days from the date of the initial notification and not more than every forty-five calendar days thereafter, send to such claimant a letter setting forth the reasons additional time is needed for investigation.

Insurers shall not continue or prolong negotiations for settlement of a claim directly with a claimant who is neither an attorney nor represented by an attorney until the claimant's rights may be affected by a statute of limitations or a policy or contract time limit, without giving the claimant written notice that the time limit may be expiring and may affect the claimant's rights. Such notice shall be given to first-party claimants thirty working days and to third party claimants sixty calendar days before the date on which such time limit may expire.

Insurers shall mail or deliver claim checks or drafts to claimants within ten working days after the claims are processed, all claim investigations are completed and said claim files are closed and ready for payment.

CALIFORNIA

For details on cancellation procedures for the standard policy, refer to the Standard Policy section.

COMMERCIAL LINES
BOP; C. ASSETS; C. AUTO; CRIME; CGL (CGL; LIQUOR LIABILITY; MARKET SEGMENTS; POLLUTION LIABILITY; PRODUCTS & COMPLETED OPERATIONS); CIM; C. PROP.; EQUIPMENT BREAKDOWN; FARM; PROF. LIAB.

Cal. Ins. Code §§670, 675.5, 676, 676.2, 677, 677.2 and 678.1

Cancellation during the Underwriting Period

Length of Underwriting Period: Sixty days.

Length of Notice: Ten days for nonpayment of premium; ten days for fraud or material misrepresentation in obtaining the policy or in pursuing a claim; thirty days for any other reason.

Reason for Cancellation: Not required except for when reason is nonpayment.

Proof Required: Proof of mailing.

Cancellation after the Underwriting Period

The policy may be cancelled **only** for the following reasons:

1. Nonpayment of premium (including payment due on a prior policy issued by the insurer and due during the current policy term covering the same risks).

2. Conviction of the named insured of a crime having as one of its necessary elements an act materially increasing any hazard insured against.

3. Fraud or material misrepresentation by the insured or a representative in obtaining the policy or in pursuing a claim.

4. Discovery of willful or grossly negligent acts or omissions, or any violations of state laws or regulations establishing safety standards, by the insured or a representative that materially increase any of the risks insured against.

5. Failure by the insured or a representative to implement reasonable loss control requirements that were agreed to as a condition of policy issuance or was a condition

precedent to the use by the insurer of a particular rate or rating plan, if the failure materially increases any of the risks insured against.

6. A determination by the commissioner that the loss of, or changes in, the insurer's reinsurance covering all or part of the risk would threaten the insurer's financial integrity or solvency.

7. A determination by the commissioner that a continuation of the policy coverage would place the insurer in violation of the laws of this state or the state of its domicile or that the continuation of coverage would threaten the solvency of the insurer.

8. A change by the named insured or his or her representative in the activities or property of the commercial or industrial enterprise that results in a material added risk.

Length of Notice: Ten days for nonpayment and for reason 3 above; thirty days for any other reason.

Reason for Cancellation: Required on the notice.

Proof Required: Proof of mailing.

Nonrenewal

Length of Notice: At least sixty; but not more than 120 days prior to the end of the policy period.

Reason for Nonrenewal: Required on the notice.

Proof Required: Proof of mailing.

Other Cancellation/Nonrenewal Provisions

Notice of nonrenewal is not required under the following conditions:

1. If the insurer renews the policy—without changes—in another company in its group.

2. If the insurer extends the policy for ninety days or less if it has given proper notice.

3. If the named insured obtains—or agrees to obtain—replacement coverage within sixty days of the termination of the policy.

4. If the policy is for a period of no more than sixty days and the insurer notifies the named insured at the time the policy is issued that it will not be renewed.

CALIFORNIA

5. If the named insured requests a change in the terms or conditions or risks covered by the policy within sixty days of the end of the policy period.

6. The insurer has made a written offer to the insured, to renew the policy under changed terms and conditions or at a changed premium rate.

Beginning on January 1, 2019, California law will no longer allow commercial policyholders to be electronically notified of conditional renewals. (Cal. Ins. Code § 678.1(g); Amended 2013 Cal SB 251).

A thirty-day notice is required if the insurer increases premiums, reduces limits or changes conditions coverage. The notice must state the effective date of and reasons for the increase, reduction or change. The increase, reduction or change is not effective unless it is based upon one of the following reasons:

1. Discovery of willful or grossly negligent acts or omissions, or any violations of state laws or regulations establishing safety standards by the named insured that materially increase any of the risks or hazards insured against.

2. The named insured fails to implement reasonable loss control requirements that are agreed to as a condition of policy issuance or were conditions precedent to the use of a particular rate, if the failure materially increases any of the risks insured against.

3. The commissioner determines that loss of or changes in an insurer's reinsurance covering the risk covered by the policy would threaten the financial integrity or solvency of the insurer unless the change is permitted.

4. A change by the named insured in the activities or property of the commercial or industrial enterprise that results in a materially added, increased or changed risk, unless the added, increased or changed risk is included in the policy.

5. With respect to a change in the rate of a policy of professional liability insurance for a health care provider, the insurer's offer of renewal notifies the policyholder that the insurer has an application filed pursuant to Section 1861.05 pending with the commissioner for approval of a change in the rate upon which the premium is based, and the commissioner subsequently approves the rate change or some different amount for the policy period.

California law allows lienholders to be notified electronically of policy terminations.

In the event that an insurer fails to give the named insured either an offer of renewal or notice of nonrenewal, the existing policy, with no change in its terms and conditions, shall remain in effect for forty-five days from the date that either the offer to renew or the notice of nonrenewal is delivered or mailed to the named insured.

CALIFORNIA

An admitted insurer licensed to issue motor vehicle liability policies shall neither cancel or refuse to renew a motor vehicle liability insurance policy covering drivers hired to drive by a commercial business establishment, nor execute the agreement specified in Cal. Ins. Code §11580.1(d)(1) with respect to those drivers because those drivers have been convicted of violations of the Vehicle Code or the traffic laws of any subdivision of the state that were committed while operating private passenger vehicles not owned or leased by their employer.

BUSINESSOWNERS, C. PROPERTY, & FARM

(Applies to properties primarily used for residential purposes)

Cal. Ins. Code §§675, 675.5, 676.2, 677, 677.2, 678.1, and 678.5

Cancellation during the Underwriting Period

Length of Underwriting Period: Sixty days.

During the underwriting period the insurer may **not** cancel because:

1. The insured has purchased earthquake coverage.

2. Corrosive soil conditions exist on the premises if the policy contains an exclusion for payment of loss for such conditions.

3. The insured has terminated policy from the California Earthquake Authority (CEA).

Length of Notice: Ten days for nonpayment or for fraud and material misrepresentation; thirty days for any other reason.

Reason for Cancellation: Required on the notice.

Proof Required: Proof of mailing.

Cancellation after the Underwriting Period

The policy may be cancelled **only** for the following reasons:

1. Nonpayment of premium (including payment due on a prior policy issued by the insurer and due during the current policy term covering the same risks).

2. Conviction of a state or federal law that materially increases any of the risks insured against.

CALIFORNIA

3. Discovery of fraud or material misrepresentation.

4. Discovery of willful or grossly negligent acts or omissions.

5. Failure by the insured or a representative to implement reasonable loss control requirements that condition that were agreed to as a condition of policy issuance or was a condition precedent to the use by the insurer of a particular rate or rating plan, if the failure materially increases any of the risks insured against.

6. A determination by the commissioner that the loss of the insurer's reinsurance covering all or part of the risk would threaten the insurer's financial integrity or solvency.

7. A determination by the commissioner that a continuation of the policy coverage would place the insurer in violation of the laws of this state or the state of its domicile.

8. A change by the named insured or his or her representative in the activities or property of the commercial or industrial enterprise that results in a material added risk.

Length of Notice: Ten days for nonpayment of premium and fraud or material misrepresentation; twenty days for any other reason. (See Cal. Ins. Code §677.4).

Reason for Cancellation: Required on the notice.

Proof Required: Proof of mailing.

Nonrenewal

Length of Notice: At least sixty, but not more than 120 days.

Reason for Nonrenewal: Required on the notice.

Proof Required: Proof of mailing.

Other Cancellation/Nonrenewal Provisions

Notice of nonrenewal is not required under the following conditions:

1. If the insurer renews the policy—without changes—in another company in its group.

2. If the insurer extends the policy for ninety days or less, if it has given proper notice.

CALIFORNIA

3. If the named insured obtains—or agrees to obtain—replacement coverage, within sixty days of the termination of the policy.

4. If the policy is for a period of no more than sixty days and the insurer notifies the named insured at the time the policy is issued that it will not be renewed.

5. If the first named insured requests a change in the terms or conditions or risks covered by the policy within sixty days of the end of the policy period.

6. If the insurer makes a written offer to the first named insured to renew the policy under changed terms or conditions or at an increased premium rate, when the increase exceeds 25 percent.

7. Insurers may not cancel, or refuse to renew, a motor vehicle liability insurance policy covering drivers hired to drive by a commercial business for the reason that those drivers have been convicted of violations of the vehicle code or the traffic laws of any subdivision of the state that were committed while operating private passenger vehicles not owned or leased by their employer.

The insurer may not cancel or nonrenew a BOP, commercial property, or farm policy if the named insured has accepted an offer of earthquake coverage or has cancelled or not renewed a policy of earthquake insurance from the California Earthquake Authority (CEA). However, if the insured has a policy from the CEA and does not pay any applicable surcharge on that policy, then the BOP, commercial property, or farm policy may be cancelled.

The insurer may not cancel or nonrenew a BOP, commercial property, or farm policy with all risk perils, solely due to corrosive soil conditions on the insured property.

The insurer may not nonrenew a BOP, commercial property, or farm policy if the named insured has accepted an offer of earthquake coverage, unless:

1. The nonrenewal is based on sound underwriting principles that are consistent with the filed underwriting guide.

2. The commissioner finds that such an exposure will threaten the insurer's solvency.

3. The insurer has lost a substantial amount of its reinsurance or experienced a substantial increase in premium for its reinsurance.

A thirty-day notice is required if the insurer increases premiums, reduces limits or changes conditions coverage. The notice must state the effective date of and reasons for the increase,

CALIFORNIA

reduction or change. The increase, reduction or change is not effective unless it is based upon one of the following reasons:

1. Discovery of willful or grossly negligent acts or omissions, or any violations of state laws or regulations establishing safety standards by the named insured that materially increase any of the risks or hazards insured against.

2. The named insured fails to implement reasonable loss control requirements that are agreed to as a condition of policy issuance or were conditions precedent to the use of a particular rate, if the failure materially increases any of the risks insured against.

3. The commissioner determines that loss of or changes in an insurer's reinsurance covering the risk covered by the policy would threaten the financial integrity or solvency of the insurer unless the change is permitted.

4. A change by the named insured in the activities or property of the commercial or industrial enterprise that results in a materially added, increased or changed risk, unless the added, increased or changed risk is included in the policy.

5. With respect to a change in the rate of a policy of professional liability insurance for a health care provider, the insurer's offer of renewal notifies the policyholder that the insurer has an application filed pursuant to Section 1861.05 pending with the commissioner for approval of a change in the rate upon which the premium is based, and the commissioner subsequently approves the rate change or some different amount for the policy period.

CGL (OCP; RAILROAD PROTECTIVE; UNDERGROUND STORAGE TANKS)

Cal. Ins. Code §§675.5, 676.2, 677, 677.2, and 678.1

Cancellation during the Underwriting Period

Length of Underwriting Period: Sixty days.

Length of Notice: Ten days for nonpayment or for fraud or material misrepresentation in obtaining the policy or in pursuing a claim; sixty days for any other reason; thirty days for OCP.

Reason for Cancellation: Required on the notice.

Proof Required: Proof of mailing; certified mail for UST policies.

CALIFORNIA

Cancellation after the Underwriting Period

The policy may be cancelled **only** for the following reasons:

1. Nonpayment of premium including nonpayment of premium due on a previous policy.

2. A judgment by a court or an administrative tribunal that insured has violated any law of this state or of the United States having as one of its necessary elements an act that materially increases any of the risks insured against.

3. Discovery of fraud or material misrepresentation.

4. Discovery of willful or grossly negligent acts or omissions.

5. Failure by the insured or a representative to implement reasonable loss control requirements that were agreed to as a condition of policy or was a condition precedent to the use by the insurer of a particular rate or rating plan, if the failure materially increases any of the risks insured against.

6. A determination by the commissioner that the loss of the insurer's reinsurance covering would threaten the insurer's financial integrity or solvency.

7. A determination by the commissioner that a continuation of the policy coverage would place the insurer in violation of the laws of this state.

8. A change by the named insured or his or her representative in the activities or property of the commercial or industrial enterprise that results in a material added risk.

Length of Notice: Ten days for nonpayment and material misrepresentation or fraud; sixty days for any other reason; thirty days for OCP.

Reason for Cancellation: Required on the notice.

Proof Required: Certified mail for underground storage tanks, proof of mailing for all other.

Nonrenewal

Length of Notice: At least sixty, but not more than 120 days.

Reason for Nonrenewal: Required on the notice.

Proof Required: Proof of mailing; certified mail for underground storage tanks.

CALIFORNIA

Other Cancellation/Nonrenewal Provisions

Notice of nonrenewal is not required under the following conditions:

1. If the insurer renews the policy, without changes, in another company in its group.

2. If the insurer extends the policy for ninety days or less if it has given proper notice.

3. If the named insured and the contractor obtain—or agree to obtain—replacement coverage, within sixty days of the termination of the policy.

4. If the policy is for a period of no more than sixty days and the insurer notifies the named insured and the contractor at the time the policy is issued that it will not be renewed.

5. If the first named insured and the contractor request a change in the terms or conditions or risks covered by the policy within sixty days of the end of the policy period.

6. If the insurer makes a written offer to the first named insured and the contractor to renew the policy under changed terms or conditions or at an increased premium rate when the increase exceeds 25 percent.

For OCP, all notices of cancellation and nonrenewal must be sent to the first named insured and the contractor.

For Railroad Protective, all notices of cancellation and nonrenewal must be sent to:

1. The named insured.

2. The producer of record.

3. The contractor.

4. Any involved government authorities.

5. Any other contracting parties designated in the declarations.

COMMERCIAL UMBRELLA

Cal. Ins. Code §§675.5, 676.2, 676.6, 677, 677.2, 678, and 678.1

Cancellation during the Underwriting Period

Length of Underwriting Period: Sixty days.

CALIFORNIA

Length of Notice: Ten days for nonpayment or for fraud or material misrepresentation in obtaining the policy or in pursuing a claim; thirty days for any other reason.

Reason for Cancellation: Required on the notice.

Proof Required: Proof of mailing.

Cancellation after the Underwriting Period

The policy may be cancelled **only** for the following reasons:

1. Nonpayment of premium (including nonpayment of premium due on a previous policy).

2. Fraud or material misrepresentation in obtaining the policy or in pursuing a claim.

3. Conviction under a state or federal law for an act that materially increases any of the risks insured against.

4. Willful or grossly negligent acts or omissions or violations of state safety laws or regulations that materially increase any of the risks insured against.

5. Failure by the insured to implement reasonable loss control requirements, agreed to as a condition of policy issuance.

6. A determination by the commissioner of insurance that the loss of, or changes in, the insurer's reinsurance covering all or part of the risk would threaten the insurer's financial integrity or solvency.

7. An increased or changed risk, unless the added, increased, or changed risk is included in the policy.

8. If an underlying policy is cancelled or nonrenewed.

9. If the financial rating of any of the underlying insurers is downgraded by a rating agency.

Length of Notice: Ten days for nonpayment and fraud or material misrepresentation; thirty days for any other reason.

Reason for Cancellation: Required on the notice.

Proof Required: Proof of mailing.

CALIFORNIA

Nonrenewal

Length of Notice: At least sixty, but not more than 120 days.

Reason for Nonrenewal: Required on the notice.

Proof Required: Proof of mailing.

WORKERS COMPENSATION

Cal. Ins.Code §§676.8 and 11664

Cancellation

The policy may be cancelled **only** for the following reasons:

1. Nonpayment of premium.

2. Failure to report payroll.

3. Failure to permit the insurer to audit its payroll required by the terms of the current or previous policy issued by the same insurer.

4. Failure to pay any additional premium resulting from an audit of payroll as required by the terms of the current or previous policy issued by the same insurer.

5. Material misrepresentation by the policyholder or its agent.

6. Failure to cooperate with the insurer in the investigation of a claim.

7. Failure to comply with federal or state safety orders.

8. Failure to comply with written recommendations from the insurer's loss control representatives.

9. The occurrence of a material change in the ownership of the insured business.

10. The occurrence of any change in the operations of the business that materially increases the hazard for frequency or severity of loss.

11. The occurrence of any change in the business or operation that requires additional or different classification for premium calculation.

CALIFORNIA

12. The occurrence of any change in the business or operation which contemplates an activity excluded by the insurer's reinsurance treaties.

Length of Notice: Ten days for nonpayment of premium and reasons 2 through 6, above; thirty days for any other allowable reason.

Reason for Cancellation: Required on the notice.

Proof Required: Proof of mailing.

Nonrenewal

Length of Notice: At least thirty, but not more than 120 days.

Reason for Nonrenewal: Required.

Proof Required: Proof of mailing.

Other Cancellation/Nonrenewal Provisions

The NCCI Cancellation Endorsement (WC 04 06 01 A) for California contains nothing about nonrenewal. However, the provisions outlined above are contained in the Cal. Ins. Code, section 11664.

SURPLUS LINES
Cal. Ins. Code §§675.5, 679.6; §1764.5

The California cancellation and nonrenewal laws do not apply to surplus lines. However, if insurance results from a transaction in which any provision of Sections 1764.2 to 1764.4 of the Cal. Ins. Code are violated, such insurance is subject to cancellation by the insured or by order of the commissioner. Such cancellation shall be without penalty to the insured.

FINANCED PREMIUMS
Cal. Ins. Code §673

If the insured has transferred his or her rights to the finance company via power of attorney (or other document), then the finance company may request cancellation on behalf of the insured if the insured is delinquent in his or her payments. The lender is to send a letter to the insurer specifying a date five or more days following the date of mailing. The insurer then processes cancellation as of the effective date and returns any unearned premium to the finance company.

CALIFORNIA

PERSONAL LINES
DWELLING FIRE & HOMEOWNERS

Cal. Ins. Code §§675.1, 676, 676.1, 676.7, 677, 677.4, 678, 678.5, 2071, and 2074.8

Cancellation during the Underwriting Period

Length of Underwriting Period: Sixty days.

Length of Notice: Twenty days for any reason, except as noted below.

Reason for Cancellation: Required on the notice.

However, the insurer may not cancel during the underwriting period when:

1. The insured has purchased earthquake coverage.

2. Corrosive soil conditions exist on the premises.

3. The insured has terminated a policy from the California Earthquake Authority (CEA) unless, the insured has accepted a new or renewal policy issued by the CEA that included an earthquake policy premium surcharge, but failed to pay the earthquake policy premium surcharge.

Proof Required: Proof of mailing.

Cancellation after the Underwriting Period

The policy may be cancelled **only** for the following reasons:

1. Nonpayment of premium.

2. Conviction of a crime for an act that increases any hazard insured against.

3. Fraud or material misrepresentation in obtaining the policy or pursuing a claim.

4. Grossly negligent acts or omissions that increase any of the hazards insured against.

5. Physical changes in the property that makes it uninsurable.

6. Nonpayment of the earthquake surcharge on a policy issued by the CEA.

Length of Notice: Ten days for nonpayment; twenty days for any other reason.

CALIFORNIA

Reason for Cancellation: Required on the notice.

Proof Required: Proof of mailing.

Nonrenewal

Length of Notice: Forty-five days.

Reason for Nonrenewal: Required on the notice.

Proof Required: Proof of mailing.

Other Cancellation/Nonrenewal Provisions

An insurer may not cancel solely because the insured is licensed to operate a family daycare center. An insurer also may not cancel solely because the insured is a foster family or an approved resource family. Coverage for foster children must be the same as that provided for a natural child. (2016 Cal AB 1997 amending Cal. Ins. Code § 676.7).

The insurer shall not cancel coverage while the primary insured structure is being rebuilt nor use the fact that the primary insured structure is in damaged condition as a result of the total loss as the sole basis for a decision to cancel the policy.

If the policy is a Form 3 or a condominium policy or a dwelling policy with the Special Coverage Endorsement, any of which exclude loss caused by corrosive soil condition, an insurer may not cancel or nonrenew because:

1. The insured has accepted the insurer's offer of earthquake coverage.

2. Corrosive soil conditions exist on the residence premises.

PERSONAL AUTO

Cal. Ins. Code §§657, 660 through 664, 666 and 11580.1

Cancellation during the Underwriting Period

Length of Underwriting Period: N/A.

Length of Notice: Ten days for any reason.

Reason for Cancellation: Not required, except for nonpayment.

Proof Required: Proof of mailing.

CALIFORNIA

Cancellation after the Underwriting Period

The policy may be cancelled **only** for the following reasons:

1. Nonpayment of premium.

2. License suspension of the named insured or any person who customarily uses the insured vehicle if the suspension occurs within the policy period or within sixty days of the most recent renewal or effective date. Under this provision, cancellation cannot be effective if suspension or revocation is removed prior to the effective date of cancellation.

3. The policy was obtained through material misrepresentation of any of the following information, and the correct information is not furnished within twenty days of receipt of notice of cancellation:

    a. safety record;

    b. annual miles driving in prior years;

    c. number of years of driving experience;

    d. record of prior automobile insurance claims, if any; or

    e. any other factor found by the commissioner of insurance to have a substantial relationship to the risk of loss.

4. A substantial increase in the hazard insured against. This provision is not included in ISO's amendatory endorsement (PP 01 69). Insurers using the ISO form should seek legal counsel before using this as a reason for cancellation.

5. Discovery of fraud by the named insured in pursuing a claim under the policy provided the insurer does not rescind the policy.

Length of Notice: Ten days for nonpayment of premium; twenty days for any other reason.

Reason for Cancellation: If the reason neither accompanies nor is included in the notice of cancellation, the notice of cancellation shall state that upon written request of the named insured, the insurer will specify the reason for the cancellation no less than fifteen days prior to the effective date of cancellation. See Cal. Ins. Code §§662 and 666.

Proof Required: Proof of mailing.

CALIFORNIA

Nonrenewal

Length of Notice: Thirty days.

Reason for Nonrenewal: Not required.

Proof Required: Proof of mailing.

Other Cancellation/Nonrenewal Provisions

An insurer may not nonrenew a personal auto policy solely on the basis of the age of the insured or on the grounds that a claim is pending under the policy.

Notices of cancellation and nonrenewal must contain a statement that the reason for cancellation or nonrenewal will be provided upon request.

Every written request for information from an insurer to an insured shall contain a prominent notice, in both English and Spanish, advising the insured that his or her failure to provide requested information within the time required (thirty days) may result in the cancellation or nonrenewal of his or her policy.

An insurer or agent who declines a submission must, upon request, furnish the reason(s) for the declination within thirty days.

Notice must be given to the named insured, lienholder or additional interest. Electronic notification is permitted.

In the event that an insurer fails to give the named insured either an offer of renewal or notice of nonrenewal, the existing policy, with no change in its terms and conditions, shall remain in effect for thirty days from the date that either the offer to renew or the notice of nonrenewal is delivered or mailed to the named insured.

An agreement made by the insurer and any named insured more than sixty days following the inception of the policy excluding a designated person by name shall be effective from the date of the agreement and shall, with the signature of a named insured, be conclusive evidence of the validity of the agreement. That agreement shall remain in force as long as the policy remains in force, and shall apply to any continuation, renewal, or replacement of the policy by the named insured, or reinstatement of the policy within thirty days of any lapse thereof.

Modification of automobile physical damage coverage by the inclusion of a deductible not exceeding $100 shall not be deemed a cancellation of the coverage or of the policy. See Cal. Ins. Code §661.

CALIFORNIA

When a policy of automobile liability is canceled (other than for nonpayment) or in the event of failure to renew a policy, the insurer must notify the named insured of his or her possible eligibility for automobile liability insurance through the automobile liability assigned risk plan. See Cal. Ins. Code §665.

PERSONAL UMBRELLA

Cal. Ins. Code §§675, 676, 677, 677.4, 678

Cancellation during the Underwriting Period

Length of Underwriting Period: Sixty days.

Length of Notice: Ten days for any reason.

Reason for Cancellation: Not required, except when reason is nonpayment of premium.

Proof Required: Proof of mailing.

Cancellation after the Underwriting Period

Length of Notice: Ten days for nonpayment of premium; thirty days for any other reason.

Reason for Cancellation: Not required.

Proof Required: Proof of mailing.

Nonrenewal

Length of Notice: Forty-five days.

Reason for Cancellation: Required on the notice.

Proof Required: Proof of mailing.

FRAUD

Cal. Ins. Code §§1871, 1872, 1873

General Information and Definitions

"Fraud occurs when someone knowingly lies to obtain some benefit or advantage to which they are not otherwise entitled or someone knowingly denies some benefit that is due and to which someone is entitled. Depending on the specific issues involved, an alleged wrongful act may be handled as an administrative action by the department or the fraud division may handle it as a criminal matter."

CALIFORNIA

"The California Insurance Fraud Division is charged with enforcing the provisions of Chapter 12 of the Cal. Ins. Code, commonly referred to as the "Insurance Frauds Prevention Act," California Penal Code, §§549-550 and California Labor Code, §3700.5. Current law requires the fraud division to investigate various felony provisions of the Penal and Insurance Codes. Most often, investigations conducted by the fraud division involve some aspect of a "Suspected Fraudulent Claim" or other related crimes.

"Cases investigated by the fraud division most often involve criminal acts involving automobile property and personal injury, workers' compensation, health insurance and residential and commercial property claims." (California Department of Insurance).

For more information, please consult the California Department of Insurance Fraud Division at http://www.insurance.ca.gov/0300-fraud/0100-fraud-division-overview/.

Reporting Requirements

Any company licensed to write insurance in this state that reasonably believes or knows that a fraudulent claim is being made shall, within sixty days after determination by the insurer that the claim appears to be a fraudulent claim, send to the fraud division, on a form prescribed by the department, the information requested by the form and any additional information relative to the factual circumstances of the claim and the parties claiming loss or damages that the commissioner may require. The fraud division shall review each report and undertake further investigation it deems necessary and proper to determine the validity of the allegations. Whenever the commissioner is satisfied that fraud, deceit, or intentional misrepresentation of any kind has been committed in the submission of the claim, he or she shall report the violations of law to the insurer, to the appropriate licensing agency, and to the district attorney of the county in which the offenses were committed. If the commissioner is satisfied that fraud, deceit, or intentional misrepresentation has not been committed, he or she shall report that determination to the insurer. If prosecution by the district attorney concerned is not begun within sixty days of the receipt of the commissioner's report, the district attorney shall inform the commissioner and the insurer as to the reasons for the lack of prosecution regarding the reported violations.

The fraud division has established a method for insurers to report suspected insurance fraud. Notification of insurance fraud may be made anonymously. Insurers may contact any of the Fraud Division Regional Offices directly responsible for a particular county. Other types of complaints may be directed to the department's Consumer Services Division.

In the absence of fraud or malice, no insurer, or the employees or agents of any insurer, shall be subjected to civil liability for libel, slander or any other relevant cause of action by virtue of providing information concerning a suspected fraudulent claim to law enforcement, including the California Department of Insurance, Fraud Division.

CALIFORNIA

To file a suspected fraudulent claim electronically, visit the following web site and submit the Suspected Fraud Claim Form eFD-1: https://interactive.web.insurance.ca.gov/efd1/!efd1.main, or email fraud@insurance.ca.gov or electronicsubmissionfd-1@insurance.ca.gov.

To file a suspected fraudulent claim by mail, review the reporting instructions and complete the FD-1 Referral Form (available on the Web site). Completed forms and any attachments should be mailed to the following address:

> California Department of Insurance
> Enforcement Branch Headquarters
> Intake Unit
> 9342 Tech Center Dr., Ste. 100
> Sacramento, CA 95826

Penalties and Statute of Limitations

Every person who is convicted of insurance fraud shall be punished by imprisonment in the county jail for one year, or in the state prison, for two, three, or five years, or by a fine not exceeding one hundred fifty thousand dollars ($150,000) or double the value of the fraud, whichever is greater, or by both imprisonment and fine. Restitution shall be ordered, including restitution for any medical evaluation or treatment services obtained or provided. The court shall determine the amount of restitution and the person or persons to whom the restitution shall be paid. A person convicted under this section may be charged the costs of investigation at the discretion of the court.

Antifraud Provisions

Any insurer that prints, reproduces, or furnishes a form to any person upon which that person gives notice to the insurer of a claim under any contract of insurance or makes a claim against the insurer for any loss, damage, liability, or other covered event shall cause to be printed or displayed, in comparative prominence compared to other contents, the following statement: "Any person who knowingly presents a false or fraudulent claim for the payment of a loss is guilty of a crime and may be subject to fines and confinement in state prison." The statement shall be preceded by the words: "For your protection California law requires the following to appear on this form" or other explanatory words of similar meaning.

An insurer doing business in this state shall pay an annual special purpose assessment to be determined by the commissioner, not to exceed five thousand one hundred dollars ($5,100), to be used exclusively for the support of the fraud division. All moneys received by the commissioner from insurers pursuant to this section shall be transmitted to the Treasurer to be deposited in the State Treasury to the credit of the Insurance Fund.

CALIFORNIA

FAIR CLAIMS PROCESSING

Cal. Ins. Code §790, 10 CCR §§2695.5 and 2695.7

Upon receiving any communication from a claimant, regarding a claim, that reasonably suggests that a response is expected, every licensee shall immediately, but in no event more than fifteen calendar days after receipt of that communication, furnish the claimant with a complete response based on the facts as then known by the licensee.

Upon receiving proof of claim, every insurer shall immediately, but in no event more than forty calendar days later, accept or deny the claim, in whole or in part. The amounts accepted or denied shall be clearly documented in the claim file unless the claim has been denied in its entirety.

If more time is required to determine whether a claim should be accepted and/or denied in whole or in part, every insurer shall provide the claimant with written notice of the need for additional time. This written notice shall specify any additional information the insurer requires in order to make a determination and state any continuing reasons for the insurer's inability to make a determination. Thereafter, the written notice shall be provided every thirty calendar days until a determination is made or notice of legal action is served. If the determination cannot be made until some future event occurs, then the insurer shall comply with this continuing notice requirement by advising the claimant of the situation and providing an estimate as to when the determination can be made.

Except where a claim has been settled by payment, every insurer shall provide written notice of any statute of limitation or other time period requirement upon which the insurer may rely to deny a claim. Such notice shall be given to the claimant not less than sixty days prior to the expiration date; except, if notice of claim is first received by the insurer within that sixty days, then notice of the expiration date must be given to the claimant immediately. With respect to a first party claimant in a matter involving an uninsured motorist, this notice shall be given at least thirty days prior to the expiration date; except, if notice of claim is first received by the insurer within that thirty days, then notice of the expiration date must be given to the claimant immediately.

No insurer shall attempt to settle a claim by making a settlement offer that is unreasonably low.

Upon acceptance of the claim in whole or in part and, when necessary, upon receipt of a properly executed release, every insurer, shall immediately, but in no event more than thirty calendar days later, tender payment or otherwise take action to perform its claim obligation.

California maintains a web site detailing fair claims processing at: http://www.insurance.ca.gov/01-consumers/130-laws-regs-hearings/05-CCR/fair-claims-regs.cfm.

COLORADO

For details on cancellation procedures for the standard policy, refer to the Standard Policy section. For details on state fraud provisions and fair claims processing procedures, refer to the end of this section.

COMMERCIAL LINES
AGRICULTURAL CAPITAL ASSETS; BOP; C. ASSETS; C. AUTO; CRIME; F. INST; CGL (CGL, LIQUOR, OCP, PRODUCTS); CIM; C. PROP.; C. UMB.; E-COM; EQUIPMENT BREAKDOWN; AND FARM

Colorado Revised Statutes §§ 10-4-109.7, 10-4-110, and 10-4-110.5

Cancellation during the Underwriting Period

Length of Underwriting Period: N/A.

Length of Notice: Ten days for nonpayment; forty-five days for any other reason.

Reason for Cancellation: Not required, except for nonpayment.

Proof Required: Proof of mailing.

Cancellation after the Underwriting Period

The policy may be cancelled **only** for the following reasons:

1. Nonpayment of premium.

2. If the insured knowingly makes a false statement on the application.

3. A substantial change in the exposure or risk, other than that indicated in the application and underwritten as of the effective date of the policy unless the insured has notified the insurer of the change and the insurer accepts such change.

Length of Notice: Ten days for nonpayment; forty-five days for any other reason.

Reason for Cancellation: Required on the notice for nonpayment.

Proof Required: Proof of mailing.

Nonrenewal

Length of Notice: Forty-five days.

COLORADO

Reason for Nonrenewal: Not required.

Proof Required: Proof of mailing.

Other Cancellation/Nonrenewal Provisions

A forty-five-day written notice with reason shown (proof of mailing) is required if the insurer decides to increase the premium unilaterally or decrease the coverage on renewal. An insurer may decrease coverage only for the reasons that allow midterm cancellation.

On OCP, ISO's CG 28 65 specifies that notice of cancellation or nonrenewal must also be sent to the contractor designated on the declarations.

CGL (RAILROAD PROTECTIVE)
Colorado Revised Statutes §§ 10-4-109.7, 10-4-110, and 10-4-110.5

Cancellation during the Underwriting Period

Length of Underwriting Period: N/A.

Length of Notice: Sixty days for any reason.

Reason for Cancellation: Not required, except for nonpayment.

Proof Required: Proof of mailing.

Cancellation after the Underwriting Period

The policy may be cancelled **only** for the following reasons:

1. Nonpayment of premium.

2. If the insured knowingly makes a false statement on the application.

3. A substantial change in the exposure or risk unless the insured has notified the insurer of the changes and the insurer accepts such change.

Length of Notice: Ten days for nonpayment; forty-five days for any other reason.

Reason for Cancellation: Required on the notice for nonpayment of premium.

Proof Required: Proof of mailing.

COLORADO

Nonrenewal

Length of Notice: Forty-five days.

Reason for Nonrenewal: Not required on the notice.

Proof Required: Proof of mailing.

Other Cancellation/Nonrenewal Provisions

A forty-five-day written notice (proof of mailing) is required if the insurer decides to increase the premium unilaterally or decrease the coverage on renewal. An insurer may decrease coverage only for the reasons that allow midterm cancellation.

ISO's CG 28 66 specifies that all notices must be mailed to the named insured, the contractor, and any involved governmental authority or other contracting party designated in the declarations.

CGL (UNDERGROUND STORAGE TANKS)

Colorado Revised Statutes §§10-4-109.7, 10-4-110, and 10-4-110.5

Cancellation during the Underwriting Period

Length of Underwriting Period: Sixty days.

Length of Notice: Ten days after receipt for nonpayment; sixty days after receipt for any other reason.

Reason for Cancellation: Not required, except for nonpayment.

Proof Required: Certified mail.

Cancellation after the Underwriting Period

The policy may be cancelled **only** for the following reasons:

1. Nonpayment of premium.

2. If the insured knowingly made a false statement on the application.

3. A substantial change in the exposure or risk, unless the insured has notified the insurer of the changes and the insurer accepts such change.

COLORADO

Length of Notice: Ten days after receipt for nonpayment; forty-five days after receipt for reason 2, above; sixty days after receipt for reason 3, above.

Reason for Cancellation: Not required, except for nonpayment.

Proof Required: Certified mail.

Nonrenewal

Length of Notice: Sixty days.

Reason for Nonrenewal: Not required.

Proof Required: Certified mail.

Other Cancellation/Nonrenewal Provisions

Statute allows insurers to cancel by sending notice by first-class mail. Insurers using ISO's CG 30 05 must use certified mail.

A forty-five-day written notice, sent first class mail, is required if the insurer decides to increase the premium unilaterally or decrease the coverage on renewal. An insurer may decrease coverage only for the reasons that allow midterm cancellation.

PROFESSIONAL LIABILITY (HOSPITAL PROFESSIONAL LIABILITY; PHYSICIANS, SURGEONS, AND DENTISTS PROFESSIONAL LIABILITY)

Colorado Revised Statutes §§ 10-4-107, 10-4-108, and -109.5

Cancellation During the Underwriting Period

Length of Underwriting Period: Sixty days.

Length of Notice: Ten days for nonpayment; thirty days for any other reason.

Reason for Cancellation: Not required, except for nonpayment.

Proof Required: Proof of mailing.

Cancellation after the Underwriting Period

The policy may be cancelled **only** for the following reasons:

1. Nonpayment of premium.

2. The license of the insured health care provider has been suspended or revoked by the appropriate state regulatory authority.

COLORADO

3. If the insured knowingly made a false statement on the application.

4. Substantial change in the exposure or risk other than that indicated in the application and underwritten as of the effective date of the policy, unless the insured notified the insurer of the change and the insurer accepts the change.

Length of Notice: Ten days for nonpayment; ninety days for any other reason.

Reason for Cancellation: Not required, except for nonpayment, but when not provided the notice must be accompanied by a statement that, upon written request of the named insured mailed or delivered to the insurer not less than fifteen days prior to the effective date of cancellation, the insurer will specify the reasons for such cancellation.

Proof Required: Proof of mailing.

Nonrenewal

Length of Notice: Ninety days.

Reason for Nonrenewal: Not required.

Proof Required: Proof of mailing.

Other Cancellation/Nonrenewal Provisions

A unilateral increase in premium or a decrease in coverage require a ninety-day notice and may be based only on nonpayment of premium or cancellation reasons 2 and 3, above. The reason for the increase in premium or reduction in coverage must be stated.

ISO's PR 02 26 specifies that the reason for cancellation must be on the notice; however, statute states, "When the reason for cancellation [or nonrenewal] does not accompany or is not included in the notice of cancellation, the insurer shall, upon written request of the named insured mailed or delivered to the insurer not less than fifteen days prior to the effective date of cancellation, specify in writing the reason for such cancellation. Such reason shall be mailed or delivered to the named insured within five days after receipt of such request."

WORKERS COMPENSATION

Colorado Revised Statutes §8-44-110

Even though Colorado makes no changes from the standard policy, Colorado statutes require a thirty-day notice for all reasons other than fraud, material misrepresentation, nonpayment of premium, or any other reason approved by the commissioner of insurance.

COLORADO

Cancellation Notice Requirements:

1. Thirty days, except notice may be less than thirty days for the following:

    a. Fraud.

    b. Material misrepresentation.

    c. Nonpayment of premium.

    d. Any other reason approved by the commissioner.

    Colorado statutes are silent on the specific number of days that must be given for exceptions.

2. Reason for cancellation not required on the notice.

3. Certified mail.

SURPLUS LINES

Colorado Revised Statutes §10-5-118

The Colorado cancellation and nonrenewal laws do not apply to surplus lines policies.

FINANCED PREMIUMS

Colorado Revised Statutes §§5-3-503

The finance company must request that the insurer cancel the policy. Within two business days of receiving the request, the insurer must send a notice of cancellation as required by the policy to the insured. Within ten days after the cancellation is effective, the insurer must pay the finance company any unearned premium.

PERSONAL LINES

DWELLING FIRE

Colorado Revised Statutes §§10-4-110.6 through 10-4-110.8

Cancellation during the Underwriting Period

Length of Underwriting Period: Thirty business days.

Length of Notice: Ten days for nonpayment; thirty days for any other reason.

Reason for Cancellation: The reason must be stated on the notice.

Proof Required: Proof of mailing.

COLORADO

Cancellation after the Underwriting Period

The policy may be cancelled **only** for the following reasons:

1. Nonpayment of premium.

2. Material misrepresentation on the application.

3. Substantial change in the risk.

Nonrenewal

Length of Notice: Thirty business days.

Reason for Cancellation: The reason must be stated on the notice.

Proof Required: Proof of mailing.

Other Cancellation/Nonrenewal Provisions

If the policy is written for a period of more than one year, the insurer may cancel on the anniversary date with a thirty-day written notice.

HOMEOWNERS

Colorado Revised Statutes §§ 10-4-110.7 and 10-4-110.8

Cancellation during the Underwriting Period

Length of Underwriting Period: Thirty business days.

Length of Notice: Ten days for nonpayment; thirty days for any other reason.

Reason for Cancellation: Required on the notice.

Proof Required: Proof of mailing.

Cancellation after the Underwriting Period

The policy may be cancelled **only** for the following reasons:

1. Nonpayment of premium.

2. Material misrepresentation on the application.

3. Substantial change in the risk.

COLORADO

Length of Notice: Ten days for nonpayment; thirty calendar days for any other reason.

Reason for Cancellation: Required on the notice.

Proof Required: First class mail. ISO's HO 01 05 specifies that proof of mailing is sufficient proof.

Nonrenewal

Length of Notice: Thirty days.

Reason for Nonrenewal: Required on the notice.

Proof Required: Proof of mailing.

Other Cancellation/Nonrenewal Provisions

If an insurer uses underwriting criteria based on an individual's credit score, the claims history of the property, or the claims history of the applicant, the insurer shall notify the applicant of the use of such criteria during the application process.

If a binder is issued, and coverage is later declined, the insurer must notify the applicant of the decision within the thirty business day binder period.

An insurer may not cancel or fail to renew coverage of an insured solely because the insured inquires about coverage for homeowner's insurance and the inquiry is not related to an actual claim to the property insured.

PERSONAL AUTO

Colorado Revised Statutes §§10-4-601 to 10-4-609 (as amended by HB 16-1025 and 2017 Colo. SB 249), and 10-4-628 to 10-4-629; 3 CCR 702-5; and Regulation 5-2-12

Cancellation during the Underwriting Period

Length of Underwriting Period: Sixty days.

Length of Notice: Ten days for any reason.

Reason for Cancellation: Where the reason for cancellation does not accompany or is not included in the notice of cancellation, the insurer shall, upon written request of the named insured, mailed or delivered to the insurer not less than fifteen days prior to the effective date of cancellation, specify in writing the reason for such cancellation. Such reason shall be mailed or delivered to the named insured within five days after receipt of such request.

Proof Required: Proof of mailing.

COLORADO

Cancellation after the Underwriting Period

The policy may be cancelled **only** for the following reasons:

1. Nonpayment of premium.

2. Revocation or suspension of the driver's license of the named insured.

3. Revocation or suspension of the driver's license of any driver who lives with the named insured or customarily uses the named insured's auto.

    Such revocation or suspension must have occurred during the policy period. If the policy period is other than one year, the revocation/suspension must have occurred since the last anniversary of the original effective date. Colorado law also allows for cancellation if the revocation or suspension occurred during the 180 days prior to a renewal date.

4. If the insured knowingly made a false statement on the application. Colorado law also allows for midterm cancellation if an insured knowingly and willfully made a false material statement regarding a claim submitted under the policy.

Length of Notice: Ten days for nonpayment; thirty days for any other reason.

Reason for Cancellation: Where the reason for cancellation does not accompany or is not included in the notice of cancellation, the insurer shall, upon written request of the named insured, mailed or delivered to the insurer not less than fifteen days prior to the effective date of cancellation, specify in writing the reason for such cancellation. Such reason shall be mailed or delivered to the named insured within five days after receipt of such request.

Proof Required: Proof of mailing.

Nonrenewal

Length of Notice: Thirty days.

Reason for Nonrenewal: Must be provided if requested by insured.

Proof Required: Proof of mailing.

Other Cancellation/Nonrenewal Provisions

If the policy is written for a term of less than six months, the insurer may nonrenew every six months, beginning six months after the original effective date.

COLORADO

If the policy is written for a term of one year or longer, the insurer may nonrenew only at each anniversary of the original effective date.

Upon request of the insured, the reasons for cancellation must be provided within fifteen days of such request; the reasons for nonrenewal, within twenty days.

If cancelled for a reason other than nonpayment or if nonrenewed, the insured must be notified of the availability of the assigned risk plan.

"Premium due date" means the date that a premium that has been previously paid is fully earned.

An insurer may not rescind (i.e., cancel retroactively) a policy or void such coverage except in case of fraud.

Whenever the insurer chooses to cancel a policy, the earned premium shall be determined on a pro-rata basis, including cancellation for nonpayment of premium.

Insurers renewing a policy excluding a named driver shall renotify the named insured by printed notice at the time of each policy renewal. Failure to renotify the named insured of the excluded driver shall make the exclusion void for all policy coverages.

Issuing a policy from an admitted company within the same insurance group as the previous policy counts as renewal so long as all other renewal requirements have been met.

PERSONAL UMBRELLA

Colorado makes no changes to the standard policy.

FRAUD

Colorado Revised Statutes §§8-43-402; 10-1-128 and 10-1-129; 10-4-1001 through 10-4-1009 (as amended by 2017 Colo. HB. 1048); 18-13-119 and 18-13-119.5; Colorado Insurance Bulletins 6-5-1, B-1.8, B-1.10, and B-1.11

General Information and Definitions

"A fraudulent insurance act is committed if a person knowingly and with intent to defraud presents, causes to be presented, or prepares with knowledge or belief that it will be presented to or by an insurer, a purported insurer, or any producer thereof any written statement as part or in support of an application for the issuance or the rating of an insurance policy or a claim for payment or other benefit pursuant to an insurance policy that she knows to contain false information concerning any fact material thereto or if she knowingly and with intent to defraud or mislead conceals information concerning any fact material thereto." C.R.S. §10-1-128 Title 10, Article 4, Part 10 is known Colorado's "Fraudulent Claims and Arson Information Reporting Act".

COLORADO

Reporting Requirements

When an insurer has reason to believe that a claim may be fraudulent or a fire loss has been caused by nonaccidental means an authorized agency must be notified. Any relevant information concerning such loss, claim or act must be reported to an authorized agency for the purpose of detecting, prosecuting, or preventing fraudulent insurance claims. Reporting of said information is confidential and not part of the public record. (C.R.S. §10-4-1003).

Any authorized agency may require insurers to release relevant information or evidence deemed important, which may include: insurance policy information, policy premium payment records, history of previous claims made by the insured, and any other material relating to the investigation of the loss. (C.R.S. §10-4-1003).

Any agency or insurer which receives information provided by the Fraudulent Claims and Arson Reporting Act must hold the information in confidence. Any authorized agency or employee may be required to testify in any proceeding in which the named party is the insurer. (C.R.S. §10-4-1004).

Fraudulent acts may be reported by using the reporting form provided in Bulletin B-1.8, available at http://www.dora.state.co.us/insurance/regs/B-1.8.pdf. If the provided form is not used, the reporting entity should include the following information in a fraudulent referral: the reporting party's information, insurer information, detailed suspect information, locations, and summary of allegations.

The report may be mailed to:

> Suspected Fraudulent Claim
>
> State of Colorado – Fraud Division
>
> Department of Insurance and Department of Law
>
> 1560 Broadway, Suite 850
>
> Denver, CO 80202

Insurers must report the fraudulent insurance act within sixty days after the date its investigation is complete and there is reasonable suspicion a reportable act occurred, or within sixty days of the receipt of a judgment or settlement. (Colorado Insurance Bulletin 6-5-1(3)(B)(4)(b)). Use the form attached to Bulletin B-1.10 to report judgements and settlements. (available at https://drive.google.com/file/d/0BwMmWVFE3YMsM0otNmNXUEdCX0k/view). Forms may be emailed to dora_ins_fraudreporting@state.co.us.

COLORADO

Penalties and Statute of Limitations

1. It is a class two misdemeanor for any person who violates any provision of the Fraudulent Claims and Arson Information Reporting Act. (C.R.S. §10-4-1007).

2. It is a class two misdemeanor for any insurance company, or agent, employee, representative, or other person acting on behalf of the insurance company to knowingly accept a rebate or gift, cash, or thing of value from any person who provides repairs, goods, or services in connection with any claim under an insurance policy which insures for property damage. (C.R.S. §18-13-119.5(4)-(5)).

3. It is a class five felony for any person to willfully make a false statement or representation material to a claim, either for self-gain or for the benefit of any other person, for the purpose of obtaining any order, benefit, award, compensation, or payment under articles 40 to 47 of Title 8 of the Colorado Revised Statutes, C.R.S. §8-43-402. Note: This statute applies to workers compensation claims.

4. A class two misdemeanor is punishable by three to twelve months imprisonment, or $250 – $1,000 fine, or both. A class five felony is punishable by one to three years imprisonment, or $1,000 – $100,000 fine, or both. (C.R.S. §§18-1.3-401 and 501).

5. Civil actions for fraud, misrepresentation, concealment, or deceit must be commenced within three years after the cause of action accrues, and not thereafter. The exception is for fraudulent acts dealing in used or salvageable vehicles, which limits the commencement of a civil case to two years after the cause of action accrues. (C.R.S. §13-80-101 as amended by 2017 Colo. SB 294).

6. Fraudulent criminal actions deemed felonies must be prosecuted within three years after the commission of the offense; misdemeanors must be prosecuted within eighteen months after the commission of the offense, and petty offenses must be prosecuted within six months after the commission of the offense. For insurance fraud pursuant to section 18-5-211, this period begins to run when the criminal act is discovered. (C.R.S. §16-5-401 as amended by 2017 Colo. HB. 1048).

Antifraud Procedures

Every entity regulated by the insurance division must pay an annual fee, not exceeding $3,000, due on or before March 1, to fund the investigation and prosecution of allegations of insurance fraud. Based upon the appropriations made to the department of law from the insurance fraud cash fund and the recommendation of the attorney general, the commissioner of insurance shall set the fee so that the revenue generated from the fee approximates the direct and indirect costs of the investigation and prosecution of allegations of insurance fraud. (C.R.S. §24-31-104.5 as amended by 2017 Colo. SB 233).

COLORADO

Every insurance company shall provide the following written notice on all printed applications for insurance, or on all insurance policies, or on all claim forms, whether printed or electronically transmitted.

It is unlawful to knowingly provide false, incomplete, or misleading facts or information to an insurance company for the purpose of defrauding or attempting to defraud the company. Penalties may include imprisonment, fines, denial of insurance and civil damages. Any insurance company or agent of an insurance company who knowingly provides false, incomplete, or misleading facts or information to a policyholder or claimant for the purpose of defrauding or attempting to defraud the policyholder or claimant with regard to a settlement or award payable from insurance proceeds shall be reported to the Colorado division of insurance within the department of regulatory agencies. (C.R.S. §10-1-128).

Note: The above written notice requirement is not applicable to reinsurance contracts, reinsurance agreements, or reinsurance claims transactions.

Every licensed insurance company doing business in Colorado shall prepare, implement, and maintain an antifraud plan. This requirement is not applicable to entities whose principle business is reinsurance, reinsurance agreements, or reinsurance claims transactions. The antifraud plan must outline procedures to:

1. Prevent, detect and investigate all forms of insurance fraud.

2. Educate appropriate employees about fraud detection and the company's antifraud plan.

3. Hire or contract for fraud investigators.

4. Report suspected or actual insurance fraud to the appropriate entities.

Every licensed insurance company, on or before the first day in March in each year, must provide a summary of its antifraud efforts as part of its annual report required by (C.R.S. §10-3-109). Bulletin B-1.11 provides answers to frequently asked questions on the department's annual summary reporting requirements. It is available at https://drive.google.com/file/d/0B7EeY5Lrg3_qcGlicEp0LTl2VXc/view.

FAIR CLAIMS PROCESSING
3 CCR 702-5:5-1-14

Insurers must make a decision on claims and/or pay benefits due within sixty days after receipt of a valid and complete claim unless there is a reasonable dispute between the parties concerning the claim, provided the insurer has complied with policy provisions.

COLORADO

Failure to make a decision and/or pay benefits due within sixty days may result in the following penalties:

1. If claim is $100 or less, the penalty shall not exceed $20.

2. If claim is greater than $100, the penalty shall be 8 percent annual interest on the amount of benefits due.

3. Civil penalty against insurer of $100 per day for each day if benefits are delayed more than sixty days.

A valid and complete claim is deemed received when:

1. All information and documents necessary to prove the insured's claim have been received by the insurer.

2. A reasonable investigation of the information submitted has been completed by the insurer, in compliance with §10-3-104, C.R.S.

3. The terms and conditions of the policy have been complied with by the insured.

4. Coverage under the policy for the insured has been established for the claim submitted.

5. There are no indicators on the claim requiring additional investigation before a decision can be made.

6. All repairs have been satisfactorily completed and the insured has given authorization to pay.

7. Negotiations or appraisals to determine the value of the claim have been completed.

8. Any litigation on the claim has been finally and fully adjudicated.

A reasonable dispute may include, but is not limited to:

1. Information necessary to make a decision on the claim has not been submitted or obtained.

2. Conflicting information is submitted or obtained and additional investigation is necessary.

COLORADO

3. The insured is not in compliance with the terms and conditions of the policy.

4. Coverage under the policy for the loss claimed has not been determined.

5. Indicators are present in the application or submission of the claim and additional investigation is necessary.

6. Litigation is commenced on the claim.

7. Negotiations or appraisals are in process to determine the value of the claim.

An insurer shall not fail to promptly settle claims, where liability has become reasonably clear, under one portion of the insurance policy in order to influence settlements under other portions of the insurance policy coverage, pursuant to §10-3-1104(1)(h)(XIII), C.R.S.

A good faith offer by the insurer to the insured within sixty days after the receipt of a valid and complete claim satisfies the requirements under this regulation.

CONNECTICUT

For details on cancellation procedures for the standard policy, refer to the Standard Policy section.

COMMERCIAL LINES
C. AUTO; CRIME; CGL; CIM; EQUIPMENT BREAKDOWN

Connecticut General Statutes §§38a-323 to 38a-326, 38a-330, and 47-255(g)

Cancellation during the Underwriting Period

Length of Underwriting Period: Sixty days.

Length of Notice: Ten days for nonpayment; thirty days for any other reason.

Reason for Cancellation: Required on the notice.

Proof Required: Registered mail, certified mail, or post office certificate of mailing.

Cancellation after the Underwriting Period

The policy may be cancelled **only** for the following reasons:

1. Nonpayment of premium.

2. Conviction of a crime arising out of acts that increase the hazard insured against.

3. Fraud or material misrepresentation in obtaining the policy or in making a claim.

4. Any willful or reckless act or omission by the insured that increases the hazard.

5. Physical changes in the property that increases the hazard.

6. The commissioner rules that continuation of the policy would place the insurer in violation of the law.

7. A material increase in the hazard insured against.

8. The insurer suffers a substantial loss of reinsurance on any of these lines.

Length of Notice: Ten days for reasons 1 through 5, above; sixty days for reasons 6 through 8, above.

CONNECTICUT

Reason for Cancellation: Required on the notice.

Proof Required: Registered mail, certified mail, or post office certificate.

Nonrenewal

Length of Notice: Sixty days.

Reason for Nonrenewal: Required on the notice.

Proof Required: Registered mail, certified mail, post office certificate of mailing, or, beginning on October 1, 2019, by electronic means, if agreed upon by the insurer and the named insured. (Connecticut General Statutes §38a-323, revised June 13, 2018 by 2018 Ct. HB 5206).

Other Cancellation/Nonrenewal Provisions

The insurer does not need to send a nonrenewal notice if the insured does not pay any advance premium required for renewal.

Whenever a commercial automobile or general liability insurance policy is nonrenewed or cancelled for whatever reason, the insurer shall furnish the insured with written reports for the insured portion of the period beginning four years prior to the nonrenewal or cancellation date and ending six months prior to that date. Such reports shall include the following:

1. Each policy number.

2. Each period of coverage provided.

3. Evidence that the reports are furnished by the insurer.

4. Written premiums.

5. Pricing information as specified by regulations.

6. A detailed listing of incurred losses.

If the policy is nonrenewed or cancelled by the insurer for reasons other than those permitting cancellation upon ten days' notice, such reports shall be provided to the insured first named in the policy or the insured's authorized producer, not later than the date of notice of nonrenewal or cancellation. If the policy is nonrenewed or cancelled by the insured, or cancelled by the insurer for any reason for which ten days' notice of cancellation is required, such reports shall be provided not later than thirty days of receipt of the written request from the insured first named in the policy or the insured's authorized producer.

CONNECTICUT

When a CGL form covers a condominium or townhouse association, notices of cancellation or nonrenewal must be sent to the first named insured, each unit owner, and each holder of a security interest to whom the insurer issued a certificate or memorandum of insurance.

For an OCP policy, all notices must be mailed to the named insured and the contractor named in the declarations. If the cancellation is for nonpayment, the contractor may avoid the cancellation by paying the premium prior to the effective date of the cancellation.

For Railroad Protective, all notices must be sent to the named insured, contractor, any involved governmental authority, and any other contracting party designated in the declarations. If the cancellation is for nonpayment, the contractor may avoid the cancellation by paying the premium prior to the effective date of the cancellation.

Failure of the insurer or its agent to provide the insured with the required notice of nonrenewal or premium billing shall entitle the insured to: 1) Renewal of the policy for a term of not less than one year, and 2) the privilege of pro rata cancellation at the lower of the current or previous year rates if exercised by the insured within sixty days from the renewal date or anniversary date. Renewal of a policy shall not constitute a waiver or estoppel with respect to grounds for cancellation that existed before the effective date of such renewal.

Transfer of any policy to an affiliate as a result of a merger or acquisition of control, shall provide notice to policyholders at least sixty days prior to the effective date of transfer. Such transfer is not considered a nonrenewal or cancellation of the policy.

Notice of nonrenewal must be given to the insured a minimum number of days in advance of the effective nonrenewal date for personal and commercial policies, including workers comp. Compliance with the minimum notice standards is determined by counting the number of calendar days beginning with the first day after the date of mailing of the transaction up to, but not including, the date the transaction is effective.

1. If an insurer intends to continue to insure a risk, either commercial or personal, but under terms or conditions less favorable than previously provided, the insurer must notify the insured by either sending a notice of nonrenewal or a conditional renewal notice. The conditional renewal notice must clearly state or be accompanied by a clear statement that identifies terms or conditions that may be less favorable to the insured under the ensuing policy.

2. Any significant reduction of coverage requires either a notice of nonrenewal or a conditional renewal notice. Some examples where conditional renewal notices are appropriate are:

   An increase in the policy's deductible or retention.

   A decrease in the limits of coverage.

   A new exclusion or deletion of coverage.

CONNECTICUT

3. The conditional renewal notice must comply with the advance number of days required by statute for nonrenewal of the particular type of policy. The conditional renewal notice must be sent by (a) registered or certified mail; (b) by mail evidenced by a United States Post Office certificate of mailing; or (c) delivered by the insurer to the insured by the required date.

4. The Department will not consider an insurer to be in violation of the requirements of Conn. Gen. Stat. § 38a-323 if the insurer provides a conditional renewal notice that gives the insured the advance number of days required by statute for nonrenewal, together with the statement of less favorable terms or conditions. (Bulletin PC-66).

AGRICULTURAL CAPITAL ASSETS; BOP;CAPITAL ASSETS; C. PROP; FARM

Connecticut General Statutes §§38a-323, 38a-324, and 38a-330

Cancellation during the Underwriting Period

Length of Underwriting Period: Sixty days.

Length of Notice: Ten days for nonpayment; thirty days for any other reason.

Reason for Cancellation: Required on the notice for all reasons other than nonpayment.

Proof Required: Registered mail, certified mail, or post office certificate.

Cancellation after the Underwriting Period

The policy may be cancelled **only** for the following reasons:

1. Nonpayment of premium.

2. Conviction of a crime arising out of acts that increase the hazard insured against.

3. Discovery of fraud or material misrepresentation by the insured in obtaining the policy or in perfecting any claim thereunder.

4. Any willful or reckless act or omission by the insured that increases the hazard.

5. Physical changes in the property that increases the hazard.

6. The commissioner rules that continuation of the policy would place the insurer in violation of the law.

CONNECTICUT

7. A material increase in the hazard insured against.

8. The insurer suffers a substantial loss of reinsurance on any of these lines.

Length of Notice: Ten days for reasons 1 through 5, above; sixty days for reasons 6 through 8, above.

Reason for Cancellation: Required on the notice for all reasons other than nonpayment of premium.

Proof Required: Registered mail, certified mail, or post office certificate.

Nonrenewal

Length of Notice: Sixty days.

Reason for Nonrenewal: Required on the notice.

Proof Required: Registered mail, certified mail, post office certificate or, beginning on October 1, 2019, by electronic means, if agreed upon by the insurer and the named insured. (Connecticut General Statutes §38a-323, revised June 13, 2018 by 2018 Ct. HB 5206).

Other Cancellation/Nonrenewal Provisions

Failure of the insurer or its agent to provide the insured with the required notice of nonrenewal or premium billing shall entitle the insured to: 1) renewal of the policy for a term of not less than one year, and 2) the privilege of pro-rata cancellation at the lower of the current or previous year rates if exercised by the insured within sixty days from the renewal date or anniversary date. Renewal of a policy shall not constitute a waiver or estoppel with respect to grounds for cancellation that existed before the effective date of such renewal.

If a loss is made payable to a designated mortgage holder who is not named in the policy as the insured, such interest in the policy may be cancelled by giving the mortgage holder a ten-day notice of cancellation.

PROFESSIONAL LIABILITY

Connecticut General Statutes §§38a-323, 38a-324, 38a-325, 38a-393 and 38a-395

Cancellation during the Underwriting Period

Length of Underwriting Period: Sixty days.

Length of Notice: Forty-five days for any reason.

CONNECTICUT

Reason for Cancellation: Required on the notice.

Proof Required: Certified mail, registered mail, or post office certificate of mailing.

Cancellation after the Underwriting Period

The policy may be canceled **only** for the following reasons:

1. Nonpayment of premium.

2. Conviction of a crime arising out of acts that increase the hazard insured against.

3. Discovery of fraud or material misrepresentation by the insured in obtaining the policy or in submitting a claim.

4. Any willful or reckless act or omission by the insured that increases the hazard.

5. Physical changes in the property that increases the hazard.

6. The commissioner rules that continuation of the policy would place the insurer in violation of the law.

7. A material increase in the hazard insured against.

8. The insurer suffers a substantial loss of reinsurance on any of these lines.

Length of Notice: Ninety days.

Reason for Cancellation: Required on the notice.

Proof Required: Certified mail, registered mail, or post office certificate of mailing.

Nonrenewal

Length of Notice: Ninety days.

Reason for Nonrenewal: Required on the notice.

Proof Required: Registered mail, certified mail, post office certificate or, beginning on October 1, 2019, by electronic means, if agreed upon by the insurer and the named insured. (Connecticut General Statutes §38a-323, revised June 13, 2018 by 2018 Ct. HB 5206).

CONNECTICUT

Other Cancellation/Nonrenewal Provisions

Insurance companies are required to report the number of cancellations and refusals to renew professional liability insurance policies for the preceding year by March first each year.

Failure of the insurer or its agent to provide the insured with the required notice of nonrenewal or premium billing shall entitle the insured to: 1) renewal of the policy for a term of not less than one year, and 2) the privilege of pro rata cancellation at the lower of the current or previous year rates if exercised by the insured within sixty days from the renewal date or anniversary date. Renewal of a policy shall not constitute a waiver or estoppel with respect to grounds for cancellation that existed before the effective date of such renewal.

For policies issued on a claims made basis only: Policies delivered, issued for delivery, or renewed shall contain: 1) a provision for the purchase of prior acts coverage, and 2) a contractual right of the insured to purchase at any time during the policy period and not later than thirty days after termination of such policy period equivalent coverage for all claims occurring during an insured policy period regardless of when made.

Individuals, partnerships, corporations, or unincorporated associations providing professional liability insurance for its employees must provide forty-five days' notice preceding the effective date of cancellation or discontinuation. If notice is not given, the individual or entity shall be liable for benefits to the same extent as the professional liability insurer would have been liable.

WORKERS COMPENSATION

Connecticut General Statutes §§31-321, 31-348, and 38a-323

Cancellation Notice Requirements

Length of Notice: Cancellation shall not become effective until fifteen days after notice of such cancellation has been filed with the Chairman of the Workers Compensation Commission.

Reason for Cancellation: Required on the notice.

Proof Required: Proof of mailing.

Nonrenewal Notice Requirements

Length of Notice: Sixty days.

Reason for Nonrenewal: Required on the notice.

CONNECTICUT

Proof Required: Registered mail, certified mail, post office certificate or, beginning on October 1, 2019, by electronic means, if agreed upon by the insurer and the named insured. (Connecticut General Statutes §38a-323, revised June 13, 2018 by 2018 Ct. HB 5206).

SURPLUS LINES

Connecticut General Statutes §§38a-323 and 38a-324

Surplus lines insurers must follow the cancellation and nonrenewal requirements for admitted companies.

Premium billing notices shall be provided by any surplus lines insurer to the insured at least sixty days in advance of the renewal or anniversary date of the policy. Notices of nonrenewal or premium billing may be provided by the surplus lines insurer or its duly authorized representative.

Failure of any surplus lines insurer to provide the insured with the required notice of nonrenewal or premium billing shall entitle the insured to an extension of the policy for a period of ninety days after the renewal or anniversary date of such policy, provided if the surplus lines insurer fails to provide the required notice on or before the renewal or anniversary date of such policy. In the event of such a ninety-day extension of coverage, the premium for the extended period of coverage shall be the current rate or the previous rate, whichever is lower.

FINANCED PREMIUMS

Connecticut General Statutes §38a-170

If the premium finance agreement contains a power of attorney enabling the insurance company to cancel any insurance contract or contracts listed in the agreement on account of any default on the part of the insured, the insurance contract or contracts shall not be cancelled by the insurance premium finance company unless such cancellation is in accordance with the provisions in this section. Not less than ten-days' written notice shall be mailed by first class mail to the insured, at his last known address, of the intent of the insurance premium finance company to cancel the insurance contract unless the default is cured within such ten-day period. After expiration of the ten day period the finance company may request, in the name of the insured, cancellation of such insurance contract by mailing to the insurer a notice of cancellation, and the insurance contract may be cancelled as if such notice of cancellation had been submitted by the insured himself, but without requiring the return of the insurance contract or contracts. The cancellation is processed as of the finance company's original default date. All statutory, regulatory, and contractual provisions or restrictions providing that the insurance contract may not be cancelled unless notice is given to a governmental agency, mortgagee, or other third party shall apply where cancellation is effected under the provisions of this section. The insurer shall give the prescribed notice on behalf of itself or the insured to any such governmental agency,

CONNECTICUT

mortgagee or other third party on or before the second business day after the day it receives the notice of cancellation from the insurance premium finance company and shall determine the effective date of cancellation taking into consideration the number of days' notice required to complete the cancellation. Return of the policy by the insured is not required. Whenever an insurance contract is cancelled in accordance with the provisions of this section, the insurer shall return whatever gross unearned premiums are due under the insurance contract to the insurance premium finance company effecting the cancellation for crediting to the account of the insured. In the event that the crediting of return premiums to the account of the insured results in a surplus over the amount due from the insured to the insurance premium finance company, such company shall refund such excess to the insured, provided no such refund shall be required if the surplus amounts to less than one dollar.

PERSONAL LINES

DWELLING & HOMEOWNERS

Connecticut General Statutes §§38a-307, 38a-323, 38a-323a to 38a-323c, and 38a-975 to 38a-999

Cancellation during the Underwriting Period

Length of Underwriting Period: Sixty days.

Length of Notice: Ten days for nonpayment; thirty days for any other reason.

Reason for Cancellation: Required on the notice.

Proof Required: Registered mail, certified mail, or certificate of mailing.

Cancellation after the Underwriting Period

The policy may be cancelled **only** for the following reasons:

1. Nonpayment of premium.

2. Material misrepresentation on the application.

3. Substantial change in the risk.

Length of Notice: Ten days for nonpayment; thirty days for any other reason.

Reason for Cancellation: Required on the notice.

Proof Required: Registered mail, certified mail, or certificate of mailing.

CONNECTICUT

Nonrenewal

Length of Notice: Sixty days.

Reason for Nonrenewal: Required on the notice.

Proof Required: Registered mail, certified mail, post office certificate or, beginning on October 1, 2019, by electronic means, if agreed upon by the insurer and the named insured. (Connecticut General Statutes §38a-323, revised June 13, 2018 by 2018 Ct. HB 5206).

Other Cancellation/Nonrenewal Provisions

The only cancellation requirements written into the Connecticut General Statutes say that the policy may be cancelled at any time and for any reason with a thirty-day notice (ten days for nonpayment). If an insurer adopts the ISO amendatory endorsements (DP 01 06 and HO 01 06), it must abide by the provisions in those endorsements.

Each insured aged fifty-five or over has the right to designate a third party to receive copies of notices of cancellation or nonrenewal. Notices to the third party are the same provisions as those going to the named insured. The designated person must provide written acceptance to the insurer. When a third party is so designated, all such notices and copies shall be mailed in an envelope clearly marked on its face with the following: "IMPORTANT INSURANCE POLICY INFORMATION: OPEN IMMEDIATELY". The copy of the notice of cancellation or nonrenewal transmitted to the third party shall be governed by the same law and policy provisions that govern the notice being transmitted to the senior citizen insured. The designation of a third party shall not constitute acceptance of any liability on the part of the third party or insurer for services provided to the senior citizen insured.

Failure of the insurer or its agent to provide the insured with the required notice of nonrenewal or premium billing shall entitle the insured to: 1) renewal of the policy for a term of not less than one year, and 2) the privilege of pro rata cancellation at the lower of the current or previous year rates if exercised by the insured within sixty days from the renewal date or anniversary date. Renewal of a policy shall not constitute a waiver or estoppel with respect to grounds for cancellation that existed before the effective date of such renewal.

PERSONAL AUTO

Connecticut General Statutes §§38a-323, 38a-341 through 38a-345, and 38a-358

Cancellation during the Underwriting Period

Length of Underwriting Period: Sixty days.

Length of Notice: Fifteen days for nonpayment of the first premium of a new policy; ten days for nonpayment of any other premium or material misrepresentation; forty-five days for any other reason.

CONNECTICUT

Reason for Cancellation: Required on the notice. The amendatory endorsement (PP 01 54) does not contain the requirement for the reason for cancellation to be shown, implying that the reason is not required. However, the Connecticut code is clear that it must be shown.

Proof Required: Registered mail, certified mail, or certificate of mailing.

Cancellation after the Underwriting Period

The policy may be cancelled **only** for the following reasons:

1. Nonpayment of premium.

2. Revocation or suspension of the driver's license or registration of the named insured.

3. Revocation or suspension of the driver's license or registration of any driver who lives with the named insured or customarily operates an automobile insured under the policy.

   Such revocation or suspension must have occurred during the policy period. If the policy period is other than one year, the revocation/suspension must have occurred since the last anniversary of the original effective date.

Length of Notice: Ten days for nonpayment; forty-five days for any other allowable reason.

Reason for Cancellation: Required on the notice. The amendatory endorsement (PP 01 54) does not contain the requirement that the reason for cancellation to be shown, implying that the reason is not required. However, the Connecticut code is clear that it must be shown.

Proof Required: Registered mail, certified mail, or certificate of mailing.

Nonrenewal

Length of Notice: Sixty days.

Reason for Nonrenewal: Required on the notice. The amendatory endorsement (PP 01 54) does not contain the requirement that the reason for nonrenewal to be shown, implying that the reason is not required. However, the Connecticut code is clear that it must be shown.

Proof Required: Registered mail, certified mail, post office certificate or, beginning on October 1, 2019, by electronic means, if agreed upon by the insurer and the named insured. (Connecticut General Statutes §38a-323, revised June 13, 2018 by 2018 Ct. HB 5206).

CONNECTICUT

Other Cancellation/Nonrenewal Provisions

1. If the policy is written for a term of less than six months, the insurer may nonrenew every six months, beginning six months after the original effective date.

2. If the policy is written for a term of one year or longer, the insurer may nonrenew only at each anniversary of the original effective date.

3. Each insured aged fifty-five or over has the right to designate a third party to receive copies of notices of cancellation or nonrenewal. Notices to the third party are the same provisions as those going to the named insured. The designated person must provide written acceptance to the insurer. When a third party is so designated, all such notices and copies shall be mailed in an envelope clearly marked on its face with the following: "IMPORTANT INSURANCE POLICY INFORMATION: OPEN IMMEDIATELY". The copy of the notice of cancellation or nonrenewal transmitted to the third party shall be governed by the same law and policy provisions that govern the notice being transmitted to the senior citizen insured. The designation of a third party shall not constitute acceptance of any liability on the part of the third party or insurer for services provided to the senior citizen insured.

4. Failure of the insurer or its agent to provide the insured with the required notice of nonrenewal or premium billing shall entitle the insured to:

    a. Renewal of the policy for a term of not less than one year.

    b. The privilege of pro-rata cancellation at the lower of the current or previous year rates if exercised by the insured within sixty days from the renewal date or anniversary date. Renewal of a policy shall not constitute a waiver or estoppel with respect to grounds for cancellation that existed before the effective date of such renewal.

5. The commissioner may require each insurance company to provide monthly policy information required for purposes of the Online Insurance Verification System.

Declinations

In Connecticut, an insurer may not base a declination, cancellation or nonrenewal on any of the following reasons:

1. The race, religion, nationality, or ethnicity of the applicant or named insured.

2. Solely on the lawful occupation or profession of the applicant or named insured, except that this provision shall not apply to any insurer that limits its market to one lawful occupation or profession or to several related lawful occupations or professions.

CONNECTICUT

3. On the principal location of the insured motor vehicle unless such decision is for a business purpose that is not a mere pretext for unfair discrimination.

4. Solely on the age, sex, or marital status of an applicant or an insured, except that this subdivision shall not apply to an insurer in an insurer group if one or more other insurers in the group would not decline an application for essentially similar coverage based upon such reasons.

5. On the fact that the applicant or named insured previously obtained insurance coverage through a residual market.

6. On the fact that another insurer previously declined to insure the applicant or terminated an existing policy in which the applicant was the named insured.

7. The first or second accident within the current experience period in relation to which the applicant or insured was not convicted of a moving traffic violation and was not at fault.

8. Solely on information contained in an insured's or applicant's credit history or credit rating or solely on an applicant's lack of credit history. For the purposes of this subdivision (8) of this section, an insurer shall not be deemed to have declined, cancelled or nonrewewed a policy if coverage is available through an affiliated insurer.

PERSONAL UMBRELLA

Connecticut General Statutes §38a-323

Cancellation during the Underwriting Period

Length of Underwriting Period: Sixty days.

Length of Notice: Ten days for nonpayment; thirty days for any other reason.

Reason for Cancellation: Required on the notice.

Proof Required: Registered mail, certified mail, or certificate of mailing.

Cancellation after the Underwriting Period

The policy may be cancelled **only** for:

1. Nonpayment of premium.

2. Material misrepresentation on the application.

3. Substantial change in the risk.

CONNECTICUT

Length of Notice: Ten days for nonpayment; thirty days for any other reason.

Reason for Cancellation: Required on the notice.

Proof Required: Registered mail, certified mail, or certificate of mailing.

Nonrenewal

Length of Notice: Sixty days.

Reason for Cancellation: Required on the notice.

Proof Required: Registered mail, certified mail, post office certificate or, beginning on October 1, 2019, by electronic means, if agreed upon by the insurer and the named insured. (Connecticut General Statutes §38a-323, revised June 13, 2018 by 2018 Ct. HB 5206).

Other Cancellation/Nonrenewal Provisions

Each insured aged fifty-five or over has the right to designate a third party to receive copies of notices of cancellation or nonrenewal. Notices to the third party are the same provisions as those going to the named insured. The designated person must provide written acceptance to the insurer.

Failure of the insurer or its agent to provide the insured with the required notice of nonrenewal or premium billing shall entitle the insured to:

1. Renewal of the policy for a term of not less than one year.

2. The privilege of pro-rata cancellation at the lower of the current or previous year rates if exercised by the insured within sixty days from the renewal date or anniversary date. Renewal of a policy shall not constitute a waiver or estoppel with respect to grounds for cancellation that existed before the effective date of such renewal.

FRAUD

Connecticut General Statutes §§38a-356, 53a-215

General Information and Definitions

A person is guilty of insurance fraud when the person, with the intent to injure, defraud or deceive any insurance company:

1. Presents or causes to be presented to any insurance company, any written or oral statement including computer-generated documents as part of, or in support of, any application for any policy of insurance or a claim for payment or other benefit

pursuant to such policy of insurance, knowing that such statement contains any false, incomplete, or misleading information concerning any fact or thing material to such application or claim.

2. Assists, abets, solicits, or conspires with another to prepare or make any written or oral statement that is intended to be presented to any insurance company in connection with, or in support of, any application for any policy of insurance or any claim for payment or other benefit pursuant to such policy of insurance, knowing that such statement contains any false, incomplete, or misleading information concerning any fact or thing material to such application or claim for the purposes of defrauding such insurance company.

"Statement" includes, but is not limited to, any notice, statement, invoice, account, estimate of property damages, bill for services, test result, or other evidence of loss, injury, or expense.

"Insurer" or "insurance company" includes any person or combination of persons doing any kind or form of insurance business other than a fraternal benefit society, and shall include a receiver of any insurer when the context reasonably permits.

Reporting Requirements

The Connecticut Department of Insurance Fraud Unit (the "Unit") uses the NAIC Uniform Suspected Insurance Fraud Reporting Form available on both the NAIC web site as well as the Connecticut's Fraud Unit Web site at: http://www.ct.gov/cid/cwp/view.asp?q=254424.

In addition, on or before March 31 of each year, each insurance company must provide the insurance commissioner annual reports detailing all information received or investigations conducted by such company during the past year concerning insurance fraud in any claim under a motor vehicle policy.

To assist in this reporting, the unit has posted the designated report form and the instructions to complete it on its web site at the above address. Completed forms should be emailed to cid.fraud@ct.gov.

Any questions or further guidance needed in completing the report should be sent to the above email address.

Penalties and Statute of Limitations

Insurance fraud is a class D felony which carries a term of imprisonment not less than one year nor more than five years or a fine in an amount not to exceed $5,000 dollars, or both fine and imprisonment within the given parameters. (C.G.S.A. § 53a-41 and C.G.S.A. §53a-35a).

CONNECTICUT

There is a three year statute of limitations for tort actions in Connecticut. (C.G.S.A. §52-577).

Antifraud Procedures

The Connecticut Department of Insurance Fraud Unit has a comprehensive guide to combating insurance and arson fraud located on its Web site at: http://www.ct.gov/cid/cwp/view.asp?q=254424.

This guide defines and provides procedures to reasonably prevent multiple types of fraud, such as: arson fraud, auto insurance fraud, health insurance fraud, life insurance fraud, financial services fraud, workers' compensation fraud, and property and casualty fraud.

FAIR CLAIMS PROCESSING

Connecticut General Statutes §38a-816

Unfair claim practices are included with all unfair methods of competition and unfair and deceptive acts or practices are defined as follows. For in-depth explanation, refer to statute.

1. Misrepresenting pertinent facts or policy provisions;

2. Failing to acknowledge and act with reasonable promptness upon communications regarding claims;

3. Failing to adopt and implement reasonable standards for investigation of claims;

4. Refusing to pay claims without conducting a reasonable investigation;

5. Failing to affirm or deny coverage within a reasonable time after receipt of proof of loss statements;

6. Not attempting in good faith to promptly, fairly and equitably settle claims in which liability is clear;

7. Compelling insureds to litigate to recovered amounts due by offering substantially less than amounts ultimately recovered;

8. Attempting to settle for less than a reasonable man would have expected based on written or printed advertising material accompanying or made part of an application;

9. Attempting to settle a claim on the basis of an application altered without insured's knowledge;

CONNECTICUT

10. Making payments without statement identifying what coverage the payment is being made;

11. Making claimants aware of company's practice of appealing arbitration awards in favor of insureds in order to compel them to accept lower settlements;

12. Delaying investigation by requiring proof of loss that is substantially the same as original proof of loss;

13. Failing to promptly settle claims under one portion of policy when liability is reasonably clear in order to influence settlement under another portion;

14. Failure to promptly provide reasonable explanation of denial of claim;

15. Using as a basis for cash settlement with a first party auto claim an amount that is less than what the insurer would pay for repairs unless agreed to by the insured or provided by the policy.

DELAWARE

For details on cancellation procedures for the standard policy, refer to the Standard Policy section.

COMMERCIAL LINES
BUSINESSOWNERS; C. PROP.

18 Delaware Code §§3911, 4120 through 4124; I.S.O. CP 02 99 06 07

Cancellation during the Underwriting Period

Length of Underwriting Period: Sixty days.

Length of Notice: Ten days for nonpayment; sixty days for any other reason.

Reason for Cancellation: Required.

Proof Required: Certified mail.

Cancellation after the Underwriting Period

The policy may be cancelled **only** for the following reasons:

1. Nonpayment of premium.

2. Fraud or material misrepresentation in obtaining the policy, or in presenting a claim under the policy.

3. Willful or reckless acts or omissions that increase any hazard insured against.

4. The occurrence of a change in the risk that substantially increases any hazard insured against after insurance coverage has been issued or renewed.

5. A violation of any local fire, health, safety, building, or construction regulation or ordinance with respect to any covered property or its occupancy that substantially increases any hazard insured against.

6. A determination by the insurance commissioner that the continuation of the policy would place the insurer in violation of the Delaware insurance laws.

7. Real property taxes owing on the insured property have been delinquent for two or more years and continue to be delinquent at the time notice of cancellation is issued.

DELAWARE

Reasons 8 through 14 below are included as part of an ISO endorsement and are not statutory.

8. The building has been vacant or unoccupied for sixty consecutive days. This provision does not apply to:

    a. seasonal unoccupancy; or

    b. buildings in the course of construction, renovation, or addition.

    c. buildings in which the Vacancy Permit endorsement applies.

9. If 65 percent of the rental units in a building are unoccupied or if 65 percent of its floor space is vacant, the building is considered vacant or unoccupied.

10. If, after a covered loss, the insured has not begun (and contracted for) repairs within thirty days after the insurer's initial payment.

11. If the building has been ordered vacated, demolished, or has been declared unsafe by a governmental authority.

12. If "fixed and salvageable" items are being removed from the building and not being replaced. Again, this doesn't apply during remodeling or renovation.

13. If the insured does not furnish utility service to the building for thirty consecutive days (other than during seasonal unoccupancy).

14. If the insured is more than one year behind in payment of property taxes on the building. This provision does not apply if the insured is involved in a "bona fide dispute" with the taxing authority.

Length of Notice: Ten days for nonpayment; sixty days for any other reason. The ISO endorsement indicates a minimum five day notification requirement.

Reason for Cancellation: Required.

Proof Required: Certified mail.

Nonrenewal

Length of Notice: Sixty days.

Reason for Cancellation: Required.

Proof Required: Certified mail.

DELAWARE

Other Cancellation/Nonrenewal Provisions

Proof of mailing must be retained for not less than one year.

The declination or termination may not be based on any of the following:

1. The race, religion, nationality, ethnic group, age, sex, or marital status of the applicant or named insured.

2. The lawful occupation or profession of the applicant or named insured. (This provision does not apply to insurers, agents, or brokers who limit their markets to one lawful occupation or group of occupations).

3. The age or location of the residence of the applicant or named insured unless such decision is for a business purpose that is not a mere pretext for unfair discrimination.

4. A previous declination or termination of the applicant.

5. The fact that the applicant or named insured was previously covered through a residual market insurance mechanism.

COMMERCIAL AUTOMOBILE

18 Delaware Code §§3903, 3904, 3905 and 3911

Cancellation during the Underwriting Period

Length of Underwriting Period: Sixty days.

Length of Notice: No less than twenty days for any reason.

Reason for Cancellation: Required on the notice.

Proof Required: Certified mail or USPS Intelligent Mail barcode (IMb). Proof of mailing must be retained for at least a year.

Cancellation after the Underwriting Period

1. Nonpayment of premium.

2. The policy was obtained through a material misrepresentation.

3. Any insured violated any of the terms and conditions of the policy.

DELAWARE

4. The named insured knowingly failed to disclose fully his/her motor vehicle accidents and moving traffic violations, or his/her losses covered under any automobile physical damage or comprehensive coverage, for the preceding thirty-six months, if called for in the application.

5. As to renewal of the policy, if the insured at any time while the policy was in force failed to disclose fully to the insurer, upon request therefore, facts relative to accidents and losses incurred material to underwriting of the risk.

6. Any insured made a false or fraudulent claim or knowingly aided or abetted another in the presentation of such a claim.

7. The named insured or any other operator who either resides in the same household or customarily operates an automobile insured under such policy:

    a. Has, within the thirty-six months prior to the notice of cancellation or nonrenewal, had a driver's license under suspension or revocation, except a child whose license has been revoked or suspended for a nondriving-related drug offense.

    b. Has a history of and is subject to epilepsy or heart attacks, and such individual cannot produce a certificate from a physician testifying to his unqualified ability to operate a motor vehicle safely.

    c. Has an accident record, conviction record (criminal or traffic), physical, mental or other condition which is such that her operation of an automobile might endanger the public safety.

    d. Has, while the policy is in force, engaged in a competitive speed contest while operating an automobile insured under the policy.

    e. Is addicted to or uses narcotics or other drugs.

    f. Uses alcoholic beverages to excess thereby impairing his ability to operate a motor vehicle.

    g. Has been convicted or forfeited bail, during the thirty-six months immediately preceding the notice of cancellation or nonrenewal, for:

        (1) Any felony.

        (2) Criminal negligence resulting in death, homicide or assault arising out of the operation of a motor vehicle.

DELAWARE

      (3) Operating a motor vehicle while in an intoxicated condition or while under the influence of drugs.

      (4) Leaving the scene of an accident without stopping to report.

      (5) Theft or unlawful taking of a motor vehicle.

      (6) Making false statements in an application for a driver's license.

  h. Has been convicted of, or forfeited bail, for three or more violations, the point total for which exceeds eight points, or three at fault accidents in which claims are paid in excess of $250 per accident within the thirty-six months immediately preceding the notice of cancellation or nonrenewal, of any law, ordinance or regulation limiting the speed of motor vehicles or any of the provisions of the motor vehicle laws of any state, violation of which constitutes a dangerous moving violation whether or not the violations were repetitions of the same offense or different offenses.

8. The insured automobile is:

  a. So mechanically defective that its operation might endanger public safety.

  b. Used in carrying passengers for hire or compensation, except that the use of an automobile for a car pool shall not be considered use of an automobile for hire or compensation.

  c. Used in the business of transportation of flammables or explosives.

  d. An authorized emergency vehicle.

  e. Modified or changed in condition during the policy period so as to increase the risk substantially.

  f. Subject to an inspection law and has not been inspected or, if inspected fails to qualify.

Length of Notice: Ten days for nonpayment; thirty days for any other reason.

Reason for Cancellation: Required on the notice. Even though the amendatory endorsement is silent on the matter, the reason must be shown because the Delaware Code requires it.

Proof Required: Certified mail or USPS Intelligent Mail barcode (IMb). Proof of mailing must be retained for at least a year. The amendatory endorsement indicates proof of mailing is sufficient proof, however, statute requires certified mail or IMb.

DELAWARE

Nonrenewal

Length of Notice: Thirty days.

Reason for Nonrenewal: Required on the notice. Even though the amendatory endorsement is silent on the matter, indicating no restrictions on the allowable reasons for nonrenewal, the Delaware Code limits nonrenewal to the same eight reasons allowable for cancellation after the underwriting period. The Delaware Code also requires that the reason for nonrenewal must be shown on the notice.

Proof Required: Certified mail or USPS Intelligent Mail barcode (IMb). Proof of mailing must be retained for at least a year.

Other Cancellation/Nonrenewal Provisions

For other Cancellation and Nonrenewal Provisions, please contact the Delaware Department of Insurance.

CRIME

Delaware makes no changes from the standard policy.

AGRICULTURAL CAPITAL ASSETS; CAPITAL ASSETS; COMMERCIAL GENERAL LIABILITY (CGL; LIQUOR; POLLUTION; PRODUCTS/COMPLETED OPERATIONS)

Code of Delaware Regulations 18 2100 – 2102, found at http://regulations.delaware.gov/AdminCode/title18/2100/2102.pdf

The only change shown on the Delaware amendatory endorsement is that a sixty-day notice of nonrenewal is required. The notice must be sent via certified mail.

Cancellation during the Underwriting Period

Length of Underwriting Period: Sixty days.

Length of Notice: Ten days.

Reason for Cancellation: Not required.

Proof Required: Certified mail; regular mail for nonpayment of premium.

Cancellation after the Underwriting Period

The policy may be cancelled **only** for the following reasons:

1. Nonpayment of premium.

DELAWARE

2. Material misrepresentation on the application.

3. Increased hazard or material change in the risk.

4. Substantial breaches of contractual duties.

5. Fraudulent acts by the insured against the insurer.

6. The insured does not cooperate with the insurer in loss control efforts.

7. Loss of, or reduction in, reinsurance.

8. Material increase in exposure due to changes in case law.

9. Loss of, or reduction in, insurance capacity.

Length of Notice: Ten days for nonpayment; sixty days for any other reason.

Reason for Cancellation: Required on the notice.

Proof Required: Certified mail; regular mail for nonpayment.

Nonrenewal

Length of Notice: Sixty days.

Reason for Nonrenewal: Required on the notice.

Proof Required: Certified mail.

Other Provisions

Mid-term premium increases: No mid-term premium increases are allowed unless the insurer and insured agree after good faith negotiations, or the insurer has written approval from the Commissioner.

COMMERCIAL GENERAL LIABILITY
(OCP; RAILROAD PROTECTIVE; UNDERGROUND STORAGE TANKS)

The only change shown on the Delaware amendatory endorsement is that a sixty-day notice of nonrenewal is required. The notice must be sent via certified mail. Railroad Protective: ISO Form CG 00 35 12 07 Underground Storage Tanks: ISO Form CG 00 42 12 04.

Cancellation during the Underwriting Period

Length of Underwriting Period: Sixty days.

Length of Notice: Ten days; UST policy requires a sixty-day notice.

DELAWARE

Reason for Cancellation: Not required.

Proof Required: Certified mail; regular mail for nonpayment.

Cancellation after the Underwriting Period

The policy may be cancelled **only** for the following reasons:

1. Nonpayment of premium.
2. Material misrepresentation on the application.
3. Increased hazard or material change in the risk.
4. Substantial breaches of contractual duties.
5. Fraudulent acts by the insured against the insurer.
6. The insured does not cooperate with the insurer in loss control efforts.
7. Loss of, or reduction in, reinsurance.
8. Material increase in exposure due to changes in case law.
9. Loss of, or reduction in, insurance capacity.

Length of Notice: Ten days for nonpayment or material misrepresentation; sixty days for any other reason. (CG 00 42 12 04)

Reason for Cancellation: Not required.

Proof Required: Certified mail; regular mail for nonpayment.

Nonrenewal

Length of Notice: Sixty days.

Reason for Cancellation: Required on the notice.

Proof Required: Certified mail.

Other Cancellation/Nonrenewal Provisions

Marine and transportation policies may cover underground storage tanks. (18 Del. Admin. Code 2101-3.0).

DELAWARE

For other Cancellation and Nonrenewal Provisions, please contact the Delaware Department of Insurance.

COMMERCIAL INLAND MARINE

Delaware makes no changes from the standard policy.

COMMERCIAL PROPERTY; & FARM

18 Delaware Code §§4122 through 4124

Declinations

In addition to outright declination, the term also includes the offering of coverage with another company in the same group that is different than the one requested on the application. Declination also includes the offering of insurance upon different terms than requested on the application.

If an insurer, an agent, or a broker declines a submission, it must provide the reason(s) for the declination or an explanation that the reasons will be provided within twenty-one days upon request from the applicant. The applicant must make such a request within ninety days.

An insurer making a declination must also make the reason(s) known, in writing, to its agent or broker. If the agent or broker cannot secure coverage for the applicant in the admitted market (other than in the residual market), the agent or broker must send the applicant a written explanation.

All agents, brokers, and direct-writing insurers must, upon request, provide a prospective customer with an application for property coverage.

Cancellation during the Underwriting Period

Length of Underwriting Period: Sixty days.

Length of Notice: Ten days for nonpayment; thirty days for any other reason.

Reason for Cancellation: Required on the notice.

Proof Required: Certified mail. Proof of mailing must be retained for at least one year.

Cancellation after the Underwriting Period

The policy may be cancelled **only** for the following reasons:

1. Nonpayment of premium.

2. Fraud or material misrepresentation on the application or in presenting a claim under the policy.

DELAWARE

3. Willful or reckless acts or omissions that increase any hazard insured against.

4. A change in the risk that substantially increases any hazard insured against.

5. Violation of local codes (such as local fire or building codes) with respect to any covered property or its occupancy that substantially increases any hazard insured against.

6. The commissioner determines that to continue the policy would place the insurer in violation of Delaware laws.

7. Real property taxes on the insured property have been delinquent for two or more years.

Length of Notice: Ten days for nonpayment; thirty days for any other reason.

Reason for Cancellation: Required on the notice.

Proof Required: Certified mail. Proof of mailing must be retained for at least one year.

Nonrenewal

Length of Notice: Thirty days.

Reason for Nonrenewal: Required on the notice.

Proof Required: Certified mail. Proof of mailing must be retained for at least one year.

Other Cancellation/Nonrenewal Provisions

The declination or termination may not be based on any of the following:

1. The race, religion, nationality, ethnic group, age, sex, or marital status of the applicant or named insured.

2. The lawful occupation or profession of the applicant or named insured.

    This provision does not apply to insurers, agents, or brokers who limit their markets to one lawful occupation or group of occupations.

3. The age or location of the residence of the applicant or named insured unless such decision is for a business purpose that is not a mere pretext for unfair discrimination.

DELAWARE

4. A previous declination or termination of the applicant.

5. The fact that the applicant or named insured was previously covered through a residual market insurance mechanism.

COMMERCIAL UMBRELLA, FARM UMB., & PROF. LIAB.
18 Delaware Code §531
Cancellation during the Underwriting Period

Length of Underwriting Period: Sixty days.

Length of Notice: Ten days for any reason.

Reason for Cancellation: Required on the notice.

Proof Required: Certified mail.

Cancellation after the Underwriting Period

The policy may be cancelled or nonrenewed **only** for the following reasons:

1. Nonpayment of premium.

2. Material misrepresentation or nondisclosure to the company of a material fact at the time of acceptance of the risk.

3. Increased hazard or material change in the risk assumed which could not have been reasonably contemplated by the parties at the time of the application.

4. Substantial breach of contractual duties, conditions or warranties that materially affect the nature and/or insurability of the risk.

5. Fraudulent acts against the company by the insured or its representatives that materially affect the nature of the risk insured.

6. Lack of cooperation from the insured on loss control matters affecting insurability of the risk.

7. Bona fide loss of or substantial changes in applicable reinsurance.

8. Material increase in exposure arising out of changes in statutory or case law subsequent to the issuance of the insurance contract.

DELAWARE

9. Bona fide loss of or reduction in available insurance capacity.

10. Any other reasons approved by the commissioner.

Length of Notice: Ten days for nonpayment; for all other reasons, notices must be sent at least sixty days but not more than 120 days prior to the effective date.

Reason for Cancellation: Required on the notice.

Proof Required: Certified mail. The amendatory endorsement does not mention certified mail.

Nonrenewal

Length of Notice: At least sixty days but not more than 120 days prior to the effective date.

Reason for Nonrenewal: Required on the notice.

Proof Required: Certified mail.

Other Cancellation/Nonrenewal Provisions

All notices of cancellation, except those for nonpayment of premium, must contain a statement advising the insured that the insured may file a written complaint about the cancellation with the Delaware Insurance Department.

Even though the amendatory endorsement (CU 02 16) is silent on the matter, the Delaware Code requires that the reason must be shown.

CRIME

Delaware makes no changes from the standard policy.

EQUIPMENT BREAKDOWN

Delaware makes no changes from the standard policy.

MANAGEMENT PROTECTION

The only changes Delaware makes from the standard policy are to require a sixty-day notice by certified mail for nonrenewal and to require the company to provide at least five days' notice to the agent or broker who wrote the policy before sending notice to the named organization.

DELAWARE

WORKERS' COMPENSATION

Delaware Code 19, §2378; 18, §408

Length of Underwriting Period: The standard workers' compensation policy allows the insurer to cancel the policy at any time for any reason.

Length of Notice: Ten days.

Reason for Cancellation: Not required.

Proof Required: The standard policy does not indicate that any proof of mailing is necessary.

Nonrenewal

Length of Notice: Sixty days.

Reason for Cancellation: Not required.

Proof Required: Certified mail.

SURPLUS LINES

The Delaware cancellation and nonrenewal laws do not apply to surplus lines.

FINANCED PREMIUMS

18 Delaware Code §4809

If the premium finance agreement contains a power of attorney, the finance company may request, in the name of the insured, that the insurer cancel the policy due to nonpayment. The finance company must first give the insured ten days to pay. If the insured fails to make payment within that ten day period, then the finance company mails the notice of cancellation to the insurer and the cancellation is processed as of the finance company's original default date. Return of the policy by the insured is not required. The insurer shall return whatever gross unearned premiums are due under the contract, but in no event shall the period for payment exceed ninety days after the effective date of the cancellation. Certified mail is required.

A premium finance agreement may provide for the payment of a delinquency charge per installment of at least $1 but may not exceed a maximum charge of 5 percent of the delinquent installment of $5, whichever is less, for each installment which is in default for a period of ten days or more. If the default results in the cancellation of any insurance contract listed in the agreement, the agreement may provide for the payment by the insured of a cancellation

DELAWARE

charge equal to the difference between any delinquency charge imposed in respect to the installment in default as permitted hereinabove and the sum of $5. No other penalties may be imposed. (CDR 18-2000-2001).

PERSONAL LINES
DWELLING FIRE & HOMEOWNERS
18 Delaware Code §§4122 and 4123

Declinations

In addition to outright declination, the term also includes the offering of coverage with another company in the same group that is different than the one requested on the application. Declination also includes the offering of insurance upon different terms than requested on the application.

If an insurer, an agent, or a broker declines a submission, it must provide the reason(s) for the declination or an explanation that the reasons will be provided upon request from the applicant. The applicant must make such a request within ninety days.

An insurer making a declination must also make the reason(s) known, in writing, to its agent or broker. If the agent or broker cannot secure coverage for the applicant in the admitted market (other than in the residual market), the agent or broker must send the applicant a written explanation.

All agents, brokers, and direct-writing insurers must, upon request, provide a prospective customer with an application for property coverage.

Cancellation during the Underwriting Period

Length of Underwriting Period: Sixty days.

Length of Notice: Ten days for any reason.

Reason for Cancellation: Required on the notice.

Proof Required: Certified mail. Proof must be retained for at least one year.

Cancellation after the Underwriting Period

The policy may be cancelled **only** for the following reasons:

1. Nonpayment of premium.

2. Fraud or material misrepresentation in obtaining the policy, continuing the policy or in presenting a claim under the policy.

DELAWARE

3. Substantial change in the risk since the policy was issued or renewed.

4. The building has been vacant or unoccupied for sixty or more consecutive days. This provision does not apply to:

    a. Seasonal unoccupancy.

    b. Buildings in the course of construction, renovation, or addition.

    c. Buildings to which the Vacancy Permit endorsement applies.

    A building fits this provision if 65 percent of its rental units are unoccupied or 65 percent of its floor space is vacant.

5. If, after a covered loss, the insured has not begun (or contracted for) repairs within thirty days after the insurer's initial payment.

6. If the building has been ordered vacated, demolished, or declared unsafe by a governmental authority.

7. If fixed and salvageable items are being removed from the building and not being replaced. This does not apply during remodeling or renovation.

8. If the insured does not furnish utility service to the building for thirty consecutive days or more (other than during seasonal unoccupancy).

9. If the insured is more than one year behind in payment of property taxes on the building. The Delaware Code says two years.

The Delaware Code is silent on reasons 4 through 9, above. Before cancelling for those reasons, an insurer should get a legal opinion on such a cancellation. The Code does, however, allow cancellation for the following reasons that are not on the amendatory endorsement:

1. Willful or reckless acts or omissions that increase any hazard insured against.

2. Violation of any local fire, health, or safety building or construction regulation or ordinance which substantially increases any hazard insured against.

3. If the commissioner determines that to continue the policy would violate the laws of Delaware.

DELAWARE

However, if the insurer has adopted the ISO amendatory endorsements (DP 01 07 & HO 01 07), it may not cancel for the above three reasons, since they are not on that endorsement.

Length of Notice: Ten days for nonpayment; thirty days for material misrepresentation or substantial change in the risk; five days for all other reasons.

Reason for Cancellation: Required on the notice. Even though the amendatory endorsements are silent on this matter—implying that a reason is not required—the code clearly calls for a reason to be shown.

Proof Required: Certified mail. Proof must be retained for at least one year.

Nonrenewal

Length of Notice: Thirty days.

Reason for Nonrenewal: Required on the notice.

Proof Required: Certified mail. Proof must be retained for at least one year.

Other Cancellation/Nonrenewal Provisions

Proof of mailing must be retained for not less than one year.

The declination or termination may not be based on any of the following:

1. The race, religion, nationality, ethnic group, age, sex, or marital status of the applicant or named insured.

2. The lawful occupation or profession of the applicant or named insured.

    This provision does not apply to insurers, agents, or brokers who limit their markets to one lawful occupation or group of occupations.

3. The age or location of the residence of the applicant or named insured unless such decision is for a business purpose that is not a mere pretext for unfair discrimination.

4. A previous declination or termination of the applicant.

5. The fact that the applicant or named insured was previously covered through a residual market insurance mechanism.

DELAWARE

PERSONAL AUTO
18 Delaware Code §§3903 through 3910

Cancellation during the Underwriting Period

Length of Underwriting Period: Sixty days.

Length of Notice: Ten days for any reason.

Reason for Cancellation: Required on the notice.

Proof Required: Certified mail or USPS Intelligent Mail barcode (IMb). Proof must be retained for at least one year.

Cancellation after the Underwriting Period

Insurers using ISO's Amendment of Policy Provisions (PP 01 52) are limited to the following reasons for cancellation after the underwriting period:

1. Nonpayment of premium.

2. Suspension or revocation of the driver's license of:

    a. The named insured.

    b. Any driver who lives with the named insured or who customarily uses the insured auto.

    The suspension or revocation must have occurred during the preceding thirty-six months. The policy may not be cancelled if the license of a person under age eighteen was suspended or revoked. The policy may not be cancelled due to the suspension of a minor's license due to underage consumption/ possession of alcohol while the minor is not driving a vehicle.

3. Material misrepresentation on the application.

However, the Delaware Code allows midterm cancellation for any of the following reasons:

1. Nonpayment of premium.

2. The policy was obtained through a material misrepresentation.

DELAWARE

3. Any insured violated any of the terms and conditions of the policy.

4. The named insured knowingly failed to disclose fully his motor vehicle accidents and moving traffic violations, or his losses covered under any automobile physical damage or comprehensive coverage, for the preceding thirty-six months, if called for in the application.

5. As to renewal of the policy, if the insured at any time while the policy was in force failed to disclose fully to the insurer, upon request therefore, facts relative to accidents and losses incurred material to underwriting of the risk.

6. Any insured made a false or fraudulent claim or knowingly aided or abetted another in the presentation of such a claim.

7. The named insured or any other operator who either resides in the same household or customarily operates an automobile insured under such policy:

   a. Has, within the thirty-six months prior to the notice of cancellation or nonrenewal, had a driver's license under suspension or revocation, except a child whose license has been revoked or suspended for a nondriving-related drug offense.

   b. Has a history of and is subject to epilepsy or heart attacks, and such individual cannot produce a certificate from a physician testifying to his/her unqualified ability to operate a motor vehicle safely.

   c. Has an accident record, conviction record (criminal or traffic), physical, mental or other condition which is such that his/her operation of an automobile might endanger the public safety.

   d. Has, while the policy is in force, engaged in a competitive speed contest while operating an automobile insured under the policy.

   e. Is addicted to or uses narcotics or other drugs.

   f. Uses alcoholic beverages to excess thereby impairing his/her ability to operate a motor vehicle.

   g. Has been convicted or forfeited bail, during the thirty-six months immediately preceding the notice of cancellation or nonrenewal, for:

      (1) Any felony.

      (2) Criminal negligence resulting in death, homicide or assault arising out of the operation of a motor vehicle.

DELAWARE

      (3) Operating a motor vehicle while in an intoxicated condition or while under the influence of drugs.

      (4) Leaving the scene of an accident without stopping to report.

      (5) Theft or unlawful taking of a motor vehicle.

      (6) Making false statements in an application for a driver's license.

  h. Has been convicted of, or forfeited bail, for three or more violations, the point total for which exceeds eight points, or three at fault accidents in which claims are paid in excess of $250 per accident within the thirty-six months immediately preceding the notice of cancellation or nonrenewal, of any law, ordinance or regulation limiting the speed of motor vehicles or any of the provisions of the motor vehicle laws of any state, violation of which constitutes a dangerous moving violation whether or not the violations were repetitions of the same offense or different offenses.

8. The insured automobile is:

  a. So mechanically defective that its operation might endanger public safety.

  b. Used in carrying passengers for hire or compensation, except that the use of an automobile for a car pool shall not be considered use of an automobile for hire or compensation.

  c. Used in the business of transportation of flammables or explosives.

  d. An authorized emergency vehicle.

  e. Modified or changed in condition during the policy period so as to increase the risk substantially.

  f. Subject to an inspection law and has not been inspected or, if inspected fails to qualify.

If an insurer has adopted the ISO amendatory endorsement (PP 01 52), it is restricted to the reasons that appear on that endorsement.

Length of Notice: Ten days for nonpayment; thirty days for any other reason.

Reason for Cancellation: Required on the notice. Even though the amendatory endorsement is silent on the matter, the reason must be shown because the Delaware code requires it.

DELAWARE

Proof Required: Certified mail or USPS Intelligent Mail barcode (IMb). Proof must be retained for at least one year. The amendatory endorsement indicates proof of mailing is sufficient proof, however, statute requires certified mail or IMb.

Nonrenewal

Length of Notice: Thirty days.

Reason for Nonrenewal: Required on the notice. Even though the amendatory endorsement is silent on the matter, indicating no restrictions on the allowable reasons for nonrenewal, the Delaware code limits nonrenewal to the same eight reasons allowable for cancellation after the underwriting period. The Delaware code also requires that the reason for nonrenewal must be shown on the notice.

Proof Required: Certified mail or USPS Intelligent Mail barcode (IMb). Proof must be retained for at least one year.

Other Cancellation/Nonrenewal Provisions

For other Cancellation and Nonrenewal Provisions, please contact the Delaware Department of Insurance.

PERSONAL UMBRELLA

Cancellation during the Underwriting Period

Length of Underwriting Period: Sixty days.

Length of Notice: Ten days.

Reason for Cancellation: Required on the notice.

Proof Required: Certified mail.

Cancellation after the Underwriting Period

Length of Notice: Ten days for nonpayment; thirty days for any other reason.

Reason for Cancellation: Required on the notice.

Proof Required: Certified mail.

DELAWARE

Nonrenewal

Length of Notice: Thirty days.

Reason for Cancellation: Required on the notice.

Proof Required: Certified mail.

FRAUD
11 Delaware Code §913; 11 §4205; 18, §§2401 through 2415
General Information and Definitions

A person is guilty of insurance fraud when, with the intent to injure, defraud or deceive any insurer the person:

1. Presents or causes to be presented to any insurer, any written or oral statement including computer-generated documents as part of, or in support of, a claim for payment or other benefit pursuant to an insurance policy, knowing that such statement contains false, incomplete or misleading information concerning any fact or thing material to such claim.

2. Assists, abets, solicits or conspires with another to prepare or make any written or oral statement that is intended to be presented to any insurer in connection with, or in support of, any claim for payment or other benefit pursuant to an insurance policy, knowing that such statement contains any false, incomplete or misleading information concerning any fact or thing material to such claim.

"Statement" includes, but is not limited to, any notice statement, proof of loss, bill of lading, receipt for payment, invoice, account, estimate of property damages, bill for services, diagnosis, prescription, hospital or doctor records, X rays, test result or other evidence of loss, injury or expense; "insurer" shall include, but is not limited to, an authorized insurer, self-insurer, reinsurer, broker, producer or any agent thereof; and "insurance policy" shall include, but is not limited to, the subscriber and members contracts of health service corporations and health maintenance organizations.

An insurer, or insurance employee, is guilty of insurance fraud when, with intent to injure, defraud, or deceive any claimant the person:

1. Present or cause to be presented to any claimant false, incomplete or misleading information regarding the nature, extent and terms of insurance coverage which may or might be available to such claimant.

DELAWARE

2. Present or cause to be presented to any insurance claimant false, incomplete or misleading information regarding or affecting in any fashion the extent of any claimant's right to benefit under, or to make a claim against, any policy. (18 Delaware Code §2407).

Reporting Requirements

Any insurer which has a reasonable belief that an act of insurance fraud is being, or has been, committed shall send to the Bureau, on a form prescribed by the Bureau, any and all information and such additional information relating to such act as the Bureau may require.

The Delaware Department of Insurance uses the NAIC Uniform Suspected Insurance Fraud Reporting Form. The form and instructions are available on the Delaware Department of Insurance web site at http://insurance.delaware.gov/reportfraud/.

Penalties and Statute of Limitations

Insurance fraud is a class G felony.

Upon a showing by a preponderance of evidence that a violation of this chapter has occurred, the commissioner may impose an administrative penalty of not more than $10,000 for each act of insurance fraud and up to two years in level V incarceration. An act of insurance fraud may be one of several such acts which taken together comprise a fraudulent insurance scheme. Assessment of the administrative penalty shall be determined by the nature, circumstances, extent and gravity of the act or acts of insurance fraud, any prior history of such act or acts, the degree of culpability and such other matters as justice may require.

Delaware has a three-year statute of limitations on tort claims.

Antifraud Procedures

All insurance claims forms shall contain a statement that clearly states in substance the following:

> "Any person who knowingly, and with intent to injure, defraud or deceive any insurer, files a statement of claim containing any false, incomplete or misleading information is guilty of a felony."

The lack of such a statement shall not constitute a defense against prosecution under this section.

The costs of administration and operation of the Delaware Insurance Fraud Prevention Bureau shall be borne by all of the insurance companies admitted or authorized to transact

DELAWARE

the business of insurance in this state. The commissioner shall assess $900 annually against each insurance company to provide the funds necessary for the operation of the Bureau. (18 Delaware Code §2415).

Individuals who know of or suspect possible insurance fraud can report it. All calls and tips are investigated. All calls and tips are confidential unless the individual should choose otherwise. Individuals can report suspected insurance fraud by:

> Calling 1-800-632-5154 toll-free in Delaware or (302) 674-7350
> Sending an email to fraud@state.de.us
> Mailing a report to:
> Fraud Prevention
> 841 Silver Lake Blvd.
> Dover, DE 19904

FAIR CLAIMS PROCESSING
18 Delaware Code §2304

Unfair claim settlement practices. No person shall commit or perform with such frequency as to indicate a general business practice any of the following:

1. Failing to acknowledge and act reasonably promptly upon communication with respect to claims arising under insurance policies.

2. Failing to adopt and implement reasonable standards for the prompt investigation of claims arising under insurance policies.

3. Refusing to pay claims without conducting a reasonable investigation based upon all available information.

4. Failing to affirm or deny coverage of claims within a reasonable time after proof of loss statements have been completed.

5. Not attempting in good faith to effectuate prompt, fair and equitable settlements of claims in which liability has become reasonably clear.

6. Attempting to settle a claim for less than the amount to which a reasonable person would have believed that person's own self was entitled by reference to written or printed advertising material accompanying or made part of an application.

7. Attempting to settle claims on the basis of an application which was altered without notice to or knowledge or consent of the insured.

8. Making claims payments to insureds or beneficiaries not accompanied by a statement setting forth the coverage under which the payments are being made.

DELAWARE

9. Delaying the investigation or payment of claims by requiring an insured, claimant or the physician of either to submit a preliminary claim report and then requiring the subsequent submission of formal proof of loss forms, both of which submissions contain substantially the same information.

10. Failing to promptly settle claims, where liability has become reasonably clear under one portion of the insurance policy coverage in order to influence settlements under other portions of the insurance policy coverage.

11. Failing to promptly provide a reasonable explanation of the basis in the insurance policy in relation to the facts or applicable law for denial of a claim or for the offer of a compromise settlement.

12. Misrepresenting pertinent facts or insurance policy provisions relating to coverages at issue.

13. Compelling insureds to institute litigation to recover amounts due under an insurance policy by offering substantially less than the amounts ultimately recovered in actions brought by such insureds.

14. Making known to insureds or claimants a policy of appealing from arbitration awards in favor of insureds or claimants for the purpose of compelling them to accept settlements or compromises less than the amount awarded in arbitration.

DISTRICT OF COLUMBIA

For details on cancellation procedures for the standard policy, refer to the Standard Policy section.

COMMERCIAL LINES
AGRICULTURAL CAPITAL ASSETS; CAPITAL ASSETS; BOP; CRIME; CGL (CGL, EMPLOYMENT PRACTICES, LIQUOR, MARKET SEGMENTS, OCP, POLLUTION, PRODUCTS/COMPLETED OPERATIONS, RAILROAD PROTECTIVE); CIM; C. PROP; EQUIPMENT BREAKDOWN; & PROF. LIAB.

D.C. Mun. Regs. tit. 26-A §§300, 301, 306

Cancellation during the Underwriting Period

Length of Underwriting Period: Thirty days.

Length of Notice: Thirty days for any reason.

Reason for Cancellation: Not required.

Proof Required: Proof of mailing.

Cancellation after the Underwriting Period

The policy may be cancelled **only** for the following reasons:

1. Nonpayment of premium.

2. Material and willful misstatement or omission of fact on the application or in a claim.

3. If the named insured has transferred the property to a person other than his beneficiary unless the transfer is permissible under the terms of the policy.

Length of Notice: Thirty days.

Reason for Cancellation: The notice of cancellation or nonrenewal shall set forth a reasonable explanation of the ground or grounds relied upon by the insurer as the basis of cancellation or nonrenewal.

Proof Required: Proof of mailing.

DISTRICT OF COLUMBIA

Nonrenewal

Length of Notice: Thirty days.

Reason for Nonrenewal: The notice of cancellation or nonrenewal shall set forth a reasonable explanation of the ground or grounds relied upon by the insurer as the basis of cancellation or nonrenewal.

Proof Required: Proof of mailing.

Other Cancellation/Nonrenewal Provisions

Written notice of cancellation or nonrenewal must be given to the agent or broker who wrote the policy, at least five days before the notice is sent to the insured.

The envelope containing the notice shall be labeled "Important Insurance Notice" in at least eighteen-point or larger type.

For cancellation for reasons other than nonpayment; thirty days prior to the date of cancellation.

For OCP policy, notice must also be sent to the contractor designated on the policy.

For Railroad Protective, notice must also be sent to the contractor designated on the policy and to any involved governmental authority. §A-301.3

COMMERCIAL AUTO & COMMERCIAL UMBRELLA

D.C. Code Ann. §§31-2406, 31-2409; D.C. Mun. Regs. tit. 26-A §§300, 301, 305, 306, 500

Cancellation during the Underwriting Period

Length of Underwriting Period: Thirty days, sixty days for auto.

Length of Notice: Thirty days for any reason.

Reason for Cancellation: Not required.

Proof Required: Post Office receipt or certified mail.

Cancellation after the Underwriting Period

The policy may be cancelled **only** for the following reasons:

DISTRICT OF COLUMBIA

1. Nonpayment of premium.

2. Suspension or revocation of the registration of an auto designated in the policy, resulting in no auto described in the policy being validly registered.

3. Suspension or revocation of the driver's license of the named insured during the policy period.

4. Material or willful misstatement or omission of fact on the application or in a claim.

5. The motor vehicle or other interest of the insured shall have been transferred to a person other than the insured or beneficiary unless the transfer is permissible under the terms of the policy.

6. Material change in the interest or use of the motor vehicle with respect to its insurability.

Reasons 1-3 are applicable to all motor vehicles. Reasons 4-6 are only applicable to motor vehicles not subject to the Compulsory/No-Fault Motor Vehicle Insurance Act of 1982, as amended. D.C. Code Ann. §31-2406.

Length of Notice: Thirty days. Fifteen days for auto (failure to pay premium).

Reason for Cancellation: The notice of cancellation or nonrenewal shall set forth a reasonable explanation of the ground or grounds relied upon by the insurer as the basis of cancellation or nonrenewal.

Proof Required: Post Office receipt or certified mail.

Nonrenewal

Length of Notice: Thirty days. Fifteen days for auto (failure to pay premium).

Reason for Nonrenewal: The notice of cancellation or nonrenewal shall set forth a reasonable explanation of the ground or grounds relied upon by the insurer as the basis of cancellation or nonrenewal.

Proof Required: Post Office receipt or certified mail.

Other Cancellation/Nonrenewal Provisions

At least five days' notice of cancellation or nonrenewal must be given to the agent or broker who wrote the policy.

DISTRICT OF COLUMBIA

The envelope containing the notice shall be labeled "Important Insurance Notice" in at least eighteen-point or larger type.

For cancellation for reasons other than nonpayment; thirty days prior to the date of cancellation.

The notice shall advise the insured of his or her appeal rights and possible eligibility in the District of Columbia Automobile Insurance Plan, or other similar plans at the time of the notice.

Fifteen days' notice may be given for nonpayment of premium. However, ISO's amendatory endorsement (CA 02 63) makes no provision for any cancellation with less than a thirty-day notice. This notice must also provide information to the insured about residual markets available to the insured according to D.C. regulations.

CGL (UNDERGROUND STORAGE TANKS)

D.C. Mun. Regs. tit. 26-A §§300, 301, 305, 306; 20 D.C. Mun. Regs. tit.20 § Appendix 67-4

Cancellation during the Underwriting Period

Length of Underwriting Period: Thirty days.

Length of Notice: Ten days for nonpayment or material misrepresentation; sixty days for any other reason.

Reason for Cancellation: Not required.

Proof Required: Certified mail.

Cancellation after the Underwriting Period

The policy may be cancelled **only** for the following reasons:

1. Nonpayment of premium.

2. Material and willful misstatement or omission of fact on the application or in a claim.

3. If the named insured has transferred the property to a person other than his beneficiary unless the transfer is permissible under the terms of the policy.

Length of Notice: Thirty days for nonpayment of premium and Reason 2, above; sixty days for Reason 3.

DISTRICT OF COLUMBIA

Reason for Cancellation: The notice of cancellation or nonrenewal shall set forth a reasonable explanation of the ground or grounds relied upon by the insurer as the basis of cancellation or nonrenewal.

Proof Required: Certified mail.

Nonrenewal

Length of Notice: Thirty days.

Reason for Nonrenewal: The notice of cancellation or nonrenewal shall set forth a reasonable explanation of the ground or grounds relied upon by the insurer as the basis of cancellation or nonrenewal.

Proof Required: Proof of mailing.

Other Cancellation/Nonrenewal Provisions

At least five days' notice of cancellation or nonrenewal must be given to the agent or broker who wrote the policy.

A copy of any cancellation or nonrenewal notice must also be sent to the DC Director of the Department of Health.

The envelope containing the notice shall be labeled "Important Insurance Notice" in at least eighteen-point or larger type.

FARM

The District of Columbia makes no changes from the standard policy.

MANAGEMENT PROTECTION

D.C. Mun. Regs. tit. 26-A §§300 and 306

Cancellation after the Underwriting Period

The policy may be cancelled **only** for the following reasons:

1. Nonpayment of premium.

2. Material and willful misstatement or omission of fact on the application or in a claim.

3. If the named insured has transferred the property to a person other than his beneficiary unless the transfer is permissible under the terms of the policy.

Length of Notice: Ten days for nonpayment; thirty days for any other reason.

DISTRICT OF COLUMBIA

Reason for Cancellation: The notice of cancellation or nonrenewal shall set forth a reasonable explanation of the ground or grounds relied upon by the insurer as the basis of cancellation or nonrenewal.

Proof Required: Proof of mailing.

Nonrenewal

Length of Notice: Thirty days.

Reason for Nonrenewal: The notice of cancellation or nonrenewal shall set forth a reasonable explanation of the ground or grounds relied upon by the insurer as the basis of cancellation or nonrenewal.

Proof Required: Proof of mailing.

Other Cancellation/Nonrenewal Provisions

Companies must also provide at least five days' notice to the agent or broker who wrote the policy before sending a cancellation or nonrenewal notice to the Named Organization.

The envelope containing the notice shall be labeled "Important Insurance Notice" in at least eighteen-point or larger type.

For cancellation for reasons other than nonpayment; thirty days prior to the date of cancellation.

WORKERS COMPENSATION

DC ST §32-1538; D.C. Code Ann. § 32-1513; D.C. Mun. Regs. tit. 7, § 216; D.C. Mun. Regs. tit. 26-A, § 311

Cancellation during the Underwriting Period

Length of Underwriting Period: N/A.

Length of Notice: Thirty days for any reason.

Reason for Cancellation: The notice of cancellation or nonrenewal shall set forth a reasonable explanation of the ground or grounds relied upon by the insurer as the basis of cancellation or nonrenewal.

DISTRICT OF COLUMBIA

Cancellation notices shall advise the insured of:

1. Appeal rights and procedures.

2. Reason(s) relied upon for the action.

3. Possible eligibility for residual a market plan or similar plan.

Proof Required: Proof of mailing. Carriers must file by certified mail, return receipt requested.

Cancellation after the Underwriting Period

Length of Notice: Thirty days.

Reason for Cancellation: The notice of cancellation or nonrenewal shall set forth a reasonable explanation of the ground or grounds relied upon by the insurer as the basis of cancellation or nonrenewal.

Proof Required: Proof of mailing. Carriers must file by certified mail, return receipt requested.

Nonrenewal

Length of Notice: Thirty days.

Reason for Nonrenewal: The notice of cancellation or nonrenewal shall set forth a reasonable explanation of the ground or grounds relied upon by the insurer as the basis of cancellation or nonrenewal.

Nonrenewal notices shall advise the insured of:

1. Appeal rights and procedures.

2. Possible eligibility for a residual market plan or similar plan.

Proof Required: Proof of mailing. Carriers must file by certified mail, return receipt requested.

Other Cancellation/Nonrenewal Provisions

Carriers must serve a copy of the Termination Notice upon the employer when termination is for one of the following reasons: Request of carrier or agency; no employees; or change of carrier.

DISTRICT OF COLUMBIA

Carriers, upon filing Termination Notice, must retain the copy labeled "Reinstatement" in their file. If at a later date they reinstate coverage they must file this Reinstatement Notice with the Office.

Carriers must notify the Office of Workers Compensation whenever they intend to cease providing coverage to an employer on the Termination Notice.

The following are reasonable explanations for termination: change of carrier, out of business, business sold, no employees, non-payment of premium, and request of carrier or agency.

SURPLUS LINES

D.C. Mun. Reg. tit. 26-A §301; D.C. Code Ann. §31-2231.01; D.C. Code Ann. 31-2502.40

The District of Columbia cancellation and nonrenewal requirements do not apply to surplus lines policies.

FINANCED PREMIUMS

D.C. Code Ann. §31-1111

If the premium finance agreement contains a power of attorney, the finance company may request, in the name of the insured, that the insurer cancel the policy due to nonpayment. The finance company must first give the insured ten days to pay. If the insured fails to make payment within that ten-day period, then the finance company mails the notice of cancellation to the insurer and the cancellation is processed as of the finance company's original default date. Return of the policy by the insured is not required. The insurer is not required to notify the insured of the cancellation. D.C. Code Ann. §§35-1561, 35-1561(c), 35-2109, and 35-2109(b).

All statutory, regulatory, and contractual restrictions providing that the insurance contract may not be cancelled unless notice is given to a governmental agency, mortgagee, or other third party shall apply where cancellation is effected under the provisions of this section. The insurer shall give the prescribed notice on behalf of itself or the insured to any governmental agency, mortgagee, or other third-party on or before the second business day after the day it receives the notice of cancellation from the premium finance company and shall determine the effective date of cancellation taking into consideration the number of days' notice required to complete the cancellation.

PERSONAL LINES
DWELLING FIRE & HOMEOWNERS

D.C. Code Ann. §31-5001; D.C. Mun. Regs. tit. 26-A §§300.2, 301, 306, 5000,

Cancellation during the Underwriting Period

Length of Underwriting Period: Thirty days.

Length of Notice: Ten days for nonpayment; thirty days for any other reason.

DISTRICT OF COLUMBIA

Reason for Cancellation: Not required.

Proof Required: Proof of mailing.

Cancellation after the Underwriting Period

The policy may be cancelled **only** for the following reasons:

1. Nonpayment of premium.

2. Material and willful misstatement or omission of fact on the application or in a claim.

3. If the named insured has transferred the property to a person other than his beneficiary, unless the transfer is permissible under the terms of the policy.

Length of Notice: Thirty days.

Reason for Cancellation: The notice of cancellation or nonrenewal shall set forth a reasonable explanation of the ground or grounds relied upon by the insurer as the basis of cancellation or nonrenewal.

Cancellation notices shall advise the insured of:

1. Appeal rights and procedures.

2. Possible eligibility for a residual market plan or similar plan.

Proof Required: Proof of mailing.

Nonrenewal

Length of Notice: Thirty days.

Reason for Nonrenewal: The notice of cancellation or nonrenewal shall set forth a reasonable explanation of the ground or grounds relied upon by the insurer as the basis of cancellation or nonrenewal.

Nonrenewal notices shall advise the insured of:

1. Appeal rights and procedures.

2. Possible eligibility for a residual market plan or similar plan.

Proof Required: Proof of mailing.

DISTRICT OF COLUMBIA

Other Cancellation/Nonrenewal Provisions

Thirty days' notice is required for nonpayment of premium. Notice to insured must contain information on the availability of residual markets according to D.C. regulations.

The envelope containing the notice shall be labeled "Important Insurance Notice" in at least eighteen-point or larger type.

All notices of cancellation/nonrenewal for homeowners insurance must contain pertinent information when referring insureds to the District of Columbia Property Insurance Facility. The address and telephone number of each agency must appear on all notices of cancellation/nonrenewal:

>District of Columbia Property Insurance Facility
>Farragut Square Business Center
>1025 Connecticut Avenue, NW, Suite 1000
>Washington, DC 20036

(As of June 1, 2014 this is the new address to obtain Application Forms and make payments.)

>Postal Address
>3290 N. Ridge Road, Suite 210
>Ellicott City, MD 21043
>1-800-492-5670
>Fax 410-244-7268
>E-mail: infor@dcpif.org

Please see the Consumer Information Sheet at www.dcpif.org for more information and regulations.

All new and renewal business should be issued a Notice of Cancellation/Nonrenewal with the required information. Failure to comply with this requirement will render the notice of cancellation and nonrenewal defective.

An insurer shall not refuse to renew a policy of homeowners insurance solely due to claim or loss frequency unless there have been two or more claims during the most recent three-year experience period. Additionally, the insurer shall not consider:

1. The first claim for a loss caused by weather, unless the insurer can provide evidence that the insured unreasonably failed to maintain the property and such failure to maintain contributed to the loss.

2. The first claim that was reported to the agent or insurer for which no payment was made by the insurer.

DISTRICT OF COLUMBIA

3. A loss where there was no investigation or other claim activity.

4. Any losses caused by a catastrophic event. A catastrophic event shall be a manmade or natural event that causes $25 million or more in insured property losses, and affects a significant number of property and casualty policyholders and insurers.

5. On the basis of the loss history of the previous owner of the property.

    An insurer shall provide a notice to its homeowners' insurance policyholders that the insurer considers claims history in determining whether to renew the policy. Such notice may be on the declarations page or on a separate notice that accompanies the policy so long as the notice is conspicuous and includes the following statement: "Your insurer may consider your claims and loss history when determining whether to renew your policy."

    If insurer attempts to cancel or nonrenew a policy of homeowner's insurance based on an insured's claims or loss history, the insurer shall specify the reasons for such action, including: the date of the claim or loss, the amount of the claim or loss, the type of insurance applicable to the claim or loss, the name of the insurer of the claim or loss, and a brief statement of circumstances that caused the claim or loss. The specifications of reasons must be sufficiently thorough in order that the insured can have an adequate basis of refuting the accuracy of any claim or loss history specified as reasons for the cancellation or nonrenewal decision of the insurer. (D.C. Mun. Reg. tit. 26-A §§5000.4 and 5000.5).

PERSONAL AUTO

D.C. Code Ann. §§31-2406, 31-2409; D.C. Mun. Regs. tit. 26-A §§300, 301, 305, 306, 500

Cancellation during the Underwriting Period

Length of Underwriting Period: Sixty days.

Length of Notice: Thirty days for any reason.

Reason for Cancellation: Required on the notice.

Proof Required: Proof of mailing.

Cancellation after the Underwriting Period

The policy may be cancelled **only** for the following reasons:

1. Nonpayment of premium.

DISTRICT OF COLUMBIA

2. Suspension or revocation of the registration of an auto designated in the policy, resulting in no auto described in the policy being validly registered.

3. Suspension or revocation of the driver's license of the named insured during the policy period.

4. Material or willful misstatement or omission of fact on the application or in a claim.

5. The motor vehicle or other interest of the insured shall have been transferred to a person other than the insured or beneficiary, unless the transfer is permissible under the terms of the policy.

6. Material change in the interest or use of the motor vehicle with respect to its insurability.

Reasons 1-3 are applicable to all motor vehicles. Reasons 4-6 are only applicable to motor vehicles not subject to the Compulsory/No-Fault Motor Vehicle Insurance Act of 1982, as amended (D.C. Code Ann. §31-2406).

Length of Notice: Fifteen days (failure to pay premium). Otherwise thirty days.

Reason for Cancellation: Required on the notice. The D.C. Administrative Code indicates that the reason must be shown.

Cancellation notices shall advise the insured of:

1. Appeal rights and procedures.
2. Possible eligibility for a residual market plan or similar plan.

Proof Required: Proof of mailing.

Nonrenewal

Length of Notice: Fifteen days (failure to pay premium). Otherwise thirty days.

Reason for Nonrenewal: Required on the notice. Even though the amendatory endorsement says nothing about showing the reason for nonrenewal, the D.C. Administrative Code says that the reason must be shown.

Nonrenewal notices shall advise the insured of:

1. Appeal rights and procedures.

Proof Required: Proof of mailing.

DISTRICT OF COLUMBIA

Other Cancellation/Nonrenewal Provisions

An insurer may not decline, cancel, or nonrenew in D.C. based on race, color, religion, national origin, sex, marital status, personal appearance, sexual orientation, family responsibilities, disability, matriculation, political affiliation, lawful occupation, gender identity, or location within the geographical area of the District of Columbia.

Any notice of cancellation or nonrenewal must have information on the availability of residual markets, a statement that other insurance may be available to the insured through the agent, through another insurer, or through the District of Columbia Assigned Risk Plan, that the insured's motor vehicle registration will be cancelled or revoked due to failure to maintain insurance and of the right to have the insurance commissioner review the action, according to D.C. regulations.

The envelope containing the notice shall be labeled "Important Insurance Notice" in at least eighteen-point or larger type.

All notices of cancellation/nonrenewal for Personal Automobile insurance must contain pertinent information when referring insureds to the District of Columbia Automobile Insurance Plan. The address and telephone number of each agency must appear on all notices of cancellation/nonrenewal:

> District of Columbia Automobile Insurance Plan
> P.O. Box 6530
> Providence, RI 02940-6530
> 1-888-820-0170
> Fax: 1800-516-1923
> E-mail: dcaip@aipso.com
> www.aipso.com

All new and renewal business should be issued a notice of cancellation/nonrenewal with the required information. Failure to comply with this requirement will render the notice of cancellation and nonrenewal defective. (See https://disb.dc.gov/publication/notice-cancellationnon-renewal-homeowners-and-personal-automobile-insurance.)

Written notice of cancellation or nonrenewal must be given to the agent or broker who wrote the policy, at least five days before the notice is sent to the insured.

An insurer may not refuse to insure, refuse to continue to insure, limit coverage available to, or charge a disadvantageous rate to any person seeking to obtain insurance required by this act because that person had not been previously insured. If the policy term is less than six months, the insurer may nonrenew every six months, beginning six months after the original effective date.

DISTRICT OF COLUMBIA

For cancellation for reasons other than nonpayment; thirty days prior to the date of cancellation.

If the policy term is one year or longer, the insurer may nonrenew the policy at each anniversary of the original effective date.

Automatic termination is allowed only if the insured obtains similar insurance on the car. It is not allowed for nonpayment of the renewal premium.

Regulations restrict the underwriting period to thirty days.

PERSONAL UMBRELLA

D.C. Mun. Regs. tit. 26-A §§300, 301, 306

Cancellation during the Underwriting Period

Length of Underwriting Period: Thirty days.

Length of Notice: Thirty days for any reason.

Reason for Cancellation: Not required.

Proof Required: Proof of mailing.

Cancellation after the Underwriting Period

The policy may be cancelled **only** for the following reasons:

1. Nonpayment of premium.

2. The insured has made a material and willful misstatement or omission of fact to us in connection with any application to or claim.

3. The insured property or other interest has been transferred to another person, unless the transfer is permissible under the terms of the policy.

Length of Notice: Thirty days.

Reason for Cancellation: Must be shown on the notice.

Cancellation notices shall advise the insured of:

1. Appeal rights and procedures.

DISTRICT OF COLUMBIA

2. Possible eligibility for a residual market plan or similar plan.

Proof Required: Proof of mailing.

Nonrenewal

Length of Notice: Thirty days.

Reason for Nonrenewal: The notice of cancellation or nonrenewal shall set forth a reasonable explanation of the ground or grounds relied upon by the insurer as the basis of cancellation or nonrenewal.

Nonrenewal notices shall advise the insured of:

1. Appeal rights and procedures.

2. Possible eligibility for a residual market plan or similar plan.

Proof Required: Proof of mailing.

Other Cancellation/Nonrenewal Provisions

Written notice of cancellation or nonrenewal must be given to the agent or broker who wrote the policy, at least five days before the notice is sent to the insured.

The envelope containing the notice shall be labeled "Important Insurance Notice" in at least eighteen-point or larger type.

FRAUD

D.C. Code Ann. §§22-3225.01 through 22-3225.15; D.C. Code Ann. § 22-3571.01

General Information and Definitions

A person commits the offense of insurance fraud in the first degree if that person knowingly engages in any of the conduct specified in D.C. Code Ann. §22-3225.02 with the intent to defraud or to fraudulently obtain property of another and thereby obtains property of another or causes another to lose property and the value of the property obtained or lost is $1,000 or more. Such actions include but are not limited to presenting false information or concealing information in an application or claim for payment, application for a license, application for premium finance transaction; tampering with records, or embezzlement.

A person commits the offense of insurance fraud in the second degree if that person knowingly engages in conduct specified in D.C. Code Ann. §22-3225.02 with the intent to defraud or to fraudulently obtain property of another and the value of the property which

DISTRICT OF COLUMBIA

is sought to be obtained is $1,000 or more. A person commits the offense of misdemeanor insurance fraud if that person knowingly engages in conduct specified in D.C. Code Ann. §22-3225.02 with the intent to defraud or to fraudulently obtain property of another.

Reporting Requirements

Based upon a reasonable belief, an insurer, insurance professional, and any other pertinent person, shall report to the Metropolitan Police Department or the Department of Insurance, Securities, and Banking, actions that may constitute the commission of insurance fraud, and assist in the investigation of insurance fraud by reasonably providing information when required by an investigating authority.

Each insurer and health maintenance organization licensed in the District shall file an annual antifraud activity report on March thirty-first of each year with the commissioner, which shall contain information about the special investigation unit's insurance fraud activities during the preceding calendar year. Annual antifraud activity reports filed with the commissioner shall be kept confidential.

Forms, instructions, and contact information are available on the Enforcement and Investigation Bureau of the District of Columbia Department of Insurance, Securities and Banking Web site at: https://disb.dc.gov/es/service/file-complaint-or-report-fraud.

Criminal Penalties and Statute of Limitations

1. Any person convicted of insurance fraud in the first degree shall be fined not more than $37,500 or imprisoned for not more than fifteen years, or both.

2. Any person convicted of insurance fraud in the second degree shall be fined not more than $12,500 or imprisoned for not more than five years, or both.

3. Any person convicted of insurance fraud in the second degree who has been convicted previously of insurance fraud, or a felony conviction based on similar grounds in any other jurisdiction, shall be fined not more than $25,000 or imprisoned for not more than ten years, or both.

4. Any person convicted of misdemeanor insurance fraud shall be fined not more than $1,000 or imprisoned for not more than 180 days, or both.

5. A person convicted of a felony violation of this subchapter shall be disqualified from engaging in the business of insurance.

6. An organization that has been found guilty of an offense may be fined twice the maximum amount specified for an individual.

DISTRICT OF COLUMBIA

Civil Liability

Any person injured by insurance fraud can bring suit for restitution plus punitive damages. Punitive damages must be between $500 and $50,000. Suit must be filed within three years of the act constituting the offense or within three years of the time the plaintiff discovered or with reasonable diligence could have discovered the act, whichever is later. (D.C. Code Ann. §22-3225.05).

Antifraud Provisions

Every insurer licensed in the District shall submit to the Department of Insurance and Securities Regulation, an insurance fraud prevention and detection plan ("plan"). The plan shall indicate specific procedures for the accomplishment of the following:

1. Prevention, detection, and investigation of insurance fraud.

2. Orientation of employees on insurance fraud prevention and detection.

3. Employment of fraud investigators.

4. Reporting of insurance fraud to the appropriate authorities.

5. Collection of restitution for financial loss caused by insurance fraud.

An insurer who fails to submit an insurance prevention and detection plan, or the warning provision detailed below, shall be subject to a fine of $500 per day, not to exceed $25,000.

All insurance application forms and all claim forms shall contain a conspicuous warning in language the same or substantially similar to the following:

WARNING

"It is a crime to provide false or misleading information to an insurer for the purpose of defrauding the insurer or any other person. Penalties include imprisonment and/or fines. In addition, an insurer may deny insurance benefits if false information materially related to a claim was provided by the applicant."

None of the above requirements apply to reinsurers, reinsurance contracts, reinsurance agreements, or reinsurance claims transactions.

FAIR CLAIMS PROCESSING

D.C. Code Ann. §31-2231.17

No person shall commit or perform with such frequency as to indicate a general business practice, including but not limited to, any of the following:

1. Knowingly misrepresent pertinent facts or insurance policy provisions relating to the claim at issue.

DISTRICT OF COLUMBIA

2. Refuse to pay a claim for a reason that is arbitrary or capricious based on all available information.

3. Attempt to settle a claim on the basis of an application which is altered without notice to, or the knowledge or consent of, the insured.

4. Fail to include with a claim paid to an insured or beneficiary a statement setting forth the coverage under which payment is being made.

5. Fail to settle a claim promptly whenever liability is reasonably clear under one portion of a policy in order to influence settlements under other portions of the policy.

6. Fail promptly upon request to provide a reasonable explanation of the basis for a denial of a claim.

7. Knowingly misrepresent pertinent facts or insurance policy provisions relating to coverage at issue.

8. Fail to acknowledge and act reasonably promptly upon communication with respect to claims arising under insurance policies.

9. Fail to adopt and implement reasonable standards for the prompt investigation of claims arising under insurance policies.

10. Refuse to pay claims without conducting a reasonable investigation.

11. Fail to affirm or deny coverage of claims within a reasonable time after proof of loss statements have been completed or after having completed its investigation related to the claims.

12. Not attempt in good faith to effectuate prompt, fair, and equitable settlement of claims submitted in which liability has become reasonably clear.

13. Compel insureds or beneficiaries to institute suits to recover amounts due under its policies by offering substantially less than the amounts ultimately recovered in actions brought by the insureds or beneficiaries.

14. Attempt to settle a claim for less than the amount to which a reasonable person would believe the insured or beneficiary was entitled by reference to written or printed advertising material accompanying or made part of an application or policy.

DISTRICT OF COLUMBIA

15. Attempt to settle claims on the basis of an application which was materially altered without notice to or knowledge or consent of the insured.

16. Make claims payments to an insured or beneficiary without indicating the coverage under which each payment is being made.

17. Make known to insureds or claimants of a policy of appealing from arbitration awards in favor of insureds or claimants for the purpose of compelling them to accept settlements or compromises of less than the amount awarded in arbitration.

18. Unreasonably delay the investigation or payment of claims by requiring both a formal proof of loss form and subsequent verification that would result in duplication of information and verification appearing in the formal proof of loss form.

19. Fail, in the case of claims denials or offers of compromise settlement, to promptly provide a reasonable and accurate explanation of the basis for such action.

20. Make false or fraudulent statements or representations on, or relative to an application for, a policy, for the purpose of obtaining a fee, commission, money, or other benefit from a provider or individual person.

The commissioner may impose a penalty for each violation. Items 1 – 6 carry a maximum penalty of $1000. For items 7 – 20, the commissioner may impose a penalty or revoke or suspend the license.

FLORIDA

For details on cancellation procedures for the standard policy, refer to the Standard Policy.

COMMERCIAL LINES
CAPITAL ASSETS; CIM; C. PROP.; CRIME; EQUIPMENT BREAKDOWN; FARM

Florida Statutes Annotated §§627.4025, 627.4091, and 627.4133

Cancellation during the Underwriting Period

Length of Underwriting Period: Ninety days.

Length of Notice: Immediate cancellation for material misstatement or misrepresentation, or failure to comply with underwriting requirements; ten days for nonpayment; twenty days for any other reason.

Reason for Cancellation: Required on the notice.

Proof Required: United States Postal Service proof of mailing form or use of certified or registered mail services showing the name of the insured, the policy number and date mailed.

During the underwriting period, the insurer may not cancel on the basis of:

1. Claims that are the result of an act of God, unless the insurer proves that the insured has not taken the necessary steps (as requested by the insurer) to prevent recurrence of damage to the insured property.

2. On the basis of a single claim which is the result of water damage, unless the insurer can demonstrate the insured failed to take action reasonably requested by the insurer to prevent a future similar occurrence of damage to the insured property.

Cancellation after the Underwriting Period

The policy may be cancelled **only** for the following reasons:

1. Nonpayment of premium.

2. Material misstatement on the application.

3. If the insured does not comply with underwriting requirements within ninety days of the effective date of coverage.

FLORIDA

4. Substantial change in the risk.

5. If the insurer is cancelling all insureds under such policies.

6. On the basis of property insurance claims that are the result of an act of God, if the insurer can show that the insured has failed to take action reasonably necessary, as requested, to prevent recurrence of damage to the insured property.

7. On the basis of a single claim which is the result of water damage, if the insurer can demonstrate that the insured has failed to take action reasonably requested by the insurer to prevent a future similar occurrence of damage to the insured property.

Length of Notice: Ten days for nonpayment; forty-five days for the reasons listed above if the policy does **not** cover a residential structure or its contents; 120 days for the reasons listed above if the policy covers a residential structure or its contents; 120 days for the reasons listed above if the policy covers a residential structure or its contents and the structure has been insured by the insurer or an affiliate for five years or longer immediately prior to the notice.

Reason for Cancellation: Required on the notice.

Proof Required: United States Postal Service proof of mailing form or use of certified or registered mail services showing the name of the insured, the policy number and date mailed.

Nonrenewal

The policy may not be nonrenewed on the basis of:

1. Claims that are the result of an act of God, unless the insurer proves that the insured has not taken the necessary steps (as requested by the insurer) to prevent recurrence of damage to the insured property.

2. On the basis of a single claim which is the result of water damage, unless the insurer can demonstrate the insured failed to take action reasonably requested by the insurer to prevent a future similar occurrence of damage to the insured property.

Restrictions on cancellation or nonrenewal of residential property in the event of hurricane or wind loss:

1. The insurer may not cancel or nonrenew a policy until at least ninety days after repairs to the residential structure have been substantially completed so that it is restored to the extent that it is insurable by another insurer writing policies in Florida. If the

insurer elects to not renew the policy, it will provide at least 120 days' notice of its intent to nonrenew ninety days after the substantial completion of repairs.

2. With respect to a policy covering a residential structure or its contents, any cancellation or nonrenewal that would otherwise take effect during the duration of a hurricane will not take effect until the end of the duration of such hurricane, unless a replacement policy has been obtained and is in effect for a claim occurring during the duration of the hurricane. The insurer may collect premium for the period of time for which the policy period is extended.

3. A hurricane is defined as a storm system that has been declared to be a hurricane by the National Hurricane Center of the National Weather Service (hereafter referred to as NHC). The hurricane occurrence begins at the time a hurricane watch or hurricane warning is issued for any part of Florida by the NHC, and ends seventy-two hours after the termination of the last hurricane watch or hurricane warning issued for any part of Florida by the NHC.

Length of Notice: Forty-five days if the policy does **not** cover a residential structure or its contents; 120 days if the policy covers a residential structure or its contents; 120 days if the residential structure has been insured by the insurer or an affiliate for five years or longer immediately prior to the notice.

Reason for Nonrenewal: Required on the notice.

Proof Required: United States Postal Service proof of mailing form or use of certified or registered mail services showing the name of the insured, the policy number and date mailed.

Other Cancellation/Nonrenewal Provisions

Insurers of commercial residential property, including farm owners, condominium associations, condominium unit owner's, apartment buildings or other policies covering a residential structure or its contents are required to provide at least 120 days' written notice.

The specific reason for a declination must accompany the declination.

1. A forty-five-day notice of the renewal premium is required for residential property coverage.

2. If the insured cancels the policy the insurer must return any unearned premium within thirty days.

3. If the insurer cancels the policy, any unearned premium must be returned within fifteen days.

FLORIDA

If an insurer fails to provide the forty-five-day or twenty-day written notice required under this section, the coverage provided to the named insured shall remain in effect until forty-five days after the notice is given or until the effective date of replacement coverage obtained by the named insured, whichever occurs first. The premium for the coverage shall remain the same during any such extension period except that, in the event of failure to provide notice of nonrenewal, if the rate filing then in effect would have resulted in a premium reduction, the premium during such extension of coverage shall be calculated based upon the later rate filing.

State law provides that in an emergency area, an insurer may not cancel/nonrenew a property policy with damage resulting from hurricane/wind loss until ninety days after the property has been repaired. Insurer must offer certain hurricane deductibles on all commercial property policies issued or renewed on or after January 1, 2006.

If policy is cancelled, the return premium must be sent within fifteen days after the date of cancellation.

Nonpayment of premium includes a check dishonored by the bank. If a dishonored check represents the initial premium payment, the contract and all contractual obligations shall be void ab initio unless the nonpayment is cured within the earlier of five days after actual notice by certified mail is received by the applicant or fifteen days after notice is sent to the applicant by certified mail or registered mail. If the contract is void, any premium received by the insurer from a third-party must be refunded to that party in full. (Fla. Stat. Ann. §627.4133).

With respect to a policy covering a residential structure or its contents, any cancellation or nonrenewal that would otherwise take effect during the duration of a hurricane will not take effect until the end of the duration of such hurricane, unless a replacement policy has been obtained and is in effect for a claim occurring during the duration of the hurricane. The insurer may collect premiums for the period of time for which the policy period is extended. A hurricane is defined as a storm system declared to be a hurricane by the National Hurricane Center of the National Weather Service (hereafter referred to as NHC). The hurricane occurrence begins at the time a hurricane watch or hurricane warning is issued for any part of Florida by the NHC, and ends seventy-two hours after the termination of the last hurricane watch or hurricane warning issued for any part of Florida by the NHC.

COMMERCIAL AUTO

Florida Statutes Annotated §§627.4133, 627.7277 through 627.7283

Cancellation during the Underwriting Period

Length of Underwriting Period: Ninety days.

Length of Notice: Ten days for nonpayment; forty-five days for any other reason.

FLORIDA

Reason for Cancellation: Required on the notice.

Proof Required: United States postal proof of mailing, or registered or certified mail.

During the underwriting period, a policy which provides personal injury protection and liability coverage:

1. May not be cancelled by the named insured except for one of the following reasons:

   a. The covered "auto" is completely destroyed such that it is no longer operable.

   b. Ownership of the covered "auto" is transferred.

   c. The named insured has purchased another policy covering the motor vehicle insured under this policy.

2. The insurer may not cancel for nonpayment of premium during the first sixty days following the date of policy issuance unless a check used to pay is dishonored for any reason.

Cancellation after the Underwriting Period

The policy may be cancelled for any reason.

Length of Notice: Ten days for nonpayment of premium; forty-five days for any other reason.

Reason for Cancellation: Required on the notice.

Proof Required: United States postal proof of mailing, or registered or certified mail.

Nonrenewal

Length of Notice: Forty-five days.

Reason for Nonrenewal: Required on the notice.

Proof Required: United States Postal Service proof of mailing or registered or certified mail.

Other Cancellation/Nonrenewal Provisions

The specific reason for a declination must accompany the declination.

A thirty-day notice of the renewal premium is required. If the insured does not pay the renewal premium, the policy automatically terminates. If the insurer fails to provide thirty

FLORIDA

days' notice of a renewal premium that results in a premium increase, the coverage under the policy remains in effect at existing rates until thirty days after notice is given or until the effective date of replacement coverage obtained by the insured, whichever occurs first.

Florida shall suspend the registration of a motor carrier who operates a commercial motor vehicle or permits it to be operated in Florida during the registration period without having in full force and effect liability insurance, a surety bond, or a valid self-insurance certificate that complies with the law. The liability insurance policy or surety bond may not be cancelled on less than thirty days' written notice by the insurer to the insurance department; such thirty days' notice to commence from the date notice is received by the department.

If the insured cancels the policy the insurer must return any unearned premium within thirty days. The insurer may retain up to 10 percent of the unearned premium and must refund at least 90 percent of the unearned premium. However, the insured may elect to apply the unearned portion of any premium paid to unpaid balances of other policies with the same insurer or insurer group. (MOTOR VEHICLE INSURANCE—RATES AND CHARGES—DISCRIMINATION, 2016 Fla. Sess. Law Serv. Ch. 2016-133 (C.S.C.S.H.B. 659)).

If the insurer cancels the policy, any unearned premium must be returned within fifteen days. The insurer must refund 100 percent of the unearned premium. However, the insured may elect to apply the unearned portion of any premium paid to unpaid balances of other policies with the same insurer or insurer group.

If the unearned premium is not mailed within the applicable period, or applied to the unpaid balance of other policies, the insurer must pay to the insured 8 percent interest on the amount due. If the unearned premium is not mailed within forty-five days after the applicable period, the insured may bring an action against the insurer.

The cancellation law applies to binders that exceed sixty days.

COMMERCIAL GENERAL LIABILITY (CGL); ELECTRONIC DATA; LIQUOR; POLLUTION; PRODUCTS WITHDRAWAL; PRODUCTS & COMPLETED OPERATIONS; OCP; RAILROAD PROTECTIVE; E-COMMERCE; MGT. PROT.

Florida Statutes Annotated §§627.4091 and 627.4133

Cancellation during the Underwriting Period

Length of Underwriting Period: Ninety days.

Length of Notice: Immediate cancellation for material misstatement or misrepresentation, or for failure to comply with underwriting requirements; ten days for nonpayment; twenty days for any other reason.

FLORIDA

Reason for Cancellation: Required on the notice.

Proof Required: United States Postal Service proof of mailing form or use of certified or registered mail services showing the name of the insured, the policy number and date mailed.

Cancellation after the Underwriting Period

The policy may be cancelled **only** for the following reasons:

1. Nonpayment of premium.

2. Material misrepresentation of fact.

3. Failure to comply with underwriting requirements established by the insurer within ninety days of the effective date.

4. Substantial change in the risk.

5. All insureds under such policies for a given class of insureds are being cancelled.

Length of Notice: Ten days for nonpayment; forty-five days for any other allowable reason.

Reason for Cancellation: Required on the notice.

Proof Required: United States Postal Service proof of mailing form or use of certified or registered mail services showing the name of the insured, the policy number and date mailed.

Nonrenewal

Length of Notice: Forty-five days.

Reason for Nonrenewal: Required on the notice.

Proof Required: United States Postal Service proof of mailing form or use of certified or registered mail services showing the name of the insured, the policy number and date mailed.

Other Cancellation/Nonrenewal Provisions

The specific reason for a declination must accompany the declination.

For OCP, all notices must be sent to the named insured and to the contractor shown in the declarations.

FLORIDA

For Railroad Protective, all notices of cancellation must be mailed to the named insured, the contractor, any involved governmental authority, or other contracting party designated in the declarations. ISO CG 00 35 requires the notice be mailed at least sixty days before the effective date of cancellation, and proof of mailing is sufficient proof of notice. Additionally, CG 00 35 requires only a thirty-day notice of nonrenewal.

A forty-five-day notice of the renewal premium is required.

If the insured cancels the policy the insurer must return any unearned premium within thirty days.

If the insurer cancels the policy, any unearned premium must be returned within fifteen days.

Nonpayment of premium includes a check dishonored by the bank. If a dishonored check represents the initial premium payment, the contract and all contractual obligations shall be void ab initio unless the nonpayment is cured within the earlier of five days after actual notice by certified mail is received by the applicant or fifteen days after notice is sent to the applicant by certified mail or registered mail. If the contract is void, any premium received by the insurer from a third-party must be refunded to that party in full.

COMMERCIAL GENERAL LIABILITY (UNDERGROUND STORAGE TANKS)

Florida Statutes Annotated §§627.4091 and 627.4133

Cancellation during the Underwriting Period

Length of Underwriting Period: Ninety days.

Length of Notice: Ten days for nonpayment or material misstatement; forty-five days for any other reason. The Florida Code requires only a forty-five-day notice, however, if an insurer has adopted the ISO amendatory endorsement (CG 00 42), it must give a ten day notice for nonpayment or material misstatement and a sixty-day notice for all other reasons.

Reason for Cancellation: Required on the notice.

Proof Required: Certified mail.

Cancellation after the Underwriting Period

The policy may be cancelled **only** for the following reasons:

1. Nonpayment of premium.

FLORIDA

2. Material misrepresentation of fact.

3. Failure to comply with underwriting requirements established by the insurer within ninety days of the effective date.

4. Substantial change in the risk.

5. All insureds under such policies for a given class of insureds are being cancelled.

Length of Notice: Ten days for nonpayment; forty-five days for reason 2 above; sixty days for all other allowable reasons. The Florida Code requires only a forty-five-day notice. However, if an insurer has adopted the ISO amendatory endorsement, it must give a sixty-day notice (CG 30 15).

Reason for Cancellation: Required on the notice.

Proof Required: Certified mail.

Nonrenewal

Length of Notice: Forty-five days. However, if an insurer has adopted the ISO amendatory endorsement, it must give a sixty-day notice.

Reason for Nonrenewal: Required on the notice.

Proof Required: Certified mail.

Other Cancellation/Nonrenewal Provisions

The specific reason for a declination must accompany the declination.

A forty-five-day notice of the renewal premium is required.

If the insured cancels the policy the insurer must return any unearned premium within thirty days.

If the insurer cancels the policy, any unearned premium must be returned within fifteen days.

Nonpayment of premium includes a check dishonored by the bank. If a dishonored check represents the initial premium payment, the contract and all contractual obligations shall be void ab initio unless the nonpayment is cured within the earlier of five days after actual notice

FLORIDA

by certified mail is received by the applicant or fifteen days after notice is sent to the applicant by certified mail or registered mail. If the contract is void, any premium received by the insurer from a third-party must be refunded to that party in full.

BOP; COMMERCIAL UMBRELLA; FARM UMB.

Florida Statutes Annotated §§627.4091 and 627.4133

Cancellation during the Underwriting Period

Length of Underwriting Period: Ninety days.

Length of Notice: Immediate cancellation for material misstatement or misrepresentation, or for failure to comply with underwriting requirements; ten days for nonpayment; twenty days for any other reason. Florida statutes only require twenty days' notice for other reasons, but insurers using ISO's CX 02 09 or CU 02 03 must provide forty-five days' notice.

Reason for Cancellation: Required on the notice.

Proof Required: United States Postal Service proof of mailing form or use of certified or registered mail services showing the name of the insured, the policy number and date mailed.

Cancellation after the Underwriting Period

The policy may be cancelled **only** for the following reasons:

1. Nonpayment of premium.

2. Material misrepresentation of fact.

3. Failure to comply with underwriting requirements established by the insurer within ninety days of the effective date.

4. Substantial change in the risk.

5. All insureds under such policies for a given class of insureds are being cancelled.

Length of Notice: Ten days for nonpayment; twenty days for any other allowable reason. Florida statutes only require twenty days' notice for other reasons, but insurers using ISO's CX 02 09 or CU 02 03 must provide forty-five days' notice.

Reason for Cancellation: Required on the notice.

Proof Required: United States Postal Service proof of mailing form or use of certified or registered mail services showing the name of the insured, the policy number and date mailed.

FLORIDA

Nonrenewal

Length of Notice: Forty-five days.

Reason for Nonrenewal: Required on the notice.

Proof Required: United States Postal Service proof of mailing form or use of certified or registered mail services showing the name of the insured, the policy number and date mailed.

PROFESSIONAL LIABILITY
Florida Statutes Annotated §§627.4133 and 627.4147
Cancellation during the Underwriting Period

Length of Underwriting Period: Ninety days.

Length of Notice: Immediate cancellation for material misstatement or misrepresentation, or for failure to comply with underwriting requirements; ten days for nonpayment of premium, or loss of license; ninety days for any other reason.

Reason for Cancellation: Required on the notice.

Proof Required: United States Postal Service proof of mailing form or use of certified or registered mail services showing the name of the insured, the policy number and date mailed.

Cancellation after the Underwriting Period

The policy may be cancelled **only** for the following reasons:

1. Nonpayment of premium.

2. Material misrepresentation on the application.

3. Failure to comply with underwriting requirements established by the insurer within ninety days of the policy's effective date.

4. Substantial change in the risk.

5. If the insurer is cancelling all insureds under such policies in a given class.

Length of Notice: Ten days for nonpayment of premium or loss of license; ninety days for any other allowable reason.

FLORIDA

Reason for Cancellation: Required on the notice.

Proof Required: United States Postal Service proof of mailing form or use of certified or registered mail services showing the name of the insured, the policy number and date mailed.

Nonrenewal

Length of Notice: Ten days for nonpayment or loss of license; ninety days for any other reason.

Reason for Nonrenewal: United States Postal Service proof of mailing form or use of certified or registered mail services showing the name of the insured, the policy number and date mailed.

Proof Required: Proof of mailing.

Other Cancellation/Nonrenewal Provisions

For insurers following ISO standards, the required length of notice may be less for other professions, including lawyers, real estate agents and brokers. Please refer to ISO forms for the appropriate notice requirements.

A sixty day notice is required for any increase in premium rate.

The specific reason for a declination must accompany the declination.

If the policy is cancelled, the insurer must return any unearned premium within fifteen days.

Nonpayment of premium includes a check dishonored by the bank. If a dishonored check represents the initial premium payment, the contract and all contractual obligations shall be void *ab initio* unless the nonpayment is cured within the earlier of five days after actual notice by certified mail is received by the applicant or fifteen days after notice is sent to the applicant by certified mail or registered mail. If the contract is void, any premium received by the insurer from a third-party must be refunded to that party in full.

WORKERS COMPENSATION

Florida Statutes Annotated §627.4133.; Fla. Admin. Code Ann. r. 69O-189.011 and 69L-56.200

Although the Florida policy makes no changes from the standard cancellation provisions, the statute cited requires the insurer to give the named insured at least forty-five days' advance written notice of nonrenewal. If the policy is not to be renewed, the written notice shall state the reason or reasons as to why the policy is not to be renewed. This requirement applies

FLORIDA

only if the insured has furnished all of the necessary information so as to enable the insurer to develop the renewal premium prior to the expiration date of the policy to be renewed.

The Florida Administrative Code requires a thirty-day notice of cancellation except when cancellation is for the following reasons:

1. The policy has been rewritten by the same company, with the same effective date.

2. Prior to the effective date of the policy, the employer had sold his business or otherwise was out of business and thereafter had no employees.

3. The Division of Workers' Compensation, Department of Financial Services and the employer were given such notice of termination prior to the effective date of the policy.

4. When the employer sells his business or otherwise goes out of business during the effective period of the policy and thereafter has no person in his employment covered by the provisions of such policy, same may be terminated as of the date the employer ceased having any person in his employment by filing such notice of termination with the Division of Worker's Compensation stating therein the reason for termination, and serving a copy thereof upon the employer in person or by mail.

5. When duplicate or dual coverage exists by reason of two different insurers having issued policies to the same employer, effective the same date, securing the same liability, as evidenced by certificates of insurance on file with the Division of Worker's Compensation one of the policies may be cancelled as of the date the notice of termination is filed with the Division of Worker's Compensation and a copy thereof served upon the employer; provided that the terminating insurer may effect retroactive cancellation by filing with the Division of Worker's Compensation a written statement from the other insurer that it assumes full liability in connection with the insured from the cancellation date of the policy which is to be terminated.

6. Where duplicate or dual coverage exists by reason of two different insurers having issued policies of insurance with different effective dates to the same employer, covering the same liability, the insurer which was first on the risk may terminate its coverage upon the effective date of the later coverage of the other insurer by giving notice to the Division of Worker's Compensation and to the employer. Where the policy with the later effective date has already been terminated by filing official notice of termination, it will be presumed that the employer is without coverage in the absence of a replacement certificate of insurance.

7. When an employer is not (no longer) required by the Workers' Compensation Law to secure the payment of compensation to his employee(s) and the employer has

FLORIDA

so advised the insurer in writing that such coverage is not required by the Act, nor desired, during the remainder of the policy period, the insurer may terminate said coverage effective upon filing notice of such termination with the Division of Worker's Compensation stating therein the reason for termination and serving a copy thereof upon the employer in person or by mail.

8. When forty-five days' notice otherwise is required pursuant to Florida Statutes Section 627.4133, and the policy has been in effect for ninety days, no such policy shall be cancelled by the insurer except when there has been a material misstatement, a nonpayment of premium, a failure to comply with underwriting requirements established by the insurer within ninety days of the date of effectuation of coverage, or a substantial change in the risk covered by the policy or when the cancellation is for all insureds under such policies for a given class of insureds.

Reason for Cancellation: Required on the notice.

Proof Required: United States Postal Service proof of mailing form or use of certified or registered mail services showing the name of the insured, the policy number and date mailed.

Special Provisions Required By Fla. Admin. Code Ann. r. 69L-56.200

Except for cancellation for nonpayment, or cancellation or nonrenewal at the request of the insured, an insurer shall not cancel or nonrenew any workers' compensation insurance policy, contract of insurance, or renewal until at least thirty days have elapsed after the insurer has electronically filed a cancellation or nonrenewal with the Division, either directly or through a third-party vendor. When an insurer files an electronic cancellation or nonrenewal directly with the Division for any reason other than nonpayment of premium or when cancellation or nonrenewal is requested by the insured, the thirty-day notice period shall be calculated from the first day following the date on which the electronic cancellation or nonrenewal was filed with the Division. If the insurer files an electronic cancellation or nonrenewal through a third-party vendor for any reason other than nonpayment of premium, or when cancellation or nonrenewal is requested by the insured, the thirty-day notice period shall be calculated from the first day following the "Jurisdiction Designee Received Date". The specific reason for a declination must accompany the declination.

SURPLUS LINES

Florida Statutes Annotated §626.9201

An insurer issuing a policy providing coverage for property, casualty, surety, or marine insurance shall give the named insured at least forty-five days' advance written notice of cancellation or nonrenewal. The written notice shall state the reason or reasons as to why the policy is not to be renewed.

FLORIDA

When cancellation is for nonpayment, at least ten days' written notice of cancellation accompanied by the reason shall be given.

When a cancellation or termination occurs during the first ninety days and the insurance is canceled or terminated for reasons other than nonpayment, at least twenty days' written notice of cancellation or termination accompanied by the reason shall be given except where there has been a material misstatement or misrepresentation or failure to comply with the underwriting requirements established by the insurer.

United States postal proof of mailing or certified or registered mailing of notice of cancellation, of intention not to renew, or of reasons for cancellation, or of the intention of the insurer to issue a policy by an insurer under the same ownership or management, to the named insured at the address shown in the policy shall be sufficient proof of notice. If an insurer fails to provide the required forty-five-day or twenty-day written notice of cancellation or nonrenewal, the coverage provided to the named insured shall remain in effect until forty-five days after the notice is given or until the effective date of replacement coverage obtained by the named insured, whichever occurs first. The premium for the coverage shall remain the same during any such extension period.

FINANCED PREMIUMS
Florida Statutes Annotated §627.848

If the premium finance agreement contains a power of attorney, the finance company may request, in the name of the insured, that the insurer cancel the policy due to nonpayment. The finance company must first give the insured ten days to pay. If the insured fails to make payment within that ten-day period, then the finance company mails the notice of cancellation to the insurer and the cancellation is processed as of the finance company's original default date. However, all statutory, regulatory, and contractual restrictions providing that the insured may not cancel her insurance contract unless she or the insurer first satisfies such restrictions by giving a prescribed notice to a governmental agency, the insurance carrier, a mortgagee, an individual, or a person designated to receive such notice for such governmental agency, insurance carrier, or individual shall apply when cancellation is effected under the provisions of a finance agreement. The insurer is required to give such notice on behalf of itself or the insured, shall give notice to such governmental agency, person, mortgagee, or individual; and it shall determine and calculate the effective date of cancellation from the day it receives the copy of the notice of cancellation from the premium finance company. Return of the policy by the insured is not required. Whenever a financed insurance contract is cancelled, the insurer must return the unpaid balance due to the premium finance company and return any remaining unearned premium to the agent or the insured within thirty days. The premium finance company must return any overpayment within fifteen days.

FLORIDA

PERSONAL LINES
DWELLING FIRE & HOMEOWNERS

Florida Statutes Annotated §§627.4025, 627.4091, 627.4133, and 627.70161; Fla. Admin. Code Ann. r. 69O-167.001

Cancellation during the Underwriting Period

Length of Underwriting Period: Ninety days.

Length of Notice: Immediate cancellation for material misstatement or misrepresentation or for failure to comply with underwriting requirements; ten days for nonpayment; twenty days for any other reason, except as noted below.

Reason for Cancellation: Required on the notice.

Proof Required: United States Postal Service proof of mailing form or use of certified or registered mail services showing the name of the insured, the policy number and date mailed.

During the underwriting period the insurer may not cancel on the basis of:

1. Claims that are the result of an act of God, unless the insurer proves that the insured has not taken the necessary steps (as requested by the insurer) to prevent recurrence of damage to the insured property.

2. A single claim which is the result of water damage, unless the insurer can demonstrate that the insured has failed to take action reasonably requested by the insurer to prevent a future similar occurrence of damage to the insured property.

Cancellation after the Underwriting Period

The policy may be cancelled **only** for the following reasons:

1. Nonpayment of premium.

2. Material misstatement.

3. Substantial change in the risk.

4. If the insured does not comply with underwriting requirements within ninety days of the effective date of coverage.

5. If the insurer is cancelling all insureds under such policies.

FLORIDA

6. On the basis of property insurance claims that are the result of an act of God if the insurer can show that the insured has failed to take action reasonably necessary, as requested, to prevent recurrence of damage to the insured property.

7. On the basis of a single claim which is the result of water damage, if the insurer can demonstrate that the insured has failed to take action reasonably requested by the insurer to prevent a future similar occurrence of damage to the insured property.

Length of Notice: Ten days for nonpayment; 120 days for any other allowable reason; 120 days if the structure has been insured by the insurer or an affiliate for five years or longer immediately prior to the notice.

Reason for Cancellation: Required on the notice.

Proof Required: United States Postal Service proof of mailing form or use of certified or registered mail services showing the name of the insured, the policy number and date mailed.

Nonrenewal

Length of Notice: Forty-five days' notice of renewal premium, 120 days' notice of nonrenewal; 120 days' notice if the residential structure has been insured by the insurer or an affiliate for five years or longer immediately prior to the notice.

Reason for Nonrenewal: Required on the notice.

Proof Required: United States Postal Service proof of mailing form or use of certified or registered mail services showing the name of the insured, the policy number and date mailed.

Other Cancellation/Nonrenewal Provisions

Residential property insurance coverage should not be canceled, denied, or nonrenewed solely on the basis of the family day care services at the residence.

An insurer may cancel or nonrenew with at least forty-five days' notice if the office finds that early cancellation of some or all of the insurer's policies is necessary to protect the best interests of the public or policyholders and the office approves the insurer's plan for early cancellation or nonrenewal of some or all of its policies.

Insurers are required to provide at least 120 days' written notice, for any reason other than nonpayment of premium.

FLORIDA

Any insurer planning to nonrenew more than 10,000 residential property insurance policies in this state within a twelve-month period shall give notice in writing to the Office of Insurance Regulation for informational purposes ninety days before the issuance of any notices of nonrenewal. The notice provided to the office must set forth the insurer's reasons for such action, the effective dates of nonrenewal, and any arrangements made for other insurers to offer coverage to affected policyholders.

Unless otherwise provided in the contract, upon cancellation by the company or the insured, the insurer must return any unearned premium within fifteen days.

The specific reason for a declination must accompany the declination.

If a state of emergency is declared by the Governor and the Commissioner of Insurance Regulation files an Emergency Order, and the "residence premises" has been damaged as a result of a hurricane or wind loss that is the subject of the declared emergency; then during the period beginning from the date the state of emergency is declared to the expiration of ninety days following the repairs to the dwelling or other structure located on the residence premises, the insurer may not cancel or nonrenew. If the insurer elects to nonrenew a policy covering a property that has been damaged, the insurer must provide at least ninety days' notice to the insured of intent to nonrenew the property ninety days after the dwelling or residential property has been repaired. The insurer or agent may cancel or nonrenew prior to the repair of the dwelling or residential property:

1. Upon ten days' notice for nonpayment of premium.

2. There has been a material misstatement or fraud related to the claim, with forty-five days' notice.

3. The insurer determines that the insured has unreasonably caused a delay in the repair of the dwelling or other structure, with forty-five days' notice.

4. The insurer has paid policy limits, with forty-five days' notice.

If the date of nonrenewal becomes effective during a "hurricane occurrence":

1. The expiration date of this policy will not become effective until the end of the "hurricane occurrence."

2. The insurer is entitled to collect additional premium for the period the policy remains in effect at prior rates or rates then in effect.

FLORIDA

The insurer may not nonrenew for these reasons:

1. On the basis of property insurance claims that are the result of an act of God unless the insurer can show that the insured has failed to take action reasonably necessary, as requested, to prevent recurrence of damage to the insured property.

With respect to a policy covering a residential structure or its contents, any cancellation or nonrenewal that would otherwise take effect during the duration of a hurricane will not take effect until the end of the duration of such hurricane, unless a replacement policy has been obtained and is in effect for a claim occurring during the duration of the hurricane. The insurer may collect premiums for the period of time for which the policy period is extended. A hurricane is defined as a storm system declared to be a hurricane by the National Hurricane Center of the National Weather Service (hereafter referred to as NHC). The hurricane occurrence begins at the time a hurricane watch or hurricane warning is issued for any part of Florida by the NHC, and ends seventy-two hours after the termination of the last hurricane watch or hurricane warning issued for any part of Florida by the NHC.

PERSONAL AUTO

Florida Statutes Annotated §§627.4091; 627.7277 through 627.7283; 627.7295

Cancellation during the Underwriting Period

Length of Underwriting Period: Sixty days.

The policy may be cancelled **only** for the following reasons:

1. The covered auto has been totally destroyed so that it is no longer operable.

2. The named insured transfers ownership of "your covered auto".

3. The named insured obtains other insurance on the covered auto.

4. If a check used for payment is dishonored for any reason.

Length of Notice: Ten days for any reason. ISO provides that cancellation for nonpayment occurs if a check is dishonored or any other type of premium payment is rejected or invalid (PP 01 84).

Reason for Cancellation: Required on the notice.

Proof Required: United States postal proof of mailing, or registered or certified mail to the first named insured at the address shown in the policy.

FLORIDA

Cancellation after the Underwriting Period

The policy may be cancelled **only** for the following reasons:

1. Nonpayment of premium.

2. Revocation or suspension of the driver's license or motor vehicle registration of the named insured or of any driver who lives with the named insured or customarily uses the named insured's auto. Such revocation or suspension must have occurred during the policy period, if the policy is a renewal, or 180 days prior to the original effective date.

3. Fraud or material misrepresentation on the application.

Length of Notice: Ten days for nonpayment; forty-five days for any other allowable reason.

Reason for Cancellation: Required on the notice.

Proof Required: United States Postal Service proof of mailing, or registered or certified mail, mailed to the first named insured and the first named insured's insurance agent.

Nonrenewal

Length of Notice: Forty-five days.

Reason for Nonrenewal: Required on the notice.

Proof Required: United States postal proof of mailing or registered or certified mail, mailed to the first named insured at the address shown in the policy and to the first named insured's insurance agent at their business address.

Other Cancellation/Nonrenewal Provisions

The specific reason for a declination must accompany the declination.

A thirty-day notice of the renewal premium is required. If the insured does not pay the renewal premium, the policy automatically terminates. If the insurer fails to provide a thirty days' notice of a renewal premium that results in a premium increase, the coverage under the policy remains in effect at existing rates until thirty days after notice is given or until the effective date of replacement coverage obtained by the insured, whichever occurs first.

Instead of cancelling or nonrenewing, an insurer may, upon expiration of the policy term, transfer a policy to another insurer under the same ownership or management as the

FLORIDA

transferring insurer, by giving the first named insured at least forty-five days' advance notice of its intent to transfer the policy and of the premium and the specific reasons for any increase in the premium.

No later than ten business days after termination of a policy, the insurer must send written or electronic notice of the termination to all holders of liens on the subject vehicle which lienholders are known to the insurer. Electronic notice is valid when there is a prior agreement between the insurer and the lienholder.

If the policy term is less than six months, the insurer may nonrenew every six months, beginning six months after the original effective date.

Nonpayment of premium includes a check dishonored by the bank. If a dishonored check represents the initial premium payment, the contract and all contractual obligations shall be void ab initio unless the nonpayment is cured within the earlier of five days after actual notice by certified mail is received by the applicant or fifteen days after notice is sent to the applicant by certified mail or registered mail. If the contract is void, any premium received by the insurer from a third-party must be refunded to that party in full.

If the policy term is one year or longer, the insurer may nonrenew the policy at each anniversary of the original effective date.

Except for nonpayment cancellation or nonrenewal of the policy, the notice of cancellation must contain the following wording: "You are permitted by law to appeal this cancellation. An appeal must be filed no later than twenty days before the effective date of cancellation set forth in this notice. Forms for such appeal and the regulations pertaining thereto may be obtained from the office. The office does not have the authority to extend the effective date of cancellation; therefore you should obtain replacement coverage prior to the effective date of cancellation."

If the insured cancels the policy the insurer must mail any unearned premium within thirty days after the effective date of the policy cancellation or receipt of notice or request for cancellation, whichever is later.

If the insurer cancels the policy, any unearned premium must be returned to the insured within fifteen days after the effective date of the policy cancellation. Failure to mail the unearned premium within the applicable period will result in the insurer paying to the insured 8 percent interest on the amount due. Failure to mail the unearned premium within forty-five days after the applicable period permits the insured to bring action against the insurer. However, the insured may elect to apply the unearned portion of any premium paid to unpaid balances of other policies with the same insurer or insurer group.

FLORIDA

If the insured cancels, the insurer may retain up to 10 percent of the unearned premium and must refund at least 90 percent. If the insurer cancels, the insurer must refund 100 percent of the unearned premium. However, the insured may elect to apply the unearned portion of any premium paid to unpaid balances of other policies with the same insurer or insurer group. (MOTOR VEHICLE INSURANCE—RATES AND CHARGES—DISCRIMINATION, 2016 Fla. Sess. Law Serv. Ch. 2016-133 (C.S.C.S.H.B. 659)).

The insurer must refund 100 percent of the unearned premium if the insured is called to active duty or transferred by the United States Armed Forces to a location where the insurance is not required. Unearned premium must be pro rata. Insurer is permitted to require a written verification of orders.

The insurer may not nonrenew solely because the insured was convicted of one or more traffic violations that did not result in an accident or in the insured's driver's license being suspended or revoked.

However, the insurer may nonrenew if the named insured was convicted of:

1. Two such traffic violations within an eighteen-month period.

2. Three or more such traffic violations within a thirty-six-month period.

3. Exceeding the lawful speed limit by more than fifteen miles per hour.

The insurer may also not nonrenew solely because the insured has had an accident. However, the insurer may nonrenew if the named insured has had two or more at-fault accidents, or three or more accidents regardless of fault, within the current three-year period.

When a policy is terminated for reasons other than nonpayment, the insurer shall notify the insured of possible eligibility in the Automobile Joint Underwriting Association.

PERSONAL UMBRELLA

Florida Statutes Annotated §§627.4133, and 627.4091

Cancellation during the Underwriting Period

Length of Underwriting Period: Ninety days.

Length of Notice: Immediate cancellation for material misstatement or misrepresentation, or failure to comply with underwriting requirements; ten days for nonpayment; twenty days for any other reason. (ISO Amendatory Endorsement DL 98 75 requires a ten-day

FLORIDA

notice for material misstatement or representation or failure to comply with underwriting requirements).

Reason for Cancellation: Required on the notice.

Proof Required: United States Postal Service proof of mailing form or use of certified or registered mail services showing the name of the insured, the policy number and date mailed.

Cancellation after the Underwriting Period

The policy may be cancelled **only** for the following reasons:

1. Nonpayment of premium.

2. A material misstatement.

3. The risk has changed substantially since the policy was issued.

4. The insured's failure to comply with underwriting requirements established by the insurer within ninety days of the effective date of coverage.

5. If the cancellation is for all insureds under policies of this type for a given class of insureds.

Length of Notice: Ten days for nonpayment; forty-five days for any other allowable reason.

Reason for Cancellation: Required on the notice.

Proof Required: United States Postal Service proof of mailing form or use of certified or registered mail services showing the name of the insured, the policy number and date mailed.

Nonrenewal

Length of Notice: Forty-five days.

Reason for Nonrenewal: Required on the notice.

Proof Required: United States Postal Service proof of mailing form or use of certified or registered mail services showing the name of the insured, the policy number and date mailed.

FLORIDA

FRAUD

Florida Statutes Annotated §§817.234; 400.991; 626.989; 626.9891; 626.9892; 775.082; 775.084

General Information and Definitions

A person commits insurance fraud if that person, with the intent to injure, defraud, or deceive any insurer presents a claim for payment knowing that such claim contains any false, incomplete, or misleading information concerning any fact or thing material to such claim; or if a person presents false, incomplete or misleading information or statement as part of or in support of an application for the issuance of or rating of an insurance policy; or if that person knowingly submits:

   a. A false, misleading, or fraudulent application or other document when applying for licensure as a health care clinic, seeking an exemption from licensure as a health care clinic, or demonstrating compliance with part X of chapter 400 with an intent to use the license, exemption from licensure, or demonstration of compliance to provide services or seek reimbursement under the Florida Motor Vehicle No–Fault Law.

   b. A claim for payment or other benefit pursuant to a personal injury protection insurance policy under the Florida Motor Vehicle No–Fault Law if the person knows that the payee knowingly submitted a false, misleading, or fraudulent application or other document when applying for licensure as a health care clinic, seeking an exemption from licensure as a health care clinic, or demonstrating compliance with part X of chapter 400 (Fla. Stat. Ann. §626.989). All claims and application forms must contain a statement that is approved by the Office of Insurance Regulation of the Financial Services Commission which clearly states in substance the following:

   "Any person who knowingly and with intent to injure, defraud, or deceive any insurer files a statement of claim or an application containing any false, incomplete, or misleading information is guilty of a felony of the third degree." This paragraph shall not apply to reinsurance contracts, reinsurance agreements, or reinsurance claims transactions.

   Additionally, all agency forms for licensure application or exemption from licensure for health care clinics must contain the following Insurance Fraud Notice statement:

   "A person who knowingly submits a false, misleading, or fraudulent application or other document when applying for licensure as a health care clinic, seeking an exemption from licensure as a health care clinic, or demonstrating compliance with part X of chapter 400, Florida Statutes, with the intent to use the license, exemption from licensure, or demonstration of compliance to provide services or seek reimbursement under the Florida Motor Vehicle No–Fault Law, commits

FLORIDA

a fraudulent insurance act, as defined in s. 626.989, Florida Statutes. A person who presents a claim for personal injury protection benefits knowing that the payee knowingly submitted such health care clinic application or document, commits insurance fraud, as defined in s. 817.234, Florida Statutes". (Fla. Stat. Ann. §400.991).

Penalties

If the value of any property involved in a violation of this section is less than $20,000, the offender commits a felony of the third degree, punishable by a term of imprisonment not exceeding five years, a fine of $5,000, or both; if the value of property involved is $20,000 or more, but less than $100,000, the offender commits a felony of the second degree, punishable by a term of imprisonment not exceeding fifteen years, a fine of $10,000, or both; if the property involved is $100,000 or more, the offender commits a felony of the first degree, punishable by a term of imprisonment not exceeding thirty years or, when specifically provided by statute, by imprisonment of a term of years not exceeding life imprisonment, a fine of $10,000, or both.

In addition to any criminal liability, a person convicted of violating any provision of this section for the purpose of receiving insurance proceeds from a motor vehicle insurance contract is subject to a civil penalty. The civil penalty will be a fine up to $5,000 for a first offense; a fine greater than $5,000, but not to exceed $10,000, for a second offense; and a fine greater than $10,000, but not to exceed $15,000, for a third or subsequent offense.

Reporting Requirements

Florida has an Anti-Fraud Reward Program in place. The department may pay rewards of up to $25,000 to persons providing information leading to the arrest and conviction of persons committing crimes investigated by the Division of Insurance Fraud arising from insurance fraud.

Antifraud Provisions

Every insurer admitted to do business in this state who at any time during the previous calendar year that had $10 million or more in direct premiums written must establish and maintain a unit or division within the company to investigate possible fraudulent claims by insureds or by persons making claims for services or repairs against policies held by insureds; or contract with others to investigate possible fraudulent claims for services or repairs against policies held by insureds. The commissioner may impose fines if an insurer fails to establish and maintain an adequate plan. An adequate plan includes:

1. A description of the procedures for detecting and investigating fraud.

2. A description of procedures for mandatory reporting.

3. A description of antifraud education and training.

FLORIDA

4. A written description or chart outlining the organizational arrangement of antifraud personnel (Florida Statutes Annotated §626.9891).

FAIR CLAIMS PROCESSING
Florida Statutes Annotated §626.9541

The following are unfair claim settlement practices:

Attempting to settle claims on the basis of an application, when serving as a binder or intended to become a part of the policy, or any other material document which was altered without notice to, or knowledge or consent of, the insured;

A material misrepresentation made to an insured or any other person having an interest in the proceeds payable under the contract or policy, for the purpose and with the intent of effecting settlement of claims, loss, or damage under the contract or policy on less favorable terms that those provided in, and contemplated by, such contract or policy; or

Committing or performing with such frequency as to indicate a general business practice any of the following constitutes and unfair and unlawful business practice:

1. Failing to adopt and implement standards for the proper investigation of claims.

2. Misrepresenting pertinent facts or insurance policy provisions relating to coverages at issue.

3. Failing to acknowledge and act promptly upon communications with respect to claims.

4. Denying claims without conducting reasonable investigations based upon available information.

5. Failing to affirm or deny full or partial coverage of claims, and, as to partial coverage, the dollar amount or extent of coverage, or failing to provide a written statement that the claim is being investigated, upon the written request of the insured within thirty days after proof-of-loss statements have been completed.

6. Failing to promptly provide a reasonable explanation in writing to the insured of the basis in the insurance policy, in relation to the facts or applicable law, for denial of a claim or for the offer of a compromise settlement.

7. Failing to promptly notify the insured of any additional information necessary for the processing of a claim.

FLORIDA

8. Failing to clearly explain the nature of the requested information and the reasons why such information is necessary.

9. Willfully failing to comply with Florida Statute 627.64194 with such frequency as to indicate a general business practice. 627.64194 relates to coverage requirements for services provided by nonparticipating providers and payment collection limitations.

10. Failing to pay personal injury protection insurance claims within the time periods required by 627.736(4)(b).

   (2016 Fla. Sess. Law Serv. Ch. 2016-222 (C.S.C.S.C.S.H.B. 221)).Failing to pay undisputed amounts of partial or full benefits owed under first-party property insurance policies within ninety days after an insurer receives notice of a residential property insurance claim, determines the amounts of partial or full benefits, and agrees to coverage, unless payment of the undisputed benefits is prevented by an act of God, prevented by the impossibility of performance, or due to actions by the insured or claimant that constitute fraud, lack of cooperation, or intentional misrepresentation regarding the claim for which benefits are owed is considered an unfair and unlawful business practice.

GEORGIA

For details on cancellation procedures for the standard policy, refer to the Standard Policy section.

COMMERCIAL LINES
AGRICULTURAL CAPITAL ASSETS

Ga. Code Ann. §§33-24-44; 33-24-47; 33-39-11

Georgia makes no changes from the standard policy. However, legal advice is suggested where such policy may be affected by provisions of Georgia law applicable to other farm and capital assets policies.

CAPITAL ASSETS; C. AUTO; CRIME; CGL (ELECTRONIC DATA; EMPLOYMENT, LIQUOR, OCP, POLLUTION, & PRODUCTS, RAILROAD PROTECTIVE); CIM; C. PROP.; C. UMB.; EQUIPMENT BREAKDOWN; FARM; & PRO. LIAB.

Ga. Code Ann. §§33-24-44; 33-24-47; 33-39-11

Cancellation during the Underwriting Period

Length of Underwriting Period: Sixty days.

Length of Notice: Ten days for any reason.

Reason for Cancellation: Required on the notice.

Proof Required: Proof of mailing.

Cancellation after the Underwriting Period

The policy may be cancelled for any reason.

Length of Notice: Ten days for nonpayment; thirty days for any other reason.

Reason for Cancellation: Not required, but must be provided upon request.

Proof Required: Proof of mailing.

Nonrenewal

Length of Notice: Forty-five days.

Reason for Nonrenewal: Not required, but must be provided upon request.

Proof Required: Proof of mailing.

GEORGIA

Other Cancellation/Nonrenewal Provisions

A forty-five-day notice prior to expiration is required if the insurer decides to increase the premium by more than 15 percent, or to limit or restrict coverage.

For OCP, all notices must be mailed to the named insured and the contractor shown in the declarations.

For Railroad Protective, all notices must be mailed to the named insured, the contractor, and any involved governmental authority or other contracting party shown on the declarations.

Unearned premium must be returned on or before effective date of cancellation either to the insured or to the agent. This shall not apply where an audit or rate investigation is required or if the premiums are financed by a premium finance company. If the insurer elects to return unearned premium to the insured via the insured's agent of record, such agent shall return the unearned premium to the insured in person or by mail within ten working days of receipt of the unearned premium, or within ten working days of notification from the insurer of the amount of return of unearned premium due, or on the effective date of cancellation, whichever is later. If the insured has an open account with the agent, return of unearned premium may be applied to any outstanding balance and any remaining unearned premium shall be returned to the insured in person or by mail, in accordance with the standards aforementioned.

If by statute, regulation, or contract the policy may not be cancelled unless notice is given to a governmental agency, mortgagee or other third-party, the insurer will mail or deliver at least ten days' notice to the first named insured and the third-party as soon as practicable after receiving the first named insured's request for cancellation. The notice will state the effective date of cancellation, which will be the later of the ten days from the date of mailing or delivering our notice, or the effective date of cancellation stated in the first named insured's notice to the insurer.

Electronic notification to lienholders is allowed, with lienholders' consent.

BOP

Ga. Code Ann. §§33-24-44; 33-24-47

Businessowners has no changes from the basic policy except in the case of Pest Applicators. In the event of cancellation, the Structural Pest Control Section of the Department of Agriculture must receive a copy of the notice at least thirty days prior to the date of cancellation. (Ga. Code Ann. §43-45-9(f)).

GEORGIA

Other Cancellation/Nonrenewal Provisions

A forty-five-day notice prior to expiration is required if the insurer decides to increase the premium by more than 15 percent, or to limit or restrict coverage.

If the notice of nonrenewal does not provide the reasons for the action, the notice must include a statement that reasons will be furnished upon request.

Unearned premium must be returned on or before effective date of cancellation either to the insured or to the agent.

Electronic notification to lienholders is allowed, with lienholders consent.

COMMERCIAL GENERAL LIABILITY (UNDERGROUND STORAGE TANKS)

Ga. Code Ann. §§33-24-44; 33-24-47; 33-39-11; ISO Endorsement CG 30 08

Cancellation during the Underwriting Period

Length of Underwriting Period: Sixty days.

Length of Notice: Ten days for any reason.

Reason for Cancellation: Required on the notice.

Proof Required: Certified mail.

Cancellation after the Underwriting Period

The policy may be cancelled for any reason.

Length of Notice: Ten days for nonpayment; thirty days for any other reason.

Reason for Cancellation: Not required on the notice, but must be provided upon request.

Proof Required: Certified mail.

If an insurer has adopted the ISO Endorsement entitled "Georgia Changes–Cancellation and Nonrenewal, Underground Storage Tank Policy," Form number CG 30 08, the following provisions shall apply in place of the Georgia Code:

Length of Notice: Ten days for nonpayment; sixty days for any other reason.

GEORGIA

Reason for Cancellation: Not required on the notice.

Proof Required: Certified mail.

Nonrenewal

Length of Notice: The Georgia Code requires a forty-five-day notice of nonrenewal.

Reason for Nonrenewal: Not required, but must be provided upon request.

Proof Required: Certified mail.

If an insurer has adopted the ISO Endorsement entitled "Georgia Changes–Cancellation and Nonrenewal, Underground Storage Tank Policy," Form number CG 30 08, the following provisions shall apply in place of the Georgia Code:

Length of Notice: Sixty days.

Reason for Nonrenewal: Not required.

Proof Required: Certified mail.

Other Cancellation/Nonrenewal Provisions

A forty-five-day notice prior to expiration is required if the insurer decides to nonrenew, increases the premium by more than 15 percent, other than any increase due to change in risk, exposure or experience modification or resulting from an audit of auditable coverages, or limits or restricts coverage. Unearned premium must be returned on or before effective date of cancellation either to the insured or to the agent. If cancelled by the insured, the insurer shall send the first named insured any premium refund due. If insurer cancels, the refund will be pro rata, except if the cancellation results from failure of the first named insured to pay, when due, any premium to us or any amount, when due, under a premium finance agreement, then the refund may be less than pro rata. Calculation of the return premium at less than pro rata represents a penalty charged on unearned premium. If the first named insured cancels, the refund may be less than pro rata.

The cancellation will be effective even if the insurer has not made or offered a refund. Any insurer or agent failing to return any unearned premium as prescribed in the above sections shall pay to the insured a penalty equal to 25 percent of the amount of the return of the unearned premium and interest equal to 18 percent per-annum until such time that proper return has been made, which penalty and interest must be paid at the time the return is made. However, the maximum amount of such penalty and interest shall not exceed 50 percent of the amount of the refund due.

Electronic notification to lienholders is allowed, with lienholders consent.

GEORGIA

CAPITAL ASSETS; COMMERCIAL PROPERTY; FARM
(Applicable only when named insured is a natural person)
Ga. Code Ann. §§33-24-44; 33-24-36; 33-24-47; 33-39-11

Cancellation during the Underwriting Period

Length of Underwriting Period: Sixty days.

Length of Notice: Ten days for any reason.

Reason for Cancellation: Required on the notice.

Proof Required: Proof of mailing.

Cancellation after the Underwriting Period

The policy may be cancelled **only** for the following reasons:

1. Nonpayment of premium.

2. Fraud or material misrepresentation on the application, in continuing the policy or in pursuing a claim.

3. A substantial increase in any hazard insured against.

4. If any insured violates any of the material terms or conditions of the policy.

Length of Notice: Ten days for nonpayment; thirty days for any other reason.

Reason for Cancellation: Required on the notice.

Proof Required: Proof of mailing.

Nonrenewal

Length of Notice: Forty-five days.

Reason for Nonrenewal: Not required, but must be provided upon request.

Proof Required: Proof of mailing.

GEORGIA

Other Cancellation/Nonrenewal Provisions

A forty-five-day notice prior to expiration is required if the insurer decides to increase the premium by more than 15 percent, other than any increase due to change in risk, exposure or experience modification or resulting from an audit of auditable coverages, or to limit or restrict coverage.

Unearned premium must be returned on or before effective date of cancellation either to the insured or to the agent. If cancelled by the insured, the insurer shall send the first named insured any premium refund due. If insurer cancels, the refund will be pro rata, except if the cancellation results from failure of the first named insured to pay, when due, any premium to us or any amount, when due, under a premium finance agreement, then the refund may be less than pro rata. Calculation of the return premium at less than pro rata represents a penalty charged on unearned premium. If the first named insured cancels, the refund may be less than pro rata.

The cancellation will be effective even if the insurer has not made or offered a refund. Any insurer or agent failing to return any unearned premium as prescribed in the above sections shall pay to the insured a penalty equal to twenty-five percent of the amount of the return of the unearned premium and interest equal to eighteen percent per-annum until such time that proper return has been made, which penalty and interest must be paid at the time the return is made. However, the maximum amount of such penalty and interest shall not exceed fifty percent of the amount of the refund due.

Electronic notification to lienholders is allowed, with lienholders consent.

WORKERS COMPENSATION

Ga. Code Ann. §§33-24-44; 33-24-44.1; 33-24-47

Cancellation during the Underwriting Period

Length of Underwriting Period: Sixty days.

Length of Notice: Ten days for any reason.

Reason for Cancellation: Required on the notice.

Proof Required: Certified mail.

Cancellation after the Underwriting Period

The policy may be cancelled for any reason.

Length of Notice: Ten days for nonpayment; seventy-five days for any other reason.

GEORGIA

Reason for Cancellation: Not required on the notice.

Proof Required: Certified mail.

Nonrenewal

Length of Notice: Seventy-five days.

Reason for Nonrenewal: Required on the notice.

Proof Required: Certified mail.

Other Cancellation/Nonrenewal Provisions

A forty-five-day notice prior to expiration is required if the insurer increases the premium by more than fifteen percent (other than any increase due to change in risk, exposure or experience modification, or resulting from an audit of auditable coverages), or limits or restricts coverage. The dollar amount of premium increase must be specified.

The Georgia Court of Appeals has held that a workers' compensation insurer was not required to provide notice to insured of nonrenewal of policy, where insurer offered to renew policy, but coverage was terminated because of nonpayment of renewal premium. *Riley v. Taylor Orchards*, 226 Ga. App. 394, 486 S.E.2d 617 (1997). When the named insured desires cancellation of the policy, the insured may cancel the policy by mailing or delivering advance notice to the insurer stating a future date on which the policy is to be cancelled, subject to the following specifications:

1. If only the insured's interest is affected, the policy shall be cancelled on the date the returned policy or written request is received by the insurer or the date specified in the written request, whichever is later. Upon receipt of a written request for cancellation from an insured, an insurer may waive the future date requirement by confirming the date and time of cancellation in writing to the insured.

2. If by statute, regulation, or contract the insurance policy may not be cancelled unless notice is given to a governmental agency, mortgagee, or other third-party, the insurer shall mail or deliver such notice stating the date cancellation shall become effective, but such date shall not be less than ten days from the date of mailing or delivery of the notice.

SURPLUS LINES
Ga. Code Ann. §33-5-21.1

Length of Underwriting Period: Sixty days.

Length of Notice: Ten days for any reason.

GEORGIA

Reason for Cancellation: Required on the notice.

Proof Required: Proof of mailing.

Cancellation after the Underwriting Period

The policy may be cancelled for any reason.

Length of Notice: Ten days for nonpayment; thirty days for any other reason.

Reason for Cancellation: Not required, but must be provided upon request.

Proof Required: Proof of mailing.

Nonrenewal

Length of Notice: Forty-five days.

Reason for Nonrenewal: Not required, but must be provided upon request.

Proof Required: Proof of mailing.

FINANCED PREMIUMS

Ga. Code Ann. §§33-22-13; 33-24-44

If the premium finance agreement contains a power of attorney, the finance company may request, in the name of the insured, that the insurer cancel the policy due to nonpayment. The finance company must first give the insured ten days to pay. If the insured fails to make payment within that ten-day period, then the finance company mails the notice of cancellation to the insurer and the cancellation is processed as of the finance company's original default date. Return of the policy by the insured is not required.

For cancellations after the underwriting period, notice to the insured shall not be required where a policy is cancelled by an insurance premium finance company under a power of attorney contained in an insurance premium finance agreement if notification of the existence of the premium finance agreement has been given to the insurer. Such agreement shall substantially comply with the following form:

> "Your insurance policy premiums have been financed and are payable on a monthly payment basis. If you do not pay each payment on or before the date due or within fifteen days of the date due, we have the right to CANCEL your insurance policy or policies which are financed under the premium finance agreement.

GEORGIA

To avoid cancellation of your policy or policies, MAKE YOUR PAYMENTS ON TIME." (Ga. Code Ann. §§33-24-46(h) [updated March 13, 2015 but this part still accurate] and 33-22-12.1).

Even where notice to the insured is waived, however, the insurer must still give the prescribed notice on behalf of itself or the insured to any governmental agency, mortgagee, or other third-party on or before the second business day after the day it receives the notice of cancellation from the premium finance company and shall determine the effective date of cancellation taking into consideration the number of days required to complete the cancellation.

PERSONAL LINES
DWELLING FIRE & HOMEOWNERS

Ga. Code Ann. §§33-24-46; 33-24-47; 33-39-11

Cancellation during the Underwriting Period

Length of Underwriting Period: Sixty days.

Length of Notice: Ten days for any reason.

Reason for Cancellation: Required on the notice.

Proof Required: Proof of mailing.

Cancellation after the Underwriting Period

The policy may be cancelled **only** for the following reasons:

1. Nonpayment of premium.

2. Fraud, concealment of material fact, or material misrepresentation on the application or in pursuing a claim.

3. A substantial increase in any hazard insured against.

4. If any insured violates any of the material terms or conditions of the policy.

Length of Notice: Ten days for nonpayment; thirty days for any other reason.

Reason for Cancellation: Required on the notice.

Proof Required: Proof of mailing.

GEORGIA

Nonrenewal

Length of Notice: Thirty days.

Reason for Nonrenewal: Required on the notice.

Proof Required: Proof of mailing.

Other Cancellation/Nonrenewal Provisions

The following must appear on the nonrenewal notice:

NOTICE

"Code Section 33-24-46 of the Official Code of Georgia Annotated provides that this insurer must, upon request, furnish you with the reasons for the failure to renew this policy. If you wish to assert that the nonrenewal is unlawful, you must file a written notice with this insurer before the time at which the nonrenewal becomes effective. The notice must specify the manner in which the failure to renew is alleged to be unlawful. If you do not file the written notice, you may not later assert a claim or action against this insurer based upon an unlawful nonrenewal."

If by statute, regulation or contract the policy may not be cancelled unless notice is given to a governmental agency, mortgagee or other third-party. The insurer will mail or deliver at least ten days' notice to the first named insured and the third-party as soon as practicable after receiving the first named insured's request for cancellation. The notice will state the effective date of cancellation, which will be the later of the ten days from the date of mailing or delivering our notice, or the effective date of cancellation stated in the first named insured's notice to the insurer.

If the policy is being nonrenewed because the agent no longer represents the insurer, the following must appear on the nonrenewal notice: Your policy has not been renewed because your present agent no longer represents this insurer. You have the option of procuring coverage through your present agent or retaining this policy by applying through another agent of this insurer. Code Section 33-24-46 of the Official Code of Georgia Annotated provides that if you will locate another agent of the insurer and apply for this policy before the time at which the nonrenewal becomes effective, this insurer will treat the application as a renewal and not as an application for a new policy.

Unearned premium must be returned on or before effective date of cancellation either to the insured or to the agent. If cancelled by the insured, the insurer shall send the first named insured any premium refund due. If insurer cancels, the refund will be pro rata, except if the cancellation results from failure of the first named insured to pay, when due, any premium

GEORGIA

to us or any amount, when due, under a premium finance agreement, then the refund may be less than pro rata. Calculation of the return premium at less than pro rata represents a penalty charged on unearned premium. If the first named insured cancels, the refund may be less than pro rata.

The cancellation will be effective even if the insurer has not made or offered a refund. Any insurer or agent failing to return any unearned premium as prescribed in the above sections shall pay to the insured a penalty equal to twenty-five percent of the amount of the return of the unearned premium and interest equal to eighteen percent per-annum until such time that proper return has been made, which penalty and interest must be paid at the time the return is made. However, the maximum amount of such penalty and interest shall not exceed fifty percent of the amount of the refund due.

When cancelling for reasons other than nonpayment, the insurer must provide notification of possible eligibility for coverage through the Georgia Fair Access to Insurance Requirements "FAIR" plan. The notice shall accompany or be included in the notice of cancellation or the notice of intent not to renew or not to continue the policy and shall state that such notice availability of the FAIR Plan is given. Included in the notice shall be the address by which the FAIR Plan might be contacted in order to determine eligibility.

PERSONAL AUTO

Ga. Code Ann. §§33-24-44; 33-24-45; 33-24-46; 33-39-11

Cancellation during the Underwriting Period

Length of Underwriting Period: Sixty days.

Length of Notice: Ten days for any reason.

Reason for Cancellation: Required on the notice. Even though the amendatory endorsement does not require that the reason for cancellation be shown, Georgia law requires that the reason be shown.

Proof Required: Proof of mailing.

Cancellation after the Underwriting Period

Georgia Statutes allow mid-term cancellation for the following reasons:

1. Nonpayment of premium. Such notice of cancellation issued to an insured, who is paying on a monthly basis, may be included with the bill issued to the insured, provided that the bill is mailed to the insured at least ten days prior to the due date.

2. Material misrepresentation on the application.

GEORGIA

3. Violation by any insured of any of the terms and conditions of the policy.

4. If called for in the application, the named insured does not fully disclose his or her driving record for the preceding thirty-six months.

5. If the named insured does not disclose the information necessary for the acceptance or proper rating of the risk.

6. If the named insured made a false or fraudulent claim.

7. The named insured or any other operator either resident in the same household or who customarily operates an automobile insured under such policy:

    a. Has the driver's license under suspension or revocation within the previous thirty-six months.

    b. Is or becomes subject to heart attacks or epilepsy. However, such an individual may produce a certificate from a physician testifying to that individual's ability to operate a motor vehicle.

    c. Has an accident record, a conviction record, criminal or traffic, or a physical, mental, or other condition that is such that his operation of an automobile might endanger the public safety.

    d. Has within the previous three years been addicted to the use of narcotics or other drugs.

    e. Has been convicted during the thirty-six months immediately preceding the effective date of the policy or during the policy period of:

        (1) A felony.
        (2) Criminal negligence resulting in death, homicide, or assault, and arising out of the operation of a motor vehicle.
        (3) Operating a motor vehicle while intoxicated or under the influence of drugs.
        (4) Being intoxicated while in or about an automobile or while having custody of an automobile.
        (5) Leaving the scene of the accident.
        (6) Theft or unlawful taking of an automobile.
        (7) Making false statements in an application for a driver's license.

    f. Has been convicted of or forfeited bail for three or more violations, within the last thirty-six months of any law, ordinance, or regulation limiting the speed of

GEORGIA

motor vehicles or any of the provisions of the motor vehicle laws of any state, violation of which constitutes a misdemeanor, whether or not the violations were repetitions of the same offense or different offenses.

8. If the insured auto is so mechanically defective that its operation might endanger public safety, is used to carry passengers for hire or compensation or; is used to carry flammables or explosives, is an authorized emergency vehicle or the insured auto has changed so much as to substantially increase the risk.

Length of Notice: Ten days for nonpayment; thirty days for any other allowable reason.

Reason for Cancellation: Required on the notice. Even though the amendatory endorsement does not require that the reason for cancellation be shown, Georgia law requires that the reason be shown.

Proof Required: Proof of mailing.

Nonrenewal

Length of Notice: Thirty days.

Reason for Nonrenewal: Required on the notice. Georgia law specifies that the reason must be shown. (Ga. Code Ann. §33-39-11).

Proof Required: Proof of mailing.

Other Cancellation/Nonrenewal Provisions

An insurer may not nonrenew due to:

1. Lack of supporting business.

2. A change in its underwriting rules, unless the change has been approved by the commissioner.

3. One or two of the following incidents within a thirty-six month period:

    a. Not-at-fault accidents.

    b. Uninsured or underinsured motorist claims.

    c. Comprehensive claims.

    d. Towing claims.

GEORGIA

4. Age, sex, location of residence address within the state, race, creed, national origin, ancestry, or marital status.

5. Lawful occupation if the insured automobile is not used in the occupation.

6. Named insured entry into military service, as long as his or her legal residence does not change from Georgia.

7. The number of years of driving experience of anyone in the household or any customary operator of the insured auto.

8. Accidents or violations that occurred more than thirty-six months prior to the expiration date.

9. Accidents in the previous thirty-six months that total less than $750 in damages.

10. One at-fault accident if the policy has been in force for at least thirty-six months.

11. Two at-fault accidents if the policy has been in force for at least seventy-two months.

12. Factors that do not relate to the claims record, driving record, or driving ability of any operator.

All notices of nonrenewal must contain the following provisions in a form substantially similar to the following:

> "Code Section 33-24-45 of the Official Code of Georgia Annotated provides that this insurer must, upon request, furnish you with the reasons for the failure to renew this policy. If you wish to assert that the nonrenewal is unlawful, you must file a written notice with this insurer before the time at which the nonrenewal becomes effective. The notice must specify the manner in which the failure to renew is alleged to be unlawful. If you do not file the written notice, you may not later assert a claim or action against this insurer based upon an unlawful nonrenewal."

If an insured is being nonrenewed because the agent's contract with the insurer has been terminated, the notice of nonrenewal must contain the following wording:

> "Your policy has not been renewed because your present agent no longer represents this insurer. You have the option of procuring coverage through your present agent or retaining this policy by applying through another agent of this insurer. Code Section 33-24-45 of the Official Code of Georgia Annotated provides that if you

GEORGIA

apply for this policy before the time at which the nonrenewal becomes effective, this insurer will treat the application as a renewal and not as an application for a new policy."

If by statute, regulation or contract the policy may not be cancelled unless notice is given to a governmental agency, mortgagee or other third-party, the insurer will mail or deliver at least ten days' notice to the first named insured and the third-party as soon as practicable after receiving the first named insured's request for cancellation. The notice will state the effective date of cancellation, which will be the later of the ten days from the date of mailing or delivering our notice, or the effective date of cancellation stated in the first named insured's notice to the insurer.

In the event of termination for reasons other than nonpayment, the insurer must provide notification of possible eligibility for insurance through the Georgia Assigned Insurance Plan.

Unearned premium must be returned on or before the effective date of cancellation either to the insured or to the agent. If cancelled by the insured, the insurer shall send the first named insured any premium refund due. If insurer cancels, the refund will be pro rata, except if the cancellation results from failure of the first named insured to pay, when due, any premium to us or any amount, when due, under a premium finance agreement, then the refund may be less than pro rata. Calculation of the return premium at less than pro rata represents a penalty charged on unearned premium. If the first named insured cancels, the refund may be less than pro rata.

The cancellation will be effective even if the insurer has not made or offered a refund. Any insurer or agent failing to return any unearned premium as prescribed in the above sections shall pay to the insured a penalty equal to twenty-five percent of the amount of the return of the unearned premium and interest equal to eighteen percent per annum until such time that proper return has been made, which penalty and interest must be paid at the time the return is made. However, the maximum amount of such penalty and interest shall not exceed fifty percent of the amount of the refund due.

Electronic notification to lienholders is allowed, with lienholders consent.

PERSONAL UMBRELLA

Ga. Code Ann. §§33-24-45 and 33-24-46

Cancellation during the Underwriting Period

Length of Underwriting Period: Sixty days.

Length of Notice: Ten days for any reason.

GEORGIA

Reason for Cancellation: Required on the notice.

Proof Required: Proof of mailing.

Cancellation after the Underwriting Period

Length of Notice: Ten days for nonpayment; thirty days for any other reason.

Reason for Cancellation: Required on the notice.

Proof Required: Proof of mailing.

Nonrenewal

Length of Notice: Thirty days.

Reason for Cancellation: Required on the notice.

Proof Required: Proof of mailing.

Other Cancellation/Nonrenewal Provisions

If by statute, regulation or contract the policy may not be cancelled unless notice is given to a governmental agency, mortgagee or other third-party, the insurer will mail or deliver at least ten days' notice to the first named insured and the third-party as soon as practicable after receiving the first named insured's request for cancellation. The notice will state the effective date of cancellation, which will be the later of the ten days from the date of mailing or delivering our notice, or the effective date of cancellation stated in the first named insured's notice to the insurer.

A notice of nonrenewal for residential real property must contain the following statement:

> "Code Section 33-24-46 of the Official Code of Georgia Annotated provides that this insurer must, upon request, furnish you with the reasons for the failure to renew this policy. If you wish to assert that the nonrenewal is unlawful, you must file a written notice with this insurer before the time at which the nonrenewal becomes effective. The notice must specify the manner in which the failure to renew is alleged to be unlawful. If you do not file the written notice, you may not later assert a claim or action against this insurer based upon an unlawful nonrenewal." (Ga. Code Ann. §33-24-46).

A notice of nonrenewal for a policy covering automobiles must also provide this notice, except that it would refer to Code Section 33-24-45, instead of 33-24-46, but would otherwise be identically worded.

GEORGIA

FRAUD

Ga. Code Ann. §§33-1-9; 33-1-16; 33-1-17

General Information and Definitions

Any person who knowingly or willingly makes or aids in the making of false/fraudulent statements or representations of any material fact or thing in any written statement or certificate, the filing of a claim, the making of an application for an insurance policy, the receiving of an application for insurance, or receives money for the sake of submitting an application for the purpose of submitting a false claim, receives money for purchasing insurance and converts it to a person's own benefit, issues fake or counterfeit policies, certificates of insurance, identification cards or quotes, or makes false/fraudulent representations as to the death/disability of a policyholder for the purpose of fraudulently obtaining money or benefit from an insurer commits insurance fraud.

Likewise anyone who knowingly or willfully solicits, negotiates, procures insurance or annuity contracts, solicits, negotiates, procures any contract relating to benefits or services, disseminates information as to coverage or rates, forwards applications, delivers policies, inspects risks, fixes rates, investigates or adjusts claims or losses, collects or forwards premiums, or in any other way acts as an agent, representative, or on behalf of an insured not authorized to transact business in this state commits fraud.

Knowingly and willingly with intent to defraud makes any annual or other statement required by law to be filed with the commissioner containing any material statements which are false commits fraud.

Penalties

Any person convicted of a violation of this code section shall be guilty of a felony and shall be punished by imprisonment for not less than two nor more than ten years, or by a fine of not more than $10,000 or both.

Reporting Requirements

Any insurer, agent, or other person licensed under this title, or an employee thereof, having knowledge of or who believes that a fraudulent insurance act is being or has been committed shall send to the commissioner a report or information pertinent to such knowledge or belief and such additional information relative thereto as the commissioner or his employees or agents may require. Visit https://www.oci.ga.gov/Fraud/Report.aspx for detailed instructions and contact information for reporting.

Antifraud Provisions

A Special Insurance Fraud Fund is established for the purpose of funding the investigation and prosecution of insurance fraud. The commissioner shall annually prepare a separate budget request to the General Assembly which sets forth the anticipated cost and expense of funding the investigation and prosecution of fraud for the ensuing twelve months.

Insurers shall make any personnel involved in investigating insurance fraud and any files relating to fraud investigations available to the commissioner, attorney general, local prosecuting officials, special prosecuting attorneys, or other law enforcement agencies as needed in order to further the investigation and prosecution of insurance fraud. (Ga. Code Ann. §33-1-17).

FAIR CLAIMS PROCESSING
Ga. Code Ann. §33-6-34

Any of the following acts of an insurer when committed as provided in Code Section 33-6-33 shall constitute an unfair claims settlement practice:

1. Knowingly misrepresenting to claimants and insureds relevant facts or policy provisions relating to coverages at issue.

2. Failing to acknowledge with reasonable promptness pertinent communications with respect to claims arising under its policies.

3. Failing to adopt and implement procedures for the prompt investigation and settlement of claims arising under its policies.

4. Not attempting in good faith to effectuate prompt, fair, and equitable settlement of claims submitted in which liability has become reasonably clear.

5. Compelling insureds or beneficiaries to institute suits to recover amounts due under its policies by offering substantially less than the amounts ultimately recovered in suits brought by them.

6. Refusing to pay claims without conducting a reasonable investigation.

7. When requested by the insured in writing, failing to affirm or deny coverage of claims within a reasonable time after having completed its investigation related to such claim or claims.

8. When requested by the insured in writing, making claims payments to an insured or beneficiary without indicating the coverage under which each payment is being made.

GEORGIA

9. Unreasonably delaying the investigation or payment of claims by requiring both a formal proof of loss and subsequent verification that would result in duplication of information and verification appearing in the formal proof of loss form; provided, however, this paragraph shall not preclude an insurer from obtaining sworn statements if permitted under the policy.

10. When requested by the insured in writing, failing in the case of claims denial or offers of compromise settlement to provide promptly a reasonable and accurate explanation of the basis for such actions. In the case of claims denials, such denials shall be in writing.

11. Failing to provide forms necessary to file claims within fifteen calendar days of a request with reasonable explanations regarding their use.

12. Failing to adopt and implement reasonable standards to assure that the repairs of a repairer owned by the insurer are performed in a workmanlike manner.

13. Indicating to a first-party claimant on a payment, draft check, or accompanying letter that said payment is final or a release of any claim unless the policy limit has been paid or there has been a compromise settlement agreed to by the first-party claimant and the insurer as to coverage and amount payable under the contract.

14. Issuing checks or drafts in partial settlement of a loss or claim under a specific coverage which contain language which releases the insurer or its insured from its total liability.

GUAM

For details on cancellation procedures for the standard policy, refer to the Standard Policy section.

COMMERCIAL LINES
AGRICULTURAL CAPITAL ASSETS

Guam makes no changes from the standard policy.

BUSINESSOWNERS

Guam makes no changes from the standard policy.

CAPITAL ASSETS (OUTPUT POLICY)

Guam makes no changes from the standard policy.

COMMERCIAL AUTO

(Insurers may adopt ISO's CA 02 78 10 01)

Cancellation during the Underwriting Period

Length of Underwriting Period: Sixty days.

Length of Notice: Ten days for nonpayment; thirty days for any other reason.

Reason for Cancellation: Not required on the notice, but must be provided upon request of the insured.

Proof Required: Proof of mailing.

Cancellation after the Underwriting Period

Length of Notice: Fifteen days for nonpayment or suspension or revocation of the named insured's license or registration; thirty days for any other reason.

Reason for Cancellation: Not required on the notice.

Proof Required: Proof of mailing.

GUAM

Nonrenewal

Length of Notice: Thirty days.

Reason for Nonrenewal: Not required on the notice but must be provided upon request.

Proof Required: Proof of mailing, an affidavit by the insurer setting forth the facts of such mailing is prima facie evidence of such mailing.

COMMERCIAL CRIME

Guam makes no changes from the standard policy except an affidavit by the insurer setting forth the facts of such mailing is prima facie evidence of such mailing.

COMMERCIAL GENERAL LIABILITY

Guam makes no changes from the standard policy except an affidavit by the insurer setting forth the facts of such mailing is prima facie evidence of such mailing.

COMMERCIAL INLAND MARINE

Guam makes no changes from the standard policy except an affidavit by the insurer setting forth the facts of such mailing is prima facie evidence of such mailing.

COMMERCIAL PROPERTY

Guam makes no changes from the standard policy except an affidavit by the insurer setting forth the facts of such mailing is prima facie evidence of such mailing.

COMMERCIAL UMBRELLA

Guam makes no changes from the standard policy except an affidavit by the insurer setting forth the facts of such mailing is prima facie evidence of such mailing.

E-COMMERCE

Guam makes no changes from the standard policy except an affidavit by the insurer setting forth the facts of such mailing is prima facie evidence of such mailing.

EQUIPMENT BREAKDOWN

Guam makes no changes from the standard policy except an affidavit by the insurer setting forth the facts of such mailing is prima facie evidence of such mailing.

GUAM

FARM

Guam makes no changes from the standard policy.

MANAGEMENT PROTECTION

Guam makes no changes from the standard policy except an affidavit by the insurer setting forth the facts of such mailing is prima facie evidence of such mailing.

PROFESSIONAL LIABILITY

Guam makes no changes from the standard policy except an affidavit by the insurer setting forth the facts of such mailing is prima facie evidence of such mailing.

WORKERS COMPENSATION

Guam makes no changes from the standard policy.

SURPLUS LINES

Surplus lines policies in Guam are not subject to regulation for cancellation and nonrenewal.

PERSONAL LINES
DWELLING FIRE & HOMEOWNERS

Guam makes no changes from the standard policy.

PERSONAL AUTO

(Insurers may adopt ISO's PP 01 49 01 05)

Cancellation during the Underwriting Period

16 Guam Code Ann. §§21104 and 21105

Length of Underwriting Period: Sixty days.

Length of Notice: Fifteen days for nonpayment; thirty days for all other reasons.

Reason for Cancellation: Not required on the notice.

Proof Required: Proof of mailing.

GUAM

Cancellation after the Underwriting Period

The policy may be cancelled **only** for the following reasons:

1. Nonpayment.

2. If your driver's license or that of:

    a. Any driver who lives with you.

    b. Any driver who customarily uses "your covered auto".

    Has been suspended or revoked. This must have occurred:

    a. During the policy period.

    b. Since the last anniversary of the original effective date if the policy period is other than one year.

    However, in the event this policy insures more than one person as:

    a. Named insured.

    b. Person living in the named insured's household.

    c. Driver who customarily uses "your covered auto"; and at least one person, other than a named insured, has had their driver's license suspended or revoked, before canceling this policy the insurer will offer to continue the policy with a provision excluding coverage when the person or persons who have had their driver's license suspended or revoked are operating any auto or "trailer". If such offer is accepted, the insurer will issue an endorsement to that effect.

Length of Notice: Fifteen days for nonpayment; thirty days for any other allowable reason.

Reason for Cancellation: Not required on the notice. However, notice must state that the reason for the notice will be provided upon request.

Proof Required: Proof of mailing.

Nonrenewal

Length of Notice: Thirty days.

Reason for Nonrenewal: Not required on the notice.

Proof Required: Proof of mailing.

GUAM

Other Cancellation/Nonrenewal Provisions

1. When the name of the person intended to be insured is specified in a policy, it can only be applied to his own interest.

2. Subject to the notice requirement, if the policy period is other than one year, insurers will have the right not to renew or continue a policy at each anniversary of its original effective date. If the insurer offers to renew or continue and the insured or insured's representative do not accept, this policy will automatically terminate at the end of the current policy period. Failure to pay the required renewal or continuation premium when due shall be considered a rejection of insurer's offer. If insured obtains other insurance on "your covered auto", any similar insurance provided by this policy will terminate as to that auto on the effective date of the other insurance.

3. If policy is cancelled, insured may be entitled to a premium refund. However, note that the insurer's making or offering to make the refund is not a condition of cancellation.

4. If insured requests reason for cancellation or nonrenewal it must be sent within five days of receipt of request.

PERSONAL UMBRELLA

Guam makes no changes from the standard policy.

FRAUD

22 Guam Code Ann. §§12109; 12111.1; 12112

General Information and Definitions

No person shall make or issue, nor cause to be made or issued, any written statement misrepresenting or making incomplete comparisons as to the terms, conditions or benefits contained in any policy for the purpose of inducing, or attempting to induce, the policyholder to lapse, forfeit, surrender, retain, exchange or convert any insurance policy.

No person shall:

1. Make, issue, circulate, or cause to be made, issued or circulated, any estimate, circular or statement misrepresenting the terms of any policy issued, or to be issued, or the benefits or advantages promised thereby, or the dividends or share of the surplus to be received thereon.

2. Make any false or misleading statement as to the dividends or share of surplus previously paid on similar policies.

GUAM

3. Make any misleading representation or any misrepresentation as to the financial condition of any insurer, or as to the legal reserve upon which any life insurer operates.

4. Use any name or title of any policy or class of policies misrepresenting the true nature thereof.

Reporting Requirements

There are no reporting requirements in Guam.

Penalties

Any person found to be in violation of the Guam insurance statutes by engaging in any of the fraudulent conduct listed above, or any lawful order of the commissioner, for which a penalty is not otherwise specifically provided, shall be guilty of a misdemeanor.

Antifraud Provisions

There are no antifraud provisions in Guam.

Application Fraud Statement

There are no application fraud statement provisions in Guam.

FAIR CLAIMS PROCESSING
22 Guam Code Ann. §§18602; 18603; 18608

An insurer is not liable for a loss caused by the willful act of the insured; but he is not exonerated by the negligence of the insured or of the insured's agents or others.

Failure to give notice of loss covered by marine or fire insurance within any period provided for by the policy or otherwise, shall not exonerate the insurer if the notice is given within a reasonable time after the insured loss has or should have first knowledge of said loss. In all other classes of insurance, the insured shall have at least twenty days after the event within which to give notice of loss. No requirement of notice within a lesser period is valid.

In all cases where loss occurs and the insurer liable therefore shall fail to pay the same within the time specified in the policy, after demand made therefore, such insurer shall be liable to pay the holder of such policy, in addition to the amount of such loss, 12 percent damages upon the amount of such loss, together with all reasonable attorney's fees for the prosecution and collection of said loss; said attorney's fees to be taxed by the court where the same is heard on original action, by appeal or otherwise, and to be taxed as a part of the costs therein, and collected as other costs are or may be by law collected; and writs of attachment or garnishment filed or issued after proof of loss or death has been received by the insurer shall not defeat the provisions of this section, provided the insurer desiring to pay the amount of the claim as shown in the proof of loss or death may pay said amount into the registry of the court after issuance of writs of attachment and garnishment, in which event there shall be no further liability on the part of said insurer. (Guam Government Code §43407; *U.S. for use of Getz Bros. & Co. v. Markowitz Bros*. 383 F.2d. 595 (9th Cir. 1967)).

Statutes cited: 22 G.C.A. § 12209, 22 G.C.A. § 15113, 22 G.C.A. § 18402, 16 G. C. A. §§21104 and 21105, 22 G. C. A. §§12109; 12111.1; 12112, 22 G. C. A. §§18602; 18603; 18608.

HAWAII

For details on cancellation procedures for the standard policy, refer to the Standard Policy section.

COMMERCIAL LINES

All commercial lines policies are subject to the cancellation and nonrenewal provisions of Haw. Rev. Stat. Ann. §431:10-226.5.

Cancellation: Length of notice is not fewer than ten days.

Nonrenewal: Length of notice is not fewer than thirty days.

Proof Required: Proof of mailing.

If under Title 24 or by the terms of the policy, a longer time period is required for a notice of cancellation or nonrenewal for the policy, the longer period shall be applicable.

AGRICULTURAL CAPITAL ASSETS

Hawaii makes no changes from the standard policy.

BOP; CGL (CGL, EMPLOYMENT, LIQUOR, MARKET SEGMENTS, OCP, POLLUTION, PRODUCTS/COMPLETED OPS, RR PROT.); & FARM (FARM LIAB.)

Cancellation during the Underwriting Period

Length of Underwriting Period: N/A.

Length of Notice: N/A.

Reason for Cancellation: N/A.

Proof Required: N/A.

Cancellation after the Underwriting Period

The policy may be cancelled **only** for the following reasons:

1. Nonpayment of premium.

2. Fraud or material misrepresentation.

HAWAII

3. Substantial increase in hazard.

4. Substantial breaches of contractual duties, conditions, or warranties.

5. Violation of any local fire, health, or safety statute or ordinance.

6. If the named insured is convicted of a crime that increases any hazard insured.

7. If the insurance commissioner determines that to continue the policy would violate Hawaii statutes.

8. Any good faith reason with the insurance commissioner's approval.

9. Conviction of the named insured for a crime having as one of its necessary elements, an act increasing any hazard that is insured against.

Length of Notice: Thirty days for any allowable reason.

Reason for Cancellation: Not required.

Proof Required: Proof of mailing.

Nonrenewal

Length of Notice: Forty-five days.

Reason for Nonrenewal: Required on the notice.

Proof Required: Proof of mailing.

Other Cancellation/Nonrenewal Provisions

Cancellation or nonrenewal shall not be deemed valid unless evidence of mailing is provided.

For BOP policies, the insurance is void in any case of fraud by the insured as it relates to coverage whether before or after a loss and concealment or misrepresentation, whether before or after a loss, shall prevent a recovery under this insurance if it was made with actual intent to deceive; or materially affects either the acceptance of the risk or the hazard assumed by the insurer.

For OCP policies, all notices must also be sent to the contractor designated on the declarations.

HAWAII

For Railroad Protective policies, all notices must also be sent to the contractor, any involved governmental authority, or other contracting party shown on the declarations.

(ISO Endorsement CU 02 19 and ISO Endorsement IL 02 65).

CAPITAL ASSETS

Hawaii makes no changes from the standard policy.

COMMERCIAL AUTO

Hawaii Revised Statutes §§431:10c-111 and -112, -110, -110.5, -111.5, 109

Cancellation during the Underwriting Period

Length of Underwriting Period: Sixty days.

Length of Notice: Twenty days for nonpayment; thirty days for any other reason.

Reason for Cancellation: Required.

Proof Required: Proof of mailing.

Cancellation after the Underwriting Period

The policy may be cancelled **only** for the following reasons:

1. Nonpayment after reasonable demand therefore.

2. Suspension or revocation of the operator's license of the principal operator.

Length of Notice: Twenty days for nonpayment; thirty days for any other reason.

Reason for Cancellation: Required.

Proof Required: Proof of mailing.

Nonrenewal

Length of Notice: Thirty days.

Reason for Nonrenewal: Required on the notice.

Proof Required: Proof of mailing.

HAWAII

Other Cancellation/Nonrenewal Provisions

An insurer may nonrenew **only** for the following reasons:

1. Nonpayment.

2. Suspension or revocation of the operator's license of the principal operator.

3. The commissioner determines that the insurer's financial soundness would be impaired by writing additional insurance.

4. The insurer stops writing in Hawaii.

5. As otherwise permitted by the Hawaii statutes.

Cancellation or nonrenewal shall not be deemed valid unless evidence of mailing is provided.

When an insurer rejects an application, it must immediately notify the applicant of the availability of the assigned risk plan.

If the insurer offers a renewal policy, but the insured does not pay the renewal premium prior to the end of the previous policy term, the renewal automatically terminates.

Insurers may only issue notices to nonrenew, or conditionally renew with reduced coverage, up to 2 percent of their policies in force at last year end in each rating category. This number is determined on a calendar year basis. Insurers nonrenewing one policy which equates to more than 2 percent in one rating category are allowed to issue the one notice. For every two new insurance policies issued in each rating territory, the insurer may nonrenew or conditionally renew one additional policy in that rating territory above the 2 percent threshold.

An insurer is exempt from the above provisions governing cancellation and nonrenewal of motor vehicle insurance if:

1. The insurer offers to replace the policy through an affiliate or subsidiary.

2. The replacement policy is effective upon the expiration of the existing policy.

3. The replacement policy provides the same or better coverage, terms, and conditions at a lower premium compared to the existing policy.

HAWAII

4. The insurer provides at least thirty days' notice of the replacement, unless the insured waives this notice requirement.

5. The insured accepts the replacement policy.

COMMERCIAL CRIME

Hawaii makes no changes from the standard policy.

COMMERCIAL GENERAL LIABILITY (UNDERGROUND STORAGE TANKS)

ISO Endorsement CG 00 42, Haw. Rev. Stat. Ann. §431:10-211.3

Cancellation during the Underwriting Period

Length of Underwriting Period: N/A.

Length of Notice: N/A.

Reason for Cancellation: N/A.

Proof Required: N/A.

Cancellation after the Underwriting Period

The policy may be cancelled **only** for the following reasons:

1. Nonpayment of premium.

2. Fraud or material misrepresentation.

3. Substantial increase in hazard.

4. Substantial breaches of contractual duties, conditions, or warranties.

5. Violation of any local fire, health, or safety statute or ordinance.

6. If the named insured is convicted of a crime that increases any hazard insured.

7. If the insurance commissioner determines that to continue the policy would violate Hawaii statutes.

8. Any good faith reason with the insurance commissioner's approval.

HAWAII

Length of Notice: Thirty days for nonpayment and fraud or material misrepresentation; sixty days for all other reasons.

Reason for Cancellation: Not required.

Proof Required: Proof of mailing.

Nonrenewal

Length of Notice: Sixty days.

Reason for Nonrenewal: Required on the notice.

Proof Required: Certified mail.

Commercial General Liability Extended Reporting Requirements

Any policy for commercial general liability coverage wherein the insurer shall offer and the insured may elect to purchase an extended reporting period for claims arising during the expiring policy period shall provide that:

1. In the event of a cancellation, there shall be a thirty-day period during which the insured may elect to purchase coverage for the extended reporting period.

2. The limit of liability in the policy aggregate for the extended reporting period shall be 100 percent of the expiring policy aggregate.

3. The insurer shall provide the following loss information to the first named insured within thirty days of the insured's request or upon any notice of cancellation or nonrenewal:

    a. All information on closed claims including the date and description of occurrence and amount of payments, if any.

    b. All information on open claims including the date and description of occurrence, amount of payment, if any, and amount of reserves, if any.

    c. All information on notices of occurrence including the date and description of occurrence and amount of resources, if any.

COMMERCIAL INLAND MARINE

Hawaii makes no changes from the standard policy.

HAWAII

COMMERCIAL PROPERTY

ISO Endorsement CU 02 19 and ISO Endorsement IL 02 65

Cancellation during the Underwriting Period

Length of Underwriting Period: N/A.

Length of Notice: N/A.

Reason for Cancellation: N/A.

Proof Required: N/A.

Cancellation after the Underwriting Period

The policy may be cancelled for any reason.

Length of Notice: Ten days for nonpayment; thirty days for any other reason.

Reason for Cancellation: Not required.

Proof Required: Proof of mailing.

Nonrenewal

Length of Notice: Forty-five days.

Reason for Nonrenewal: Required on the notice.

Proof Required: Proof of mailing.

Other Cancellation/Nonrenewal Provisions

Cancellation or nonrenewal shall not be deemed valid unless evidence of mailing is provided.

When insurance is provided under the policy for Legal Liability Coverage Form or Mortgageholders Errors and Omissions Coverage Form, the policy may **only** be cancelled for one or more of the following reasons:

1. Nonpayment of premium.

2. Fraud or material misrepresentation.

3. Substantial increase in the risk hazard, except to the extent that the insurer should have reasonably foreseen the change when entering into the contract.

4. Substantial breaches of contractual duties, conditions or warranties.

5. Violation of any local fire, health or safety statute or ordinance.

6. Conviction of the named insured for a crime having as one of its necessary elements, an act increasing any hazard that is insured against.

7. Determination by the insurance commissioner that the continuation of the policy places the insurer in violation of Hawaii Statutes.

8. Any good faith reason with the approval of the insurance commissioner.

COMMERCIAL UMBRELLA

ISO Endorsement CU 02 19

Cancellation during the Underwriting Period

Length of Underwriting Period: N/A.

Length of Notice: N/A.

Reason for Cancellation: N/A.

Proof Required: N/A.

Cancellation after the Underwriting Period

After the underwriting period, the policy may **only** be cancelled for any of the following reasons:

1. Nonpayment of premium.

2. Fraud or material misrepresentation.

3. Substantial increase in the risk hazard, except to the extent that the insurer should have reasonably foreseen the change when entering into the contract.

4. Substantial breaches of contractual duties, conditions or warranties by the insured.

5. Violation of any local fire, health or safety statute or ordinance.

HAWAII

6. Conviction of the named insured for a crime having as one of its necessary elements, an act increasing any hazard that is insured against.

7. Determination by the insurance commissioner that the continuation of the policy places the insurer in violation of Hawaii Statutes.

8. Any good faith reason with the approval of the insurance commissioner.

9. The driver's license of the principal operator of a "covered auto" is under suspension or revocation.

Length of Notice: Thirty days for any reason.

Reason for Cancellation: Not required.

Proof Required: Proof of mailing.

Nonrenewal

Length of Notice: Forty-five days.

Reason for Nonrenewal: Not required.

Proof Required: Proof of mailing.

Other Cancellation/Nonrenewal Provisions

Cancellation or nonrenewal shall not be deemed valid unless evidence of mailing is provided.

If the policy insures autos, the insurer has the right not to renew or continue this policy **only** if:

1. One or more of the reasons listed under cancellation exists.

2. The Hawaii insurance commissioner determines that the insurer's financial soundness would be impaired by the writing of additional policies of insurance.

3. The insurer ceases to write any new policies of insurance of any kind in the State of Hawaii.

4. The insurer is otherwise permitted by the laws of the State of Hawaii to terminate the policy.

The insurer must specify the reason for cancellation on the notice.

HAWAII

CRIME

Hawaii makes no changes from the standard policy.

E-COMMERCE

Hawaii makes no changes from the standard policy.

EQUIPMENT BREAKDOWN

Hawaii makes no changes from the standard policy.

FARM
(Other than Farm Liability)

Hawaii makes no changes from the standard policy.

PROFESSIONAL LIABILITY

Hawaii makes no changes from the standard policy.

WORKERS COMPENSATION
Hawaii Revised Statutes §386-127

Hawaii makes no changes from the standard policy.

SURPLUS LINES

Cancellation and nonrenewal laws in Hawaii do not apply to surplus lines policies.

PERSONAL LINES
DWELLING FIRE
Hawaii Revised Statutes §§431:10-210 and 431:10-226.5

Hawaii makes no changes from the standard policy.

HOMEOWNERS
Hawaii Revised Statutes §§431:10-210 and 431:10-226.5

Although Hawaii makes no changes from the standard policy, insurers using the ISO forms are limited to cancellation for nonpayment, material misrepresentation on the application, and

HAWAII

substantial change in the risk. Statutes do not limit the reasons for cancellation or nonrenewal. Legal advice is suggested.

Other Cancellation/Nonrenewal Provisions

Cancellation or nonrenewal shall not be deemed valid unless evidence of mailing is provided.

PERSONAL AUTO

Hawaii Revised Statutes §§431:10c-110.5, 431: 10c-111 and 431:10c-112;

Haw. Code R. §16-23-13

Cancellation during the Underwriting Period

Length of Underwriting Period: Sixty days.

Length of Notice: Twenty days for nonpayment; thirty days for any other reason.

Reason for Cancellation: Required on the notice.

Proof Required: Proof of mailing.

Cancellation after the Underwriting Period

The policy may be cancelled **only** for the following reasons:

1. Nonpayment.

2. The vehicle's principal operator's driver's license is under suspension or revocation.

Length of Notice: Twenty days for nonpayment of premium; thirty days for any other allowable reason.

Reason for Cancellation: Not required.

Proof Required: Proof of mailing.

Nonrenewal

Length of Notice: Thirty days.

Reason for Nonrenewal: Not required.

Proof Required: Proof of mailing.

HAWAII

Other Cancellation/Nonrenewal Provisions

Cancellation or nonrenewal shall not be deemed valid unless evidence of mailing is provided.

An insurer may nonrenew in Hawaii **only** under the following conditions:

1. Nonpayment.

2. The vehicle's principal operator's driver's license is under suspension or revocation.

3. If the insurance commissioner determines that further writings would impair the insurer's financial condition.

4. If the insurer ceases to do business in Hawaii.

5. If the laws of Hawaii permit.

Automatic termination for nonpayment of a renewal is allowed if the renewal is sent to the insured at least thirty days ahead of time.

An insurer, including a general agent, subagent, or solicitor, shall within fifteen working days of a request for an appointment service the applicant; provided service shall mean provide an application and rate quote for a motor vehicle insurance policy. Failure to service an applicant within the fifteen working day period shall be deemed a rejection. Upon rejection of an application for motor vehicle insurance policy or optional additional insurance by the affirmative act of the insurer or by a failure to service the applicant within fifteen working days, an insurer, including a general agent, subagent, or solicitor, at a meeting within ten working days of the rejection shall immediately offer to place the requested insurance coverage with the joint underwriting plan.

An insurer is exempt from the above provisions governing cancellation and nonrenewal of motor vehicle insurance if:

1. The insurer offers to replace the policy through an affiliate or subsidiary.

2. The replacement policy is effective upon the expiration of the existing policy.

3. The replacement policy provides the same or better coverage, terms, and conditions at a lower premium compared to the existing policy.

4. The insurer provides at least thirty day-notice of the replacement, unless the insured waives this notice requirement.

5. The insured accepts the replacement policy.

HAWAII

PERSONAL UMBRELLA

Hawaii Revised Statutes §431:10-226.5

Cancellation during the Underwriting Period

Length of Underwriting Period: Sixty days.

Length of Notice: Ten days for any reason.

Reason for Cancellation: Not required.

Proof Required: Proof of mailing.

Cancellation after the Underwriting Period

Length of Notice: Ten days for nonpayment of premium; thirty days for any other reason.

Reason for Cancellation: Not required.

Proof Required: Proof of mailing.

Nonrenewal

Length of Notice: Thirty days.

Reason for Cancellation: Not required.

Proof Required: Proof of mailing.

Other Cancellation/Nonrenewal Provisions

Cancellation or nonrenewal shall not be deemed valid unless evidence of mailing is provided.

FRAUD

Hawaii Revised Statutes §§431:2-401 through 431:2-410

General Information and Definitions

A person commits the offense of insurance fraud if the person intentionally or knowingly misrepresents or conceals material facts, opinions, intention, or law to obtain or attempt to obtain coverage, benefits, recovery, or compensation when presenting:

1. An application for the issuance or renewal of an insurance policy or reinsurance contract.

HAWAII

2. False information on a claim for payment.

3. A claim for the payment of a loss.

4. Multiple claims for the same loss or injury, including knowingly presenting such multiple and duplicative claims to more than one insurer.

5. To a person, insurer, or other licensee false, incomplete, or misleading information to obtain coverage or payment otherwise available under an insurance policy.

6. To a person or producer, information about a person's status as a licensee that induces a person or insurer to purchase an insurance policy or reinsurance contract.

Reporting Requirements

Within sixty days of an insurer or other licensee's employee or agent discovering credible information indicating insurance fraud, or as soon thereafter as practicable, the insurer or licensee shall provide to the branch information, including documents and other evidence, regarding the alleged fraud. The insurance fraud investigations branch (the "Branch") shall work with the insurer or licensee to determine what information shall be provided.

Penalties and Statute of Limitations

Insurance fraud is a criminal offense and shall constitute:

1. A class B felony if the value of the benefits, recovery, or compensation obtained or attempted to be obtained exceeds $20,000.

2. A class C felony if the value of the benefits, recovery, or compensation obtained or attempted to be obtained exceeds $750.

3. A misdemeanor if the value of the benefits, recovery, or compensation obtained or attempted to be obtained is not in excess of $750.

Insurance fraud may be prosecuted under any applicable statute or common law, and all such remedies shall be cumulative.

In addition to or in lieu of criminal penalties, any person who commits insurance fraud may be subject to the administrative penalties. Specifically, if a person is found to have knowingly committed insurance fraud, the commissioner may assess any or all of the following penalties:

1. Restitution to any insurer or any other person of benefits or payments fraudulently received or other damages or costs incurred.

HAWAII

2. A fine of not more than $10,000 for each violation.

3. Reimbursement of attorneys' fees and costs of the party sustaining a loss under this part; provided that the State shall be exempt from paying attorneys' fees and costs to other parties.

Statute of Limitations

Administrative actions brought for insurance fraud under this part shall be brought within six years after the insurance fraud is discovered or by exercise of reasonable diligence should have been discovered and, in any event, no more than ten years after the date on which a violation is committed.

Antifraud Provisions

The Hawaii Insurance Department's investigations branch has the power to:

1. Conduct a statewide program for the prevention of insurance fraud; provided that the branch shall not have jurisdiction over workers' compensation.

2. Notwithstanding any other law to the contrary, investigate and prosecute in administrative hearings and courts of competent jurisdiction all persons involved in insurance fraud violations.

3. Promote public and industry-wide education about insurance fraud.

In addition, the Branch may review and take appropriate action on complaints relating to insurance fraud.

Funding for the branch shall come from the compliance resolution fund.

FAIR CLAIMS PROCESSING

Hawaii Revised Statutes §431:13-103

Unfair claim settlement practices is committing or performing with such frequency as to indicate a general business practice any of the following:

1. Misrepresenting pertinent facts or insurance policy provisions relating to coverages at issue.

2. With respect to claims arising under its policies, failing to respond with reasonable promptness, in no case more than fifteen working days, to communications received from:

    a. The insurer's policyholder.

    b. Any other persons, including the commissioner.

HAWAII

    c. The insurer of a person involved in an incident in which the insurer's policyholder is also involved.

    The response shall be more than an acknowledgment that such person's communication has been received, and shall adequately address the concerns stated in the communication.

3. Failing to adopt and implement reasonable standards for the prompt investigation of claims arising under insurance policies.

4. Refusing to pay claims without conducting a reasonable investigation based upon all available information.

5. Failing to affirm or deny coverage of claims within a reasonable time after proof of loss statements have been completed.

6. Failing to offer payment within thirty calendar days of affirmation of liability, if the amount of the claim has been determined and is not in dispute.

7. Failing to provide the insured, or when applicable the insured's beneficiary, with a reasonable written explanation for any delay, on every claim remaining unresolved for thirty calendar days from the date it was reported.

8. Not attempting in good faith to effectuate prompt, fair, and equitable settlements of claims in which liability has become reasonably clear.

9. Compelling insureds to institute litigation to recover amounts due under an insurance policy by offering substantially less than the amounts ultimately recovered in actions brought by the insureds.

10. Attempting to settle a claim for less than the amount to which a reasonable person would have believed the person was entitled by reference to written or printed advertising material accompanying or made part of an application.

11. Attempting to settle claims on the basis of an application which was altered without notice, knowledge, or consent of the insured.

12. Failing to promptly settle claims, where liability has become reasonably clear, under one portion of the insurance policy coverage to influence settlements under other portions of the insurance policy coverage.

HAWAII

13. Failing to promptly provide a reasonable explanation of the basis in the insurance policy in relation to the facts or applicable law for denial of a claim or for the offer of a compromise settlement.

14. Indicating to the insured on any payment draft, check, or in any accompanying letter that the payment is "final" or "a release" of any claim if additional benefits relating to the claim are probable under coverages afforded by the policy; unless the policy limit has been paid or there is a bona fide dispute over either the coverage or the amount payable under the policy.

IDAHO

For details on cancellation procedures for the standard policy, refer to the Standard Policy section.

COMMERCIAL LINES
AGRICULTURAL CAPITAL ASSETS; BOP; CAPITAL ASSETS; C. AUTO; CRIME; CGL (CGL, EMPLOYMENT, LIQUOR, MARKET SEGMENTS, OCP, POLLUTION, PRODUCTS/COMPLETED OPERATIONS, RR PROTECTIVE); CIM; C. PROP.; E-COMMERCE; EQUIPMENT BREAKDOWN; FARM; FINANCIAL; MGT; PROFESSIONAL LIABILITY

Idaho Code §41-1842

Cancellation during the Underwriting Period

Length of Underwriting Period: Sixty days.

Length of Notice: Ten days for nonpayment, however, the ten-day notification period begins five days following the date of postmark. The notice must state the effective date of the cancellation; thirty days for any other reason.

Reason for Cancellation: Not required, but must be provided upon request of the insured.

Proof Required: Proof of mailing.

Cancellation after the Underwriting Period

The policy may be cancelled **only** for the following reasons:

1. Nonpayment.

2. Fraud or material misrepresentation on the application, in continuing the policy, or in presenting a claim.

3. Acts or omissions by the insured that increase any hazard insured against.

4. A change in the risk that materially increases any hazard insured against.

5. If the insurer loses part or all of its reinsurance on the risk.

6. If the Director determines that the continuation of the policy would jeopardize the insurer's solvency or place the insurer in violation of the insurance laws of Idaho or any other state.

IDAHO

7. If the insured violates any policy terms or conditions other than nonpayment of premium.

Length of Notice: Ten days for nonpayment, however, the ten-day notification period begins five days following the date of postmark. The notice must state the effective date of the cancellation; thirty days for all other allowable reasons.

Reason for Cancellation: Not required, except for nonpayment. In all other cases, the reason must be provided upon request.

Proof Required: Proof of mailing.

Nonrenewal

Length of Notice: Forty-five days.

Reason for Nonrenewal: Not required but must be provided upon request.

Proof Required: Proof of mailing.

Other Cancellation/Nonrenewal Provisions

If the insurer does not mail the notice at least forty-five days before the expiration or anniversary date of the policy, the policy remains in effect until forty-five days after notice is mailed. Earned premium for the extended period of coverage is at the rates applicable to the expiring policy.

The insurer must give a thirty-day notice prior to any of the following:

1. A premium increase of more than 10 percent.
2. A change in deductible.
3. A reduction in limits.
4. A reduction in coverage.

For OCP policies all notices must be mailed to the named insured and the contractor shown on the declarations.

For Railroad Protective policies all notices must be mailed to the first named insured, the contractor, any involved governmental authority, or other contracting party shown on the declarations.

IDAHO

Any insurer intending to implement block cancellations or block nonrenewals of insurance policies shall provide the director written notice of such intentions no later than one hundred twenty days prior to such intended action. (Idaho Code Ann. §41-1841).

COMMERCIAL GENERAL LIABILITY
(Underground Storage Tank Policy)
Idaho Code §41-1842

Cancellation during the Underwriting Period

Length of Underwriting Period: Sixty days.

Length of Notice: Ten days for nonpayment, however, the ten-day notification period begins five days following the date of postmark. The notice must state the effective date of the cancellation; thirty days for fraud or material misrepresentation; sixty days for any other reasons. The sixty-day requirement is not contained in the Idaho code. However, if an insurer has adopted the ISO amendatory endorsement (CG 30 09), it must follow this provision.

Reason for Cancellation: Not required on the notice, except for nonpayment. In all other cases, the reason must be provided upon request.

Proof Required: Certified mail.

Cancellation after the Underwriting Period

The policy may be cancelled **only** for the following reasons:

1. Nonpayment.

2. Fraud or material misrepresentation on the application, in continuing the policy, or in presenting a claim.

3. Acts or omissions by the insured that increase any hazard insured against.

4. A change in the risk that materially increases any hazard insured against.

5. If the insurer loses part or all of its reinsurance on the risk.

6. If the Director determines that the continuation of the policy would jeopardize the insurer's solvency or place the insurer in violation of the insurance laws of Idaho or any other state.

7. If the insured violates any policy terms or conditions other than paying the premium.

IDAHO

Length of Notice: Ten days for nonpayment, however, the ten-day notification period begins five days following the date of postmark. The notice must state the effective date of the cancellation; thirty days for fraud or material misrepresentation; sixty days for all other allowable reasons. The sixty-day requirement is not contained in the Idaho code. However, if an insurer has adopted the ISO amendatory endorsement (CG 30 09), it must follow this provision.

Reason for Cancellation: Not required on the notice, except for nonpayment. In all other cases, the reason must be provided upon request.

Proof Required: Certified mail.

Nonrenewal

Length of Notice: Sixty days. The sixty-day requirement is not contained in the Idaho Code, which requires only a forty-five-day notice of nonrenewal for commercial policies. However, if an insurer has adopted the ISO amendatory endorsement (CG 30 09), it must follow this provision.

Reason for Nonrenewal: Not required.

Proof Required: Certified mail.

Other Cancellation/Nonrenewal Provisions

If the insurer does not mail the notice at least sixty days before the expiration or anniversary date of the policy, the policy remains in effect until sixty days after notice is mailed. Earned premium for the extended period of coverage is at the rates applicable to the expiring policy.

Any insurer intending to implement block cancellations or block nonrenewals of insurance policies shall provide the director written notice of such intentions no later than one hundred twenty days prior to such intended action. (Idaho Code Ann. §41-1841).

The insurer must give a thirty-day notice prior to any of the following:

1. A premium increase of more than 10 percent.

2. A change in deductible.

3. A reduction in limits.

4. A reduction in coverage.

IDAHO

COMMERCIAL UMBRELLA

Idaho makes no changes from the standard policy.

WORKERS COMPENSATION

Idaho Code §72-311

Cancellation

Length of Notice: Ten days if cancelled at the request of the policy holder, for failure to pay, for material misrepresentation, due to substantial unforeseen changes to risk, or due to substantial breaches of contractual duties. Sixty days for any other reason.

Reason for Cancellation: Not specified in statute.

Proof Required: Certified mail. Notice must be filed with the contracting party at the last known address and also with the industrial commission. For purposes of this section, service by certified mail is complete either on acknowledgement of receipt or refusal of the notice by the contracting party or the fifteenth day after the date the postal authority first attempts to deliver the certified mail as evidenced by P.S. form 3849 or other similar document.

Nonrenewal

Length of Notice: Ten days if nonrenewed at the request of the policy holder, for failure to pay, for material misrepresentation, due to substantial unforeseen changes to risk, or due to substantial breaches of contractual duties. Sixty days for any other reason.

Reason for Nonrenewal: Note specified in statute.

Proof Required: Certified mail. Notice must be filed with the contracting party at the last known address and also with the industrial commission. For purposes of this section, service by certified mail is complete either on acknowledgement of receipt or refusal of the notice by the contracting party or the fifteenth day after the date the postal authority first attempts to deliver the certified mail as evidenced by P.S. form 3849 or other similar document.

Other Cancellation/Nonrenewal Provisions

No statement in an application for such a policy, contract or bond shall void the policy, contract or bond as between the surety and employer unless such statement shall be false and would materially have affected the acceptance of the risk if known by the surety. In no case shall the holding of the policy, contract or bond void between the surety and employer affect the surety's obligation to the employer's employees or their dependents to pay compensation

IDAHO

and to discharge other obligations under this law. In such case, the surety shall have a right of action against the employer for any amounts for which the surety is liable under such policy, contract or bond. (Idaho Code Ann. § 72-310).

Every such policy, contract or bond shall contain a provision to the effect that the insolvency or bankruptcy of the employer and his discharge therein shall not relieve the surety from the payment of compensation for injuries received or occupational diseases contracted or death sustained by an employee during the life of such policy or contract. (Idaho Code Ann. § 72-308).

SURPLUS LINES
Idaho Code § 41-1842

The Idaho cancellation laws do not apply to surplus lines policies.

FINANCED PREMIUMS
Idaho Code §28-44-401

The insured may give the finance company the authority to cancel the policy. The finance company must give the insured fifteen days to pay. The finance company then refunds any unearned loan finance charge to the insured.

If the insurance contract cancelled provides motor vehicle liability insurance the notice of cancellation shall briefly inform the debtor of the consequences under the laws of this state of operating a motor vehicle without liability insurance; and a copy of the notice of cancellation shall be sent to the Idaho Transportation Department.

PERSONAL LINES
DWELLING FIRE & HOMEOWNERS
Idaho Code §41-2401

The only change from the standard policy provisions is the statutory requirement that the ten-day notification period for nonpayment begins five days following the date of postmark and is accompanied by the reason for the cancellation.

PERSONAL AUTO
Idaho Code §§41-2506 through 41-2512
Cancellation during the Underwriting Period

Length of Underwriting Period: Sixty days.

Length of Notice: Ten days for nonpayment of premium; twenty days for all other reasons.

IDAHO

Reason for Cancellation: Not required on the notice, except for nonpayment. In all other cases, the reason must be provided upon request.

Proof Required: Proof of mailing.

Cancellation after the Underwriting Period

The policy may be cancelled **only** for the following reasons:

1. Nonpayment.

2. Material misrepresentation on the application.

3. Any insured violated any terms and conditions of the policy.

4. If the named insured did not fully disclose accidents, tickets, or physical damage claims for the preceding thirty-six months if asked for in the application.

5. While the policy was in force failed to fully disclose upon written request, facts relative to accidents and losses incurred material to underwriting the risk.

6. Any insured made a false or fraudulent claim or knowingly helps someone else to make such a claim.

7. If the named insured, resident driver, or any customary operator of the insured auto:

    a. Has had his or her driver's license suspended or revoked within the previous thirty-six months.

    b. Has a history of and is subject to epilepsy or heart attacks. (Not applicable if the person provides a certificate from a physician testifying to his or her ability to drive).

    c. Has an accident, traffic, or criminal record; a physical, mental, or other condition that might endanger the public safety, with that person driving.

    d. Takes part in a prearranged competitive speed contest—either as a driver or a passenger—in the insured auto during the policy period.

    e. Has been addicted to the use of narcotics and other drugs within the previous thirty-six months.

    f. Uses alcohol to excess.

IDAHO

    g. Was convicted or forfeited bail for any of the following in the preceding thirty-six months:

        (1) Any felony.
        (2) Criminal negligence resulting in death, homicide, or assault as a result of an auto accident.
        (3) Driving while intoxicated or under the influence of drugs.
        (4) Leaving the scene of an accident without stopping to report.
        (5) Theft or unlawful taking of a motor vehicle.
        (6) Making fraudulent statements when applying for a driver's license.

    h. Is convicted of three or more moving violations within the previous thirty-six months.

8. If the insured's auto is:

    a. So mechanically defective that its operation might endanger public safety.

    b. Used to carry passengers for compensation.

    c. Used to transport flammables or explosives.

    d. An authorized emergency vehicle.

    e. Changed in a way that substantially increases the risk.

    f. Not inspected, when required, or fails the inspection.

Length of Notice: Ten days for nonpayment; twenty days for all other reasons.

Reason for Cancellation: Not required except for nonpayment. However, notice must state that the reason for the notice will be provided upon request.

Proof Required: Proof of mailing.

Nonrenewal

Nonrenewal is allowed **only** under the following circumstances:

1. One of the reasons for midterm cancellation exists.

2. If, at any time during the policy period, the named insured, a resident relative, or regular operator of the insured auto fails to fully disclose facts relative to an accident.

IDAHO

3. If the laws of Idaho allow for nonrenewal.

4. If the insured auto is now registered in a jurisdiction other than Idaho.

Length of Notice: Thirty days.

Reason for Nonrenewal: Not required. However, notice must state that the reason will be provided upon request.

Proof Required: Proof of mailing.

Other Cancellation/Nonrenewal Provisions

A renewal policy automatically terminates if the insured does not pay the renewal premium when due. When the policy is terminated for reasons other than nonpayment, the insurer must notify the insured of possible eligibility for insurance through the automobile assigned risk plan.

An insurer shall have the right to exclude, cancel or refuse to renew coverage under an automobile insurance policy as to designated individuals. Any such cancellation or refusal to renew shall be acknowledged by the signature of the named insured.

PERSONAL UMBRELLA

Cancellation during the Underwriting Period

Length of Underwriting Period: Sixty days.

Length of Notice: Ten days for any reason.

Reason for Cancellation: Not required.

Proof Required: Proof of mailing.

Cancellation after the Underwriting Period

Length of Notice: Ten-day notice for nonpayment; thirty-day notice for any other reason.

Reason for Cancellation: Not required.

Proof Required: Proof of mailing.

IDAHO

Nonrenewal

Length of Notice: Thirty days.

Reason for Nonrenewal: Not required.

Proof Required: Proof of mailing.

FRAUD

Idaho Code §§41-268; 41-290; 41-293; 41-1305

General Information and Definitions

Any person who, with the intent to defraud or deceive an insurer for the purpose of obtaining any money or benefit, presents or causes to be presented to any insurer, producer, practitioner or other person, any statement as part of, or in support of, a claim for payment or other benefit, knowing that such statement contains false, incomplete, or misleading information concerning any fact or thing material to such claim.

No person shall make or issue, or cause to be made or issued, any written or oral statement misrepresenting or making incomplete comparisons as to the terms, conditions, or benefits contained in any policy for the purpose of inducing or attempting or tending to induce the policyholder to lapse, forfeit, surrender, lease, retain, exchange, or convert, or otherwise use or dispose of any insurance policy, or any right or option thereunder, or in connection with any such statement and for like purpose fail to disclose all reasonably material facts, or a material fact necessary to make the statements made, in the light of the circumstances under which they are made, not misleading.

Reporting Requirements

Any insurer which has facts to support a belief that a fraudulent claim is being or has been made shall, within sixty days of the receipt of such notice, send to the Director of Insurance, on a form prescribed by the Director, the information requested and such additional information relative to the claim and the parties claiming loss or damages as the Director may require. The Director of the Department of Insurance shall review such reports and select such claims as, in his judgment, may require further investigation. He shall then cause an independent examination of the facts surrounding such claim to be made to determine the extent, if any, to which fraud, deceit, or intentional misrepresentation of any kind exists in the submission of the claim. The Director of the Department of Insurance shall report any alleged violations of law which his investigations disclose to the appropriate licensing agency and prosecuting authority having jurisdiction with respect to any such violation.

Penalties

Any violator of this section is guilty of a felony and shall be subject to a term of imprisonment not to exceed fifteen years, or a fine not to exceed $15,000, or both and shall be ordered to make restitution to the insurer or any other person for any financial loss sustained as a result of a violation of this section. Each instance of violation may be considered a separate offense.

Antifraud Provisions

There is hereby created an account in the agency asset fund in the state treasury, to be designated the "arson, fire and fraud prevention account." The account shall be used by the Director of the Department of Insurance for enforcement of this act, investigation of alleged cases of arson, fraud and related alleged violations of the laws of this state, and prevention of fire, explosions and other conditions necessary for the public safety, health, peace and welfare.

FAIR CLAIMS PROCESSING
Idaho Code §§41-1329; 41-1329A; 41-5602

Unfair claims processing consists of committing or performing any of the following acts or omissions intentionally, or with such frequency as to indicate a general business practice:

1. Misrepresenting pertinent facts or insurance policy provisions relating to coverages at issue.

2. Failing to acknowledge and act reasonably and promptly upon communications with respect to claims arising under insurance policies.

3. Failing to adopt and implement reasonable standards for the prompt investigation of claims arising under insurance policies.

4. Refusing to pay claims without conducting a reasonable investigation based upon all available information.

5. Failing to affirm or deny coverage of claims within a reasonable time after proof of loss statements have been completed.

6. Not attempting in good faith to effectuate prompt, fair and equitable settlements of claims in which liability has become reasonably clear.

7. Compelling insureds to institute litigation to recover amounts due under an insurance policy by offering substantially less than the amounts ultimately recovered in actions brought by such insureds.

8. Attempting to settle a claim for less than the amount to which a reasonable man would have believed he was entitled by reference to written or printed advertising material accompanying or made part of an application.

IDAHO

9. Attempting to settle claims on the basis of an application which was altered without notice to, or knowledge or consent of the insured.

10. Making claims payments to insureds or beneficiaries not accompanied by a statement setting forth the coverage under which the payments are being made.

11. Making known to insureds or claimants a policy of appealing from arbitration awards in favor of insureds or claimants for the purpose of compelling them to accept settlements or compromises less than the amount awarded in arbitration.

12. Delaying the investigation or payment of claims by requiring an insured, claimant, or the physician of either to submit a preliminary claim report and then requiring the subsequent submission of formal proof of loss forms, both of which submissions contain substantially the same information.

13. Failing to promptly settle claims, where liability has become reasonably clear, under one portion of the insurance policy coverage in order to influence settlements under other portions of the insurance policy coverage.

14. Failing to promptly provide a reasonable explanation of the basis in the insurance policy in relation to the facts or applicable law for denial of a claim or for the offer of a compromise settlement.

An insurer shall process a claim for payment for health care services rendered by a practitioner or facility to a beneficiary in accordance with this section.

1. If a beneficiary, practitioner or facility submits an electronic claim to an insurer within thirty days of the date on which service was delivered, an insurer shall pay or deny the claim not later than thirty days after receipt of the claim.

2. If a beneficiary, practitioner or facility submits a paper claim for payment to an insurer within forty-five days of the date on which service was delivered, an insurer shall pay or deny the claim not later than forty-five days after receipt of the claim.

3. If an insurer denies the claim or needs additional information to process the claim, the insurer shall notify the practitioner or facility and the beneficiary in writing within thirty days of receipt of an electronic claim or within forty-five days of receipt of a paper claim. The notice shall state why the insurer denied the claim.

4. If the claim was denied because more information was required to process the claim, the notice shall specifically describe all information and supporting documentation

IDAHO

needed to evaluate the claim for processing. If the practitioner or facility submits the information and documentation identified by the insurer within thirty days of receipt of the written notice, the insurer shall process and pay the claim within thirty days of receipt of the additional information or, if appropriate, deny the claim.

If claims processing is found to be unfair, the Director may impose an administrative penalty not to exceed $10,000 and may, in addition to the fine, or in the alternative to the fine, refuse to continue or suspend or revoke an insurer's certificate of authority.

ILLINOIS

For details on cancellation procedures for the standard policy, refer to the Standard Policy section.

COMMERCIAL LINES

Cancellation and nonrenewal notices may be provided electronically to mortgagees, lienholders, and brokers or agents of record. (215 Ill. Comp. Stat. Ann. 5/143.16).

BOP; CAPITAL ASSETS; COMMERCIAL PROPERTY; & FARM; COMMERCIAL INLAND MARINE

(Applicable to Real Property other than Residential Properties that are occupied by four families or less.)

215 ILCS 5/141.01, 5/143.10, and 5/143.11 et seq., 5/143.16a, 5/143.17a; 5/143.20a, 5/143.21.1

Cancellation during the Underwriting Period

Length of Underwriting Period: Sixty days.

Length of Notice: Ten days for nonpayment and reasons 7 through 10 below; thirty days for all other allowable reasons.

Reason for Cancellation: Required on the notice.

Proof Required: Proof of mailing to the named insured and the last known mortgagees or lienholders at the last mailing address known by the company. Proof of mailing includes a recognized U.S. Post Office form or a form acceptable to the United States Post Office or other commercial mail delivery service. A copy of all notices shall be sent to the insured's broker or agent of record if known at the last mailing address known to the company. Certified and regular mail to insured for reasons 4-8 below.

Cancellation after the Underwriting Period

The policy may be cancelled **only** for the following reasons:

1. Nonpayment.

2. When a policy was obtained by misrepresentation.

3. The insured violated the terms of the policy.

ILLINOIS

4. For any act which measurably increases the risk originally accepted.

5. Certification by the Director of loss of reinsurance.

6. If the Director determines that to continue on the policy could place the insurer in violation of the Illinois Insurance Code.

7. If the insured does not start repairs to a building within sixty days after adjustment of a fire loss, unless the delay is caused by labor dispute or weather.

8. If the building is unoccupied for sixty or more consecutive days. (Not applicable to seasonal unoccupancy or buildings under repair, construction, or reconstruction if properly secured against unauthorized entry).

9. If the building has been declared unsafe in accordance with the law or if it has either an outstanding order to vacate or an outstanding demolition order.

10. If utility services have not been connected to the building for thirty consecutive days or more.

Length of Notice: Ten days for nonpayment and reasons 7 through 10 listed above; sixty days for all other reasons.

Reason for Cancellation: Required on the notice.

Proof Required: Proof of mailing to the named insured and the last known mortgagees or lienholders at the last mailing address known by the company. Proof of mailing includes a recognized U.S. Post Office form or a form acceptable to the U.S. Post Office or other commercial mail delivery service. A copy of all notices shall be sent to the insured's broker or agent of record if known at the last mailing address known to the company. Certified and regular mail required to insured for reasons 7-10 listed above.

Nonrenewal

Length of Notice: Thirty days, unless the policy has been in force for five years or longer, then a sixty day notice is required.

Reason for Nonrenewal: Required on the notice.

Proof Required: Proof of mailing to the named insured and the last known mortgagees or lienholders at the last mailing address known by the company. Proof of mailing includes a recognized U.S. Post Office form or a form acceptable to the U.S. Post Office or other

ILLINOIS

commercial mail delivery service. A copy of all notices shall be sent to the insured's broker or agent of record if known at the last mailing address known to the company.

Other Cancellation/Nonrenewal Provisions

A Business owners Policy may be voided in the event of policyholder concealment, misrepresentation or fraud.

An insurer may not cancel or refuse to issue or renew a policy based solely on a previous insurer's cancellation, refusal to issue, or nonrenewal.

Automatic termination as of the renewal date is allowed if the insured does not pay the renewal premium.

A sixty-day notice is required prior to renewal under any of the following conditions: a premium increase of 30 percent or more, any change in deductibles, or any other change that materially alters the policy. Note that this requirement does not appear on the Illinois Amendatory Endorsement.

Insurance companies may not cancel or nonrenew policies for the sole reason that their contract with the agent of record has terminated.

If an agent, broker or other representative or employee of any insurance company or agency recommends, advises, suggests or requires the cancellation of a policy at any time other than the policy anniversary or expiration date, the insured must be informed in writing of the additional cost of such cancellation before the cancellation or termination of the policy. This only applies to the short rate cancellations.

COMMERCIAL PROPERTY

(Applicable to residential properties occupied by four families or less. These policies are treated as Personal Line Dwelling Fire and Homeowners.)

215 ILCS 5/141.01, 5/143.10, and 5/143.11 et seq.,5/143.16a 5/143.17a

Cancellation during the Underwriting Period

Length of Underwriting Period: Sixty days.

Length of Notice: Ten days for nonpayment; thirty days for all other reasons.

Reason for Cancellation: Required on the notice.

Proof Required: Proof of mailing to the named insured and the last known mortgagees or lienholders at the last mailing address known by the company. Proof of mailing includes

ILLINOIS

a recognized U.S. Post Office form or a form acceptable to the U.S. Post Office or other commercial mail delivery service. A copy of all notices shall be sent to the insured's broker or agent of record if known at the last mailing address known to the company.

Allowable Reasons for Cancellation

The policy may be cancelled **only** for the following reasons:

1. Nonpayment.

2. Material misrepresentation on the application.

3. Measurable increase in risk.

Length of Notice: Ten days for nonpayment; thirty days for all other reasons.

Reason for Cancellation: Required on the notice.

Proof Required: Proof of mailing to the named insured and the last known mortgagees or lienholders at the last mailing address known by the company. Proof of mailing includes a recognized U.S. Post Office form or a form acceptable to the U.S. Post Office or other commercial mail delivery service. A copy of all notices shall be sent to the insured's broker or agent of record if known at the last mailing address known to the company.

Nonrenewal

Length of Notice: Sixty days.

Reason for Nonrenewal: Required on the notice.

Proof Required: Proof of mailing to the named insured and the last known mortgagees or lienholders at the last mailing address known by the company. Proof of mailing includes a recognized U.S. Post Office form or a form acceptable to the U.S. Post Office or other commercial mail delivery service. A copy of all notices shall be sent to the insured's broker or agent of record if known at the last mailing address known to the company.

The policy may also be nonrenewed for either of the following reasons:

1. Material misrepresentation on the application.

2. Measurable increase in risk.

ILLINOIS

Other Cancellation/Nonrenewal Provisions

An insurer may not cancel or refuse to issue or renew a policy based solely on a previous insurer's cancellation, refusal to issue, or nonrenewal.

Automatic termination as of the renewal date is allowed if the insured does not pay the renewal premium.

A sixty-day notice is required prior to renewal under any of the following conditions: a premium increase of 30 percent or more, any change in deductibles, or any other change that materially alters the policy. Note that this requirement does not appear on the Illinois Amendatory Endorsements (IL 02 84 and BP 01 54).

Insurance companies may not cancel or nonrenew policies for the sole reason that their contract with the agent of record has terminated.

If an agent, broker or other representative or employee of any insurance company or agency recommends, advises, suggests or requires the cancellation of a policy at any time other than the policy anniversary or expiration date, the insured must be informed in writing of the additional cost of such cancellation before the cancellation or termination of the policy. This only applies to the short rate cancellations.

COMMERCIAL AUTO

215 ILCS 5/141.01, 5/143.10, and 5/143.11 et seq.,5/143.16a, 5/143.17a

Cancellation during the Underwriting Period

Length of Underwriting Period: Sixty days.

Length of Notice: Ten days for nonpayment; thirty days for all other reasons.

Reason for Cancellation: Required on the notice.

Proof Required: Proof of mailing to the named insured, and lienholder or loss payee at the last mailing address known by the company. Proof of mailing includes a recognized U.S. Post Office form or a form acceptable to the U.S. Post Office or other commercial mail delivery service. A copy of all notices shall be sent to the insured's broker or agent of record if known at the last mailing address known to the company.

Cancellation after the Underwriting Period

The policy may be cancelled **only** for the following reasons:

1. Nonpayment.

2. Material misrepresentation on the application.

ILLINOIS

3. If any insured violates any of the terms and conditions of the policy.

4. Measurable increase in risk.

5. If the insurer loses part or all of its reinsurance on the risk.

6. If the Director otherwise determines that to continue on the policy could place the insurer in violation of the Illinois Insurance Code.

Length of Notice: Ten days for nonpayment; sixty days for all other allowable reasons.

Reason for Cancellation: Required on the notice.

Proof Required: Proof of mailing to the named insured, and the loss payee at the last mailing address known by the company. Proof of mailing includes a recognized U.S. Post Office form or a form acceptable to the U.S. Post Office or other commercial mail delivery service. A copy of all notices shall be sent to the insured's broker or agent of record if known at the last mailing address known to the company.

Nonrenewal

Length of Notice: Sixty days.

Reason for Nonrenewal: Required on the notice.

Proof Required: Proof of mailing to the named insured, and the loss payee at the last mailing address known by the company. Proof of mailing includes a recognized U.S. Post Office form or a form acceptable to the U.S. Post Office or other commercial mail delivery service. A copy of all notices shall be sent to the insured's broker or agent of record if known at the last mailing address known to the company.

Other Cancellation/Nonrenewal Provisions

An insurer may not cancel or refuse to issue or renew a policy based solely on a previous insurer's cancellation, refusal to issue, or nonrenewal.

Automatic termination as of the renewal date is allowed if the insured does not pay the renewal premium.

A sixty-day notice is required prior to renewal under any of the following conditions: a premium increase of 30 percent or more, any change in deductibles, or any other change that materially alters the policy. Note that this requirement does not appear on the Illinois Amendatory Endorsement (CA 02 70).

ILLINOIS

Insurance companies may not cancel or nonrenew policies for the sole reason that their contract with the agent of record has terminated.

If an agent, broker or other representative or employee of any insurance company or agency recommends, advises, suggests or requires the cancellation of a policy at any time other than the policy anniversary or expiration date, the insured must be informed in writing of the additional cost of such cancellation before the cancellation or termination of the policy. This only applies to the short rate cancellations.

COMMERCIAL CRIME COVERAGE FORM; COMMERCIAL CRIME POLICY; EMPLOYEE THEFT; GOVERNMENT CRIME COVERAGE FORM; GOVERNMENT CRIME POLICY; KIDNAP/RANSOM AND EXTORTION COVERAGE FORM; KIDNAP/RANSOM & EXTORTION POLICY

215 ILCS 5/141.01, 5/143.10, and 5/143.11 et seq., 5/143.16a, 5/143.17a

Cancellation during the Underwriting Period

Length of Underwriting Period: Sixty days.

Length of Notice: Ten days for nonpayment; thirty days for all other reasons.

Reason for Cancellation: Required on the notice.

Proof Required: Proof of mailing at the last mailing address known by the company. Proof of mailing includes a recognized U.S. Post Office form or a form acceptable to the U.S. Post Office or other commercial mail delivery service. A copy of all notices shall be sent to the insured's broker or agent of record if known at the last mailing address known to the company.

Cancellation after the Underwriting Period

The policy may be cancelled **only** for the following reasons:

1. Nonpayment.

2. Material misrepresentation on the application.

3. If any insured violates any of the terms and conditions of the policy.

4. Measurable increase in risk.

5. If the insurer loses part or all of its reinsurance on the risk.

6. If the Director determines that to continue on the policy could place the insurer in violation of the Illinois Insurance Code.

ILLINOIS

Length of Notice: Ten days for nonpayment; sixty days for all other reasons.

Reason for Cancellation: Required on the notice.

Proof Required: Proof of mailing at the last mailing address known by the company. Proof of mailing includes a recognized U.S. Post Office form or a form acceptable to the U.S. Post Office or other commercial mail delivery service. A copy of all notices shall be sent to the insured's broker or agent of record if known at the last mailing address known to the company.

Nonrenewal

Length of Notice: Sixty days.

Reason for Nonrenewal: Required on the notice.

Proof Required: Proof of mailing at the last mailing address known by the company. Proof of mailing includes a recognized U.S. Post Office form or a form acceptable to the U.S. Post Office or other commercial mail delivery service. A copy of all notices shall be sent to the insured's broker or agent of record if known at the last mailing address known to the company.

Other Cancellation/Nonrenewal Provisions

An insurer may not cancel or refuse to issue or renew a policy based solely on a previous insurer's cancellation, refusal to issue, or nonrenewal.

Automatic termination as of the renewal date is allowed if the insured does not pay the renewal premium.

A sixty-day notice is required prior to renewal under any of the following conditions: a premium increase of 30 percent or more, any change in deductibles, or any other change that materially alters the policy. Note that this requirement does not appear on the Illinois Amendatory Endorsement (CR 02 02).

Insurance companies may not cancel or nonrenew policies for the sole reason that their contract with the agent of record has terminated.

If an agent, broker or other representative or employee of any insurance company or agency recommends, advises, suggests or requires the cancellation of a policy at any time other than the policy anniversary or expiration date, the insured must be informed in writing of the additional cost of such cancellation before the cancellation or termination of the policy. This only applies to the short rate cancellations.

ILLINOIS

COMMERCIAL GENERAL LIABILITY
(CGL, LIQUOR, MARKET SEGMENTS, OCP, POLLUTION, PRODUCTS)

215 ILCS 5/141.01, 5/143.10, and 5/143.11 et seq.,5/143.16a, 5/143.17a

Cancellation during the Underwriting Period

Length of Underwriting Period: Sixty days.

Length of Notice: Ten days for nonpayment; thirty days for all other reasons.

Reason for Cancellation: Required on the notice.

Proof Required: Proof of mailing at the last mailing address known by the company. Proof of mailing includes a recognized U.S. Post Office form or a form acceptable to the U.S. Post Office or other commercial mail delivery service. A copy of all notices shall be sent to the insured's broker or agent of record if known at the last mailing address known to the company.

Cancellation after the Underwriting Period

The policy may be cancelled **only** for the following reasons:

1. Nonpayment.

2. Material misrepresentation on the application.

3. If any insured violates any of the terms and conditions of the policy.

4. Measurable increase in risk.

5. If the insurer loses part or all of its reinsurance on the risk.

6. If the Director determines that to continue on the policy could place the insurer in violation of the Illinois Insurance Code.

Length of Notice: Ten days for nonpayment; sixty days for all other reasons.

Reason for Cancellation: Required on the notice.

Proof Required: Proof of mailing at the last mailing address known by the company. Proof of mailing includes a recognized U.S. Post Office form or a form acceptable to the U.S. Post Office or other commercial mail delivery service. A copy of all notices shall be sent to the insured's broker or agent of record if known at the last mailing address known to the company.

ILLINOIS

Nonrenewal

Length of Notice: Sixty days.

Reason for Nonrenewal: Required on the notice.

Proof Required: Proof of mailing at the last mailing address known by the company. Proof of mailing includes a recognized U.S. Post Office form or a form acceptable to the U.S. Post Office or other commercial mail delivery service. A copy of all notices shall be sent to the insured's broker or agent of record if known at the last mailing address known to the company.

Other Cancellation/Nonrenewal Provisions

All notices must be mailed to the named insured and the contractor or governmental authority shown in the declarations.

An insurer may not cancel or refuse to issue or renew a policy based solely on a previous insurer's cancellation, refusal to issue, or nonrenewal.

Automatic termination as of the renewal date is allowed if the insured does not pay the renewal premium.

A sixty-day notice is required prior to renewal under any of the following conditions: a premium increase of 30 percent or more, any change in deductibles, or any other change that materially alters the policy. Note that this requirement does not appear on the Illinois Amendatory Endorsements (CG 02 00, or CG 30 18).

Insurance companies may not cancel or nonrenew policies for the sole reason that their contract with the agent of record has terminated.

If an agent, broker or other representative or employee of any insurance company or agency recommends, advises, suggests or requires the cancellation of a policy at any time other than the policy anniversary or expiration date, the insured must be informed in writing of the additional cost of such cancellation before the cancellation or termination of the policy. This only applies to the short rate cancellations.

COMMERCIAL GENERAL LIABILITY
(Railroad Protective)

215 ILCS 5/141.01, 5/143.10, and 5/143.11 et seq.,5/143.16a, 5/143.17a

Cancellation during the Underwriting Period

Length of Underwriting Period: Sixty days.

Length of Notice: Ten days for nonpayment; thirty days for all other reasons.

ILLINOIS

Reason for Cancellation: Required on the notice.

Proof Required: Proof of mailing at the last mailing address known by the company. Proof of mailing includes a recognized U.S. Post Office form or a form acceptable to the U.S. Post Office or other commercial mail delivery service. A copy of all notices shall be sent to the insured's broker or agent of record if known at the last mailing address known to the company.

Cancellation after the Underwriting Period

The policy may be cancelled **only** for the following reasons:

1. Nonpayment.

2. Material misrepresentation on the application.

3. If any insured violates any of the terms and conditions of the policy.

4. Measurable increase in risk.

5. If the insurer loses part or all of its reinsurance on the risk.

6. If the Director determines that to continue on the policy could place the insurer in violation of the Illinois Insurance Code.

Length of Notice: Ten days for nonpayment; sixty days for all other allowable reasons.

Reason for Cancellation: Required on the notice.

Proof Required: Proof of mailing at the last mailing address known by the company. Proof of mailing includes a recognized U.S. Post Office form or a form acceptable to the U.S. Post Office or other commercial mail delivery service. A copy of all notices shall be sent to the insured's broker or agent of record if known at the last mailing address known to the company.

Nonrenewal

Length of Notice: Sixty days.

Reason for Nonrenewal: Required on the notice.

Proof Required: Proof of mailing at the last mailing address known by the company. Proof of mailing includes a recognized U.S. Post Office form or a form acceptable to the U.S. Post Office or other commercial mail delivery service. A copy of all notices shall be sent to the insured's broker or agent of record if known at the last mailing address known to the company.

ILLINOIS

Other Cancellation/Nonrenewal Provisions

All notices must be mailed to the named insured, the contractor, any involved government authorities, or other contracting parties shown in the declarations.

An insurer may not cancel or refuse to issue or renew a policy based solely on a previous insurer's cancellation, refusal to issue, or nonrenewal.

Automatic termination as of the renewal date is allowed if the insured does not pay the renewal premium.

A sixty-day notice is required prior to renewal under any of the following conditions: a premium increase of 30 percent or more, any change in deductibles, or any other change that materially alters the policy. Note that this requirement does not appear on the Illinois Amendatory Endorsement (CG 29 06).

Insurance companies may not cancel or nonrenew policies for the sole reason that their contract with the agent of record has terminated.

The statute does not require a sixty-day notice for reasons other than nonpayment during the first sixty days, however, insurers using ISO's CG 29 06 must comply with the terms of the policy.

If an agent, broker or other representative or employee of any insurance company or agency recommends, advises, suggests or requires the cancellation of a policy at any time other than the policy anniversary or expiration date, the insured must be informed in writing of the additional cost of such cancellation before the cancellation or termination of the policy.

COMMERCIAL GENERAL LIABILITY
(Underground Storage Tank Policy)

215 ILCS 5/141.01, 5/143.10, and 5/143.11 et seq., 5/143.16a, 5/143.17a

Cancellation during the Underwriting Period

Length of Underwriting Period: Sixty days.

Length of Notice: Ten days for nonpayment; thirty days for all other reasons.

Reason for Cancellation: Required on the notice.

Proof Required: Proof of mailing at the last mailing address known by the company. Proof of mailing includes a recognized U.S. Post Office form or a form acceptable to the U.S. Post Office or other commercial mail delivery service. A copy of all notices shall be sent to the insured's broker or agent of record if known at the last mailing address known to the company.

ILLINOIS

Cancellation after the Underwriting Period

The policy may be cancelled **only** for the following reasons:

1. Nonpayment.

2. Material misrepresentation on the application.

3. If any insured violates any of the terms and conditions of the policy.

4. Measurable increase in risk.

5. If the insurer loses part or all of its reinsurance on the risk.

6. If the Director determines that to continue on the policy could place the insurer in violation of the Illinois Insurance Code.

Length of Notice: Ten days for nonpayment; sixty days for all other reasons. The ISO Amendatory Endorsement CG 00 42 allows for a ten-day notice for misrepresentation.

Reason for Cancellation: Required on the notice.

Proof Required: Proof of mailing at the last mailing address known by the company. Proof of mailing includes a recognized U.S. Post Office form or a form acceptable to the U.S. Post Office or other commercial mail delivery service. A copy of all notices shall be sent to the insured's broker or agent of record if known at the last mailing address known to the company.

Nonrenewal

Length of Notice: Sixty days.

Reason for Nonrenewal: Required on the notice.

Proof Required: Proof of mailing at the last mailing address known by the company. Proof of mailing includes a recognized U.S. Post Office form or a form acceptable to the U.S. Post Office or other commercial mail delivery service. A copy of all notices shall be sent to the insured's broker or agent of record if known at the last mailing address known to the company.

Other Cancellation/Nonrenewal Provisions

Use of certified mail is not a statutory requirement. However, insurers using ISO's CG 00 42 must comply with the policy requirement.

ILLINOIS

An insurer may not cancel or refuse to issue or renew a policy based solely on a previous insurer's cancellation, refusal to issue, or nonrenewal.

Automatic termination as of the renewal date is allowed if the insured does not pay the renewal premium.

A sixty-day notice is required prior to renewal under any of the following conditions: a premium increase of 30 percent or more, any change in deductibles, or any other change that materially alters the policy. Note that this requirement does not appear on the Illinois Amendatory Endorsement (CG 30 18).

Insurance companies may not cancel or nonrenew policies for the sole reason that their contract with the agent of record has terminated.

If an agent, broker or other representative or employee of any insurance company or agency recommends, advises, suggests or requires the cancellation of a policy at any time other than the policy anniversary or expiration date, the insured must be informed in writing of the additional cost of such cancellation before the cancellation or termination of the policy. This only applies to the short rate cancellations.

COMMERCIAL UMBRELLA

215 ILCS 5/141.01, 5/143.10, and 5/143.11 et seq., 5/143.16a, 5/143.17a

Cancellation during the Underwriting Period

Length of Underwriting Period: Sixty days.

Length of Notice: Ten days for nonpayment; thirty days for all other reasons.

Reason for Cancellation: Required on the notice.

Proof Required: Proof of mailing at the last mailing address known by the company. Proof of mailing includes a recognized U.S. Post Office form or a form acceptable to the U.S. Post Office or other commercial mail delivery service. A copy of all notices shall be sent to the insured's broker or agent of record if known at the last mailing address known to the company.

Cancellation after the Underwriting Period

The policy may be cancelled **only** for the following reasons:

1. Nonpayment.

2. Material misrepresentation on the application.

3. If any insured violates any of the terms and conditions of the policy.

ILLINOIS

4. Measurable increase in risk.

5. If the insurer loses part or all of its reinsurance on the risk.

6. If the Director determines that to continue on the policy could place the insurer in violation of the Illinois Insurance Code.

Length of Notice: Ten days for nonpayment; sixty days for all other reasons.

Reason for Cancellation: Required on the notice.

Proof Required: Proof of mailing at the last mailing address known by the company. Proof of mailing includes a recognized U.S. Post Office form or a form acceptable to the U.S. Post Office or other commercial mail delivery service. A copy of all notices shall be sent to the insured's broker or agent of record if known at the last mailing address known to the company.

Nonrenewal

Length of Notice: Thirty days.

Reason for Nonrenewal: Required on the notice.

Proof Required: Proof of mailing at the last mailing address known by the company. Proof of mailing includes a recognized U.S. Post Office form or a form acceptable to the U.S. Post Office or other commercial mail delivery service. A copy of all notices shall be sent to the insured's broker or agent of record if known at the last mailing address known to the company.

Other Cancellation/Nonrenewal Provisions

An insurer may not cancel or refuse to issue or renew a policy based solely on a previous insurer's cancellation, refusal to issue, or nonrenewal.

Automatic termination as of the renewal date is allowed if the insured does not pay the renewal premium.

A sixty-day notice is required prior to renewal under any of the following conditions: a premium increase of 30 percent or more, any change in deductibles, or any other change that materially alters the policy. Note that this requirement does not appear on the Illinois Amendatory Endorsement (CM 02 04).

Insurance companies may not cancel or nonrenew policies for the sole reason that their contract with the agent of record has terminated.

ILLINOIS

PROFESSIONAL LIABILITY

215 ILCS 5/141.01, 5/143.10, and 5/143.11 et seq., 5/143.16a, 5/143.17a

Cancellation during the Underwriting Period

Length of Underwriting Period: Sixty days.

Length of Notice: Ten days for nonpayment; thirty days for all other reasons.

Reason for Cancellation: Required on the notice.

Proof Required: Proof of mailing at the last mailing address known by the company. Proof of mailing includes a recognized U.S. Post Office form or a form acceptable to the U.S. Post Office or other commercial mail delivery service. A copy of all notices shall be sent to the insured's broker or agent of record if known at the last mailing address known to the company.

Cancellation after the Underwriting Period

The policy may be cancelled **only** for the following reasons:

1. Nonpayment.

2. Material misrepresentation on the application.

3. If any insured violates any of the terms and conditions of the policy.

4. Measurable increase in risk.

5. If the insurer loses part or all of its reinsurance on the risk.

6. If the Director determines that to continue on the policy could place the insurer in violation of the Illinois Insurance Code.

Length of Notice: Ten days for nonpayment; sixty days for all other reasons.

Reason for Cancellation: Required on the notice.

Proof Required: Proof of mailing at the last mailing address known by the company. Proof of mailing includes a recognized U.S. Post Office form or a form acceptable to the U.S. Post Office or other commercial mail delivery service. A copy of all notices shall be sent to the insured's broker or agent of record if known at the last mailing address known to the company.

ILLINOIS

Nonrenewal

Length of Notice: Sixty days.

Reason for Nonrenewal: Required on the notice.

Proof Required: Proof of mailing at the last mailing address known by the company. Proof of mailing includes a recognized U.S. Post Office form or a form acceptable to the U.S. Post Office or other commercial mail delivery service. A copy of all notices shall be sent to the insured's broker or agent of record if known at the last mailing address known to the company.

Other Cancellation/Nonrenewal Provisions

An insurer may not cancel or refuse to issue or renew a policy based solely on a previous insurer's cancellation, refusal to issue, or nonrenewal.

Automatic termination as of the renewal date is allowed if the insured does not pay the renewal premium.

A sixty-day notice is required prior to renewal under any of the following conditions: a premium increase of 30 percent or more, any change in deductibles, or any other change that materially alters the policy. Note that this requirement does not appear on the Illinois Amendatory Endorsement (CM 02 04).

Insurance companies may not cancel or nonrenew policies for the sole reason that their contract with the agent of record has terminated.

EQUIPMENT BREAKDOWN

215 ILCS 5/141.01, 5/143.10, and 5/143.11 et seq., 5/143.16a, 5/143.17a

Cancellation during the Underwriting Period

Length of Underwriting Period: Sixty days.

Length of Notice: Ten days for nonpayment; thirty days for any other reasons.

Reason for Cancellation: Required on the notice.

Proof Required: Proof of mailing to named insured and lienholder or loss payee at the last mailing address known by the company. Proof of mailing includes a recognized U.S. Post Office form or a form acceptable to the U.S. Post Office or other commercial mail delivery service. A copy of all notices shall be sent to the insured's broker or agent of record if known at the last mailing address known to the company.

ILLINOIS

Cancellation after the Underwriting Period

The policy may be cancelled **only** for the following reasons:

1. Nonpayment.

2. Material misrepresentation on the application.

3. If any insured violates any of the terms and conditions of the policy.

4. Measurable increase in the risk.

5. If the insurer certifies to the Director that it has lost all or part of its reinsurance on the risk.

6. If the director determines that continuation of the policy would place the insurer in violation of Illinois law.

Length of Notice: Ten days for nonpayment; sixty days for all other allowable reasons.

Reason for Cancellation: Required on the notice.

Proof Required: Proof of mailing to named insured and lienholder or loss payee at the last mailing address known by the company. Proof of mailing includes a recognized U.S. Post Office form or a form acceptable to the U.S. Post Office or other commercial mail delivery service. A copy of all notices shall be sent to the insured's broker or agent of record if known at the last mailing address known to the company.

Nonrenewal

Length of Notice: At least sixty days.

Reason for Nonrenewal: Required on the notice.

Proof Required: Proof of mailing to named insured and lienholder or loss payee at the last mailing address known by the company. Proof of mailing includes a recognized U.S. Post Office form or a form acceptable to the U.S. Post Office or other commercial mail delivery service. A copy of all notices shall be sent to the insured's broker or agent of record if known at the last mailing address known to the company.

Other Cancellation/Nonrenewal Provisions

An insurer may not cancel or refuse to issue or renew a policy based solely on a previous insurer's cancellation, refusal to issue, or nonrenewal.

ILLINOIS

A copy of any termination notice must be sent to the broker or agent.

Automatic termination as of the renewal date is allowed if the insured does not pay the renewal premium.

A sixty-day notice is required prior to renewal when a premium increase of 30 percent or more, any change in deductibles, or any other change that materially alters the policy. This requirement does not appear on the Illinois Amendatory Endorsement (EB 01 03).

Insurance companies may not cancel or nonrenew policies for the sole reason that their contract with the agent of record has terminated.

If an agent, broker or other representative or employee of any insurance company or agency recommends, advises, suggests or requires the cancellation of a policy at any time other than the policy anniversary or expiration date, the insured must be informed in writing of the additional cost of such cancellation before the cancellation or termination of the policy. This only applies to the short rate cancellations.

WORKERS COMPENSATION

215 ILCS 5/141.01, 5/143.10, 5/143.11 et seq. 5/143.16a, and 5/143.14-17a

Cancellation during the Underwriting Period

Length of Underwriting Period: Sixty days.

Length of Notice: Thirty days for any reason. Statute allows for ten-day notification for nonpayment; however insurers using NCCI's WC 12 06 01 C must provide thirty-day notification for any cancellation.

Reason for Cancellation: Required on the notice.

Proof Required: Proof of mailing at the last mailing address known by the company. Proof of mailing includes a recognized U.S. Post Office form or a form acceptable to the U.S. Post Office or other commercial mail delivery service. A copy of all notices shall be sent to the insured's broker or agent of record if known at the last mailing address known to the company. Notice also must be given to the Illinois Workers Compensation Commission.

The policy may be cancelled **only** for the following reasons:

1. Nonpayment.

2. Material misrepresentation on the application.

3. If any insured violates any of the terms and conditions of the policy.

ILLINOIS

4. Measurable increase in the risk.

5. If the insurer certifies to the Director that it has lost all or part of its reinsurance on the risk.

6. If the Director determines that continuation of the policy would place the insurer in violation of any Illinois insurance laws.

Length of Notice: Sixty days for any reasons. Statute allows for ten-day notification for nonpayment; however insurers using NCCI's WC 12 06 01 C must provide a thirty-day notice for any cancellation.

Reason for Cancellation: Required on the notice.

Proof Required: Proof of mailing at the last mailing address known by the company. Proof of mailing includes a recognized U.S. Post Office form or a form acceptable to the U.S. Post Office or other commercial mail delivery service. A copy of all notices shall be sent to the insured's broker or agent of record if known at the last mailing address known to the company. Notice must also be given to the Illinois Industrial Commission.

Nonrenewal

Length of Notice: Sixty days.

Reason for Nonrenewal: Required on the notice.

Proof Required: Proof of mailing at the last mailing address known by the company. Proof of mailing includes a recognized U.S. Post Office form or a form acceptable to the U.S. Post Office or other commercial mail delivery service. A copy of all notices shall be sent to the insured's broker or agent of record if known at the last mailing address known to the company.

Other Cancellation/Nonrenewal Provisions

If a nonrenewal notice does not give at least thirty-one days, the policy is extended for another year.

An insurer may not cancel or refuse to issue or renew a policy based solely on a previous insurer's cancellation, refusal to issue, or nonrenewal.

A sixty-day notice is required prior to renewal under any of the following conditions: a premium increase of 30 percent or more, any change in deductibles, or any other change that materially alters the policy. This provision does not appear on the NCCI amendatory endorsement for Illinois, but the Illinois Code requires such a notice.

ILLINOIS

SURPLUS LINES
215 ILCS 5/143.11 and 5/445

The Illinois cancellation and nonrenewal requirements do not apply to surplus lines policies.

FINANCED PREMIUMS
215 ILCS 5/513a11, 5/143.14

If the premium finance agreement contains a power of attorney, the insurer must honor the date of cancellation as set forth in the finance company's notice. Written notice of the intent to cancel for nonpayment of premium must be mailed to the named insured at least ten days in advance. At the end of the ten-day period, the premium finance company may request, in the name of the named insured, cancellation. A copy of the request must be mailed to the named insured at their last known address.

The insurer must notify any mortgagee, governmental agency, or other third-party that is designated on or before the fifth business day after it receives the premium finance company's notice of cancellation.

PERSONAL LINES
DWELLING FIRE & HOMEOWNERS
215 ILCS 5/141.01, 5/143.10, 5/143.11, 5/143.13, 5/143.16a, and 5/143.17

Cancellation during the Underwriting Period

Length of Underwriting Period: Sixty days.

Length of Notice: Ten days for nonpayment; thirty days for all other reasons.

Reason for Cancellation: Required on the notice.

Proof Required: Proof of mailing to the named insured and the last known mortgagees or lienholders at the last mailing address known by the company. Proof of mailing includes a recognized U.S. Post Office form or a form acceptable to the U.S. Post Office or other commercial mail delivery service. A copy of all notices shall be sent to the insured's broker or agent of record if known at the last mailing address known to the company.

Cancellation after the Underwriting Period

The policy may be cancelled **only** for the following reasons:

1. Nonpayment.

ILLINOIS

2. Misrepresentation or fraud on the application.

3. Measurable increase in the risk.

Length of Notice: Ten days for nonpayment; thirty days for all other reasons.

Reason for Cancellation: Required on the notice.

Proof Required: Proof of mailing to the named insured and the last known mortgagees or lienholders at the last mailing address known by the company. Proof of mailing includes a recognized U.S. Post Office form or a form acceptable to the U.S. Post Office or other commercial mail delivery service. A copy of all notices shall be sent to the insured's broker or agent of record if known at the last mailing address known to the company.

Nonrenewal

Length of Notice: Thirty days if policy was in force less than five years; sixty days if policy was in force five years or more.

Reason for Nonrenewal: Required on the notice.

Proof Required: Proof of mailing at the last mailing address known by the company. Proof of mailing includes a recognized U.S. Post Office form or a form acceptable to the U.S. Post Office or other commercial mail delivery service. A copy of all notices shall be sent to the insured's broker or agent of record if known at the last mailing address known to the company.

Other Cancellation/Nonrenewal Provisions

If the insured has had the policy for five or more years, the insurer may nonrenew with a thirty-day notice only for the same reasons as allowed for midterm cancellation. Otherwise, the insurer must give sixty days' notice of nonrenewal.

An insurer may not cancel or refuse to issue or renew a policy based solely on a previous insurer's cancellation, refusal to issue, or nonrenewal.

Automatic termination as of the renewal date is allowed if the insured does not pay the renewal premium.

A sixty-day notice is required prior to renewal under any of the following conditions: a premium increase of 30 percent or more, any change in deductibles, or any other change that materially alters the policy. Note that this requirement does not appear on the Illinois Amendatory Endorsement.

ILLINOIS

Insurance companies may not cancel or nonrenew policies for the sole reason that their contract with the agent of record has terminated.

If an agent, broker or other representative or employee of any insurance company or agency recommends, advises, suggests or requires the cancellation of a policy at any time other than the policy anniversary or expiration date, the insured must be informed in writing of the additional cost of such cancellation before the cancellation or termination of the policy. This only applies to the short rate cancellations.

No insurance company authorized to do business in the state that issues policies for personal multiperil property coverage, commonly known as homeowners insurance, may refuse to issue or renew a homeowners insurance policy to the owner or tenant of any single family dwelling, or to any owner of or tenant residing in a multiunit residential dwelling which contains from two to four units in a single buildings, solely on the grounds that a space heater is being used inside the dwelling.

PERSONAL AUTO
215 ILCS 5/141.01, 5/143.10, 5/143.11, 5/143.13, 5/143.16a and 5/143.17, 5/143.19

Cancellation during the Underwriting Period

Length of Underwriting Period: Sixty days.

Length of Notice: Ten days for nonpayment; thirty days for all other reasons.

Reason for Cancellation: Required on the notice.

Proof Required: Proof of mailing to the named insured and lienholder or loss payee at the last mailing address known by the company. Proof of mailing includes a recognized U.S. Post Office form or a form acceptable to the U.S. Post Office or other commercial mail delivery service. A copy of all notices shall be sent to the insured's broker or agent of record if known at the last mailing address known to the company.

Cancellation after the Underwriting Period

The policy may be cancelled **only** for nonpayment or for any of the following reasons:

Illinois law allows all of the following reasons for midterm cancellation.

1. Nonpayment of premium.

2. The policy was obtained through a material misrepresentation.

3. Any insured violated any of the terms and conditions of the policy.

ILLINOIS

4. The named insured failed to disclose fully his motor vehicle accidents and moving traffic violations for the preceding thirty-six months if called for in the application.

5. Any insured made a false or fraudulent claim of knowingly aiding or abetting another in the presentation of such a claim.

6. The named insured or any other operator who either resides in the same household or customarily operates an automobile insured under such policy:

    a. Has, within the twelve months prior to the notice of cancellation, had his driver's license under suspension or revocation.

    b. Is or becomes subject to epilepsy or heart attacks, and such individual does not produce a certificate from a physician testifying to his unqualified ability to operate a motor vehicle safely.

    c. Has an accident record, conviction record (criminal or traffic), physical, or mental condition which is such that his operation of an automobile might endanger the public safety.

    d. Has, within the thirty-six months prior to the notice of cancellation, been addicted to the use of narcotics or other drugs.

    e. Has been convicted, or forfeited bail, during the thirty-six months immediately preceding the notice of cancellation, for any felony, criminal negligence resulting in death, homicide or assault arising out of the operation of a motor vehicle, operating a motor vehicle while in an intoxicated condition or while under the influence of drugs, being intoxicated while in, or about, an automobile or while having custody of an automobile, leaving the scene of an accident without stopping to report, theft or unlawful taking of a motor vehicle, making false statements in an application for an operator's or chauffeur's license or has been convicted or forfeited bail for three or more violations within the twelve months immediately preceding the notice of cancellation, of any law, ordinance, or regulation limiting the speed of motor vehicles or any of the provisions of the motor vehicle laws of any state, violation of which constitutes a misdemeanor, whether or not the violations were repetitions of the same offense of different offenses.

7. The insured automobile is:

    a. So mechanically defective that its operation might endanger public safety.

    b. Used in carrying passengers for hire or compensation (the use of an automobile for a car pool shall not be considered use of an automobile for hire or compensation).

ILLINOIS

    c. Used in the business of transportation of flammables or explosives.

    d. An authorized emergency vehicle.

    e. Changed in shape or condition during the policy period so as to increase the risk substantially.

    f. Subject to an inspection law and has not been inspected or, if inspected, has failed to qualify.

An insurer using the ISO's PP 01 74, is restricted to the reasons listed below.

1. Nonpayment of premium.

2. Revocation or suspension of the driver's license of the named insured or any driver who lives with the named insured or customarily uses the named insured's auto. Such revocation or suspension must have occurred during the preceding twelve months.

3. Material misrepresentation on the application.

Length of Notice: Ten days for nonpayment; thirty days for all other reasons.

Reason for Cancellation: Required on the notice.

Proof Required: Proof of mailing to the named insured and lienholder or loss payee at the last mailing address known by the company. Proof of mailing includes a recognized U.S. Post Office form or a form acceptable to the U.S. Post Office or other commercial mail delivery service. A copy of all notices shall be sent to the insured's broker or agent of record if known at the last mailing address known to the company.

Nonrenewal

Length of Notice: Thirty days if policy is in force less than five years; sixty days if policy has been in force for five years or more.

Reason for Nonrenewal: Required on the notice.

Proof Required: Proof of mailing to the named insured and lienholder or loss payee at the last mailing address known by the company. Proof of mailing includes a recognized U.S. Post Office form or a form acceptable to the U.S. Post Office or other commercial mail delivery service. A copy of all notices shall be sent to the insured's broker or agent of record if known at the last mailing address known to the company.

ILLINOIS

Other Cancellation/Nonrenewal Provisions

If the policy has been in force for five or more years, the insurer may only nonrenew for one or more of the statutory reasons allowed for midterm cancellation. An insurer may not cancel or refuse to issue or renew a policy based solely on a previous insurer's cancellation, refusal to issue, or nonrenewal.

Automatic termination as of the renewal date is allowed if the insured does not pay the renewal premium.

A sixty-day notice is required prior to renewal under any of the following conditions: a premium increase of 30 percent or more, any change in deductibles, or any other change that materially alters the policy. Note that this requirement does not appear on the Illinois Amendatory Endorsement.

Insurance companies may not cancel or nonrenew policies for the sole reason that their contract with the agent of record has terminated.

Policies may not be nonrenewed solely for claims against the policy, or for claims that were closed without payment.

If an agent, broker or other representative or employee of any insurance company or agency recommends, advises, suggests or requires the cancellation of a policy at any time other than the policy anniversary or expiration date, the insured must be informed in writing of the additional cost of such cancellation before the cancellation or termination of the policy. This only applies to the short rate cancellations. (215 ILCS 5/143.12).

Insurer must provide notice of possible eligibility for coverage in Illinois Automobile Insurance Plan with any notice of termination for reasons other than nonpayment of premium. Such notice shall accompany or be included in the notice of cancellation or in the notice of intent not to renew. (215 ILCS 5/143.20).

PERSONAL UMBRELLA

215 ILCS 5/141.01, 5/143.10, 5/143.11, 5/143.13, and 5/143.17

Cancellation during the Underwriting Period

Length of Underwriting Period: Sixty days.

Length of Notice: Ten days.

Reason for Cancellation: Reason for notice must be stated.

ILLINOIS

Proof Required: Proof of mailing at the last mailing address known by the company. Proof of mailing includes a recognized U.S. Post Office form or a form acceptable to the U.S. Post Office or other commercial mail delivery service. A copy of all notices shall be sent to the insured's broker or agent of record if known at the last mailing address known to the company.

Cancellation after the Underwriting Period

Length of Notice: Ten-day notice for nonpayment; thirty-day notice for any other reason.

Reason for Cancellation: Reason for notice must be stated.

Proof Required: Proof of mailing at the last mailing address known by the company. Proof of mailing includes a recognized U.S. Post Office form or a form acceptable to the U.S. Post Office or other commercial mail delivery service. A copy of all notices shall be sent to the insured's broker or agent of record if known at the last mailing address known to the company.

Nonrenewal

Length of Notice: Thirty days.

Reason for Nonrenewal: Reason for notice must be stated.

Proof Required: Proof of mailing at the last mailing address known by the company. Proof of mailing includes a recognized U.S. Post Office form or a form acceptable to the U.S. Post Office or other commercial mail delivery service. A copy of all notices shall be sent to the insured's broker or agent of record if known at the last mailing address known to the company.

Other Cancellation/Nonrenewal Provisions

A copy of any termination notice must be sent to the agent or broker.

Insurance companies may not cancel or nonrenew policies for the sole reason that their contract with the agent of record has terminated.

If an agent, broker or other representative or employee of any insurance company or agency recommends, advises, suggests or requires the cancellation of a policy at any time other than the policy anniversary or expiration date, the insured must be informed in writing of the additional cost of such cancellation before the cancellation or termination of the policy. This only applies to the short rate cancellations.

ILLINOIS

FRAUD

740 ILCS 92/1 through 92/45; 720 ILCS 5/17-10.5

General Information and Definitions

Insurance Fraud. A person commits insurance fraud when he or she knowingly obtains, attempts to obtain, or causes to be obtained, by deception, control over the property of an insurance company or self-insured entity by the making of a false claim or by causing a false claim to be made on any policy of insurance issued by an insurance company or by the making of a false claim or by causing a false claim to be made to a self-insured entity, intending to deprive an insurance company or self-insured entity permanently of the use and benefit of that property.

Health Care Benefits Fraud. A person commits health care benefits fraud against a provider, other than a governmental unit or agency, when he or she knowingly obtains or attempts to obtain, by deception, health care benefits and that obtaining or attempt to obtain health care benefits does not involve control over property of the provider.

Aggravated Insurance Fraud. A person commits aggravated insurance fraud on a private entity when he or she commits insurance fraud three or more times within an eighteen-month period arising out of separate incidents or transactions.

Aggravated Insurance Fraud Conspiracy. A person commits to being an organizer of an aggravated insurance fraud on a private entity conspiracy if aggravated insurance fraud on a private entity forms the basis for a charge of conspiracy and the person occupies a position of organizer, supervisor, financer, or other position of management within the conspiracy.

Reporting Requirements

Any person may report allegations of insurance noncompliance and fraud to the Department of Insurance's fraud and insurance noncompliance unit whose duty it shall be to investigate the report. The unit shall notify the Commission of reports of insurance noncompliance.

Penalties and Statute of Limitations

1. A violation relating to insurance fraud in which the value of the property obtained, attempted to be obtained, or caused to be obtained is $300 or less is a Class A misdemeanor.

2. A violation relating to insurance fraud in which the value of the property obtained, attempted to be obtained, or caused to be obtained is more than $300 but not more than $10,000 is a Class 3 felony.

ILLINOIS

3. A violation of insurance fraud in which the value of the property obtained, attempted to be obtained, or caused to be obtained is more than $10,000 but not more than $100,000 is a Class 2 felony.

4. A violation of insurance fraud in which the value of the property obtained, attempted to be obtained, or caused to be obtained is more than $100,000 is a Class 1 felony.

5. A violation relating to health care benefits fraud is a Class A misdemeanor.

6. A violation relating to aggravated insurance fraud is a Class 1 felony, regardless of the value of the property obtained, attempted to be obtained, or caused to be obtained.

7. A violation relating to aggravated insurance fraud conspiracy is a Class X felony.

8. Civil Liability. A person who knowingly obtains, attempts to obtain, or causes to be obtained, by deception, control over the property of any insurance company by the making of a false claim or by causing a false claim to be made on a policy of insurance issued by an insurance company, or by the making of a false claim or by causing a false claim to be made to a self-insured entity, intending to deprive an insurance company or self-insured entity permanently of the use and benefit of that property, shall be civilly liable to the insurance company or self-insured entity that paid the claim or against whom the claim was made or to the subrogee of that insurance company or self-insured entity in an amount equal to either three times the value of the property wrongfully obtained or, if no property was wrongfully obtained, twice the value of the property attempted to be obtained, whichever amount is greater, plus reasonable attorney's fees.

9. An action in response to insurance fraud may not be filed more than three years after the discovery of the facts constituting the grounds for commencing the action.

10. An action may be filed pursuant to this Act within not more than eight years after the commission of an act constituting a violation relating to insurance fraud.

Antifraud Provisions

The Illinois Department of Insurance maintains a web site that details insurance fraud and how to prevent it from occurring at http://insurance.illinois.gov.

FAIR CLAIMS PROCESSING
50 Ill. Adm. Code 919.50 and 919.60

Insurance companies shall affirm or deny liability on claims within a reasonable time and shall offer payment within thirty days after affirmation of liability, if the amount of the claim

ILLINOIS

is determined and not in dispute. For those portions of the claim which are not in dispute and for which the payee is known, the company shall tender payment within said thirty days.

On first-party claims if a settlement of a claim is less than the amount claimed, or if the claim is denied, the insurance company shall provide to the insured a reasonable written explanation of the basis of the lower offer or denial within thirty days after the investigation and determination of liability is completed. This explanation shall clearly set forth the policy definition, limitation, exclusion or condition upon which denial was based. Notice of Availability of the Department of Insurance shall accompany this explanation.

Within thirty days after the initial determination of liability is made, if the claim is denied, the insurance company shall provide the third party a reasonable written explanation of the basis of the denial.

No insurance company shall deny a claim upon information obtained in a telephone conversation or personal interview with any source unless such telephone conversation or personal interview is documented in the claim file.

The insurance company's standards for claims processing shall be such that notice of claim and proofs of loss submitted against one policy issued by that company shall fulfill the insured's obligation under any and all similar policies issued by that company and specifically identified by the insured to said company to the same degree that the same form would be required under any similar policy. If additional information is required to fulfill the insured's obligation under other similar policies, the company may request the additional information. When it is apparent to the company that additional benefits would be payable under an insured's policy upon receipt of additional proofs of loss from the insured, the company shall communicate to and cooperate with the insured in determining the extent of the company's additional liability.

No company shall indicate to an insured on a payment draft, check or in any accompanying letter that said payment is "final" or "a release" of any claim unless the policy limit has been paid or there is a bonafide dispute either over coverage or the amount payable under the policy. No company shall make any statement, written or oral, requiring an insured to complete a proof of loss in less time than is provided in the policy. No company shall make any statement requiring an insured to give written notice of loss within a specified time so that the company is relieved of its obligations under a policy if such time limit is not complied with, unless such a statement is made after the insured's unreasonable failure to give written notice. No company shall request or require any insured to submit to a polygraph examination. The use of examinations under oath, sworn statements or similar procedures shall not be so restricted, if authorized under the applicable insurance contracts.

These are the general standards of fair claims processing in Illinois. Note that specific types of insurance have additional fair claims rules. For additional rules for automobile and casualty and property see 50 Ill. Adm. Code 919.80 through 919.100. For additional rules for life, accident, and health see 919.70. These are in addition to the general rules listed above, not instead of them.

INDIANA

For details on cancellation procedures for the standard policy, refer to the Standard Policy section.

COMMERCIAL LINES
AGRICULTURAL CAPITAL ASSETS; BOP; CAPITAL ASSETS; COMM. AUTO; CRIME; CGL (CGL, EMPLOYMENT, LIQUOR, OCP; POLLUTION, ELECTRONIC LIABILITY, PRODUCTS/COMP. OPS., RR PROT); CIM; C. PROP.; C. UMB.; E-COMMERCE; EQUIPMENT BREAKDOWN; FARM; FIN. INST; MGT. PROT; & PROF. LIABILITY

Ind. Code Ann. §§27-1-31-1, 27-1-31-2, 27-1-31-2.5, and 27-1-31-3

Cancellation during the Underwriting Period

Length of Underwriting Period: Ninety days.

Length of Notice: Ten days for nonpayment; twenty days for fraud or misrepresentation; thirty days for any other reason.

Reason for Cancellation: Not required.

Proof Required: Proof of mailing delivered or mailed to the named insured at the last known address of the named insured.

Cancellation after the Underwriting Period

The policy may be cancelled **only** for any of the following reasons:

1. Nonpayment.

2. Fraud or material misrepresentation.

3. A substantial change in the risk.

4. If the reinsurance on the risk is cancelled.

5. If the insured does not comply with the insurer's safety recommendations.

Length of Notice: Ten days for nonpayment; twenty days for fraud or material misrepresentation; forty-five days for all other allowable reasons.

Reason for Cancellation: Not required.

INDIANA

Proof Required: Proof of mailing delivered or mailed to the named insured at the last known address of the named insured.

Nonrenewal

Length of Notice: Forty-five days before the expiration date if the coverage is one year or less, or before the anniversary date of the policy if the coverage is for more than one year.

Reason for Nonrenewal: Not required.

Proof Required: Proof of mailing delivered or mailed to the named insured at the last known address of the named insured.

Other Cancellation/Nonrenewal Provisions

A nonrenewal notice is not required if the insured's coverage is being transferred to an affiliated insurer as the result of a merger, acquisition, or restructuring in the incumbent insurance company if the transfer results in the same or broader coverage and the insured approves of the transfer.

COMMERCIAL GENERAL LIABILITY
(Underground Storage Tanks)

Ind. Code Ann. §§27-1-31-1, 27-1-31-2, 27-1-31-2.5, and 27-1-31-3

Cancellation during the Underwriting Period

Length of Underwriting Period: Ninety days.

Length of Notice: Ten days for nonpayment; twenty days for fraud or misrepresentation; sixty days for any other reason. Even though the Indiana statute calls for only a thirty-day notice for any other reason, sixty days must be given if the insurer has adopted ISO's amendatory endorsement (CG 30 23).

Reason for Cancellation: Not required.

Proof Required: Certified mail.

Cancellation after the Underwriting Period

The policy may be cancelled **only** for the following reasons:

1. Nonpayment.

2. Fraud or material misrepresentation.

INDIANA

3. Substantial change in the risk.

4. Reinsurance on the risk is cancelled.

5. If the insured does not comply with the insurer's safety recommendations.

Length of Notice: Ten days for nonpayment; twenty days for fraud or misrepresentation; sixty days for any other reason. Even though the Indiana statute calls for only a forty-five-day notice for any other reason, sixty days must be given if the insurer has adopted ISO's amendatory endorsement (CG 30 23).

Reason for Cancellation: Not required.

Proof Required: Certified mail.

Nonrenewal

Length of Notice: Sixty days. Even though the Indiana statute calls for only a forty-five-day notice of nonrenewal before the expiration date if the coverage is one year or less, or before the anniversary date of the policy if the coverage is for more than one year, sixty days must be given if the insurer has adopted ISO's amendatory endorsement (CG 30 23).

Reason for Nonrenewal: Not required.

Proof Required: Certified mail.

Other Cancellation/Nonrenewal Provisions

A nonrenewal notice is not required if the insured's coverage is being transferred to an affiliated insurer as the result of a merger, acquisition, or restructuring in the incumbent insurance company if the transfer results in the same or broader and the insured approves of the transfer.

PROFESSIONAL LIABILITY

Ind. Code Ann. §§27-1-31-1 through 27-1-31-3, 34-18-13-4

Cancellation during the Underwriting Period

Length of Underwriting Period: Ninety days.

Length of Notice: Thirty days.

Reason for Cancellation: Not required.

INDIANA

Proof Required: Proof of mailing delivered or mailed to the named insured at the last known address of the named insured.

Cancellation after the Underwriting Period

The policy may be cancelled **only** for any of the following reasons:

1. Nonpayment.

2. Fraud or material misrepresentation.

3. A substantial change in the risk.

4. If the reinsurance on the risk is cancelled.

5. If the insured does not comply with the insurer's safety recommendations.

Length of Notice: As required by the Indiana Code, a ten day notice is required for nonpayment and twenty days for fraud and material misrepresentation. However, if the insurer has adopted ISO amendatory endorsement (PR 02 10), it must give the following number of days: thirty days for nonpayment; thirty days for fraud or material misrepresentation; forty-five days for all other reasons. Legal advice is suggested.

Reason for Cancellation: Not required.

Proof Required: Proof of mailing delivered or mailed to the named insured at the last known address of the named insured.

Nonrenewal

Length of Notice: Forty-five days before the expiration date if the coverage is one year or less, or before the anniversary date of the policy if the coverage is for more than one year.

Reason for Nonrenewal: Not required.

Proof Required: Proof of mailing delivered or mailed to the named insured at the last known address of the named insured.

Other Cancellation/Nonrenewal Provisions

A nonrenewal notice is not required if the insured's coverage is being transferred to an affiliated insurer as the result of a merger, acquisition, or restructuring in the incumbent

INDIANA

insurance company if the transfer results in the same or broader and the insured approves of the transfer.

A termination of the medical malpractice coverage policy is not effective for patients claiming against the insured covered by the policy unless at least thirty days before effect of the cancellation, a written notice giving the date upon which termination becomes effective has been received by the commissioner at the commissioner's office.

WORKERS COMPENSATION

Ind. Code Ann. §22-3-7-34

The Indiana Code requires a thirty-day notice to the state's workers compensation board. Legal advice is suggested if an amendatory endorsement meeting this requirement is not attached to a workers compensation policy.

SURPLUS LINES

Ind. Code Ann. §27-1-31-1

Surplus lines insurers must follow the cancellation and nonrenewal requirements for admitted companies.

FINANCED PREMIUMS

Ind. Code Ann. §27-7-12-2

Indiana equates nonpayment of premium with nonpayment to a finance company and does not specify that cancellation and nonrenewal procedures differ from nonfinanced policy requirements.

PERSONAL LINES
DWELLING FIRE & HOMEOWNERS

Ind. Code Ann. §§27-7-12-1 through 27-7-12-7

Cancellation during the Underwriting Period

Length of Underwriting Period: Sixty days.

Length of Notice: Ten days for any reason.

Reason for Cancellation: Not required, but notice must state that reason will be provided upon written request.

Proof Required: Proof of mailing delivered or mailed to the named insured at the last known address of the named insured.

INDIANA

Cancellation after the Underwriting Period

The policy may be cancelled **only** for the following reasons:

1. Nonpayment.

2. Fraud or material misrepresentation made by or with the knowledge of the named insured in obtaining or continuing the policy, or presenting a claim under the policy.

3. Substantial change in the risk since the policy was issued.

Note: The Indiana Code also allows for mid-term cancellation for the following reasons. However, these reasons do not appear on the ISO amendatory endorsements. If an insurer has adopted the ISO amendatory endorsements (DP 01 13 and HO 01 13), it may not use these reasons to cancel a policy:

1. Willful or reckless acts or omissions on the part of the named insured that increase a hazard insured against.

2. Change in the risk that substantially increases a hazard insured against after coverage has been issued or renewed.

3. Violations of any local codes such as fire, health, safety, building, or construction.

4. If the insurance commissioner determines that continuation of the policy would place the insurer in violation of the law.

5. If the insured is more than two years delinquent in the payment of property taxes.

Length of Notice: Ten days for nonpayment; twenty days for any other allowable reason.

Reason for Cancellation: Not required, but notice must state that reason will be provided upon written request.

Proof Required: Proof of mailing delivered or mailed to the named insured at the last known address of the named insured.

Nonrenewal

Length of Notice: Twenty days.

Reason for Nonrenewal: Not required, but notice must state that reason will be provided upon written request.

INDIANA

Proof Required: Proof of mailing delivered or mailed to the named insured at the last known address of the named insured.

Other Cancellation/Nonrenewal Provisions

If the policy is written for a period of more than one year, the insurer may cancel on the anniversary date with a twenty-day written notice.

If the reason for cancellation is not stated, the insurer must provide a written explanation of the specific reasons for the cancellation upon request.

An insurer may not cancel or nonrenew a homeowner policy based on any of the following:

1. The race, religion, nationality, ethnic group, age, sex, or marital status of the applicant or named insured.

2. Solely upon the lawful occupation or profession of the applicant or named insured. This provision does not apply to an insurer that limits its market to one lawful occupation or profession or to several related lawful occupations or professions.

3. The age or location of the residence of the applicant or named insured.

4. The fact that another insurer previously declined to insure the applicant or terminated an existing policy in which the applicant was the named insured.

5. The fact that the applicant or named insured previously obtained insurance coverage through a residual market insurance mechanism.

If the policy was procured by an independent insurance producer licensed in Indiana, the insurer must deliver or mail notice of cancellation to the insurance producer not less than ten days before the insurer delivers or mails the notice to the named insured, unless the obligation to notify the insurance producer is waived in writing by the insurance producer.

If an insurer mails or delivers to an insured a renewal notice, bill, certificate, or policy indicating the insurer's willingness to renew a policy and the insured does not respond, the insurer is not required to provide to the insured notice of intention not to renew.

PERSONAL AUTO

Ind. Code Ann. §§27-7-6-1 through 27-7-6-12

Cancellation during the Underwriting Period

Length of Underwriting Period: Sixty days.

Length of Notice: Ten days for any reason.

INDIANA

Reason for Cancellation: Not required.

Proof Required: Proof of mailing to the named insured at the address shown in the policy is sufficient proof of notice.

Cancellation after the Underwriting Period

The policy may be cancelled **only** for any of the following reasons:

1. Nonpayment.

2. Suspension or revocation of the driver's license of:

    a. The named insured.

    b. Any driver who lives with the named insured or who customarily uses the insured auto. The suspension or revocation must occur during the policy period or since the last anniversary date.

3. Fraud, willful misrepresentation or concealment, by any insured in respect to a material fact or circumstance relating to the issuance or continuation of the policy.

Even though the Indiana statute allows the following as acceptable reasons for midterm cancellation, insurers using ISO's amendatory endorsement (PP 01 66) are limited to the more restrictive provisions:

1. If the named insured or any resident or regular operator of the car is under treatment for epilepsy or heart disease and cannot produce a certificate from a doctor testifying to the insured's unqualified ability to operate a motor vehicle safely or the insured uses drugs or alcohol to excess.

2. Violation of any terms or conditions of the contract.

3. If the insured moves to a state or country where the insurer is not licensed.

A change or substitution in policy form is not deemed a cancellation.

Length of Notice: Ten days for nonpayment accompanied by the reason; twenty days for all other reasons.

Reason for Cancellation: Not required, but when not given, notice must state that reason will be provided upon written request.

INDIANA

Proof Required: Proof of mailing to the named insured at the address shown in the policy is sufficient proof of notice.

Nonrenewal

Length of Notice: Twenty days.

Reason for Nonrenewal: Not required.

Proof Required: Proof of mailing to the named insured at the address shown in the policy is sufficient proof of notice.

Other Cancellation/Nonrenewal Provisions

When a personal auto policy is cancelled for any reason other than nonpayment or in the event of failure to renew a policy providing automobile liability coverage, the insurer must notify the named insured of the availability of the assigned risk plan. Such notice must accompany or be included in the notice of cancellation or the notice of intent not to renew.

A nonrenewal notice is not required if the insured's coverage is being transferred to an affiliated insurer as the result of a merger, acquisition, or restructuring in the incumbent insurance company if the transfer results in the same or broader coverage and the insured approves of the transfer.

The notice of cancellation shall state or be accompanied by a statement that upon written request of the named insured, mailed or delivered to the insurer not less than fifteen days prior to the effective date of cancellation, the insurer will specify in writing the reason for such cancellation. Such reason must be mailed or delivered to the named insured within five days after receipt of such request.

An insurer may not refuse to issue, cancel or refuse to renew a disabled person who holds a valid driver's license or renew the policy solely because of the disability, or cancel, fail to renew, or refuse to issue a policy under conditions less favorable to disabled persons than to nondisabled persons.

An insurer may use credit information in underwriting or rating a customer. If an insurer chooses to use credit information, the insurer must disclose to the consumer its intention to use credit information.

An insurer shall not deny, cancel, or decline to renew an insurance policy, or base a renewal rate, solely based on credit information.

An insurer that utilizes credit information to underwrite or rate risks shall, at annual renewal, re-underwrite or re-rate an insured's personal insurance policy based on a current

INDIANA

credit report or insurance score if requested by the insured. Exceptions apply. See Ind. Code Ann. §27-2-21-16(a).

If the policy was procured by an insurance producer, notice of intent to cancel or decision not to renew must be mailed or delivered to the insurance producer at least ten days prior to the cancellation mailing or delivery to the named insured unless such notice of intent is or has been waived in writing by the insurance producer.

A policy period or term of six months or less and any policy with no fixed expiration date will be considered as if written for a policy period or term of six months. Any policy written for a term longer than one year will be considered as if written for successive policy periods or terms of one year, and such policy may be terminated by the insurer at the expiration of any annual period after giving twenty days' notice of cancellation prior to such anniversary date.

PERSONAL UMBRELLA

Ind. Code Ann. §27-1-41-10 and ISO Endorsement DL 98 01

Cancellation during the Underwriting Period

Length of Underwriting Period: Sixty days.

Length of Notice: Ten days for any reason.

Reason for Notice: Not required.

Proof Required: Proof of mailing.

Cancellation after the Underwriting Period

Length of Notice: Ten day for nonpayment; thirty days for any other reason.

Reason for Notice: Not required.

Proof Required: Proof of mailing.

Nonrenewal

Length of Notice: Thirty days.

Reason for Notice: Not required.

Proof Required: Proof of mailing.

INDIANA

Other Cancellation/Nonrenewal Provisions

An insurer may cancel or refuse to renew an individual certificate while maintaining in force the master policy and other individual certificates issued under the master policy. An insurer that cancels or refuses to renew a master policy shall, within a period determined by the commissioner, provide: (1) to the group administrator; and (2) to each individual participating group member; written notice of the cancellation or refusal to renew. (Ind. Code Ann. §27-1-41-10).

FRAUD

Ind. Code Ann. §§35-43-5-4.5 and 27-1-3-22

General Information and Definitions

A person who, knowingly and with intent to defraud, makes, utters, presents, or causes to be presented to an insurer or an insurance claimant, a claim statement that contains false, incomplete, or misleading information concerning the claim or presents, causes to be presented, or prepares with the knowledge or belief that it will be presented to or by an insurer, an oral, a written, or an electronic statement that the person knows to contain materially false information as part of, in support of, or concerning a fact that is material to:

1. The rating of an insurance policy.

2. A claim for payment or benefit under an insurance policy.

3. Premiums paid on an insurance policy.

4. Payments made in accordance with the terms of an insurance policy.

5. An application for a certificate of authority.

6. The financial condition of an insurer.

7. The acquisition of an insurer.

8. Commits insurance fraud.

Or conceals any information concerning a subject set forth in clauses (1) through (8); or commits other violations listed in Ind. Code Ann. §35-43-5-4.5 commits insurance fraud.

Reporting Requirements

Indiana does not have any mandatory insurance fraud reporting and instead relies on submission of suspected insurance fraud through the NAIC or by contacting the Deputy Commissioner Enforcement Division below.

INDIANA

For information regarding fraudulent insurance activity, please contact:

> Debra Webb
> Deputy Commissioner Enforcement Division
> 317-233-9431 dwebb@idoi.in.gov

A person who acts without malice, fraudulent intent, or bad faith is not subject to civil liability for filing a report or furnishing, orally or in writing, other information concerning a suspected, anticipated, or completed fraudulent insurance act if the report or other information is provided to or received from any of the following:

1. The department or an agent, employee or designee of the department.

2. Law enforcement officials or an agent or employee of a law enforcement official.

3. The National Association of Insurance Commissioners.

4. Any agency or bureau of federal or state government established to detect and prevent fraudulent insurance acts.

5. Any other organization established to detect and prevent fraudulent insurance acts.

6. An agent, employee, or designee of an entity referred to in (3)-(5).

This section does not abrogate or modify common law or statutory privilege or immunity.

Penalties

Insurance fraud is a Level 6 felony. However, an insurance fraud offense is a Level 5 felony if:

1. The person who commits the offense has a prior unrelated conviction under this section.

2. The value of property, services, or other benefits obtained or attempted to be obtained by the person as a result of the offense; or the economic loss suffered by another person as a result of the offense is at least $2,500.

3. A person who knowingly and with intent to defraud makes a material misstatement in support of an application for the issuance of an insurance policy commits insurance application fraud, a Class A misdemeanor.

INDIANA

FAIR CLAIMS PROCESSING
Ind. Code Ann. §27-4-1-4.5

The following are unfair claim settlement practices:

1. Misrepresenting pertinent facts or insurance policy provisions relating to coverages at issue.

2. Failing to acknowledge and act reasonably and promptly upon communications with respect to claims arising under insurance policies.

3. Failing to adopt and implement reasonable standards for the prompt investigation of claims arising under insurance policies.

4. Refusing to pay claims without conducting a reasonable investigation based upon all available information.

5. Failing to affirm or deny coverage of claims within a reasonable time after proof of loss statements have been completed.

6. Not attempting in good faith to effectuate prompt, fair, and equitable settlements of claims in which liability has become reasonably clear.

7. Compelling insureds to institute litigation to recover amounts due under an insurance policy by offering substantially less than the amounts ultimately recovered in actions brought by such insureds.

8. Attempting to settle a claim for less than the amount to which a reasonable individual would have believed the individual was entitled by reference to written or printed advertising material accompanying or made part of an application.

9. Attempting to settle claims on the basis of an application that was altered without notice to or knowledge or consent of the insured.

10. Making claims payments to insureds or beneficiaries not accompanied by a statement setting forth the coverage under which the payments are being made.

11. Making known to insureds or claimants a policy of appealing from arbitration awards in favor of insureds or claimants for the purpose of compelling them to accept settlements or compromises less than the amount awarded in arbitration.

12. Delaying the investigation or payment of claims by requiring an insured, a claimant, or the physician of either to submit a preliminary claim report and then requiring the subsequent submission of formal proof of loss forms, both of which submissions contain substantially the same information.

13. Failing to promptly settle claims, where liability has become reasonably clear, under one portion of the insurance policy coverage in order to influence settlements under other portions of the insurance policy coverage.

14. Failing to promptly provide a reasonable explanation of the basis in the insurance policy in relation to the facts or applicable law for denial of a claim or for the offer of a compromise settlement.

15. In negotiations concerning liability insurance claims, ascribing a percentage of fault to a person seeking to recover from an insured party, in spite of an obvious absence of fault on the part of that person.

16. The unfair claim settlement practices defined in Ind. Code Ann. §27-4-1.5.

IOWA

For details on cancellation procedures for the standard policy, refer to the Standard Policy section.

COMMERCIAL LINES
AGRICULTURAL CAPITAL ASSETS; BOP; CAPITAL ASSETS; C. AUTO; CRIME; CIM; CGL (CGL, EMPLOYMENT, LIQUOR, MARKET SEGMENTS, OCP, POLLUTION, PRODUCTS/ COMPLETED OPS, RR PROT); C. PROP.; EQUIPMENT BREAKDOWN; FARM; & PROF. LIAB.

Iowa Code §§515.127 through 515.128A

Cancellation during the Underwriting Period

Length of Underwriting Period: Sixty days.

Length of Notice: Thirty days for loss of reinsurance (if the commissioner determines that the cancellation is justified); ten days for any other reason.

Reason for Cancellation: Required on the notice.

Proof Required: Certificate of mailing. A post office department certificate of mailing to the named insured at the address shown in the policy or contract is proof of receipt of the mailing (no proof required for cancellation due to nonpayment).

Cancellation after the Underwriting Period

The policy may be cancelled **only** for the following reasons:

1. Nonpayment.

2. Fraud or material misrepresentation in obtaining the policy, in pursuing a claim, or in renewing the policy.

3. Acts or omissions that substantially increase or change the risk.

4. A determination by the commissioner of insurance that the continuation of the policy coverage would:

    a. Place the insurer in violation of Iowa law or the laws of any other state.
    b. Threaten the insurer's solvency.

IOWA

5. If the insured breaches any policy term or condition.

6. Loss of reinsurance (with the commissioner's approval).

Length of Notice: Thirty days for loss of reinsurance (if the commissioner determines that the cancellation is justified); ten days for any other reason.

Reason for Cancellation: Required on the notice.

Proof Required: Certificate of mailing. A post office department certificate of mailing to the named insured at the address shown in the policy or contract is proof of receipt of the mailing (no proof required for cancellation due to nonpayment).

Nonrenewal

Length of Notice: Forty-five days.

Reason for Nonrenewal: Not required, but must be provided upon request.

Proof Required: Certificate of mailing. A post office department certificate of mailing to the named insured at the address shown in the policy or contract is proof of receipt of the mailing. A notice of nonrenewal is not effective unless mailed or delivered by the insurer to the named insured and any loss payee.

Other Cancellation/Nonrenewal Provisions

The Iowa statute says that the following are to be treated as nonrenewal: an increase in premium or deductible of 25 percent or more or a material reduction in limits or coverage. §515.128A.

A nonrenewal notice is not required if the insured fails to pay a renewal premium or any advance premium required by the insurer for renewal. A notice of nonrenewal is not required if the insured is transferred from an insurer to an affiliate for future coverage as a result of a merger, acquisition, or company restructuring and if the transfer results in the same or broader coverage. §515.128.

For OCP policies all notices must be mailed to the first named insured and the contractor shown in the declarations.

For Railroad Protective policies all notices must be mailed to the named insured, the contractor, any involved governmental authority, or other contracting party shown in the declarations.

For Property policies, ten days' notice of cancellation also must be given to a mortgagee.

IOWA

A notice of nonrenewal is not required if the insured is transferred to an affiliate insurer because of a merger, acquisition, or company restructuring if the coverage is the same or broader than expiring.

In 2005, provisions of the Iowa Standard Fire Policy regarding voiding of the policy were changed to state that the entire policy is void if an insured willfully concealed or misrepresented any material fact or fraud. Before the change, the provision for voiding a property policy for fraud and material misrepresentation referred to the insured.

An insurance company organized under chapter 515 (Insurance Other Than Life) that contracts with an independent (noncaptive) insurance producer or MGA must provide 180 day notice prior the termination of the contract unless it contains a written provision expressly reserving to the insurer all right, title, and interest to the ownership or the use of insurance business written. I.C.A. §515.106.

COMMERCIAL GENERAL LIABILITY
(Underground Storage Tank Policy)

Iowa Code §§515.127 through 515.128A

Cancellation during the Underwriting Period

Length of Underwriting Period: Sixty days.

Length of Notice: Thirty days for loss of reinsurance; ten days for any other reason.

Reason for Cancellation: Required.

Proof Required: Certified mail.

Cancellation after the Underwriting Period

The policy may be cancelled **only** for the following reasons:

1. Nonpayment.

2. Misrepresentation or fraud on the application, in the renewal process, or in making a claim.

3. Acts or omissions by the insured that substantially change or increase the risk insured.

4. If the commissioner determines that to continue the policy would jeopardize the insurer's solvency or be in violation of any state's insurance laws.

IOWA

5. Breach of a policy term or condition.

6. If the insurer loses its reinsurance on the risk (with the commissioner's approval).

Length of Notice: Ten days for nonpayment and misrepresentation or fraud; sixty days for all other allowable reasons.

Reason for Cancellation: Required.

Proof Required: Certified mail.

Nonrenewal

Length of Notice: Forty-five days.

Reason for Nonrenewal: Required.

Proof Required: Certified mail.

Other Cancellation/Nonrenewal Provisions

If insurers do not give notice the insured has the option of continuing the policy for the remainder of the notice period plus an additional thirty days.

The requirement of ISO's amendatory endorsement (CG 30 29 11 94) for sixty-day notification and certified mail do not appear to be required by Iowa statute. Legal advice is suggested.

The Iowa statute says that the following are to be treated as nonrenewal: an increase in premium or deductible of 25 percent or more or a material reduction in limits or coverage.

A notice of nonrenewal is not required if the insured is transferred to an affiliate insurer because of a merger, acquisition, or company restructuring if the coverage is the same or broader than expiring.

An insurance company organized under chapter 515 (Insurance Other Than Life) that contracts with an independent (noncaptive) insurance producer or MGA must provide 180 day notice prior to the termination of the contract unless it contains a written provision expressly reserving to the insurer all right, title, and interest to the ownership or the use of insurance business written. I.C.A. §515.106.

IOWA

COMMERCIAL UMBRELLA

Iowa Code §515.127 and 515.129

Cancellation during the Underwriting Period

Length of Underwriting Period: Sixty days.

Length of Notice: Ten days for any reason.

Reason for Cancellation: Required on the notice.

Proof Required: Certificate of mailing to insured and any loss payees. Proof of mailing not required for nonpayment.

Cancellation after the Underwriting Period

The policy may be cancelled **only** for the following reasons:

1. Nonpayment.

2. Fraud or material misrepresentation in obtaining the policy, in pursuing a claim, or in renewing the policy.

3. Acts or omissions that substantially increase or change the risk.

4. A determination by the commissioner of insurance that the continuation of the policy coverage would:

    a. Place the insurer in violation of Iowa law or the laws of any other state.
    b. Threaten the insurer's solvency.

5. Loss of reinsurance (with the commissioner's approval).

6. If the insured breaches any policy condition.

7. Cancellation or nonrenewal of one of the underlying policies.

8. A material change in the underlying policies.

9. A reduction of the financial strength rating of one of the underlying carriers.

IOWA

Length of Notice: Ten days.

Reason for Cancellation: Required on the notice.

Proof Required: Certificate of mailing to the insured and any loss payees. Proof of mailing is not required for nonpayment.

Nonrenewal

Length of Notice: Forty-five days.

Reason for Nonrenewal: Not required on the notice.

Proof Required: Certificate of mailing to the insured and any loss payees.

Other Cancellation/Nonrenewal Provisions

A nonrenewal notice is not required if the insured fails to pay a renewal premium.

A notice of nonrenewal is not required if the insured is transferred to an affiliate insurer because of a merger, acquisition, or company restructuring if the coverage is the same or broader than expiring.

If the policy is conditionally renewed based on requirements regarding underlying insurance, the conditional renewal notice may stand as an effective notice of nonrenewal if the conditions are not met as of the renewal date or thirty days after the conditional renewal notice was given.

Statute permits a commercial umbrella in force less than sixty days to be cancelled at the time notice is mailed or delivered. However, insurers using the ISO forms (CU 02 20) may not use this provision.

An insurance company organized under chapter 515 (Insurance Other Than Life) that contracts with an independent (noncaptive) insurance producer or MGA must provide 180 day notice prior the termination of the contract unless it contains a written provision expressly reserving to the insurer all right, title, and interest to the ownership or the use of insurance business written. I.C.A. §515.106.

WORKERS COMPENSATION
Iowa Code §§515.127 through 515.128A

Although the NCCI policy has no endorsement amending the cancellation provisions, Iowa statutes appear to place the same cancellation and nonrenewal requirements on workers compensation policies as on all other commercial lines policies (see above).

IOWA

SURPLUS LINES

Iowa Code §§507A.3 and 515.126

Surplus lines insurers must follow the same cancellation and nonrenewal requirements as admitted companies.

FINANCED PREMIUMS

Iowa equates nonpayment of premium with nonpayment to a finance company.

PERSONAL LINES
DWELLING FIRE & HOMEOWNERS

Iowa Code §§515.129A and 515.129B

Cancellation during the Underwriting Period

Length of Underwriting Period: Sixty days.

Length of Notice: Ten days for nonpayment; thirty days for all other reasons.

Reason for Cancellation: Not required, but must be provided upon request.

Proof Required: Proof of mailing. A post office department certificate of mailing to the named insured at the address shown in the policy or contract is proof of receipt of the mailing.

Cancellation after the Underwriting Period

The policy may be cancelled **only** for the following reasons:

1. Nonpayment of premium.

2. Failure to pay dues or fees where payment of dues or fees is a prerequisite to obtaining or continuing insurance coverage in force.

3. Fraud or material misrepresentation.

4. Actions by the insured which substantially change or increase the risk insured.

5. Violation of a term or condition of the insurance policy or contract.

6. A change in the risk that substantially increases a hazard insured against.

IOWA

Length of Notice: Ten days for nonpayment; thirty days for all other reasons.

Reason for Cancellation: Not required on the notice, but must be provided upon request.

Proof Required: Proof of mailing. A post office department certificate of mailing to the named insured at the address shown in the policy or contract is proof of receipt of the mailing.

Nonrenewal

Length of Notice: Thirty days.

Reason for Nonrenewal: Required.

Proof Required: Proof of mailing, electronic transmission, or delivery to the first named insured's last known address.

Other Cancellation/Nonrenewal Provisions

If the policy is written for a period of more than one year, the insurer may cancel on the anniversary date with a thirty-day written notice.

A notice of nonrenewal is not required if the insured is transferred to an affiliate insurer because of a merger, acquisition, or company restructuring if the coverage is the same or broader than expiring.

PERSONAL AUTO

Iowa Code §§515D.4 to 515D.7 and 515D.11

(Less than four autos)

Cancellation during the Underwriting Period

Length of Underwriting Period: Sixty days.

Length of Notice: Ten days for nonpayment; thirty days for any other reason.

Reason for Cancellation: Not required, but must be provided upon request. A statement of reason must be mailed or delivered to the named insured within five days after receipt of a request.

Proof Required: Proof of mailing. A post office department certificate of mailing to the named insured at the address shown in the policy will be proof of receipt of such mailing.

IOWA

Cancellation after the Underwriting Period

The Iowa amendatory endorsement indicates that the policy may be cancelled **only** for the following reasons:

1. Nonpayment of premium or dues where payment of dues as a prerequisite to obtaining or continued insurance.

2. Suspension or revocation of the driver's license of:

    a. The named insured.
    b. Any driver who lives with the named insured or who customarily uses the insured auto.
    The suspension or revocation must occur during the policy period or, if the policy period is a renewal, during its term or the 180 days immediately preceding its effective date.

3. Material misrepresentation or fraud affecting the policy or the presentation of a claim on the application. The Iowa statute lists the following as allowable reasons for cancellation, even though they are not on the amendatory endorsement (PP 01 98). If an insurer has adopted the amendatory endorsement, it may not cancel for these reasons:

    1. If the insured violates the terms of the contract.

    2. If the named insured or any resident or regular operator of the car engages in a competitive speed contest.

    3. If the named insured or anyone who resides in the same household or regularly uses the covered auto is or has been convicted or forfeited bail for any of the following during the thirty-six months immediately preceding the effective date of the policy or during the policy period:

        a. Criminal negligence resulting in death, homicide, or assault, and arising out of the operation of a motor vehicle.
        b. Operating a motor vehicle while intoxicated or under the influence of drugs.
        c. Leaving the scene of the accident.

Length of Notice: Twenty days for the reasons above and within fifteen days of receipt of delivery of a statement of reason.

IOWA

Reason for Cancellation: A statement of reason must be mailed or delivered to the named insured within five days after receipt of a request.

Proof Required: Proof of mailing. A post office department certificate of mailing to the named insured at the address shown in the policy will be proof of receipt of such mailing.

Nonrenewal

Length of Notice: Thirty days.

Reason for Nonrenewal: Not required, but must be provided upon request. A statement of reason must be mailed or delivered to the named insured within ten days after receipt of a request.

Proof Required: Proof of mailing. A post office department certificate of mailing to the named insured at the address shown in the policy will be proof of receipt of such mailing.

Other Cancellation/Nonrenewal Provisions

If the policy term is less than six months, the insurer may nonrenew every six months, beginning six months after the original effective date.

If the policy term is six months or longer but less than one year, the insurer may nonrenew at the end of the policy period.

If the policy term is one year or longer, the insurer may nonrenew the policy at each anniversary of the original effective date.

A nonrenewal notice is not required if the insured fails to pay a renewal premium.

If the policy is cancelled or nonrenewed for a reason other than nonpayment of premium, the insurer must advise the insured of possible eligibility under the Iowa's automobile insurance plan. Such notice must accompany the notice of cancellation or intent not to renew.

Insurers are prohibited from refusing to renew a policy solely because of age, residence, sex, race, color, creed, or occupation of an insured.

Insurers are prohibited from requiring a physical examination of a policyholder as a condition for renewal solely on the basis of age or other arbitrary reason. In the event that an insurer requires a physical examination of a policyholder, the burden of proof in establishing reasonable and sufficient grounds for such requirement shall rest with the insurer and the expenses incident to such examination shall be borne by the insurer.

A notice of exclusion of a person under a policy is not effective unless written notice is mailed or delivered to the named insured at least twenty days prior to the effective date

IOWA

of the exclusion. The written notice shall state the reason for the exclusion, together with notification of the right to a hearing before the commissioner within fifteen days of receipt or delivery of a statement of reason.

During the policy period, a modification of automobile physical damage coverage, other than coverage for loss caused by collision, where provision is made for the application of a deductible amount not exceeding one hundred dollars, will not be deemed a cancellation of the coverage or of the policy.

An insurance company organized under chapter 515 (Insurance Other Than Life) that contracts with an independent (noncaptive) insurance producer or MGA must provide 180 day notice prior the termination of the contract unless it contains a written provision expressly reserving to the insurer all right, title, and interest to the ownership or the use of insurance business written. I.C.A. § 515.106.

PERSONAL UMBRELLA

Iowa Code §§515.125; 515.129A and 515.129B

Cancellation during the Underwriting Period

Length of Underwriting Period: Sixty days.

Length of Notice: Ten days for nonpayment; thirty days for any other reason.

Reason for Cancellation: Not required, but must be provided upon request.

Proof Required: Proof of mailing. A post office department certificate of mailing to the named insured at the address shown in the policy or contract is proof of receipt of the mailing.

Cancellation after the Underwriting Period

Length of Notice: Ten-day notice for nonpayment; thirty-day notice for any other reason.

Reason for Cancellation: Not required, but must be provided upon request.

Proof Required: Proof of mailing. A post office department certificate of mailing to the named insured at the address shown in the policy or contract is proof of receipt of the mailing.

Nonrenewal

Length of Notice: Thirty days.

Reason for Nonrenewal: Not required, but must be provided upon request.

IOWA

Proof Required: Proof of mailing, electronic transmission, or delivery to the last known address of the first named insured.

FRAUD

Iowa Code §§507E.3 through 507E.7

General Information and Definitions

A person commits a class "D" felony if the person, with the intent to defraud an insurer, does any of the following:

1. Presents or causes to be presented to an insurer, any written document or oral statement, including a computer-generated document, as part of, or in support of, a claim for payment or other benefit pursuant to an insurance policy, knowing that such document or statement contains any false information concerning a material fact.

2. Assists, abets, solicits, or conspires with another to present or cause to be presented to an insurer, any written document or oral statement, including a computer-generated document, that is intended to be presented to any insurer in connection with, or in support of, any claim for payment or other benefit pursuant to an insurance policy, knowing that such document or statement contains any false information concerning a material fact.

3. Presents or causes to be presented to an insurer, any written document or oral statement, including a computer-generated document, as part of, or in, an application for insurance coverage, knowing that such document or statement contains false information concerning a material fact.

"Statement" includes, but is not limited to, any notice, statement, proof of loss, bill of lading, receipt for payment, invoice, account, estimate of property damage, bill for services, diagnosis, prescription, hospital or physician record, x-ray, test result, or other evidence of loss, injury, or expense.

Reporting Requirements

An insurer who believes that a fraudulent claim or application for insurance coverage is being made shall provide, within sixty days of the receipt of such claim or application, written notification to the bureau of the claim or application on a form prescribed by the bureau, including any additional information requested by the bureau related to the claim or application or the party making the claim or application.

A person acting without malice, fraudulent intent, or bad faith is immune from civil liability as a result of filing a report or furnishing, orally or in writing, other information concerning

IOWA

alleged acts in violation of Iowa insurance fraud rules, if the report or information is provided to or received from any of the following:

1. Law enforcement officials, their agents and employees.

2. The National Association of Insurance Commissioners, the insurance division, a federal or state governmental agency or bureau established to detect and prevent fraudulent insurance acts, or any other organization established for such purpose, and their agents, employees, or designees.

3. An authorized representative of an insurer.

Note: That this section does not affect in any way any common law or statutory privilege or immunity applicable to such person or entity. Insurance companies can submit an online report to the Iowa Insurance Fraud Bureau through the National Association of Insurance Commissioner's fraud reporting system at https://eapps.naic.org/ofrs/.

Insurance companies can also download a reporting form and send the completed form to the bureau. Forms and instructions are available at the Iowa Insurance Fraud Bureau's Web site at http://www.iid.state.ia.us/insurance_fraud.

Penalties

Insurance fraud is a Class "D" felony in the State of Iowa, which is punishable by up to five years in prison and a fine up to $7,500.

FAIR CLAIMS PROCESSING

Iowa Admin. Code r. 191-15.41(507B)

15.41(1) An insurer shall fully disclose to first-party claimants all pertinent benefits, coverages or other provisions of a policy or contract under which a claim is presented.

15.41(2) Within thirty days after receipt by the insurer of properly executed proofs of loss, the first-party property claimant shall be advised of the acceptance or denial of the claim by the insurer. No insurer shall deny a claim on the grounds of a specific policy provision, condition or exclusion unless reference to such provision, condition, or exclusion is included in the denial. The denial must be given to the claimant in writing, and the claim file of the insurer shall contain documentation of the denial.

When there is a reasonable basis supported by specific information available for review by the commissioner that the first-party claimant has fraudulently caused or contributed to the loss, the insurer is relieved from the requirements of this sub-rule. However, the claimant shall be advised of the acceptance or denial of the claim within a reasonable time for full investigation after receipt by the insurer of a properly executed proof of loss.

15.41(3) If the insurer needs more time to determine whether a first-party claim should be accepted or denied, the insurer shall so notify the first-party claimant within thirty days after receipt of the proof of loss and give the reasons more time is needed. If the investigation remains incomplete, the insurer shall–forty-five days from the initial notification and every forty-five days thereafter–send to the claimant a letter setting forth the reasons additional time is needed for investigation.

When there is a reasonable basis supported by specific information available for review by the commissioner for suspecting that the first-party claimant has fraudulently caused or contributed to the loss, the insurer is relieved from the requirements of this sub-rule. However, the claimant shall be advised of the acceptance or denial of the claim by the insurer within a reasonable time for full investigation after receipt by the insurer of a properly executed proof of loss.

15.41(4) Insurers shall not fail to settle first-party claims on the basis that responsibility for payment should be assumed by others except as may otherwise be provided by policy provisions.

15.41(5) No insurer shall make statements indicating that the rights of a third-party claimant may be impaired if a form or release, other than a release to obtain medical records, is not completed within a given period of time unless the statement is given for the purpose of notifying the third-party claimant of the provision of a statute of limitations.

15.41(6) The insurer shall affirm or deny liability on claims within a reasonable time and shall tender payment within thirty days of affirmation of liability, if the amount of the claim is determined and not in dispute. In claims where multiple coverages are involved, payments which are not in dispute under one of the coverages and where the payee is known should be tendered within thirty days if such payment would terminate the insurer's known liability under that coverage.

15.41(7) No producer shall conceal from a first-party claimant benefits, coverages or other provisions of any insurance policy or insurance contract when such benefits, coverages or other provisions are pertinent to a claim.

15.41(8) A claim shall not be denied on the basis of failure to exhibit property unless there is documentation of breach of the policy provisions to exhibit or cooperate in the claim investigation.

IOWA

15.41(9) No insurer shall deny a claim based upon the failure of a first-party claimant to give written notice of loss within a specified time limit unless the written notice is a written policy condition. An insurer may deny a claim if the claimant's failure to give written notice after being requested to do so is so unreasonable as to constitute a breach of the claimant's duty to cooperate with the insurer.

15.41(10) No insurer shall indicate to a first-party claimant on a payment draft, check or in any accompanying letter that said payment is "final" or "a release" of any claim unless the policy limit has been paid or there has been a compromise settlement agreed to by the first-party claimant and the insurer as to coverage and amount payable under the contract.

15.41(11) No insurer shall request or require any insured to submit to a polygraph examination unless authorized under the applicable insurance contracts and state law.

KANSAS

For details on cancellation procedures for the standard policy, refer to the Standard Policy section.

COMMERCIAL LINES
AGRICULTURAL CAPITAL ASSETS; BOP; CAPITAL ASSETS; CRIME; COMMERCIAL AUTO; C. UMBRELLA; FARM UMBRELLA; CGL (other than UNDERGROUND STORAGE TANKS) COMMERCIAL INLAND MARINE; COMMERCIAL PROPERTY; EQUIPMENT BREAKDOWN; FARM; PROFESSIONAL LIABILITY; & WORKERS COMPENSATION

Kan. Stat. Ann. §§40-2,120 to 40-2,122; Kan. Admin. Regs. § 40-3-15

Cancellation during the Underwriting Period

Length of Underwriting Period for New Business: Ninety days.

Length of Notice: Ten days for nonpayment; thirty days for any other reason.

Reason for Cancellation: Required on the notice.

Proof Required: Proof of mailing. United States Post Office certificate of mailing to last mailing address known to insurer. Proof of mailing is sufficient proof of notice.

Cancellation after the Underwriting Period

The policy may be cancelled **only** for the following reasons:

1. Nonpayment.

2. Material misrepresentation on the application.

3. If any insured violates any of the material terms and conditions of the policy.

4. If the insurer discovers unfavorable underwriting factors about the named insured that did not exist at policy inception.

5. If the insurance commissioner determines that continuation of the policy would place the insurer in a hazardous financial condition or in violation of Kansas law.

6. If the insurance commissioner determines that the insurer no longer has adequate reinsurance.

KANSAS

Length of Notice: Ten days for nonpayment; thirty days for all other reasons.

Reason for Cancellation: Required on the notice.

Proof Required: Proof of mailing. United States Post Office certificate of mailing to last mailing address known to insurer. Proof of mailing is sufficient proof of notice.

Nonrenewal

Length of Notice: Sixty days.

Reason for Nonrenewal: Required on the notice.

Proof Required: Proof of mailing to the named insured at such person's last known address of the insurance company's intention not to renew such policy.

Other Cancellation/Nonrenewal Provisions

For OCP policies all notices must be sent to the named insured and the contractor shown in the declarations.

For Railroad Protective policies all notices must be sent to the named insured, the contractor, any involved governmental authority, and any other contracting party shown in the declarations.

The company may satisfy the obligation to provide notice to the policyholder by causing such notice to be given by a licensed agent.

COMMERCIAL AUTO

Kan. Stat. Ann. §§40-2,120 to 40-2,122, and Kan. Admin. Regs. 40-3-15

Cancellation during the Underwriting Period

Length of Underwriting Period for New Business: Ninety days.

Length of Notice: Ten days for nonpayment; thirty days for all other reasons.

Reason for Cancellation: Required on the notice.

Proof Required: Certified or registered mail. (ISO requires certified or registered mail, or United States Post Office certificate of mailing to last mailing address known to insurer. Proof of mailing is sufficient proof of notice.)

KANSAS

Cancellation after the Underwriting Period

The policy may be cancelled **only** for the following reasons:

1. Nonpayment.

2. Material misrepresentation on the application.

3. If any insured violates any of the terms and conditions of the policy.

4. If the insurer discovers unfavorable underwriting factors about the named insured that did not exist at policy inception.

5. If the insurance commissioner determines that continuation of the policy would place the insurer in a hazardous financial condition or in violation of Kansas law.

6. If the insurance commissioner determines that the insurer no longer has adequate reinsurance.

Length of Notice: Ten days for nonpayment; thirty days for any other reason.

Reason for Cancellation: Required on the notice.

Proof Required: Certified or registered mail. (ISO requires certified or registered mail, or United States Post Office certificate of mailing to last mailing address known to insurer. Proof of mailing is sufficient proof of notice).

Nonrenewal

Length of Notice: Sixty days.

Reason for Nonrenewal: Required on the notice.

Proof Required: Certified or registered mail. (ISO requires certified or registered mail, or United States Post Office certificate of mailing to last mailing address known to insurer. Proof of mailing is sufficient proof of notice.)

Other Cancellation/Nonrenewal Provisions

If an insurer is using the ISO endorsement (CA 02 65), the following apply:

1. If the insured is a vehicle dealer or a mobile home dealer, the insurer must also send a thirty-day notice of cancellation to the Kansas Director of Vehicles.

2. The company may satisfy the obligation to provide notice to the policyholder by causing such notice to be given by a licensed agent.

KANSAS

COMMERCIAL GENERAL LIABILITY
(Underground Storage Tank Policy)

Kan. Stat. Ann. §§40-2,120 to 40-2,122; Kan. Admin. Regs. §40-3-15

Cancellation during the Underwriting Period

Length of Underwriting Period for New Business: Ninety days.

Length of Notice: Ten days for nonpayment; thirty days for material misrepresentation; sixty days for any other reason. The requirement for a sixty-day notice in all other cases is not contained in the K. S. T. However, if an insurer adopts the ISO amendatory endorsement (CG 30 33), it must give the sixty-day notice.

Reason for Cancellation: Required on the notice.

Proof Required: Certified mail.

Cancellation after the Underwriting Period

The policy may be cancelled **only** for the following reasons:

1. Nonpayment.

2. Material misrepresentation on the application.

3. If any other insured violates any of the material terms and conditions of the policy.

4. If the insurer discovers unfavorable underwriting factors about the named insured that did not exist at policy inception.

5. If the insurance commissioner determines that continuation of the policy would place the insurer in a hazardous financial condition or in violation of Kansas law.

6. If the insurance commissioner determines that the insurer no longer has adequate reinsurance.

Length of Notice: Ten days for nonpayment; thirty days for material misrepresentation; sixty days for any other reason. The requirement for a sixty-day notice in all other cases is not contained in the K. S. T. However, if an insurer adopts the ISO amendatory endorsement (CG 30 33), it must give the sixty-day notice.

Reason for Cancellation: Required on the notice.

Proof Required: Certified mail.

KANSAS

Nonrenewal

Length of Notice: Sixty days.

Reason for Nonrenewal: Required on the notice.

Proof Required: Certified mail.

SURPLUS LINES

The surplus lines insurance policy allows the insurer to cancel the policy at any time for any reason, since their rates, rules and forms are not subject to department approval.

FINANCED PREMIUMS

Kan. Stat. Ann. §40-2612

If the premium finance agreement contains a power of attorney, the finance company may request, in the name of the insured, that the insurer cancel the policy due to nonpayment. The finance company must first give the insured notice of the intent to cancel and ten days to pay. If the insured fails to make payment within that ten-day period, the finance company mails the notice of cancellation to the insurer and the insured. The insurer also must give notice to applicable third parties (e.g., mortgagees) on or before the second business day after the day it receives the notice of cancellation from the premium finance company. The effective date of cancellation will take into consideration the number of days' notice that is required. Return of the policy by the insured is not required. Whenever a financed insurance contract is cancelled, the insurer shall, within twenty days of the effective date of cancellation, return whatever gross unearned premiums are due under the insurance contract to the premium finance company, either directly or via the agent or agency writing the insurance, where an assignment of such funds is included in the premium finance agreement for the account of the insured or insureds. Except as provided in KSA 40-411 or KSA 40-420, KAR 40-1-10 states each form shall provide at least five days written notice for cancellation to an insured before the policy may be cancelled as a result of a premium installment nonpayment.

PERSONAL LINES
DWELLING FIRE & HOMEOWNERS

(Applicable only to owner-occupied dwellings) Kan. Admin. Regs. §40-3-15;

Kan. Stat. Ann. §40-2,112 (b)(1) and (d).

Cancellation during the Underwriting Period

Length of Underwriting Period for New Business: Sixty days.

Length of Notice: Ten days for nonpayment; thirty days for any other reason.

KANSAS

Reason for Cancellation: Required on the notice.

Proof Required: Proof of mailing. Refund must accompany cancellation or be returned within ten days.

Nonrenewal

Length of Notice: Thirty days.

Reason for Nonrenewal: Required on the notice.

Proof Required: Proof of mailing.

DWELLING FIRE

(Applicable only to nonowner-occupied dwellings)

Kan. Admin. Regs. §40-3-15

Cancellation during the Underwriting Period

Length of Underwriting Period for New Business: Sixty days.

Length of Notice: Ten days for nonpayment; thirty days for any other reason.

Reason for Cancellation: Required on the notice.

Proof Required: Proof of mailing.

Nonrenewal

Length of Notice: Thirty days.

Reason for Nonrenewal: Required on the notice.

Proof Required: Proof of mailing.

PERSONAL AUTO

Kan. Stat. Ann. §§40-276 to 40-278; Kan. Admin. Regs. §40-3-31

Cancellation during the Underwriting Period

Length of Underwriting Period: Sixty days.

Length of Notice: Ten days for nonpayment; thirty days for all other reasons.

KANSAS

Reason for Cancellation: Required on the notice.

Proof Required: Certified or registered mail or United States Post Office certificate of mailing to the named insured shown in the Declarations at the latest address filed with the insurer by or on behalf of the named insured.

Cancellation after the Underwriting Period

The policy may be cancelled **only** for the following reasons:

1. Nonpayment.

2. Fraudulent misrepresentation on the application.

3. Violation by any insured of any of the terms and conditions of the policy.

4. If the named insured or any other driver who regularly uses the covered auto:

    a. Has his or her license suspended or revoked during the policy period.

    b. Is or becomes subject to heart attacks or epilepsy. However, such an individual may produce a certificate from a physician testifying to that individual's ability to operate a motor vehicle.

    c. Is or has been convicted during the thirty-six months immediately preceding the effective date of the policy or during the policy period for:

    (1) Any felony.
    (2) Criminal negligence resulting in death, homicide, or assault, and arising out of the operation of a motor vehicle.
    (3) Operating a motor vehicle while intoxicated or under the influence of drugs.
    (4) Leaving the scene of the accident without stopping to report.
    (5) Theft of a motor vehicle.
    (6) Making false statements in an application for a driver's license.
    (7) Three moving violations within eighteen months.

Length of Notice: Ten days for nonpayment; thirty days for all other reasons.

Reason for Cancellation: Required on the notice.

Proof Required: Certified or registered mail or United States Post Office certificate of mailing to the named insured shown in the Declarations at the latest address filed with the insurer by or on behalf of the named insured.

KANSAS

Nonrenewal

Length of Notice: Thirty days.

Reason for Nonrenewal: Required on the notice.

Proof Required: Certified or registered mail or United States Post Office certificate of mailing to the named insured shown in the Declarations at the latest address filed with the insurer by or on behalf of the named insured.

Nonrenewal Provisions

The insurer may also deny renewal for the following reasons:

1. When company has been permitted by commissioner to reduce its premium volume in order to preserve the financial integrity of the insurer.

2. When insurance company ceases to transact business in this state.

3. When insurance company is able to show competent medical evidence that insured has physical or mental disablement that impairs his ability to drive in a safe and reasonable manner.

4. When unfavorable underwriting factors pertinent to the risk are existent, and of a substantial nature, which could not have reasonably been ascertained by the company at the initial issuance of the policy or last renewal.

5. When the policy has been in effect for five years.

6. When any reason specified as a reason for cancellation in K.S.A. 40-277 exists.

The insurer may only nonrenew when any of the allowable reasons for cancellation exist or as permitted by the commissioner. No insurance company may refuse to renew a policy until after June 30, 2002, based on an insured's failure to maintain membership in a bona fide association, until both the insurance company and bona fide association have complied with the requirements of K.S.A. 40-276a(b).

When an insurer cancels or nonrenews for any reason other than nonpayment, it must notify the insured of the availability of the Kansas Automobile Plan. Such notice must accompany or be included in the notice of cancellation, or nonrenewal given by the insurer.

Within ten days after receiving a written request, a company must furnish the reason for the cancellation or nonrenewal in writing. This statement is required only when reasons for cancellation or nonrenewal are not sent with the cancellation or nonrenewal notice.

KANSAS

PERSONAL UMBRELLA

Cancellation during the Underwriting Period

Length of Underwriting Period for New Business: Sixty days.

Length of Notice: Ten days for any reason.

Reason for Cancellation: Within ten days after receiving a written request, the company will furnish the reason for the cancellation or nonrenewal in writing. This statement is required only when reasons for cancellation or nonrenewal are not sent with the cancellation or nonrenewal notice.

Proof Required: Proof of mailing delivered or mailed to the insured at the mailing address shown in the Declarations.

Cancellation after the Underwriting Period

Length of Notice: Ten days notice for nonpayment; thirty days notice for any other reason.

Reason for Cancellation: Within ten days after receiving a written request, the company will furnish the reason for the cancellation or nonrenewal in writing. This statement is required only when reasons for cancellation or nonrenewal are not sent with the cancellation or nonrenewal notice.

Proof Required: Proof of mailing delivered or mailed to the insured at the mailing address shown in the Declarations.

Nonrenewal

Length of Notice: Thirty days.

Reason for Nonrenewal: Within ten days after receiving a written request, the company will furnish the reason for the cancellation or nonrenewal in writing. This statement is required only when reasons for cancellation or nonrenewal are not sent with the cancellation or nonrenewal notice.

Proof Required: Proof of mailing delivered or mailed to the insured at the mailing address shown in the Declarations.

FRAUD

Kan. Stat. Ann. §40-2,120; §§40-2,118, 40-2,118a, and 40-2,119

General Information and Provisions

For purposes of this act a "fraudulent insurance act" means an act committed by any person who, knowingly and with intent to defraud, presents, causes to be presented or prepares

KANSAS

with knowledge or belief that it will be presented to or by an insurer, purported insurer, broker or any agent thereof, any written, electronic, electronic impulse, magnetic, oral or telephonic commission statement as part of, or in support of, an application for the issuance of, or the rating of an insurance policy for personal or commercial insurance, or a claim for payment or other benefit pursuant to an insurance policy for commercial or personal insurance which such person knows to contain materially false information concerning any fact material thereto; or conceals, for the purpose of misleading, information concerning any fact material thereto.

Reporting Requirements

An insurer that has knowledge or a good faith belief that a fraudulent insurance act is being or has been committed shall provide to the commissioner, on a form prescribed by the commissioner, any and all information and such additional information relating to such fraudulent insurance act as the commissioner may require.

Any other person that has knowledge or a good faith belief that a fraudulent insurance act is being or has been committed may provide to the commissioner, on a form prescribed by the commissioner, any and all information and such additional information relating to such fraudulent insurance act as the commissioner may request.

A person who acts without malice, fraudulent intent, or bad faith is not subject to civil liability for filing a report or furnishing, orally or in writing, other information concerning a suspected, anticipated, or completed fraudulent insurance act if the report or other information is provided to or received from any of the following:

1. The department or an agent, an employee, or a designee of the department.

2. Law enforcement officials or an agent or employee of a law enforcement official.

3. The National Association of Insurance Commissioners.

4. Any agency or bureau of federal or state government established to detect and prevent fraudulent insurance acts.

5. Any other organization established to detect and prevent fraudulent insurance acts.

6. An agent, an employee, or a designee of an entity referred to in subdivisions (3) through (5).

Note: This paragraph does not abrogate or modify in any way any common law or statutory privilege or immunity.

KANSAS

Penalties

A fraudulent insurance act shall constitute a severity level 6, nonperson felony if the amount involved is $25,000 or more; a severity level 7, nonperson felony if the amount is at least $5,000 but less than $25,000; a severity level 8, nonperson felony if the amount is at least $1,000 but less than $5,000; and a class C nonperson misdemeanor if the amount is less than $1,000. Any combination of fraudulent acts as defined in subsection (a) which occurs in a period of six consecutive months which involves $25,000 or more shall have a presumptive sentence of imprisonment regardless of its location on the sentencing grid block.

In addition to any other penalty, a person who violates this statute shall be ordered to make restitution to the insurer or any other person or entity for any financial loss sustained as a result of such violation. An insurer shall not be required to provide coverage or pay any claim involving a fraudulent insurance act.

Antifraud Provisions

Each insurer shall have antifraud initiatives reasonably calculated to detect fraudulent insurance acts. Antifraud initiatives may include: fraud investigators, who may be insurer employees or independent contractors; or an antifraud plan submitted to the commissioner. Each insurer that submits an anti-fraud plan shall notify the commissioner of any material change in the information contained in the antifraud plan within thirty days after such change occurs. Such insurer shall submit to the commissioner in writing the amended antifraud plan.

The requirement for submitting any antifraud plan, or any amendment thereof, to the commissioner shall expire on July 1, 2016.

FAIR CLAIMS PROCESSING

Kan. Admin. Regs. 40-1-34

The Kansas Insurance Department uses the NAIC Unfair Claims Settlement Practices Model Regulation as a basis for its rules relating to fair claims processing.

KENTUCKY

For details on cancellation procedures for the standard policy, refer to the Standard Policy section.

COMMERCIAL LINES
AGRICULTURAL CAPITAL ASSETS; BOP; CAPITAL ASSETS; C. AUTO; CRIME; CGL (CGL, LIQUOR, MARKET SEGMENTS, OCP, POLLUTION, RODS./COMPLETED OPS.); CIM; C. PROP.; C. UMB.; E-COMMERCE; EQUIPMENT BREAKDOWN; FARM; & PRO. LIABILITY

KRS §§304.14-010 and 304.20-300 to 304.20-350, 806 KAR 20:010

Declinations

Definition: In addition to refusal to issue based on an application, a declination also includes:

1. The offering of coverage in a company in the group of insurers that differs from the company requested on the nonbinding application or written request for coverage.

2. The offering of coverage terms that differ from those requested on the application.

3. The refusal of an agent or broker to submit a nonbinding application or written request for coverage.

If the applicant makes a written request for the reason(s) for the declination, the insurer is required to provide a prompt written response to such inquiries.

Cancellation during the Underwriting Period

Length of Underwriting Period: Sixty days.

Length of Notice: Fourteen days for any reason.

Reason for Cancellation: Required on the notice. Shall be a statement reasonably calculated to inform the applicant or insured of the reason for the declination, cancellation or nonrenewal. The insurer shall provide specific grounds and shall not rely on "underwriting reasons" in general.

Proof Required: Proof of mailing of notice of cancellation or of reasons for cancellation to the named insured at the address shown in the policy is sufficient proof of notice.

KENTUCKY

Cancellation after the Underwriting Period

The policy may be cancelled **only** for the following reasons:

1. Nonpayment.

2. Fraud or material misrepresentation in obtaining the policy, in pursuing a claim, or in continuing the policy.

3. Willful or reckless acts or omissions that increase any hazard insured against.

4. A change in the risk that substantially increases any hazard insured against after insurance coverage has been issued or renewed.

5. A violation of any local fire, health, safety, building or construction regulation or ordinance that substantially increases any hazard insured against.

6. If the insurer is unable to obtain reinsurance on the risk.

7. If the insurance commissioner determines that the continuation of the policy would place the insurer in violation of the Kentucky insurance laws or regulations.

Length of Notice: Fourteen days for nonpayment; seventy-five days for all other allowable reasons.

Reason for Cancellation: Required on the notice. Shall be a statement reasonably calculated to inform the applicant or insured of the reason for the declination, cancellation or nonrenewal. The insurer shall provide specific grounds and shall not rely on "underwriting reasons" in general.

Proof Required: Proof of mailing of notice of cancellation or of reasons for cancellation to the named insured at the address shown in the policy is sufficient proof of notice.

Nonrenewal

Length of Notice: Seventy-five days.

Reason for Nonrenewal: Required on the notice. Shall be a statement reasonably calculated to inform the applicant or insured of the reason for the declination, cancellation or nonrenewal. The insurer shall provide specific grounds and shall not rely on "underwriting reasons" in general.

Proof Required: Proof of mailing of notice of intention not to renew or of reasons for nonrenewal to the named insured at the address shown in the policy is sufficient proof of notice.

KENTUCKY

Other Cancellation/Nonrenewal Provisions

If the insurer has manifested its willingness to renew by mailing or delivering a renewal notice, bill, certificate, or policy to the first named insured at his last known address at least thirty days before the end of the current policy period with the amount of the renewal premium charge and its due date clearly set forth within, then the policy expires and terminates without further notice to the insured on the due date unless the renewal premium is received on or before that date. When any policy terminates in this manner, the insurer must, within fifteen days, deliver or mail to the first named insured at his last known address a notice that the policy was not renewed and the date coverage ceased to exist.

A premium increase of more than 25 percent requires a seventy-five-day notice.

On OCP policies all notices must be mailed to the named insured and the contractor shown in the declarations.

COMMERCIAL GENERAL LIABILITY
(Railroad Protective)

KRS §§304.14-010 and 304.20-310 through 304.20-350, 806 KAR 20:010

Declinations

Definition: In addition to refusal to issue based on an application, a declination also includes:

1. The offering of coverage in a company in the group of insurers that differs from the company requested on the application.

2. The offering of coverage terms that differ from those requested on the application.

3. The refusal of an agent or broker to submit a nonbinding application or written request for coverage.

If the applicant makes a written request for the reason(s) for the declination, the insurer is required to provide a prompt written response to such inquiries.

Cancellation during the Underwriting Period

Length of Underwriting Period: Sixty days.

Length of Notice: Fourteen days. Note: even though the Kentucky code only requires a fourteen-day notice for cancellations in the underwriting period, an insurer must give a fourteen-day notice for nonpayment and sixty-day notice for any other reason if it has adopted ISO's amendatory endorsement (CG 28 87).

KENTUCKY

Reason for Cancellation: Required on the notice. Shall be a statement reasonably calculated to inform the applicant or insured of the reason for the declination, cancellation or nonrenewal. The insurer shall provide specific grounds and shall not rely on "underwriting reasons" in general.

Proof Required: Proof of mailing of notice of cancellation or of reasons for cancellation to the named insured at the address shown in the policy is sufficient proof of notice.

Cancellation after the Underwriting Period

The policy may be cancelled **only** for the following reasons:

1. Nonpayment.

2. Fraud or material misrepresentation in obtaining the policy, in pursuing a claim, or in continuing the policy.

3. Willful or reckless acts or omissions that increase any hazard insured against.

4. A change in the risk that substantially increases any hazard insured against after insurance coverage has been issued or renewed.

5. A violation of any local fire, health, safety, building or construction regulation or ordinance that substantially increases any hazard insured against.

6. If the insurer is unable to obtain reinsurance on the risk.

7. If the insurance commissioner determines that the continuation of the policy would place the insurer in violation of the Kentucky insurance laws or regulations.

Length of Notice: Fourteen days for nonpayment; seventy-five days for all other allowable reasons.

Reason for Cancellation: Required on the notice. Shall be a statement reasonably calculated to inform the applicant or insured of the reason for the declination, cancellation or nonrenewal. The insurer shall provide specific grounds and shall not rely on "underwriting reasons" in general.

Proof Required: Proof of mailing of notice of cancellation or of reasons for cancellation to the named insured at the address shown in the policy is sufficient proof of notice.

KENTUCKY

Nonrenewal

Length of Notice: Seventy-five days.

Reason for Nonrenewal: Required on the notice. Shall be a statement reasonably calculated to inform the applicant or insured of the reason for the declination, cancellation or nonrenewal. The insurer shall provide specific grounds and shall not rely on "underwriting reasons" in general.

Proof Required: Proof of mailing. Mailing of notice of intention not to renew or of reasons for nonrenewal to the named insured at the address shown in the policy is sufficient proof of notice.

Other Cancellation/Nonrenewal Provisions

All notices must be mailed to the named insured, contractor, any involved governmental authority, and any other contracting party shown on the declarations.

A premium increase of more than 25 percent requires a seventy-five-day notice.

The department may disapprove any form filed if the form "contains or incorporates by reference…any inconsistent, ambiguous, or misleading clauses, or exceptions and conditions which deceptively affect the risk purported to be assumed in the general coverage of the contract." (K.R.S. 304.14-130(1) (b)).

COMMERCIAL GENERAL LIABILITY

(Underground Storage Tank Policy)

KRS §§304.14-010 and 304.20-310 through 304.20-350

Declinations

Definition: In addition to refusal to issue based on an application, a declination also includes:

1. The offering of coverage in a company in the group of insurers that differs from the company requested on the application.

2. The offering of coverage terms that differ from those requested on the application.

3. The refusal of an agent or broker to submit a nonbinding application or written request for coverage.

KENTUCKY

If the applicant makes a written request for the reason(s) for the declination, the insurer is required to provide a prompt written response to such inquiries.

Cancellation during the Underwriting Period

Length of Underwriting Period: Sixty days.

Length of Notice: Fourteen days. **Note:** Even though the Kentucky code only requires a fourteen-day notice for cancellations in the underwriting period, an insurer must give fourteen days notice for nonpayment, fraud, or material misrepresentation; sixty days notice for any other reason if it has adopted ISO's amendatory endorsement (CG 30 38).

Reason for Cancellation: Required on the notice. Shall be a statement reasonably calculated to inform the applicant or insured of the reason for the declination, cancellation or nonrenewal. The insurer shall provide specific grounds and shall not rely on "underwriting reasons" in general.

Proof Required: Certified mail. Even though the Kentucky statute only requires proof of standard mailing of notice of cancellation or of reasons for cancellation to the named insured at the address shown in the policy is sufficient proof of notice, an insurer must use certified mail if it has adopted ISO's amendatory endorsement.

Cancellation after the Underwriting Period

The policy may be cancelled only for the following reasons:

1. Nonpayment.

2. Fraud or material misrepresentation in obtaining the policy, in pursuing a claim, or in continuing the policy.

3. Willful or reckless acts or omissions that increase any hazard insured against.

4. A change in the risk that substantially increases any hazard insured against after insurance coverage has been issued or renewed.

5. A violation of any local fire, health, safety, building or construction regulation or ordinance that substantially increases any hazard insured against.

6. If the insurer is unable to obtain reinsurance on the risk.

7. If the insurance commissioner determines that the continuation of the policy would place the insurer in violation of the Kentucky insurance laws or regulations.

KENTUCKY

Length of Notice: Fourteen days after receipt for nonpayment; seventy-five days after receipt for all other reasons.

Reason for Cancellation: Required on the notice. Shall be a statement reasonably calculated to inform the applicant or insured of the reason for the declination, cancellation or nonrenewal. The insurer shall provide specific grounds and shall not rely on "underwriting reasons" in general.

Proof Required: Certified mail. Kentucky statute only requires proof of standard mailing of notice of cancellation or of reasons for cancellation to the named insured at the address shown in the policy is sufficient proof of notice. An insurer must use certified mail if it has adopted ISO's amendatory endorsement (CG 30 38).

Nonrenewal

Length of Notice: Seventy-five days.

Reason for Nonrenewal: Required on the notice. Shall be a statement reasonably calculated to inform the applicant or insured of the reason for the declination, cancellation or nonrenewal. The insurer shall provide specific grounds and shall not rely on "underwriting reasons" in general.

Proof Required: Certified mail. Kentucky statute only requires proof of standard mailing; mailing of notice of intention not to renew or of reasons for nonrenewal to the named insured at the address shown in the policy is sufficient proof of notice. An insurer must use certified mail if it has adopted ISO's amendatory endorsement (CG 30 38).

Other Cancellation/Nonrenewal Provisions

A premium increase of more than 25 percent requires a seventy-five-day notice.

The department may disapprove any form filed if the form "contains or incorporates by reference…any inconsistent, ambiguous, or misleading clauses, or exceptions and conditions which deceptively affect the risk purported to be assumed in the general coverage of the contract." (K.R.S. 304.14-130(1)(b)).

WORKERS COMPENSATION

KRS §§304.14-010, 304.20-300 through 304.20-350, 342.340, and 803 KAR 25:175

Cancellation during the Underwriting Period

Length of Underwriting Period: Sixty days.

Length of Notice: Fourteen days for any reason.

KENTUCKY

Reason for Cancellation: Required on the notice. Shall be a statement reasonably calculated to inform the applicant or insured of the reason for the declination, cancellation or nonrenewal. The insurer shall provide specific grounds and shall not rely on "underwriting reasons" in general.

Proof Required: Proof of mailing of notice of cancellation or of reasons for cancellation to the named insured at the address shown in the policy is sufficient proof of notice.

Cancellation after the Underwriting Period

The policy may be cancelled **only** for the following reasons:

1. Nonpayment.

2. Discovery of fraud or material misrepresentation by or with the insured's knowledge in obtaining the policy, continuing the policy, in presenting a claim under the policy.

3. Discovery of willful or reckless acts or omissions increasing any hazard originally insured against.

4. Change in conditions after the effective date of the policy or any renewal substantially increasing any hazard originally insured.

5. A violation of any local fire, health, or safety, building or construction regulation or ordinance at any covered work places substantially increasing any hazard originally insured.

6. The insurer's involuntary loss of reinsurance for the policy.

7. A determination by the Commissioner of Insurance that the continuation of the policy would place the insurer in violation of the Kentucky insurance laws.

Length of Notice: Fourteen days for nonpayment; seventy-five days for all other reasons.

Reason for Cancellation: Required on the notice. Shall be a statement reasonably calculated to inform the applicant or insured of the reason for the declination, cancellation or nonrenewal. The insurer shall provide specific grounds and shall not rely on "underwriting reasons" in general.

Proof Required: Proof of mailing of notice of cancellation or of reasons for cancellation to the named insured at the address shown in the policy is sufficient proof of notice.

KENTUCKY

Nonrenewal

Length of Notice: Seventy-five days.

Reason for Nonrenewal: Required on the notice. Shall be a statement reasonably calculated to inform the applicant or insured of the reason for the declination, cancellation or nonrenewal. The insurer shall provide specific grounds and shall not rely on "underwriting reasons" in general.

Proof Required: Proof of mailing. Mailing of notice of intention not to renew or of reasons for nonrenewal to the named insured at the address shown in the policy is sufficient proof of notice.

Other Cancellation/Nonrenewal Provisions

A premium increase of more than 25 percent requires a seventy-five-day notice to the insured. The insurer may comply with this requirement by extending the period of coverage of the current policy at the expiring premium.

If the insurer fails to provide the notice of nonrenewal as required, the policy will be deemed to be renewed for the ensuing policy period upon payment of the appropriate premium, and coverage will continue until the insured has accepted replacement coverage with another insurer, until the insured has agreed to the nonrenewal, or until the policy is cancelled.

The Department of insurance may disapprove any form filed if the form "contains or incorporates by reference…any inconsistent, ambiguous, or misleading clauses, or exceptions and conditions which deceptively affect the risk purported to be assumed in the general coverage of the contract." (K.R.S. 304.14-130(1)(b)).

Every employer who cancels its insurance or its membership in an approved self-insured group must immediately notify the Commissioner of Workers Claims of the cancellation, the date thereof and the reasons therefor. Every insurance carrier or self-insured group must notify the Commissioner of Workers Claims of each new policy or change or termination, issuance of a new policy, change or of any policy issued by it, except that the carrier or self-insured group need not set forth its reasons therefore unless requested by the commissioner. Notice shall be provided electronically. Termination of any policy must take effect no more than ten days before the receipt of the notification by the commissioner unless the employer obtained other insurance and the commissioner is notified of that fact by the insurer assuming the risk.

The insurer or self-insured group must also notify a named additional insured at the address listed on the evidence of coverage under a workers' compensation insurance policy upon cancellation, lapse, termination, expiration, or nonrenewal. (KRS 342.340 and 803 KAR 25:175. KRS 342.340 and 803 KAR 25:175).

KENTUCKY

SURPLUS LINES
KRS §304.14-010

The Kentucky Department of Insurance does not license nonadmitted insurers, and has jurisdiction over surplus lines brokers only. The Department does not specifically prescribe cancellation/nonrenewal provisions in policies issued by nonadmitted insurers.

FINANCED PREMIUMS
KRS §304.30-110 and 806 KAR 30:090

If the premium finance agreement contains a power of attorney, the finance company may request, in the name of the insured, that the insurer cancel the policy due to nonpayment. The finance company must first give the insured ten days to pay. If the insured fails to make payment within that ten-day period, then the finance company mails the notice of cancellation to the insurer and the cancellation is processed as of the finance company's original default date. The premium finance company also must mail the notice of cancellation to the insured at their last known address. Insurers must notify appropriate third parties of the cancellation by the second business day after receiving notice from the premium finance company, determining the date of cancellation by considering the required number of days' notice. Return of the policy by the insured is not required.

Premium finance companies are required to maintain written proof of mailing of notices of cancellation. The written proof shall be a receipt provided by the United States Postal Service. If a premium finance company does not maintain the proof of mailing, the purported notice is void.

PERSONAL LINES
DWELLING FIRE & HOMEOWNERS
KRS §§304.14-010, 304.20-300 through 304.20-350, and 806 KAR 20:010

Declinations

Definition: In addition to refusal to issue based on an application, a declination also includes:

1. The offering of coverage in a company in the group of insurers that differs from the company requested on the application.

2. The offering of coverage terms that differ from those requested on the application.

3. The refusal of an agent or broker to submit a nonbinding application or written request for coverage.

KENTUCKY

If the applicant makes a written request for the reason(s) for the declination, the insurer is required to provide a prompt written response to such inquiries.

Cancellation during the Underwriting Period

Length of Underwriting Period: Sixty days.

Length of Notice: Fourteen days.

Reason for Cancellation: Required on the notice. The Kentucky statute requires a reason to be shown. This provision does not appear on ISO's amendatory endorsements (DP 01 16 or HO 01 16).

Proof Required: Proof of mailing of notice of cancellation or of reasons for cancellation to the named insured at the address shown in the policy is sufficient proof of notice.

Cancellation after the Underwriting Period

The policy may be cancelled **only** for the following reasons:

1. Nonpayment.
2. Fraud or material misrepresentation in obtaining the policy, in pursuing a claim, or in continuing the policy.
3. Willful or reckless acts that increase any hazard insured against.
4. A change in the risk that substantially increases any hazard insured against.
5. A violation of any local fire, health, or safety code that substantially increases any hazard insured against.
6. If the insurer is unable to obtain reinsurance on the risk.

The Kentucky statute allows the insurer to cancel if the insurance commissioner determines that the continuation of the policy would place the insurer in violation of the Kentucky insurance laws. However, because this provision does not appear on the amendatory endorsement, an insurer may not use it to cancel a policy if it has adopted the ISO amendatory endorsements.

Length of Notice: Fourteen days for nonpayment; seventy-five days for all other allowable reasons.

Reason for Cancellation: Required on the notice. Although not stated as a requirement in ISO's amendatory endorsements, Kentucky statute requires a reason to be shown.

KENTUCKY

Shall be a statement reasonably calculated to inform the applicant or insured of the reason for the declination, cancellation or nonrenewal. The insurer shall provide specific grounds and shall not rely on "underwriting reasons" in general.

Proof Required: Proof of mailing of notice of cancellation or of reasons for cancellation to the named insured at the address shown in the policy is sufficient proof of notice.

Nonrenewal

Length of Notice: Seventy-five days.

Reason for Nonrenewal: Required on the notice. Although not stated as a requirement in ISO's amendatory endorsements, Kentucky statute requires a reason to be shown. Shall be a statement reasonably calculated to inform the applicant or insured of the reason for the declination, cancellation or nonrenewal. The insurer shall provide specific grounds and shall not rely on "underwriting reasons" in general.

Proof Required: Proof of mailing. Mailing of notice of intention to not renew or of reasons for nonrenewal to the named insured at the address shown in the policy is sufficient proof of notice.

Other Cancellation/Nonrenewal Provisions

A premium increase of more than 25 percent requires a seventy-five-day notice.

A reason for cancellation or nonrenewal which does not appear in the notice of cancellation or nonrenewal shall not be a basis for cancellation or nonrenewal.

The department may disapprove any form filed if the form "contains or incorporates by reference…any inconsistent, ambiguous, or misleading clauses, or exceptions and conditions which deceptively affect the risk purported to be assumed in the general coverage of the contract." (K.R.S. 304.14-130(1)(b)).

PERSONAL AUTO

KRS §304.20-040, 806 KAR 20:020, 806 KAR 20:010

Declinations

Definition: In addition to refusal to issue based on an application, a declination also includes:

1. The offering of coverage in a company in the group of insurers that differs from the company requested on the application.

2. The offering of coverage terms that differ from those requested on the application.

KENTUCKY

3. The refusal of an agent or broker to submit a nonbinding application or written request for coverage.

If the applicant makes a written request for the reason(s) for the declination, the insurer is required to provide a prompt written response to such inquiries.

Cancellation during the Underwriting Period

Length of Underwriting Period: Sixty days.

Length of Notice: Fourteen days.

Reason for Cancellation: Required on the notice. Shall be a statement reasonably calculated to inform the applicant or insured of the reason for the declination, cancellation or nonrenewal. The insurer shall provide specific grounds and shall not rely on "underwriting reasons" in general.

Proof Required: Proof of mailing of notice of cancellation or of reasons for cancellation to the named insured at the address shown in the policy is sufficient proof of notice.

Cancellation after the Underwriting Period

The policy may be cancelled **only** for:

1. Nonpayment.

2. For suspension or revocation of the driver's license or motor vehicle registration of the named insured or any driver who lives with the named insured or who customarily uses the insured auto. The suspension must have occurred during the policy period, or if the policy is a renewal during the policy period or the preceding 180 days.

3. Discovery of fraud or material misrepresentation made by or with the knowledge of the named insured in obtaining the policy, continuing the policy, or in presenting a claim under the policy.

4. Discovery of willful acts or omissions on the part of the named insured that increase any hazard insured against.

5. If the insurance commissioner determines that the continuation of the policy would place the insurer in violation of the Kentucky insurance laws.

However, if an insurer uses the ISO amendatory endorsement, reasons 4 and 5 may not be used. Reason 2 on the ISO amendatory endorsement does not permit cancellation because of suspension or revocation of the motor vehicle registration (PP 01 53). Legal advice is suggested.

KENTUCKY

Length of Notice: Fourteen days for nonpayment; twenty days for all other allowable reasons.

Reason for Cancellation: Required on the notice. Even though the ISO's Kentucky Amendatory endorsement is silent on this, Kentucky statute requires the reason to be shown. Shall be a statement reasonably calculated to inform the applicant or insured of the reason for the declination, cancellation or nonrenewal. The insurer shall provide specific grounds and shall not rely on "underwriting reasons" in general.

Proof Required: Proof of mailing of notice of cancellation or of reasons for cancellation to the named insured at the address shown in the policy is sufficient proof of notice.

Nonrenewal

Length of Notice: Seventy-five days.

Reason for Nonrenewal: Required on the notice. ISO's Kentucky amendatory endorsement (PP 01 53) does not specify that the reason must be shown; however, it is required by Kentucky statute. Shall be a statement reasonably calculated to inform the applicant or insured of the reason for the declination, cancellation or nonrenewal. The insurer shall provide specific grounds and shall not rely on "underwriting reasons" in general.

Proof Required: Proof of mailing. Mailing of notice of intention not to renew or of reasons for nonrenewal to the named insured at the address shown in the policy is sufficient proof of notice.

Other Cancellation/Nonrenewal Provisions

If a policy is cancelled for any reason other than nonpayment or if it is nonrenewed, the insurer must tell the insured of the availability of the Kentucky automobile assigned risk plan. The Kentucky automobile insurance plan created per K.R.S. §304.13-151(6) is the residual market and assigns the risks upon receipt of applications. When a renewal policy terminates because the renewal premium was not received on or before the due date, the insurer shall, within fifteen days, deliver or mail to the first-named insured at his last known address a notice that the policy was not renewed and the date on which the coverage under it ceased to exist. No insurer or agent shall decline, refuse to renew, or cancel a policy of automobile insurance solely because:

1. Of the credit history, or lack of credit history, or the following extraordinary life circumstances that directly influence the credit history of the applicant or insured:

    a. Catastrophic event, as declared by the federal or state government.
    b. Serious illness or injury, or serious illness or injury to an immediate family member.

KENTUCKY

      c.   Death of a spouse, child, or parent.
      d. Divorce or involuntary interruption of legally owed alimony or support payments.
      e.   Identity theft.
      f.   Temporary loss of employment for a period of three months or more, if it results from involuntary termination.
      g. Military deployment overseas.
      h. Other events, as determined by the insurer.

2. The applicant or insured has previously obtained automobile coverage through a residual market mechanism or from a carrier providing nonstandard coverage.

3. The applicant or insured has sustained one or more losses that immediately result from a natural cause without the intervention of any person and that could not have been prevented by the exercise of prudence, diligence, and care.

4. Of the race, religion, nationality, ethnic group, age, sex, or marital status of the applicant or named insured.

5. Another insurer previously declined to insure the applicant or terminated an existing policy in which the applicant was the named insured.

A reason for cancellation or nonrenewal which does not appear in the notice of cancellation or nonrenewal shall not be a basis for cancellation or nonrenewal.

The department may disapprove any form filed if the form "contains or incorporates by reference…any inconsistent, ambiguous, or misleading clauses, or exceptions and conditions which deceptively affect the risk purported to be assumed in the general coverage of the contract." (K.R.S. 304.14-130(1)(b)).

PERSONAL UMBRELLA

KRS §§304.14-010, 304.20-300 through 304.20-350

Cancellation during the Underwriting Period

Length of Underwriting Period: Sixty days.

Length of Notice: Fourteen days for any reason.

Reason for Cancellation: Required on the notice. Kentucky statute requires the reason to be stated. However, ISO's amendatory endorsement (DL 98 64) does not specify that the reason must be shown. Shall be a statement reasonably calculated to inform the applicant or

KENTUCKY

insured of the reason for the declination, cancellation or nonrenewal. The insurer shall provide specific grounds and shall not rely on "underwriting reasons" in general.

Proof Required: Proof of mailing of notice of cancellation or of reasons for cancellation to the named insured at the address shown in the policy is sufficient proof of notice.

Cancellation after the Underwriting Period

1. Nonpayment.

2. Upon discovery of fraud or material misrepresentation made by, or with the knowledge of, the named insured in obtaining or continuing this policy, or in presenting a claim under this policy.

3. Upon discovery of willful or reckless acts or omissions on the part of the named insured which increase any hazard insured against.

4. Upon the occurrence of a change in the risk which substantially increases any hazard insured against after insurance coverage has been issued or renewed.

5. If there is a violation of any local fire, health, safety, building or construction regulation or ordinance with respect to any insured property or the occupancy of such property which substantially increases any hazard insured against.

6. If we are unable to reinsure the risk covered by the policy.

Length of Notice: Fourteen-day notice for nonpayment; seventy-five-day notice for any other allowable reason.

Reason for Cancellation: Reason for notice must be stated. Kentucky statute requires the reason to be stated. However, ISO's amendatory endorsement (DL 98 64) does not specify that the reason must be shown. Shall be a statement reasonably calculated to inform the applicant or insured of the reason for the declination, cancellation or nonrenewal. The insurer shall provide specific grounds and shall not rely on "underwriting reasons" in general.

Proof Required: Proof of mailing of notice of cancellation or of reasons for cancellation to the named insured at the address shown in the policy is sufficient proof of notice.

Nonrenewal

Notice Requirements: Seventy-five days.

KENTUCKY

Reason for Nonrenewal: Required on the notice. Kentucky statute requires the reason to be stated. However, ISO's amendatory endorsement (DL 98 64) does not specify that the reason must be shown. Shall be a statement reasonably calculated to inform the applicant or insured of the reason for the declination, cancellation or nonrenewal. The insurer shall provide specific grounds and shall not rely on "underwriting reasons" in general.

Proof Required: Proof of mailing. Mailing of notice of intention to not renew or of reasons for nonrenewal to the named insured at the address shown in the policy is sufficient proof of notice.

Other Cancellation/Nonrenewal Provisions

If a renewal notice is mailed to the insured at least thirty days before the end of the policy period, stating the renewal premium and its due date, the policy will terminate without further notice unless the renewal premium is received by the insurer or its authorized agent by the due date.

The department may disapprove any form filed if the form "contains or incorporates by reference…any inconsistent, ambiguous, or misleading clauses, or exceptions and conditions which deceptively affect the risk purported to be assumed in the general coverage of the contract." (K.R.S. 304.14-130(1)(b)).

FRAUD

KRS §§304.47-020 and 304.47-050; 806 KAR 47:010

General Information and Definitions

A person or entity commits a fraudulent insurance act if he engages in any of the following, including but not limited to matters relating to workers' compensation:

1. Knowingly and with intent to defraud or deceive presents, causes to be presented, or prepares with the knowledge or belief that it will be presented to an insurer, Board of Claims, Special Fund or any agency thereof, any oral or written statement as part of, in support of a claim for payment or other benefit pursuant to an insurance policy knowing that the statement contains false, incomplete, or misleading information concerning any fact or thing material to a claim.

2. Knowingly and with intent to defraud or deceive presents, causes to be presented, or prepares with the knowledge or belief that it will be presented to an insurer, Board of Claims, Special Fund or any agency thereof, any statement as part of or in support of an application for an insurance policy for renewal, reinstatement, replacement of insurance or in support of an application to a lender for money to pay a premium, knowing that the statement contains any false or misleading information concerning any fact or thing material to the application.

3. Knowingly and willingly transacts any contract, agreement, or instrument which violates this title; or with intent to defraud or deceive receives money for purchasing insurance and fails to do so; knowingly and with intent to defraud or deceive fails to make payment or disposition of money or voucher as required by agreement or legal obligation, that comes into his or her possession while acting as a licensee under this chapter; issues fake or counterfeit policies, certificates of insurance, identification cards, binders, or other documents that evidence insurance; makes any false or fraudulent representation as to the death or disability of a policy or certificate holder in any written statement or certificate for the purpose of fraudulently obtaining money or benefit from an insurer; engages in unauthorized insurance; knowingly and with intent to defraud or deceive presents, causes to be presented, or prepares any statement knowing it contains any false, incomplete, or misleading information to an insurer or commissioner to support the rating of a policy, the financial condition of an insurer, the formation, acquisition, merger, reconsolidation, dissolution, or withdrawal from one or more lines of insurance, a document filed with the commissioner; knowingly and with intent to defraud or deceive engages in solicitation of new or renewal insurance risks on behalf of an insolvent insurer, removes, conceals, alters, tampers with, or destroys any money, records, or any other property or assets of an insurer; or assists, abets, solicits or conspires with another to commit a fraudulent insurance act.

Every insurer shall designate at least two but no more than four primary contact persons who shall communicate with the Insurance Fraud Unit on matters relating to the reporting, investigation, and prosecution of suspected fraudulent insurance acts as defined in K.R.S. §304.47-020.

Penalties

A person convicted of fraud shall be guilty of a misdemeanor where the aggregate of the claim, benefit or money is less than or equal to $500 shall be punished by imprisonment for not more than one year; a fine per occurrence of not more than $1,000 per individual nor $5,000 per corporation or twice the amount of gain received as a result of the violation, whichever is greater; or both imprisonment and fines. If 2017 KY B.R. 313 is passed the amount of the fine will increase from $500 to $1,500.

Fraud of over $500 is guilty of a felony and is punished by imprisonment for more than one but less than five years; a fine per occurrence of not more than $10,000 per individual nor $100,000 per corporation or twice the amount of gain received as a result of the violation; or imprisonment and fines.

Any person, with the purpose to establish or maintain a criminal syndicate, or to facilitate any of its activities is guilty of engaging in organized crime, a Class B felony, and will be punished by imprisonment for not less than ten years but less than twenty years; a fine,

KENTUCKY

per occurrence, of not more than $10,000 per individual or $100,000 per corporation, or twice the amount of gain received as a result of the violation, whichever is greater; or both imprisonment and a fines.

In addition to imprisonment, fines or both, a person convicted in violation of this section may be ordered to make restitution to any victim who suffered a monetary loss due to any actions by that person that resulted in the adjudication of guilt, and to the division for the cost of any investigation. The amount of restitution will equal the monetary value of the actual loss or twice the amount of gain received as a result of the violation, whichever is greater.

Reporting

The following, having knowledge or belief that a fraudulent insurance act has been committed shall send to the division a report or information pertinent to the knowledge or belief and any additional information the commissioner or commissioner's employees may require: any professional practitioner licensed or regulated by the commonwealth except as provided by law; any private medical review committee; any insurer, agent, or other person licensed under this chapter; and employees of said practitioners.

In the absence of malice, fraud, or gross negligence, no insurer or agent authorized by an insurer to act on its behalf, law enforcement agency, the Department of Workers' Claims, their respective employees, or an insured will be subject to any civil liability for libel, slander, or related cause of action by virtue of filing reports or for releasing or receiving any information pursuant to this subsection.

FAIR CLAIM PROCESSING
KRS §§304.12-230 and 304.12-235

All claims under any contract of insurance shall be paid to the named insured or health care provider no more than thirty days from the date of notice and proof of claim are provided to the insurer. If an insurer fails to make a good faith attempt to settle a claim within the time prescribed, the value of the final settlement shall bear interest at the rate of 12 percent per annum from and after the expiration of the thirty-day period. Likewise if a claim is not settled within the time prescribed and the delay was without reasonable foundation, the insured person or health care provider is entitled to be reimbursed for his reasonable attorney's fees incurred. This does not apply to Workers' Compensation claims.

It is an unfair claims settlement practice for any person to commit or perform any of the following acts or omissions:

1. Misrepresenting pertinent facts or insurance policy provisions relating to coverages at issue.

KENTUCKY

2. Failing to acknowledge and act reasonably promptly upon communications with respect to claims arising under insurance policies.

3. Failing to adopt and implement reasonable standards for the prompt investigation of claims arising under insurance policies.

4. Refusing to pay claims without conducting a reasonable investigation based upon all available information.

5. Failing to affirm or deny coverage of claims within a reasonable time after proof of loss statements have been completed.

6. Not attempting in good faith to effectuate prompt, fair and equitable settlements of claims in which liability has become reasonably clear.

7. Compelling insureds to institute litigation to recover amounts due under an insurance policy by offering substantially less than the amounts ultimately recovered in actions brought by such insureds.

8. Attempting to settle a claim for less than the amount to which a reasonable man would have believed he was entitled by reference to written or printed advertising material accompanying or made part of an application.

9. Attempting to settle claims on the basis of an application which was altered without notice to, or knowledge or consent of the insured.

10. Making claims payments to insureds or beneficiaries not accompanied by statement setting forth the coverage under which the payments are being made.

11. Making known to insureds or claimants a policy of appealing from arbitration awards in favor of insureds or claimants for the purpose of compelling them to accept settlements or compromises less than the amount awarded in arbitration.

12. Delaying the investigation or payment of claims by requiring an insured, claimant, or the physician of either to submit a preliminary claim report and then requiring the subsequent submission of formal proof of loss forms, both of which submissions contain substantially the same information.

13. Failing to promptly settle claims, where liability has become reasonably clear, under one portion of the insurance policy coverage in order to influence settlements under other portions of the insurance policy coverage.

KENTUCKY

14. Failing to promptly provide a reasonable explanation of the basis in the insurance policy in relation to the facts or applicable law for denial of a claim or for the offer of a compromise settlement.

15. Failing to comply with the decision of an independent review entity to provide coverage for a covered person as a result of an external review in accordance with K.R.S. 304.17A-621, 304.17A-623, and 304.17A-625.

16. Knowingly and willfully failing to comply with the provisions of K.R.S. 304.17A-714 when collecting claim overpayments from providers.

17. Knowingly and willfully failing to comply with the provisions of K.R.S. 304.17A-708 on resolution of payment errors and retroactive denial of claims.

LOUISIANA

COMMERCIAL LINES
AGRICULTURAL CAPITAL ASSETS; BOILER/EQUIPMENT BREAKDOWN; CAP. ASSETS; C. AUTO; CRIME; CGL (CGL, EMPLOYMENT, LIQUOR, OCP, POLLUTION, & PRODUCTS/COMPLETED OPS.); CIM; C. PROP.; C. UMB.; FARM; FIN. INST.; MGT. PROT.; and PROF. LIABILITY

Louisiana Revised Statutes §§22:887, 22:1265 through 22:1267

For all lines of business: When payment of unearned premium is made to the insured's agent, carriers are required to provide notice to the insured, at the time of cancellation, that the cancellation may generate a return of unearned premium. (La. R.S. § 22:887).

Cancellation during the Underwriting Period

Length of Underwriting Period: Sixty days. (La. R.S. § 22:1266).

Length of Notice: Ten days for nonpayment; sixty days for any other reason. (La. R.S. § 22:1266).

Reason for Cancellation: Not required, but the insurer must provide the reason in writing if requested by the insured. (La. R.S. § 22:1266).

Proof Required: Proof of mailing. The affidavit of the individual making or supervising such a mailing shall constitute prima facie evidence. Certified mail is required if cancellation is based on the insured's check or other negotiable instrument being uncollectible for any reason. (La. R.S. § 22:1266).

Cancellation after the Underwriting Period

The policy may be cancelled only for the following reasons:

1. Nonpayment. (La. R.S. § 22:1267).

2. Fraud or material misrepresentation on the application, in continuing the policy, or in presenting a claim under the policy. (La. R.S. § 22:1267).

3. Acts or omissions by the named insured that change or increase any hazard insured against. (La. R.S. § 22:1267).

4. A change in the risk that increases risk of loss after insurance coverage has been issued or renewed, including an increase in exposure due to regulation, legislation, or court decision. (La. R.S. § 22:1267).

LOUISIANA

5. The insurance commissioner determines that the continuation of the policy would place the insurer in violation of the any state's insurance laws. (La. R.S. § 22:1267).

6. If the insured violates or breaches any policy terms or conditions. (La. R.S. § 22:1267).

7. Any other reasons that are approved by the commissioner. (La. R.S. § 22:1267).

Length of Notice: Ten days for nonpayment; thirty days for all other reasons. When cancellation is based on an uncollectible negotiable instrument, the effective date of cancellation may be the date premium was due. (La. R.S. § 22:1267).

Reason for Cancellation: Not required, but the insurer must provide the reason in writing if the insured requests. (La. R.S. § 22:1267).

Proof Required: Proof of mailing. Certified mail is required if cancellation is based on the insured's check or other negotiable instrument being uncollectible for any reason. (La. R.S. § 22:1266).

Nonrenewal

Length of Notice: Sixty days. (La. R.S. § 22:887).

Reason for Nonrenewal: Not required, but the insurer must provide the reason in writing if requested by the insured. Nonrenewal notices must include loss information for the prior three years. If a proper notice is given, and the insurer then extends the policy for ninety days or less, no new notice is needed for the extension. (La. R.S. § 22:887).

Proof Required: Proof of mailing. The affidavit of the individual making or supervising such a mailing shall constitute prima facie evidence. (La. R.S. § 22:887).

Other Cancellation/Nonrenewal Provisions

On OCP policies all notices must be mailed to the first named insured and the contractor shown in the declarations. (Louisiana Revised Statute §1267).

On policies covering condominium associations, notices must also be mailed to each unit owner holding a certificate of insurance. (La. R.S. § 9:1123.112).

A thirty day notice is required in the event of any rate increase, change in deductible, reduction in limits, or reduction in coverage. This provision does not apply for changes in a rate or plan that is filed with the state and applies to an entire class of business.

Commercial excess and umbrella policies are exempted from the Louisiana cancellation statute for commercial lines. (Louisiana Revised Statute §1267).

LOUISIANA

Notification must be given to mortgage holders, pledgees or other persons known to have an insurable interest of at least ten days in the case of nonpayment and thirty days for any other reason or sixty days' notice in the case of nonrenewal. (La. R.S. § 22:887).

The nonrenewal notice must include loss information for the policy period the policy has been in force or up to three years whichever period of time is greater. (La. R.S. § 22:887).

EXCLUDED DRIVER

Louisiana Revised Statutes §32:900

A driver may be excluded from a commercial policy if the owner obtains and maintains in force another policy of motor vehicle insurance which provides coverage for the excluded person equal to that policy from which the person was excluded.

BUSINESSOWNERS

Louisiana Revised Statutes §§22:1265 through 22:1267

Cancellation during the Underwriting Period

Length of Underwriting Period: Sixty days. (La. R.S. § 22:1266).

Length of Notice: Ten days for nonpayment; sixty days for any other reason. When cancellation is based on an uncollectible negotiable instrument, the effective date of cancellation may be the date premium was due. (La. R.S. § 22:1266).

Reason for Cancellation: Not required, but the insurer must provide the reason in writing if requested by the insured. (La. R.S. § 22:1266).

Proof Required: Proof of mailing. The affidavit of the individual making or supervising such a mailing shall constitute prima facie evidence. (La. R.S. § 22:887).

Cancellation after the Underwriting Period

Length of Notice: Ten days for nonpayment; thirty days for all other reasons. When cancellation is based on an uncollectible negotiable instrument, the effective date of cancellation may be the date premium was due. (La. R.S. § 22:1266).

Reason for Cancellation: Not required, but the insurer must provide the reason in writing if the insured requests. The policy may only be cancelled for the following reasons: nonpayment, fraud or misrepresentation, changes or increases in hazards, a determination of illegality by the insurance commissioner, a violation of the policy terms by the insured, or any other reason approved by the commissioner. (La. R.S. § 22:1266).

Proof Required: Proof of mailing. (La. R.S. § 22:1266).

LOUISIANA

Nonrenewal

Length of Notice: Sixty days. (La. R.S. § 22:1267).

Reason for Nonrenewal: Not required, but the insurer must provide the reason in writing if requested by the insured. Nonrenewal notices must include loss information for the prior three years. If a proper notice is given, and the insurer then extends the policy for ninety days or less, no new notice is needed for the extension. (La. R.S. § 22:1267).

Proof Required: Proof of mailing. The affidavit of the individual making or supervising such a mailing shall constitute prima facie evidence. Nonrenewal notices must include loss information for the prior three years. (La. R.S. § 22:1267).

Other Cancellation/Nonrenewal Provisions

On policies covering condominium associations, notices must also be mailed to each unit owner holding a certificate of insurance.

A thirty-day notice is required in the event of any rate increase, change in deductible, reduction in limits, or reduction in coverage. This provision does not apply for changes in a rate or plan that is filed with the state and applies to an entire class of business. (La. R.S. § 9:1123.112).

Notification must be given to mortgage holders, pledgees or other persons known to have an insurable interest in the policy.

The nonrenewal notice must include loss information for the policy period the policy has been in force or up to three years which ever period of time is greater.

COMMERCIAL GENERAL LIABILITY
(Railroad Protective)

Louisiana Revised Statutes §22:1267

Cancellation during the Underwriting Period

Length of Underwriting Period: Sixty days.

Length of Notice: Ten days for nonpayment; sixty days for any other reason. When cancellation is based on an uncollectible negotiable instrument, the effective date of cancellation may be the date premium was due.

Reason for Cancellation: Not required, but the insurer must provide the reason in writing if the insured requests. (La. R.S. § 22:1267).

LOUISIANA

Proof Required: Proof of mailing. The affidavit of the individual making or supervising such a mailing shall constitute prima facie evidence. Certified mail is required if cancellation is based on the insured's check or other negotiable instrument being uncollectible for any reason. A ten-day notice is permitted in this case. (La. R.S. § 22:1267).

Cancellation after the Underwriting Period

Length of Notice: Ten days for nonpayment; thirty days for all other reasons. When cancellation is based on an uncollectible negotiable instrument, the effective date of cancellation may be the date the premium was due. (La. R.S. § 22:1267).

Reason for Cancellation: Not required, but the insurer must provide the reason in writing if the insured requests. The policy may only be cancelled for the following reasons: nonpayment, fraud or misrepresentation, changes or increases in hazards, change in risk, a determination of illegality by the insurance commissioner, a violation of the policy terms by the insured, or any other reason approved by the commissioner. (La. R.S. § 22:1267).

Proof Required: Proof of mailing. The affidavit of the individual making or supervising such a mailing shall constitute prima facie evidence. Certified mail is required if cancellation is based on the insured's check or other negotiable instrument being uncollectible for any reason. (La. R.S. § 22:1267).

Nonrenewal

Length of Notice: Sixty days. (La. R.S. § 22:1267).

Reason for Nonrenewal: Not required, but the insurer must provide the reason in writing if requested by the insured. Nonrenewal notices must include loss information for the prior three years. If a proper notice is given, and the insurer then extends the policy for ninety days or less, no new notice is needed for the extension. (La. R.S. § 22:1267).

Proof Required: Proof of mailing. The affidavit of the individual making or supervising such a mailing shall constitute prima facie evidence. (La. R.S. § 22:1267).

Other Cancellation/Nonrenewal Provisions

All notices must be mailed to the named insured, the contractor, any involved governmental authority, or any other contracting party designated in the Declarations.

A thirty-day notice is required in the event of any rate increase, change in deductible, reduction in limits, or reduction in coverage. This provision does not apply for changes in a rate or plan that is filed with the state and applies to an entire class of business.

The nonrenewal notice must include loss information for the policy period the policy has been in force or up to three years, whichever period of time is greater.

LOUISIANA

COMMERCIAL GENERAL LIABILITY
(Underground Storage Tank Policy)

Louisiana Revised Statutes §22:1267

La. Admin Code. tit. 33, pt. XI, §1115

Cancellation during the Underwriting Period

Length of Underwriting Period: Sixty days. (La. R.S. § 22:1267).

Length of Notice: Thirty days for nonpayment; sixty days for any other reason. Louisiana statute allows for a ten-day notice for nonpayment, an insurer must give thirty days for any reason if it has adopted the ISO amendatory endorsement (CG 30 19). When cancellation is based on an uncollectible negotiable instrument, the effective date of cancellation may be the date the premium was due. (La. R.S. § 22:1267).

Reason for Cancellation: Not required, but the insurer must provide the reason in writing if requested by the insured. (La. R.S. § 22:1267).

Proof Required: Certified mail.

Cancellation after the Underwriting Period

The policy may be cancelled **only** for the following reasons:

1. Nonpayment. (La. R.S. § 22:1267).

2. Fraud or material misrepresentation on the application, in continuing the policy, or in presenting a claim under the policy. (La. R.S. § 22:1267).

3. Acts or omissions by the named insured that change or increase any hazard insured against. (La. R.S. § 22:1267).

4. A change in the risk increases the hazard. This includes an increase in exposure due to regulation, legislation, or court decision. (La. R.S. § 22:1267).

5. The insurance commissioner determines that the continuation of the policy would place the insurer in violation of the state's insurance laws. (La. R.S. § 22:1267).

6. If the insured violates or breaches any policy terms or conditions. (La. R.S. § 22:1267).

7. Any other reasons that are approved by the commissioner. (La. R.S. § 22:1267).

LOUISIANA

Length of Notice: Ten days for nonpayment; thirty days for fraud or misrepresentation; sixty days for all other allowable reasons. Notice period begins when notice is actually received by the insured. (La. R.S. § 22:1267).

Reason for Cancellation: Not required, but the insurer must provide the reason in writing if the insured requests. (La. R.S. § 22:1267).

Proof Required: Certified mail. (La. R.S. § 22:1267).

Nonrenewal

Length of Notice: Sixty days. (La. R.S. § 22:1267).

Reason for Nonrenewal: Not required, but the insurer must provide the reason in writing if requested by the insured. Nonrenewal notices will include loss information for the prior three years. If a proper notice is given, and the insurer then extends the policy for ninety days or less, no new notice is needed for the extension. (La. R.S. § 22:1267).

Proof Required: Certified mail. (La. R.S. § 22:1267).

Other Cancellation/Nonrenewal Provisions

The nonrenewal notice must include loss information for the policy period the policy has been in force or up to three years which ever period of time is greater.

The insurance covers claims for any occurrence that commenced during the term of the policy that is discovered and reported to the insurer within six months of the effective date of the cancellation or termination of the policy.

WORKERS COMPENSATION

Louisiana Revised Statutes §22:1267

Cancellation during the Underwriting Period

Length of Underwriting Period: Sixty days. (La. R.S. § 22:1267).

Length of Notice: Ten days for nonpayment; sixty days for any other reason. When cancellation is based on an uncollectible negotiable instrument, the effective date of cancellation may be the date premium was due. (La. R.S. § 22:1267).

Reason for Cancellation: Required on the notice. (La. R.S. § 22:1267).

Proof Required: Proof of mailing. The affidavit of the individual making or supervising such a mailing shall constitute prima facie evidence. (La. R.S. § 22:1267).

LOUISIANA

Cancellation after the Underwriting Period

The policy may be cancelled only for the following reasons:

1. Nonpayment. (La. R.S. § 22:1267).

2. Fraud or material misrepresentation on the application, in continuing the policy, or in presenting a claim under the policy. (La. R.S. § 22:1267).

3. Acts or omissions by the named insured that change or increase any hazard insured against. (La. R.S. § 22:1267).

4. If a change in the risk increases the hazard. This includes an increase in exposure due to regulation, legislation, or court decision. (La. R.S. § 22:1267).

5. If the insurance commissioner determines that the continuation of the policy would place the insurer in violation of the state's insurance laws. (La. R.S. § 22:1267).

6. If the insured violates or breaches any policy terms or conditions. (La. R.S. § 22:1267).

7. Any other reasons that are approved by the commissioner. (La. R.S. § 22:1267).

Length of Notice: Ten days for nonpayment; thirty days for all other reasons. (La. R.S. § 22:1267).

Reason for Cancellation: Not required, but the insurer must provide the reason in writing if the insured requests. (La. R.S. § 22:1267).

Proof Required: Proof of mailing. (La. R.S. § 22:1267).

Nonrenewal

Length of Notice: Sixty days. (La. R.S. § 22:1267).

Reason for Nonrenewal: Not required, but the insurer must provide the reason in writing if the insured requests. If a proper notice is given, and the insurer then extends the policy for ninety days or less, no new notice is needed for the extension. (La. R.S. § 22:1267).

Proof Required: Proof of mailing. The affidavit of the individual making or supervising such a mailing shall constitute prima facie evidence. (La. R.S. § 22:1267).

LOUISIANA

Other Cancellation/Nonrenewal Provisions

A thirty-day notice is required in the event of any rate increase, change in deductible, reduction in limits, or reduction in coverage. This provision does not apply for changes in a rate or plan that is filed with the state and applies to an entire class of business. (La. R.S. § 22:1267).

Nonrenewal notices must include loss information for the prior three years. (La. R.S. § 22:1267).

If the nonrenewal notice is sent less than sixty days prior to the expiration date, coverage remains in effect under the same terms and conditions until sixty days after the notice is mailed or delivered. (La. R.S. § 22:1267).

The nonrenewal notice must include loss information for the policy period the policy has been in force or up to a maximum of three years. (La. R.S. § 22:1267).

SURPLUS LINES

Louisiana Revised Statutes §§22:431-446, 1267

The Louisiana cancellation and nonrenewal statutes do not apply to surplus lines. All cancellation and nonrenewal terms are governed by the terms of the policy.

FINANCED PREMIUMS

Louisiana Revised Statutes §§9:3550, 22:1266

A premium finance company may cancel a policy for nonpayment so long as it has a power of attorney to do so. The finance company must send a notice of cancellation to the insured. This can be done via mail or electronically. The insured then has ten days to make payment (fourteen days if the finance company is located outside Louisiana). If the insured makes payment, the finance company must send a notice of rescission to the insured within three days of the payment. If the insured fails to make payment, the finance company may effect cancellation. Within five days of effecting cancellation, the finance company must send to the insurer: (La. R.S. § 9:3550).

1. A copy of the notice of cancellation.

2. A statement certifying that the finance agreement contains a valid power of attorney. (La. R.S. § 9:3550).

3. A statement certifying that the finance agreement is in default and has not been paid. (La. R.S. § 9:3550).

4. A statement certifying that the notice of cancellation was sent to the insured, this must also specify the date the notice was sent. (La. R.S. § 9:3550).

LOUISIANA

5. A statement certifying that copies of the notice of cancellation were sent to all interested parties in the finance agreement, specifying their names and addresses. (La. R.S. § 9:3550).

The insurer shall treat this as though cancellation has been requested by the insured and may proceed to cancel. Return of the insurance contract is not required. The effective date of cancellation shall be as of 12:01 a.m. on the tenth day after the date specified in the statement (item 4 above) as the date the finance company sent notice to the insured. The insurer must give notice to any parties listed in the insurer's records as requiring notice. The insurer does not need to provide notice to the parties that were given notice by the finance company as listed in the finance company's statement (item 5 above). The insurer must give notice on or before the fifth business day after the day it receives a copy of the notice of cancellation from the insurance premium finance company. The insurer shall determine the effective date of cancellation taking into consideration the number of days' notice required to complete the cancellation if such notice is given by the insurer, otherwise the effective date of cancellation shall be calculated from the date the premium finance company sent the notice taking into consideration the number of days' notice required to complete the cancellation. The insurer must return unearned premiums and commissions to the insurance premium finance company no later than sixty days after the effective date of cancellation. (La. R.S. § 9:3550).

PERSONAL LINES
DWELLING FIRE

Louisiana Revised Statutes §§22:1265 and 22:1266

Louisiana makes no changes from the standard dwelling fire policy. However, recent changes in Louisiana law require that a thirty-day notice must be delivered or mailed to each mortgagee, pledgee, or other known person shown by the policy to have an interest in any loss which may occur. "Delivered" includes electronic transmittal, facsimile, or personal delivery. (La. R.S. § 22:1266).

HOMEOWNERS

Louisiana Revised Statutes §§22:887, 22:1265 and 22:1266

Cancellation during the Underwriting Period

Length of Underwriting Period: Sixty days. (La. R.S. § 22:887).

Length of Notice: Ten days for nonpayment; thirty days for all other reasons. When cancellation is based on an uncollectible negotiable instrument, the effective date of cancellation may be the date premium was due. (La. R.S. § 22:1266).

Reason for Cancellation: Must be provided upon written request within six months of the cancellation or nonrenewal. (La. R.S. § 22:1266).

LOUISIANA

Proof Required: First-class mail. The affidavit of the individual making or supervising such a mailing shall constitute prima facie evidence. Certified mail is required if cancellation is based on the insured's check or other negotiable instrument being uncollectible for any reason. (La. R.S. § 22:1266).

Cancellation after the Underwriting Period

Policies in force three years or less may be cancelled only for the following reasons:

1. Nonpayment. (La. R.S. § 22:1266).

2. Material misrepresentation on the application or at any time since the policy was issued. (La. R.S. § 22:1266).

3. Substantial change in the risk. (La. R.S. § 22:1266).

When the policy has been in effect and renewed for more than three years, the insurer may cancel or nonrenew only for the following reasons: (La. R.S. § 22:1265).

1. The named insured commits fraud with intent to deceive, at any time since the policy was issued. (La. R.S. § 22:1265).

2. There is a material change in the risk. (La. R.S. § 22:1265).

3. The named insured files two or more claims within a three-year period of time within the five years preceding the current policy renewal rate, that are not the result of an incident due entirely to the forces of nature and exclusively without human intervention. Statute specifies that the incident will be considered a claim when there has been a demand for payment by the insured under the terms of the policy. (La. R.S. § 22:1265).

4. The continuation of the policy endangers the insurer's solvency. (La. R.S. § 22:1265).

Length of Notice: Ten days for nonpayment; thirty days for all other allowable reasons. When cancellation is based on an uncollectible negotiable instrument, the effective date of cancellation may be the date premium was due. (La. R.S. § 22:1266).

Reason for Cancellation: Not required. (La. R.S. § 22:1266)

Proof Required: Proof of mailing. Certified mail is required if cancellation is based on the insured's check or other negotiable instrument being uncollectible for any reason. (La. R.S. § 22:1266).

LOUISIANA

Nonrenewal

Length of Notice: Thirty days.

Reason for Nonrenewal: Must be provided upon written request within six months of the cancellation or nonrenewal.

Proof Required: Proof of mailing. The affidavit of the individual making or supervising such a mailing shall constitute prima facie evidence.

Other Cancellation/Nonrenewal Provisions

1. Policies written for a period of more than one and up to three years may be cancelled on the anniversary date with a thirty-day notice. (La. R.S. § 22:1266).

2. When the policy has been in force for more than three years, nonrenewal is restricted to the same reasons allowed for cancellation. (La. R.S. § 22:1265).

3. An insurer may not cancel, nonrenew, or refuse to issue based solely on the fact that the insured (applicant) owns an All-Terrain Vehicle (ATV), but the ATV may be excluded from coverage. A thirty-day notice is required in the event of any rate increase, change in deductible, reduction in limits, or reduction in coverage. This provision does not apply for changes in a rate or plan that is filed with the state and applies to an entire class of business. (La. R.S. § 22:1265).

4. Written explanation of the reason for cancellation must be provided upon written request of the named insured. (La. R.S. § 22:1265).

5. A thirty-day notice must be delivered or mailed to each mortgagee, pledgee, or other known person shown by the policy to have an interest in any loss which may occur. "Delivered" includes electronic transmittal, facsimile, or personal delivery. (La. R.S. § 22:887).

6. Louisiana statutes specify that an incident shall be deemed a claim only when there is a demand for payment by the insured or the insured's representative under the terms of the policy. A report of a loss or a question relating to coverage shall not independently establish a claim. The phrase "two or more claims within a period of three years" shall not include any loss incurred or arising from an "Act of God" incident which is due directly to forces of nature and exclusively without human intervention. (La. R.S. § 22:1265).

7. When a cancellation is based on an uncollectible negotiable instrument, the cancellation notice must advise that the policy will be reinstated effective from the date the premium payment was due, if the insured provides a cashier's check or money order for the full

＃ LOUISIANA

amount of the returned check or other negotiable instrument within ten days of the date that the cancellation was mailed. (La. R.S. § 22:1266).

PERSONAL AUTO

Louisiana Revised Statutes §§22:1265 and 22:1266; 32:900

(Policies insuring four or fewer vehicles.)

Cancellation during the Underwriting Period

Length of Underwriting Period: Sixty days. (La. R.S. § 22:1266).

Length of Notice: Ten days for nonpayment; thirty days for any other reason. (La. R.S. § 22:1266).

Reason for Cancellation: Not required. (La. R.S. § 22:1266).

Proof Required: Proof of mailing. (La. R.S. § 22:1266).

Cancellation after the Underwriting Period

The policy may be cancelled **only** for the following reasons:

1. Nonpayment. (La. R.S. § 22:1266).

2. Suspension or revocation of the driver's license of:

    a. The named insured.
    b. Any driver who lives with the named insured or who customarily uses an insured auto.
    The suspension or revocation must occur during the policy period or within 180 days prior to the renewal date. (La. R.S. § 22:1266).

3. Fraud or material misrepresentation when making a claim. (La. R.S. § 22:1266).

Statute permits cancellation if the insurer does not receive an application after a valid binder has been issued. However, this reason is not available to insurers using ISO's PP 01 95. (La. R.S. § 22:1266).

Length of Notice: Ten days for nonpayment; thirty days for all other reasons. (La. R.S. § 22:1266).

Reason for Cancellation: Not required. (La. R.S. § 22:1266).

Proof Required: Certified mail; proof of mailing for nonpayment of premium. (La. R.S. § 22:1266).

LOUISIANA

Nonrenewal

Length of Notice: Twenty days. (La. R.S. § 22:1266).

Reason for Nonrenewal: Not required. (La. R.S. § 22:1266).

Proof Required: Certified mail (not required for nonpayment of premium). (La. R.S. § 22:1266).

Other Cancellation/Nonrenewal Provisions

A thirty-day notice is required in the event of any rate increase, change in deductible, reduction in limits, or reduction in coverage. This provision does not apply for changes in a rate or plan that is filed with the state and applies to an entire class of business.

Nonrenewal based solely on: 1) the insured's attained age, and 2) that the insured has submitted a single claim for damage to the auto is prohibited. A legitimate reason, such as physical or mental infirmity, is allowed. (La. R.S. § 22:1266).

An insurer and an insured may by written agreement exclude from coverage the named insured, the named insured's spouse, or any other named person who is a resident of the same household as the named insured at the time the written agreement is entered into. The exclusion is valid for the life of the policy and a new form is not required upon renewal, reinstatement, substitute, or amendment of policy. (La. R.S. § 32:900).

When a cancellation is based on an uncollectible negotiable instrument, the cancellation notice must advise that the policy will be reinstated effective from the date the premium payment was due, if the insured provides a cashier's check or money order for the full amount of the returned check or other negotiable instrument within ten days of the date that the cancellation was mailed. (La. R.S. § 22:1266).

PERSONAL UMBRELLA

Louisiana Revised Statutes §§22:1265 and 22:1266

Cancellation during the Underwriting Period

Length of Underwriting Period: Sixty days. (La. R.S. § 22:1266).

Length of Notice: Ten days for nonpayment; thirty days for any other reason. When cancellation is based on an uncollectible negotiable instrument, the effective date of cancellation may be the date premium was due. (La. R.S. § 22:1266).

Reason for Cancellation: Not required. (La. R.S. § 22:1266).

LOUISIANA

Proof Required: Proof of mailing. The affidavit of the individual making or supervising such a mailing shall constitute prima facie evidence. (La. R.S. § 22:1266).

Cancellation after the Underwriting Period

Length of Notice: Ten days for nonpayment; thirty days for any other reason. When cancellation is based on an uncollectible negotiable instrument, the effective date of cancellation may be the date premium was due. (La. R.S. § 22:1266).

Reason for Cancellation: Not required. (La. R.S. § 22:1266).

Proof Required: Proof of mailing. The affidavit of the individual making or supervising such a mailing shall constitute prima facie evidence. (La. R.S. § 22:1266).

Nonrenewal

Length of Notice: Thirty days. (La. R.S. § 22:1265).

Reason for Nonrenewal: Reason for notice is not required. (La. R.S. § 22:1265).

Proof Required: Proof of mailing. The affidavit of the individual making or supervising such a mailing shall constitute prima facie evidence. (La. R.S. § 22:1265).

Other Cancellation/Nonrenewal Provisions

When a cancellation is based on an uncollectible negotiable instrument, the cancellation notice must advise that the policy will be reinstated effective from the date the premium payment was due, if the insured provides a cashier's check or money order for the full amount of the returned check or other negotiable instrument within ten days of the date that the cancellation was mailed. (La. R.S. § 22:1266).

FRAUD

Louisiana Revised Statutes §§22:572.1; 22:1923; 22:1924; 22:1926

General Information and Definitions

A fraudulent insurance act is defined as acts or omissions committed by any person who, knowingly and with intent to defraud: (La. R.S. § 22:1923).

> Presents, causes to be presented, or prepares with knowledge or belief that it will be presented to an insurer, broker, or agent thereof any oral or written statement that he knows to contain materially false information as part of or in support of any fact material to an application for insurance, rating for any insurance policy, claim for

LOUISIANA

payment, premiums paid, payments made in accordance with terms of any policy, financial condition of any insurer, or reinsurer, acquisition of any insurer/reinsurer. Solicits or accepts new or renewal business for an insolvent insurer, removes or attempts to remove records from the home office of an insurer/reinsurer, diverts funds in connection with insurance transactions, conduction of insurance business, formation of insurance entities, supplies false documents to the Department of Insurance, or makes fraudulent proof of insurance documents. (La. R.S. § 22:1923).

Antifraud Provisions

Each authorized insurer and health maintenance organization shall prepare, implement, and maintain an insurance antifraud plan. The plan shall be filed with the commissioner and shall outline specific procedures, actions, and safeguards that are applicable, relevant, and appropriate to the type of insurance the insurer writes or the type of coverage offered by the health maintenance organization.

The plan will include how the insurer/organization will detect, investigate and prevent fraud, educate employees on fraud detection and the insurer/organization's antifraud plan, report a fraudulent insurance act as defined in Louisiana Revised Statutes §22:1923(1), to the Department of Insurance as well as appropriate loss enforcement, and pursue restitution for financial loss. The plan and any summary report must be filed with the commissioner by April first of each calendar year. The commissioner may choose to require the insurer to file a summary report at other intervals as well.

Reporting Requirements

Any person, company or other legal entity including but not limited to those engaged in the business of insurance, including agents, brokers, and adjusters, which believes that a fraudulent claim is being made, shall within sixty days of receipt of said notice send, on a form prescribed by the section on insurance fraud, the information requested and such additional information relative to the claim and the parties claiming loss or damage because of an occurrence or accident as the section may require. (La. R.S. § 22:1926).

The section of insurance fraud shall report any alleged violations of law which it investigates to the appropriate licensing agency, Insurance Fraud Division of the Office of State Police, the Insurance Fraud Division of the Department of Justice, and the prosecutorial authority having jurisdiction. (La. R.S. § 22:1926).

Penalties

Any person who commits an act of insurance fraud is guilty of a felony and shall be subject to a term of imprisonment, with or without hard labor, not to exceed five years, or a fine not to exceed $5,000 or both, on each count and payment of restitution to the victim company of any

LOUISIANA

payments to the defendant that the court determines was not owed and the costs incurred by the victim of evaluation, defense, investigation, attorney and court fees. (La. R.S. § 22:1924).

Application Fraud Statement

All applications for insurance and all claim forms must contain a statement that clearly states in substance the following: (La. R.S. § 22:1924).

> "Any person who knowingly presents a false or fraudulent claim for payment of a loss or benefit or knowingly presents false information in an application for insurance is guilty of a crime and may be subject to fines and confinement in prison."

FAIR CLAIMS PROCESSING

Louisiana Revised Statutes §§22:1892, 22:1811, 22:1821, and 22:1973

Payment of Claims

Insurers shall pay the amount of any claim, with the exception of death claims, due any insured within thirty days after receipt of satisfactory proof of loss from the insured or any party in interest. Insurers shall pay the amount of any death claim due within sixty days of receipt of proof of death. The producer of record shall be notified of any such payments. Third-party claimants shall be paid the same way. (La. R.S. § 22:1892 and § 22:1811).

Except in event of a catastrophic loss, the insurer shall initiate adjustment of property or injury claims within fourteen days after notification of loss by the claimant. In the case of catastrophic loss, initiation shall take place within thirty days from the notice of loss except that the commissioner may extend the required time for damages arising from a presidentially declared emergency or disaster or a gubernatorial declared emergency or disaster up to an additional thirty days. (La. R.S. § 22:1892).

Failure to make such payment within thirty days after receipt of satisfactory notice of loss or failure to make a written offer to settle any property damage claim, or failure to make such payment within thirty days after written agreement or settlement when such failure is found to be arbitrary, capricious, or without probable cause, shall subject the insurer to a penalty in addition to the amount of the loss of 50 percent damages on the amount found to be due from the insurer to the insured, or $1,000, whichever is greater, payable to the insured, as well as reasonable attorney fees and costs. The penalty does not apply to losses from fire when the loss was related to arson and the state fire marshal or other state/local investigative bodies have the loss under arson investigation. (La. R.S. § 22:1892).

Duty Owed

1. An insurer, including but not limited to a foreign line and surplus line insurer, owes to his insured a duty of good faith and fair dealing. The insurer has an affirmative duty to

LOUISIANA

adjust claims fairly and promptly and to make a reasonable effort to settle claims with the insured or the claimant, or both. Any insurer who breaches these duties shall be liable for any damages sustained as a result of the breach. (La. R.S. § 22:1973).

2. Any one of the following acts, if knowingly committed or performed by an insurer, constitutes a breach of the insurer's duties imposed in Subsection 1:

   a. Misrepresenting pertinent facts or insurance policy provisions relating to any coverages at issue. (La. R.S. § 22:1973).
   b. Failing to pay a settlement within thirty days after an agreement is reduced to writing. (La. R.S. § 22:1973).
   c. Denying coverage or attempting to settle a claim on the basis of an application which the insurer knows was altered without notice to, or knowledge or consent of, the insured. (La. R.S. § 22:1973).
   d. Misleading a claimant as to the applicable prescriptive period. (La. R.S. § 22:1973).
   e. Failing to pay the amount of any claim due any person insured by the contract within sixty days after receipt of satisfactory proof of loss from the claimant when such failure is arbitrary, capricious, or without probable cause. (La. R.S. § 22:1973).
   f. Failing to pay claims pursuant to Louisiana Revised Statutes §22:1893 (claims involving immovable property) when such failure is arbitrary, capricious, or without probable cause. (La. R.S. § 22:1973).

3. In addition to any general or special damages to which a claimant is entitled for breach of the imposed duty, the claimant may be awarded penalties assessed against the insurer in an amount not to exceed two times the damages sustained or five thousand dollars, whichever is greater. Such penalties, if awarded, shall not be used by the insurer in computing either past or prospective loss experience for the purpose of setting rates or making rate filings. (La. R.S. § 22:1973).

4. The provisions of this section shall not be applicable to claims made under health and accident insurance policies. (La. R.S. § 22:1973).

5. The Insurance Guaranty Association Fund, as provided in Louisiana Revised Statutes §22:2051 *et seq.*, shall not be liable for any special damages awarded under the provisions of this section. (La. R.S. § 22:1973).

MAINE

For details on cancellation procedures for the standard policy, refer to the Standard Policy section.

COMMERCIAL LINES
AGRICULTURAL CAPITAL ASSETS; BOP; C. AUTO; CRIME; CGL (CGL, EMPLOYMENT, LIQUOR, MARKET SEGMENTS, OCP, POLLUTION, PRODUCTS/COMPLETED OPS., RR PROT); CIM; C. PROP.; C. UMB.; EQUIPMENT BREAKDOWN; FARM; & PROFESSIONAL LIABILITY

Maine Revised Statutes, tit. 24-A, §§2908 and 3007

Cancellation during the Underwriting Period

Length of Underwriting Period: Sixty days.

Length of Notice: Ten days after receipt by the named insured for any reason.

Reason for Cancellation: Required on the notice.

Proof Required: A post office certificate of mailing is considered conclusive proof of receipt on the third calendar day after mailing.

Cancellation after the Underwriting Period

The policy may be cancelled **only** for the following reasons:

1. Nonpayment.

2. Fraud or material misrepresentation made by or with the knowledge of the named insured in obtaining the policy, continuing the policy, or in presenting a claim under the policy.

3. Substantial change in the risk increasing the risk of loss after insurance coverage has been issued or renewed. This includes without limitation an increase in exposure due to regulation, legislation, or court decision.

4. The insured's failure to comply with reasonable loss control measures.

5. Substantial breach of contractual duties, conditions, or warranties.

MAINE

6. Determination by the superintendent of insurance that the continuation of a class or block of business to which the policy belongs will jeopardize the insurer's solvency or will place the insurer in violation of the states' insurance laws.

These first five reasons for cancellation must be listed in all policies issued and in all renewals.

Length of Notice: Ten days after receipt by the named insured for any reason.

Reason for Cancellation: Required on the notice.

Proof Required: A post office certificate of mailing is considered conclusive proof of receipt on the third calendar day after mailing.

Nonrenewal

Length of Notice: Thirty days after receipt by the named insured.

Reason for Nonrenewal: Required on the notice.

Proof Required: A post office certificate of mailing is considered conclusive proof of receipt on the third calendar day after mailing.

Other Cancellation/Nonrenewal Provisions

Any insured who has received notice of an insurer's intent to cancel may request a hearing before the superintendent within forty-five days of the receipt of the notice. The burden of proof for the reason of cancellation shall be upon the insurer. The superintendent has the authority to order that the policy remain in effect.

On OCP policies all notices must be sent to the named insured and to any designated contractor. Although this is not a statutory requirement in Maine, it is a typical contractual requirement.

On railroad protective policies all notices must be sent to the named insured, any governmental authority, and to any contractor shown in the declarations. Although this is not a statutory requirement in Maine, it is a typical contractual requirement.

A thirty day notice is required if the insurer intends to renew the policy on less favorable terms to the named insured or at a higher rate. This provision does not apply to rate plans filed with the commissioner and applying to an entire class of business.

For policies providing automobile physical damage coverage, like notice of cancellation or nonrenewal must also be given to any party named in the loss payable clause. (24-A M.R.S.A. §2908(5)). See Bulletin 372 at https://www.maine.gov/pfr/insurance/legal/bulletins/pdf/372.pdf.

MAINE

COMMERCIAL GENERAL LIABILITY
(Underground Storage Tank Policy)

Maine Revised Statutes, tit. 24-A, §§2908

Cancellation during the Underwriting Period

Length of Underwriting Period: Sixty days.

Length of Notice: Maine statutes allow cancellation as soon as ten days after receipt of notice. If ISO Maine Changes-Cancellation and Nonrenewal (CG 30 24) is used, ten days after receipt by the named insured for nonpayment; sixty days after receipt by the named insured for all other reasons.

Reason for Cancellation: Required on the notice.

Proof Required: A post office certificate of mailing is considered conclusive proof of receipt on the third calendar day after mailing. If the insurer is using ISO forms, it must send notice by certified mail.

Cancellation after the Underwriting Period

The policy may be cancelled **only** for the following reasons:

1. Nonpayment.

2. Fraud or material misrepresentation made by or with the knowledge of the named insured in obtaining the policy, continuing the policy, or in presenting a claim under the policy.

3. Substantial change in the risk which increases the risk of loss after insurance coverage has been issued or renewed. Such a change may include an increase in exposure due to regulation, legislation, or court decision.

4. The named insured's failure to comply with reasonable loss control recommendations.

5. Substantial breach of contractual duties, conditions, or warranties.

6. Determination by the superintendent of insurance that the continuation of the class or block of business to which the policy belongs will jeopardize the insurer's solvency or will place it in violation of the laws of any state.

These first five reasons must be listed in all policies issued and in all policy renewals.

MAINE

Length of Notice: Ten days after receipt by the named insured for nonpayment; sixty days after receipt by the named insured for all other reasons if ISO Maine Changes – Cancellation and Nonrenewal endorsement used.

Reason for Cancellation: Required on the notice.

Proof Required: A post office certificate of mailing is considered conclusive proof of receipt on the third calendar day after mailing. If the insurer is using ISO forms, it must send notice by certified mail.

Nonrenewal

Length of Notice: Thirty days.

Reason for Nonrenewal: Not required unless the policy says otherwise.

Proof Required: A post office certificate of mailing is considered conclusive proof of receipt on the third calendar day after mailing. If the insurer is using the ISO forms, it must send notice by certified mail.

Other Cancellation/Nonrenewal Provisions

Any insured who has received notice of an insurer's intent to cancel may request a hearing before the superintendent within forty-five days of the receipt of the notice. The burden of proof for the reason of cancellation shall be upon the insurer. The superintendent has the authority to order that the policy remain in effect.

A thirty-day notice is required if the insurer intends to renew the policy on less favorable terms to the named insured or at a higher rate. This provision does not apply to rate plans filed with the superintendent and applying to an entire class of business.

DWELLING FIRE

(Applicable only to a one through four family dwelling not occupied in any part by the named insured.)

Maine Revised Statutes, tit. 24-A, §§3002, 3005, and 3007

Cancellation during the Underwriting Period

Length of Underwriting Period: Sixty days.

Length of Notice: Ten days after receipt by the named insured.

Reason for Cancellation: Required on the notice.

MAINE

Proof Required: A post office certificate of mailing is considered conclusive proof of receipt on the third calendar day after mailing.

Cancellation after the Underwriting Period

The policy may be cancelled **only** for the following reasons:

1. Nonpayment.

2. Fraud or material misrepresentation made by or with the knowledge of the named insured in obtaining the policy, continuing the policy, or presenting a claim under the policy.

3. Substantial change in the risk which increases the risk of loss after insurance coverage has been issued or renewed, including an increase in exposure due to regulation, legislation, or court decision.

4. Failure to comply with reasonable loss control recommendations.

5. Substantial breach of contractual duties, conditions, or warranties.

6. Determination by the superintendent that the continuation of a class or block of business to which the policy belongs will jeopardize a company's solvency or will place the insurer in violation of the insurance laws of Maine or any other state.

The first five reasons must be listed in all policies issued and in all policy renewals.

Length of Notice: Ten days after receipt by the named insured.

Reason for Cancellation: Required on the notice.

Proof Required: A post office certificate of mailing is considered conclusive proof of receipt on the third calendar day after mailing.

Nonrenewal

Length of Notice: Thirty days.

Reason for Nonrenewal: Not required.

Proof Required: A post office certificate of mailing is considered conclusive proof of receipt on the third calendar day after mailing.

MAINE

Other Cancellation/Nonrenewal Provisions

A thirty-day notice is required if the insurer intends to renew the policy on less favorable terms to the insured or at a higher rate. This provision does not apply to rate plans filed with the superintendent and applying to an entire class of business.

Maine statutes require that notice time frame is after receipt by the named insured.

WORKERS' COMPENSATION

Maine Revised Statutes, tit. 24-A §§2901, 2908, and 39-A §403(1)

Cancellation during the Underwriting Period

Length of Underwriting Period: Sixty days.

Length of Notice: Thirty days for any reason, and notice must be sent to the Workers Compensation Board as well as the named insured.

Reason for Cancellation: Required on the notice.

Proof Required: A post office certificate of mailing is conclusive proof of receipt on the third calendar day after mailing.

Cancellation after the Underwriting Period

The policy may be cancelled **only** for the following reasons:

1. Nonpayment.

2. Fraud or a material misrepresentation made by or with the knowledge of the named insured in obtaining the policy, continuing the policy, or presenting a claim under the policy.

3. Substantial change in the risk which increases risk of loss after insurance coverage has been issued or renewed, including, but not limited to, an increase in exposure due to rules, legislation, or court decision.

4. Failure of the insured to comply with reasonable loss control measures.

5. A substantial breach of contractual duties, conditions, or warranties under the policy.

MAINE

6. The superintendent has determined that the continuation of a class or block of business to which the policy belongs will jeopardize a company's solvency or will place the insurer in violation of the laws of Maine or any other state.

The first five reasons must be listed in all policies issued and in all policy renewals.

Length of Notice: Thirty days' notice must be sent to the Workers Compensation Board as well as the named insured.

Reason for Cancellation: Required on notice.

Proof Required: A post office certificate of mailing is conclusive proof of receipt on the third calendar day after mailing.

Nonrenewal

Length of Notice: Thirty days' notice must be sent to the Workers Compensation Board as well as the named insured.

Reason for Nonrenewal: Not required.

Proof Required: A post office certificate of mailing is conclusive proof of receipt on the third calendar day after mailing.

Other Cancellation/Nonrenewal Provisions

The Workers Compensation Board must be notified of all policy cancellations and nonrenewals.

A thirty-day notice is required if the insurer intends to renew the policy on less favorable terms to the named insured or at a higher rate. This provision does not apply to rate plans filed with the superintendent and applying to an entire class of business.

SURPLUS LINES

Maine Revised Statutes, tit. 24-A, §2009-A

Surplus lines insurers must send fourteen-day notices of cancellation and nonrenewal. When cancellation is for nonpayment of premium, a ten-day notice is required. A post office certificate of mailing is considered conclusive proof of notification on the fifth calendar day after mailing. Surplus lines coverage is not subject to the cancellation and nonrenewal terms described in sections 2908 or 3007. Personal lines dwelling fire (owner-occupied), and

MAINE

homeowners policies written by surplus lines insurers are subject to the requirements of the Maine Property Insurance Cancellation Control Act.

FINANCED PREMIUMS

Maine Revised Statutes, tit. 24-A, §§2908, 2912(3), 3007 and 3049.

Maine equates nonpayment to a finance company with nonpayment of premium.

PERSONAL LINES
DWELLING FIRE & HOMEOWNERS

Maine Revised Statutes, tit. 24-A, §§3048, 3049, 3050, 3051, 3055-A and 3057

(Applicable to policies that cover a one through four family dwelling used solely for residential purposes and occupied in whole or in part by the named insured.)

Cancellation during the Underwriting Period

Length of Underwriting Period: Ninety days or 120 days if the policy covers a secondary residence that is expected to be continuously unoccupied for three or more months in an annual period. Notice must be received by the named insured prior to the ninetieth day or 120th day.

Length of Notice: Ten days for nonpayment; twenty days for all other reasons.

Reason for Cancellation: Maine statutes do not require a reason to be shown for policies that have been in effect less than ninety or 120 days, however, a reason must be shown if the insurer has adopted ISO's amendatory endorsement (HO 01 18).

Proof Required: A post office certificate of mailing is considered conclusive proof of receipt on the fifth calendar day after mailing.

Cancellation after the Underwriting Period

The policy may be cancelled **only** for the following reasons:

1. Nonpayment of premium.

2. Conviction of the named insured of a crime having as one of its necessary elements an act increasing any hazard insured against.

3. Fraud or material misrepresentation by the insured or the insured's representative in obtaining the insurance, or by the named insured in pursuing a claim under the policy.

MAINE

4. Discovery of a failure to disclose a material fact in relation to the application for insurance that would, if known, substantially alter the terms of coverage.

   4-A. Violation of terms or conditions of the policy.

5. Discovery of negligent acts or omissions by the insured which substantially increase any hazard insured against.

6. Physical changes in the property that makes it uninsurable.

7. Vacancy of the property and custodial care is not maintained.

8. Presence of a trampoline if the insured is notified that the policy will be cancelled if the trampoline is not removed and the trampoline remains on the property thirty or more days after the date of notice.

9. Presence of a swimming pool that is not fenced, in accordance with the standards established in 22 M.R.S. §1631, if the pool remains in noncompliance with those standards for thirty days after notice by the insurer of the defective condition and intent to cancel.

10. A loss caused by a dog bite unless, after notice, the dog is removed.

11. Failure to comply with reasonable loss control recommendations within ninety days of notice.

Length of Notice: Ten days for nonpayment; twenty days for all other allowable reasons. Must include a notice of the named insureds right to apply for a hearing before the superintendent within thirty days.

Reason for Cancellation: Required on the notice.

Proof Required: A post office certificate of mailing is considered conclusive proof of receipt on the fifth calendar day after mailing.

Nonrenewal

Length of Notice: Thirty days. Must include a notice of the named insured's right to apply for a hearing before the superintendent within thirty days.

Reason for Nonrenewal: Required on the notice. The reason for nonrenewal must be a good faith reason and related to the insurability of the property, or a ground for cancellation

MAINE

under Section 3049, or a ground for nonrenewal under Section 3055-A. Grounds for cancellation under Section 3049 are listed above in items 1-11 If an insurer files a plan to discontinue business in a line of insurance, the superintendent may authorize the nonrenewal of policies in that line of business if there is similar coverage available in the admitted market. (24-A M.R.S.A §3055-A). The reason or reasons given must be explicit.

Proof Required: A post office certificate of mailing is considered conclusive proof of receipt on the third calendar day after mailing.

Other Cancellation/Nonrenewal Provisions

Any party named in a loss payable clause on the policy must receive like notice. A thirty-day notice is required if the insurer intends to renew the policy on less favorable terms to the named insured or at a higher rate. This provision does not apply to rate plans filed with the superintendent and applying to an entire class of business.

Age of a dwelling without consideration of its current condition may not be used as the sole basis of cancellation or nonrenewal.

Maine statutes specify that the notice time frame is after receipt by the named insured.

An insurance company may not refuse to issue a property insurance policy for the sole reason that the previous owner of the property submitted claims for losses to that property. (24-A M.R.S.A §3058).

An insurer may not refuse to issue or renew coverage the primary residence of a family child care provider unless denial of care is based solely on underwriting factors other than the use of the family property. (24-A M.R.S.A §3060).

PERSONAL AUTO

Maine Revised Statutes, tit, 24-A, §§2908, 2913, 2914, 2915, 2916, 2916-A, 2916-B, 2916-C and 2917

(Pertains to Four or Fewer Vehicles.)

Cancellation during the Underwriting Period

Length of Underwriting Period: Sixty days.

Length of Notice: Ten days for nonpayment; twenty days for any other reason.

Reason for Cancellation: Not required.

MAINE

Proof Required: A post office certificate of mailing is considered conclusive proof of the named insured's receipt on the fifth calendar day after mailing.

Cancellation after the Underwriting Period

The policy may be cancelled **only** for the following reasons:

1. Nonpayment.

2. Fraud or material misrepresentation that affects the policy or a claim under it.

3. Violation of the terms or conditions of the policy.

4. Suspension or revocation of the driver's license of:

    a. The named insured.

    b. Any driver who lives with the named insured or who customarily uses the insured auto.

    The suspension or revocation must occur during the policy period or during the 180 days prior to the policy's effective date if the policy is a renewal.

However, this provision does not apply with respect to:

1. A first or second suspension of an adult provisional driver's license resulting from a moving motor vehicle violation.

2. A first or second suspension of a juvenile provisional license resulting from a moving motor vehicle violation other than:

    a. A conviction for operating under the influence of intoxicants or with an excessive blood alcohol level.

    b. Operation of a motor vehicle with any amount of alcohol in the blood.

3. A suspension of the driver's license of a minor resulting from the illegal transportation of liquor in a motor vehicle.

Length of Notice: Ten days for nonpayment; twenty days for all other reasons. Must include a notice of the named insured's right to apply within thirty days for a hearing before the superintendent.

MAINE

Reason for Cancellation: Required on the notice. Even though ISO's amendatory endorsement (PP 01 75) is silent on this matter, the Maine insurance code specifies that the reason must be shown.

Proof Required: A post office certificate of mailing is considered conclusive proof of the named insured's receipt on the fifth calendar day after mailing.

Notice also must be given to any party mentioned in the loss payable clause if physical damage coverage is affected.

Nonrenewal

Length of Notice: Thirty days. Must include a notice of the insured's right to apply within thirty days for a hearing before the superintendent.

Reason for Nonrenewal: Specific reasons are required on the notice. The ISO amendatory endorsement (PP 01 75) is silent on this matter. However, the Maine insurance code specifies that the reason must be shown.

Proof Required: A post office certificate of mailing is considered conclusive proof of the named insured's receipt on the third calendar day after mailing.

Nonrenewal Provisions

Maine statutes permit nonrenewal for any of the cancellation reasons set forth in Section 2914, and for any of the following reasons:

1. If the named insured or any operator who resides in the same household or who customarily operates an insured vehicle is convicted of any of the following within thirty-six months prior to the policy yearly anniversary (this provision also applies to B and C below):

    a. Driving under the influence of alcohol or drugs.

    b. Vehicular homicide or assault, criminal negligence in use or operation of a motor vehicle resulting in the injury or death of another person, or use or operation of a motor vehicle directly or indirectly in the commission of a felony.

    c. Operating a vehicle at an excessive speed or in a reckless manner where injury or death results.

    d. Three or more violations for speeding or reckless operation.

MAINE

    e.   Operating a motor vehicle without a valid license or registration, or during a period of revocation or suspension of a license, or in violation of limitations set forth on the operator's license.

    f.   Operating a motor vehicle while attempting to avoid apprehension or arrest by a law enforcement officer.

    g.   Filing or attempting to file a false or fraudulent automobile insurance claim or knowingly abetting in the filing or attempted filing of any such claim.

    h.   Leaving the scene of an accident without reporting it.

    i.   Filing false documents with the Secretary of State or the Bureau of Motor Vehicles or using a license or registration obtained by filing a false document.

    j.   Operating a motor vehicle in a race or speed test.

    k.   Knowingly letting an unlicensed driver operate a vehicle insured under the policy.

2.   When a named insured or other person who operates a vehicle insured under the policy is individually or aggregately involved in two or more vehicle accidents while operating a motor vehicle insured under the policy, or under another policy issued by the same insurer for a motor vehicle in the same household, resulting in either bodily injury or death to a person or apparent property damage of the amount defined in 29-A M.R.S. § 2551 as a reportable accident.

3.   There is a material change in the type of motor vehicle which so substantially increases the hazard insured against as to render the vehicle uninsurable in accordance with the insurer's underwriting standards in effect at the time the policy was issued or last renewed; provided that if the vehicle is uninsurable for physical damages coverage only, the insurer shall offer to renew the policy without the physical damage coverages.

Other Cancellation/Nonrenewal Provisions

A thirty-day notice is required if the insurer intends to renew the policy on less favorable terms to the insured or at a higher rate. This provision does not apply to rate plans filed with the superintendent and applying to an entire class of business.

Effective ninety days after the end of the First Regular Session of the 128th Maine Legislature, the Legislature has amended 24-A M.R.S. § 2916 to prohibit insurers from refusing to issue, cancelling, nonrenewing, reducing liability limits, or increasing the premium solely because an applicant, a person to whom the policy has been issued or another insured driver has reached a certain age.

MAINE

Maine statutes specify that the notice time frame is after receipt by the named insured.

Individuals who present an unreasonable risk and whose continued inclusion provide grounds for cancellation or nonrenewal of the policy may be excluded from coverage upon mutual agreement between the insured and the named insured. (24-A M.R.S. §2916-B).

An insurer may choose not to renew policies if that insurer files a plan with the superintendent to discontinue business in that line of insurance but only if the insurer can demonstrate that there is substantially similar coverage in the market and only if the superintendent authorizes the insurer to do so.

Whenever a policy is cancelled for reasons other than nonpayment, the insured must be notified of the availability of the Maine Automobile Insurance Plan.

Whenever a policy is nonrenewed, or cancelled after the initial underwriting period, the named insured must be notified of the right to appeal the action to the superintendent of insurance within thirty days.

For policies providing automobile physical damage coverage, like notice of cancellation or nonrenewal must also be given to any party named in the loss payable clause (24-A M.R.S.A. §2908(5)).

PERSONAL UMBRELLA

Maine Revised Statutes, tit. §§24-A 2908

Cancellation during the Underwriting Period

Length of Underwriting Period: Sixty days.

Length of Notice: Ten days.

Reason for Cancellation: Not required.

Proof Required: A post office certificate of mailing is considered conclusive proof of receipt on the third calendar day after mailing.

Cancellation after the Underwriting Period

The policy may be cancelled **only** for the following reasons:

1. Nonpayment.

MAINE

2. Fraud or material misrepresentation made by or with the knowledge of the named insured in obtaining the policy, continuing the policy or in presenting a claim under the policy.

3. Substantial change in the risk which increases the risk of loss after insurance coverage has been issued or renewed, including, but not limited to, an increase in exposure due to rules, legislation or court decision.

4. Failure to comply with reasonable loss control recommendations.

5. Substantial breach of contractual duties, conditions or warranties.

6. Determination by the superintendent that the continuation of a class or block of business to which the policy belongs will jeopardize a company's solvency or will place the insurer in violation of the insurance laws of Maine or any other state.

The first five reasons must be listed in all policies issued and in all policy renewals.

Length of Notice: Ten days for any reason.

Reason for Cancellation: The notice must state the effective date of and the reason or reasons for cancellation.

Proof Required: A post office certificate of mailing is considered conclusive proof of receipt on the third calendar day after mailing.

Nonrenewal

Length of Notice: Thirty days.

Reason for Nonrenewal: Not required.

Proof Required: A post office certificate of mailing is considered conclusive proof of receipt on the third calendar day after mailing.

FRAUD

Maine Revised Statutes, tit. 24-A §2186

Definition

A fraudulent insurance act is defined as any of the following acts or omissions when committed knowingly and with intent to defraud:

MAINE

1. Presenting, causing to be presented, or preparing any information containing false information as to a material fact with knowledge or belief that the information will be presented on or behalf of an insured, claimant, or applicant to an insurer concerning an application, rating of a policy, a claim for payment, payments made in accordance with a policy or premiums paid.

2. Presenting false information to an insurer or insurance producer concerning a document filed with an insurance regulatory officer.

3. Presenting false information concerning the formation, acquisition, merger of one or more lines of insurance in this state by an insurer.

4. Soliciting or accepting new or renewal insurance risks on behalf of an insurer or other person engaged in the business of insurance by a person who knows or should know that the insurer or other person responsible for the risk is insolvent at the time of the transaction.

5. Removing, concealing, altering or destroying the assets or records of an insurer or other person engaged in the business of insurance or other person engaged in the business of insurance.

6. Embezzling, purloining or converting money, funds, premiums, credits or other property of an insurer or other person engaged in the business of insurance.

7. Transacting the business of insurance in violation of laws requiring a license, certificate of authority, or other legal authority.

8. Attempting to commit, aiding or abetting in the commission of, or conspiring to commit any of these acts.

Reporting

Insurers are to file a fraud report annually to the superintendent on or before March 1, listing acts the insurer knew or reasonably believed to have been committed during the previous year.

Antifraud Plan

Insurers are to prepare and implement an antifraud plan. The plan must outline procedures to prevent, detect and investigate insurance fraud, educate appropriate employees on the plan and fraud detection, provide for the hiring of fraud investigators, report insurance fraud to law enforcement and regulatory authorities in the investigation and prosecution of fraud.

MAINE

Penalties

Any violation of this section is subject to civil penalties and other remedies as provided in 24-A M.R.S.A. §12-A.

Application Fraud Statement

All applications and claim forms for insurance must contain the following statement or a substantially similar statement:

> "It is a crime to knowingly provide false, incomplete or misleading information to an insurance company for the purpose of defrauding the company. Penalties may include imprisonment, fines or a denial of insurance benefits."

UNFAIR CLAIMS PRACTICES
24-A M.R.S.A. §2164-D

It is an unfair claims practice for any insurer doing business in Maine to commit any unfair claims practice if it has been committed in conscious disregard of the statute or it has been committed with a frequency that indicates it is a general business practice to participate in that type of conduct.

An unfair claims practice consists of any of the following:

1. Knowingly misrepresenting to claimants and insureds relevant facts or policy provisions related to coverages at issue.

2. Failing to acknowledge with reasonable promptness pertinent written communications with respect to claims arising under its policies.

3. Failing to adopt and implement reasonable standards for the prompt investigation and settlement of claims arising under its policies.

4. Failing to develop and maintain documented claim files supporting decisions made regarding liability.

5. Refusing to pay claims without conducting a reasonable investigation.

6. Failing to affirm coverage or deny coverage, reserving any appropriate defenses, within a reasonable time after having completed its investigation related to a claim.

7. Attempting to settle or settling claims on the basis of an application that was materially altered without notice to, or knowledge or consent of, the insured.

MAINE

8. Making claim payments to an insured or beneficiary without indicating the coverage under which each payment is being made.

9. Unreasonably delaying the investigation or payment of claims by requiring both a formal proof of loss and subsequent verification when subsequent verification would result in duplication of information appearing in the formal proof of loss.

10. Failing, in the case of claims denials or offers of compromise settlement, to promptly provide an accurate written explanation of the basis for those actions.

11. Failing to provide forms, accompanied by reasonable explanations for their use, necessary to present claims within fifteen calendar days of such a request. This paragraph does not apply when there is an extraordinary loss or series of losses resulting from a catastrophe as determined by the superintendent.

12. Failing to adopt and implement reasonable standards to ensure that the repairs of a repairer owned by or required to be used by the insurer are performed in a professional manner.

    It is an unfair claims practice for any insurer in Maine to compel their insured to seek lawsuits to recover amounts due under its policies by offering substantially less than the amounts recovered in suits brought by them with a frequency to indicate a general business practice. This does not apply when an insurer has a reasonable basis to dispute the amount of damages, the extent of injuries claimed, or their liability.

    It is an unfair claims practice for an insurer practicing in Maine to not act in good faith to resolve claims without good cause and with a frequency to indicate a good business practice.

MARYLAND

For details on cancellation procedures for the standard policy, refer to the Standard Policy section.

COMMERCIAL LINES

BINDERS

Md. INSURANCE Code Ann. §12-106

This section applies only to a binder. An insurer may cancel a binder or policy during the underwriting period if the risk does not meet the underwriting standards of the insurer. A notice of cancellation applicable to a binder shall:

1. Be in writing.

2. Have an effective date of not less than:

    a. Fifteen days after mailing for underwriting reasons.
    b. Ten days after mailing for nonpayment.

3. State clearly and specifically the insurer's actual reason for the cancellation.

4. Be sent by a first-class mail tracking method to the named insured's last known address.

When an insurer issues a binder or policy it must also provide written notice of its ability to cancel the binder or policy during the underwriting period with a fifteen-day notice, stating the actual reason for the action. Lienholders and mortgage holders must receive written notice at least fifteen days before the effective date of cancellation. Binders must be replaced by a policy within forty-five days unless cancelled.

BOP; CAPITAL ASSETS; COMMERCIAL AUTO; CGL (All Except RR Prot. & Underground Storage Tanks); CRIME; CIM; C. PROP.; FARM; & PROF. LIAB.

Md. INSURANCE Code Ann. §§12-106; 27-603 and 27-605

Cancellation during the Underwriting Period

Length of Underwriting Period: Forty-five days.

Length of Notice: Ten days for nonpayment; fifteen days for any other reason.

MARYLAND

Reason for Cancellation: Must state clearly and specifically the actual reason for cancellation.

Proof Required: Must be sent to the insured's last known address by a first-class mail tracking method which requires a certificate of mail and an electronic mail tracking system used by the United States Postal Service. A certificate of bulk mailing does not fulfill the requirements.

Cancellation after the Underwriting Period

A policy may not be cancelled midterm except for the following reasons:

1. Nonpayment.

2. Material misrepresentation or fraud in connection with the application, policy, or presentation of a claim.

3. A matter or issue that constitutes a threat to public safety.

4. A change in the condition of the risk that increases the hazard insured against.

5. Due to the revocation or suspension of the driver's license or motor vehicle registration of the named insured or covered driver, or due to driving record related reasons.

Length of Notice: Ten days for nonpayment; forty-five days for any other reason.

Reason for Cancellation: Must state clearly and specifically the actual reason for cancellation if for any reason other than nonpayment of premium.

Proof Required: Must be sent to the insured's last known address by a first-class mail tracking method which requires a certificate of mail and an electronic mail tracking system used by the United States Postal Service. A certificate of bulk mailing does not fulfill the requirements.

Nonrenewal

Length of Notice: Forty-five days.

Reason for Nonrenewal: Must state clearly and specifically the actual reason for nonrenewal.

Proof Required: Must be sent to the insured's last known address via a first-class mail tracking method, which includes a certificate of mail and an electronic mail tracking system used by the United States Postal Service. A certificate of bulk mailing does not fulfill the requirements.

MARYLAND

Other Cancellation/Nonrenewal Provisions

On OCP policies all notices must be sent to the first named insured and the contractor shown in the declarations.

A forty-five day written notice is required (on policies other than automobile) if the renewal premium will increase by 20 percent or more unless the increase results from: an increase in the units of exposure, the application of an experience rating plan or a retrospective rating plan, a premium audit done in accordance with the policy terms, a change made by the insured that increases exposure to the risk, a request made by the insured to change coverage. (MD Code, Ins. §27-608; Md. Code Regs. 31.15.13.02). Currently, this notice is required to be sent by first class mail. If proposed legislation (2015 MD S.B. 434(NS) and 2015 MD H.B. 699(NS)) is enacted, then it will also be acceptable to send this notice electronically.

If an insurer provides a renewal policy and notice of premium due to an insured at least forty-five days before the renewal date of the policy and the insured fails to make the required payment by the renewal date, the insurer may terminate the policy on the renewal date for nonpayment of premium after sending to the insured, by certificate of mail, a written offer to reinstate the renewal policy without lapse in coverage. An offer to reinstate shall provide not less than ten days for the insured to make the required premium payment.

Exempt commercial policyholders do not need forty-five days' notice if the policy requires thirty days' notice. An exempt commercial policy holder is one that pays a total of $25,000 a year or more in total commercial premiums and meets any two of the following criteria: generates annual revenues or sales in excess of $10 million; possesses a net worth in excess of $5 million; employs at least twenty-five full-time employees; is a nonprofit or public body with an annual budget of at least $10 million; or is a municipal corporation with a population of at least 15,000. (MD Code, Ins. §§27-608 and 11-206(j)).

Insurers issuing a cancellation or nonrenewal notice must advise the insured of the possible right to replace the insurance under the Maryland Property Insurance Availability Act or through another plan for which the insured may be eligible.

An insurer may not refuse to issue or renew a contract of property insurance solely because the subject of the risk or the applicant's or insured's address is located in a certain geographic area of the state unless both:

1. At least sixty days before the refusal, the insurer has filed with the commissioner a written statement designating the geographic area.

2. The designation has an objective basis and is not arbitrary or unreasonable. (MD Code, Ins. §19-107).

MARYLAND

COMMERCIAL AUTO; & C. UMB.

Md. INSURANCE Code Ann. §§12-106, 19-107, 27-609, 27-613

Cancellation during the Underwriting Period

Length of Underwriting Period: Forty-five days.

Length of Notice: Ten days for nonpayment; fifteen days for any other reason.

Reason for Cancellation: The insurer's statement of actual reason for cancellation or nonrenewal must be clear and specific and include a brief statement of the basis for the action, including, at a minimum:

1. If the action of the insurer is due wholly or partly to an accident:

    a. The name of the driver.
    b. The date of the accident.
    c. If fault is a material factor for the insurer's action, a statement that the driver was at fault.

2. If the action of the insurer is due wholly or partly to a violation of the Maryland Vehicle Law or the vehicle laws of another state or territory of the United States:

    a. The name of the driver.
    b. The date of the violation.
    c. A description of the violation.

3. If the action of the insurer is due wholly or partly to the claims history of an insured, a description of each claim.

4. Whether the insurer's action is based on a violation of law, policy terms or conditions, or the insurer's underwriting standards.

5. Whether the insurer's action is based on a material misrepresentation.

6. Any other information that is the basis for the insurer's action.

Proof Required: Must be sent to the insured's last known address via a first-class mail tracking method, which requires a certificate of mail and an electronic mail tracking system used by the United States Postal Service. A certificate of bulk mailing does not fulfill the requirements.

MARYLAND

Cancellation after the Underwriting Period

The policy may be cancelled **only** for the following reasons:

1. Nonpayment.

2. Revocation or suspension of the driver's license of the named insured.

3. Revocation or suspension of the driver's license of any covered driver on the policy.

    Such revocation or suspension must have occurred during the policy period. The insurer must first offer to exclude such a driver, with such exclusion resulting in coverage for other drivers being continued.

4. Material misrepresentation or fraud in connection with the application, policy, or presentation of a claim.

5. Matter or issue related to the risk that constitutes a threat to public safety.

6. Change in condition of the risk that results in an increase in the hazard insured against.

Length of Notice: Ten days for nonpayment; forty-five days for any other reason.

Reason for Cancellation: Must state clearly and specifically the actual reason for cancellation.

Proof Required: Must be sent to the insured's last known address by a first-class mail tracking method which requires a certificate of mail and an electronic mail tracking system used by the United States Postal Service. A certificate of bulk mailing does not fulfill the requirements.

Nonrenewal

Length of Notice: Forty-five days.

Reason for Nonrenewal: Must state clearly and specifically the actual reason for nonrenewal.

Proof Required: Must be sent to the insured's last known address by a first-class mail tracking method which requires a certificate of mail and an electronic mail tracking system used by the United States Postal Service. A certificate of bulk mailing does not fulfill the requirements.

Other Cancellation/Nonrenewal Provisions

Maryland makes no statutory distinction between personal and commercial auto insurance. Mandatory endorsement forms for personal auto policies from ISO however, all provide that

MARYLAND

personal auto policies exclude commercial activity from coverage including, but not limited to livery or transport, the business of selling, repairing, or servicing, or delivery of newspaper, postal, or food delivery.

The insurer shall notify the insured of the possible right to replace the insurance under the Maryland Property Insurance Availability Act, through the Maryland Automobile Insurance Fund, or through another plan for which the insured may be eligible.

If an insurer is allowed to cancel, nonrenew, or increase the premiums on a policy of automobile liability insurance because of the claim experience or driving record of one or more but less than all of the individuals insured under the policy, the insurer, instead of cancellation, nonrenewal, or premium increase, is required to offer to continue or renew the insurance, but to exclude all coverage when a motor vehicle is operated by the specifically named excluded individual or individuals whose claim experience or driving record could have justified the cancellation, nonrenewal, or premium increase.

If an insurer legally could refuse to issue a policy of automobile liability insurance under which more than one individual is insured because of the claim experience or driving record of one or more but less than all of the individuals applying to be insured under the policy, the insurer may issue the policy but exclude all coverage when a motor vehicle is operated by the specifically named excluded individual or individuals whose claim experience or driving record could have justified the refusal to issue. (MD Code, Ins. §27-609).

An insurer may not refuse to issue or renew a contract of motor vehicle insurance solely because the subject of the risk or the applicant's or insured's address is located in a certain geographic area of the state unless:

1. At least sixty days before the refusal, the insurer has filed with the commissioner a written statement designating the geographic area.

2. The designation has an objective basis and is not arbitrary or unreasonable.

COMMERCIAL GENERAL LIABILITY

(Railroad Protective)

Md. INSURANCE Code Ann. §§12-106, 27-603, 27-605, and 27-608.

Cancellation during the Underwriting Period

Length of Underwriting Period: Forty-five days.

Length of Notice: Ten days for nonpayment; fifteen days for any other reason.

MARYLAND

Reason for Cancellation: Must state clearly and specifically the actual reason for cancellation.

Proof Required: Must be sent to the insured's last known address by a first-class mail tracking method which requires a certificate of mail and an electronic mail tracking system used by the United States Postal Service. A certificate of bulk mailing does not fulfill the requirements.

Cancellation after the Underwriting Period

A policy may not be cancelled midterm except for the following reasons:

1. Nonpayment.

2. Material misrepresentation or fraud in connection with the application, policy, or presentation of a claim.

3. A matter or issue that constitutes a threat to public safety.

4. A change in the condition of the risk that increases the hazard insured against.

5. Due to the revocation or suspension of the driver's license or motor vehicle registration of the named insured or covered driver due to driving record related reasons.

Length of Notice: Ten days for nonpayment; forty-five days for any other reason.

Reason for Cancellation: Must state clearly and specifically the actual reason for cancellation.

Proof Required: Must be sent to the insured's last known address by a first-class mail tracking method which requires a certificate of mail and an electronic mail tracking system used by the United States Postal Service. A certificate of bulk mailing does not fulfill the requirements.

Nonrenewal

Length of Notice: Forty-five days.

Reason for Nonrenewal: Must state clearly and specifically the actual reason for nonrenewal.

Proof Required: Must be sent to the insured's last known address by a first-class mail tracking method which requires a certificate of mail and an electronic mail tracking system used by the United States Postal Service. A certificate of bulk mailing does not fulfill the requirements.

MARYLAND

Other Cancellation/Nonrenewal Provisions

All notices must also be sent to the contractor and any involved governmental authority. (ISO Form CG 29 70).

A forty-five day written notice is required (on policies other than automobile) if the renewal premium will increase by 20 percent or more.

COMMERCIAL GENERAL LIABILITY (UNDERGROUND STORAGE TANKS)

Md. INSURANCE Code Ann. §§12-106, 27-603, and 27-605

Cancellation during the Underwriting Period

Length of Underwriting Period: Forty-five days.

Length of Notice: Ten days for nonpayment; forty-five days for misrepresentation; sixty days for any other reason. The Maryland code does not indicate the sixty-day requirement for cancellation due to other reasons. However, if an insurer has adopted ISO's amendatory endorsement (CG 30 37), it must give the sixty-day notice.

Reason for Cancellation: Must state clearly and specifically the actual reason for cancellation.

Proof Required: Must be sent to the insured's last known address by a first-class mail tracking method which requires a certificate of mail and an electronic mail tracking system used by the United States Postal Service. A certificate of bulk mailing does not fulfill the requirements.

Cancellation after the Underwriting Period

A policy may not be cancelled midterm except for the following reasons:

1. Nonpayment.

2. Material misrepresentation or fraud in connection with the application, policy, or presentation of a claim.

3. A matter or issue that constitutes a threat to public safety.

4. A change in the condition of the risk that increases the hazard insured against.

Length of Notice: Ten days for nonpayment; forty-five days for material misrepresentation; sixty days for any other reason. The Maryland code does not indicate the sixty-day requirement

MARYLAND

for cancellation due to other reasons. However, if an insurer has adopted the ISO amendatory endorsement (CG 30 37), it must give the sixty-day notice.

Reason for Cancellation: Must state clearly and specifically the actual reason for cancellation.

Proof Required: Must be sent to the insured's last known address by a first-class mail tracking method which requires a certificate of mail and an electronic mail tracking system used by the United States Postal Service. A certificate of bulk mailing does not fulfill the requirements.

Nonrenewal

Length of Notice: Forty-five days.

Reason for Nonrenewal: Must state clearly and specifically the actual reason for nonrenewal.

Proof Required: Must be sent to the insured's last known address by a first-class mail tracking method which requires a certificate of mail and an electronic mail tracking system used by the United States Postal Service. A certificate of bulk mailing does not fulfill the requirements.

Other Cancellation/Nonrenewal Provisions

A forty-five day written notice is required (on policies other than automobile) if the renewal premium will increase by 20 percent or more.

EQUIPMENT BREAKDOWN

Md. INSURANCE Code Ann. §§12-106, 27-603, and 27-605

Cancellation during the Underwriting Period

Length of Underwriting Period: Forty-five days.

Length of Notice: Ten days for nonpayment; fifteen days for any other reason.

Reason for Cancellation: Must state clearly and specifically the actual reason for cancellation.

Proof Required: Must be sent to the insured's last known address by a first-class mail tracking method which requires a certificate of mail and an electronic mail tracking system used by the United States Postal Service. A certificate of bulk mailing does not fulfill the requirements.

Cancellation after the Underwriting Period

A policy may not be cancelled midterm except for the following reasons:

1. Nonpayment.

MARYLAND

2. Material misrepresentation or fraud in connection with the application, policy, or presentation of a claim.

3. A matter or issue that constitutes a threat to public safety.

4. A change in the condition of the risk that increases the hazard insured against.

5. Due to the revocation or suspension of the driver's license or motor vehicle registration of the named insured or covered driver due to driving record related reasons.

Length of Notice: Ten days for nonpayment; forty-five days for any other reason.

Reason for Cancellation: Must state clearly and specifically the actual reason for cancellation.

Proof Required: Must be sent to the insured's last known address by a first-class mail tracking method which requires a certificate of mail and an electronic mail tracking system used by the United States Postal Service. A certificate of bulk mailing does not fulfill the requirements.

Nonrenewal

Length of Notice: Forty-five days.

Reason for Nonrenewal: Must state clearly and specifically the actual reason for nonrenewal.

Proof Required: Must be sent to the insured's last known address by a first-class mail tracking method which requires a certificate of mail and an electronic mail tracking system used by the United States Postal Service. A certificate of bulk mailing does not fulfill the requirements.

Other Cancellation/Nonrenewal Provisions

If an insurer provides a renewal policy and notice of premium due to an insured at least forty-five days before the renewal date of the policy and the insured fails to make the required payment by the renewal date, the insurer may terminate the policy on the renewal date for nonpayment of premium after sending to the insured, by certificate of mail, a written offer to reinstate the renewal policy without lapse in coverage. An offer to reinstate shall provide not less than ten days for the insured to make the required premium payment.

The insurer shall notify the insured of the possible right to replace the insurance under the Maryland Property Insurance Availability Act, through the Maryland Automobile Insurance Fund, or through another plan for which the insured may be eligible.

MARYLAND

WORKERS COMPENSATION

Md. INSURANCE Code Ann. §19-406(Amended by 2015 Maryland Laws Ch. 88 (H.B. 358), which will take effect January 1, 2016)

Length of Notice: Ten days for nonpayment; thirty days for any other reason until January 1, 2016. Forty-five days for any other reason after January 1, 2016. Nonrenewal requires a thirty day notice until January 1, 2016, and a forty-five day notice after January 1, 2016.

Reason for Action: The actual reason for cancellation must be stated.

Proof Required: Nonpayment requires certificate of mailing; any other termination requires certified mail or personal service.

A copy of the notice must be filed with the State Workers Compensation Commission's designee.

Even though the NCCI Cancellation and Nonrenewal Endorsement, WC 19 06 01 C, is silent on the matter—implying that the reason does not have to be shown—the Maryland Insurance Code Section §19-406 requires the notice to include the insurer's actual reason for the cancellation or nonrenewal of the policy.

SURPLUS LINES

The Maryland cancellation and nonrenewal laws do not apply to surplus lines. (*Smith v. Underwriters at Lloyd's of London*, 326 Md. 600, 606 A.2d 273 (1992)).

FINANCED PREMIUMS

Md. INSURANCE Code Ann. §§23-401 through 23-406 and Md. Code Regs. 31.16.05.01.

The insurer must send the insured a ten-day notice of its intent to cancel due to nonpayment. If the insured fails to make payment within that ten-day period, then the finance company mails the notice of cancellation to the insurer and the cancellation is processed as of the finance company's original default date. If the insurer receives the notice from the premium finance company within thirty days of the requested date, that date is to be used. If the insurer receives the notice more than thirty days after the effective date, the policy is cancelled as of the date the insurer receives the notice.

An insurer may not honor a cancellation request by a premium finance company unless it is accompanied by a signed power of attorney or other valid authority to cancel the insurance, or unless a signed authority to cancel has been previously submitted to the insurer.

With respect to commercial automobile, fire, or liability insurance, the insured may request that notice be sent by personal delivery, first-class mail, electronic mail, or facsimile

MARYLAND

transmission. The insurer must adhere to this request. Return of the policy is not required. Pro rata return of the gross unearned premiums is required within forty-five days of: receipt by the insurer of a notice from the premium finance company; the date the insurer cancels; or completion of any payroll audit necessary to determine the earned amount.

PERSONAL LINES BINDERS

Md. INSURANCE Code Ann. §12-106

This section applies only to a binder. An insurer may cancel a binder or policy during the underwriting period if the risk does not meet the underwriting standards of the insurer. A notice of cancellation applicable to a binder shall:

1. Be in writing.

2. Have an effective date of not less than:

    a. Fifteen days for underwriting reasons.
    b. Ten days for nonpayment.

3. State clearly and specifically the insurer's actual reason for the cancellation.

4. Must be sent to the insureds last known address by a first-class mail tracking method which requires a certificate of mail and an electronic mail tracking system used by the United States Postal Service. A certificate of bulk mailing does not fulfill the requirements.

When an insurer issues a binder or policy it must also provide written notice of its ability to cancel the binder or policy during the underwriting period with a fifteen-day notice, stating the actual reason for the action. Lienholders and mortgage holders must receive written notice at least fifteen days before the effective date of cancellation. Binders must be replaced by a policy within forty-five days unless cancelled.

DWELLING FIRE & HOMEOWNERS

Code of Maryland §§12-106; 27-602 and 27-607, Proposed legislation (2015 Maryland House Bill No. 647)

Cancellation during the Underwriting Period

Length of Underwriting Period: Forty-five days.

Length of Notice: Ten days for nonpayment; fifteen days for any other reason.

MARYLAND

Reason for Cancellation: Must state clearly and specifically the actual reason for cancellation.

Proof Required: Must be sent to the named insured's last known address by a first-class mail tracking method which requires a certificate of mail and an electronic mail tracking system used by the United States Postal Service. A certificate of bulk mailing does not fulfill the requirements.

Cancellation after the Underwriting Period

The policy may be cancelled **only** for the following reasons:

1. Nonpayment.

2. Material misrepresentation on the application.

3. Substantial change in the risk.

4. Matter or issue related to the risk that constitutes a threat to public safety.

Maryland statutes also permit cancellation for a conviction:

1. Within the preceding five year period, of arson.

2. Within the preceding three year period, of a crime which directly increases the hazard insured against. (MD Code, Ins. §27-501).

However, insurers who use ISO's amendatory endorsements (DP 01 19 & HO 01 19) are prohibited from using these reasons.

Length of Notice: Ten days for nonpayment; forty-five days for all other allowable reasons.

Reason for Cancellation: Required on the notice. Statute requires that the reason be clear and specific.

Proof Required: Must be sent to the insured's last known address by a first-class mail tracking method which requires a certificate of mail and an electronic mail tracking system used by the United States Postal Service. A certificate of bulk mailing does not fulfill the requirements.

Nonrenewal

Length of Notice: Forty-five days.

Reason for Nonrenewal: Must state clearly and specifically the actual reason for nonrenewal.

MARYLAND

Proof Required: Must be sent to the insured's last known address by a first-class mail tracking method which requires a certificate of mail and an electronic mail tracking system used by the United States Postal Service. A certificate of bulk mailing does not fulfill the requirements.

Other Cancellation/Nonrenewal Provisions

1. If the policy is written for a period of more than one year, the insurer may cancel on the anniversary date with a forty-five day written notice.

2. A notice of cancellation must include the current address and phone number of the Maryland Property Insurance Availability Fund.

3. An insurer may not refuse to issue or renew a contract of property insurance solely because the subject of the risk or the applicant's or insured's address is located in a certain geographic area of the State unless:

    a. At least sixty days before the refusal, the insurer has filed with the commissioner a written statement designating the geographic area.

    b. The designation has an objective basis and is not arbitrary or unreasonable.

4. A binder must be issued or cancelled within forty-five days. If cancelled, the cancellation must be in writing.

5. The name and address of a mortgage holder must be listed on a binder. If the binder is cancelled, the mortgage holder must be given at least fifteen days advance notice.

6. Maryland statutes prohibit:

    a. Underwriting based on claims that occurred more than three years before the effective date of a new or renewal policy.

    b. Underwriting based on credit information that occurred more than five years before the effective date of a new or renewal policy.

    c. Use of credit information in determining a particular payment plan.

A forty-five day written notice is required (by first-class mail) stating both the amount of the renewal policy premium and the amount of the expiring policy premium.

MARYLAND

PERSONAL AUTO

Md. INSURANCE Code Ann. §§12-106; 27-602, 27-604, 27-609 and 27-613

Cancellation during the Underwriting Period

Length of Underwriting Period: Forty-five days.

Length of Notice: Ten days for nonpayment; fifteen days for any other reason.

Reason for Cancellation: Must state clearly and specifically the actual reason for cancellation.

Even though ISO's amendatory endorsement (PP 01 68) is silent on the matter—implying that the reason does not have to be shown—the Maryland Insurance Code requires the reason to be stated on all cancellation notices.

Proof Required: Must be sent to the insured's last known address by a first-class mail tracking method which requires a certificate of mail and an electronic mail tracking system used by the United States Postal Service. A certificate of bulk mailing does not fulfill the requirements.

Cancellation after the Underwriting Period

The policy may be cancelled **only** for the following reasons:

1. Nonpayment.

2. Revocation or suspension of the driver's license of the named insured.

3. Revocation or suspension of the driver's license of any driver who lives with the named insured or customarily uses the named insured's auto.

    Such revocation or suspension must have occurred during the policy period or since the last anniversary of the original effective date if the policy period is other than one year. The insurer must offer to continue the policy excluding such a driver.

4. Material misrepresentation on the application.

5. A matter or issue that constitutes a threat to public safety.

6. A change in the condition of the risk that increases the hazard insured against.

Length of Notice: Ten days for nonpayment; forty-five days for all other reasons.

MARYLAND

Reason for Cancellation: The insurer's statement of actual reason for cancellation or nonrenewal must be clear and specific and include a brief statement of the basis for the action, including, at a minimum:

1. If the action of the insurer is due wholly or partly to an accident:

    a. The name of the driver.
    b. The date of the accident.
    c. If fault is a material factor for the insurer's action, a statement that the driver was at fault.

2. If the action of the insurer is due wholly or partly to a violation of the Maryland Vehicle Law or the vehicle laws of another state or territory of the United States:

    a. The name of the driver.
    b. The date of the violation.
    c. A description of the violation.

3. If the action of the insurer is due wholly or partly to the claims history of an insured, a description of each claim.

4. Whether the insurer's action is based on a violation of law, policy terms or conditions, or the insurer's underwriting standards.

5. Whether the insurer's action is based on a material misrepresentation.

6. Any other information that is the basis for the insurer's action.

Proof Required: Must be sent to the insured's last known address by a first-class mail tracking method which requires a certificate of mail and an electronic mail tracking system used by the United States Postal Service. A certificate of bulk mailing does not fulfill the requirements.

Nonrenewal

Length of Notice: Forty-five days.

Reason for Nonrenewal: Must state clearly and specifically the actual reason for nonrenewal.

Proof Required: Must be sent to the insured's last known address by a first-class mail tracking method which requires a certificate of mail and an electronic mail tracking system used by the United States Postal Service. A certificate of bulk mailing does not fulfill the requirements.

MARYLAND

Other Cancellation/Nonrenewal Provisions

1. All notices must be in triplicate and on a form approved by the commissioner.

2. A forty-five day notice is required if coverage is being reduced with certificate of mailing.

3. The insurer must provide a forty-five day notice prior to renewal if premium is being increased and state the reasons for the action. The notice must advise the insured of the right to file a protest with the commissioner and request a hearing.

4. A notice of cancellation must include the current address and phone number of the Maryland Automobile Insurance Fund.

5. If an insurer is allowed to cancel, nonrenew, or increase the premiums on a policy of automobile liability insurance because of the claim experience or driving record of one or more but less than all of the individuals insured under the policy, the insurer, instead of cancellation, nonrenewal, or premium increase, is required to offer to continue or renew the insurance, but to exclude all coverage when a motor vehicle is operated by the specifically named excluded individual or individuals whose claim experience or driving record could have justified the cancellation, nonrenewal, or premium increase.

6. If an insurer legally could refuse to issue a policy of automobile liability insurance under which more than one individual is insured because of the claim experience or driving record of one or more but less than all of the individuals applying to be insured under the policy, the insurer may issue the policy but exclude all coverage when a motor vehicle is operated by the specifically named excluded individual or individuals whose claim experience or driving record could have justified the refusal to issue.

7. An insurer may not refuse to issue or renew a contract of motor vehicle insurance solely because the subject of the risk or the applicant's or insured's address is located in a certain geographic area of the state unless:

    a. At least sixty days before the refusal, the insurer has filed with the commissioner a written statement designating the geographic area.
    b. The designation has an objective basis and is not arbitrary or unreasonable.

    A binder must be issued or cancelled within forty-five days.

    The name and address of any lienholders must be listed on a binder. If the binder is cancelled, the lienholders must be given at least fifteen days advance notice.

MARYLAND

8. Maryland statutes prohibit:

    a. Underwriting based on accident or driving history that occurred more than three years before the effective date of the new or renewal policy.
    b. Underwriting based on adverse credit information that occurred more than five years before the effective date of the new or renewal policy.
    c. Use of credit information in determining a particular payment plan.

PERSONAL UMBRELLA

Md. INSURANCE Code Ann. §§12-106; 27-602, 27-604, and 27-607

Length of Underwriting Period: Forty-five days.

Length of Notice: Ten days for nonpayment; fifteen days for any other reason.

Reason for Notice: Must state clearly and specifically the actual reason for cancellation.

Proof Required: Must be sent to the insured's last known address by a first-class mail tracking method which requires a certificate of mail and an electronic mail tracking system used by the United States Postal Service. A certificate of bulk mailing does not fulfill the requirements.

Cancellation after the Underwriting Period

Length of Notice: Ten-day notice for nonpayment; forty-five day notice for any other reason.

Reason for Notice: Must state clearly and specifically the actual reason for nonrenewal.

Proof Required: Must be sent to the insured's last known address by a first-class mail tracking method which requires a certificate of mail and an electronic mail tracking system used by the United States Postal Service. A certificate of bulk mailing does not fulfill the requirements.

Nonrenewal

Length of Notice: Forty-five days.

Reason for Notice: Must state clearly and specifically the actual reason for cancellation.

Proof Required: Must be sent to the insured's last known address by a first-class mail tracking method which requires a certificate of mail and an electronic mail tracking system used by the United States Postal Service. A certificate of bulk mailing does not fulfill the requirements.

MARYLAND

Other Cancellation/Nonrenewal Provisions

A forty-five day written notice is required (by first-class mail) stating both the amount of the renewal policy premium and the amount of the expiring policy premium.

FRAUD

Md. INSURANCE Code Ann. §§§27-801 through 27-805

Definition

"Insurance fraud" means:

1. A violation of Md. INSURANCE Code Ann. §§27-401 through 27-408.

2. Theft, as set out in §§7-101 through 7-104 of the Criminal Law Article:

   a. From a person regulated under this article.
   b. By a person regulated under this article or an officer, director, agent, or employee of a person regulated under this article.

3. Any other fraudulent activity that is committed by or against a person regulated under this article and is a violation of:

   a. Title 1, Subtitle 3 of the Agriculture Article.
   b. Title 19, Subtitle 2 or Subtitle 3 of the Business Regulation Article.
   c. Title 14, Subtitle 29, §11-810 or §14-1317 of the Commercial Law Article.
   d. The Criminal Law Article other than Title 8, Subtitle 2, Part II or §10-614.
   e. Title 12, Subtitle 9 of the Financial Institutions Article.
   f. §14-127 of the Real Property Article.
   g. §6-301 of the Alcoholic Beverages Article
   h. §109 of the Code of Public Local Laws of Caroline County.
   i. §4-103 of the Code of Public Local Laws of Carroll County.
   j. §8A-1 of the Code of Public Local Laws of Talbot County.

Reporting Requirements

An authorized insurer, its employees, fund producers, insurance producers, viatical settlement providers or brokers who in good faith believe that insurance fraud has been or is being committed shall report the fraud in writing to the commissioner, the Fraud Division, or the appropriate federal, state or local law enforcement authorities. Independent insurance producers and premium finance companies must report in writing to the Fraud Division.

MARYLAND

Antifraud Plan

Insurers must establish an antifraud plan that includes procedures to prevent insurance fraud, report fraud to appropriate law enforcement authorities, cooperate with the prosecution of insurance fraud cases, and report fraud-related data to the commissioner and Fraud division. The insurer must notify the commissioner in writing within thirty days after the insurer institutes or modifies the plan.

Application Fraud Statement

All applications for insurance and all claim forms must contain the following statement or a substantially similar statement:

> "Any person who knowingly or willfully presents a false or fraudulent claim for payment of a loss or benefit or who knowingly or willfully presents false information in an application for insurance is guilty of a crime and may be subject to fines and confinement in prison."

FAIR CLAIMS PROCESSING

Md. INSURANCE Code Ann. §27-303; Md. Code Regs. 31.15.07.04

It is an unfair claim settlement practice and a violation of this subtitle for an insurer or nonprofit health service plan to:

1. Misrepresent pertinent facts or policy provisions that relate to the claim or coverage at issue.

2. Refuse to pay a claim for an arbitrary or capricious reason based on all available information.

3. Attempt to settle a claim based on an application that is altered without notice to, or the knowledge or consent of, the insured.

4. Fail to include with each claim paid to an insured or beneficiary a statement of the coverage under which payment is being made.

5. Fail to settle a claim promptly whenever liability is reasonably clear under one part of a policy, in order to influence settlements under other parts of the policy.

6. Fail to provide promptly on request a reasonable explanation of the basis for a denial of a claim.

7. Fail to meet the requirements of Title 15, Subtitle 10B of this article for preauthorization for a health care service.

8. Fail to comply with the provisions of Title 15, Subtitle 10A of this article.

9. Fail to act in good faith, as defined under §27-1001 of this title, in settling a first-party claim under a policy of property and casualty insurance.

10. Fail to comply with the provisions of §16-118 of this article.

First-party claims should be investigated within forty-five days of notification; if not, the insurer shall notify the claimant in writing of the actual reason that additional time for the investigation is needed. Notice shall be sent every forty-five days until the insurer either affirms or denies coverage.

When a first-party claimant is neither an attorney or represented by one, the insurer shall—upon receipt of claim—inform the claimant that there may be a statute of limitations which may bar a claimant's rights in the future.

When an insurer denies a claim on the grounds of a specific policy provision, condition, or exclusion, the insurer shall notify the claimant as to the provision, condition, or exclusion on which the denial is based.

When there is a reasonable basis, supported by specific information available for review by the commissioner, that the first-party claimant has fraudulently caused or contributed to the loss, the insurer is relieved of the requirements to notify the claimant of the reason for a need for additional time for investigation.

PENALTIES

MD Code, Insurance, §27-305

For violation of the unfair claim practices act, a penalty not to exceed $2,500 shall be imposed.

For failure to act in good faith as listed in item 9 above, a penalty not to exceed $125,000 shall be imposed. Restitution of actual damages not to exceed policy limits, expenses and litigation costs, including reasonable attorney's fees, and interest on actual damages, expenses and litigation costs from the date on which the claim would have been paid had the insurer acted in good faith, may be required.

MASSACHUSETTS

For details on cancellation procedures for the standard policy, refer to the Standard Policy section.

ALL POLICIES IN MASSACHUSETTS

Mass. Gen. Laws Ann. ch.175 §§99, 111A, 111B and 113A

A written notice is required prior to renewal if the insurer intends to eliminate or reduce policy coverages, conditions, or definitions. The insurer must attach a printed notice setting forth what has been changed.

COMMERCIAL LINES
BUSINESSOWNERS; CAPITAL ASSETS; COMMERCIAL PROPERTY

Mass. Gen. Laws Ann. ch. 175, §§99, 113F, 187C, 187D, and 193P

Cancellation during the Underwriting Period

Length of Underwriting Period: Sixty days.

Length of Notice: Ten days for nonpayment; five days for any other reason. Mortgagees always receive twenty days' notice.

Reason for Cancellation: Required on the notice.

Proof Required: First-class mail with certificate of mailing receipt.

Cancellation after the Underwriting Period

The policy may be cancelled **only** for the following reasons:

1. Nonpayment.

2. If the insured is convicted of a crime arising out of an act which increases the chances of loss under the policy.

3. Fraud or material misrepresentation by the insured on the application.

4. Willful or reckless acts or omissions by the insured that increase the hazard insured against.

5. Physical changes in the property that results in the property becoming uninsurable.

6. If the commissioner determines that continuation of the policy would violate the law.

MASSACHUSETTS

Length of Notice: Ten days for nonpayment; five days for any other reason. Mortgagees always receive twenty days' notice.

Reason for Cancellation: Required on the notice.

Proof Required: Certificate of mailing.

Nonrenewal

Length of Notice: Forty-five days.

Reason for Nonrenewal: Required on the notice.

Proof Required: Certificate of mailing.

Other Cancellation/Nonrenewal Provisions

1. The nonrenewal provision applies **only** to policies that:

   a. Cover real property used as a residence, if the property consists of not more than four dwelling units.

   b. Cover personal property of a person residing in such real property.

2. If the policy was procured in part or in whole through the use of an agent or broker, the nonrenewal notice is sent only to the agent or broker. The agent or broker must, within fifteen days, send a copy of the nonrenewal notice to the named insured.

3. When the reason for cancellation is nonpayment, the insured may continue coverage and avoid the effect of the cancellation by payment at any time prior to the effective date of cancellation.

BOP; LIQUOR LIABILITY

Mass. Gen. Laws Ann. ch. 175, §112B

Cancellation during the Underwriting Period

Length of Underwriting Period: Sixty days.

Length of Notice: Ten days for nonpayment; thirty days for any other reason.

Reason for Cancellation: Required on the notice.

Proof Required: First-class mail with certificate of mailing receipt.

MASSACHUSETTS

Cancellation after the Underwriting Period

Length of Notice: Ten days for nonpayment; thirty days for named insured's loss of license; sixty days for any other reason.

Reason for Cancellation: Required on the notice.

Proof Required: Certificate of mailing.

Nonrenewal

Length of Notice: Sixty days.

Reason for Nonrenewal: Required on the notice.

Proof Required: Certificate of mailing.

Other Cancellation/Nonrenewal Provisions

1. If the policy has been in effect for sixty days or more, notice must also be sent to the licensing authorities, and the alcoholic beverages control commission.

2. If policy is issued pursuant to §§64A, 64B or 67 of Mass. Gen. Law Ann. Chapter 138, cancellation for nonpayment requires a thirty-day notice.

COMMERCIAL AUTO

Mass. Gen. Laws Ann. ch. 90, §34K; ch. 175, §§22C and 113A, 113F, 113H

Massachusetts does not use the ISO policy.

Cancellation during the Underwriting Period

Length of Underwriting Period: Ninety days.

Length of Notice: Ten days for any reason.

Reason for Cancellation: Required on the notice. When cancellation is for nonpayment, the amount owed must also be stated. Cancellation statutes are the same for commercial and personal lines.

Proof Required: Certificate of mailing.

MASSACHUSETTS

Cancellation after the Underwriting Period

The policy may be cancelled **only** for the following reasons:

1. Nonpayment.

2. Fraud or material misrepresentation on the application in the renewal process.

3. Suspension or revocation of the driver's license of the named insured or a resident who normally operates a vehicle or of their registration during the policy period.

4. Insured fail to comply with a request for inspection of his vehicle by insurer.

Comprehensive and collision may be cancelled on a vehicle if:

1. It is owned or driven by anyone who has been convicted of vehicular homicide, auto related fraud, or auto theft in the last five years.

2. It is owned or driven by anyone who has made a material misrepresentation under these coverages within the last five years.

3. It is owned or driven by anyone convicted of driving under the influence of alcohol or drugs in the last three years.

4. The Registrar of Motor Vehicles has issued a salvage title for it (and a new title has not been issued).

5. It is classified as a high-theft vehicle and it does not have a minimum antitheft or auto recovery device.

Collision may be cancelled on a vehicle if the owner or operator has been involved in four at-fault accidents within three years.

Comprehensive may be cancelled on a vehicle if the owner or operator has two or more total auto theft or fire claims within three years.

Towing and labor may be cancelled during the first ninety days of the policy.

Length of Notice: Twenty days for any reason.

Reason for Cancellation: Required on the notice. When cancellation is for nonpayment, the amount owed must also be stated.

Proof Required: Certificate of mailing.

MASSACHUSETTS

Nonrenewal

Length of Notice: Forty-five days.

Reason for Nonrenewal: N/A.

Proof Required: N/A.

Other Cancellation/Nonrenewal Provisions

1. All cancellation notices must also be sent to the Registrar of Motor Vehicles.

2. When notice is sent to an agent or broker that placed the coverage, the agent or broker must send a copy to the insured within fifteen days of receipt unless coverage has been replaced.

3. Company must refund any unearned premium as result of cancellation within thirty days.

4. Statutes require the insured to provide a twenty-day written notice to the insurer in order to cancel the policy.

5. In order to cancel the rights of any secured lender, a notice of cancellation must also be sent to the secured lender in the same manner as to the insured.

COMMERCIAL CRIME; CGL; CIM; C. UMB.; FARM

Mass. Gen. Laws Ann. ch. 175, §§187C, 187D

The only change Massachusetts makes from the standard policy is to add the requirement of a forty-five day notice for nonrenewal.

EQUIPMENT BREAKDOWN

Mass. Gen. Laws Ann. ch. 175, §§187C, 187D

Massachusetts makes no changes from the standard policy.

WORKERS COMPENSATION

Mass. Gen. Laws Ann. ch. 152, §§25K; 55A; 65B and 211 Code of Mass. Regs. 111.07

The insurer may cancel only for nonpayment, fraud or material misrepresentation affecting the policy, or a substantial increase in hazard insured against. Such cancellation shall not be effective until ten days after written notice is given by us to the insured and The Workers' Compensation Rating and Inspection Bureau of Massachusetts, or until notice has been received by the Bureau that you have secured insurance from another insurance company, whichever occurs first.

Any violation of 211 CMR 111.04 or 111.05 shall be considered fraud or material misrepresentation pursuant to M.G.L. c. 152, §55A, as added by St. 1991, c. 398, §84, and grounds for cancellation or nonrenewal, provided that the employee leasing company has been provided thirty days to cure the violation.

Individual members of a workers' compensation self-insurance group are subject to cancellation by the group pursuant to the group's bylaws. Cancellation by the insured requires delivering advance written notice to the insurer requesting cancellation. The group must notify the commissioner of insurance and the division of industrial accidents of the termination or cancellation of a member within ten days and must maintain coverage of each cancelled member responsible for thirty days after such notice, with the member responsible for the premium for this period, unless the workers' compensation agency notifies the group that the member has procured workers' compensation insurance, has become a self-insurer, or has become a member of another group. A member of a group who elects to terminate its membership or is cancelled remains jointly and severally liable for the workers' compensation obligations of the group which were incurred during the cancelled or terminated member's period of membership.

An insurer may nonrenew a policy for any reason.

The notice of nonrenewal must state: "Your policy will terminate on the policy expiration date (the exact expiration date must be given, e.g. 11/30/03)". The notice of nonrenewal must be sent in enough time so that the insured and the WCRIBMA receive the notice at least ten days prior to the expiration date of the current policy. The assigned carrier shall obtain for its records, at a minimum, a certificate of mailing receipt from the United States Postal Service showing the name and address of the insured to which the notice of nonrenewal was mailed. The carrier will always provide the reason for nonrenewal on any notice sent to the WCRIBMA or the insured employer. Pool carriers should refer to the sample notice of nonrenewal in statute.

If an assigned carrier does not receive the deposit premium prior to the expiration date of the current policy, it shall not issue a renewal policy. A copy of any notice sent to the insured employer should also be sent to the producer of record. The carrier should always be able to produce a copy or other exact reproduction of the documents(s) sent to the insured employer.

SURPLUS LINES

It appears that the Massachusetts cancellation and nonrenewal provisions do not apply to surplus lines policies.

MASSACHUSETTS

FINANCED PREMIUMS

Mass. Gen. Laws Ann. ch. 90, §34K

Motor Vehicle Policies

If the premium finance agreement contains a power of attorney, the finance company may request, in the name of the insured, that the insurer cancel the policy due to nonpayment. The finance company must first give notice of the intent to cancel by registered or certified mail and must give the insured ten days to pay. If the insured fails to make payment within that ten day period, then the finance company mails the notice of cancellation to the insurer along with a notice of compliance with Mass. Gen. Laws Ann. ch. 90, §34K. The cancellation is processed as of the finance company's original default date. Return of the policy by the insured is not required.

Other Policies

A premium finance company may give notice of cancellation to the insured by sending it by first-class mail. The agency must obtain a certificate of mailing as proof that notice was sent.

PERSONAL LINES
DWELLING FIRE & HOMEOWNERS

Mass. Gen. Laws Ann. ch. 175, §§99, 187C, 187D, 193P

Cancellation during the Underwriting Period

Length of Underwriting Period: Sixty days.

Length of Notice: Ten days for nonpayment; five days for any other reason. Twenty days to mortgagee for any reason.

Reason for Cancellation: Required on the notice.

Proof Required: First-class mail with certificate of mailing receipt.

Cancellation after the Underwriting Period

The policy may be cancelled **only** for the following reasons:

1. Nonpayment.

2. If the insured is convicted of an act which increases the chances of loss under the policy.

MASSACHUSETTS

3. Fraud or material misrepresentation on the application.

4. Willful or reckless acts or omissions that increase the hazard insured against.

5. Physical changes in the property that results in the property becoming uninsurable.

6. If the commissioner determines that continuation of the policy would violate the law.

Length of Notice: Ten days for nonpayment; five days for all other allowable reasons. Twenty days to mortgagee for any reason.

Reason for Cancellation: Required on the notice.

Proof Required: Certificate of mailing.

Nonrenewal

Length of Notice: Forty-five days.

Reason for Nonrenewal: Required on the notice.

Proof Required: Certificate of mailing

Other Cancellation/Nonrenewal Provisions

1. If the policy is written for a period of more than one year, the insurer may cancel on the anniversary date with a thirty-day written notice. If the policy was procured in part or in whole through the use of an agent or broker, the nonrenewal notice is sent only to the agent or broker. The agent or broker must, within fifteen days, send a copy of the nonrenewal notice to the named insured.

2. When the reason for cancellation is nonpayment, the insured may continue coverage and avoid the effect of the cancellation by payment at any time prior to the effective date of cancellation.

PERSONAL AUTO

*Mass. Gen. Laws Ann. ch. 175, §§22C, 22D, 113A, 113F, 113H,
211 Mass. Code Regs. 97.03, 97.06*

Cancellation during the Underwriting Period

Length of Underwriting Period: Ninety days.

Length of Notice: Ten days for nonpayment; thirty days for all other reasons.

MASSACHUSETTS

Reason for Cancellation: Required on the notice. When cancellation is for nonpayment, the amount owed must also be stated.

Proof Required: Registered or certified mail.

Cancellation after the Underwriting Period

The policy may be cancelled **only** for the following reasons:

1. Nonpayment.

2. Suspension or revocation of the driver's license of the named insured or a resident who normally operates a vehicle or of their registration during the policy period.

3. Fraud or material misrepresentation on the application on in the renewal process.

4. Failure to furnish a completed renewal application thirty days prior to expiration.

5. Failure to comply with the insurer's request for any inspection.

Comprehensive and collision may be cancelled on a vehicle if:

1. It is owned or driven by anyone who has been convicted of vehicular homicide, auto related fraud, or auto theft in the last five years.

2. It is owned or driven by anyone who has made a material misrepresentation under these coverages within the last five years.

3. It is owned or driven by anyone convicted of driving under the influence of alcohol or drugs in the last three years.

4. The Registrar of Motor Vehicles has issued a salvage title for it (and a new title has not been issued).

5. It is classified as a high-theft vehicle and it does not have a minimum antitheft or auto recovery device.

Collision may be cancelled on a vehicle if the owner or operator has been involved in four at-fault accidents within three years.

Comprehensive may be cancelled on a vehicle if the owner or operator has two or more total auto theft or fire claims within three years.

Towing and labor may be cancelled during the first ninety days of the policy.

MASSACHUSETTS

Length of Notice: Twenty days.

Reason for Cancellation: Required on the notice. When cancellation is for nonpayment, the amount owed must also be stated.

Proof Required: Certificate of mailing.

Nonrenewal

Length of Notice: Forty-five days.

Reason for Nonrenewal: Required on the notice.

Proof Required: Certificate of mailing.

Other Cancellation/Nonrenewal Provisions

1. For someone whose driver's license or auto registration is under suspension or revocation the insurer may suspend coverage for that person under any of the optional insurance parts of the policy. The insurer may also reduce the limits available for that person under BI, PD, and UM to state minimum limits.

2. All cancellation notices must also be sent to the Registrar of Motor Vehicles.

3. When notice is sent to an agent or broker that placed the coverage, the agent or broker must send a copy to the insured within fifteen days of receipt unless coverage has been replaced.

4. Company must refund any unearned premium as result of cancellation within thirty days.

5. Statutes require the insured to provide a twenty-day written notice to the insurer to cancel the policy.

6. In order to cancel the rights of any secured lender, a notice of cancellation must also be sent to the secured lender in the same manner as to the insured.

7. In the event a company eliminates or reduces certain coverages, conditions, or definitions in a motor vehicle policy, the company must attach a printed notice on each policy explaining what coverages, conditions or definitions have been eliminated or reduced. Otherwise, the reductions or eliminations will not take effect.

MASSACHUSETTS

PERSONAL UMBRELLA
ISO amendatory endorsement DL 99 13

Length of Underwriting Period: Sixty days.

Length of Notice: Ten days.

Reason for notice: Required on the notice.

Proof Required: Certificate of mailing.

Cancellation after the Underwriting Period

Length of Notice: Ten days for nonpayment; thirty days for any other reason.

Reason for notice: Required on the notice.

Proof Required: Certificate of mailing.

Nonrenewal

Length of Notice: Thirty days.

Reason for notice: Required on the notice.

Proof Required: Certificate of mailing.

Termination

A policy may be terminated by the insured by returning the policy to the insurer or giving the insurer an advance written notice of the date cancellation is to take effect.

FRAUD
Mass. Gen. Laws Ann. ch. 175, §186

General Information and Definitions

Oral or written misrepresentations made in the negotiation of a policy of insurance by the insured or on his behalf shall be deemed material or shall defeat or avoid the policy only if the misrepresentation is made with actual intent to deceive, or unless the matter misrepresented or made a warranty increased the risk of loss, or the lack of knowledge due to the misrepresentation or warranty would otherwise have influenced the insurer in making the contract at all.

MASSACHUSETTS

FAIR CLAIMS PROCESSING
Mass. Gen. Laws Ann. ch. 176D, §3

Unfair claim settlement practices: An unfair claim settlement practice shall consist of any of the following acts or omissions:

1. Misrepresenting pertinent facts or insurance policy provisions relating to coverages at issue.

2. Failing to acknowledge and act reasonably and promptly upon communications with respect to claims arising under insurance policies.

3. Failing to adopt and implement reasonable standards for the prompt investigation of claims arising under insurance policies.

4. Refusing to pay claims without conducting a reasonable investigation based upon all available information.

5. Failing to affirm or deny coverage of claims within a reasonable time after proof of loss statements have been completed.

6. Failing to effectuate prompt, fair and equitable settlements of claims in which liability has become reasonably clear.

7. Compelling insureds to institute litigation to recover amounts due under an insurance policy by offering substantially less than the amounts ultimately recovered in actions brought by such insureds.

8. Attempting to settle a claim for less than the amount to which a reasonable man would have believed he was entitled by reference to written or printed advertising material accompanying or made part of an application.

9. Attempting to settle claims on the basis of an application which was altered without notice to, or knowledge or consent of the insured.

10. Making claims payments to insured or beneficiaries not accompanied by a statement setting forth the coverage under which payments are being made.

11. Making known to insured or claimants a policy of appealing from arbitration awards in favor of insureds or claimants for the purpose of compelling them to accept settlements of compromises less than the amount awarded in arbitration.

MASSACHUSETTS

12. Delaying the investigation or payment of claims by requiring that an insured or claimant, or the physician of either, submit a preliminary claim report and then requiring the subsequent submission of formal proof of loss forms, both of which submissions contain substantially the same information.

13. Failing to settle claims promptly, where liability has become reasonably clear, under one portion of the insurance policy coverage in order to influence settlements under other portions of the insurance policy coverage.

14. Failing to provide promptly a reasonable explanation of the basis in the insurance policy in relation to the facts or applicable law for denial of a claim or for the offer of a compromise settlement.

MICHIGAN

For details on cancellation procedures for the standard policy, refer to the Standard Policy section.

COMMERCIAL LINES
AGRICULTURAL CAPITAL ASSETS;
BUSINESSOWNERS; CAPITAL ASSETS; & C. PROP.

Michigan Compiled Laws Annotated §§500.2027, 500.2833, 500.3020

Cancellation during the Underwriting Period

The policy may be cancelled for any reason that does not conflict with MCLA §500.2027(a) and (b).

Length of Underwriting Period: N/A.

Length of Notice: At least ten days prior to cancellation, or longer if stated in the policy contract. Also, federal or state regulatory agencies such as the Departments of Transportation and the Michigan Public Service Commission may require a greater number of days notice of cancellation.

Reason for Cancellation: Not required.

Proof Required: N/A.

Cancellation after the Underwriting Period

The policy may be cancelled for any reason that does not conflict with MCLA §500.2027(a) and (b).

Length of Notice: At least ten days prior to cancellation, or longer if stated in the policy contract. Also, federal or state regulatory agencies such as the Departments of Transportation and the Michigan Public Service Commission may require a greater number of days notice of cancellation.

Reason for Cancellation: Not required.

Proof Required: Proof of mailing.

Nonrenewal

The policy may be terminated for any reason that does not conflict with MCLA §500.2027(a) and (b).

MICHIGAN

Length of Notice: At least ten days prior to termination, or longer if stated in the policy contract. Also, federal or state regulatory agencies such as the Departments of Transportation and the Michigan Public Service Commission may require a greater number of days notice of termination.

Reason for Nonrenewal: N/A.

Proof Required: N/A.

Other Cancellation/Nonrenewal Provisions

The policy may be cancelled for any reason that does not conflict with MCLA §500.2027(a) and (b).

Minimum earned premium is $25. Termination notices must be sent to mortgage holders.

COMMERCIAL CRIME; FARM; CGL (All Coverage Parts); CIM; FARM; E. COMMERCE; EQUIPMENT BREAKDOWN; MGT. PROT.; & PROF. LIAB.

Michigan Compiled Laws Annotated §§500.2027, 500.2123, 500.2833, and 500.3020

Cancellation during the Underwriting Period

The policy may be cancelled for any reason that does not conflict with MCLA §500.2027(a) and (b).

Length of Underwriting Period: N/A.

Length of Notice: At least ten days prior to cancellation, or longer if stated in the policy contract. Also, federal or state regulatory agencies such as the Departments of Transportation and the Michigan Public Service Commission may require a greater number of days notice of cancellation.

Reason for Cancellation: N/A.

Proof Required: N/A.

Cancellation after the Underwriting Period

The policy may be cancelled for any reason that does not conflict with MCLA §500.2027(a) and (b).

Length of Notice: At least ten days prior to cancellation, or longer if stated in the policy contract. Also, federal or state regulatory agencies such as the Departments of Transportation

MICHIGAN

and the Michigan Public Service Commission may require a greater number of days notice of cancellation.

Per requirements of federal or state regulatory agencies, Underground Storage Tank and Railroad Protective Liability policies may require at least sixty days.

Reason for Cancellation: Not required.

Proof Required: Proof of mailing.

Nonrenewal

The policy may be terminated for any reason that does not conflict with MCLA §500.2027(a) and (b).

Length of Notice: At least ten days prior to termination, or longer if stated in the policy contract. Also, federal or state regulatory agencies such as the Departments of Transportation and the Michigan Public Service Commission may require a greater number of days notice of termination.

Per requirements of federal or state regulatory agencies, Underground Storage Tank policies may require at least sixty days notice of cancellation for reasons other than nonpayment of premium.

Reason for Nonrenewal: Not required.

Proof Required: Proof of mailing.

Other Cancellation/Nonrenewal Provisions

1. Minimum earned premium is $25. Nonrenewal notice must be sent to the first named insured.

2. On Liquor Liability policies all notices must also be sent to the Michigan Liquor Control Commission. (Mich. Comp. Laws §436.1807).

3. Michigan Compiled Laws §§500.2833 and 500.3020 specify ten days notice of cancellation, but ISO amendatory endorsements (CG 30 10 and IL 00 17) require either thirty or sixty days notice as indicated for cancellation due to reasons other than nonpayment of premium. Insurers using the ISO forms must comply with policy terms.

MICHIGAN

COMMERCIAL AUTO

Michigan Compiled Laws Annotated §§500.2027, 500.2833, 500.2123, 500.3020, 500.3220 500.3224 and 500.3204

Cancellation during the Underwriting Period

The policy may be cancelled for any reason that does not conflict with MCLA §500.2027(a) and (b).

Length of Underwriting Period: Fifty-five days.

Length of Notice: At least twenty days after the date of mailing or delivery of the notice, or longer if stated in the policy contract. Also, federal or state regulatory agencies such as the Departments of Transportation and the Michigan Public Service Commission may require a greater number of days notice of cancellation.

Reason for Cancellation: Not required.

Proof Required: Proof of mailing.

Cancellation after the Underwriting Period

The policy may be cancelled for any reason that does not conflict with MCLA §500.2027(a) and (b).

The policy may be cancelled **only** for nonpayment or if the driver's license of the named insured, any resident or any regular operator is suspended or revoked and the suspension or revocation is final.

Length of Notice: At least twenty days prior to cancellation, or longer if stated in the policy contract. Also, federal or state regulatory agencies such as the Departments of Transportation and the Michigan Public Service Commission may require a greater number of days notice of cancellation.

Reason for Cancellation: Not required.

Proof Required: Certified mail; regular mail, with proof of mailing for nonpayment.

Nonrenewal

Length of Notice: Twenty days.

Reason for Nonrenewal: Not required.

Proof Required: Certified mail.

MICHIGAN

Other Cancellation/Nonrenewal Provisions

The minimum earned premium is $25.

COMMERCIAL UMBRELLA; FARM EXCESS LIABILITY

Michigan Compiled Laws Annotated §§500.2027, 2833 and 500.3020

Cancellation during the Underwriting Period

The policy may be cancelled for any reason that does not conflict with MCLA §500.2027(a) and (b).

Length of Underwriting Period: N/A.

Length of Notice: At least ten days prior to cancellation, or longer if stated in the policy contract. Also, federal or state regulatory agencies such as the Departments of Transportation and the Michigan Public Service Commission may require a greater number of days notice of cancellation.

Reason for Cancellation: Not required.

Proof Required: Proof of mailing.

Cancellation after the Underwriting Period

The policy may be cancelled for any reason that does not conflict with MCLA §500.2027(a) and (b).

Length of Notice: At least ten days prior to cancellation, or longer if stated in the policy contract. Also, federal or state regulatory agencies such as the Departments of Transportation and the Michigan Public Service Commission may require a greater number of days notice of cancellation.

Reason for Cancellation: Not required.

Proof Required: Proof of mailing.

Nonrenewal

The policy may be terminated for any reason that does not conflict with MCLA §500.2027(a) and (b).

Length of Notice: Thirty days.

Reason for Nonrenewal: Not required.

Proof Required: Proof of mailing.

MICHIGAN

Other Cancellation/Nonrenewal Provisions

Minimum earned premium is $25. Nonrenewal must be sent to the first named insured.

WORKERS COMPENSATION
Michigan Compiled Laws Annotated §§418.621, 500.2016, 500.2027

The policy may be terminated for any reason that does not conflict with MCLA §500.2027(a) and (b) and MCLA §500.2116(1) (b) and (c).

Cancellation is not effective until twenty days after the notice is received by the Michigan Bureau of Workers Compensation Agency.

FINANCED PREMIUMS
Michigan Compiled Laws Annotated §500.1511

If the premium finance agreement contains a power of attorney, the finance company may request, in the name of the insured, that the insurer cancel the policy due to nonpayment. The finance company must first give the insured ten days to pay. If the insured fails to make payment within that ten-day period, then the finance company mails the notice of cancellation to the insurer and the cancellation is processed as of the finance company's original default date. Return of the policy by the insured is not required. All statutory, regulatory and contractual restrictions providing that the insurance contract may not be cancelled unless notice is given to a governmental agency, mortgagee or other third party shall apply where cancellation is effected by the finance company. The insurer shall give the prescribed notice on behalf of itself or the insured to any governmental agency, mortgagee or other third party on or before the second business day after the day it receives the notice of cancellation from the premium finance company and shall determine the effective date of cancellation taking into consideration the number of days' notice required to complete the cancellation.

SURPLUS LINES
Michigan Compiled Laws Annotated §§500.1904

Rates used by unauthorized insurers shall not be subject to this code, except that a rate shall not be unfairly discriminatory.

Forms used by unauthorized insurers pursuant to this chapter shall not be subject to this code, except that a policy shall not contain language which misrepresents the true nature of the policy or class of policies.

MICHIGAN

PERSONAL LINES
DWELLING FIRE

Michigan Compiled Laws Annotated §§500.2027, 500.2833 and 500.3020

Cancellation during the Underwriting Period

The policy may be cancelled for any reason that does not conflict with MCLA §500.2027(a) and (b).

Length of Underwriting Period: N/A.

Length of Notice: At least ten days prior to cancellation, or longer if stated in the policy contract.

Reason for Cancellation: Not required.

Proof Required: Proof of mailing.

Cancellation after the Underwriting Period

The policy may be cancelled for any reason that does not conflict with MCLA §500.2027(a) and (b).

After the underwriting period, the policy may be cancelled only for the following reasons:

1. Nonpayment.
2. Material misrepresentation on the application.
3. Substantial change in the risk.

Length of Notice: At least ten days prior to cancellation, or longer if stated in the policy contract.

Reason for Cancellation: Not required.

Proof Required: Proof of mailing.

Nonrenewal

The policy may be terminated for any reason that does not conflict with MCLA §500.2027(a) and (b).

Length of Notice: At least ten days prior to nonrenewal, or longer if stated in the policy contract.

MICHIGAN

Reason for Nonrenewal: Not required.

Proof Required: Proof of mailing.

Other Cancellation/Nonrenewal Provisions

If the policy is written for a period of more than one year, the insurer may cancel on the anniversary date with a thirty-day written notice. The minimum earned premium is $25.

HOMEOWNERS
Michigan Compiled Laws Annotated §§500.2027, 500.2102, 500.2103, 500.2113, 500.2117, 500.2122, 500.2123, and 500.2833

The policy may be cancelled only if the insurer finds that the policyholder is not an eligible person according to its eligibility rules filed in accordance with MCLA §§500.2117 and 500.2103(2) and (3).

The notice shall contain the reasons for cancellation and shall state that, pursuant to MCLA §500.2113 the policyholders have a right to a private, informal managerial-level conference with the insurer and to a review before the Insurance Department, if the conference fails to resolve the dispute.

Length of Underwriting Period: Fifty-five days.

Length of Notice: Ten days for nonpayment; twenty days for all other reasons.

Reason for Cancellation: Required on the notice.

Proof Required: Proof of mailing.

Cancellation after the Underwriting Period

The policy may be cancelled only if the person is not an "eligible person" pursuant to MCLA §§500.2117 and 500.2103(2) and (3). Eligibility requirements include but are not limited to owner/occupant of the dwelling, condition of the residence, and claims history.

After the underwriting period, the policy may be cancelled **only** for the following reasons:

1. Nonpayment.

2. Material misrepresentation on the application.

3. Substantial change in the risk.

MICHIGAN

Length of Notice: As provided in the policy for nonpayment; thirty days for all other reasons.

Reason for Cancellation: Not required.

Proof Required: Proof of mailing.

Nonrenewal

The policy may be terminated only if the person is not an "eligible person" pursuant to MCLA §§500.2117 and 500.2103(2) and (3).

Length of Notice: Thirty days.

Reason for Nonrenewal: Required on the notice.

Proof Required: Proof of mailing.

Allowable Reasons for Nonrenewal

ISO endorsements are silent on restrictions to nonrenewal. However, Michigan statutes permit nonrenewal of homeowner policies when:

1. There has been one or more of the following:

    a. Three paid claims within the immediately preceding three-year period totaling $3,000.00 or more, exclusive of weather-related claims.

    b. Three paid claims within the immediately preceding three-year period totaling $4,000.00 or more, including weather-related claims.

    c. After written notice from the insurer, the insured fails to correct a physical condition that is directly related to a paid claim or that presents a clear risk of significant loss under the property or liability portions of a homeowners policy.

2. A history of three or more paid claims within an immediately preceding three-year period if the insurer meets all of the following:

    a. Has an underwriting rule allowing consideration of paid claim history in effect.

    b. The underwriting rule is for a paid claim history that totals not less than $3,000 or more exclusive of weather-related claims and totals not less than $4,000 including weather-related claims.

MICHIGAN

    c. The underwriting rule must apply to an insured that has had a homeowner policy with the insurer for a continuous minimum period of time as determined by the insurer that may be any period of time between five and ten years.

3. The number of residences within the dwelling is inconsistent with the policy forms approved by the commissioner for the insurer.

4. The unoccupancy of a dwelling for more than sixty days, if there is evidence of an intent to vacate or keep the premises vacant or unoccupied, as to the applicant or insured.

5. The existence of an adjacent physical hazard, if the hazard presents a significant risk of loss directly related to the perils insured or to be insured against for which a rate surcharge is not applicable. Nonrenewal based upon an adjacent physical hazard must be due to a change in the hazard from that which existed at the original date of issuance of the policy.

6. The failure of the insured or applicant to purchase an amount of insurance in excess of 80 percent of the replacement cost of the property if both:

    a. The purchase of an amount of insurance in excess of 80 percent of the replacement cost is a condition for sale of the policy.

    b. The insurer offers at least one form of a replacement cost policy for which the insurer requires only a minimum amount of insurance equal to 80 percent of the replacement cost of the dwelling as a condition of purchase.

7. There were one or more incidents involving a threat, harassment, or physical assault by the insured or applicant for insurance on an insurer employee, agent, or agent employee while acting within the scope of his or her employment so long as a report of the incident was filed with an appropriate law enforcement agency.

Other Cancellation/Nonrenewal Provisions

Definition: In addition to refusal to issue based on an application, a declination also includes:

1. Refusal by an agent to submit an application on behalf of an applicant to any of the insurers represented by the agent.

2. Refusal by an insurer to issue insurance to a person upon receipt of an application for insurance.

MICHIGAN

3. Offering insurance at higher rates with a different insurer than that requested by a person.

4. Offering coverage with less favorable terms or conditions than those requested by a person.

An insurer shall not refuse to insure, refuse to continue to insure, or limit coverage available to an eligible person for automobile insurance, except in accordance with its filed underwriting rules which must be in accordance with MCLA §§500.2117 and 500.2103(2) and (3).

Notice to the Applicant: An insurer or agent, upon making a declination of insurance, must inform the applicant of each specific reason for the declination. If the application or request for coverage was made in writing, the insurer or agent must provide the explanation of reasons in writing. If the application or request for coverage was made orally, the insurer or agent may provide the applicant with an oral explanation instead of a written explanation, and must offer to provide a written explanation if the applicant requests a written explanation within ninety days. Minimum earned premium is $25. (MCLA §500.2122)

PERSONAL AUTO

Michigan Compiled Laws §§500.2027, 500.2103, 500.2104, 500.2105, 500.2113, 500.2116a, 500.2118, 500.2120, 500.2122, 500.2123, 500.3020, 500.3204, 500.3206, 500.3212, 500.3220, and 500.3224

Cancellation during the Underwriting Period

The policy may be cancelled only if the insurer finds that the policyholder is not an eligible person according to its eligibility rules filed in accordance with MCLA §§500.2103(1) and (4), 500.2105(2), 500.2116a, 500.2118, and/or 500.2120.

For group-rated programs, the notice shall contain the reasons for the cancellation and shall state in bold type that the insured has the statutory right within seven days from the date of mailing to appeal to the state Insurance Department. There is no right to appeal if the cancellation is based on nonpayment of premium.

For nongroup-rated program, the notice shall contain the reasons for cancellation and shall state that the policyholders have a right to a private, informal managerial-level conference with the insurer and to a review before the Insurance Department, if the conference fails to resolve the dispute.

Length of Underwriting Period: Fifty-five days.

Length of Notice: Ten days for nonpayment; twenty days for any other reason.

MICHIGAN

Reason for Cancellation: Required on notice.

Proof Required: Certified mail.

Cancellation after the Underwriting Period

The policy may be cancelled only if the insurer finds that the policyholder is not an eligible person according to its eligibility rules filed in accordance with MCLA §§500.2103(1) and (4), 500.2105(2), 500.2116a, 500.2118, and/or 500.2120.

For group-rated programs, the notice shall contain the reasons for the cancellation and shall state in bold type that the insured has the statutory right within seven days from the date of mailing to appeal to the state Insurance Department. There is no right to appeal if the cancellation is based on nonpayment of premium.

The policy may be cancelled **only** for the following reasons:

1. Nonpayment.

2. Suspension or revocation of the driver's license of the following persons:

    a. The named insured.

    b. Any driver who lives with the named insured or who customarily uses the insured auto.

    The suspension or revocation must occur during the policy period or since the last anniversary date of the original effective date if the policy period is other than one year.

Length of Notice: Ten days for nonpayment; thirty days for all other reasons.

Reason for Cancellation: Required on the notice.

Proof Required: For group-rated coverage, certified mail return receipt requested. For nongroup-rated coverage, proof of mailing.

Nonrenewal

The policy may be terminated only if the insurer finds that the policyholder is not an eligible person according to its eligibility rules filed in accordance with MCLA §§500.2118, 500.2103(1) and (4), 500.2105(2), 500.2120, and/or 500.2116a.

MICHIGAN

Length of Notice: Thirty days.

Reason for Nonrenewal: Required on the notice.

Proof Required: Proof of mailing.

Other Cancellation/Nonrenewal Provisions

In addition to refusal to issue based on an application, a declination also includes:

1. Refusal by an agent to submit an application on behalf of an applicant to any of the insurers represented by the agent.

2. Refusal by an insurer to issue insurance to a person upon receipt of an application for insurance.

3. Offering insurance at higher rates with a different insurer than that requested by a person.

4. Offering coverage with less favorable terms or conditions than those requested by a person.

An insurer shall not refuse to insure, refuse to continue to insure, or limit coverage available to an eligible person for automobile insurance, except in accordance with its filed underwriting rules, which must include the following provisions in accordance with MCLA §§500.2105(2), 500.2013(1) and (4), 500.2116a, 500.2118, and/or 500.2120:

1. The insurance eligibility point accumulation in excess of the amounts established by law.

2. With respect to a vehicle, substantial modifications from the vehicle's original manufactured state for purposes of increasing the speed or acceleration capabilities of the vehicle.

3. Failure by the person to provide proof that insurance was maintained in force with respect to any vehicle that was both owned by the person and driven or moved by the person or by a member of the household of the person during the six month period immediately preceding application.

4. Type of vehicle insured or to be insured, based on one of the following, without regard to the age of the vehicle:

    a. The vehicle is of limited production or of custom manufacture.

    b. The insurer does not have a rate lawfully in effect for the type of vehicle.

MICHIGAN

    c. The vehicle represents exposure to extraordinary expense for repair or replacement under comprehensive or collision coverage.

5. Use of a vehicle insured or to be insured for transportation of passengers for hire, for rental purposes, or for commercial purposes.

6. For purposes of requiring comprehensive deductibles of not more than $150.00, or of refusing to insure if the person refuses to accept a required deductible, the claim experience of the person with respect to comprehensive coverage.

7. An insurer shall not utilize an underwriting rule based on total abstinence from the consumption of alcoholic beverages unless the insurer has been authorized to transact automobile insurance in Michigan prior to January 1, 1981, and has consistently utilized such an underwriting rule as part of the insurer's automobile insurance underwriting since that time.

8. One or more incidents involving a threat, harassment, or physical assault by the insured or applicant for insurance on an insurer employee, agent, or agent employee while acting within the scope of his or her employment so long as a report of the incident was filed with an appropriate law enforcement agency.

Notice to the Applicant: An insurer or agent, upon making a declination of insurance, must inform the applicant of each specific reason for the declination. If the application or request for coverage was made in writing, the insurer or agent must provide the explanation of reasons in writing. If the application or request for coverage was made orally, the insurer or agent may provide the applicant with an oral explanation instead of a written explanation, and must offer to provide a written explanation if the applicant requests one within ninety days.

An insured may not appeal cancellation of the policy within the fifty-five day underwriting period.

The notice of cancellation must advise the insured of the right to appeal reasons for cancellation or nonrenewal (other than nonpayment).

Automatic termination is not allowed due to the insured's purchase of other insurance.

PERSONAL UMBRELLA

(ISO Form DL 24 02, MCLA §500.2027)

Cancellation during the Underwriting Period

The policy may be cancelled for any reason that does not conflict with MCLA §500.2027(a) and (b).

MICHIGAN

Length of Underwriting Period: N/A.

Length of Notice: At least ten days prior to cancellation, or longer if stated in the policy contract.

Reason for Notice: Not required.

Proof Required: Proof of mailing.

Cancellation after the Underwriting Period

The policy may be cancelled for any reason that does not conflict with MCLA §500.2027(a) and (b).

Length of Notice: Ten days for nonpayment of premium, thirty days for any other reason.

Reason for Notice: Not required.

Proof Required: Proof of mailing.

Nonrenewal Notice Requirements

The policy may be terminated for any reason that does not conflict with MCLA §500.2027(a) and (b).

Length of Notice: Thirty days

Reason for Notice: Not required.

Proof Required: Proof of mailing.

Other Cancellation/Nonrenewal Provisions

The minimum earned premium is $25.

FRAUD

Michigan Compiled Laws Annotated §§500.4503, 500.4507 and 500.4511

General Information and Definitions

A fraudulent insurance act includes, but is not limited to, acts or omissions committed by any person who knowingly, and with an intent to injure, defraud, or deceive presents any statement knowing that the statement contains any false information concerning any fact material to an application for the issuance of an insurance policy; presents a statement

MICHIGAN

as part of, or in support of, a claim for payment or other benefit pursuant to an insurance policy, knowing that the statement contains false information concerning any fact or thing material to the claim.

Penalties

A person who commits a fraudulent insurance act is guilty of a felony punishable by imprisonment for not more than four years or a fine of not more than $50,000, or both, and will be ordered to pay restitution. A person who enters into an agreement or conspiracy is punishable by imprisonment for not more than ten years or a fine of $50,000, or both, and will be ordered to pay restitution.

Reporting Requirements

If an insurer knows or reasonably believes it knows the identity of a person who it has reason to believe committed a fraudulent insurance act or has knowledge of a suspected fraudulent insurance act that is reasonably believed not to have been reported to an authorized agency, then for the purpose of notification and investigation, the insurer or an agent authorized by an insurer to act on its behalf may notify an authorized agency of the knowledge or belief and provide any additional information requested.

Application Fraud Statement

Michigan does not require application fraud statements.

FAIR CLAIMS PROCCESSING

Michigan Compiled Laws Annotated §500.2006

Timely Basis. An insurer must pay claims on a timely basis to its insured, an individual or entity directly entitled to benefits under its insured's contract of insurance, or a third party tort claimant, the benefits provided under the terms of its policy. Failure to pay claims on a timely basis is an unfair trade practice unless the claim is reasonably in dispute.

Proof of Loss. An insurer must specify in writing the materials that constitute a satisfactory proof of loss not later than thirty days after receipt of a claim unless the claim is settled within the thirty days. If proof of loss is not supplied as to the entire claim, the amount supported by proof of loss is considered paid on a timely basis if paid within sixty days after receipt of proof of loss by the insurer.

Interest. If benefits are not paid on a timely basis the benefits paid will bear simple interest from a date sixty days after satisfactory proof of loss was received by the insurer at the rate of 12 percent per annum, if the claimant is the insured or an individual or entity directly entitled to benefits under the insured's contract of insurance. If the claimant is a third party tort claimant, then the benefits paid will bear interest from a date sixty days after satisfactory proof of loss was received by the insurer at the rate of 12 percent per annum if the liability of the insurer for the claim is not reasonably in dispute, the insurer has refused payment in bad faith and the bad faith was determined by a court of law. The interest must be paid in addition to and at the time of payment of the loss. If the loss exceeds the limits of insurance coverage available, interest must be payable based upon the limits of insurance coverage rather than the amount of the loss. If payment is offered by the insurer but is rejected by the claimant, and the claimant does not subsequently recover an amount in excess of the amount offered, interest is not due. Interest paid pursuant to this section will be offset by any award of interest that is payable by the insurer pursuant to the award.

MINNESOTA

For details on cancellation procedures for the standard policy, refer to the Standard Policy section.

COMMERCIAL LINES
BOP; CAPITAL ASSETS; C. AUTO; CRIME; CGL (other than Underground Storage Tanks); CIM; COMMERCIAL PROPERTY; C. UMB; E-COMMERCE; EQUIPMENT BREAKDOWN; FARM; MANAGEMENT PROTECTION; & PROFESSIONAL LIABILITY

Minn. Stat. Ann. §§60A.36, 60A.37, 60A.38, and 60A.351

Cancellation during the Underwriting Period

Length of Underwriting Period: Ninety days.

Length of Notice: Ten days for nonpayment; companies using ISO's amendatory endorsements (CA 02 18, CG 29 07, CG 33 10, CU 01 06, EC 02 21, IL 02 45 or MP 02 45) must comply with their policy provisions requiring thirty days' notice for reasons other than nonpayment.

Reason for Cancellation: Not required.

Proof Required: Proof of mailing.

Cancellation after the Underwriting Period

The policy may be cancelled **only** for the following reasons:

1. Nonpayment of premium.

2. Misrepresentation or fraud by the named insured in obtaining the policy or in pursuing a claim under the policy.

3. Acts or omissions by the named insured that substantially increase or change the risk insured.

4. Refusal by the named insured to eliminate known conditions that increase the potential for loss after notification by the insurer.

5. Substantial change in the risk.

6. Loss of reinsurance by the insurer.

MINNESOTA

7. Determination by the commissioner that the continuation of the policy could place the insurer in violation of Minnesota insurance law.

8. Nonpayment of dues to an association or organization, where payment of dues is a prerequisite to obtaining or continuing such insurance. (Not applicable to retired individuals sixty-two or older, or who are disabled according to Social Security standards).

Length of Notice: Ten days for nonpayment; sixty days for all other allowable reasons.

Reason for Cancellation: Required on the notice.

Proof Required: Proof of mailing.

Nonrenewal

Length of Notice: Sixty days.

Reason for Nonrenewal: Not required.

Proof Required: Proof of mailing.

Other Cancellation/Nonrenewal Provisions

1. A cancellation for nonpayment cannot be effective if payment is received prior to the effective date of cancellation.

2. For Commercial Umbrella policies, ISO's amendatory endorsement, CU 01 06 indicates a thirty-day notice for nonrenewal, however, statute requires sixty days.

3. If cancellation is for loss of reinsurance, the notice must give the insured ten days to appeal the cancellation to the commissioner. The commissioner must rule on the appeal within thirty days of receipt.

4. On OCP policies all notices must also be sent to the first named insured and to any designated contractor shown in the declarations.

5. On Railroad Protective policies all notices must be sent to the named insured, the contractor shown in the declarations, and any governmental authority shown in the declarations.

6. On all policies providing commercial liability and property coverage, a thirty-day written notice prior to renewal is required if the insurer intends to renew with less favorable terms

MINNESOTA

as to dollar amount of coverages, deductibles, or rates. This provision does not apply if the changes relate to guide "a" rates or if there has been a change in the risk insured.

7. On all policies covering liquor liability, the Minnesota Liquor Control Division must be notified of any termination.

COMMERCIAL AUTO

(Applicable only to an individual with fewer than five private passenger autos; and a plan of reparation security that insures fewer than five autos rated on a commercial or fleet basis.)

Minn. Stat. Ann. §§65B.14, 65B.15, 65B.16, 65B.17, 65B.18, 65B.19 and Minn. R. 2770.7800

Cancellation during the Underwriting Period

Length of Underwriting Period: Sixty days.

Length of Notice: Ten days for nonpayment (Minn. Stat. Ann. §60B.16 allows a ten-day notice for any reason during the underwriting period, but ISO's amendatory endorsement (CA 02 18) requires thirty days for reasons other than nonpayment of premium.)

Reason for Cancellation: Required on the notice.

Proof Required: Proof of mailing.

Cancellation after the Underwriting Period

The policy may be cancelled **only** for the following reasons:

1. Nonpayment.

2. The policy was obtained through a material misrepresentation.

3. Any insured makes a false or fraudulent claim or knowingly aided or abetted another in the presentation of such a claim.

4. The named insured failed to fully disclose accidents or violations for the preceding thirty-six months if called for on the application.

5. The named insured does not disclose the information necessary to rate the risk.

6. The named insured does not give proper notice of loss or does not cooperate with the insurer in settling a claim.

MINNESOTA

7. The named insured or any other driver living with the named insured or who customarily uses the insured vehicle:

   a. Has had his driver's license suspended or revoked within the previous thirty-six months, because of a moving violation or that person's refusal to be tested for driving under the influence.

   b. Is or becomes subject to heart attacks or epilepsy and does not produce a certificate from a physician testifying to that individual's ability to safely operate a motor vehicle.

   c. Has an accident record, a conviction record, or a physical or mental condition that his operation of an automobile might endanger the public safety.

   d. Has been convicted, or forfeited bail, during the twenty-four months immediately preceding the notice of cancellation for criminal negligence in the use or operation of an auto, or assault arising out of the use of an auto or operating an auto while in an intoxicated condition or while under the influence of drugs; or leaving the scene of an accident without stopping to report; or making false statements in an application for a driver's license, or theft or unlawful taking of an auto.

   e. Has been convicted or forfeited bail for one or more moving violations within the eighteen months immediately preceding the cancellation date which justifies a revocation of a driver's license.

8. The insured auto is:

   a. So mechanically defective that its operation might endanger public safety.

   b. Used to carry passengers for hire or compensation (does not include car pools).

   c. Used to carry flammables or explosives.

   d. Is an authorized emergency vehicle.

   e. Subject to an inspection law and has not been inspected or it fails inspection.

   f. Substantially changed in type or condition during the policy period so as to give clear evidence of a use other than the original use.

MINNESOTA

Length of Notice: Ten days for nonpayment; thirty days for all other reasons.

Reason for Cancellation: Required on the notice.

Proof Required: Proof of mailing.

Nonrenewal

Length of Notice: Sixty days.

Reason for Nonrenewal: Required on the notice.

Proof Required: Proof of mailing.

Other Cancellation/Nonrenewal Provisions

1. A cancellation for nonpayment cannot be effective if payment is received prior to the effective date of cancellation.

2. Information regarding tickets and accidents must be specifically requested on the application in order for an insurer to cancel during the underwriting period.

3. Auto policies may be nonrenewed if an insured equals or exceeds the relevant number of points stated in Minn. R. 2770.8000 or if the insured fails to provide necessary underwriting information after two written requests from the insurer. The deductible amount under physical damage may be increased if three or more comprehensive claim payments have been made during the experience period or two or more comprehensive claim payments during the most recent twelve-month period. The physical damage portion may be nonrenewed if there have been a total of three payments for a single insured vehicle or four payments for multiple vehicles for various combinations of comprehensive and collision payments. (Minn. R. 2770.7800).

COMMERCIAL GENERAL LIABILITY
(Underground Storage Tanks)

Minn. Stat. Ann. §§60A.35, 60A.351, 60A.36, 60A.37, and 60A.38

Cancellation during the Underwriting Period

Length of Underwriting Period: Ninety days.

Length of Notice: Ten days for nonpayment; thirty days for fraud or misrepresentation; sixty days for any other reason. The policy may be rescinded in the case of material

MINNESOTA

misrepresentation or fraud on the part of the insured in obtaining the coverage or pursuing a claim under the policy. However, insurers using ISO's CG 30 30 must comply with the more restrictive notification requirement.

Reason for Cancellation: Not required on the notice.

Proof Required: Certified mail. Certified mail is not a requirement of statute, however, insurers using ISO's CG 30 30 must comply with the certified mail requirement.

Cancellation after the Underwriting Period

The policy may be cancelled **only** for the following reasons:

1. Nonpayment.

2. Misrepresentation or fraud by the named insured in obtaining the policy or in pursuing a claim under the policy.

3. An act or omission by the named insured that substantially increases or changes the risk insured.

4. Refusal by the named insured to eliminate known conditions that increase the potential for loss after notification by the insurer that the condition must be removed.

5. Substantial change in the risk, except to the extent that it should have reasonably been foreseen.

6. Loss of reinsurance on the risk.

7. Determination by the commissioner that the continuation of the policy could place the insurer in violation of Minnesota insurance law.

8. Nonpayment of dues to an association or organization, where payment of dues is a prerequisite to obtaining or continuing such insurance. (Not applicable to retired individuals sixty-two or older, or who are disabled according to Social Security standards).

Length of Notice: Ten days for nonpayment; sixty days for all other reasons.

Reason for Cancellation: Required on the notice.

Proof Required: Proof of mailing.

MINNESOTA

Nonrenewal

Length of Notice: Sixty days.

Reason for Nonrenewal: Not required on the notice.

Proof Required: Proof of mailing.

Other Cancellation/Nonrenewal Provisions

1. A cancellation for nonpayment cannot be effective if payment is received prior to the effective date of cancellation.

2. On all policies providing commercial liability and or property coverage, a thirty-day written notice prior to renewal is required if the insurer intends to renew with less favorable terms as to dollar amount of coverages, deductibles, or rates. This provision does not apply if the changes relate to guide "a" rates or if there has been a change in the risk insured.

FARM
(Applicable to policies covering residential buildings)
Minn. Stat. Ann. §§65A.01, 65A.29 and 65A.351

Declination

Once a person has completed an application for coverage, he is entitled to the insurer's offer of coverage or a written declination, including the reasons for the declination. A written notice must be provided to all applicants for homeowners' insurance, at the time the application is submitted, containing the following language in bold print:

> **"THE INSURER MAY ELECT TO CANCEL COVERAGE AT ANY TIME DURING THE FIRST 59 DAYS FOLLOWING ISSUANCE OF THE COVERAGE FOR ANY REASON WHICH IS NOT SPECIFICALLY PROHIBITED BY STATUTE."**

If the insurer provides the notice on the insurer's Web site, the insurer or agent may advise the applicant orally or in writing of its availability for review on the insurer's Web site in lieu of providing a written notice, if the insurer advises the applicant of the availability of a written notice upon the applicant's request. The insurer shall provide the notice in writing if requested by the applicant. An oral notice shall be presumed delivered if the agent or insurer makes a contemporaneous notation in the applicant's record of the notice having been delivered or if the insurer or agent retains an audio recording of the notification provided to the applicant.

MINNESOTA

Cancellation during the Underwriting Period

Length of Underwriting Period: Sixty days.

Length of Notice: Twenty days.

Reason for Cancellation: Required on the notice.

Proof Required: Proof of mailing.

Cancellation after the Underwriting Period

The policy may be cancelled **only** for the following reasons:

1. Nonpayment.

2. Misrepresentation or fraud on the application or in pursuing a claim.

3. Acts or omissions by the named insured that materially increase the risk.

4. Physical changes in the insured property (not corrected or restored by the named insured within a reasonable time) that makes the property uninsurable.

Length of Notice: Thirty days for any reason.

Reason for Cancellation: Required on the notice.

Proof Required: Proof of mailing.

Nonrenewal

Length of Notice: Sixty days.

Reason for Nonrenewal: Required on the notice.

Proof Required: Proof of mailing.

Other Cancellation/Nonrenewal Provisions

A cancellation for nonpayment cannot be effective if payment is received prior to the effective date of cancellation.

On all policies providing commercial liability and or property coverage, a thirty-day written notice prior to renewal is required if the insurer intends to renew with less favorable

MINNESOTA

terms as to dollar amount of coverages, deductibles, or rates. This provision does not apply if the changes relate to guide "a" rates or if there has been a change in the risk insured.

WORKERS COMPENSATION
Minn. Stat. Ann. §§60A.35 to 60A.38, 176.185 and 176.421
Cancellation during the Underwriting Period

Length of Underwriting Period: N/A.

Length of Notice: Thirty days for nonpayment; sixty days for any other reason.

Reason for Cancellation: Required on the notice.

Proof Required: First class mail.

Cancellation after the Underwriting Period

The policy may be cancelled **only** for the following reasons:

1. Nonpayment.

2. Misrepresentation or fraud by the named insured in obtaining the policy or in pursuing a claim under the policy.

3. An act or omission by the named insured that substantially increases or changes the risk insured.

4. Refusal of the insured to eliminate known conditions that increase the potential for loss after notification by the insurer that the condition must be removed.

5. Substantial change in the risk assumed, except to the extent that the insurer should reasonably have foreseen the change or contemplated the risk in writing the policy.

6. Loss of reinsurance by us which provided coverage to us for a significant amount of the underlying risk insured. Any notice of cancellation pursuant to this item shall advise you that you have ten days from the date of receipt of the notice to appeal the cancellation to the commissioner of commerce and that the commissioner will render a decision as to whether the cancellation is justified because of the loss of reinsurance within thirty business days after receipt of the appeal.

7. A determination by the commissioner that the continuation of the policy could place the insurer in violation of Minnesota insurance laws.

MINNESOTA

8. Nonpayment of dues to an association or organization, where payment of dues is a prerequisite to obtaining or continuing such insurance. (Not applicable to retired individuals sixty-two or older, or who are disabled according to Social Security standards).

Length of Notice: Thirty days for nonpayment; sixty days for any other allowable reason.

Reason for Cancellation: Required on the notice.

Proof Required: First class mail.

Nonrenewal

Length of Notice: Sixty days.

Reason for Nonrenewal: Not required on the notice.

Proof Required: First class mail.

Other Cancellation/Nonrenewal Provisions

1. A notice for nonpayment shall state the amount of premium due and the due date, and shall state the effect of nonpayment by the due date. Cancellation shall not be effective if a payment is made prior to the due date.

2. On all policies other than those applying to ocean marine, accident and health, or reinsurance, a sixty-day written notice prior to renewal is required if the insurer intends to renew with less favorable terms as to dollar amount of coverages, deductibles, or rates. This provision does not apply if the changes relate to guide "a" rates or if there has been a change in the risk insured.

3. Cancellation or termination notices also must be sent within ten days after their effective dates to the commissioner.

SURPLUS LINES

Minn. Stat. Ann. §60A.35

The Minnesota cancellation laws do not apply to surplus lines policies.

FINANCED PREMIUMS

Minn. Stat. Ann. §59A.11

If the premium finance agreement contains a power of attorney, the finance company may request, in the name of the insured, that the insurer cancel the policy due to nonpayment.

MINNESOTA

The finance company must first give the insured ten days to pay. The insurance agent or broker listed on the agreement also must be notified as indicated on the premium finance agreement of the potential cancellation. If the insured fails to make payment within that ten-day period, the finance company mails the notice of cancellation to the insurer and the cancellation is processed as of the finance company's original default date. Return of the policy by the insured is not required.

Where statutory, regulatory or contractual restrictions provide that the insurance contract may not be canceled unless notice is given to a governmental agency, mortgagee, or other third-party, the insurer shall give the prescribed notice on behalf of itself or the insured to the governmental agency, mortgagee or other third-party within ten days after the day it receives the notice of cancellation from the premium finance company. When the above restrictions require the continuation of insurance beyond the effective date of cancellation specified by the premium finance company, the insurance shall be limited to the coverage to which the restrictions relate and to the persons they are designed to protect.

PERSONAL LINES
DWELLING FIRE & HOMEOWNERS

Minn. Stat. Ann. §§65A.01 through 65A.11, 65A.29;
Minn. R. 2880.0200 through 2880.0400

Declination

Once a person has completed an application for coverage, he is entitled to the insurer's offer of coverage or a written declination, including the reasons for the declination. A written notice must be provided to all applicants for homeowners' insurance, at the time the application is submitted, containing the following language in bold print:

"THE INSURER MAY ELECT TO CANCEL COVERAGE AT ANY TIME DURING THE FIRST 60 DAYS FOLLOWING ISSUANCE OF THE COVERAGE FOR ANY REASON WHICH IS NOT SPECIFICALLY PROHIBITED BY STATUTE."

If the insurer provides the notice on the insurer's Web site, the insurer or agent may advise the applicant orally or in writing of its availability for review on the insurer's Web site in lieu of providing a written notice, if the insurer advises the applicant of the availability of a written notice upon the applicant's request. The insurer shall provide the notice in writing if requested by the applicant. An oral notice shall be presumed delivered if the agent or insurer makes a contemporaneous notation in the applicant's record of the notice having been delivered or if the insurer or agent retains an audio recording of the notification provided to the applicant.

MINNESOTA

Cancellation during the Underwriting Period

Length of Underwriting Period: Sixty days.

Length of Notice: Twenty days for any reason.

Reason for Cancellation: Required on the notice.

Proof Required: Proof of mailing.

Cancellation after the Underwriting Period

The policy may be cancelled **only** for the following reasons:

1. Nonpayment.

2. Misrepresentation or fraud on the application or in pursuing a claim.

3. Acts or omissions by the named insured that materially increase the risk.

4. Physical changes in the insured property which are not corrected or restored by the named insured within a reasonable time that make the property uninsurable.

Length of Notice: Thirty days for any allowable reason.

Reason for Cancellation: Required on the notice. Even though the ISO endorsement Special Provisions-Minnesota is silent on this matter—implying that the reason is not required—the reason for cancellation must be shown.

Proof Required: Proof of mailing.

Nonrenewal

Length of Notice: Sixty days.

Reason for Nonrenewal: Required on the notice.

Proof Required: Proof of mailing.

Permissible Reasons For Nonrenewal

The items noted above as permissible reasons for cancellation:

1. Use of the premises for an illegal activity.

MINNESOTA

2. The termination of an agency contract, unless the insurer assigns the terminated agent's book of business to another agent.

2. Violations of local laws or ordinances that increase the possibility of loss.

3. Refusal of the insured to eliminate known conditions that increase the potential for loss after being notified of the conditions. The insurer must give two written requests to eliminate the hazards before nonrenewing.

4. A substantial change in the quality or availability of fire protection services.

5. If the insured has two or more losses during the experience period, not including losses caused by natural causes, losses for which no payment was made, or losses in which the insurer recovers 80 percent or more of the payment through subrogation.

6. If the insurer withdraws from writing homeowners insurance in Minnesota.

7. Failure of the named insured to provide requested and necessary underwriting information.

8. Delinquent property taxes for two or more years.

9. If the named insured no longer owns or resides at the insured location, unless the spouse resides there and retains ownership.

10. If an insurer has grounds to nonrenew a homeowner policy on a primary residence of the named insured, homeowner policies on secondary residences of the insured also may be nonrenewed. (Minn. R. 2880.0200).

Other Cancellation/Nonrenewal Provisions

1. A cancellation for nonpayment cannot be effective if payment is received prior to the effective date of cancellation.

2. On all policies other than those applying to ocean marine, accident and health, or reinsurance, a sixty-day written notice prior to renewal is required if the insurer intends to renew with less favorable terms as to dollar amount of coverages, deductibles, or rates. This provision does not apply if the changes relate to guide "a" rates or if there has been a change in the risk insured.

3. Nonrenewal notices must include a statement advising the insured of the right of complaint within thirty days of receiving the notice and of the availability of insurance from the Minnesota Property Insurance Placement Facility.

MINNESOTA

4. Insurers must keep a record of nonrenewals and company initiated cancellations for three years. This record must be made available to the commissioner at the company's place of business.

PERSONAL AUTO

Minn. Stat. Ann. §§65B.14 through 65B.19; Minn. R. 2770.7800

Cancellation during the Underwriting Period

Length of Underwriting Period: Fifty-nine days.

Length of Notice: Ten days.

Reason for Cancellation: Required on the notice.

Proof Required: Proof of mailing.

Cancellation after the Underwriting Period

The policy may be cancelled **only** for the following reasons:

1. Nonpayment.

2. The policy was obtained through a material misrepresentation.

3. Any insured makes a false or fraudulent claim or knowingly aided or abetted another in the presentation of such a claim.

4. The named insured failed to fully disclose accidents or violations for the preceding thirty-six months if called for on the application.

5. The named insured does not disclose the information necessary to rate the risk.

6. The named insured does not give proper notice of loss or does not cooperate with the insurer in settling a claim.

7. The named insured or any other driver lives with the named insured or customarily uses the insured vehicle:

    a. Has had his driver's license suspended or revoked within the previous thirty-six months, because of a moving violation or that person's refusal to be tested for driving under the influence.

MINNESOTA

    b. Is or becomes subject to heart attacks or epilepsy and does not produce a certificate from a physician testifying to that individual's ability to safely operate a motor vehicle.

    c. Has an accident record, a conviction record, or a physical or mental condition that his operation of an automobile might endanger the public safety.

    d. Has been convicted, or forfeited bail, during the twenty-four months immediately preceding the notice of cancellation for criminal negligence in the use or operation of an auto, or assault arising out of the use of an auto or operating an auto while in an intoxicated condition or while under the influence of drugs; or leaving the scene of an accident without stopping to report; or making false statements in an application for a driver's license, or theft or unlawful taking of an auto.

    e. Has been convicted or forfeited bail for one or more moving violations within the eighteen months immediately preceding the cancellation date which justify a revocation of a driver's license.

8. The insured auto is:

    a. So mechanically defective that its operation might endanger public safety.

    b. Used to carry passengers for hire or compensation (does not include car pools).

    c. Used to carry flammables or explosives.

    d. Is an authorized emergency vehicle.

    e. Subject to an inspection law and has not been inspected or it fails inspection.

    f. Substantially changed in type or condition during the policy period so as to give clear evidence of a use other than the original use. However, since these reasons are not on PP 01 60, insurers using that form are restricted to the reasons listed above.

Length of Notice: Ten days for nonpayment; thirty days for all other reasons.

Reason for Cancellation: Required on the notice.

Proof Required: Proof of mailing.

MINNESOTA

Nonrenewal

Length of Notice: Sixty days.

Reason for Nonrenewal: Required on the notice.

Proof Required: Proof of mailing.

Other Cancellation/Nonrenewal Provisions

1. A cancellation for nonpayment cannot be effective if payment is received prior to the effective date of cancellation.

2. Auto policies may be nonrenewed if an insured equals or exceeds the relevant number of points stated in Minn. R. 2770.8000 or if the insured fails to provide necessary underwriting information after two written requests from the insurer. The deductible amount under physical damage may be increased if three or more comprehensive claim payments have been made during the experience period or two or more comprehensive claim payments during the most recent twelve-month period. The physical damage portion may be nonrenewed if there have been a total of three payments for a single insured vehicle or four payments for multiple vehicles for various combinations of comprehensive and collision payments.

PERSONAL UMBRELLA

Minn. Stat. Ann. §§65B.15, 65B.16, and 65B.19

Cancellation during the Underwriting Period

Length of Underwriting Period: Sixty days.

Length of Notice: Ten days

Reason for Notice: Not required.

Proof Required: Proof of mailing.

Cancellation after the Underwriting Period

The policy may be cancelled **only** for the following reasons:

1. Nonpayment.

2. Misrepresentation or fraud by the named insured in obtaining the policy or in pursuing a claim under the policy.

MINNESOTA

3. Acts or omissions by the named insured that substantially increase or change the risk insured.

4. Refusal by the named insured to eliminate known conditions that increase the potential for loss after notification by the insurer.

5. Substantial change in the risk.

6. Loss of reinsurance by the insurer.

7. Determination by the commissioner that the continuation of the policy could place the insurer in violation of Minnesota insurance law.

8. Nonpayment of dues to an association or organization, where payment of dues is a prerequisite to obtaining or continuing such insurance. (Not applicable to retired individuals sixty-two or older, or who are disabled according to Social Security standards).

Length of Notice: Ten days for nonpayment; thirty days for any other reason.

Reason for Notice: Not required.

Proof Required: Proof of mailing.

Nonrenewal

Length of Notice: Thirty days.

Reason for Notice: Not required.

Proof Required: Proof of mailing.

FRAUD

Minn. Stat. Ann. §§60A.951 through 60A. 956

General Information and Definitions

"Insurance fraud" occurs when a person presents or causes to be presented to any insurer, or prepares with knowledge or belief that it will be so presented, a written or oral statement, including a computer-generated document, an electronic claim filing, or other electronic transmission, that contains materially false or misleading information, or a material and misleading omission, concerning an application for the issuance of an insurance policy; the rating of an insurance policy; a claim for payment, reimbursement, or benefits payable under an insurance policy to an insured, a beneficiary, or a third-party, premiums on an insurance policy, or payments made in accordance with the terms of an insurance policy.

Reporting Requirements

Any person engaged in the business of insurance having knowledge or a reasonable suspicion that a fraudulent insurance act is being, will be, or has been committed must provide to the Division of Insurance Fraud Prevention. If insurers, agents, or authorized persons report such information, they are immune from any liability for the release of the information.

Antifraud Provisions

An insurer must institute, implement, and maintain an antifraud plan. This does not apply to reinsurers, the Workers' Compensation Reinsurance Association, self-insurers, and excess insurers. Within thirty days after instituting or modifying an antifraud plan, the insurer must notify the commissioner in writing. The notice must include the name of the person responsible for administering the plan. An antifraud plan must establish procedures to prevent insurance fraud, including: internal fraud involving the insurer's officers, employees, or agents; fraud resulting from misrepresentations on applications for insurance; and claims fraud; report insurance fraud to appropriate law enforcement authorities; and cooperate with the prosecution of insurance fraud cases.

Viatical settlements contracts and purchase agreement forms and applications for viatical settlements, regardless of the form of transmission, must contain the following statement or a substantially similar statement:

> "Any person who knowingly presents false information in an application for insurance or viatical settlement contract or a viatical settlement purchase agreement is guilty of a crime and may be subject to fines and confinement in prison."

Application Fraud Statement

Minnesota does not require fraud statements on applications for insurance, but it does require the following language on all claims forms:

> "A person who files a claim with intent to defraud or helps commit a fraud against an insurer is guilty of a crime."

FAIR CLAIMS PROCESSING

Minn. Stat. Ann. §72A.201

The following acts by an insurer, an adjuster, a self-insured, or a self-insurance administrator constitute unfair settlement practices:

MINNESOTA

1. Except for claims made under a health insurance policy, after receiving notification of claim from an insured or a claimant, failing to acknowledge receipt of the notification of the claim within ten business days, and failing to promptly provide all necessary claim forms and instructions to process the claim, unless the claim is settled within ten business days.

2. Failing to reply, within ten business days of receipt, to all other communications about a claim from an insured or a claimant that reasonably indicate a response is requested or needed.

3. Failing to complete its investigation and inform the insured or claimant of acceptance or denial of a claim within thirty business days after receipt of notification of claim unless the investigation cannot be reasonably completed within that time.

4. Where evidence of suspected fraud is present, the requirement to disclose their reasons for failure to complete the investigation within the time period set forth need not be specific. The insurer must make this evidence available to the Department of Commerce if requested.

5. Failing to notify an insured who has made a notification of claim of all available benefits or coverages which the insured may be eligible to receive under the terms of a policy and of the documentation which the insured must supply in order to ascertain eligibility.

6. Unless otherwise provided by law or in the policy, requiring an insured to give written notice of loss or proof of loss within a specified time, and thereafter seeking to relieve the insurer of its obligations if the time limit is not complied with, unless the failure to comply with the time limit prejudices the insurer's rights and then only if the insurer gave prior notice to the insured of the potential prejudice.

7. Advising an insured or a claimant not to obtain the services of an attorney or an adjuster, or representing that payment will be delayed if an attorney or an adjuster is retained by the insured or the claimant.

8. Failing to advise in writing an insured or claimant who has filed a notification of claim known to be unresolved, and who has not retained an attorney, of the expiration of a statute of limitations at least sixty days prior to that expiration. For the purposes of this clause, any claim on which the insurer has received no communication from the insured or claimant for a period of two years preceding the expiration of the applicable statute of limitations shall not be considered to be known to be unresolved and notice need not be sent pursuant to this clause.

9. Demanding information which would not affect the settlement of the claim.

MINNESOTA

10. Unless expressly permitted by law or the policy, refusing to settle a claim of an insured on the basis that the responsibility should be assumed by others.

11. Failing, within sixty business days after receipt of a properly executed proof of loss, to advise the insured of the acceptance or denial of the claim by the insurer. No insurer shall deny a claim on the grounds of a specific policy provision, condition, or exclusion unless reference to the provision, condition, or exclusion is included in the denial. The denial must be given to the insured in writing with a copy filed in the claim file.

12. Denying or reducing a claim on the basis of an application which was altered or falsified by the agent or insurer without the knowledge of the insured.

13. Failing to notify the insured of the existence of the additional living expense coverage when an insured under a homeowners policy sustains a loss by reason of a covered occurrence and the damage to the dwelling is such that it is not habitable.

14. Failing to inform an insured or a claimant that the insurer will pay for an estimate of repair if the insurer requested the estimate and the insured or claimant had previously submitted two estimates of repair.

MISSISSIPPI

For details on cancellation procedures for the standard policy, refer to the Standard Policy section.

COMMERCIAL LINES
AGRICULTURAL CAPITAL ASSETS; BOP; C. ASSETS; C. AUTO; CGL (CGL, EMPLOYMENT, LIQUOR, POLLUTION, & PRODS/COMP OPS); C. PROP.; C. UMB.; FARM; E-COMMERCE; MGT. PROT.; AND PROF. LIAB.

Mississippi Code §83-5-28

Mississippi makes the following changes from the standard policy: nonrenewal for nonpayment requires a ten-day notice, thirty days for any other reason, and a thirty-day notice of cancellation must be given to any mortgagee. A reduction in coverage requires a thirty-day advance notice. Mortgage holders must be given notice of any termination, including insured's request. Where there is a named creditor loss payee, notice of cancellation must be mailed in a manner in which a proof of mailing can be provided, or personally delivered to the named creditor loss payee not less than thirty days prior to the effective date of such cancellation, reduction or nonrenewal.

CIM; CRIME & EQUIPMENT BREAKDOWN

Mississippi makes no changes from the standard policy.

COMMERCIAL GENERAL LIABILITY (OCP, Railroad Protective, & Underground Storage Tank Policy)

Mississippi Code §83-5-28

Mississippi makes the following changes from the standard policies: nonrenewal for nonpayment requires a ten-day notice and thirty days for any other reason; notices on OCP policies must go to the named insured and the designated contractor; and notices on Railroad Protective policies must go to the named insured, the designated contractor, and any involved governmental authority. Mortgage holders must be given notice of any termination, including insured's request. Where there is a named creditor loss payee, notice of cancellation must be mailed in a manner in which a proof of mailing can be provided, or personally delivered to the named creditor loss payee.

A reduction in coverage requires a thirty-day advance notice.

MISSISSIPPI

WORKERS COMPENSATION
Mississippi Code §71-3-77

All notices of cancellation and nonrenewal must be thirty days in length and must be delivered or sent by registered mail to the insured and to the Mississippi Workers Compensation Commission.

SURPLUS LINES
Mississippi Code §83-5-3

Every insurance company, foreign or domestic, that qualifies to do business in the State of Mississippi shall be required to execute an agreement to be bound by the statute laws of the State of Mississippi pertaining to the periods of limitation prescribed by the statute law of this state.

FINANCED PREMIUMS
Mississippi Code §81-21-19

If the premium finance agreement contains a power of attorney, the finance company may request, in the name of the insured, that the insurer cancel the policy due to nonpayment. The finance company must first give the insured ten days to pay. If the insured fails to make payment within that ten-day period, then the finance company mails the notice of cancellation to the insurer and the cancellation is processed as of the finance company's original default date. Return of the policy by the insured is not required.

All statutory, regulatory and contractual restrictions providing that the insurance contract may not be cancelled unless notice is given to a governmental agency, mortgagee or third party other than the insured shall apply where cancellation is in effect. Insurer shall give the prescribed notice on behalf of itself or the insured to any governmental agency, mortgagee or other third party on or before the fifth business day after the day it receives the notice of cancellation from the premium finance company and shall determine the effective date of cancellation taking into consideration the number of days' notice required to complete the cancellation.

PERSONAL LINES
DWELLING FIRE
Mississippi Code §83-5-28

The only change from the standard policy in Mississippi is that a reduction in coverage requires a thirty-day advance notice. Where there is a named creditor loss payee, notice of cancellation must be mailed in a manner in which a proof of mailing can be provided, or personally delivered to the named creditor loss payee.

MISSISSIPPI

HOMEOWNERS

Mississippi Code §83-5-28

A thirty-day notice of cancellation for any reason other than nonpayment is required during the sixty-day underwriting period. A reduction in coverage requires a thirty-day advance notice.

All notices must be sent to named insured and any named creditor or loss payees. Where there is a named creditor loss payee, notice of cancellation must be mailed in a manner in which a proof of mailing can be provided, or personally delivered to the named creditor loss payee.

PERSONAL AUTO

Mississippi Code §§83-11-3, 83-11-5, 83-11-7, 83-11-9, and 83-11-13

Cancellation during the Underwriting Period

Length of Underwriting Period: Sixty days.

Length of Notice: Ten days for nonpayment, thirty days for any other reason.

Reason for Cancellation: Required for nonpayment; not required on the notice for any other reason, but reason must be provided upon written request of the insured.

Proof Required: Proof of mailing.

Cancellation

The policy may be cancelled **only** for the following reasons:

1. Nonpayment.

2. Suspension or revocation of the driver's license of:

    a. The named insured.

    b. Any driver who lives with the named insured or who customarily uses the insured auto.

    The suspension or revocation must occur during the policy period or since the last anniversary date of the original effective date if the policy period is other than one year.

Note Also: The Mississippi Code allows a policy to be cancelled if the insured does not pay dues to an organization "where the original issue of such policy was dependent upon membership."

MISSISSIPPI

However, this reason does not appear on the ISO amendatory endorsement, so insurer's using the unmodified ISO form cannot use this as a reason to cancel the policy.

Length of Notice: Ten days for nonpayment; thirty days for all other reasons.

Reason for Cancellation: Not required on the notice, but reason must be provided upon written request of the insured.

Proof Required: Proof of mailing.

Nonrenewal

Length of Notice: Thirty days.

Reason for Nonrenewal: Not required on the notice.

Proof Required: Proof of mailing.

Other Cancellation/Nonrenewal Provisions

1. If the policy is written for a term of less than six months, the insurer may nonrenew every six months, beginning six months after the original effective date.

2. If the policy is written for a term of one year or longer, the insurer may nonrenew only at each anniversary of the original effective date.

3. If a personal auto policy is cancelled or nonrenewed for reasons other than nonpayment of premium, the insurer must notify the insured of the availability of the Mississippi Assigned Risk Plan.

   A reduction in coverage requires a thirty-day advance notice.

   All notices must be sent to the named insured and any loss payees. Notice to the named creditor loss payee to be by certified mail, return receipt requested, or by personal delivery by the agent not less than thirty days prior to the effective date of such cancellation, reduction or nonrenewal.

PERSONAL UMBRELLA

Mississippi Code § 83-11-5

Length of Underwriting Period: Sixty days.

Length of Notice: Ten days.

Reason for Cancellation: Reason for notice not required.

MISSISSIPPI

Proof Required: Proof of mailing.

Cancellation after the Underwriting Period

Length of Notice: Ten day notice for nonpayment; thirty day notice for any other reason.

Reason for Cancellation: Reason for notice not required.

Proof Required: Proof of mailing.

Nonrenewal

Length of Notice: Thirty days.

Reason for Nonrenewal: Reason for notice is not required.

Proof Required: Proof of mailing.

FRAUD

Mississippi Code §§7-5-301, 7-5-303, 7-5-309, and 7-5-307.

General Information and Definitions

A person or entity cannot, with the intent to appropriate to himself or to another any benefit, knowingly execute, collude or conspire to execute or attempt to execute a scheme or artifice to defraud any insurance plan in connection with the delivery of, or payment for, insurance benefits, items, services or claims; or to obtain by means of false or fraudulent pretense, representation, statement or promise money, or anything of value, in connection with the delivery of or payment for insurance claims under any plan or program or state law, items or services which are in whole or in part paid for, reimbursed, subsidized by, or are a required benefit of, an insurance plan or an insurance company or any other provider.

A person or entity cannot, in any matter related to any insurance plan, knowingly and willfully falsify, conceal or omit by any trick, scheme, artifice or device a material fact, make any false, fictitious or fraudulent statement or representation or make or use any false writing or document, knowing or having reason to know that the writing or document contains any false or fraudulent statement or entry in connection with the provision of insurance programs.

Penalties

A person who violates any Mississippi insurance fraud provision is guilty of a felony and, upon conviction thereof, will be punished by imprisonment for not more than three years, or by a fine of not more than $5,000.00 or double the value of the fraud, whichever is greater, or both.

MISSISSIPPI

If the defendant found to have violated any of the Mississippi insurance fraud provisions is an organization, then it shall be subject to a fine of not more than $150,000.00 for each violation. "Organization" for purposes of this subsection means a person other than an individual. The term includes corporations, partnerships, associations, joint-stock companies, unions, trusts, pension funds, unincorporated organizations, governments and political subdivisions thereof and nonprofit organizations.

In a proceeding for violations of any of the Mississippi insurance fraud provisions, the court, in addition to the criminal penalties imposed under this section, will assess against the defendant convicted of such violation double those reasonable costs that are expended by the Insurance Integrity Enforcement Bureau of the Office of Attorney General or the district attorney's office in the investigation of such case, including, but not limited to, the cost of investigators, process service, court reporters, expert witnesses and attorney's fees. A monetary penalty assessed and levied under this section shall be deposited to the credit of the State General Fund, and the Attorney General may institute and maintain proceedings in his name for enforcement of payment in the circuit court of the county of residence of the defendant and, if the defendant is a nonresident, such proceedings shall be in the Circuit Court of the First Judicial District of Hinds County, Mississippi.

Reporting Requirements

If any workers' compensation provider, health insurance provider, employee of the Workers' Compensation Commission or other person or entity has a belief or has any information that a false or misleading statement or representation or fraud or fraudulent denial has been made in connection with or relating to a workers' compensation claim or in connection with or relating to any insurance claim in relation to an insurance plan as defined in Mississippi Code §7-5-303, such person or entity may report such belief to the Insurance Integrity Enforcement Bureau, furnish any information which may be pertinent and cooperate in an investigation conducted by the bureau. Investigators for the Insurance Integrity Enforcement Bureau are authorized law enforcement officers and they are authorized to investigate and exercise such powers as are granted to other authorized law enforcement officers; however, the Insurance Integrity Enforcement Bureau and its investigators and personnel do not have any authority to impede, interfere with or control the operations and functions of the Mississippi Workers' Compensation Commission.

Application Fraud Statement

Mississippi does not require fraud statements on insurance applications.

FAIR CLAIMS PROCESSING

Mississippi Code §§83-18-29; 7-5-301; 83-5-29 to 83-5-51

A person or entity cannot fraudulently deny the payment of an insurance claim.

MISSISSIPPI

The commissioner may, in his or her discretion, suspend or revoke the certificate of authority of an administrator if the commissioner finds that the administrator has, without just cause, refused to pay proper claims or perform services arising under its contracts or has, without just cause, caused covered individuals to accept less than the amount due them or caused covered individuals to employ attorneys or bring suit against the administrator to secure full payment or settlement of such claims.

MISSOURI

For details on cancellation procedures for the standard policy, refer to the Standard Policy section.

COMMERCIAL LINES
BOP; CGL (All Coverage Parts); CRIME; EQUIPMENT BREAKDOWN; FARM LIAB; MGT. PROT., & PRO. LIAB.

Missouri Statutes §§375.001 through 375.004; 379.882 through 379.886

Cancellation during the Underwriting Period

Length of Underwriting Period: Sixty days.

Length of Notice: Ten days for any reason.

Reason for Cancellation: Required on the notice.

Proof Required: Proof of mailing.

Cancellation after the Underwriting period

The policy may be cancelled for any statutory reason.

1. Nonpayment of premium.
2. Fraud or material misrepresentation.
3. Convicted of a crime arising out of increased hazard.
4. Physical changes in the property.

Length of Notice: Ten days for nonpayment; thirty days for the reasons listed below:

1. Nonpayment of premium.
2. Fraud or material misrepresentation affecting the policy or a claim.
3. Changes in conditions that materially increase the risk.
4. Insolvency of the insurer.
5. If the insurer involuntarily loses its reinsurance.

Sixty days for any other reason.

MISSOURI

Reason for Cancellation: Required on the notice.

Proof Required: Proof of mailing.

Nonrenewal

Length of Notice: Sixty days.

Reason for Nonrenewal: Required on the notice.

Proof Required: Proof of mailing.

Other Cancellation/Nonrenewal Provisions

1. On OCP policies all notices must also be sent to any designated contractor.

2. On Railroad Protective policies all notices must also be sent to any designated contractor and any involved governmental authority.

3. On BOP or GL policies providing coverage for liquefied petroleum gas retailers, handlers and transporters, a copy of any termination notice must also be sent to the Missouri Propane Gas Commission.

4. Insurers must send a premium alteration notification notice if premiums increase twenty-five percent or more for a commercial policy. The notice must be sent at least sixty days prior to the expiration date of the policy, except in the case of excess or umbrella insurers that rely on underlying commercial insurance policies for premium development. Such umbrella or excess insurers must provide notice of a 25 percent or more increase at least thirty days prior to the policy expiration date. If the insurer(s) fails to meet this notice requirement, the insured may continue the policy for the remainder of the notice period plus an additional thirty days at the premium rate of the existing policies.

5. Policyholders are entitled to receive three years of loss history on cancelled or nonrenewed policies within thirty days of submitting a written request for such information. If the policy has been in force for less than three years, the policyholder is entitled to total experience on the policy within thirty days of the written request.

6. Insurers may not cancel or nonrenew an entire line or class of commercial casualty insurance without providing ninety days written notice to the director of the Missouri Department of Insurance before sending notices of cancellation or nonrenewal to insureds.

MISSOURI

AGRICULTURAL CAPITAL ASSETS; CAP. ASSETS; C. PROP; & FARM

Missouri Statutes §§375.001 through 375.004; 379.321; 379.882 through 379.886

Cancellation during the Underwriting Period

Length of Underwriting Period: Sixty days.

Length of Notice: Ten days for any reason.

Reason for Cancellation: Required on the notice.

Proof Required: Proof of mailing.

Cancellation

The policy may be cancelled for any statutory reason.

Length of Notice: Ten days for nonpayment; thirty days for the reasons listed below:

1. Fraud or material misrepresentation affecting the policy or a claim.

2. Changes in conditions that materially increase the risk.

3. Insolvency of the insurer.

4. If the insurer involuntarily loses its reinsurance.

Sixty days for any other reason.

Reason for Cancellation: Required on the notice.

Proof Required: Proof of mailing.

Nonrenewal

Length of Notice: Thirty days.

Reason for Nonrenewal: Required on the notice.

Proof Required: Proof of mailing.

Other Cancellation/Nonrenewal Provisions

1. Insurers must send a premium alteration requiring notification if premiums increase twenty-five percent or more for a commercial policy. If the insurer(s) fails to meet this

MISSOURI

notice requirement, the insured may continue the policy for the remainder of the notice period plus an additional thirty days at the premium rate of the existing policies.

2. Policyholders are entitled to receive three years of loss history on cancelled or nonrenewed policies within thirty days of submitting a written request for such information. If the policy has been in force for less than three years, the policyholder is entitled to total experience on the policy within thirty days of the written request.

COMMERCIAL AUTO; C. UMB.; FARM UMB.

(Applicable to an individual, partnership, or LLC with fewer than five private passenger autos.)

Missouri Statutes §§379.110, 379.114, 379.116, 379.118, 379.120, 379.321, 379.884, and 379.886

Cancellation during the Underwriting Period

Length of Underwriting Period: Sixty days.

Length of Notice: Ten days for any reason.

Reason for Cancellation: Required on the notice.

Poof Required: Post office certificate of mailing.

Cancellation after the Underwriting Period

The policy may be cancelled **only** for:

1. Nonpayment.

2. Suspension or revocation of the named insured's driver's license during the policy period.

   However, if there is more than one named insured, the insurer may not cancel, but must offer to exclude just the person with the suspended license.

Length of Notice: Ten days for nonpayment; sixty days for all other allowable reasons (Missouri Statutes § 379.118 allows a thirty-day notice, but those adopting the ISO amendatory endorsement (CA 02 19) must comply with the sixty-day notice in the endorsement).

Reason for Cancellation: Required on the notice.

Proof Required: Post office certificate.

MISSOURI

Nonrenewal

Length of Notice: Sixty days (Missouri Statutes § 379.118 allows a thirty-day notice, but those adopting the ISO amendatory endorsement (CA 02 19) must comply with the sixty-day notice in the endorsement).

Reason for Nonrenewal: Required on the notice.

Proof Required: Post office certificate of mailing.

Other Cancellation/Nonrenewal Provisions

1. For liability umbrella policies providing coverage for liquefied petroleum gas retailers, handlers and transporters, a copy of any termination notice must also be sent to the Missouri Propane Gas Commission.

2. Insurers must send a premium alteration requiring notification if premiums increase twenty-five percent or more for a commercial policy. The notice must be sent at least sixty days prior to the expiration date of the policy, except in the case of excess or umbrella insurers that rely on underlying commercial insurance policies for premium development. Such umbrella or excess insurers must provide notice of a twenty-five percent or more increase at least thirty days prior to the policy expiration date. If the insurer(s) fails to meet this notice requirement, the insured may continue the policy for the remainder of the notice period plus an additional thirty days at the premium rate of the existing policies.

3. Policyholders are entitled to receive three years of loss history on cancelled or nonrenewed policies within thirty days of submitting a written request for such information. If the policy has been in force for less than three years, the policyholder is entitled to total experience on the policy within thirty days of the written request.

4. Insurers may not cancel or nonrenew an entire line or class of commercial casualty insurance without providing ninety days written notice to the director of the Missouri Department of Insurance before sending notices of cancellation or nonrenewal to insureds.

5. An Insurer shall provide a written notice of a reduction in coverage to the named insured no less than fifteen days prior to the effective date of the proposed reduction in coverage. (Missouri Statutes § 379.118, as amended by 2018 Mo. SB 708).

COMMERCIAL AUTO

(For commercial autos not described above)

Missouri Statutes §§379.882 through 379.886

Cancellation

The policy may be cancelled for any statutory reason.

MISSOURI

Length of Notice: Sixty days except for the reasons listed below:

1. Nonpayment of premium.

2. Fraud or material misrepresentation affecting the policy or a claim.

3. Changes in conditions that materially increase the risk.

4. Insolvency of the insurer.

5. If the insurer involuntarily loses its reinsurance.

Reason for Cancellation: Required on the notice.

Proof Required: Proof of mailing.

Nonrenewal

Length of Notice: Thirty days (Missouri Statutes § 379.118 requires a thirty-day notice. The Common Policy Conditions IL 00 17 makes no provision for nonrenewal.)

Reason for Nonrenewal: Required on the notice.

Proof Required: Post office certificate of mailing.

Other Cancellation/Nonrenewal Provisions

1. Insurers must send a premium alteration requiring notification if premiums increase 25 percent or more for a commercial policy. The notice must be sent at least sixty days prior to the expiration date of the policy, except in the case of excess or umbrella insurers that rely on underlying commercial insurance policies for premium development. Such umbrella or excess insurers must provide notice of a twenty-five percent or more increase at least thirty days prior to the policy expiration date. If the insurer(s) fails to meet this notice requirement, the insured may continue the policy for the remainder of the notice period plus an additional thirty days at the premium rate of the existing policies.

2. Policyholders are entitled to receive three years of loss history on cancelled or nonrenewed policies within thirty days of submitting a written request for such information. If the policy has been in force for less than three years, the policyholder is entitled to total experience on the policy within thirty days of the written request.

3. Insurers may not cancel or nonrenew an entire line or class of commercial casualty insurance without providing ninety days' written notice to the director of the Missouri Department of Insurance before sending notices of cancellation or nonrenewal to insureds.

MISSOURI

4. An Insurer shall provide a written notice of a reduction in coverage to the named insured no less than fifteen days prior to the effective date of the proposed reduction in coverage. (Missouri Statutes § 379.118, as amended by 2018 Mo. SB 708).

COMMERCIAL INLAND MARINE

Missouri makes no changes from the standard policy.

WORKERS COMPENSATION

Missouri Statutes §§375.001 through 375.011; Mo. Code Regs. Ann. tit. 20, § 500-6.800

Cancellation during the Underwriting Period

Length of Underwriting Period: Sixty days.

Length of Notice: Ten days for any reason.

Reason for Cancellation: Required on the notice.

Proof Required: Proof of mailing.

Cancellation

Length of Notice: Ten days for nonpayment; thirty days for any of the specified reasons listed below:

1. Nonpayment of premium.

2. Fraud or material misrepresentation affecting the policy or in the presentation of a claim under the policy.

3. Changes in conditions after the effective date of the policy materially increasing the hazards originally insured.

4. Physical change which increases hazards.

Reason for Cancellation: Required on the notice.

Proof Required: Proof of mailing.

Legal advice is suggested.

MISSOURI

Nonrenewal

Length of Notice: Sixty days.

Reason for Nonrenewal: Required on the notice.

Proof Required: Proof of mailing.

Other Cancellation/Nonrenewal Provisions

1. Insurers must send a premium alteration requiring notification if premiums increase twenty-five percent or more for a commercial policy. The notice must be sent at least sixty days prior to the expiration date of the policy, except in the case of excess or umbrella insurers that rely on underlying commercial insurance policies for premium development. Such umbrella or excess insurers must provide notice of a 25 percent or more increase at least thirty days prior to the policy expiration date. If the insurer(s) fails to meet this notice requirement, the insured may continue the policy for the remainder of the notice period plus an additional thirty days at the premium rate of the existing policies.

2. Policyholders are entitled to receive three years of loss history on cancelled or nonrenewed policies within thirty days of submitting a written request for such information. If the policy has been in force for less than three years, the policyholder is entitled to total experience on the policy within thirty days of the written request.

3. Insurers may not cancel or nonrenew an entire line or class of commercial casualty insurance without providing ninety days written notice to the director of the Missouri Department of Insurance before sending notices of cancellation or nonrenewal to insureds.

SURPLUS LINES

Missouri Statutes § 379.882

Surplus lines insurers must follow the cancellation and nonrenewal requirements for admitted companies.

FINANCED PREMIUMS

Missouri Statutes §§364.100 and 364.130

If the premium finance agreement contains a power of attorney, the finance company may request, in the name of the insured, that the insurer cancel the policy due to nonpayment. The finance company must first give the insured ten days to pay. If the insured fails to make payment within that ten-day period, then the finance company mails the notice of cancellation to the insurer and the cancellation is processed as of the finance company's original default date. Return of the policy by the insured is not required.

MISSOURI

All statutory, regulatory, and contractual restrictions providing that the insurance contract may not be canceled unless notice is given to a governmental agency, mortgagee, or other third party shall apply where cancellation is effected under the provisions of this section. The insurer shall give the prescribed notice on behalf of itself or the insured to any governmental agency, mortgagee, or other third party on or before the second business day after the day it receives the notice of cancellation from the premium finance company and shall determine the effective date of cancellation taking into consideration the number of days' notice required to complete the cancellation.

PERSONAL LINES
DWELLING FIRE & HOMEOWNERS

Missouri Statutes §§375.001 through 375.004

Cancellation during the Underwriting Period

Length of Underwriting Period: Sixty days.

Length of Notice: Ten days for any reason.

Reason for Cancellation: Required on the notice.

Proof Required: Proof of mailing.

Cancellation after the Underwriting Period

Missouri statutes limit cancellation to **only** the following reasons:

1. Nonpayment.

2. Fraud or material misrepresentation affecting the policy or in the presentation of a claim, or violation of any of the terms or conditions of the policy.

3. If the named insured or any occupant of the property is convicted of a crime arising out of acts increasing the hazard insured against.

4. Physical changes in the property which increase the hazards insured.

Length of Notice: Ten days for nonpayment; thirty days for all other reasons.

Reason for Cancellation: Required on the notice.

Proof Required: Proof of mailing.

MISSOURI

Nonrenewal

Length of Notice: Thirty days.

Reason for Nonrenewal: Required on the notice. Even though the Missouri amendatory endorsements (DL 01 24 and HO 01 24) are silent on this matter, the reason for nonrenewal must be shown on the notice.

Proof Required: Proof of mailing.

PERSONAL AUTO

Missouri Statutes §§375.001 through 375.011; 379.110 through 379.122

Cancellation during the Underwriting Period

Length of Underwriting Period: Sixty days.

Length of Notice: Ten days for any reason.

Reason for Cancellation: Required on the notice.

Proof Required: Post office certificate of mailing.

Cancellation after the Underwriting Period

The policy may be cancelled **only** for:

Nonpayment or suspension or revocation of the driver's license of the named insured. The suspension or revocation must occur during the policy period or since the last anniversary date. If there is more than one named insured, the insurer must offer to exclude the driver with the suspended or revoked license.

Length of Notice: Ten days for nonpayment; thirty days for all other allowable reasons.

Reason for Cancellation: Required on the notice. Even though the Missouri amendatory endorsement is silent on this matter, the reason for cancellation must be shown on the notice.

Proof Required: Post office certificate of mailing.

Nonrenewal

Length of Notice: Thirty days.

MISSOURI

Reason for Nonrenewal: Required on the notice. Even though ISO's Missouri amendatory endorsement (PP 01 63) is silent on this matter, the reason for nonrenewal must be shown on the notice.

Proof Required: Post office certificate of mailing.

Other Cancellation/Nonrenewal Provisions

1. Policies with a term of less than six months or with no fixed expiration date are considered as if they were written for successive terms of six months.

2. Notice must state that the insured may be eligible for coverage through the assigned risk plan if other insurance is not available.

3. These provisions are not applicable to policies covering more than four vehicles, or to policies issued through the assigned risk plan.

4. No insurer shall cancel or refuse to write or refuse to renew a policy of automobile insurance on any person with at least two years' driving experience solely because of the age, residence, race, sex, color, creed, national origin, ancestry or lawful occupation, including the military service, of anyone who is or seeks to become insured or solely because another insurer has refused to write a policy, or has canceled or has refused to renew an existing policy in which that person was the named insured, nor shall any insurance company or its agent or representative require any applicant, policyholder or operator to divulge in a written application or otherwise whether any insurer has canceled or refused to renew or issue to the applicant, policyholder or operator a policy of automobile insurance.

5. An Insurer shall provide a written notice of a reduction in coverage to the named insured no less than fifteen days prior to the effective date of the proposed reduction in cover-age. (Missouri Statutes § 379.118, as amended by 2018 Mo. SB 708).

Notice to the Applicant: If an insurer declines an application, it must send a written notice advising the applicant of the specific reasons for the declination within thirty days. The notice must advise the applicant of the availability of the assigned risk plan.

PERSONAL UMBRELLA

Cancellation during the Underwriting Period

Length of Underwriting Period: Sixty days.

Length of Notice: Ten days for any reason.

MISSOURI

Reason for Notice: Not required.

Proof Required: Proof of mailing.

Cancellation after the Underwriting Period

Cancellation is only allowed for the following reasons:

1. Nonpayment.

2. Fraud or material misrepresentation affecting the policy or in the presentation of a claim, or violation of any of the terms or conditions of the policy.

3. If the named insured or any occupant of the property is convicted of a crime arising out of acts increasing the hazard insured against.

4. Physical changes in the property which increase the hazards insured.

Length of Notice: Ten days for nonpayment; thirty days for any other reason.

Reason for Notice: Not required.

Proof Required: Proof of mailing.

Nonrenewal

The policy may be nonrenewed for any reason.

Length of Notice: Thirty days.

Reason for Notice: Required on the notice.

Proof Required: Proof of mailing.

FRAUD

Missouri Statutes §§375.991 et seq.

General Information and Definitions

A person commits a "fraudulent insurance act" if such person knowingly presents, causes to be presented, or prepares with knowledge or belief that it will be presented, to or by an insurer, purported insurer, broker, or any agent thereof, any oral or written statement including computer generated documents as part of, or in support of, an application for the issuance of, or the rating of, an insurance policy for commercial or personal insurance, or a claim for payment or other benefit pursuant to an insurance policy for commercial or personal insurance, which such person knows to contain materially false information concerning any fact material thereto or if such person conceals, for the purpose of misleading another, information concerning any fact material thereto.

A "fraudulent insurance act" also includes, but is not limited to, knowingly filing false insurance claims with an insurer, health services corporation, or health maintenance organization by engaging in any one or more of the following false billing practices:

1. "Unbundling", an insurance claim by claiming a number of medical procedures were performed instead of a single comprehensive procedure.

2. "Upcoding", an insurance claim by claiming that a more serious or extensive procedure was performed than was actually performed.

3. "Exploding", an insurance claim by claiming a series of tests was performed on a single sample of blood, urine, or other bodily fluid, when actually the series of tests was part of one battery of tests.

4. "Duplicating", a medical, hospital or rehabilitative insurance claim made by a health care provider by resubmitting the claim through another health care provider in which the original health care provider has an ownership interest.

Penalties

A fraudulent insurance act for a first offense is a class E felony. Any person who pleads guilty to or is found guilty of a fraudulent insurance act who has previously pled guilty to or has been found guilty of a fraudulent insurance act is guilty of a class D felony.

Any person who pleads guilty or is found guilty of a fraudulent insurance act will be ordered by the court to make restitution to any person or insurer for any financial loss sustained as a result of such violation. The court shall determine the extent and method of restitution.

Reporting Requirements

Any company which believes that a fraudulent claim is being made must, within sixty days of the receipt of such notice, send to the department of insurance, financial institutions and professional registration, on a form prescribed by the department, the information requested and such additional information relative to the claim and the parties claiming loss or damages because of the accident as the department may require. The department of insurance, financial institutions and professional registration will review such reports and select such claims as, in its judgment, may require further investigation. It will then cause an independent examination of the facts surrounding such claim to be made to determine the extent, if any, to which fraud,

MISSOURI

deceit, or intentional misrepresentation of any kind exists in the submission of the claim. The department of insurance, financial institutions and professional registration will report any alleged violations of law which its investigations disclose to the appropriate licensing agency and prosecuting authority having jurisdiction with respect to any such violation.

Application Fraud Statement

Missouri does not require fraud statements.

FAIR CLAIMS PROCESSING

Missouri Statutes § 375.1007

Any of the following acts by an insurer constitutes an improper claims practice:

1. Misrepresenting to claimants and insureds relevant facts or policy provisions relating to coverages at issue.

2. Failing to acknowledge with reasonable promptness pertinent communications with respect to claims arising under its policies.

3. Failing to adopt and implement reasonable standards for the prompt investigation and settlement of claims arising under its policies.

4. Not attempting in good faith to effectuate prompt, fair and equitable settlement of claims submitted in which liability has become reasonably clear.

5. Compelling insureds or beneficiaries to institute suits to recover amounts due under its policies by offering substantially less than the amounts ultimately recovered in suits brought by them.

6. Refusing to pay claims without conducting a reasonable investigation.

7. Failing to affirm or deny coverage of claims within a reasonable time after proof of loss statements have been completed and communicated to the insurer.

8. Attempting to settle a claim for less than the amount to which a reasonable person would believe the insured or beneficiary was entitled by reference to written or printed advertising material accompanying or made part of an application.

9. Attempting to settle claims on the basis of an application which was materially altered without notice to, or knowledge or consent of, the insured.

MISSOURI

10. Making a claims payment to an insured or beneficiary without indicating the coverage under which each payment is being made.

11. Unreasonably delaying the investigation or payment of claims by requiring both a formal proof of loss form and subsequent verification that would result in duplication of information and verification appearing in the formal proof of loss form.

12. Failing in the case of claims denial or offers of a compromise settlement to promptly provide a reasonable and accurate explanation of the basis for such actions.

13. Failing to provide forms necessary to present claims within fifteen calendar days of a request with reasonable explanations regarding their use.

14. Failing to adopt and implement reasonable standards to assure that the repairs of a repairer owned by or required to be used by the insurer are performed in a workmanlike manner.

15. Failing to promptly settle claims where liability has become reasonably clear under one portion of the insurance policy coverage in order to influence settlements under other portions of the insurance policy coverage.

MONTANA

For details on cancellation procedures for the standard policy, refer to the Standard Policy section.

COMMERCIAL LINES
AGRICULTURAL CAPITAL ASSETS; BOP; CAPITAL ASSETS; CRIME; CGL (CGL, EMPLOYMENT, LIQUOR, OCP, POLLUTION, RR PROT; PRODS. / COMPLETED OPS.) C. PROP.; CIM; EQUIPMENT BREAKDOWN; FARM

Montana Code §§33-15-1101 to 33-15-1121

Cancellation during the Underwriting Period

Length of Underwriting Period: Sixty days.

Length of Notice: Ten days for any reason.

Reason for Cancellation: Not required.

Proof Required: Proof of mailing.

Cancellation after the Underwriting Period

The policy may be cancelled **only** for the following reasons:

1. Nonpayment.

2. Material misrepresentation.

3. Substantial change in the risk assumed; except to the extent the insurer should reasonably have foreseen the change or contemplated the risk in writing the policy.

4. Substantial breaches of any of the contractual duties, conditions, or warranties.

5. If the commissioner determines that continuation of the policy would place the insurer in violation of the Montana Insurance Code.

6. If the insurer becomes financially impaired.

7. Any other reason approved by the commissioner.

MONTANA

Length of Notice: Ten days for any reason.

Reason for Cancellation: Required upon written request if requested within sixty days of cancellation. Reasons must be provided on written request within twenty-one days of receipt of the request. Exception is where cancellation is for nonpayment of premium.

Proof Required: Proof of mailing.

Nonrenewal

Length of Notice: Forty-five days.

Reason for Nonrenewal: Required upon written request if requested within sixty days of nonrenewal. Reasons must be provided on written request within twenty-one days of receipt of the request.

Proof Required: Proof of mailing.

Other Cancellation/Nonrenewal Provisions

Renewal on less favorable terms is treated as a nonrenewal, and has the same notice requirement of forty-five days. However, this provision does not appear on the ISO amendatory endorsement.

An insurer may not refuse to renew a property and casualty insurance policy on the basis of a single loss occurring during the policy period unless the insurer has previously disclosed in writing to the insured, at the time that the insured applied for the insurance or prior to the insured's renewal, that a single loss is among the insurer's criteria for nonrenewal.

If a policy has been issued for a term longer than one year and for additional premium consideration an annual premium has been guaranteed, the insurer may not increase the annual premium for the term of that policy.

Nonrenewal notification to the insured's producer via electronic transfer meets the requirements of a mailed or delivered copy.

For OCP policies all notices must also be sent to the designated contractor. For Railroad Protective policies all notices must also be sent to the designated contractor and to any involved governmental authority.

MONTANA

PROFESSIONAL LIABILITY

Montana Code §§33-15-1103 and 33-23-302

Cancellation during the Underwriting Period

Length of Underwriting Period: Sixty days.

Length of Notice: Sixty days for any reason.

Reason for Cancellation: Consumer must be notified he may request the reasons for cancellation.

Proof Required: Proof of mailing.

Cancellation after the Underwriting Period

The policy may be cancelled **only** for the following reasons:

1. Nonpayment.

2. Material misrepresentation.

3. Substantial change in the risk assumed; except to the extent the insurer should reasonably have foreseen the change or contemplated the risk in writing the policy.

4. Substantial breaches of any of the contractual duties, conditions, or warranties.

5. If the commissioner determines that continuation of the policy would place the insurer in violation of the Montana Insurance Code.

6. If the insurer becomes financially impaired.

7. Any other reason approved by the commissioner.

Length of Notice: Sixty days for any reason.

Reason for Cancellation: Required on the notice.

Proof Required: Proof of mailing.

MONTANA

Nonrenewal

Length of Notice: Sixty days.

Reason for Nonrenewal: Consumer must be notified he may request the reasons for cancellation.

Proof Required: Proof of mailing.

Other Cancellation/Nonrenewal Provisions

These rules apply to any dentist, registered nurse, nursing home administrator, registered physical therapist, podiatrist, licensed psychologist, osteopath, chiropractor, pharmacist, optometrist, or veterinarian, licensed under the laws of this state, or a licensed hospital or long-term care facility as the employer of any person so identified.

COMMERCIAL AUTO

Montana Code §§33-23-211 through 33-23-214

Cancellation during the Underwriting Period

Length of Underwriting Period: Sixty days.

Length of Notice: Ten days for nonpayment; forty-five days for any other reason.

Reason for Cancellation: Must be included if cancellation is for nonpayment of premium, otherwise consumer must be notified she may request the reasons for cancellation.

Proof Required: Proof of mailing.

Cancellation after the Underwriting Period

The policy may be cancelled **only** for:

1. Nonpayment.

2. Revocation or suspension of the driver's license or vehicle registration of the named insured, any driver who lives with the named insured, or one who customarily uses the named insured's auto. This must occur during the policy period, or if the policy is a renewal, during the 180 days immediately preceding the effective date.

Length of Notice: Ten days for nonpayment; forty-five days for any other allowable reason.

MONTANA

Reason for Cancellation: Must be included if cancellation is for nonpayment of premium, otherwise consumer must be notified he or she may request the reasons for cancellation.

Proof Required: Proof of mailing.

Nonrenewal

Length of Notice: Forty-five days.

Reason for Nonrenewal: Consumer must be notified he may request the reasons for cancellation.

Proof Required: Proof of mailing.

Other Cancellation/Nonrenewal Provisions

Notices must either state or offer to disclose the reason for cancellation or nonrenewal upon request.

Renewal on less favorable terms is treated as a nonrenewal, with the same notice requirements of forty-five days. This provision does not appear on ISO's amendatory endorsement (CA 02 20).

COMMERCIAL GENERAL LIABILITY
(Underground Storage Tanks)

Montana Code §§33-15-1101 to 33-15-1106

Cancellation during the Underwriting Period

Length of Underwriting Period: Sixty days.

Length of Notice: Ten days for any reason.

Reason for Cancellation: Not required.

Proof Required: Proof of mailing.

Cancellation after the Underwriting Period

The policy may be cancelled **only** for the following reasons:

1. Nonpayment.

2. Material misrepresentation.

MONTANA

3. Substantial change in the risk assumed.

4. If the insured breaches the policy's duties, conditions, or warranties.

5. If the commissioner determines that continuation of the policy would violate Montana Insurance Code.

6. Financial impairment of the insurer.

7. Any other reasons approved by the commissioner.

Length of Notice: Ten days for any reason.

Reason for Cancellation: Not required. Consumer must be notified he may request the reasons for cancellation.

Proof Required: Proof of mailing.

Nonrenewal

Length of Notice: Forty-five days.

Reason for Nonrenewal: Not required. Consumer must be notified he may request the reasons for cancellation.

Proof Required: Proof of mailing.

Other Cancellation/Nonrenewal Provisions

If a policy has been issued for a term longer than one year and if either the premium is prepaid or an agreed term, it is guaranteed in exchange for additional consideration, the insurer generally may not increase the annual premium for the term of that policy.

Renewal on less favorable terms is treated as a nonrenewal and requires forty-five days' notice. However, this provision does not appear on the ISO amendatory endorsement.

An insurer may not refuse to renew a property and casualty insurance policy on the basis of a single loss occurring during the policy period unless the insurer has previously disclosed in writing to the insured, at the time that the insured applied for the insurance or prior to the insured's renewal, that a single loss is among the insurer's criteria for nonrenewal.

MONTANA

If an insurer has adopted ISO form CG 30 39, then a sixty-day notice is required for all cancellations or nonrenewals. All notices of cancellation or nonrenewal must be sent by certified mail under the ISO form as well.

COMMERCIAL UMBRELLA

Montana Code §§33-15-1101 to 33-15-1106

Cancellation during the Underwriting Period

Length of Underwriting Period: Sixty days.

Length of Notice: Ten days for any reason.

Reason for Cancellation: Not required, but must be provided upon written request.

Proof Required: Proof of mailing.

Cancellation after the Underwriting Period

The policy may be cancelled **only** for the following reasons:

1. Nonpayment.

2. Material misrepresentation.

3. Substantial change in the risk assumed; except to the extent the insurer should reasonably have foreseen the change or contemplated the risk in writing the policy.

4. Substantial breaches of any of the contractual duties, conditions, or warranties.

5. If the commissioner determines that continuation of the policy would place the insurer in violation of the Montana Insurance Code.

6. If the insurer becomes financially impaired.

7. Any other reason approved by the commissioner.

Length of Notice: Ten days for any reason.

Reason for Cancellation: Not required, but must be provided upon written request.

Proof Required: Proof of mailing.

MONTANA

Nonrenewal Notice Requirements

Length of Notice: Forty-five days.

Reason for Nonrenewal: Not required, but must be provided upon request.

Proof Required: Proof of mailing.

Allowable Reasons for Nonrenewal

No restrictions.

Other Cancellation/Nonrenewal Provisions

Renewal on less favorable terms is treated as a nonrenewal and requires forty-five days' notice. An insurer may not refuse to renew a property and casualty insurance policy on the basis of a single loss occurring during the policy period unless the insurer has previously disclosed in writing to the insured, at the time that the insured applied for the insurance or prior to the insured's renewal, that a single loss is among the insurer's criteria for nonrenewal.

If a policy has been issued for a term longer than one year and if either the premium is prepaid or an agreed term is guaranteed for additional premium consideration, the insurer generally may not increase the annual premium for the term of that policy.

Insurers that use ISO form CX 02 34 must provide forty-five days' notice of cancellation for any reason other than nonpayment of premium.

WORKERS COMPENSATION

Montana Code §§33-15-1101 to 33-15-1107, 39-71-2205; Mont. Admin. R. 24.29.4314

Cancellation during the Underwriting Period

Length of Underwriting Period: Sixty days.

Length of Notice: Twenty days for any reason.

Reason for Cancellation: Not required.

Proof Required: Proof of mailing.

MONTANA

Cancellation

The policy may be cancelled **only** for the following reasons:

1. Nonpayment.

2. Material misrepresentation.

3. Substantial change in the risk assumed; except to the extent the insurer should reasonably have foreseen the change or contemplated the risk in writing the policy.

4. Substantial breaches of any of the contractual duties, conditions, or warranties.

5. If the commissioner determines that continuation of the policy would place the insurer in violation of the Montana Insurance Code.

6. If the insurer becomes financially impaired.

7. Any other reason approved by the commissioner.

Length of Notice: Twenty days for any reason.

Reason for Cancellation: Required upon written request if requested within sixty days of cancellation. Reasons must be provided by written request within twenty days of receipt of the request. Exception is where cancellation is for nonpayment of premium.

Proof Required: Proof of mailing.

Nonrenewal

Length of Notice: Forty-five days.

Reason for Nonrenewal: Required upon written request if requested within sixty days of nonrenewal. Reasons must be provided on written request within twenty-one days of receipt of the request.

Proof Required: Proof of mailing.

Other Cancellation/Nonrenewal Provisions

Cancellation can occur only after twenty days prior notice. Notice must be provided to the insured and to the Department of Labor and Industry.

MONTANA

SURPLUS LINES

Montana Code §33-2-302

Surplus Lines insurers are governed by the regulations of the home state of the insured. If the home state of an insured is Montana then the transaction is governed by the statutes and rules of Montana regardless of where the insured risk is located if it is a part of a multi-state risk. If the home state is Montana, the rules regarding cancellation and nonrenewal are governed by the nature of the specific risk being insured and fall under those guidelines.

FINANCED PREMIUMS

Montana Code §33-14-304

If the premium finance agreement contains a power of attorney, the finance company may request, in the name of the insured, that the insurer cancel the policy due to nonpayment. The finance company must first give the insured ten days' written notice of the cancellation via mail. If the insured fails to make payment within that ten-day period, the finance company must then mail the notice of cancellation to the insurer and the cancellation is processed as of the finance company's original default date. Return of the policy by the insured is not required.

All statutory, regulatory, and contractual restrictions providing that the insurance contract may not be canceled unless notice is given to a governmental agency, mortgagee, or other third party apply whenever cancellation is effected by a premium finance company. The insurer shall give the prescribed notice on behalf of itself or the insured to any governmental agency, mortgagee, or other third party on or before the second business day after the day it receives the notice of cancellation from the premium finance company and shall determine the effective date of cancellation taking into consideration the number of days' notice required to complete the cancellation.

PERSONAL LINES
DWELLING FIRE, HOMEOWNERS

Montana Code §§33-15-1101 to 33-15-1111, 33-23-401

Cancellation during the Underwriting Period

Length of Underwriting Period: Sixty days.

Length of Notice: Twenty days for nonpayment of premium, forty-five days for any other reason.

Reason for Cancellation: Consumer must be notified he may request the reason for cancellation.

Proof Required: Proof of mailing.

MONTANA

Cancellation after the Underwriting Period

The policy may be cancelled **only** for the following reasons:

1. Nonpayment.

2. Material misrepresentation on the application.

3. The risk has changed substantially since the policy was issued, except to the extent that the insurer should reasonably have foreseen the change when writing the risk.

4. Substantial breaches of contractual duties, conditions, or warranties.

5. If the insurance commissioner determines that to continue the policy would violate Montana statutes.

6. If the insurer becomes financially impaired.

7. Any other reason with the insurance commissioner's approval.

Length of Notice: Twenty days for nonpayment of premium; forty-five days for any other reason.

Reason for Cancellation: Consumer must be notified he may request the reason for cancellation.

Proof Required: Proof of mailing.

Nonrenewal

Length of Notice: Forty-five days. Must contain information about the insureds right to request the reason for the nonrenewal.

Reason for Nonrenewal: Required upon written request if requested within sixty days of nonrenewal. Reasons must be provided on written request within twenty-one days of receipt of request.

Proof Required: Proof of mailing.

Other Cancellation/Nonrenewal Provisions

If a policy has been issued for a term longer than one year and if either the policy's premium is prepaid or an agreed term is guaranteed by additional premium consideration, the insurer generally may not increase the annual premium for the term of that policy.

MONTANA

Nonrenewal notification to the insured's producer via electronic transfer meets the requirements of a mailed or delivered copy.

An insurer may not refuse to renew a property and casualty insurance policy on the basis of a single loss occurring during the policy period unless the insurer has previously disclosed in writing to the insured, at the time that the insured applied for the insurance or prior to the insured's renewal, that a single loss is among the insurer's criteria for nonrenewal.

An insurer may not decline, cancel, or refuse to write a homeowners policy for the principal reason that the insured operates a daycare center (as defined by code) that meets code requirements. However, the insurer may exclude or limit coverage with respect to losses related to the daycare facility.

PERSONAL AUTO

Montana Code §§33-23-211, 33-23-212, 33-23-214, and 33-15-1101 to 33-15-1106

Cancellation during the Underwriting Period

Length of Underwriting Period: Sixty days.

Length of Notice: Ten days for nonpayment; forty-five days for all other reasons.

Reason for Cancellation: Must be included if for nonpayment of premium, consumer must be notified he may request the reason for cancellation.

Proof Required: Proof of mailing.

Cancellation after the Underwriting Period

The policy may be cancelled **only** for the following reasons:

1. Nonpayment.
2. Revocation or suspension of the driver's license or vehicle registration of the named insured, any driver who lives with the named insured or one who customarily uses the named insured's auto. This must occur during the policy period, or if the policy is a renewal, during the 180 days immediately preceding the effective date.

Length of Notice: Ten days for nonpayment; forty-five days for all other reasons.

Reason for Cancellation: Must be included if for nonpayment of premium, consumer must be notified he may request the reason for cancellation.

Proof Required: Proof of mailing.

MONTANA

Nonrenewal

Length of Notice: Forty-five days.

Reason for Nonrenewal: Not required, but must be provided upon written request.

Proof Required: Proof of mailing.

Other Cancellation/Nonrenewal Provisions

1. If the policy term is less than six months, the insurer may nonrenew every six months, beginning six months after the original effective date.

2. If the policy term is one year or longer, the insurer may nonrenew the policy at each anniversary of the original effective date.

3. Notices must offer to disclose reason upon request. This provision does not appear on the ISO's amendatory endorsement (PP 01 83).

4. Renewal on less favorable terms is treated as a nonrenewal, requires forty-five days' notice.

PERSONAL UMBRELLA

Montana Code §§33-15-1101 to 33-15-1111

Cancellation during the Underwriting Period

Length of Underwriting Period: Sixty days.

Length of Notice: Ten days for any reason.

Reason for Cancellation: Consumer must be notified he may request the reason for cancellation.

Proof Required: Proof of mailing.

Cancellation after the Underwriting Period

The policy may be cancelled **only** for the following reasons:

1. Nonpayment.

2. Material misrepresentation on the application.

MONTANA

3. The risk has changed substantially since the policy was issued, except to the extent that the insurer should reasonably have foreseen the change when writing the risk.

4. Substantial breaches of contractual duties, conditions, or warranties.

5. If the insurance commissioner determines that to continue the policy would violate Montana statutes.

6. If the insurer becomes financially impaired.

7. Any other reason with the insurance commissioner's approval.

Length of Notice: Ten days for any reason.

Reason for Cancellation: Consumer must be notified he may request the reason for cancellation.

Proof Required: Proof of mailing.

Nonrenewal

Length of Notice: Forty-five days. Must contain information about the insureds right to request the reason for the nonrenewal.

Reason for Nonrenewal: Required upon written request if requested within sixty days of nonrenewal. Reasons must be provided on written request within twenty-one days of receipt of this request.

Proof Required: Proof of mailing.

FRAUD

Montana Code §§33-1-1202; 33-1-1205; 33-1-1211

General Information and Definitions

A person commits insurance fraud by presenting or causing to be presented, for pecuniary or any other benefit, to any insurer, purported insurer, producer, or administrator any written or oral statement, including computer-generated documents, containing false, incomplete, or misleading information, concerning any fact or thing material to, as part of, or in support of a claim for payment or other benefit pursuant to an insurance policy.

Other acts also constitute insurance fraud, including: assisting, abetting, soliciting or conspiring with another to prepare or make any written or oral statement containing false,

MONTANA

incomplete, or misleading information concerning any fact that is intended to be presented to any insurer or purported insurer or in connection with, material to, or in support of any claim for payment or other benefit pursuant to an insurance policy or contract.

Insurance fraud is committed when one presents or causes to be presented a materially false or altered application of insurance to or by an insurer, purported insurer, producer, or administrator. Accepting premium money while knowing that coverage will not be provided constitutes insurance fraud. A health care provider commits insurance fraud by submitting a false or altered bill or report of physical condition to an insurer. One may not offer or accept an inducement, whether direct or indirect with the intention of deceiving an insurer. Finally, one may not present counterfeit insurance documents to any person.

Penalties

Perpetrators of insurance fraud face a myriad of penalties. After a hearing, the insurance commissioner may impose a maximum fine of $25,000 but insurance producers and adjusters may not be fined more than $5,000 per violation. The commissioner may also require a guilty party to pay hearing costs. Anyone who either purposely or knowingly commits insurance fraud commits the crime of theft under Montana Code §45-6-301 and faces the corresponding penalties, including potential prison. Finally, the commissioner may require a person who commits insurance fraud to make restitution to the insurer or to any other defrauded party for the entirety of the financial loss sustained due to the insurance fraud.

Reporting Requirements

Every insurer, independent adjuster, independent administrator, independent consultant and independent producer has the duty to fully cooperate with the insurance commissioner regarding the commissioner's investigation of apparent insurance fraud. Additionally, insurers, officers or employees of the insurers, independent adjusters, independent administrators, independent consultants, or independent producers must notify the commissioner within sixty days of potential insurance fraud if they have reason to believe that insurance fraud has been or is being committed. When the alleged insurance fraud involves a claim or application submitted to the state compensation insurance fund, or a policy issued by that fund, notice must be given within sixty days to the State Fraud Detection and Prevention Unit. Individuals who contribute to or cooperate with an investigation of suspected insurance fraud generally receive immunity.

Application Fraud Statement

Montana does not require a fraud statement on applications for insurance.

MONTANA

FAIR CLAIMS PROCESSING

Montana Code §33-18-232 *Applies to health insurance as defined in §33-18-231*

Generally

An insurer must either pay or deny a claim within thirty days after receiving proof of loss unless the insurer makes a reasonable request for additional information or documents in order to evaluate the claim. If the insurer makes such a reasonable request, the insurer must pay or deny the claim within sixty days of receiving the proof of loss unless the insurer has either notified the insured, the insured's assignee, or the claimant of why the insurer did not pay the claim in full, or the insurer reasonably believes that insurance fraud has been committed and reports the suspected fraud to the insurance commissioner.

Penalty

If the insurer fails to pay a valid claim and the interest exceeds $5 according to the aforementioned timeline, the insurer must pay the claim plus 10 percent annual interest calculated from the date when the payment came due. For purposes of calculating interest, a claim is considered due thirty days after the insurer's receipt of proof of loss.

NEBRASKA

For details on cancellation procedures for the standard policy, refer to the Standard Policy section.

COMMERCIAL LINES
AGRICULTURAL CAPITAL ASSETS; BOP; CAPITAL ASSETS; CRIME; COMMERCIAL UMBRELLA; CGL (All Coverage Parts) CIM; C. PROP.; EQUIPMENT BREAKDOWN; FARM; & PROD. LIABILITY

Revised Statutes of Nebraska § 44-522

Cancellation during the Underwriting Period

Length of Underwriting Period: Sixty days.

Length of Notice: Ten days for nonpayment; sixty days for any other reason.

Reason for Cancellation: Required on the notice.

Proof Required: A United States Postal Service certificate of mailing is sufficient proof of receipt of notice on the third calendar day after the date of the certificate of mailing.

Cancellation after the Underwriting Period

The policy may be cancelled **only** for the following reasons:

1. Nonpayment of premium.

2. Material misrepresentation made in obtaining the policy.

3. Submission of a fraudulent claim.

4. Insured has violated the terms and conditions of the policy.

5. Substantial increase in risk.

6. Certification to the director of insurance of loss of reinsurance by the insurer which provided coverage to the insurer for all or a substantial part of the underlying risk insured.

7. The director of insurance determines that the continuation of the policy could violate Nebraska's insurance laws.

NEBRASKA

Length of Notice: Ten days for nonpayment; sixty days for any other reason.

Reason for Cancellation: Required on the notice.

Proof Required: A United States Postal Service certificate of mailing is sufficient proof of receipt of notice on the third calendar day after the date of the certificate of mailing.

Nonrenewal

Length of Notice: Sixty days.

Reason for Nonrenewal: Required on the notice.

Proof Required: A United States Postal Service certificate of mailing is sufficient proof of receipt of notice on the third calendar day after the date of the certificate of mailing.

Other Cancellation/Nonrenewal Provisions

On OCP policies the listed contractor must also be notified.

On Railroad Protective policies the listed contractor and any involved governmental authority must also be notified.

Cancellation and nonrenewal require certified mail for companies using ISO's CG 30 14 (Underground Storage Tank); CU 02 08 (Commercial Liability Umbrella); and FB 02 14 (Farm Umbrella Liability).

COMMERCIAL AUTO

Revised Statutes of Nebraska §44-523

Cancellation during the Underwriting Period

Length of Underwriting Period: Sixty days.

Length of Notice: Must be mailed during underwriting period.

Reason for Cancellation: Not required.

Proof Required: Proof of mailing.

Cancellation after the Underwriting Period

Length of Notice: Thirty days for reasons other than for nonpayment of premium. Nonpayment does not have a length of notice requirement.

NEBRASKA

Reason for Cancellation: Not required.

Proof Required: Registered or certified mail for any reason other than nonpayment.

Other Cancellation/Nonrenewal Provisions

No requirements for nonrenewal stated in statute.

A notice of cancellation, initiated by a premium finance company, of a policy of automobile liability insurance issued or delivered in this state shall only be effective if mailed by registered or certified mail to the named insured at the address shown in the policy at least ten days prior to the effective date of such cancellation.

WORKERS COMPENSATION

Revised Statutes of Nebraska § 48-144.03

Nebraska provides for three different classes of worker's compensation policies:

1. Worker's compensation policies other than master policies or multiple coordinated policies obtained by a professional employer organization.

2. Worker's compensation master policies obtained by a professional employer organization.

3. Worker's compensation multiple coordinated policies obtained by a professional employer organization.

Worker's Compensation Policies Other Than Master Policies or Multiple Coordinated Policies Obtained by a Professional Employer Organization

Cancellation

Length of Notice: Ten days for reasons listed below; thirty days for any other reason.

1. Notice from the employer to the insurer to cancel the policy.

2. Nonpayment.

3. Failure of the employer to reimburse deductible losses, as required under the policy.

4. Failure of the employer, if covered pursuant to the Assigned Risk Plan, to comply with Nebraska workplace safety statutes.

NEBRASKA

Reason for Cancellation: Required on the notice.

Proof Required: Certified mail.

Nonrenewal

Length of Notice: Ten days for reasons listed below; thirty days for any other reason.

1. Notice from the employer to the insurer to not renew the policy.

2. Nonpayment of premium due to the insurer under any policy written by the insurer for the employer.

3. Failure of the employer to reimburse deductible losses, as required under the policy.

4. Failure of the employer, if covered pursuant to the Assigned Risk Plan, to comply with Nebraska workplace safety statutes.

Reason for Nonrenewal: Required on the notice.

Proof Required: Certified mail.

All notices must be sent to both the compensation court and to the employer.

Workers' Compensation Master Policies Obtained by a Professional Employer Organization

Cancellation

Length of Notice: Ten days for reasons listed below; thirty days for any other reason.

1. Notice from the client to the professional organization or insurer to cancel the policy.

2. Notice from the professional employer organization of the client's nonpayment of premium.

Reason for Cancellation: Required on the notice.

Proof Required: Certified mail.

Nonrenewal

Length of Notice: Thirty days.

NEBRASKA

Reason for Nonrenewal: Required on the notice.

Proof Required: Certified mail.

All notices must be sent to both the compensation court and the professional employer organization.

Workers' Compensation Multiple Coordinated Policies Obtained by a Professional Employer Organization

Cancellation

Length of Notice: Ten days for reasons listed below; thirty days for any other reason.

1. Notice from the client to the professional organization or insurer to cancel the policy.

2. Notice from the professional employer organization of the client's nonpayment of premium or failure to reimburse deductibles.

3. Failure of the employer, if covered pursuant to the Assigned Risk Plan, to comply with Nebraska workplace safety statutes.

4. Nonpayment or failure to reimburse deductibles, if covered pursuant to the Assigned Risk Plan.

Reason for Cancellation: Required on the notice.

Proof Required: Certified mail.

Nonrenewal

Length of Notice: Ten days for reasons listed below; thirty days for any other reason.

1. Notice from the client to the professional organization or insurer to cancel the policy.

2. Notice from the professional employer organization of the client's nonpayment of premium or failure to reimburse deductibles.

Reason for Nonrenewal: Required on the notice.

Proof Required: Certified mail.

All notices must be sent to the compensation court, the professional employer organization, and the client employer.

NEBRASKA

Other Cancellation/Nonrenewal Provisions

Notices from insurers to the compensation court may be provided by electronic means if such electronic means is approved by the administrator of the compensation court. If notice is provided by electronic means, it shall be deemed given upon receipt and acceptance of said notice by the compensation court.

SURPLUS LINES

The Nebraska cancellation and nonrenewal laws do not apply to surplus lines. Nebraska does not regulate rates and forms for Surplus Lines.

FINANCED PREMIUMS

Revised Statutes of Nebraska §§44-522 and 44-523

Premium finance companies may cancel the policy for nonpayment with a ten-day notice.

PERSONAL LINES
DWELLING FIRE & HOMEOWNERS

Revised Statutes of Nebraska § 44-522

Cancellation during the Underwriting Period

Length of Underwriting Period: Sixty days.

Length of Notice: Ten days for nonpayment; sixty days for any other reason.

Reason for Cancellation: Required on the notice.

Proof Required: A United States Postal Service certificate of mailing is sufficient proof of receipt of notice on the third calendar day after the date of the certificate of mailing.

Cancellation after the Underwriting Period

The policy may be cancelled only for the following reasons:

1. Nonpayment.

2. Material misrepresentation on the application.

3. Substantial increase in the risk.

NEBRASKA

4. Submission of a fraudulent claim.

5. Any insured has violated the terms and conditions of the policy.

6. Certification to the Director of Insurance of loss of reinsurance by the insurer which provided coverage to the insurer for all or a substantial part of the underlying risk insured.

7. The Director of Insurance determines that continuation of the policy could violate Nebraska's insurance laws.

Length of Notice: Ten days for nonpayment; sixty days for any other allowable reason.

Reason for Cancellation: Required on the notice.

Proof Required: United States Postal Service certificate of mailing on the third calendar day after the date of the certificate of mailing.

Nonrenewal

Length of Notice: Sixty days.

Reason for Nonrenewal: Required on the notice.

Proof Required: United States Postal Service certificate of mailing on the third calendar day after the date of the certificate of mailing.

PERSONAL AUTO

Revised Statutes of Nebraska §§44-514 to 44-520

Cancellation during the Underwriting Period

Length of Underwriting Period: Sixty days.

Length of Notice: Ten days for any reason. Nebraska Statute does not indicate length of notice required during underwriting period.

Reason for Cancellation: Not required, but may be requested by written request of named insured.

Proof Required: Certified or registered mail. Nebraska Statute does not indicate proof required during underwriting period.

NEBRASKA

Cancellation after the Underwriting Period

The policy may be cancelled **only** for the following reasons:

1. Nonpayment.

2. The named insured or any operator, whether a resident in the same household or one who customarily operates an automobile insured under the policy:

   a. Has had his or her driver's license suspended or revoked.

   b. Has been convicted of larceny or theft of a vehicle in violation of Neb. Rev. St. § 28-516.

   c. Has been convicted of an offense for which suspension or revocation of the offender's driver's license is mandatory.

   d. Whose driver's license is subject to suspension or revocation pursuant to the provisions of Neb. Rev. St. §§ 60-4,182 to 60-4,186.

3. Fraud or material misrepresentation affecting the policy or in the presentation of a claim, or in violation of any of the terms or conditions of the policy.

Length of Notice: Ten days for nonpayment; thirty days for any other allowable reason.

Reason for Cancellation: Required for nonpayment; not required for any other reason, unless specifically requested by the insured. If the insured requests reason for cancellation, this reason must be mailed to the insured no later than five days after receipt of the request. If the insurer does not provide reason in the original cancellation, the insurer must make it clear in the notice that the insured must provide written request no later than twenty-five days prior to the date of cancellation in order to receive reason for cancellation. (Neb. Rev. St. § 44-516).

Proof Required: Registered or certified mail.

Nonrenewal

Length of Notice: Twenty days.

Reason for Nonrenewal: Not required. The insurer must mail or deliver the reason for its refusal to renew, in writing, upon written request of the insured no less than fifteen days before the effective date of its notice of intention not to renew.

Proof Required: Proof of mailing.

NEBRASKA

Other Cancellation/Nonrenewal Provisions

When the reason for cancellation or nonrenewal is not provided, the notice must specify that the reason will be provided to the insured upon request.

If the insurer offers a renewal and the insured does not pay the renewal premium, the policy will automatically terminate.

When automobile bodily injury and property damage liability coverage is canceled, other than for nonpayment of premium, or in the event of failure to renew automobile bodily injury and property damage liability coverage, the insurer shall notify the named insured of the insured's possible eligibility for automobile liability insurance through an affiliated insurer or the automobile liability assigned risk plan. Such notice shall accompany or be included in the notice of cancellation or the notice of intent not to renew.

Any policy written for a term longer than one year or any policy with no fixed expiration date shall be considered as if written for successive policy periods or terms of one year, and such policy may be terminated at the expiration of any annual period upon giving twenty days' notice of cancellation prior to such anniversary date, and such cancellation shall not be subject to any other provisions of sections 44-514 to 44-521. (Neb. Rev. St. § 44-514).

PERSONAL UMBRELLA

Revised Statutes of Nebraska § 44-522

Cancellation during the Underwriting Period

Length of Underwriting Period: Sixty days.

Notice Requirements: Ten days for nonpayment; sixty days for any other reason.

Reason for Cancellation: Not required.

Proof Required: A United States Postal Service certificate of mailing is sufficient proof of receipt of notice on the third calendar day after the date of the certificate of mailing.

Cancellation after the Underwriting Period

1. Nonpayment of premium.
2. Material misrepresentation in obtaining the policy.
3. Submission of a fraudulent claim.
4. Any insured has violated the terms and conditions of the policy.

NEBRASKA

5. Substantial increase in risk.

6. Certification to the Director of Insurance of loss of reinsurance by the insurer which provided coverage to the insurer for all or a substantial part of the underlying risk insured.

7. The Director of Insurance determines that the continuation of the policy could violate Nebraska's insurance laws.

Length of Notice: Ten day notice for nonpayment; sixty days for any other allowable reason.

Reason for Cancellation: Required on notice.

Proof Required: United States Postal Service certificate of mailing on the third calendar day after the date of the certificate of mailing.

Nonrenewal

Length of Notice: Sixty days.

Reason for Nonrenewal: Required on notice.

Proof Required: A United States Postal Service certificate of mailing is sufficient proof of receipt of notice on the third calendar day after the date of the certificate of mailing.

FRAUD

Revised Statutes of Nebraska §§44-6601 to 44-6608 and 28-631

Definition

The following acts constitute both civil and criminal insurance fraud under Nebraska law:

1. Knowingly and with the intent to either defraud or deceive, presenting, causing to be presented, or preparing with knowledge or belief that it will be presented to or by an insurer, or any agent of an insurer, any statement as part of, in support of, or in denial of a claim for payment or other benefit from an insurer or pursuant to an insurance policy knowing that the statement contains a false, incomplete, or misleading information concerning any fact or thing that is material to the claim.

2. Assisting, abetting, soliciting, or conspiring with another to prepare or make any statement that is intended to be presented to or by an insurer or person in connection with or in support of any claim for payment or other benefit from an insurer pursuant to an insurance policy while knowing that the statement contains false, incomplete, or misleading information regarding a material fact or thing regarding the claim.

NEBRASKA

3. Making false or fraudulent representations about the death or disability of a policy holder, certificate holder, or any covered person in any statement or certificate in order to fraudulently obtain money or benefit from an insurer.

4. Knowingly and willfully transacting a contract, agreement, or instrument that violates any of the provisions in this list.

5. Converting money to the holder's own benefit that was received so that the holder could purchase insurance.

6. Willfully embezzling, abstracting, taking dishonestly, or converting money, funds, premiums, credits or other of an insurer or person engaged in the business of insurance.

7. Knowingly and with the intent to defraud or deceive issuing or possessing fake or counterfeit insurance policies, certificates of insurance, insurance identification cards, or insurance binders.

8. Knowingly and with the intent to defraud or deceive, making a false entry of a material fact in or pertaining to any document or statement filed with or required by the Department of Insurance.

9. Knowingly and with the intent to defraud or deceive removing, concealing, altering, diverting, or destroying assets or records of an insurer or person engaged in the business of insurance or attempting to remove, conceal, alter, divert or destroy assets or records of an insurer or person engaged in the business of insurance.

10. Knowingly and with the intent to defraud or deceive providing false, incomplete, or misleading information to an insurer concerning the number, location, or classification of employees to lessen or reduce the premium for worker's compensation insurance.

11. Willfully operating as or aiding and abetting another operating as a discount medical plan organization in violation of subsection (1) of Neb. Rev. St. § 44-8306.

12. Willfully collecting fees for purported membership in a discount medical plan but purposefully failing to provide the promised benefits.

Please note that Nebraska's criminal and civil statutes codify these same basic elements in different sequences.

NEBRASKA

Reporting

Individuals or entities that act without malice, fraudulent intent, or bad faith enjoy immunity from civil liability for furnishing information relating to suspected fraudulent insurance acts to the officials and entities listed in Neb. Rev. St. § 44-6605.

Insurance Fraud Act Fees

By March 1st of each year, each insurer shall pay a fee to the director, which may only be appropriated to carry out the purposes of the Insurance Fraud Act. The amount of this fee will be determined by the director, not to exceed $200. (Neb. Rev. St. § 44-6606).

Penalty

Those convicted of civil insurance fraud face the following maximum civil penalties:

1. $5,000 for the first violation.

2. $10,000 for the second violation.

3. $15,000 for each subsequent violation.

Violators of Nebraska's Civil Insurance Fraud Act may have to pay expenses of the investigation or of other actions that arose out of their violation.

Those convicted under Nebraska's criminal insurance fraud statute are guilty of a felony. However, a prosecution under either the criminal or civil section of the law stands in lieu of a prosecution under the other section. (Nev. Rev. St. §44-6607).

Application Fraud Statement
Revised Statutes of Nebraska § 44-1112

Only viatical settlement contracts and applications must contain the following statement or a substantially similar statement: "Any person who knowingly presents false information in an application for insurance or viatical settlement contract is guilty of a crime and may be subject to fines and confinement in prison."

FAIR CLAIMS PROCESSING

Revised Statutes of Nebraska §§44-101, 44-1536 to 44-1545
Generally

Generally speaking, all those involved in the insurance industry have a duty to act in good faith, abstain from deceptive or misleading practices, and to keep, observe and practice the relevant principles of law and equity.

NEBRASKA

The following are unfair claims settlement practices when committed by an insurer either flagrantly and in conscious disregard of the Unfair Insurance Claims Settlement Practices Act or done in conscious disregard of the regulations adopted under that act or have been committed with such frequency as to indicate a general business practice of engaging in that type of conduct.

1. Knowingly misrepresenting to claimants and insureds relevant facts or policy provisions relating to pertinent coverage.

2. Failing to acknowledge with reasonable promptness pertinent communications regarding claims arising under the insurer's policies.

3. Failing to adopt and implement reasonable standards for promptly investigating and settling claims arising under the insurer's policies.

4. Not making a good-faith attempt to effectuate the prompt, fair, and equitable settlement of claims submitted in which liability has become reasonably clear.

5. Not making a good-faith attempt to effectuate prompt, fair, and equitable settlement of property and casualty claims in which coverage and the amount of the loss are reasonably clear and for loss of tangible personal property within real property which is insured by a policy subject to Neb. Rev. St. § 44-501.02 and which is wholly destroyed by fire, tornado, windstorm, lightning, or explosion.

6. Compelling insureds or beneficiaries to institute litigation to recover amounts due under its policies by offering substantially less than the amounts ultimately recovered in litigation brought by them.

7. Refusing to pay claims without conducting a reasonable investigation.

8. Failing to affirm or deny coverage of a claim within a reasonable time after the insurer has completed its investigation related to such claim.

9. Attempting to settle a claim for less than the amount to which a reasonable person would believe the insured or beneficiary was entitled by reference to written or printed advertising material accompanying or made part of an application.

10. Attempting to settle claims on the basis of an application which was materially altered without notice to the insured or without the insured's knowledge or consent.

11. Making a claims payment to an insured or beneficiary without signifying the coverage under which each payment is being made.

NEBRASKA

12. Unreasonably delaying the investigation or payment of claims by requiring both a formal proof-of-loss form and subsequent verification that would result in the duplication of information and verification appearing in the formal proof-of-loss form.

13. In the case of a claim denial or the offer of a compromise settlement, failing to promptly, reasonably, and accurately explain the basis for such action.

14. Failing to provide the required forms to present claims with reasonable explanations regarding their use within fifteen working days of a request.

15. Not adopting and implementing reasonable standards to assure that the repairs of a repairer that is owned by or affiliated with the insurer are performed skillfully.

16. Requiring the insured or claimant to use a particular company or location for motor vehicle repair. However, insurers may enter into discount agreements with companies and locations for motor vehicle repair or otherwise enter into any business arrangement or affiliation which reduces the cost of motor vehicle repair if the insured or claimant has the right to use a particular company or reasonably available location for motor vehicle repair.

17. Failing to provide coverage information or coordinate benefits pursuant to Neb. Rev. St. § 68-928.

18. Failing to pay interest on any proceeds due on a life insurance policy as required by Neb. Rev. St. § 44-3,143.

Automobile insurers must provide the required information for the motor vehicle insurance database stipulated in Neb. Rev. St. §§ 60-3,136 to 60-3,139. (These sections have been amended by 2015 Nebraska Laws L.B. 666 but this amendment has not changed the stated provision.)

Penalty

After determining that an insurer has engaged in an unfair claims settlement practice, the Director of Insurance will issue a cease and desist order that will prohibit the insurer from recommencing the offending practice. In addition to the order, insurers may have to pay penalties up to $1,000 for individual violations subject to a $30,000 aggregate maximum. However, insurers that commit flagrant violations in conscious disregard of the Unfair Claims Settlement Practices Act face a maximum penalty of $15,000 per violation with an aggregate maximum penalty of $150,000. Insurers who knew or reasonably should have known that

NEBRASKA

their conduct violated the Unfair Insurance Claims Settlement Practices Act may have their licenses or certificates of authority revoked.

Insurers face additional penalties for violating the terms of the Insurance Director's cease and desist order. These include maximum penalty of $30,000 per violation limited to an aggregate penalty of $150,000 and suspension of their insurer's license or certificate of authority.

NEVADA

For details on cancellation procedures for the standard policy, refer to the Standard Policy section.

COMMERCIAL LINES
AGRICULTURAL CAPITAL ASSETS; BOP; CAPITAL ASSETS; C. AUTO; CRIME; CGL (all parts except Underground Storage Tanks); CIM; C. PROP.; C. UMB.; E-COMMERCE; EQUIPMENT BREAKDOWN; & FARM

Nevada Revised Statutes §§687B.310 to 687B.340

Cancellation during the Underwriting Period

Length of Underwriting Period: Seventy days.

Length of Notice: Ten days.

Reason for Cancellation: Required on the notice.

Proof Required: Proof of delivery, first class or certified mailing, or in the case of electronic delivery, verification or acknowledgment of receipt by the policyholder within three days of delivery.

Cancellation after the Underwriting Period

The policy may be cancelled **only** for the following reasons:

1. Nonpayment of premium.

2. The insured is convicted of a crime that increases the hazard covered by the policy.

3. Fraud or material misrepresentation in obtaining the policy or presenting a claim.

4. Any act, omission or violation of any policy condition that occurred after the policy's first effective date and both substantially and materially increases the hazard covered by the policy.

5. A material change in the risk that substantially and materially increases the hazard.

6. The commissioner determines that for the insurer to continue its present volume of premiums would jeopardize its solvency or would be hazardous to the interests of policyholders, creditors, or the public.

7. The commissioner determines that continuation of the policy would violate Nevada law.

NEVADA

Length of Notice: Ten days for nonpayment; thirty days for all other allowable reasons; sixty days for cancellation on an anniversary date if policy is issued for a term of more than one year.

Reason for Cancellation: Required on the notice.

Proof Required: Proof of delivery, first class or certified mailing, or in the case of electronic delivery, verification or acknowledgment of receipt by the policyholder within three days of delivery.

Nonrenewal

Length of Notice: Sixty days.

Reason for Nonrenewal: Required on the notice.

Proof Required: Proof of delivery, first class or certified mailing, or in the case of electronic delivery, verification or acknowledgement of receipt by the policyholder within three days of delivery.

Other Cancellation/Nonrenewal Provisions

Renewal on altered terms requires a thirty-day notice.

On OCP polices all notices must be sent to the named insured and to any designated contractor.

On Railroad Protective polices, all notices must be sent to the named insured, any governmental authority, and to any contractor shown in the declarations.

On Commercial Auto policies, no policy may be cancelled, nonrenewed, or have its premium increased because of claims that were not the insured's fault. (N.R.S. §687B.385). In addition, insurers may not refuse to issue policies because of claims that were not the insured's fault. (N.R.S. §687B.385 as amended by 2017 Nevada AB 83).

Insurers may not refuse to issue, cancel, refuse to renew, or increase premiums on commercial auto policies because of "inquiries made regarding an actual or potential claim under any policy of insurance regarding:

The existence of insurance coverage for any matter; or

Any hypothetical or informational matter pertaining to insurance."

Insurers may not refuse to issue, cancel, refuse to renew, or increase premiums on commercial auto policies because of "claims made under any policy of insurance for which

NEVADA

the insurer has not made any payment or for which the insurer recovered the entirety of the insurer's payment on the claim by means of salvage, subrogation or another mechanism." (N.R.S. §687B.385 as amended by 2017 Nevada AB 83).

If an insurer fails to provide a timely notice of nonrenewal, the insurer shall provide the insured with a policy of insurance on the identical terms as in the expiring policy.

Renewed policies have no underwriting period.

If a notice of cancellation or nonrenewal does not state with reasonable precision the facts on which the insurer's decision is based, the insurer shall supply that information within six days after receipt of a written request by the policyholder. No notice is effective unless it contains adequate information about the policyholder's right to make such a request. (N.R.S. §687B.360).

Except for a notice of cancellation for failure to pay premium when due, a notice of cancellation or nonrenewal for a Commercial Auto policy must contain adequate instructions enabling the policyholder to apply for insurance through the assigned-risk plan. (N.R.S §687B.370).

An insurer which intends to withdraw from providing insurance for a particular class of insureds shall notify the Commissioner of that intention at least sixty days before the notice of cancellation or nonrenewal is delivered or mailed to the insureds. (N.R.S. §687B.410).

COMMERCIAL GENERAL LIABILITY

(Underground Storage Tanks)

N.R.S. §§687B.310 to 687B.340

Cancellation during the Underwriting Period

Length of Underwriting Period: Seventy days.

Length of Notice: Ten days for nonpayment; sixty days for any other reason. Nevada only requires a ten-day notice. However, if an insurer has adopted ISO's CG 30 43, it must give a sixty-day notice.

Reason for Cancellation: Required with the notice.

Proof Required: Proof of delivery, first class mailing, or certified mailing, or in the case of electronic delivery, verification or acknowledgment of receipt by the policyholder within three days of delivery.

NEVADA

Cancellation after the Underwriting Period

The policy may be cancelled **only** for the following reasons:

1. Nonpayment.

2. The insured is convicted of a crime that increases the hazard covered by the policy.

3. Fraud or material misrepresentation in obtaining the policy, in continuing the policy, or in pursuit of a claim.

4. Any act, omission, or violation of any policy condition, that substantially and materially increases the hazard covered by the policy.

5. A material change in the risk that occurred after the first effective date and substantially and materially increases the hazard.

6. The commissioner determines that for the insurer to continue its present volume of premiums would jeopardize its solvency or would be hazardous to the interests of policyholders, creditors, or the public.

7. The commissioner determines that continuation of the policy would violate Nevada law.

Length of Notice: Ten days for nonpayment; sixty days for all other reasons. The Nevada code only requires a thirty-day notice. If an insurer has adopted ISO's CG 30 43, it must give a sixty-day notice.

Reason for Cancellation: Required with the notice.

Proof Required: Proof of delivery, first class mailing, or certified mailing, or in the case of electronic delivery, verification or acknowledgment of receipt by the policyholder within three days of delivery.

Nonrenewal

Length of Notice: Sixty days. ISO's CG 30 43 contains no provisions for nonrenewal. However, the Nevada code requires a sixty-day notice.

Reason for Nonrenewal: Required with the notice.

Proof Required: Proof of delivery, first class mailing, or certified mailing, or in the case of electronic delivery, verification or acknowledgment of receipt by the policyholder within three days of delivery.

NEVADA

Other Cancellation/Nonrenewal Provisions

Renewal on altered terms requires a thirty-day notice.

If an insurer fails to provide a timely notice of nonrenewal, the insurer shall provide the insured with a policy of insurance on terms identical to those of the expiring policy.

Renewed policies have no underwriting period.

If a notice of cancellation or nonrenewal does not state with reasonable precision the facts on which the insurer's decision is based, the insurer shall supply that information within six days after receipt of a written request by the policyholder. No notice is effective unless it contains adequate information about the policyholder's right to make such a request. (N.R.S. §687B.360).

An insurer which intends to withdraw from providing insurance for a particular class of insureds shall notify the Commissioner of that intention at least sixty days before the notice of cancellation or nonrenewal is delivered or mailed to the insureds. (N.R.S. §687B.410).

PROFESSIONAL LIABILITY

N.R.S. §§687B.310 to 687B.340

Cancellation during the Underwriting Period

Length of Underwriting Period: Seventy days.

Length of Notice: Ten days.

Reason for Cancellation: Required with the notice.

Proof Required: Proof of delivery, first class mailing, or certified mailing, or in the case of electronic delivery, verification or acknowledgment of receipt by the policyholder within three days of delivery.

Cancellation after the Underwriting Period

The policy may be cancelled **only** for the following reasons:

1. Nonpayment of premium.

2. The insured is convicted of a crime that increases the hazard covered by the policy.

3. Fraud or material misrepresentation in obtaining the policy or in presenting a claim.

NEVADA

4. Any act, omission or violation of any policy condition that substantially and materially increases the hazard covered by the policy.

5. A material change in the risk that occurs after the effective date and substantially and materially increases the hazard that the policy originally insured.

6. The commissioner determines that for the insurer to continue its present volume of premiums would jeopardize its solvency or would be hazardous to the interests of policyholders, creditors, or the public.

7. The commissioner determines that continuing the policy would violate Nevada law.

Length of Notice: Ten days for nonpayment; thirty days for all other reasons; 120 days for cancellation on an anniversary date if policy is issued for a term of more than one year. Nevada Statute and ISO's PR 02 14 require sixty-day notice for anniversary cancellations. The 120 day cancellation is only required for insurers using ISO's PR 02 13.

Reason for Cancellation: Required with the notice.

Proof Required: Proof of delivery, first class mailing, or certified mailing, or in the case of electronic delivery, verification or acknowledgment of receipt by the policyholder within three days of delivery.

Nonrenewal

Length of Notice: One hundred twenty days. Nevada Statute and ISO's PR 02 14 require sixty-day notice. The 120-day cancellation requirement is only required for insurers using ISO's PR 02 13.

Reason for Nonrenewal: Required with the notice.

Proof Required: Proof of delivery, first class mailing, or certified mailing, or in the case of electronic delivery, verification or acknowledgment of receipt by the policyholder within three days of delivery.

Other Cancellation/Nonrenewal Provisions

Renewal on altered terms requires a thirty-day notice.

If an insurer fails to provide a timely notice of nonrenewal, the insurer shall provide the insured with a policy of insurance with terms identical to those in the expiring policy.

Renewed policies have no underwriting period.

NEVADA

If a notice of cancellation or nonrenewal does not state with reasonable precision the facts on which the insurer's decision is based, the insurer shall supply that information within six days after receipt of a written request by the policyholder. No notice is effective unless it contains adequate information about the policyholder's right to make such a request. (N.R.S. §687B.360).

An insurer which intends to withdraw from providing insurance for a particular class of insureds shall notify the Commissioner of that intention at least sixty days before the notice of cancellation or nonrenewal is delivered or mailed to the insureds. (N.R.S. §687B.410).

WORKERS COMPENSATION

Also known as Industrial Insurance in Nevada

N.R.S. §§616B.033, 687B.310 to 687B.355

Cancellation during the Underwriting Period

Length of Underwriting Period: Seventy days.

Length of Notice: Ten days for nonpayment; thirty days for any other reason.

Reason for Cancellation: Required with the notice.

Proof Required: Proof of delivery, first class mailing, or certified mailing, or in the case of electronic delivery, verification or acknowledgment of receipt by the policyholder within three days of delivery.

Cancellation after the Underwriting Period

The policy may be cancelled **only** for the following reasons:

1. Nonpayment.

2. A failure by the insured to:

    (a) Report any payroll.

    (b) Allow the insurer to audit any payroll in accordance with the terms of the policy or any previous policy issued by the same insurer.

    (c) Pay any additional premium charged because of an audit of any payroll as required by the terms of the policy or any previous policy issued by the insurer.

NEVADA

3. A material failure by the policyholder to comply with federal or state orders concerning safety or any written recommendation of the insurer's loss control representative.

4. A material change in ownership of the policyholder or any change in the policyholder's business or operations that:

    (a) Materially increases the hazard for frequency or severity of loss.

    (b) Requires additional or different classifications for the calculation of premiums.

    (c) Contemplate an activity that is excluded by any reinsurance treaty of the insurer.

5. A material misrepresentation made by the holder of the policy.

6. A failure by the policyholder to cooperate with the insurer in conducting an investigation of a claim.

    If the insured corrects the condition to the satisfaction of the insurer within the period specified in the policy of insurance, the insurer cannot cancel the policy.

Length of Notice: Ten days for nonpayment; thirty days for any other allowable reason; sixty days for cancellation on an anniversary date if policy is issued for a term of more than one year.

Reason for Cancellation: Required with the notice.

Proof Required: Proof of delivery, first class mailing, or certified mailing, or in the case of electronic delivery, verification or acknowledgment of receipt by the policyholder within three days of delivery.

Nonrenewal

Length of Notice: Sixty days.

Reason for Nonrenewal: Required with the notice.

Proof Required: Proof of delivery, first class mailing, or certified mailing, or in the case of electronic delivery, verification or acknowledgment of receipt by the policyholder within three days of delivery.

NEVADA

Other Cancellation/Nonrenewal Provisions

A written notice of cancellation is not required if the company and the insured mutually agree to cancel the policy and reissue a new policy based upon a material change in the ownership or operations of the business.

Renewal on altered terms requires a thirty-day written notice.

If an insurer fails to provide a timely notice of nonrenewal, the insurer shall provide the insured with a policy of insurance on the identical terms as in the expiring policy.

Renewed policies have no underwriting period.

If a notice of cancellation or nonrenewal does not state with reasonable precision the facts on which the insurer's decision is based, the insurer shall supply that information within six days after receipt of a written request by the policyholder. No notice is effective unless it contains adequate information about the policyholder's right to make such a request. (N.R.S. §687B.360).

Except for a notice of cancellation for failure to pay premium when due, a notice of cancellation or nonrenewal must contain adequate instructions enabling the policyholder to apply for insurance through the assigned-risk plan (N.R.S. §687B.370).

An insurer which intends to withdraw from providing insurance for a particular class of insureds shall notify the Commissioner of that intention at least sixty days before the notice of cancellation or nonrenewal is delivered or mailed to the insureds. (N.R.S. §687B.410).

FINANCED PREMIUMS
N.R.S. §686A.460

If the premium finance agreement contains a power of attorney, the finance company may request, in the name of the insured, that the insurer cancel the policy due to nonpayment. The finance company must first give the insured and the agent who submitted the agreement ten days written notice to cure the default. If the premium is not paid within that ten-day period, the company may cancel the policy if it mails a notice of cancellation containing the effective date of cancellation to the insured and the insurer. Return of the policy by the insured is not required. No insurance policy may be cancelled for nonpayment of a charge for a late payment.

SURPLUS LINES
N.R.S. §687B.010

The Nevada cancellation and nonrenewal laws can apply to surplus lines. An individual policy purchased by a Nevadan, in Nevada and delivered in Nevada is subject to notice requirements. See *Daniels v. National Home Life Assur. Co.*, 103 Nev. 674 (1987).

NEVADA

PERSONAL LINES
DWELLING FIRE & HOMEOWNERS
N.R.S. §§687B.310 to 687B.340

Cancellation during the Underwriting Period

Length of Underwriting Period: Sixty to seventy days. Nevada Statute allows for a seventy-day underwriting period. However, insurers using ISO HO 01 27 and DL 01 27 are required to use a sixty-day underwriting period.

Length of Notice: Ten days.

Reason for Cancellation: Required with the notice.

Proof Required: Proof of delivery, first class mailing, or certified mailing, or in the case of electronic delivery, verification or acknowledgment of receipt by the policyholder within three days of delivery.

Cancellation after the Underwriting Period

The policy may be cancelled **only** for the following reasons:

1. Nonpayment.

2. The insured is convicted of a crime that increases the hazard covered by the policy.

3. Fraud or material misrepresentation in obtaining the policy or presenting a claim.

4. Any act, omission or violation of any policy condition that occurred after the policy's first effective date and both substantially and materially increases the hazard covered by the policy.

5. A material change in the risk that substantially and materially increases the hazard.

6. The commissioner determines that for the insurer to continue its present volume of premiums would jeopardize its solvency or would be hazardous to the interests of policyholders, creditors, or the public.

7. The commissioner determines that continuation of the policy would violate Nevada law.

Length of Notice: Ten days for nonpayment; thirty days for all other allowable reasons. ISO's HO 01 27 is more restrictive, cancellation is allowed only for nonpayment, material

NEVADA

misrepresentation in the policy application, and substantial change in risk that would warrant substantial difference in premium.

Reason for Cancellation: Required with the notice. Even though ISO's form HO 01 27 is silent on the matter, the Nevada Code requires it.

Proof Required: Proof of delivery, first class mailing, or certified mailing, or in the case of electronic delivery, verification or acknowledgment of receipt by the policyholder within three days of delivery.

Nonrenewal

Length of Notice: Thirty days.

Reason for Nonrenewal: Required with the notice.

Proof Required: Proof of delivery, first class mailing, or certified mailing, or in the case of electronic delivery, verification or acknowledgment of receipt by the policyholder within three days of delivery.

Other Cancellation/Nonrenewal Provisions

Renewal on altered terms requires a thirty-day notice.

If an insurer fails to provide a timely notice of nonrenewal, the insurer shall provide the insured with a policy of insurance on the identical terms as in the expiring policy.

Renewed policies have no underwriting period.

If a notice of cancellation or nonrenewal does not state with reasonable precision the facts on which the insurer's decision is based, the insurer shall supply that information within six days after receipt of a written request by the policyholder. No notice is effective unless it contains adequate information about the policyholder's right to make such a request. (N.R.S §687B.360).

An insurer which intends to withdraw from providing insurance for a particular class of insureds shall notify the Commissioner of that intention at least sixty days before the notice of cancellation or nonrenewal is delivered or mailed to the insureds. (N.R.S. §687B.410).

Nevada has Home Protection Insurance, also known as a home warranty (N.R.S. §690B.100). Cancellation of a Home Protection policy is only allowed for nonpayment, fraud or misrepresentation of material facts, and if coverage is for home before sale and home was not sold. This insurance is not renewable unless its terms provide otherwise. (N.R.S. §690B.160).

NEVADA

PERSONAL AUTO

N.R.S. §§485.3092, 687B.310 to 687B.385

Cancellation during the Underwriting Period

Length of Underwriting Period: Sixty days if using ISO's PP 01 82; seventy days under Nevada Statute and ISO's PP 92 82.

Length of Notice: Ten days.

Reason for Cancellation: Required with the notice.

Proof Required: Proof of delivery, first class mailing, or certified mailing, or in the case of electronic delivery, verification or acknowledgment of receipt by the policyholder within three days of delivery.

Cancellation after the Underwriting Period

The policy may be cancelled **only** for the following reasons:

1. Nonpayment of premium.
2. Conviction of insured of a crime arising out of acts that increase the hazard covered by the policy.
3. Material misrepresentation in obtaining the policy or in presenting a claim.
4. Act, omission, or violation of any policy condition which both occurred after the policy's first effective date and materially increased the risk covered by the policy.
5. Substantial change in the risk which occurred after the policy's first effective date.
6. The Commissioner of Insurance determines that continuing the insurer's present volume of premiums would jeopardize the insurer's solvency or would be hazardous to the interests of the insurer's policyholders, creditors, or the public.
7. The Commissioner of Insurance determines that continuing the policy would violate or place the insurer in violation of Nevada law.

ISO's PP 01 82 and PP 92 82 eliminate reasons 5-7 and replace them with:

1. Suspension or revocation of the driver's license of any of the following people:

    (a) The named insured.

(b) Any driver who lives with the named insured.
(c) Any driver who customarily uses the "covered auto".

Length of Notice: Ten days for nonpayment; thirty days for all other allowable reasons. ISO's PP 01 82 does not allow cancellation for reason 2, 4, or material misrepresentation in presenting a claim.

Reason for Cancellation: Required with the notice.

Proof Required: Proof of delivery, first class mailing, or certified mailing, or in the case of electronic delivery, verification or acknowledgment of receipt by the policyholder within three days of delivery.

Nonrenewal

Length of Notice: Thirty days.

Reason for Nonrenewal: Required on the notice.

Proof Required: Proof of delivery, first class mailing, or certified mailing, or in the case of electronic delivery, verification or acknowledgment of receipt by the policyholder within three days of delivery.

Other Cancellation/Nonrenewal Provisions

If the policy is written for a term of less than six months, the insurer may nonrenew every six months, beginning six months after the original effective date. (ISO Forms PP 01 82 and PP 92 82).

If the policy is written for a term of one year or longer, the insurer may nonrenew only at each anniversary of the original effective date. (ISO Form PP 01 82 and PP 92 82).

If the policy has been certified as proof of financial responsibility, a ten-day notice must also be filed with the Department of Motor Vehicles. (N.R.S. §485.308).

No policy may be cancelled, nonrenewed, or have its premium increased because of claims that were not the insured's fault. In addition, insurers may not refuse to issue policies because of claims that were not the insured's fault. (N.R.S. §687B.385 as amended by 2017 Nevada AB 83).

NEVADA

Insurers may not refuse to issue, cancel, refuse to renew, or increase premiums on auto policies because of "inquiries made regarding an actual or potential claim under any policy of insurance regarding:

The existence of insurance coverage for any matter; or

Any hypothetical or informational matter pertaining to insurance."

Insurers may not refuse to issue, cancel, refuse to renew, or increase premiums on auto policies because of "claims made under any policy of insurance for which the insurer has not made any payment or for which the insurer recovered the entirety of the insurer's payment on the claim by means of salvage, subrogation or another mechanism." (N.R.S. §687B.385 as amended by 2017 Nevada AB 83).

Renewal on altered terms requires a thirty-day notice.

If an insurer fails to provide a timely notice of nonrenewal, the insurer shall provide the insured with a policy of insurance on the identical terms as in the expiring policy.

Failure to pay the renewal premium causes the policy to lapse as of the renewal date.

Renewed policies have no underwriting period.

If a notice of cancellation or nonrenewal does not state with reasonable precision the facts on which the insurer's decision is based, the insurer shall supply that information within six days after receipt of a written request by the policyholder. No notice is effective unless it contains adequate information about the policyholder's right to make such a request. (N.R.S. §687B.360).

Except for a notice of cancellation for failure to pay premium when due, a notice of cancellation or nonrenewal must contain adequate instructions enabling the policyholder to apply for insurance through the assigned-risk plan (N.R.S. §687B.370).

An insurer which intends to withdraw from providing insurance for a particular class of insureds shall notify the Commissioner of that intention at least sixty days before the notice of cancellation or nonrenewal is delivered or mailed to the insureds. (N.R.S. §687B.410).

Cancellation and nonrenewal based on the following reasons are prohibited: age, residence, race, color, creed, national origin, ancestry, sexual orientation, gender identity or expression, occupation, and claims for which insured is not at fault. (N.R.S. §§ 687B.385 – 687B.400).

NEVADA

PERSONAL UMBRELLA
N.R.S. §§687B.310 to 687B.440

Cancellation during the Underwriting Period

Length of Underwriting Period: Seventy days.

Length of Notice: Ten days.

Reason for Cancellation: Reason for notice must be stated.

Proof Required: Proof of delivery, first class mailing, or certified mailing, or in the case of electronic delivery, verification or acknowledgment of receipt by the policyholder within three days of delivery.

Cancellation after the Underwriting Period

The policy may be cancelled **only** for the following reasons:

1. Nonpayment of premium.

2. The insured is convicted of a crime that increases the hazard covered by the policy.

3. Fraud or material misrepresentation in obtaining the policy or in presenting a claim.

4. Any act, omission, or violation of any policy condition, that substantially and materially increases the hazard covered by the policy.

5. A material change in the risk that occurred after the policy's first effective date and both substantially and materially increases the hazard.

6. The commissioner determines that for the insurer to continue its present volume of premiums would jeopardize its solvency or would be hazardous to the interests of policyholders, creditors, or the public.

7. The commissioner determines that continuation of the policy would violate Nevada law.

Length of Notice: Ten-day notice for nonpayment; thirty-day notice for any other reason.

Reason for Cancellation: Reason for notice must be stated.

Proof Required: Proof of delivery, first class mailing, or certified mailing, or in the case of electronic delivery, verification or acknowledgment of receipt by the policyholder within three days of delivery.

NEVADA

Nonrenewal

Length of Notice: Thirty days.

Reason for Nonrenewal: Required on the notice.

Proof Required: Proof of delivery, first class mailing, or certified mailing, or in the case of electronic delivery, verification or acknowledgment of receipt by the policyholder within three days of delivery.

Other Cancellation/Nonrenewal Provisions

An insurer offering an umbrella policy to an individual shall obtain a signed disclosure statement from the individual indicating whether the umbrella policy includes uninsured or underinsured vehicle coverage.

The disclosure statement for an umbrella policy covering uninsured or underinsured vehicle coverage must be on a form provided by the Commissioner of Insurance or in a form substantially similar to that provided in N.R.S. §687B.440.

Renewal on altered terms requires a thirty-day notice.

If an insurer fails to provide a timely notice of nonrenewal, the insurer shall provide the insured with a policy of insurance on the identical terms as in the expiring policy.

Renewed policies have no underwriting period.

If a notice of cancellation or nonrenewal does not state with reasonable precision the facts on which the insurer's decision is based, the insurer shall supply that information within six days after receipt of a written request by the policyholder. No notice is effective unless it contains adequate information about the policyholder's right to make such a request. (N.R.S. §687B.360).

An insurer which intends to withdraw from providing insurance for a particular class of insureds shall notify the Commissioner of that intention at least sixty days before the notice of cancellation or nonrenewal is delivered or mailed to the insureds. (N.R.S. §687B.410).

Cancellation and nonrenewal based on the following reasons are prohibited: age, residence, race, color, creed, national origin, ancestry, sexual orientation, gender identity or expression, occupation, and claims for which insured is not at fault. (N.R.S. §§ 687B.385 – 687B.400).

NEVADA

FRAUD

N.R.S. §§686A.281 to 686A.295

Definition

Knowingly and willfully committing the following acts constitutes insurance fraud under Nevada law:

1. Presenting or causing to be presented any statement to an insurer, a reinsurer, a producer, a broker or any agent thereof, a statement that conceals or omits facts, or contains false or misleading information concerning any fact material to an application for the issuance of an insurance policy.

2. Presenting or causing to be presented any statement as a part of, or in support of, a claim for payment or other benefits under a policy of insurance that conceals or omits facts, or contains false or misleading information concerning any fact material to that claim.

3. Assisting, abetting, soliciting or conspiring with another person to present or cause to be presented any statement to an insurer, a reinsurer, a producer, a broker or any agent thereof, that conceals or omits facts, or contains false or misleading information concerning any fact material to an application for the issuance of a policy of insurance or a claim for payment or other benefits under such a policy.

4. Acting or failing to act to defraud or deceive an insurer, a reinsurer, a producer, a broker or any agent thereof, to obtain a policy of insurance pursuant to this title or any proceeds or other benefits under such a policy.

5. As a practitioner, an insurer or any agent thereof, acting to assist, conspire with or urge another person to commit any act or omission specified in this section through deceit, misrepresentation, or other fraudulent means.

6. Accepting any proceeds or other benefits under a policy of insurance, while knowing that the proceeds or other benefits are derived from any act or omission specified in this section.

7. Employing a person to procure clients, patients or other persons who obtain services or benefits under a policy of insurance for the purpose of engaging in any act or omission specified in this section. However, such insurance fraud does not include contact or communication by an insurer, agent, or representative of the insurer with a client, patient, or other person if the contact or communication is made for a lawful purpose, including, without limitation, communication by an insurer with a holder of a policy

NEVADA

of insurance issued by the insurer or with a claimant concerning the settlement of any claims against the policy.

8. Participating in, aiding, abetting, conspiring to commit, soliciting another person to commit, or permitting an employee or agent to violate any of the above provisions.

Reporting Requirements

Any person, governmental entity, insurer or insurer's authorized representative must report any information concerning insurance fraud to both the Commissioner of Insurance and the Attorney General. An insurer that reasonably suspects that a loss to an insured may have been caused by something other than an accident or a natural occurrence must notify the Commissioner of Insurance and Attorney General in writing of the suspicion. If the suspect loss is believed to be caused by fire, the insurer must also notify an investigative or law enforcement agency.

Penalties

Perpetrators of insurance fraud are guilty of a felony and are punished accordingly. Those who are convicted of insurance fraud or plead guilty, guilty but mentally ill, or nolo contendere to a charge of insurance fraud may be required to pay court costs and the costs of investigating the corresponding insurance fraud. An agent, broker, solicitor, examining physician, applicant or other person who knowingly or willfully make any false or fraudulent statement or representation in or with reference to any application for insurance is guilty of a category D felony, punishable by a prison term between one and four years, plus fines.

APPLICATION FRAUD STATEMENT

N.R.S. §688C.500

An application or contract for a viatical settlement, however transmitted, must contain a statement substantially as follows: "A person who knowingly presents false information in an application for a viatical settlement is guilty of insurance fraud and subject to fine and imprisonment."

FAIR CLAIMS PROCESSING

Partially preempted by ERISA. N.R.S. §686A.310 still applies where not preempted by 29 U.S.C.A. §§1001 - 1461.(Employee Retirement Income Security Act).

In terms of settling claims, except for claims related to the employee retirement income security act, Nevada law prohibits the following practices as unfair:

1. Misrepresenting to insureds or claimants pertinent facts or insurance policy provisions relating to any coverage at issue.

NEVADA

2. Failing to acknowledge and act reasonably promptly upon communications with respect to claims arising under insurance policies.

3. Failing to adopt and implement reasonable standards for the prompt investigation and processing of claims arising under insurance policies.

4. Failing to affirm or deny coverage of claims within a reasonable time after proof of loss requirements have been completed and submitted by the insured.

5. Failing to effectuate prompt, fair, and equitable settlements of claims in which liability of the insurer has become reasonably clear.

6. Compelling insureds to institute litigation to recover amounts due under an insurance policy by offering substantially less than the amounts ultimately recovered in actions brought by such insureds, when the insureds have made claims for amounts reasonably similar to the amounts ultimately recovered.

7. Attempting to settle a claim by an insured for less than the amount to which a reasonable person would have believed he or she was entitled by reference to written or printed advertising material accompanying or made part of an application.

8. Attempting to settle claims on the basis of an application which was altered without notice to, or knowledge or consent of, the insured, or the representative, agent or broker of the insured.

9. Failing, upon payment of a claim, to inform insureds or beneficiaries of the coverage under which payment is made.

10. Making known to insureds or claimants a practice of the insurer of appealing from arbitration awards in favor of insureds or claimants for the purpose of compelling them to accept settlements or compromises less than the amount awarded in arbitration.

11. Delaying the investigation or payment of claims by requiring an insured or a claimant, or the physician of either, to submit a preliminary claim report, and then requiring the subsequent submission of formal proof of loss forms, both of which submissions contain substantially the same information.

12. Failing to settle claims promptly, where liability has become reasonably clear, under one portion of the insurance policy coverage in order to influence settlements under other portions of the insurance policy coverage.

NEVADA

13. Failing to comply with the provisions of N.R.S. §§687B.310 to 687B.390, inclusive, or §687B.410.

14. Failing to provide promptly to an insured a reasonable explanation of the basis in the insurance policy, with respect to the facts of the insured's claim and the applicable law, for the denial of the claim or for an offer to settle or compromise the claim.

15. Advising an insured or claimant not to seek legal counsel.

16. Misleading an insured or claimant concerning any applicable statute of limitations.

    For claims relating to employee retirement income security, see 29 U.S.C.A. §§1001 – 1461.

In terms of settling claims relating to employee retirement income security, Federal law prohibits the following practices as unfair:

1. Making false statements about the financial condition or solvency of such plan or arrangement.

2. Making false statements about the benefits provided by such a plan.

3. Making false statements about the regulatory status of such a plan or other arrangement under any Federal or State law governing collective bargaining, labor management relations, or intern union affairs.

4. Making false statements about the regulatory status of such plan or other arrangement regarding exemption from state regulatory authority under this chapter. (29 U.S.C.A. §1149).

NEW HAMPSHIRE

COMMERCIAL LINES
AGRICULTURAL CAPITAL ASSETS; BOILER/EQUIPMENT BREAKDOWN; BOP; CAPITAL ASSETS; AUTO; PROP.; CIM; CRIME; E-COMMERCE; FARM; FIN. INST; CGL (CGL, LIQUOR, OWNER & CONTRACTOR'S PROTECTIVE, RAILROAD PROTECTIVE, UNDERGROUND STORAGE TANKS, POLLUTION, EMPLOYMENT PRACTICES LIABILITY, PRODS. /COMPLETED OPS.); UMB; MGT. PROTECTION; MED. PROFESSIONAL LIABILITY

New Hampshire Revised Statutes (N.H. Rev. Stat. Ann.) §§ 417-C:1 to 417-C:3 and 417-C:6

Cancellation during the Underwriting Period

Length of Underwriting Period: Sixty days.

Length of Notice: Ten days

Reason for Cancellation: Required on the notice.

Proof Required: Certified mail (or certificate of mailing for nonpayment).

Cancellation after the Underwriting Period

The policy may be cancelled **only** for the following reasons:

1. Nonpayment.

2. Fraud or material misrepresentation affecting the policy or in the presentation of a claim.

3. If the insured violates of any of the terms or conditions of the policy.

4. Substantial increase in hazard. Cancellation for this reason requires prior approval of the Commissioner.

Length of Notice: Ten days for nonpayment or substantial increase in hazard; sixty days for all other allowable reasons.

Reason for Cancellation: Required on the notice.

Proof Required: Certified mail (or certificate of mailing for nonpayment).

NEW HAMPSHIRE

Nonrenewal

Length of Notice: Sixty days unless insured fails to pay a required advance premium.

Reason for Nonrenewal: Currently not required. (N.H. Rev. Stat. Ann. § 417-C:3).

Proof Required: Proof of mailing.

Other Cancellation/Nonrenewal Provisions

Increases in premium of 25 percent or less require thirty days' notice.

Increases in premium of more than 25 percent also require sixty days' notice.

WORKERS COMPENSATION

N.H. Rev. Stat. Ann. § 281-A:9 and New Hampshire Code of Administrative Rules, Chapter Lab 300

Cancellation and Nonrenewal

Length of Notice: Thirty days for nonpayment; forty-five days any other reason.

Reason for Cancellation: Written termination notice must be filed with the Labor Commissioner and a copy of the notice sent to the employer. Reason for notice must be stated as per Lab300 (Workers' Compensation Insurance Coverage).

Proof Required: Proof of filing and proof of mailing as per Lab 300. Insurer must file a written termination with the commissioner and send a copy of the notice to the employer.

SURPLUS LINES

N.H. Rev. Stat. Ann. § 405:24

The New Hampshire cancellation and nonrenewal laws do not apply to surplus lines.

FINANCED PREMIUMS

N.H. Rev. Stat. Ann. § 415-B:9

If the premium finance agreement contains a power of attorney, the finance company may request, in the name of the insured, that the insurer cancel the policy due to nonpayment. After default, the premium finance company may cancel by mailing insurer a notice of cancellation, stating effective date of cancellation (not less than ten days after date of mailing notice). The premium finance company must also mail a copy of notice of cancellation to insured at last known address and to agent or broker.

NEW HAMPSHIRE

Insurer must give notice on behalf of itself or insured to any governmental agency, mortgagee, or other third party on or before second business day after the day it receives notice. Insurer must determine effective date of cancellation taking into consideration the number of days' notice required to complete cancellation.

Notice must state the date (not less than ten days after its mailing) that the cancellation will become effective.

PERSONAL LINES

DWELLING FIRE & HOMEOWNERS

(For policies covering dwellings that are fully or in-part owner-occupied; or that cover contents only.)

N.H. Rev. Stat. Ann. §§ 417-B:1 to 417-B:4

Cancellation during the Underwriting Period

Length of Underwriting Period: Ninety days.

Length of Notice: Ten days for any reason unless prohibited by N.H. Rev. Stat. Ann. § 417:4.

Reason for Cancellation: Required on notice or a statement that information is available on request.

Proof Required: Proof of physical delivery or proof of mailing.

Cancellation after the Underwriting Period

The policy may be cancelled **only** for the following reasons:

1. Nonpayment.

2. Conviction of a crime having as one of its necessary elements an act increasing the risk of loss.

3. Fraud or material misrepresentation by the named insured in the pursuit of a claim.

4. Grossly negligent acts or omissions by the insured that substantially increase any of the insured-against hazards.

5. Physical changes in the property which result in the property becoming uninsurable.

6. Specific request of the insured.

NEW HAMPSHIRE

Length of Notice: Ten days for nonpayment; forty-five days for all other allowable reasons.

Reason for Cancellation: Required on notice or a statement that information is available on request.

Proof Required: Proof of physical delivery or proof of mailing.

Nonrenewal

Length of Notice: Ten days for nonpayment; forty-five days for all other allowable reasons.

Reason for Nonrenewal: Required on notice or a statement that information is available on request.

Proof Required: Proof of physical delivery or proof of mailing. Electronic mailing does not count.

Other Cancellation/Nonrenewal Provisions

Requests for reasons for cancellation and nonrenewal must be made in writing and mailed or delivered to insurer at least ten days prior to effective cancellation date. The insurer will specify reason(s) within five days of receipt of request.

The nonrenewal of a homeowner's insurance policy is prohibited if the nonrenewal is based solely on the insured having filed a single valid claim within any previous or the current policy term. Inquiries about coverage on a policy do not constitute a valid claim. (N.H. Rev. Stat. § 417-B:3-a). For policies that contain no fixed expiration date or that are issued for other than annual periods a term shall be considered each 12 month anniversary from the date of policy issuance. (N.H. Rev. Stat. § 417-B:3-a).

No insurer shall cancel or refuse to write or renew a policy of insurance insuring against any of the contingencies solely because of the age, residence, race, color, creed, national origin, ancestry, marital status, or lawful occupation, including the military service, of anyone who is or seeks to become insured or solely because another insurer has refused to write a policy, or has cancelled or has refused to renew an existing policy in which that person was the named insured (N.H. Rev. Stat. § 417-B:2).

No insurer shall cancel, refuse to write, or refuse to renew a policy under this chapter solely on the basis of credit information obtained from a credit rating, a credit history, or a credit scoring model without consideration of any other applicable and permitted underwriting factor independent of credit information (N.H. Rev. Stat. § 417 B:2-a).

NEW HAMPSHIRE

PERSONAL AUTO

N.H. Rev. Stat. Ann.§§ 417-A:1 to 417-A:5

Cancellation during the Underwriting Period

Length of Underwriting Period: Sixty days.

Length of Notice: Ten days.

Reason for Cancellation: Required on the notice.

Proof Required: Proof of physical delivery or proof of mailing.

Cancellation after the Underwriting Period

The policy may be cancelled **only** for the following reasons:

1. Nonpayment.

2. Specific request of insured.

3. Failure to sign the New Hampshire residency form.

Length of Notice: Ten days for nonpayment; forty-five days for any other allowable reason.

Reason for Cancellation: Required on the notice.

Proof Required: Proof of physical delivery or proof of mailing.

Nonrenewal

Length of Notice: Ten days for nonpayment; forty-five days for any other reason.

Reason for Nonrenewal: Required on the notice.

Proof Required: Proof of physical delivery or proof of mailing.

Other Cancellation/Nonrenewal Provisions

No insurer shall cancel, refuse to write or refuse to renew a policy of automobile insurance on any person solely because of the age, residence, race, color, creed, national origin, ancestry, marital status or lawful occupation, including the military service, of anyone who is or seeks to become insured or solely because another insurer has refused to write a

NEW HAMPSHIRE

policy, or has cancelled or has refused to renew an existing policy in which that person was the named insured (N.H. Rev. Stat. § 417-A:3).

Coercion by insurer: No insurer shall refuse to renew a policy of automobile insurance previously issued to an individual solely because such individual has no other policy of insurance with said insurer (N.H. Rev. Stat. Ann. § 417-A:3-a).

No insurer shall cancel, refuse to write, or refuse to renew a policy of automobile insurance solely on the basis of credit information obtained from a credit rating, a credit history, or a credit scoring model, without consideration of any other applicable and permitted underwriting factors independent of credit information. (N.H. Rev. Stat § 417-A:3-c).

A member of a group of affiliated companies may refuse to write, cancel, or refuse to renew a particular policy consistent with N.H. Rev. Stat. Ann. § 412 and filed and approved underwriting guidelines, provided the member immediately offers a policy of insurance, including policy terms and premiums, for the applicant or insured with another member of the same group. The replacement offer and terms shall be delivered or mailed together with the notice of cancellation or nonrenewal of a particular policy. (NH AC Ins. § 1402.04).

The movement of a policy from one company to another within a group of affiliated companies, or the movement of a policy to a different tier within one company resulting in a different rate for the insured, is permitted within the underwriting period if the movement is consistent and in compliance with the company's underwriting guidelines, in accordance with the provisions of N.H. Rev. Stat. Ann. § 412, otherwise such movement can only occur on the renewal date of the policy and requires a forty-five day written notice to policyholder. The replacement offer and terms shall be delivered or mailed together with the notice of cancellation or nonrenewal of a particular policy. (NH ADC Ins. § 1402.04).

Any insured may, within ten days of the receipt by the insured of notice of cancellation or nonrenewal, request in writing to the insurance Commissioner that the Commissioner reviews the action of the insurer in cancelling or refusing to renew the policy of such insured. (N.H. Rev. Stat. § 417-A:7).

A notice of nonrenewal for nonpayment of premium on a policy written on other than a continuous basis is not required if the insurer has manifested in writing its willingness to renew by issuing or offering to issue a renewal policy certificate or other evidence of renewal or has manifested such intention in writing by other means. (N.H. Rev. Stat. § 417-A:5-a).

Notices of cancellation and nonrenewal must:

1. Be approved as to form by the commissioner prior to use.

NEW HAMPSHIRE

2. State the date on which such cancellation or refusal to renew shall become effective.

3. State the specific reasons for cancellation or nonrenewal.

4. Advise the insured that the insured has the right to request that the insurance commissioner review the insurer's decision.

5. Advise the insured of eligibility for insurance through the automobile reinsurance facility. (N.H. Rev. Stat. § 417-A:5).

FRAUD
N.H. Rev. Stat. Ann. §§ 638:20 and 417:28
Definition

A person is guilty of insurance fraud, if, such person knowingly and with intent to injure, defraud, or deceive any insurer, conceals or causes to be concealed from any insurer a material statement, or presents or causes to be presented to any insurer, or prepares with knowledge or belief that it will be so presented, any written or oral statement including computer-generated documents, knowing that such statement contains any false, incomplete or misleading information which is material to:

1. An application for the issuance of any insurance policy.

2. The rating of any insurance policy.

3. A claim for payment or benefit pursuant to any insurance policy.

4. Premiums on any insurance policy.

5. Payments made in accordance with the terms of any insurance policy.

A person is guilty as an accomplice to insurance fraud, if, with a purpose to injure, defraud or deceive any insurer, the person assists, abets, solicits or conspires with another to commit insurance fraud, as defined above.

Penalties

The penalty for insurance fraud varies depending on the pecuniary value of the fraud. If the value of the fraudulent portion of the claim exceeds $1,500, insurance fraud is a Class A felony. If the value of the fraudulent portion of the claim exceeds $1,000 but not $1,500, the insurance fraud constitutes a class B felony. If the value of the fraudulent portion of the claim does not exceed $1,000, the insurance fraud is a misdemeanor.

NEW HAMPSHIRE

Reporting Requirements

A person or entity which has reason to believe that either insurance fraud or insurance-related criminal activity has been committed must report it to the Insurance Fraud Investigation Unit within sixty days. Reports must be made on a form prescribed by the Insurance Fraud Investigation Unit. Absent fraud or malice, officials of either a public entity or an insurance company who furnish information on an insurance company's behalf, shall have immunity from civil and criminal prosecution for disclosures made to the Insurance Fraud Investigation Unit.

Application Fraud Statement

Life settlement contracts and applications must contain the following statement:

> "Any person who knowingly presents false information in an application for insurance or life settlement contract is guilty of a crime and may be subject to fines and confinement in prison."

A substantially similar statement is sufficient. (N.H. Rev. Stat. § 408-D:14).

Insurer Antifraud Initiatives

Insurers shall have antifraud initiatives reasonably calculated to detect, prosecute, and prevent fraudulent insurance acts, including a written antifraud plan submitted to the commissioner.

If a commissioner finds that the insurer licensed to do business in New Hampshire has failed to submit a plan as required, reasonably calculated to detect, prosecute, and prevent fraud, or has submitted but failed to execute the plan, the commissioner may issue a fine or suspend the right of the insurer to do business. (N.H. Rev. Stat. § 417:30).

FAIR CLAIMS PROCESSING

N.H. Rev. Stat. Ann. §§ 417:1 to 417:17

Definition

The following acts by an insurer, if committed without just cause and not merely inadvertently or accidentally, constitute unfair claim settlement practices and are prohibited:

1. Knowingly misrepresenting to claimants or insureds pertinent facts or policy provisions relating to coverages at issue.

2. Failing to acknowledge and act promptly upon communications with respect to claims arising under insurance policies.

NEW HAMPSHIRE

3. Not adopting and implementing standards for the prompt and reasonable investigating claims that arise under insurance policies.

4. Not making a good-faith attempt to effectuate prompt, fair, and equitable settlements or compromises of claims in which liability has become reasonably clear.

5. Compelling claimants to institute litigation to recover amounts due under insurance policies by offering substantially less than the amounts ultimately recovered in actions brought by them.

6. Adopting or making known to insureds or claimants a policy of appealing from arbitration awards in favor of insureds or claimants for the purpose of compelling them to accept settlements or compromises less than the amount awarded in arbitration.

7. Attempting to settle or compromise a claim on the basis of an application which was altered without notice to, or knowledge or consent of the insured.

8. Attempting to settle or compromise a claim for less than the amount which the insured had been led to believe the insured was entitled to by written or printed advertising material accompanying or incorporated into an application.

9. Attempting to delay the investigation or payment of claims by requiring an insured and the insured's physician to submit a preliminary claim report and then requiring the subsequent submission of formal proof of loss forms, both of which submissions contain substantially the same information.

10. Making a claim payment that is not accompanied by a statement setting forth the benefits included within the claim payment.

11. Failing to affirm or deny coverage of claims within a reasonable time after proof of loss forms have been submitted.

12. Refusing payment of a claim solely on the basis of an insured's request to do so without independently evaluating the insured's liability based upon all available information.

13. Failure of an insurer to maintain a complete record of all complaints which it has received, whether or not they were deemed valid, the time it took to process the complaint, and the disposition thereof and file an annual report thereof with the insurance department; or

NEW HAMPSHIRE

14. Knowingly underestimating the value of any claim by an insurer or by an adjuster representing the insurer. (wording change effective July 29, 2018)

Note: The insurance commissioner reserves the right to examine and investigate into the affairs of every person engaged in the business of insurance in New Hampshire to determine whether such person is engaged in any unfair method of competition or any unfair act or practice. (N.H. Rev. Stat. § 417:5).

Penalties

Violators of the insurance Commissioner's cease and desist order regarding an unfair claims settlement practice may have their license suspended, revoked, or not renewed. The commissioner may also impose on violators of such a cease and desist order a maximum administrative penalty of $2,500 for each method offending competition, act, or practice. (N.H. Rev. Stat. § 417:13).

NEW JERSEY

For details on cancellation procedures for the standard policy, refer to the Standard Policy section.

COMMERCIAL LINES
AGRICULTURAL CAPITAL ASSETS; BOP; CAPITAL ASSETS; C. AUTO; CRIME; CGL (CGL, EMPLOYMENT PRACTICES, LIQUOR, OCP, POLLUTION, PRODS. / COMPLETED OPS, RAILROAD PROTECTIVE) CIM; C. PROP.; C. UMB.; E. COMMERCE; EQUIPMENT BREAKDOWN; FARM; & PROF. LIABILITY

New Jersey Statutes §17:29C-1 through 17:29C-13; N.J.A.C. 11:1-20.2 through 11:1-20.6

Cancellation during the Underwriting Period

Length of Underwriting Period: Sixty days unless the policy is a renewal.

Length of Notice: Ten days for nonpayment or existence of a moral hazard as defined by N.J.A.C. 11:1-20.2(f); thirty days, but not more than 120 days, for any other reason. New Jersey FAIR Plan policies allow five-day notice in certain circumstances, see N.J.A.C. 11:1-5.2 for details.

Reason for Cancellation: Required on the notice sent to the first named insured.

Proof Required: Certified mail or both a date-stamped proof of mailing from the Post Office showing insured's name and address and that the insurer retain a duplicate copy of the mailed notice.

Cancellation after the Underwriting Period

The policy may be cancelled **only** for the following reasons:

1. Nonpayment.

2. Existence of a moral hazard, defined in N.J.A.C. 11:1-20.2(f) as:

   a. The risk, danger or probability that the insured will destroy, or permit to be destroyed, the insured property for the purpose of collecting the insurance proceeds. Any change in the circumstances of an insured that will increase the probability of such a destruction may be considered a "moral hazard."

   b. The substantial risk, danger or probability that the character, circumstances or personal habits of the insured may increase the possibility of loss or liability for which an insurer will be held responsible. Any change in the character or

NEW JERSEY

circumstances of an individual, corporate, partnership or other insured that will increase the probability of such a loss or liability may be considered a "moral hazard."

3. Material misrepresentation or nondisclosure of a material fact at the time of acceptance of the risk.

4. Increased hazard or material change in the risk which the insurer could not have reasonably contemplated at the time of assumption of the risk.

5. Substantial breaches of contractual duties, conditions, or warranties that materially affect nature and/or insurability of the risk.

6. If the insured does not cooperate with loss control measures that materially affect the insurability of the risk.

7. Fraudulent acts by the insured or the insured's representative that materially affect the nature of the risk.

8. If the insurer suffers a loss of or reduction in available insurance capacity.

9. Material increase in exposure due to subsequent changes in statutory or case law.

10. If the insurer loses all or a substantial part of its reinsurance on the risk.

11. Failure of the insured to comply with any Federal, State, or local codes (such as local fire, health, safety or building or construction regulation, law or ordinance) with respect to any covered property which substantially increases any hazard insured against after a sixty-day written notification of a violation of such law, regulation, or ordinance.

12. Failure of the insured to provide reasonable and necessary underwriting information upon written request and reasonable opportunity to respond.

13. If the agent is terminated. However, the insurer must inform the insured of his or her right to continue coverage with the current insurer. The insured must agree in writing to the cancellation of the policy.

14. Any other reason outlined in the insurer's underwriting guidelines, provided the guidelines are not arbitrary, capricious, or unfairly discriminatory. Only the guidelines which are in effect at the inception of the policy or subsequent renewal as applicable may be used.

NEW JERSEY

Note: Any underwriting guideline or standard premised on adverse loss experience shall be limited in application to nonrenewals only and shall specifically identify the type of loss experience which supports and justifies the nonrenewal action. (N.J.A.C. 11:1–20.4).

Length of Notice: Ten days for nonpayment and moral hazard; thirty days, but not more than 120 days, for all other allowable reasons. New Jersey FAIR Plan policies allow five-day notice in certain circumstances, see N.J.A.C. 11:1-5.2 for details.

Reason for Cancellation: Required on the notice sent to the first named insured. Notice must specify the reason and the factual basis upon which the insurer relied.

Proof Required: Certified mail or both a date-stamped proof of first-class mailing showing the name and the address of the insured and that the insurer retains a duplicate copy of the mailed notice.

Nonrenewal

Length of Notice: Thirty days, but not more than 120 days.

Reason for Nonrenewal: Required on the notice.

Proof Required: Certified mail or both a date-stamped proof of first-class mailing, from the Post Office, showing the name and the address of the insured and that the insurer retains a duplicate copy of the mailed notice.

Other Cancellation/Nonrenewal Provisions

New Jersey law specifies that cancellation for nonpayment will not be effective if the insured pays the amount due before the effective date set forth in the notice.

Insurer may only nonrenew for the same reasons as allowed for cancellation.

Failure to send such notice to any designated mortgagee or loss payee shall invalidate the cancellation only as to the mortgagee's or loss payee's interest.

Every policy shall contain a provision with the following language:

> "Pursuant to New Jersey law, this policy cannot be cancelled or nonrenewed for any underwriting reason or guideline which is arbitrary, capricious or unfairly discriminatory or without adequate prior notice to the insured. The underwriting reasons or guidelines that an insurer can use to cancel or nonrenew a policy must

NEW JERSEY

be maintained by the insurer in writing and must be furnished to the insured and/or the insured's lawful representative upon written request.

This provision shall not apply to any policy which has been in effect for less than sixty days at the time notice of cancellation is mailed or delivered, unless the policy is a renewal policy." (N.J.A.C. 11:1-20.3)

All notices of nonrenewal and cancellation, except those for nonpayment of premium, must contain a statement which shall be clearly and prominently set out in boldface type or another manner which draws the reader's attention advising the insured that the insured may file a written complaint about the cancellation or nonrenewal with the New Jersey Department of Banking and Insurance, Office of Consumer Protection, PO Box 325, Trenton, New Jersey 08625-0325.

With respect to payment of the renewal premium, notice of the amount of the renewal premium and any change in contract terms shall be given to the insured in writing not more than 120 days nor less than thirty days prior to the due date of the premium and shall clearly state the effect of nonpayment of the premium by the due date. If the insurer fails to provide such notice of renewal, the insured shall be entitled to continue the expiring policy at the same terms and premium until such time as the insurer shall send appropriate notice of termination or renewal.

With respect to payment of the renewal premium for medical malpractice liability insurance policies, notice of the amount of the renewal premium and any change in contract terms shall be given to the insured in writing not more than 120 days nor less than 30 days prior to the due date of the premium and shall clearly state the effect of nonpayment of the premium by the due date. If the insurer fails to provide such notice of renewal, the insured shall be entitled to continue the expiring policy at the same terms and premium until such time as the insurer shall send appropriate notice of termination or renewal. (N.J.A.C. 11:1-20.2(c) and (m)).

Pursuant to N.J.S.A. 17:29B–4.1, no inquiry by an insured for information regarding the insured's homeowners' insurance policy, or coverage for a particular loss under that policy, shall be categorized as a claim for purposes of determining adverse loss experience.

Pursuant to N.J.S.A. 17:36–5.20a, no insurer authorized to do business in this State shall cancel or nonrenew an insurance policy covering an owner occupied one-to-four family dwelling solely because of claims or losses due to weather-related damage or a third-party criminal act committed by someone who is not a resident of the insured dwelling, unless the claim or loss identifies or confirms an increase in hazard, a material change in the risk assumed or a breach of contractual duties, conditions or warranties that materially affect the nature or the insurability of the risk. (N.J.A.C. 11:1–20.4).

NEW JERSEY

COMMERCIAL GENERAL LIABILITY
(Underground Storage Tanks)

New Jersey Statutes §17:29C-1 through 17:29C-13; N.J.A.C. 11:1-20.2 through 11:1-20.6

Cancellation during the Underwriting Period

Length of Underwriting Period: Sixty days unless the policy is a renewal.

Length of Notice: Ten days for nonpayment or the existence of a moral hazard; thirty days for material misrepresentation or nondisclosure; sixty days for any other reason. Regulations allow thirty days, but not more than 120 days, for any other reasons. However, insurers using ISO's CG 30 13 must comply with the more restrictive requirements.

Reason for Cancellation: Required on the notice. Even though the ISO amendatory endorsement (CG 30 13) for New Jersey is silent on this matter the state code says that the reason and factual basis upon which the insurer relies must be provided.

Proof Required: Certified mail or both a date-stamped proof of first-class mailing from the Post Office showing the name and the address of the insured and that the insurer retains a duplicate copy of the mailed notice.

Cancellation after the Underwriting Period

The policy may be cancelled **only** for the following reasons:

1. Nonpayment.

2. Existence of a moral hazard, as defined in N.J.A.C. 11:1-20.2(f). See beginning.

3. Material misrepresentation or nondisclosure of a material fact existing at the time of the application.

4. Increased hazard or material change in the risk which the insurer could not have reasonably contemplated by the parties when they assumed the risk.

5. Substantial breaches of contractual duties, conditions, or warranties that materially affect nature and/or insurability of the risk.

6. If the insured does not cooperate with loss control measures that materially affect the insurability of the risk.

7. Fraudulent acts by the insured or the insured's representative that materially affect the nature of the risk.

NEW JERSEY

8. If the insurer suffers a loss of or reduction in available insurance capacity.

9. Material increase in exposure due to changes in the statutory or case law.

10. If the insurer loses all or a substantial part of its reinsurance on the risk.

11. Failure of the insured to comply with any federal, state, or local codes (such as local fire, health, safety or building or construction regulation, law or ordinance) with respect to any covered property which substantially increases any hazard insured against after a sixty-day written notification of a violation of such law, regulation, or ordinance.

12. Failure of the named insured to provide reasonable and necessary underwriting information upon written request and a reasonable opportunity to respond.

13. If the agent is terminated. However, the insurer must inform the insured of his or her right to continue coverage with the current insurer.

14. Any other reason outlined in the insurer's underwriting guidelines, provided the guidelines are not arbitrary, capricious, or unfairly discriminatory. Only the guidelines which are in effect at the inception of the policy or subsequent renewal as applicable may be used.

    Note: Any underwriting guideline or standard premised on adverse loss experience shall be limited in application to nonrenewals only and shall specifically identify the type of loss experience which supports and justifies the nonrenewal action. (N.J.A.C. 11:1–20.4).

Length of Notice: Ten days for nonpayment or the existence of a moral hazard; thirty days, but not more than 120 days, for material misrepresentation or nondisclosure; sixty days, but not more than 120 days, for all other allowable reasons. Regulations allow thirty days, but not more than 120 days, for all other allowable reason. However, insurers using ISO's CG 30 13 must comply with the more restrictive requirements.

Reason for Cancellation: Required on the notice, along with factual basis upon which the insurer relies.

Proof Required: Certified mail or both proof of first-class mailing from the Post Office showing the name and the address of the insured and that the insurer retains a duplicate copy of the mailed notice.

NEW JERSEY

Nonrenewal

Length of Notice: Sixty days, but not more than 120 days. Regulations allow thirty days, but not more than 120 days. However, insurers using ISO's CG 30 13 must comply with the more restrictive requirements.

Reason for Nonrenewal: Required on the notice, along with factual basis upon which the insurer relies.

Proof Required: Certified mail or both date-stamped proof of first-class mailing from the Post Office showing the name and the address of the insured and that the insurer retains a duplicate copy of the mailed notice.

Other Cancellation/Nonrenewal Provisions

Insurer may only nonrenew for the same reasons as allowed for cancellation.

Every policy shall contain a provision with the following language:

> "Pursuant to New Jersey law, this policy cannot be cancelled or nonrenewed for any underwriting reason or guideline which is arbitrary, capricious, or unfairly discriminatory or without adequate prior notice to the insured. The underwriting reasons or guidelines that an insurer can use to cancel or nonrenew a policy must be maintained by the insurer in writing and will be furnished to the insured and/or the insured's lawful representative upon written request.
>
> This provision shall not apply to any policy which has been in effect for less than sixty days at the time notice of cancellation is mailed or delivered, unless the policy is a renewal policy." (N.J.A.C. 11:1-20.3)

All notices of nonrenewal and cancellation, except those for nonpayment of premium, must contain a statement which shall be clearly and prominently set out in boldface type or other manner which draws the reader's attention advising the insured that the insured may file a written complaint about the cancellation or nonrenewal with the New Jersey Department of Banking and Insurance, Office of Consumer Protection, PO Box 325, Trenton, New Jersey 08625-0325.

Pursuant to N.J.S.A. 17:29B–4.1, no inquiry by an insured for information regarding the insured's homeowners' insurance policy, or coverage for a particular loss under that policy, shall be categorized as a claim for purposes of determining adverse loss experience.

Pursuant to N.J.S.A. 17:36–5.20a, no insurer authorized to do business in this State shall cancel or nonrenew an insurance policy covering an owner occupied one-to-four family dwelling solely because of claims or losses due to weather-related damage or a third-party criminal act committed by someone who is not a resident of the insured dwelling, unless the

NEW JERSEY

claim or loss identifies or confirms an increase in hazard, a material change in the risk assumed or a breach of contractual duties, conditions or warranties that materially affect the nature or the insurability of the risk. (N.J.A.C. 11:1–20.4).

WORKERS COMPENSATION
New Jersey Statutes §34:15-81

New Jersey makes no changes from the standard policy. Ten days' notice to the Commissioner of Banking and Insurance is required.

SURPLUS LINES
N.J.A.C. §11:1-20.1

Surplus lines insurers are not required to follow the cancellation and nonrenewal laws of New Jersey. (However, surplus lines insurers are encouraged to comply with the cancellation and nonrenewal rules applicable to standard carriers).

FINANCED PREMIUMS
New Jersey Statutes §17:16D-13

If the premium finance agreement contains a power of attorney, the finance company may request, in the name of the insured, that the insurer cancel the policy due to nonpayment. The finance company must first give the insured ten days to pay. A copy of the notice must be sent to the insurance agent or broker listed on the finance agreement. The insurer shall give the prescribed notice on behalf of itself or the insured to any governmental agency, mortgagee, or other third-party on or before the second business day after the day it receives the notice of cancellation from the premium finance company. If the insured fails to make payment within that ten-day period, then the finance company mails the notice of cancellation to the insured and to the insurer. The effective date of the cancellation shall not be earlier than three days after mailing such notice to the insured and to the insurance agent/broker. Return of the policy by the insured is not required.

PERSONAL LINES
DWELLING FIRE & HOMEOWNERS
New Jersey Statutes §17:29C-1 through 17:29C-13; N.J.A.C. 11:1-20.2 through 11:1-20.6

Cancellation during the Underwriting Period

Length of Underwriting Period: Sixty days unless the policy is a renewal.

Length of Notice: Ten days for nonpayment or moral hazard; thirty days, but not more than 120 days, for any other reasons. New Jersey FAIR Plan policies allow five-day notice in certain circumstances, see N.J.A.C. 11:1-5.2 for details.

NEW JERSEY

Reason for Cancellation: Required on the notice.

Proof Required: Certified mail or both proof of first-class mailing from the Post Office showing the name and the address of the insured and that the insurer retain a duplicate copy of the mailed notice.

Cancellation after the Underwriting Period

The policy may be cancelled **only** for the following reasons:

1. Nonpayment.

2. Existence of a moral hazard, as defined in N.J.A.C. 11:1-20.2(f). See beginning.

3. Material misrepresentation or nondisclosure of a material fact at the time of the application.

4. Increased hazard or material change in the risk which the insurer could not have reasonably contemplated at the time of assumption of the risk.

5. Substantial breaches of contractual duties, conditions, or warranties that materially affect nature and/or insurability of the risk.

6. If the insured does not cooperate with loss control measures that materially affect the insurability of the risk.

7. Fraudulent acts by the insured or the insured's representative that materially affect the nature of the insured-against risk.

8. If the insurer suffers a loss of or reduction in available insurance capacity.

9. Material increase in exposure due to changes in statutory or case law.

10. If the insurer loses all or a substantial part of its reinsurance on the risk.

11. Failure of the insured to comply with any federal, state or local codes (such as local fire, health, safety or building or construction regulation, law or ordinance) with respect to any covered property which substantially increases any hazard insured against after a sixty-day notice of a violation of such law, regulation, or ordinance.

12. Failure of the named insured to provide reasonable and necessary underwriting information upon written request and reasonable opportunity to respond.

NEW JERSEY

13. If the agent is terminated. However, the insurer must inform the insured of her right to continue coverage with the current insurer.

14. Any other reason outlined in the insurer's underwriting guidelines, provided the guidelines are not arbitrary, capricious, or unfairly discriminatory. Only the guidelines which are in effect at the inception of the policy or subsequent renewal as applicable may be used.

    Note: Any underwriting guideline or standard premised on adverse loss experience shall be limited in application to nonrenewals only and shall specifically identify the type of loss experience which supports and justifies the nonrenewal action. (N.J.A.C. 11:1–20.4).

Length of Notice: Ten days for nonpayment or moral hazard; thirty days, but not more than 120 days, for all other allowable reasons. New Jersey FAIR Plan policies allow five-day notice in certain circumstances, see N.J.A.C. 11:1-5.2 for details.

Reason for Cancellation: Required on the notice, along with factual basis upon which the insurer relies.

Proof Required: Certified mail or both a date-stamped proof of mailing from the Post Office and that the insurer retains a duplicate copy of the mailed notice.

Nonrenewal

Length of Notice: Thirty days, but not more than 120 days.

Reason for Nonrenewal: Required on the notice, along with factual basis upon which the insurer relies.

Proof Required: Certified mail or both proof of first-class mailing from the post office showing the name and the address of the insured and that the insurer retains a true duplicate copy of the mailed notice.

Other Cancellation/Nonrenewal Provisions

An insurer may only nonrenew for the same reasons as allowed for cancellation, as well as adverse loss experience. Any underwriting guideline or standard premised on adverse loss experience shall be limited in application to nonrenewals only and shall specifically identify the type of loss experience which supports and justifies the nonrenewal action.

Every policy shall contain a provision with the following language:

> "Pursuant to New Jersey law, this policy cannot be cancelled or nonrenewed for any underwriting reason or guideline which is arbitrary, capricious or unfairly

NEW JERSEY

discriminatory or without adequate prior notice to the insured. The underwriting reasons or guidelines that an insurer can use to cancel or nonrenew a policy must be maintained by the insurer in writing and will be furnished to the insured and/or the insured's lawful representative upon written request.

This provision shall not apply to any policy which has been in effect for less than sixty days at the time notice of cancellation is mailed or delivered, unless the policy is a renewal policy." (N.J.A.C. 11:1-20.3)

Insurers are required to permit senior citizens to designate a third-party to whom notices of cancellation, nonrenewal and conditional renewal are to be sent. The copy of the notice of cancellation, nonrenewal or conditional renewal transmitted to the third-party shall be governed by the same law and policy provisions which govern the notice being transmitted to the insured senior citizen. The outside of the envelope must be marked in bold face with the following: "IMPORTANT INSURANCE POLICY INFORMATION: OPEN IMMEDIATELY." (N.J.S.A. §17:29C-1.2).

All notices of nonrenewal and cancellation, except those for nonpayment of premium, must contain a statement which shall be clearly and prominently set out in boldface type or other manner which draws the reader's attention advising the insured that the insured may file a written complaint about the cancellation or nonrenewal with the New Jersey Department of Banking and Insurance, Office of Consumer Protection, PO Box 325, Trenton, New Jersey 08625-0325.

Pursuant to N.J.S.A. 17:29B–4.1, no inquiry by an insured for information regarding the insured's homeowners' insurance policy, or coverage for a particular loss under that policy, shall be categorized as a claim for purposes of determining adverse loss experience.

Pursuant to N.J.S.A. 17:36–5.20a, no insurer authorized to do business in this State shall cancel or nonrenew an insurance policy covering an owner occupied one-to-four family dwelling solely because of claims or losses due to weather-related damage or a third-party criminal act committed by someone who is not a resident of the insured dwelling, unless the claim or loss identifies or confirms an increase in hazard, a material change in the risk assumed or a breach of contractual duties, conditions or warranties that materially affect the nature or the insurability of the risk. N.J.A.C. 11:1–20.4

PERSONAL AUTO

New Jersey Statutes §§17:28-8 and 17:29C-6 through 17:29C-10;
N.J.A.C. 11:3-7.6, 11:3-8.3 through 11:3-8.10

Cancellation during the Underwriting Period

Length of Underwriting Period: Sixty days.

NEW JERSEY

Length of Notice: Fifteen days, but not more than thirty days, for nonpayment; twenty days for any other reason.

Reason for Cancellation: Required on the notice of cancellation for nonpayment; otherwise, the cancellation must be accompanied by a statement that the reasons for cancellation will be made available upon request but not less than fifteen days prior to the effective date of the cancellation. Even though the ISO amendatory endorsement for New Jersey (PP 01 81) is silent on this matter, state code says that the reason must be provided.

Proof Required: Certified mail or both a date stamped proof of mailing from the post office showing the name and address of the insured and that the insurer retain a certified true copy of the mailed notice.

Cancellation after the Underwriting Period

The policy may be cancelled **only** for the following reasons:

1. Nonpayment.

2. Revocation or suspension of the driver's license or motor vehicle registration of:

   a. The named insured.
   b. Any driver who lives with the named insured.
   c. Any driver who customarily operates an auto insured under the policy.

   Such revocation or suspension must have occurred during the policy period. If the policy period is other than one year, the revocation/suspension must have occurred since the last anniversary of the original effective date. The suspension or revocation must be for one or more of the reasons listed in NJAC 11:8.10(a) 3.

3. Providing false or misleading information regarding an application, renewal, or claim.

4. The insurer determines within sixty days of issuance of a new policy that the named insured does not meet the acceptance criteria in effect at the time of application.

Length of Notice: Fifteen days, but not more than thirty days, for nonpayment; twenty days for all other allowable reasons.

NEW JERSEY

Reason for Cancellation: Required on the notice of cancellation for nonpayment, otherwise, the cancellation must be accompanied by a statement that the reasons for cancellation will be made available upon request but not less than fifteen days prior to the effective date of the cancellation.

Proof Required: Certified mail or both a date-stamped proof of mailing from the Post Office showing the name and address of the insured and that the insurer keep a duplicate, true copy of the mailed notice. (N.J.S.A 17:29C-10)

Nonrenewal

Length of Notice: Twenty days prior to anniversary date for policies longer than one year or with no fixed expiration date. Sixty days, but not more than ninety days, for all other policies.

Reason for Nonrenewal: Required on the notice.

Proof Required: Certified mail or both a date-stamped proof of mailing showing the name and address of the insured and that the insurer keep a duplicate copy of the mailed notice.

Other Cancellation/Nonrenewal Provisions

Subject to the limitations of N.J.A.C. 11:3-8.7, an insurer may issue a notice of nonrenewal to the named insured who is an eligible person insured in the following instances:

1. When the policyholder or other person insured under the policy either has:

    a. Provided false or misleading information in connection with an application or renewal of coverage, or as part of a claim for benefits.
    b. Failed to provide the minimum information necessary to accurately rate the policy or renewal.

2. An insurer may nonrenew the policies of 2 percent of the insurer's in force voluntary market policies in each rating territory.

3. An insurer may nonrenew one automobile for each two automobiles written by the insurer during the same calendar year and in the same rating territory.

    An insurer may issue a notice of nonrenewal to any ineligible person pursuant to N.J.A.C. 11:3-34.4.

NEW JERSEY

For the purpose of determining whether a person is an eligible person pursuant to N.J.A.C. 11:3-34.4, an insurer shall consider those accidents and violations accrued only in the experience period set forth in its acceptance criteria for renewal business established in accordance with N.J.A.C. 11:3-8.12.

An insurer may issue a notice of nonrenewal to insureds who are ineligible persons for failure to meet the insurer's acceptance criteria in an amount not to exceed 2 percent of the insurer's in force voluntary market policies in each rating territory.

When a policy is nonrenewed, the insurer must advise the insured of the availability of the assigned risk plan.

Insurers are required to permit senior citizens to designate a third-party to whom notices of cancellation, nonrenewal and conditional renewal are to be sent. The copy of the notice of cancellation, nonrenewal or conditional renewal transmitted to the third-party shall be governed by the same law and policy provisions which govern the notice being transmitted to the senior citizen insured. (N.J. Stat. § 17:29C-1.2)

Named Excluded Driver

Election of a "named excluded driver" endorsement shall be in writing and signed by the named insured on a form prescribed by the Commissioner. (N.J. Stat. §17:28-8).

PERSONAL UMBRELLA

New Jersey Statutes §17:29C-1 through 17:29C-13; N.J.A.C. 11:1-20.2 through 11:1-20.6

Cancellation during the Underwriting Period

Length of Underwriting Period: Sixty days unless the policy is a renewal.

Length of Notice: Ten days for nonpayment or moral hazard; thirty days, but not more than 120 days, for any other reasons. New Jersey FAIR Plan policies allow five-day notice in certain circumstances, see N.J.A.C. 11:1-5.2 for details.

Reason for Cancellation: Required on the notice.

Proof Required: Certified mail or both proof of first class mailing from the Post Office showing the name and the address of the insured and that the insurer retains a duplicate copy of the mailed notice.

Cancellation after the Underwriting Period

The policy may be cancelled **only** for the following reasons:

1. Nonpayment.

NEW JERSEY

2. Existence of a moral hazard, as defined in NJAC 11:1-20.2(f). See beginning.

3. Material misrepresentation or nondisclosure of a material fact at the time of the application.

4. Increased hazard or material change in the risk which the insurer could not have reasonably contemplated at the time of assumption of the risk.

5. Substantial breaches of contractual duties, conditions, or warranties that materially affect nature and/or insurability of the risk.

6. If the insured does not cooperate with loss control measures that materially affect the insurability of the risk.

7. Fraudulent acts by the insured or the insured's representative that materially affect the nature of the insured-against risk.

8. If the insurer suffers a loss of or reduction in available insurance capacity.

9. Material increase in exposure due to changes in statutory or case law.

10. If the insurer loses all or a substantial part of its reinsurance on the risk.

11. Failure of the insured to comply with any federal, state or local codes (such as local fire, health, safety or building or construction regulation, law or ordinance) with respect to any covered property which substantially increases any hazard insured against after a sixty-day notice of a violation of such law, regulation, or ordinance.

12. Failure of the named insured to provide reasonable and necessary underwriting information upon written request and reasonable opportunity to respond.

13. If the agent is terminated. However, the insurer must inform the insured of his or her right to continue coverage with the current insurer.

14. Any other reason outlined in the insurer's underwriting guidelines, provided the guidelines are not arbitrary, capricious, or unfairly discriminatory. Only the guidelines which are in effect at the inception of the policy or subsequent renewal as applicable may be used.

    Note: Any underwriting guideline or standard premised on adverse loss experience shall be limited in application to nonrenewals only and shall specifically identify the type of loss experience which supports and justifies the nonrenewal action. N.J.A.C. 11:1–20.4.

NEW JERSEY

Length of Notice: Ten days for nonpayment or moral hazard; thirty days, but not more than 120 days, for all other allowable reasons. New Jersey FAIR Plan policies allow five-day notice in certain circumstances, see N.J.A.C. 11:1-5.2 for details.

Reason for Cancellation: Required on the notice, along with factual basis upon which the insurer relies.

Proof Required: Certified mail or both a date-stamped proof of mailing from the Post Office and that the insurer retains a duplicate copy of the mailed notice.

Nonrenewal

Length of Notice: Thirty days, but not more than 120 days.

Reason for Nonrenewal: Required on the notice, along with factual basis upon which the insurer relies.

Proof Required: Certified mail or both proof of first-class mailing from the Post Office showing the name and the address of the insured and that the insurer retains a true duplicate copy of the mailed notice.

Other Cancellation/Nonrenewal Provisions

An insurer may only nonrenew for the same reasons as allowed for cancellation, as well as adverse loss experience. Any underwriting guideline or standard premised on adverse loss experience shall be limited in application to nonrenewals only and shall specifically identify the type of loss experience which supports and justifies the nonrenewal action.

Every policy shall contain a provision with the following language:

> "Pursuant to New Jersey law, this policy cannot be cancelled or nonrenewed for any underwriting reason or guideline which is arbitrary, capricious or unfairly discriminatory or without adequate prior notice to the insured. The underwriting reasons or guidelines that an insurer can use to cancel or nonrenew a policy must be maintained by the insurer in writing and will be furnished to the insured and/or the insured's lawful representative upon written request.
>
> This provision shall not apply to any policy which has been in effect for less than sixty days at the time notice of cancellation is mailed or delivered, unless the policy is a renewal policy." (N.J.A.C. 11:1-20.3)

NEW JERSEY

Insurers are required to permit senior citizens to designate a third-party to whom notices of cancellation, nonrenewal and conditional renewal are to be sent. The copy of the notice of cancellation, nonrenewal or conditional renewal transmitted to the third-party shall be governed by the same law and policy provisions which govern the notice being transmitted to the insured senior citizen. (N.J.S.A. §17:29C-1.2).

All notices of nonrenewal and cancellation, except those for nonpayment of premium, must contain a statement which shall be clearly and prominently set out in boldface type or other manner which draws the reader's attention advising the insured that the insured may file a written complaint about the cancellation or nonrenewal with the New Jersey Department of Banking and Insurance, Office of Consumer Protection, PO Box 325, Trenton, New Jersey 08625-0325.

Pursuant to N.J.S.A. 17:29B–4.1, no inquiry by an insured for information regarding the insured's homeowners' insurance policy, or coverage for a particular loss under that policy, shall be categorized as a claim for purposes of determining adverse loss experience.

Pursuant to N.J.S.A. 17:36–5.20a, no insurer authorized to do business in this State shall cancel or nonrenew an insurance policy covering an owner occupied one-to-four family dwelling solely because of claims or losses due to weather-related damage or a third-party criminal act committed by someone who is not a resident of the insured dwelling, unless the claim or loss identifies or confirms an increase in hazard, a material change in the risk assumed or a breach of contractual duties, conditions or warranties that materially affect the nature or the insurability of the risk. (N.J.A.C. 11:1–20.4).

FRAUD

New Jersey Statute §§2C:21-4.6 and 17:33A-1 through 34

Definition

A person commits the crime of insurance fraud if that person knowingly makes, or causes to be made, a false, fictitious, fraudulent, or misleading statement of material fact in, or omits a material fact from, or causes a material fact to be omitted from, any record, bill, claim or other document, in writing, electronically, orally or in any other form, that a person attempts to submit, submits, causes to be submitted, or attempts to cause to be submitted as part of, in support of or opposition to or in connection with:

1. A claim for payment, reimbursement or other benefit pursuant to an insurance policy, or from an insurance company or the "Unsatisfied Claim and Judgment Fund Law."

2. An application to obtain or renew an insurance policy.

NEW JERSEY

3. Any payment made or to be made in accordance with the terms of an insurance policy or premium finance transaction.

4. An affidavit, certification, record or other document used in any insurance or premium finance transaction.

In addition, a person commits the crime of insurance fraud if that person operates a motor vehicle on the public highways of New Jersey which is insured under a policy using another state as the primary residence even though that person's principle residence is in New Jersey or the vehicle is principally garaged in New Jersey. This does not apply to people who have honestly obtained insurance in another state as a secondary residence or temporary residence. (N.J.S.A. 2C:21-4.6).

A person may violate New Jersey's separate Insurance Fraud Prevention Act in the following ways. A person or a practitioner violates this act if he:

1. Presents or causes to be presented any written or oral statement as part of, or in support of or opposition to, a claim for payment or other benefit pursuant to an insurance policy or the "Unsatisfied Claim and Judgment Fund Law," knowing that the statement contains any false or misleading information concerning any fact or thing material to the claim.

2. Prepares or makes any written or oral statement that is intended to be presented to any insurance company, the Unsatisfied Claim and Judgment Fund or any claimant thereof in connection with, or in support of or opposition to any claim for payment or other benefit pursuant to an insurance policy or the "Unsatisfied Claim and Judgment Fund Law", knowing that the statement contains any false or misleading information concerning any fact or thing material to the claim.

3. Conceals or knowingly fails to disclose the occurrence of an event which affects any person's initial or continued right or entitlement to either:

    a. Any insurance benefit or payment.
    b. The amount of any benefit or payment to which the person is entitled.

4. Prepares or makes any written or oral statement, intended to be presented to any insurance company or producer for the purpose of obtaining:

    a. A motor vehicle insurance policy, that the person to be insured maintains a principal residence in New Jersey when, in fact, that person's principal residence is in a state other than New Jersey.

NEW JERSEY

    b. An insurance policy, knowing that the statement contains any false or misleading information concerning any fact or thing material to an insurance application or contract.

5. Conceals or knowingly fails to disclose any evidence, written or oral, which may be relevant to a finding that a violation of the provisions of the preceding paragraph has or has not occurred.

6. Knowingly assists, conspires with, or urges any person or practitioner to violate any of the provisions of this act.

7. Due to the assistance, conspiracy or urging of any person or practitioner, knowingly benefits, directly or indirectly, from the proceeds derived from a violation of this act.

8. If the owner, administrator or employee of any hospital knowingly allows the use of the facilities of the hospital by any person in furtherance of a scheme or conspiracy to violate any of the provisions of this act.

9. For pecuniary gain, for himself or another, he directly or indirectly solicits any person or practitioner to engage, employ or retain either himself or any other person to manage, adjust or prosecute any claim or cause of action, against any person, for damages for negligence, or, for pecuniary gain, for himself or another, directly or indirectly solicits other persons to bring causes of action to recover damages for personal injuries or death, or for pecuniary gain, for himself or another, directly or indirectly solicits other persons to make a claim for personal injury protection benefits pursuant to P.L. 1972, c. 70 (C.39:6A-1 *et seq.*); provided, however, that this subsection shall not apply to any conduct otherwise permitted by law or by rule of the Supreme Court.

Penalties

Insurance fraud is a crime of the second degree if both:

1. The person knowingly commits five or more acts of insurance fraud.

2. The aggregate value of property, services or other benefits wrongfully obtained or sought to be obtained is at least $1,000.

    Note, that while each act of insurance fraud is a distinct offense, five or more separate acts may be aggregated for the purpose of establishing liability under the above factors.

Insurance fraud is a crime of the third degree if the aforementioned criteria are not met.

NEW JERSEY

A finding of liability under New Jersey's Insurance Fraud Prevention Act carries the following fines and costs:

1. $5,000 for the first violation.

2. $10,000 for the second violation.

3. $15,000 for each subsequent violation.

4. Court costs and reasonable attorney's fees to the Commissioner.

Insurance fraud is a crime in the fourth degree if a person makes a dishonest representation to his or her insurance provider about the principle place of residence or place of garage for the purposes of obtaining more affordable auto insurance. (N.J.S.A. 2C:21-4.6).

Violating the Insurance Fraud Prevention Act may have ramifications on one's credentials. In the case of a professional licensed or certified by a professional licensing board in the Division of Consumer Affairs of the Department of Law and Public Safety who is guilty of fraud, the Insurance Fraud Prosecutor may recommend to the appropriate board a suspension or revocation of the professional license.

In addition to any other penalty, fine or charge imposed pursuant to law, a person who is found in any legal proceeding to have committed insurance fraud shall be subject to a surcharge in the amount of $1,000. If a person is charged with insurance fraud in a legal proceeding and the charge is resolved through a settlement requiring the person to pay a sum of money, the person shall be subject to a surcharge in an amount equal to 5 percent of the settlement payment.

Reporting Requirements

Anyone who believes that a violation of this act has been or is being made must immediately notify the bureau and the Office of the Insurance Fraud Prosecutor after discovery of the alleged violation of this act and shall send to the bureau and office, on a form and in a manner jointly prescribed by the Commissioner and the Insurance Fraud Prosecutor, the information requested and such additional information relative to the alleged violation as the bureau or office may require.

No person shall be subject to civil liability for libel, violation of privacy or otherwise by virtue of the filing of reports or furnishing of other information, in good faith and without malice, required by this section or required by the bureau or the Office of the Insurance Fraud Prosecutor as a result of the authority conferred upon it by law. (N.J.S.A. §17:33A-9)

NEW JERSEY

Application Fraud Statement

Viatical settlement contracts and applications must contain the following language:

> "Any person who knowingly presents false information in an application for insurance or viatical settlement contract is guilty of a crime and may be subject to fines and confinement in prison." (N.J.S.A. §17B:30B-12).

> Insurance claim forms shall contain a statement in a form approved by the Commissioner that clearly states in substance the following: "Any person who knowingly files a statement of claim containing any false or misleading information is subject to criminal and civil penalties." (N.J.S.A. §17:33A-6).

> Insurance application forms shall contain a statement in a form approved by the Commissioner that clearly states in substance the following: "Any person who includes any false or misleading information on an application for an insurance policy is subject to criminal and civil penalties." (N.J.S.A. §17:33A-6).

FAIR PROCESSING CLAIMS

New Jersey Statute §§17:29B-4 and 17B:30-20

Definition

New Jersey law prohibits the following claim settlement practices when they are committed or performed with such frequency as to indicate a general business practice:

1. Misrepresenting pertinent facts or insurance policy provisions relating to coverages at issue.

2. Failing to acknowledge and act reasonably promptly upon communications with respect to claims arising under insurance policies.

3. Failing to adopt and implement reasonable standards for the prompt investigation of claims arising under insurance policies.

4. Refusing to pay claims without conducting a reasonable investigation based upon all available information.

5. Failing to affirm or deny coverage of claims within a reasonable time after proof of loss statements have been completed.

6. Not attempting in good faith to effectuate prompt, fair, and equitable settlements of claims in which liability has become reasonably clear.

NEW JERSEY

7. Compelling insureds to institute litigation to recover amounts due under an insurance policy by offering substantially less than the amounts ultimately recovered in actions brought by such insureds.

8. Attempting to settle a claim for less than the amount to which a reasonable man would have believed he was entitled by reference to written or printed advertising material accompanying or made part of an application.

9. Attempting to settle claims on the basis of an application which was altered without notice to, or knowledge or consent of the insured.

10. Making claims payments to insureds or beneficiaries not accompanied by a statement setting forth the coverage under which the payments are being made.

11. Making known to insureds or claimants a policy of appealing from arbitration awards in favor of insureds or claimants for the purpose of compelling them to accept settlements or compromises less than the amount awarded in arbitration.

12. Delaying the investigation or payment of claims by requiring an insured, claimant or the physician of either to submit a preliminary claim report and then requiring the subsequent submission of formal proof of loss forms, both of which submissions contain substantially the same information.

13. Failing to promptly settle claims, where liability has become reasonably clear, under one portion of the insurance policy coverage in order to influence settlements under other portions of the insurance policy coverage.

14. Failing to promptly provide a reasonable explanation of the basis in the insurance policy in relation to the facts or applicable law for denial of a claim or for the offer of a compromise settlement.

15. Requiring insureds or claimants to institute or prosecute complaints regarding motor vehicle violations in the municipal court as a condition of paying private passenger automobile insurance claims.

Penalty

Those who violate the Commissioner's cease and desist order arising out of the commission of one of the aforementioned practices must pay a fine of $5,000 for each violation. The Commissioner may revoke or suspend the license or authority of any such person.

NEW MEXICO

For details on cancellation procedures for the standard policy, refer to the Standard Policy section.

COMMERCIAL LINES

Insurance Division Bulletin No. 2012-009 dated July 17, 2012, states that certain commercial policyholders are required to provide certain state agencies with proofs of insurance that include a statement from the insurer that the insurer will notify the state agency thirty days before cancelling the insurance. In situations where this applies, insurers shall provide such a statement.

AGRICULTURAL CAPITAL ASSETS; BOP; CAPITAL ASSETS; CRIME; E-COMMERCE; CGL (All coverage parts except OCP, RR Prot. and UST.); CIM; C. PROP.; EQUIPMENT BREAKDOWN; FARM; FINANCIAL INSTITUTIONS; & PROF. LIAB.

1978 N.M.S.A. §59A-18-29. New Mexico Admin. Code §13.8.4.8 and 13.8.4.9

Cancellation during the Underwriting Period

Length of Underwriting Period: Sixty days from original issuance.

Length of Notice: Ten days. However, the effective date of termination must fall within the sixty-day underwriting period.

Reason for Cancellation: Not required.

Proof Required: Proof of delivery or proof of mailing.

Cancellation after the Underwriting Period

The policy may be cancelled **only** for the following reasons:

1. Nonpayment.

2. Substantial change in the risk since the policy was issued.

3. The policy was obtained through material misrepresentation, fraudulent statements, omissions or concealment of fact material to the acceptance of the risk or to the hazard assumed.

4. Willful and negligent acts or omissions by the insured that have substantially increased the hazard insured against.

NEW MEXICO

5. Revocation or suspension of driver's license of the named insured or other operator who either resides in the same household or customarily operates the vehicle.

6. Presentation of a claim based on fraud or material misrepresentation.

Length of Notice: Ten days for nonpayment; fifteen days for reasons 3-6; thirty days for reason 2.

Reason for Cancellation: Required on the notice to insured but not to additional insured or a lienholder.

Proof Required: Proof of delivery or proof of mailing.

Nonrenewal

Length of Notice: Thirty days.

Reason for Nonrenewal: Not required.

Proof Required: Proof of mailing.

Other Cancellation/Nonrenewal Provisions

New Mexico Insurance Regulation §13.8.4.10 requires an insurer to send a thirty-day written notice to the agent or the insured if it intends to renew with changed limits, restricted coverages, or changed deductibles.

COMMERCIAL AUTO; COMMERCIAL UMBRELLA

1978 N.M.S.A. §59A-18-29. New Mexico Admin. Code §13.8.4.8 and 13.8.4.9

Cancellation during the Underwriting Period

Length of Underwriting Period: Sixty days from original issuance.

Length of Notice: Ten days. However, the effective date of termination must fall within the sixty-day underwriting period.

Reason for Cancellation: Not required.

Proof Required: Proof of delivery or proof of mailing.

NEW MEXICO

Cancellation after the Underwriting Period

The policy may be cancelled **only** for the following reasons:

1. Nonpayment.

2. Substantial change in the risk since the policy was issued.

3. The policy was obtained through material misrepresentation, fraudulent statements, omissions or concealment of fact material to the acceptance of the risk or to the hazard assumed.

4. Willful and negligent acts or omissions by the insured that have substantially increased the hazard insured against.

5. Revocation or suspension of the driver's license of the named insured or other operator who lives in the same household or who customarily operates the insured vehicle.

6. Presentation of a claim based on fraud or material misrepresentation.

Length of Notice: Ten days for nonpayment; fifteen days for reasons 3-6; thirty days for reason 2.

Reason for Cancellation: Required on the notice to insured but not to additional insured or a lienholder.

Proof Required: Proof of delivery or proof of mailing.

Nonrenewal

Length of Notice: Thirty days.

Reason for Nonrenewal: Not required.

Proof Required: Proof of mailing.

Other Cancellation/Nonrenewal Provisions

New Mexico Insurance Regulation §13.8.4.10 requires an insurer to send a thirty-day written notice to the agent or the insured if it intends to renew with changed limits, restricted coverages, or changed deductibles.

NEW MEXICO

Exclusion of Named Driver

Any motor vehicle insurance policy may be endorsed to exclude a named driver from coverage. The endorsement shall be signed by at least one named insured. Such endorsements must be substantially similar to the model "Driver Exclusion Endorsement" form found in the statute 1978 N.M.S.A §66-5-222.

COMMERCIAL GENERAL LIABILITY-OCP

1978 N.M.S.A. §59A-18-29. New Mexico Admin. Code §13.8.4.8 and 13.8.4.9

Cancellation during the Underwriting Period

Length of Underwriting Period: Sixty days from original issuance.

Length of Notice: Ten days. However, the effective date of termination must fall within the sixty-day underwriting period.

Reason for Cancellation: Not required.

Proof Required: Proof of delivery or proof of mailing.

Cancellation after the Underwriting Period

The policy may be cancelled **only** for the following reasons:

1. Nonpayment.

2. Substantial change in the risk.

3. The policy was obtained through material misrepresentation, fraudulent statements, omissions or concealment of fact material to the acceptance of the risk or to the hazard assumed.

4. Willful and negligent acts or omission by the insured have substantially increased the hazards insured against.

5. Revocation or suspension of driver's license of the named insured or other operator who either resides in the same household or customarily operates the vehicle.

6. Presentation of a claim based on fraud or material misrepresentation.

NEW MEXICO

Length of Notice: Ten days for nonpayment; thirty days for all other reasons; fifteen days for reasons 3-6. However, insurers using ISO's form CG 28 29 must comply with the more restrictive requirements.

Reason for Cancellation: Required on the notice to insured but not to additional insured or a lienholder.

Proof Required: Proof of delivery or proof of mailing.

Nonrenewal

Length of Notice: Thirty days.

Reason for Nonrenewal: Not required.

Proof Required: Proof of mailing.

Other Cancellation/Nonrenewal Provisions

New Mexico Administrative Code §13.8.4.10 requires an insurer to send a thirty-day written notice to the agent or the insured if it intends to renew with changed limits, restricted coverages, or changed deductibles.

COMMERCIAL GENERAL LIABILITY

(Railroad Protective)

1978 N.M.S.A. §59A-18-29. New Mexico Admin. Code §13.8.4.8 and 13.8.4.9

Cancellation during the Underwriting Period

Length of Underwriting Period: Sixty days.

Length of Notice: Ten days for nonpayment; sixty days for any other reason. Statutes permit a ten-day notice for any reason. However, insurers using ISO's CG 28 30 must comply with the more restrictive requirement. Statute requires the effective date of termination must fall within the sixty days of the underwriting period. Legal advice is suggested if using ISO's CG 28 30 because effective date of termination may fall outside underwriting period.

Reason for Cancellation: Not required.

Proof Required: Proof of delivery or proof of mailing.

NEW MEXICO

Cancellation after the Underwriting Period

The policy may be cancelled **only** for the following reasons:

1. Nonpayment.

2. Substantial change in the risk since the policy was issued.

3. The policy was obtained through material misrepresentation, fraudulent statements, omissions or concealment of fact material to the acceptance of the risk or to the hazard assumed.

4. Willful and negligent acts or omission by the insured have substantially increased the hazards insured against.

5. Revocation or suspension of driver's license of the named insured or other operator who either resides in the same household or customarily operates the vehicle.

6. Presentation of a claim based on fraud or material misrepresentation.

Length of Notice: Ten days for nonpayment; thirty days for reason 2; fifteen days for reasons 3-6. However, insurers using ISO's CG 28 30 must comply with the more restrictive requirements.

Reason for Cancellation: Required on the notice to insured but not to additional insured or a lienholder.

Proof Required: Proof of delivery or proof of mailing.

Nonrenewal

Length of Notice: Thirty days.

Reason for Nonrenewal: Not required.

Proof Required: Proof of mailing.

Other Cancellation/Nonrenewal Provisions

All notices must be sent to the named insured and the contractor and any involved governmental authority designated in the declarations.

NEW MEXICO

New Mexico Administrative Code §13.8.4.10 requires an insurer to send a thirty-day written notice to the agent or the insured if it intends to renew with changed limits, restricted coverages, or changed deductibles.

COMMERCIAL GENERAL LIABILITY
(Underground Storage Tanks)

1978 N.M.S.A. §59A-18-29. New Mexico Admin. Code §13.8.4.8 and 13.8.4.9

Cancellation during the Underwriting Period

Length of Underwriting Period: Sixty days from original issuance.

Length of Notice: Ten days. However, insurers using ISO's CG 30 63 must comply with the more restrictive requirement. Statute requires the effective date of termination must fall within the sixty-day underwriting period.

Reason for Cancellation: Not required.

Proof Required: Proof of delivery or proof of mailing.

Cancellation after the Underwriting Period

The policy may be cancelled **only** for the following reasons:

1. Nonpayment.

2. Substantial change in the risk since the policy was issued.

3. The policy was obtained through material misrepresentation, fraudulent statements, omissions or concealment of fact material to the acceptance of the risk or to the hazard assumed.

4. Willful and negligent acts or omission by the insured have substantially increased the hazards insured against.

5. Presentation of a claim based on fraud or material misrepresentation.

Length of Notice: Ten days for nonpayment; fifteen days for material misrepresentation; sixty days for any other allowable reasons. Regulations permit for fifteen days for reasons 3-5 and thirty days for reason 2. However, insurers using ISO's CG 30 63 must comply with the more restrictive requirements.

NEW MEXICO

Reason for Cancellation: Required on the notice to insured but not to additional insured or a lienholder.

Proof Required: Proof of delivery or proof of mailing.

Nonrenewal

Length of Notice: Thirty days.

Reason for Nonrenewal: Not required.

Proof Required: Proof of delivery or proof of mailing.

Other Cancellation/Nonrenewal Provisions

All notices must be sent to the named insured, the contractor, and any involved governmental authority or other contracting party shown in the declarations.

New Mexico Administrative Code §13.8.4.10 requires an insurer to send a thirty-day written notice to the agent or the insured if it intends to renew with changed limits, restricted coverages, or changed deductibles. However, insurers using ISO's CG 30 63 must give sixty days' notice of such changes.

WORKERS COMPENSATION

1978 N.M.S.A. §§59A-18-12 and 59A-18-29; New Mexico Admin. Code §§13.8.4.8; 13.8.4.9 and 13.17.5.7

Cancellation during the Underwriting Period

Length of Underwriting Period: Sixty days.

Length of Notice: Ten days; however, the effective date of termination must fall within the sixty-day underwriting period.

Reason for Cancellation: Not required.

Proof Required: Proof of delivery or proof of mailing.

Cancellation after the Underwriting Period

The policy or any of its parts may be cancelled **only** for the following reasons:

1. Nonpayment.

2. Substantial change in the risk since the policy was issued.

NEW MEXICO

3. The policy was obtained through material misrepresentation, fraudulent statements, omissions or concealment of fact material to the acceptance of the risk or to the hazard assumed.

4. Willful and negligent acts or omissions by the insured that have substantially increased the hazards insured against.

5. Presentation of a claim based on fraud or material misrepresentation.

6. Any act of subterfuge, artifice, trick, device, misrepresentation or concealment, whether committed knowingly or negligently, including but not limited to:

   a. Providing false or misleading information to an insurer, its agent, a rating bureau or the assigned risk pool.

   b. Failing to disclose to the insurer or a rating bureau client's or leasing contractor's true ownership, change of ownership, or current or previous employee leasing arrangements.

   c. Failing to disclose of any employer's, client's or leasing contractor's operations, location, payrolls, worker's compensation loss experience, experience modifiers, worker classifications or other necessary rating information.

   d. Failing to disclose the existence of more than one policy covering an employer's, client's or leasing contractor's workers.

   e. Failing to disclose the identity of all former insurers and self-insurance plans providing workers compensation coverage to an employer's, client's or leasing contractor's workers, including but not limited to workers provided to any client through an employee leasing arrangement.

Length of Notice: Ten days for nonpayment; fifteen days for reasons 3-5; thirty days for reason 2 and 6.

Reason for Cancellation: Required on the notice to insured but not to additional insured or a lienholder.

Proof Required: Proof of delivery or mailing.

Nonrenewal

Length of Notice: Thirty days.

NEW MEXICO

Reason for Nonrenewal: Not required.

Proof Required: Proof of mailing.

Other Cancellation/Nonrenewal Provisions

Insurer must file notice within ten days of cancellation with the Workers' Compensation Administration.

A workers' compensation insurance policy form and risk classification must be filed with the superintendent when a worker performing work for an employer in New Mexico and the employer is not domiciled in New Mexico.

SURPLUS LINES
1978 N.M.S.A. §59A-18-1

The New Mexico cancellation and nonrenewal laws do not apply to surplus lines unless such contracts are specifically included by rule.

FINANCED PREMIUMS
1978 N.M.S.A. §59A-45-11

If the premium finance agreement contains a power of attorney, the finance company may request, in the name of the insured, that the insurer cancel the policy due to nonpayment. The finance company must mail the insured a ten-day written notice to pay. If the insured fails to make payment within that ten day period, then the finance company mails the notice of cancellation to the insurer and the cancellation is processed as of the finance company's original default date. Return of the policy by the insured is not required.

All statutory, regulatory and contractual restrictions providing that the insurance contract may not be given to a governmental agency, mortgagee or other third party shall apply where cancellation is made by the premium finance company. The insurer or its licensed agent shall give the prescribed notice on behalf of itself or the insured to any governmental agency, mortgagee, or other third party on or before the tenth business day after the day it receives the notice of cancellation from the premium finance company and shall determine the effective date of cancellation, taking into consideration the number of days' notice required to complete the cancellation.

PERSONAL LINES

Insurance Division Bulletin No. 2007-004 dated May 7, 2007, requires insurers, upon request, to provide policyholders with a detailed written explanation of the reasons why the

NEW MEXICO

premium for a homeowner, auto or other personal lines has changed or is about to change. This response must be sent with ten days of receiving a request form the policyholder. Insurers are also required to email a copy of the explanation to the Commissioner at insbureau@state.nm.us. The explanation shall include a list that itemizes the rating elements that contributed to the premium charge and the dollar amount of premium attributable to each item. (https://www.osi.state.nm.us/InsuranceBulletins/docs/Bulletin2007-004.pdf)

DWELLING FIRE & HOMEOWNERS

1978 N.M.S.A. §59A-18-29. New Mexico Admin. Code §13.8.4.8 and 13.8.4.9

Length of Underwriting Period: Sixty days from original issuance.

Length of Notice: Ten days. However, the effective date of termination must fall within the sixty-day underwriting period.

Reason for Cancellation: Not required.

Proof Required: Proof of delivery or proof of mailing.

Cancellation after the Underwriting Period

The policy may be cancelled **only** for the following reasons:

1. Nonpayment.

2. Substantial change in the risk since the policy was issued.

3. The policy was obtained through material misrepresentation, fraudulent statements, omissions or concealment of fact material to the acceptance of the risk or to the hazard assumed.

4. Willful and negligent acts or omissions by the insured that have substantially increased the hazard insured against.

5. Presentation of a claim based on fraud or material misrepresentation.

Length of Notice: Ten days for nonpayment; thirty days for reason 2 and 3. ISO's DP 01 30 and HO 01 30 do not allow reasons 4 and 5. Regulations allow for fifteen days for reasons 3-5. However, insurers using ISO's DP 01 30 and HO 01 30 must comply with the more restrictive requirements.

Reason for Cancellation: Required on the notice to insured but not to additional insured or a lienholder.

Proof Required: Proof of delivery or proof of mailing.

NEW MEXICO

Nonrenewal

Length of Notice: Thirty days.

Reason for Nonrenewal: Not required.

Proof Required: Proof of mailing.

Other Cancellation/Nonrenewal Provisions

New Mexico Insurance Regulation §13.8.4.10 requires an insurer to send a thirty-day written notice to the agent or the insured if it intends to renew with changed limits, restricted coverages, or changed deductibles.

PERSONAL AUTO

1978 N.M.S.A. §59A-18-29; New Mexico Admin. Code §13.8.4.8 and 13.8.4.9

Length of Underwriting Period: Sixty days from original issuance.

Length of Notice: Ten days. However, the effective date of termination must fall within the sixty-day underwriting period.

Reason for Cancellation: Not required.

Proof Required: Proof of delivery or proof of mailing.

Cancellation after the Underwriting Period

The policy may be cancelled **only** for the following reasons:

1. Nonpayment.

2. Substantial change in the risk since the policy was issued.

3. The policy was obtained through material misrepresentation, fraudulent statements, omissions or concealment of fact material to the acceptance of the risk or to the hazard assumed.

4. Willful and negligent acts or omissions by the insured that have substantially increased the hazard insured against.

5. Revocation or suspension of driver's license of the named insured or other operator who either resides in the same household or customarily operates the vehicle.

6. Presentation of a claim based on fraud or material misrepresentation.

NEW MEXICO

Length of Notice: Ten days for nonpayment; fifteen days for reasons 3-6; thirty days for reason 2.

Reason for Cancellation: Required on the notice to insured but not to additional insured or a lienholder.

Proof Required: Proof of delivery or proof of mailing.

Nonrenewal

Length of Notice: Thirty days.

Reason for Nonrenewal: Not required.

Proof Required: Proof of mailing.

Other Cancellation/Nonrenewal Provisions

New Mexico Insurance Regulation §13.8.4.10 requires an insurer to send a thirty-day written notice to the agent or the insured if it intends to renew with changed limits, restricted coverages, or changed deductibles.

If the policy is written for a term of six months or less, the insurer has the right to nonrenew every six months.

Exclusion of Named Driver

Any motor vehicle insurance policy may be endorsed to exclude a named driver from coverage. The endorsement shall be signed by at least one named insured. Such endorsements must be substantially similar to the model "Driver Exclusion Endorsement" form found in N. M. S. A. §66-5-222.

PERSONAL UMBRELLA

1978 N.M.S.A. §59A-18-29; New Mexico Admin. Code §13.8.4.8 and 13.8.4.9

Length of Underwriting Period: Sixty days.

Length of Notice: Ten days. However, the effective date of termination must fall within the sixty-day underwriting period.

Reason for Cancellation: Not required.

Proof Required: Proof of delivery or proof of mailing.

NEW MEXICO

Cancellation after the Underwriting Period

The policy may be cancelled **only** for the following reasons:

1. Nonpayment.

2. Substantial change in the risk since the policy was issued.

3. The policy was obtained through material misrepresentation, fraudulent statements, omissions or concealment of fact material to the acceptance of the risk or to the hazard assumed.

4. Willful and negligent acts or omission by the insured have substantially increased the hazards insured against.

5. Presentation of a claim based on fraud or material misrepresentation.

Length of Notice: Ten-day notice for nonpayment; thirty days for reason 2-4. ISO's DL 98 95 does not allow reason 5. Regulations allow for fifteen days for reasons 3-5. However, insurers using ISO's DL 98 95 must comply with the more restrictive requirements.

Reason for Cancellation: Required on the notice to insured but not to additional insured or a lienholder.

Proof Required: Proof of delivery or proof of mailing.

Nonrenewal

Length of Notice: Thirty days.

Reason for Nonrenewal: Not required.

Proof Required: Proof of mailing.

FRAUD

1978 N.M.S.A. §§59A-1-18, 59A-16c-1 through 59A-16c-16

Definition

Insurance fraud has a broad meaning under New Mexico law to include any act or practice in connection with an insurance transaction that constitutes a crime under the New Mexico criminal code or insurance code.

Fees to contribute to the insurance fraud fund are due annually. The superintendent will set the rate. The penalty for failure to pay is $1000/month. (59A-16c-14).

NEW MEXICO

Penalties

1978 N.M.S.A. §§59A-1-18 and 59A-16C-9

If any person licensed by any agency of any state or the federal government or holding credentials from any professional organization is convicted of insurance fraud in New Mexico, the superintendent of insurance shall notify the appropriate licensing or credentialing authority of the judgment for appropriate disciplinary action.

Unless classified differently, violating the insurance code constitutes a petty misdemeanor and is punishable by a fine not to exceed $500. Besides the fine, administrative penalties may be imposed for violations of New Mexico's Insurance Code. The administrative penalty is capped at $5,000 per violation unless the violation is willful and intentional, in which case, the penalty may be as high as $10,000 per violation. Besides the aforementioned statutory fines and assessments, the insurance department may bring an action to recover penalties in sums not to exceed the criminal fine for each violation of the insurance code instead of criminally prosecuting the defendant.

Reporting Requirements

1978 N.M.S.A. §§59A-16C-6 and 59A-16C-7

Every insurer or licensed insurance professional that reasonably believes that an act of insurance fraud will be, is being or has been committed shall furnish and disclose knowledge and information about it to the superintendent of insurance and must cooperate fully with any investigation conducted by the superintendent. Failure to comply with this subsection shall constitute grounds for the superintendent to impose both an administrative penalties mentioned in the preceding section and any applicable suspension, revocation or denial of a license or certificate of authority.

A person who has a reasonable belief that an act of insurance fraud will be, is being or has been committed, or any person who collects, reviews or analyzes information concerning insurance fraud, may furnish and disclose any information in his possession concerning the insurance fraud to the superintendent or to an authorized representative of an insurer that requests the information for the purpose of detecting, prosecuting or preventing insurance fraud.

Except for those who intentionally communicate false information that they actually believe to be false, no one shall be subject to liability for reporting or furnishing information concerning insurance fraud when they report such information to:

1. The Department of Insurance, the superintendent or law enforcement agencies, their officials, agents or employees.

NEW MEXICO

2. The National Association of Insurance Commissioners, a federal or state governmental agency or office established to detect and prevent insurance fraud, any other organization established for the same purpose and their agents, employees or designees; or

3. An insurer's antifraud unit.

   a. Report fraud at http://www.osi.state.nm.us/FraudBureau/fraudcontactus.aspx or call 855-4-ASK-OSI or text FRAUD to TIP411.

   b. For worker's compensation fraud, medicare/medicaid fraud, and social security fraud, do not report to the above. Instead report to the respective agencies that regulate each.

   c. Workers compensation fraud: https://workerscomp.nm.gov/Enforcement.

   d. Medicare/medicaid fraud: http://www.hsd.state.nm.us/LookingForAssistance/Report_Fraud.aspx.

   e. Social Security fraud: https://www.ssa.gov/fraudreport/oig/public_fraud_reporting/form.htm.

Application Fraud Statement
1978 N.M.S.A. §59A-16C-8

All claim forms and applications for insurance must contain a statement permanently affixed to the application or claim form which states substantially as follows:

> "Any person who knowingly presents a false or fraudulent claim for payment of a loss or benefit or knowingly presents false information in an application for insurance is guilty of a crime and may be subject to civil fines and criminal penalties."

FAIR CLAIMS PROCESSING
1978 N.M.S.A. §59A-16-20

Definition

The following practices regarding claims, when by an insurer or other person, knowingly committed or performed with such frequency as to indicate a general business practice, are prohibited under New Mexico law:

1. Misrepresenting to insureds pertinent facts or policy provisions relating to coverages at issue.

NEW MEXICO

2. Not acknowledging and acting reasonably promptly upon communications with respect to claims from insureds arising under policies.

3. Not adopting and implementing reasonable standards for promptly investigating and processing of insureds' claims arising under policies.

4. Failing to affirm or deny coverage of insureds' claims within a reasonable time after proof of loss requirements under the policy have been satisfied by the insured.

5. Not attempting in good faith to effectuate prompt, fair and equitable settlements of an insured's claims in which liability has become reasonably clear.

6. Not settling all catastrophic claims within ninety days after the assignment of a catastrophic claim number when a catastrophic loss has been declared.

7. Compelling insureds to institute litigation to recover amounts due under policy by offering substantially less than the amounts ultimately recovered in actions brought by such insureds when such insureds have made claims for amounts reasonably similar to amounts ultimately recovered.

8. Attempting to settle an insured's claim for less than the amount to which a reasonable person would expect to be entitled by reference to written or printed advertising material accompanying or incorporated into an application.

9. Attempting to settle claims on the basis of an application that was altered without notice to, or knowledge or consent of, the insured, his representative, agent, or broker.

10. Failing, after payment of a claim, to inform insureds or beneficiaries, upon request by them, of the coverage under which payment has been made.

11. Making known to insureds or claimants a practice of insurer of appealing from arbitration awards in favor of insureds or claimants for the purpose of compelling them to accept settlements or compromises less than the amount awarded in arbitration.

12. Delaying the investigation or payment of claims by requiring an insured, claimant or the physician of either to submit a preliminary claim report and then requiring the subsequent submission of formal proof of loss forms, both of which submissions contain substantially the same information.

NEW MEXICO

13. Failing to promptly settle an insured's claims where liability has become apparent under one portion of the policy coverage in order to influence settlement under other portions of the policy coverage.

14. Failing to promptly provide an insured a reasonable explanation of the basis relied on in the policy in relation to the facts or applicable law for denial of a claim or for the offer of a compromise settlement.

15. Violating a provision of the Domestic Abuse Insurance Protection Act.

NEW YORK

For details on cancellation procedures for the standard policy, refer to the Standard Policy section.

COMMERCIAL LINES

INSURANCE
COMMERCIAL RISK INSURANCE, PROFESSIONAL LIABILITY INSURANCE OR PUBLIC ENTITY INSURANCE

New York Insurance Law §§3426 and 3428

Cancellation during the Underwriting Period

Length of Underwriting Period: Sixty days.

Length of Notice: Fifteen days for reasons listed below. Twenty days for any other reason (thirty days if using ISO IL 02 68).

1. Nonpayment.

2. Conviction of a crime arising out of acts increasing the insured-against hazard.

3. Discovery of fraud or material misrepresentation in the obtaining of the policy or in the presentation of a claim.

4. Discovery of an act or omission, or a violation of any policy condition, that substantially and materially increases the hazard insured against, and which occurred subsequent to inception of the current policy period.

5. Material physical change in the property insured, occurring after issuance or last annual renewal anniversary date of the policy, which results in the property becoming uninsurable in accordance with the insurer's objective, uniformly applied underwriting standards in effect at the time the policy was issued or last renewed; or material change in the nature or extent of the risk, occurring after issuance or last annual renewal anniversary date of the policy, which causes the risk of loss to be substantially and materially increased beyond that contemplated at the time the policy was issued or last renewed.

6. A determination by the superintendent that the continuation would jeopardize the insurer's solvency or be hazardous to the interest of policyholders, creditors or the public.

NEW YORK

7. A determination by the superintendent that the continuation of the policy would violate, or would place the insurer in violation of, any provision of the New York Insurance Code.

8. Where the insurer has reason to believe, in good faith and with sufficient cause, that there is a probable risk of danger that the insured will destroy the insured property, or permit it to be destroyed, for the purpose of collecting the insurance proceeds.

Reason for Cancellation: Notice must specify the grounds for cancellation and shall contain where applicable a reference to the pertinent part of the New York Insurance Code. Notices of cancellation for nonpayment of premium must indicate the amount due.

Proof Required: Proof of delivery or proof of mailing.

Cancellation after the Underwriting Period

The policy may only be cancelled for the eight reasons listed above.

Length of Notice: Fifteen days for any allowable reason.

Reason for Cancellation: Specific reason for the action is required on the notice. Notices must reference pertinent paragraphs or subparagraphs of the New York Insurance Code. Notices of cancellation for nonpayment of premium must indicate the amount due.

Proof Required: Proof of delivery or proof of mailing.

Conditional Renewal/Nonrenewal Notice Requirements

Length of Notice: At least sixty but not more than 120 days.

Reason for Nonrenewal: Notice must include the specific reason(s) for conditional renewal, or nonrenewal including the amount of any premium increase for conditional renewal and description of any other changes.

Proof Required: Proof of delivery or proof of mailing.

Special Provisions

All notices must be sent to the first named insured at the address shown on the policy and to the authorized agent.

A conditional renewal notice is required if the insurer intends to renew under any of the following conditions: change in limits, change in or reduction of coverage, increased deductible, addition of an exclusion, or increase in premium of more than 10 percent.

NEW YORK

When property is subject to the Anti-Arson Application in accordance with 11 NY ADC 62-4.2, the insurer may cancel if the named insured fails to return the completed, signed and affirmed anti-arson application. Within forty-five days of the effective date of a new policy, the insurer may cancel the policy by giving twenty days' written notice to the insured and to the mortgage holder shown in the declarations.

In the event of a late conditional renewal notice or a late nonrenewal notice, issued prior to the expiration date of the policy, coverage shall remain in effect, on the same terms and conditions of the expiring policy and at the lower of the current rates or the prior period's rates, until sixty days after such notice is mailed or delivered, unless the insured has replaced the coverage or elects to cancel, in which case such cancellation shall be on a pro rata premium basis. However, if the insured elects to renew on the basis of the conditional renewal notice, then such terms, conditions and rates shall govern the policy upon expiration of such sixty day period unless such notice was provided at least thirty days prior to the expiration date of the policy, in which event the terms, conditions and rates set forth in the conditional renewal notice shall apply as of the renewal date.

The notice of nonrenewal or conditional renewal for an excess liability policy, or a policy issued to a jumbo risk, must be mailed at least thirty days, but not more than 120 days in advance of the expiration of such policy.

When the premium is advanced under a premium finance agreement, the insurer is entitled to retain a minimum earned premium of 10 percent of the gross premium or $60, whichever is greater.

COMMERCIAL AUTO

(Applicable to risks other than above)

New York Insurance Law §§3426 and 3428; ISO Amend. Endors. CA 02 25

Cancellation during the Underwriting Period

Length of Underwriting Period: Sixty days.

Length of Notice: Fifteen days for the reasons listed below; twenty days for any other reason.

1. Nonpayment.

2. If the insured is convicted of a crime that involves increasing an insured-against hazard.

3. Fraud or material misrepresentation on the application or in the pursuit of a claim.

NEW YORK

4. An act or omission, or violation of a policy condition, committed after the inception of the current policy period, by the insured that substantially increases the insured-against hazards.

5. Material physical change in the risk occurring after the issuance, resulting in the property becoming uninsurable.

6. Required pursuant to a determination by the superintendent that continuation of the insurer's present volume would jeopardize their solvency or be hazardous to the interest of policyholders, creditors, or the public.

7. If the Superintendent determines continuation of the policy would be a violation of the state's insurance laws.

8. If the insurer has reason to believe that the insured will destroy or permit to be destroyed the covered property. A copy of this notice must be sent to the Insurance Department.

9. Suspension or revocation of the driver's license of anyone who regularly operates a covered auto.

Reason for Cancellation: Notice must specify the grounds for cancellation and shall contain where applicable a reference to the pertinent part of the New York Insurance Code. Notices of cancellation for nonpayment of premium must indicate the amount due.

Proof Required: Proof of delivery or proof of mailing.

Cancellation after the Underwriting Period

The policy may be cancelled **only** for the reasons listed above.

Length of Notice: Fifteen days for any allowable reason.

Reason for Cancellation: Notice must specify the grounds for cancellation and shall contain where applicable a reference to the pertinent part of the New York Insurance Code. Notices of cancellation for nonpayment of premium must indicate the amount due.

Proof Required: Proof of delivery or proof of mailing.

Conditional Renewal/Nonrenewal Provisions

Length of Notice: At least sixty but not more than 120 days.

NEW YORK

Reason for Nonrenewal: Notice will include the specific reason(s) conditional renewal, or nonrenewal including the amount of any premium increase for conditional renewal and description of any other changes.

Proof Required: Proof of delivery or proof of mailing.

Other Cancellation/Nonrenewal Provisions

All notices must be sent to the first named insured and the authorized agent.

A Notice of Conditional Renewal is required if the insurer intends to renew under any of the following conditions: change in limits, change in or reduction of coverage, increased deductible, addition of an exclusion, or increase in premium of more than 10 percent. See ISO CA 02 25.

When the premium is advanced under a premium finance agreement, the insurer is entitled to retain a minimum earned premium of 10 percent of the gross premium or $60, whichever is greater.

COMMERCIAL GENERAL LIABILITY

(OCP; Special Protective & HIGHWAY)

New York Insurance Law §3426

Cancellation during the Underwriting Period

Length of Underwriting Period: Sixty days.

Length of Notice: Fifteen days for any of the reasons listed below; thirty days if using ISO Amendatory Endorsement CG 28 67, otherwise twenty days for any other reason during the underwriting period.

Reason for Cancellation: Required on the notice. Notices of cancellation for nonpayment must indicate the amount due. Notices must reference pertinent paragraphs or subparagraphs of the New York Insurance Code.

Proof Required: Proof of delivery or proof of mailing.

The policy may be cancelled **only** for the following reasons after the underwriting period:

1. Nonpayment.

2. If the insured is convicted of a crime that involves increasing an insured-against hazard.

NEW YORK

3. Fraud or material misrepresentation in obtaining the policy or in the pursuit of a claim.

4. An act or omission, or violation of a policy condition, by the insured that substantially increases the hazards insured against after the issuance of the policy or after the last renewal date.

5. Material physical change in the insured property occurring after the issuance of the policy which results in the property becoming uninsurable.

6. Required pursuant to a determination by the superintendent that continuation of the insurer's present volume would jeopardize their solvency or be hazardous to the interest of policyholders, creditors or the public.

7. If the Superintendent determines continuation of the policy would violate the state's insurance laws, would jeopardize the insurer's solvency, or would be hazardous to the interest of the insurer's policyholders, creditors, or the public.

Reason for Cancellation: Required on the notice. Notices must reference pertinent paragraphs or subparagraphs of the New York Insurance Code.

Proof Required: Proof of delivery or proof of mailing.

Cancellation after the Underwriting Period

The policy may be cancelled **only** for nonpayment or for any of the reasons listed above.

Length of Notice: Fifteen days.

Reason for Cancellation: Notice must specify the grounds for cancellation and shall contain, where applicable, a reference to the pertinent part of the New York Insurance Code. Notices of cancellation for nonpayment of premium must indicate the amount due.

Proof Required: Proof of delivery or proof of mailing.

Conditional Renewal/Nonrenewal Provisions

Length of Notice: At least sixty but not more than 120 days.

Reason for Nonrenewal: Notice will include the specific reason(s) for conditional renewal, or nonrenewal including the amount of any premium increase for conditional renewal and description of any other changes.

Proof Required: Proof of delivery or proof of mailing.

NEW YORK

Other Cancellation/Nonrenewal Provisions

All notices must be sent to the first named insured and the authorized agent.

A conditional renewal notice is required if the insurer intends to renew under any of the following conditions: change in limits, change in or reduction of coverage, increased deductible, addition of an exclusion, or increase in premium of more than 10 percent. All notices must be sent to the named insured, authorized agent and the contractor designated in the declarations.

COMMERCIAL GENERAL LIABILITY

(Railroad Protective)

New York Insurance Law §3426

Cancellation during the Underwriting Period

Length of Underwriting Period: Sixty days.

Length of Notice: Fifteen days for nonpayment; twenty days for any other reason. Sixty days if using ISO amendatory endorsement. CG 28 68.

Reason for Cancellation: Notice must specify the grounds for cancellation and shall contain where applicable a reference to the pertinent part of the New York Insurance Code. Notices of cancellation for nonpayment of premium must indicate the amount due.

Proof Required: Proof of delivery or proof of mailing.

Cancellation after the Underwriting Period

The policy may be cancelled **only** for the following reasons:

1. Nonpayment.

2. If the insured is convicted of a crime that involves increasing an insured-against hazard.

3. Fraud or material misrepresentation on the application or in the pursuit of a claim.

4. An act or omission, or violation of a policy condition, by the insured that substantially and materially increases the hazards insured against which occurred subsequent to inception of the current policy period.

5. Material change in the insured property occurring after the policy was issued.

NEW YORK

6. Required pursuant to a determination by the superintendent that continuation of the insurer's present volume would jeopardize their solvency or be hazardous to the interest of policyholders, creditors, or the public.

7. If the superintendent determines continuation of the policy would be a violation of the state's insurance laws, would jeopardize the insurer's solvency, or would be hazardous to the interest of the insurer's policyholders, creditors, or the public.

8. If the insurer has reason to believe that the insured will destroy or permit the destruction of the covered property. A copy of this notice must be sent to the Insurance Department.

Length of Notice: Fifteen days for nonpayment; twenty days for any other reason.

Reason for Cancellation: Notice must specify the grounds for cancellation and shall contain where applicable a reference to the pertinent part of the New York Insurance Code. Notices of cancellation for nonpayment of premium must indicate the amount due.

Proof Required: Proof of delivery or proof of mailing.

Conditional Renewal/Nonrenewal Provisions

Length of Notice: At least sixty but not more than 120 days.

Reason for Nonrenewal: Notice will include the specific reason(s) conditional renewal, or nonrenewal including the amount of any premium increase for conditional renewal and description of any other changes.

Proof Required: Proof of delivery or proof of mailing.

Other Cancellation/Nonrenewal Provisions

All notices must be sent to the first named insured and the authorized agent.

A conditional renewal notice is required if the insurer intends to renew under any of the following conditions: change in limits, change in or reduction of coverage, increased deductible, addition of an exclusion, or increase in premium of more than 10 percent.

All notices must be sent to the named insured, authorized agent, the contractor and any involved governmental authority designated in the declarations.

These conditions are also given in ISO amendatory endorsement CG 28 68.

NEW YORK

COMMERCIAL UMBRELLA
New York Insurance Law §3426

For commercial umbrellas applicable to other than those specified above:

Length of Underwriting Period: Sixty days.

Length of Notice: Fifteen days for nonpayment and any reason listed as allowable after the underwriting period. Twenty days for any other reason during the underwriting period.

Reason for Cancellation: Notice must specify the grounds for cancellation and shall contain where applicable a reference to the pertinent part of the New York Insurance Code. Notices of cancellation for nonpayment of premium must indicate the amount due.

Proof Required: Proof of delivery or proof of mailing.

Cancellation after the Underwriting Period

The policy may be cancelled **only** for the following reasons:

1. Nonpayment.

2. Conviction of a crime arising out of acts increasing the insured-against hazard.

3. Discovery of fraud or material misrepresentation in obtaining the policy or in presenting a claim.

4. Discovery of an act or omission, or a violation of any policy condition, that substantially and materially increases the hazard insured against, and which occurred after the inception of the current policy period.

5. Required pursuant to a determination by the superintendent that the continuation would jeopardize the insurer's solvency or be hazardous to the interest of policyholders, creditors or the public.

6. A determination by the superintendent that the continuation of the policy would violate, or would place the insurer in violation of, any provision of the New York Insurance Code.

7. Suspension or revocation during the required policy period of the driver's license of any person who continues to operate a covered auto, other than a suspension issued pursuant to subdivision (1) of section 510(b) of the Vehicle and Traffic Law or one or

NEW YORK

   more administrative suspensions arising from the same incident which has or have been terminated prior to the effective date of cancellation.

8. Cancellation of one or more of the underlying policies providing primary or intermediate coverage where such cancellation is based upon reasons 1 through 7 above; and such policies are not replaced without lapse.

Conditional Renewal/Nonrenewal Provisions

Length of Notice: Not less than thirty or more than 120 days.

Reason for Nonrenewal: Notice will include the specific reason(s) conditional renewal, or nonrenewal including the amount of any premium increase for conditional renewal and description of any other changes. Notices of cancellation for nonpayment must indicate the amount due.

Proof Required: Proof of delivery or proof of mailing.

Other Cancellation/Nonrenewal Provisions

All notices must be sent to the first named insured and the authorized agent.

A conditional renewal notice is required if the insurer intends to renew under any of the following conditions: change in limits, change in or reduction of coverage, increased deductible, addition of an exclusion, or increase in premium of more than 10 percent.

When the premium is advanced under a premium finance agreement, the insurer is entitled to retain a minimum earned premium of 10 percent of the gross premium or $60, whichever is greater.

WORKERS COMPENSATION

New York Workers' Compensation Law, Chapter 67, Article 4, §54

Cancellation

Length of Notice: Ten days for nonpayment; thirty days for any other reason. Date must be specified on notice.

Proof Required: Proof of delivery or certified mailing.

Nonrenewal

Length of Notice: Thirty days.

Proof Required: Proof of delivery or certified mailing.

NEW YORK

Other Cancellation/Nonrenewal Provisions

All notices of cancellation and nonrenewal must be filed with the Office of the Chair of the Workers Compensation Board within required time periods.

Proposed legislation (2015 New York Senate Bill No. 4399, New York Two Hundred Thirty-Eighth Legislative Session) would require notice of conditional renewal to be mailed or delivered between sixty and one-hundred-twenty days before expiration of a policy if an insurance company wishes to change anything in the policy upon renewal. It would also require the specific reasons for the conditional renewal to be stated.

SURPLUS LINES

New York Insurance Law §3426

The New York Insurance Commissioner issued an opinion bulletin stating: Pursuant to N.Y. Ins. Law §3426(L)(2), policies issued by unauthorized insurers through excess lines brokers are specifically exempted from the requirements contained in N.Y. Ins. Law §3426. However, in the case of fire insurance coverage provided under the commercial property/casualty policy, the insured must receive five days' written notice of cancellation pursuant to N.Y. Ins. Law §3404.

FINANCED PREMIUMS

New York Banking Law §576

If the premium finance agreement contains a power of attorney, the finance company may request, in the name of the insured, that the insurer cancel the policy due to nonpayment. The finance company must first mail to the insured's last known address a ten-day notice to pay. The insured must cure the default within the ten days plus an additional three days for mailing the notice. If the insured fails to make payment within that period, then the finance company mails the notice of cancellation to the insurer. Return of the policy by the insured is not required. The insurer(s) must also return any unearned premiums, excluding 10 percent or $60, whichever is greater to the premium finance company. If the premium finance company cancels a motor vehicle liability insurance policy, notification must be filed with the commissioner of motor vehicles within thirty days unless a notice of such cancellation is not required by the vehicle and traffic laws or by the regulations of the Commissioner of Motor Vehicles.

PERSONAL LINES

DWELLING FIRE & HOMEOWNERS

New York Insurance Law §3425

Cancellation during the Underwriting Period

Length of Underwriting Period: Sixty days.

NEW YORK

Length of Notice: Fifteen days for nonpayment; twenty days for any other reason. If the insurer is using ISO amendatory endorsement HO 01 31 or DP 01 31, then thirty days' notice for any other reason.

Reason for Cancellation: Specific reason(s) required on the notice. Notices of cancellation for nonpayment must indicate the amount due.

Proof Required: Proof of mailing.

Cancellation after the Underwriting Period

The policy may be cancelled only for the following reasons:

1. Nonpayment.

2. If the insured is convicted of a crime that involves increasing an insured-against hazard.

3. Fraud or material misrepresentation in obtaining a policy or in presenting a claim.

4. Willful or reckless acts or omissions that increase the insured-against hazards.

5. Physical changes in the property occurring since issuance or last renewal that makes it uninsurable.

6. If the Superintendent of Insurance determines that the continuation of the policy would be a violation of New York's insurance laws.

7. Required pursuant to a program approved by the superintendent as necessary because a continuation of the present premium volume would be hazardous to the interests of policyholders of the insurer, its creditors or the public.

   Note: In Circular Letter No. 23 (2008) dated November 19, 2008, the insurance commissioner advised that midterm cancellation of homeowner policies based upon the residence becoming unoccupied or due to a foreclosure does not constitute a physical change to the property within the meaning of §3425(c)(2)(D) or (E). Insurers seeking to terminate a policy under either of these circumstances should seek legal counsel. Supplement #1 to Circular Letter No. 23 was issued on April 7, 2009. The supplement greatly expands upon the circular letter.

Length of Notice: Fifteen days for nonpayment; twenty days for all other reasons. If the insurer is using ISO amendatory endorsement HO 01 31 or DP 01 31, then thirty days' notice for any other reason.

NEW YORK

Reason for Cancellation: Required on the notice. Notices of cancellation for nonpayment of premium must indicate the amount due.

Proof Required: Proof of mailing.

Conditional Renewal/Nonrenewal

Length of Notice: At least forty-five but not more than sixty days.

Reason for Nonrenewal: Specific reason(s) required on the notice. Change of limits or elimination of any coverages must be stated on conditional renewals.

Proof Required: Proof of mailing.

Other Cancellation/Nonrenewal Provisions

Instead of sending cancellation, the insurer may choose to amend the limits of liability or coverages with a twenty day notice.

All notices must be sent to the first named insured and the authorized agent or broker. Notice must be sent to the authorized agent or broker within seven days of the time such notice is mailed to the insured.

A homeowner policy may only be nonrenewed (for any reason) every three years.

During that three year period, nonrenewal is treated the same as cancellation.

If the property is subject to the Anti-Arson Application in accordance with 11 NYCRR §62-4.2, the insurer can cancel the entire policy giving twenty days' notice if the application is not returned within forty-five days of inception (new policy). On a renewal, failure to return the affirmed application results in a twenty day notice.

All notices of cancellation, nonrenewal or conditional renewal must inform the recipient if coverage is available through the New York Property Insurance Underwriting Program, or through a "market assistance" established to facilitate placement of homeowners insurance. See 11 NYCRR §74.2.

When the premium is advanced under a premium finance agreement, the insurer is entitled to retain a minimum earned premium of 10 percent of the gross premium or $60, whichever is greater.

NEW YORK

PERSONAL AUTO

New York Insurance Law §3425

Cancellation during the Underwriting Period

Length of Underwriting Period: Sixty days.

Length of Notice: Fifteen days for nonpayment; twenty days for any other reason.

Reason for Cancellation: Specific reason(s) required on the notice for cancellation. Notices of cancellation for nonpayment must indicate the amount due.

Proof Required: Proof of mailing.

Cancellation after the Underwriting Period

The policy may be cancelled **only** for the following reasons:

1. Nonpayment.

2. Revocation or suspension of the driver's license of the named insured or that of any driver who customarily uses the insured automobile.

    Such revocation or suspension must have occurred during the policy period. If the policy period is other than one year, the revocation/suspension must have occurred during the policy period or since the last anniversary of the original effective date if the policy period is other than one year. However, these provisions do not apply to:

    a. A suspension issued under Section 510(b)(1) of the vehicle and traffic law.
    b. One or more administrative suspensions from the same incident that terminate prior to the effective date of cancellation.

3. Fraud or material misrepresentation on the application or in making a claim.

4. Required pursuant to a program approved by the superintendent as necessary because a continuation of the present premium volume would be hazardous to the interests of policyholders of the insurer, its creditors or the public.

Length of Notice: Fifteen days for nonpayment; twenty days for any other allowable reason.

NEW YORK

Reason for Cancellation: Required on the notice. Even though the ISO amendatory endorsement (PP 01 79) is silent on the matter, the reason must be shown on the notice. Notices of cancellation for nonpayment of premium must indicate the amount due.

Proof Required: Proof of mailing.

Conditional Renewal/Nonrenewal

Length of Notice: At least forty-five days but not more than sixty days.

Reason for Nonrenewal: Specific reasons for the action are required on the notice. Change of limits or elimination of any coverages must be stated on conditional renewals.

Proof Required: Proof of mailing.

Reasons for nonrenewal include, in addition to those allowed for cancellation:

1. Where the named insured or any other person who customarily operates an auto insured under the policy is convicted of:

    a. Operating a motor vehicle while intoxicated or impaired by alcohol or a drug within the meeting of the law;
    b. Homicide or assault arising out of the vehicle's use, or criminal negligence in the use or operation of a motor vehicle resulting in the injury or death of another person, or use of the vehicle in commission of a felony;
    c. Exceeding the speed limit or in a reckless manner where death or injury results;
    d. Excess speed or recklessness or any combination of these on three or more occasions;
    e. Operating an insured vehicle without a valid license or registration, or during a period of revocation or suspension thereof, or in violation of the limitations applicable to a license issued;
    f. Fleeing from an officer while operating an insured vehicle;
    g. Filing or attempting to file a false or fraudulent automobile insurance claim, or knowingly aiding or abetting in the filing or attempted filing of any such claim;
    h. Leaving the scene of an accident without reporting;
    i. Filing false documents with the department of motor vehicles or using a license or registration obtained by filing a false document with the department of motor vehicles;

NEW YORK

    j.   Operating a motor vehicle in a race or speed test; or
    k. Knowingly permitting or authorizing an unlicensed driver to operate an insured vehicle.

2. Where the named insured or a customary operator is involved in three or more vehicle accidents (not including not at fault). This number is increased by two for each additional vehicle over one insured on the policy.

3. Where there is a material change in the type of motor vehicle which substantially increases the insured-against hazard. However, if the insured motor vehicle is uninsurable for physical damage coverages only, the insurer must offer to renew the policy without the physical damage coverages.

4. Where other uniformly applied standards as may be prescribed by the superintendent exist.

Other Cancellation/Nonrenewal Provisions

All notices must be sent to the first named insured and the authorized agent or broker. Notice must be sent to the authorized agent or broker within seven days of the time such notice is mailed to the insured.

The right to cancel applies to each and every coverage or limit afforded by the policy.

Automatic termination is not allowed in New York.

Instead of sending cancellation, the insurer may choose to amend the limits of liability or coverages with a twenty day notice. New York Insurance Law §3425(f)(1) and (2) allow additional nonrenewal provisions. Under this section, an insurer may nonrenew up to 2 percent of its total voluntary business, and it may nonrenew one policy for every two pieces of new business. These restrictions are based on year end totals and are enforced by rating territory.

Proposed legislation (2015 New York Assembly Bill No. 4944, New York Two Hundred Thirty-Eighth Legislative Session) would prohibit an insurer from cancelling or refusing to renew a policy solely because a claim is in dispute or because the insured has made a complaint against the company.

Proposed legislation (2015 New York Assembly Bill No. 4750, New York Two Hundred Thirty-Eighth Legislative Session) would prohibit conditional renewal raising premiums solely based on the insured's age.

NEW YORK

PERSONAL UMBRELLA

New York Insurance Law §3425

Cancellation during the Underwriting Period

Length of Underwriting Period: Sixty days.

Length of Notice: Fifteen days for nonpayment; twenty days for any other reason.

Reason for Cancellation: Reason for the notice is required. Notices of cancellation for nonpayment must indicate the amount due.

Proof Required: Proof of mailing.

Cancellation after the Underwriting Period

The policy may be cancelled **only** for the following reasons:

1. Nonpayment.

2. Conviction of a crime arising out of acts increasing the insured-against hazard.

3. Discovery of fraud or material misrepresentation in obtaining the policy or in the presentation of a claim thereunder.

4. Discovery of willful or reckless acts or omissions increasing the insured-against hazard.

5. Physical changes in the insured property occurring after issuance or last annual anniversary date of the policy which result in the property becoming uninsurable in accordance with our objective, uniformly applied underwriting standards in effect at the time the policy was issued or last voluntarily renewed.

6. A determination by the Superintendent of Insurance that the continuation of the policy would violate or would place us in violation of the New York Insurance Law.

7. Required pursuant to a program approved by the superintendent as necessary because a continuation of the present premium volume would be hazardous to the interests of policyholders of the insurer, its creditors or the public.

Length of Notice: Fifteen days for nonpayment; twenty days for any other reason.

NEW YORK

Reason for Nonrenewal: Reason for notice must be stated. Even though ISO's amendatory endorsement (DL 98 89) is silent on the matter, statute requires that for nonrenewal be stated. Notices of cancellation for nonpayment must indicate the amount due.

Proof Required: Proof of mailing.

Conditional Renewal/Nonrenewal

Length of Notice: At least forty-five days but not more than sixty days.

Reason for Nonrenewal: Specific reason(s) for notice must be stated. Change of limits or elimination of any coverages must be stated on conditional renewals.

Proof Required: Proof of mailing.

Other Cancellation/Nonrenewal Provisions

All notices must be sent to the first named insured and the authorized agent or broker. Notice must be sent to the authorized agent or broker within seven days of the time such notice is mailed to the insured.

FRAUD

New York Insurance Law §§401 through 411 and New York Penal Law §§176.00 through 176.70

Definition

A fraudulent insurance act is committed by anyone who, knowingly and with intent to defraud presents, causes to be presented, or prepares with knowledge or belief that it will be presented to or by an insurer, self-insurer, or purported insurer, or purported self-insurer, or any agent thereof, any written statement as part of, or in support of, an application for the issuance of, or the rating of a commercial insurance policy, or certificate or evidence of self-insurance for commercial insurance or commercial self-insurance, or a claim for payment or other benefit pursuant to an insurance policy or self-insurance program for commercial or personal insurance which the perpetrator knows to:

1. Contain materially false information concerning any material fact.

2. Conceal, for the purpose of misleading, information concerning any material fact.

Penalties

In addition to varying criminal penalties, perpetrators of fraudulent insurance acts face civil penalties not exceeding five thousand dollars plus the amount of the fraudulent claim for each

NEW YORK

fraudulent insurance act. Insurance fraud for less than $1,000 is a misdemeanor in New York, if it is a first offense. Insurance fraud for more than $1,000 is a felony in New York. Pending legislation (2015 New York Assembly Bill No. 5428, New York Two Hundred Thirty-Eighth Legislative Session) may change these dollar amounts.

Reporting Requirements

Any person licensed or registered in the insurance industry, and any person engaged in the business of insurance or life settlement in New York who is exempted from compliance with New York licensing requirements, including the state insurance fund of this state, who has reason to believe that an insurance transaction may be fraudulent, or has knowledge that a fraudulent insurance transaction is about to take place, or has taken place shall, within thirty days after discovering that the transaction appears to be fraudulent, send to the Insurance Frauds Bureau on the pertinent form, the information requested by the form and such additional information relative to the factual circumstances of the transaction and the parties involved as the superintendent of the Insurance Fraud Bureau requires. The reporting form and instructions on where to send it are available at http://www.dfs.ny.gov/insurance/frauds/fd7repoc.htm

Insurance applications must contain the following wording: "Any person who knowingly and with intent to defraud any insurance company or other person files an application for insurance or statement of claim containing any materially false information, or conceals for the purpose of misleading, information concerning any fact material thereto, commits a fraudulent insurance act, which is a crime, and shall also be subject to a civil penalty not to exceed five thousand dollars and the stated value of the claim for each such violation."

All applications and claims forms for automobile insurance must contain the following: "Any person who knowingly makes or knowingly assists, abets, solicits or conspires with another to make a false report of the theft, destruction, damage or conversion of any motor vehicle to a law enforcement agency, the department of motor vehicles or an insurance company, commits a fraudulent insurance act, which is a crime, and shall also be subject to a civil penalty not to exceed five thousand dollars and the value of the subject motor vehicle or stated claim for each violation." (New York Insurance Law §403).

Fraud Prevention Plans

Insurers must file plans with the superintendent for detection, investigation, and prevention of fraud. These plans must include details of how the plans will be implemented. Insurers must, as a part of this plan, have an investigations unit or contract with a provider for such investigations. These investigators must meet certain educational and experience qualifications. For further details of plan requirements, see New York Insurance Law §409.

NEW YORK

FAIR CLAIMS PROCESSING

New York Insurance Law §2601, and §5106

Any of the following acts by an insurer, if committed without just cause and performed with such frequency as to indicate a general business practice, shall constitute unfair claim settlement practices and are prohibited under New York law:

1. Knowingly misrepresenting to claimants pertinent facts or policy provisions relating to coverage.

2. Failing to acknowledge with reasonable promptness pertinent communications as to claims arising under its policies.

3. Not adopting and implementing reasonable standards for the prompt investigation of claims arising under its policies.

4. Not attempting in good faith to effectuate prompt, fair, and equitable settlements of claims submitted in which liability has become reasonably clear, except where there is a reasonable basis supported by specific information available for review by the Department of Insurance that the claimant has caused the loss to occur by arson. After receiving a properly executed proof of loss, the insurer shall advise the claimant of acceptance or denial of the claim within thirty working days.

5. Compelling policyholders to institute suits to recover amounts due under its policies by offering substantially less than the amounts ultimately recovered in suits brought by them.

6. Failing to promptly disclose coverage of a claim arising out of the death or bodily injury of a person pursuant to subsection (d) or subparagraph (A) of paragraph two of subsection (f) of New York Insurance Law §3420.

7. Submitting reasonably rendered claims to the independent dispute resolution process established under article six of the financial services law.

For motor vehicle insurance, fair claims processing requires payment on proven claims to be made within thirty days. (New York Insurance Law §5106).

NORTH CAROLINA

COMMERCIAL LINES

AGRICULTURAL CAPITAL ASSETS; BOILER/EQUIPMENT BREAKDOWN; BOP; CAPITAL ASSETS; CRIME; CGL (all except UNDERGROUND STORAGE TANKS); CIM; C. PROP; C. UMB.; E-COMMERCE; FARM; MGT. PROT.; PROF. LIAB.

North Carolina General Statutes §§58-41-15 through 58-41-25

Cancellation during the Underwriting Period

Length of Underwriting Period: Sixty days unless the policy is a renewal.

Length of Notice: Fifteen days for any permitted reason. If the insurer is using ISO amendatory endorsement IL 02 69, AG 01 38, BP 01 16, CG 29 01, CG 29 02, or CG 33 40, fifteen days for nonpayment; thirty days for any other reason. Legal advice is suggested.

Reason for Cancellation: Required on the notice.

Proof Required: Proof of mailing.

Cancellation after the Underwriting Period

The policy may be cancelled **only** for the following reasons:

1. Nonpayment.

2. Act or omission that constitutes material misrepresentation or nondisclosure of a material fact in obtaining the policy, in pursuing a claim, or in continuing the policy.

3. Increased hazard or material change in the risk.

4. Substantial breach of contractual duties, conditions, or warranties.

5. Fraudulent acts by the insured or the insured's representative that materially affect the insurability of the risk.

6. Willful failure by the insured or the insured's representative to implement reasonable loss control requirements that materially affect insurability after written notice from the insurer.

NORTH CAROLINA

7. If the insurer loses its facultative reinsurance or a loss of or substantial changes in applicable reinsurance as provided in N.C. Gen. Stat. Ann. §58-41-30.

8. Insured's conviction of a crime arising out of acts that materially affect the insurability of the risk.

9. A determination by the commissioner that continuation of the policy would violate the laws of North Carolina.

10. If the insurer is a fraternal insurer and the insured does not meet the charter requirements.

Length of Notice: Fifteen days for nonpayment or any other permitted reason. The North Carolina statute does not contain the thirty-day provision for cancellation for other than nonpayment that appears in the ISO amendatory endorsements (IL 02 69, AG 01 38, BP 01 16, CG 29 01, CG 29 02, and CG 33 40). Legal advice is suggested.

Reason for Cancellation: Required on the notice.

Proof Required: Proof of mailing.

Nonrenewal

Length of Notice: Forty-five days.

Reason for Nonrenewal: Required on the notice.

Proof Required: Proof of mailing.

Other Cancellation/Nonrenewal Provisions

Cancellation for nonpayment will not become effective if premium is paid before the effective date set forth in the notice of cancellation.

The company may cancel for any reason with prior written consent of the insured.

All notices must be sent to the named insured and any mortgagee or loss payee designated in the declarations.

A forty-five day notice is required if the insurer intends to renew under any of the following conditions: decrease in coverage, increase in deductibles, imposition of any kind of surcharge, or increase in the premium rate.

For OCP policies any notice must also be sent to the listed contractor.

NORTH CAROLINA

For Railroad Protective policies any notice must also be sent to the listed contractor and any involved governmental entity.

Delivery by an insurer of a policy superseding a policy previously issued by the insurer at the end of the previously issued policy period is not a refusal to renew when it is delivered by the same insurer, or an affiliate or subsidiary. (N.C. Gen. Stat. Ann. §58-41-20).

COMMERCIAL AUTO

(Applicable to policies and limits that cannot be ceded to the North Carolina Reinsurance Facility)

North Carolina General Statutes §§58-41-15 through 58-41-25

Cancellation during the Underwriting Period

Length of Underwriting Period: Sixty days unless the policy is a renewal.

Length of Notice: Fifteen days for any permitted reason. If the insurer is using ISO amendatory endorsement CA 01 26 then fifteen days for nonpayment and thirty days for any other permitted reason. Legal advice should be obtained.

Reason for Cancellation: Required on the notice.

Proof Required: Proof of mailing.

Cancellation after the Underwriting Period

The policy may be cancelled **only** for the following reasons:

1. Nonpayment.

2. An act or omission that constitutes material misrepresentation or nondisclosure of a material fact in obtaining the policy, in pursuing a claim, or in continuing the policy.

3. Increased hazard or material change in the risk.

4. Substantial breaches of contractual duties, conditions, or warranties.

5. Fraudulent acts by the insured or the insured's representative that materially affect the insurability of the risk.

6. Willful failure by the insured or the insured's representative to implement reasonable loss control requirements that materially affect the insurability of the risk after written notice by the insurer.

NORTH CAROLINA

7. If the insurer loses its facultative reinsurance or a loss of or substantial changes in applicable reinsurance as provided in N.C. Gen. Stat. Ann. §58-41-30.

8. Insured's conviction of a crime arising out of acts that materially affect the insurability of the risk.

9. A determination by the commissioner that continuation of the policy would violate the laws of North Carolina.

10. If the insurer is a fraternal insurer and the insured does not meet the charter requirements.

Length of Notice: Fifteen days for nonpayment or other permitted reason. The North Carolina statute does not contain the thirty-day provision for cancellation for other than nonpayment found in the ISO amendatory endorsement. Legal advice should be obtained.

Reason for Cancellation: Required on the notice.

Proof Required: Proof of mailing.

Nonrenewal

The policy can be nonrenewed for any reason.

Length of Notice: Forty-five days.

Reason for Nonrenewal: Required on the notice.

Proof Required: Proof of mailing.

Other Cancellation/Nonrenewal Provisions

Cancellation for nonpayment will not become effective if premium is paid before the effective date set forth in the notice of cancellation.

The company may cancel for any reason with prior written consent of the insured.

All notices must be sent to the named insured and any mortgagee or loss payee designated in the declarations.

A forty-five day notice is required if the insurer intends to renew under any of the following conditions: decrease in coverage, increase in deductibles, imposition of any kind of surcharge, or increase in the premium rate.

NORTH CAROLINA

Delivery by an insurer of a policy superseding a policy previously issued by the insurer at the end of the previously issued policy period is not a refusal to renew when it is delivered by the same insurer, or an affiliate or subsidiary. (N.C. Gen. Stat. Ann. §58-41-20).

COMMERCIAL AUTO

(Applicable to policies and limits that can be ceded to the North Carolina Reinsurance Facility.)

North Carolina General Statutes §58-37-50

The policy, any limit, or coverage may be cancelled **only** for the following reasons:

1. Nonpayment.

2. The insured becomes a nonresident of North Carolina and is not otherwise eligible for coverage through the North Carolina Motor Vehicle Reinsurance Facility.

3. A member company has terminated an agency contract for reasons other than the quality of the agent's insureds or the agent has terminated the contract and such agent represented the company in taking the original application for insurance.

4. The policy is cancelled pursuant to a power of attorney given a company licensed according to the provisions of N.C. Gen. Stat. Ann. §58-35-5.

5. The insurer is a fraternal insurer and the insured does not meet the charter requirements.

6. The named insured is no longer an eligible risk under N.C. Gen. Stat. Ann. §58-37-1.

Length of Notice: Fifteen days.

Reason for Cancellation: Required on the notice.

Proof Required: Proof of mailing.

Nonrenewal

If the insurer is using ISO amendatory endorsement CA 01 26, the policy may be nonrenewed only for one or more of the following reasons:

1. Nonpayment.

2. The insured becomes a resident of North Carolina and is not otherwise entitled to coverage through the North Carolina Motor Vehicle Reinsurance facility.

NORTH CAROLINA

3. The contract with the agent through whom the policy is written is terminated for reasons other than the quality of the agent's insureds.

4. The policy is cancelled pursuant to a power of attorney given a company licensed according to the provisions of N.C. Gen. Stat. Ann. §58-35-5

5. The insured fails to meet the requirements contained in the insurer's corporate charter, articles of incorporation, or bylaw, when the insurer is a company organized for the sole purpose of providing members of an organization with insurance coverage in North Carolina.

Length of Notice: Forty-five days.

Reason for Nonrenewal: Required on the notice.

Proof Required: Proof of mailing.

Other Cancellation/Nonrenewal Provisions

Cancellation for nonpayment will not become effective if premium is paid before the effective date.

The company may cancel for any reason with prior written consent of the insured.

All notices must be sent to the named insured and any mortgagee or loss payee designated in the declarations.

A forty-five day notice is required if the insurer intends to renew under any of the following conditions: decrease in coverage, increase in deductibles, imposition of any kind of surcharge, or increase in the premium rate.

COMMERCIAL GENERAL LIABILITY
(UNDERGROUND STORAGE TANKS)

North Carolina General Statutes §§58-41-15 through 58-41-25

Cancellation during the Underwriting Period

Length of Underwriting Period: Sixty days.

Length of Notice: Fifteen days for any permitted reason. If the insurer is using ISO amendatory endorsement CG 30 25: fifteen days for nonpayment; thirty days for material misrepresentation; sixty days for any other reason. The North Carolina statute does not contain the thirty-day

NORTH CAROLINA

provision for cancellation for material misrepresentation; nor does it contain the sixty-day provision for cancellation for any other reason. Legal advice should be obtained.

Reason for Cancellation: Required on the notice.

Proof Required: Proof of mailing.

Cancellation after the Underwriting Period

The policy, any limit or coverage may be cancelled **only** for the following reasons:

1. Nonpayment.

2. An act or omission that constitutes material misrepresentation or nondisclosure of a material fact in obtaining the policy, in pursuing a claim, or in continuing the policy.

3. Increased hazard or material change in the risk.

4. Substantial breaches of contractual duties, conditions, or warranties that materially affect the insurability of the risk.

5. Fraudulent acts by the insured or the insured's representative that materially affect the insurability of the risk.

6. Willful failure by the insured or the insured's representative to implement reasonable loss control requirements that materially affect the insurability of the risk after written notice from the insurer.

7. If the insurer loses its facultative reinsurance or a loss of or substantial changes in applicable reinsurance as provided in N.C. Gen. Stat. Ann. §58-41-30.

8. Insured's conviction of a crime arising out of acts that materially affect the insurability of the risk.

9. A determination by the commissioner that continuation of the policy would violate the laws of North Carolina.

10. If the insurer is a fraternal insurer and the insured does not meet the charter requirements.

Length of Notice: Fifteen days for any permitted reason. If the insurer is using ISO amendatory endorsement CG 30 25 then: fifteen days for nonpayment; thirty days for material misrepresentation; sixty days for any other reason. The North Carolina statute does not contain

NORTH CAROLINA

the thirty-day provision for cancellation for material misrepresentation; nor does it contain the sixty-day provision for cancellation for any other reason. Legal advice should be obtained.

Reason for Cancellation: Required on the notice.

Proof Required: Proof of mailing. If the insurer has adopted ISO's amendatory endorsement CG 30 25 then it must use certified mail.

Nonrenewal

Length of Notice: Forty-five days. If the insurer has adopted ISO's amendatory endorsement CG 30 25 then it must give sixty days' notice.

Reason for Nonrenewal: Required on the notice.

Proof Required: Proof of mailing. If the insurer has adopted ISO's amendatory endorsement CG 30 25 then it must use certified mail.

Other Cancellation/Nonrenewal Provisions

Cancellation for nonpayment will not become effective if premium is paid before the effective date.

The company may cancel for any reason with prior written consent of the insured.

All notices must be sent to the named insured and any mortgagee or loss payee designated in the declarations.

A forty-five day notice is required if the insurer intends to renew under any of the following conditions: decrease in coverage, increase in deductibles, imposition of any kind of surcharge, or increase in the premium rate.

Delivery by an insurer of a policy superseding a policy previously issued by the insurer at the end of the previously issued policy period is not a refusal to renew when it is delivered by the same insurer, or an affiliate or subsidiary. (N.C. Gen. Stat. Ann. §58-41-20).

WORKERS COMPENSATION

North Carolina General Statutes §§58-36-105 and 58-36-110

Cancellation during the Underwriting Period

Length of Underwriting Period: Sixty days unless it is a renewal.

Length of Notice: Thirty days.

NORTH CAROLINA

Reason for Cancellation: Required on the notice.

Proof Required: Mailing via registered or certified mail, with a return receipt requested.

Cancellation after the Underwriting Period

The policy may be cancelled only for the following reasons:

1. Nonpayment.

2. An act or omission that constitutes material misrepresentation or nondisclosure of a material fact in obtaining the policy, continuing the policy, or in presenting a claim under the policy.

3. Increased hazard or material change in the risk.

4. Substantial breach of contractual duties, conditions, or warranties that materially affects the insurability of the risk.

5. Fraudulent acts by the insured or the insured's representative that materially affect the insurability of the risk.

6. Willful failure by the insured or the insured's representative to implement reasonable loss control measures that materially affect the insurability of the risk after written notice from the insurer.

7. If the insurer loses its facultative reinsurance or a loss of or substantial changes in applicable reinsurance as provided in N.C. Gen. Stat. Ann. §58-41-30.

8. Insured's conviction of a crime arising out of acts that materially affect the insurability of the risk.

9. A determination by the commissioner that continuation of the policy would violate the laws of North Carolina.

10. If the insurer is a fraternal insurer and the insured does not meet the charter requirements.

Length of Notice: Fifteen days.

Reason for Cancellation: Required on the notice.

Proof Required: Mailing via registered or certified mail, with a return receipt requested.

NORTH CAROLINA

Nonrenewal

Length of Notice: Forty-five days.

Reason for Nonrenewal: Required on the notice.

Proof Required: First class mailing.

Other Cancellation/Nonrenewal Provisions

The company may cancel for any reason with prior written consent of the insured.

Failure to send a notice of nonrenewal to any person designated in the policy invalidates the nonrenewal only as to that person's interest.

A copy of all notices must be sent to the agent or broker of record by regular first-class mail.

Cancellation for nonpayment is not effective if the amount due is paid before the effective date stated in the notice of cancellation.

If an insurer, upon renewal, lowers coverage limits, raises the insured's deductible (without the insured's consent), or raises premium rates for reasons within the insurer's exclusive control (not including experience modification changes, exposure changes, or loss cost rate changes), a thirty-day written notice is required. Proof of mailing is sufficient.

Delivery by an insurer of a policy superseding a policy previously issued by the insurer at the end of the previously issued policy period is not a refusal to renew when it is delivered by the same insurer, or an affiliate or subsidiary. (N.C. Gen. Stat. Ann. §58-36-87).

SURPLUS LINES

North Carolina General Statutes §§58-41-10 and 58-21-2

The cancellation and nonrenewal statutes in North Carolina do not apply to surplus lines.

FINANCED PREMIUMS

North Carolina General Statutes §58-35-85

If the premium finance agreement contains a power of attorney, the finance company may request, in the name of the insured, that the insurer cancel the policy due to nonpayment. The finance company must first give the insured ten days to pay. If the insured fails to make payment within that ten-day period, then the finance company mails the request for cancellation to the insurer and the notice of requested cancellation to the insured. Cancellation is processed as

NORTH CAROLINA

of the insurer's receipt of a copy of the request for cancellation notice. Return of the policy by the insured is not required. Return of gross unearned premiums is required within thirty days after the effective date of cancellation.

PERSONAL LINES

DWELLING FIRE & HOMEOWNERS

North Carolina General Statutes §58-44-16 and Cancellation and Nonrenewal Provisions stipulated in the NC Homeowners Policy and the NC Dwelling Fire Policy

Cancellation during the Underwriting Period

Length of Underwriting Period: Sixty days unless the policy is a renewal.

Length of Notice: Ten days for any reason.

Reason for Cancellation: Required on the notice.

Proof Required: Proof of delivery or proof of mailing.

Cancellation after the Underwriting Period

The policy may be cancelled **only** for the following reasons:

1. Nonpayment.
2. Material misrepresentation in obtaining the policy, a fact which if known would have caused the insurer not to issue the policy.
3. If the risk has changed substantially since the policy was issued.

Length of Notice: Ten days for nonpayment and thirty days for the other stipulated reasons.

Reason for Cancellation: Required on the notice.

Proof Required: Proof of delivery or proof of mailing.

Nonrenewal

Length of Notice: Thirty days.

Reason for Nonrenewal: Required on the notice.

Proof Required: Proof of mailing.

NORTH CAROLINA

Other Cancellation/Nonrenewal Provisions

North Carolina requires the standard fire policy, which allows a policy to be cancelled with a five-day written notice for any reason.

A fifteen day notice is required whenever an insurer changes the coverage other than at the request of the insured or changes the premium rate. N.C. Gen. Stat. §58-36-45.

Delivery by an insurer of a policy superseding a policy previously issued by the insurer at the end of the previously issued policy period is not a refusal to renew when it is delivered by the same insurer, or an affiliate or subsidiary. (N.C. Gen. Stat. Ann. §58-41-20). http://www.ncdoi.com/PC/Documents/Filings/2018%20Dwelling/COMPLETE_FILING_Part1_20180207.compressed_Part2.pdf

http://www.ncdoi.com/_Publications/Consumer%20Guide%20to%20Homeowners%20Insurance_CHO1.pdf

PERSONAL AUTO

North Carolina General Statutes §§58-2-164(g), 58-36-65, 58-36-85 and 58-37-50

Length of Underwriting Period: None. North Carolina is a "take all comers" state.

Length of Notice: Fifteen days for nonpayment; sixty days for any allowable reason.

Reason for Cancellation: Required on the notice.

Proof Required: Proof of mailing.

The policy may be cancelled **only** for the following reasons:

1. An applicant provides false and misleading information as to the applicant's or any named insured's status as an eligible applicant and that fraudulent information makes the applicant or any named insured appear to be an eligible applicant when that person is in fact not an eligible applicant.

2. An applicant for the issuance or renewal of a nonfleet private passenger motor vehicle insurance policy knowingly makes a material misrepresentation of the years of driving experience or the driving record of any named insured or of any other operator who resides in the same household and who customarily operates a motor vehicle to be insured under the policy.

3. Nonpayment.

NORTH CAROLINA

4. If the insured becomes a nonresident of North Carolina and is not otherwise eligible for coverage.

5. If the agent's contract with the insurer is terminated for reasons other than the quality of the agent's insureds or the agent has terminated the contract and such agent represented the company in taking the original application for insurance.

6. If the policy is cancelled pursuant to a power of attorney given a company licensed according to N.C. Gen. Stat. Ann. §58-35-5.

7. If the insurer is a fraternal insurer and the insured does not meet the charter requirements.

8. The insured is no longer an eligible risk under N.C. Gen. Stat. Ann. §58-37-1.

Nonrenewal

The only allowable reasons for nonrenewal are the same as for cancellation.

Length of Notice: Fifteen days for nonpayment; sixty days for any allowable reason.

Reason for Nonrenewal: Required on the notice.

Proof Required: Proof of mailing.

Other Cancellation/Nonrenewal Provisions

An insurer may not cancel or nonrenew types or limits of coverage, to the extent that they can be placed in the Reinsurance Facility.

A written termination notice must include or be accompanied by a statement that advises the insured of the penalty for driving a vehicle without insurance and that the insured has the right to request the Department of Insurance to review the termination.

Delivery by an insurer of a policy superseding a policy previously issued by the insurer at the end of the previously issued policy period is not a refusal to renew when it is delivered by the same insurer, or an affiliate or subsidiary. (N.C. Gen. Stat. Ann. §58-36-87).

PERSONAL UMBRELLA

North Carolina General Statutes §§58-41-15 and 58-41-20

Cancellation during the Underwriting Period

Length of Underwriting Period: Sixty days.

NORTH CAROLINA

Length of Notice: Fifteen days.

Reason for Cancellation: Required on the notice.

Proof Required: Proof of mailing.

Cancellation after the Underwriting Period

The policy may be cancelled **only** for the following reasons:

1. Nonpayment.

2. An act or omission that constitutes material misrepresentation or nondisclosure of a material fact in obtaining the policy, in pursuing a claim, or in continuing the policy.

3. Increased hazard or material change in the risk.

4. Substantial breach of contractual duties, conditions, or warranties that materially affects the insurability of the risk.

5. Fraudulent acts by the insured or the insured's representative that materially affects the insurability of the risk.

6. Willful failure by the insured or the insured's representative to institute reasonable loss control measures that materially affect the insurability of the risk after written notice from insurer.

7. If the insured loses its facultative reinsurance or a loss of or substantial changes in applicable reinsurance as provided in N.C. Gen. Stat. Ann. §58-41-30.

8. Insured's conviction of a crime arising out of acts that materially affect the insurability of the risk.

9. A determination by the commissioner that continuation of the policy would violate the laws of North Carolina.

10. If the insurer is a fraternal insurer and the insured does not meet the charter requirements.

Length of Notice: Fifteen days.

Reason for Cancellation: Required on the notice.

Proof Required: Proof of mailing.

NORTH CAROLINA

Nonrenewal

Length of Notice: Forty-five days.

Reason for Nonrenewal: Required on the notice.

Proof Required: Proof of mailing.

Other Cancellation/Nonrenewal Provisions

Failure to send this notice to the agent or broker of record does not invalidate the cancellation.

Cancellation for nonpayment is not effective if the amount due is paid before the effective date stated in the notice of cancellation

The policy may be cancelled for any reason with the prior written consent of the insured.

FRAUD

North Carolina General Statutes §§58-2-160 through 58-2-164

Definition

No North Carolina statute explicitly defines insurance fraud. However, the North Carolina General Statutes prohibit the following fraudulent activity.

The following acts are prohibited when they are conducted by any person who, with the intent to injure, defraud, or deceive an insurer or insurance claimant:

1. Presenting or causing to be presented a written or oral statement, including computer-generated documents as part of, in support of, or in opposition to, a claim for payment or other benefit pursuant to an insurance policy, knowing that the statement contains false or misleading information concerning any fact or matter material to the claim.

2. Assisting, abetting, soliciting, or conspiring with another person to prepare or make any written or oral statement that is intended to be presented to an insurer or insurance claimant in connection with, in support of, or in opposition to, a claim for payment or other benefit pursuant to an insurance policy, knowing that the statement contains false or misleading information concerning a fact or matter material to the claim.

Violators of this provision may have to pay compensatory damages, attorneys' fees, costs, and reasonable investigative costs.

It is a felony for any insurance agent, broker, or administrator to embezzle or fraudulently convert to his own use, or, with intent to use or embezzle, take, secret, or otherwise dispose

NORTH CAROLINA

of, or fraudulently withhold, appropriate, lend, invest, or otherwise use or apply any money, negotiable instrument, or other consideration received by him in his performance as an agent, broker, or administrator.

An individual commits the misdemeanor of insurance fraud or rate evasion by:

1. Presenting or causing to be presented a written or oral statement in support of an application for auto insurance or for vehicle registration pursuant to N.C. Gen. Stat. Ann. §20-52(a)(4) and (a)(5), knowing that the application contains false or misleading information that states the applicant is an eligible risk when the applicant is not an eligible risk.

2. Assisting, abetting, soliciting, or conspiring with another person to prepare or make any written or oral statement that is intended to be presented to an insurer in connection with or in support of an application for auto insurance or for vehicle registration pursuant to N.C. Gen. Stat. Ann. §20-52(a)(4) and (a)(5), if the person knows that the statement contains false or misleading information that states the applicant is an eligible risk when the applicant is not an eligible risk.

In addition to any other authorized penalties, a violation of this subsection may be punishable by a maximum fine of $1,000 for each violation.

Anyone who willfully makes a false statement to the commissioner is guilty of a class I felony and the entity on whose behalf the false statement or oath was made will be fined between $2,000 and $10,000. (N.C. Gen. Stat. Ann. §58-2-180).

Reporting Requirements

Whenever any insurance company, or employee or representative of such company, or any other person licensed or registered under the North Carolina insurance laws knows or has reasonable cause to believe that any other person has violated N.C. Gen. Stat. Ann. §§58-2-161, 58-2-162, 58-2-164, 58-2-180, 58-8-1, 58-24-180(e), or whenever any insurance company, or employee or representative of such company, or any other person licensed or registered under the North Carolina insurance laws knows or has reasonable cause to believe that any entity licensed by the commissioner is financially impaired, it is the duty of such person, upon acquiring such knowledge, to notify the commissioner and provide the commissioner with a complete statement of all of the relevant facts and circumstances. Such report is a privileged communication, and when made without actual malice does not subject the person making the same to any liability whatsoever. The commissioner may suspend, revoke, or refuse to renew the license of any licensee who willfully fails to comply with this section. Report fraud at http://www.ncdoi.com/Investigations/Report_Insurance_Fraud.aspx

NORTH CAROLINA

Application Fraud Statement

Viatical settlement contracts and applications must contain the following, or a substantially similar statement:

> "Any person who knowingly presents false information in an application for insurance or viatical settlement contract or a viatical settlement purchase agreement is guilty of a felony and may be subject to fines and confinement in prison." (N.C. Gen. Stat. Ann. §58-58-267).

FAIR CLAIMS PROCESSING

North Carolina General Statutes §§58-63-10 through 58-63-60

Definition

The following practices in settling claims are prohibited under North Carolina law when they are committed or performed with such frequency as to indicate a general business practice of any of the following:

1. Misrepresenting pertinent facts or insurance policy provisions relating to coverages at issue.

2. Failing to acknowledge and act reasonably promptly upon communications regarding claims arising under insurance policies.

3. Failing to adopt and implement reasonable standards for the prompt investigation of claims arising under insurance policies.

4. Refusing to pay claims without conducting a reasonable investigation based upon all available information.

5. Failing to affirm or deny coverage of claims within a reasonable time after proof-of-loss statements have been completed.

6. Not attempting in good faith to effectuate prompt, fair, and equitable settlements of claims in which liability has become reasonably clear.

7. Compelling the insured to institute litigation to recover amounts due under an insurance policy by offering substantially less than the amounts ultimately recovered in actions brought by such insured.

8. Attempting to settle a claim for less than the amount to which one reasonably believed one was entitled.

NORTH CAROLINA

9. Attempting to settle claims based on an application which was altered without notice to, or knowledge or consent of, the insured.

10. Making claims payments to insureds or beneficiaries not accompanied by a statement setting forth the coverage under which the payments are being made.

11. Making known to insureds or claimants a policy of appealing from arbitration awards in favor of insureds or claimants for the purpose of compelling them to accept settlements or compromises less than the amount awarded in arbitration.

12. Delaying the investigation or payment of claims by requiring an insured claimant, or the physician, of or either, to submit a preliminary claim report and then requiring the subsequent submission of formal proof-of-loss forms, both of which submissions contain substantially the same information.

13. Failing to promptly settle claims where liability has become reasonably clear, under one portion of the insurance policy coverage in order to influence settlements under other portions of the insurance policy coverage.

14. Failing to promptly provide a reasonable explanation of the basis in the insurance policy in relation to the facts or applicable law for denial of a claim or for the offer of a compromise settlement.

Proposed legislation (2015 North Carolina Senate Bill No. 451) would add:

15. Improper actions related to copayment; and

16. Failure to review, adjust, or remove maximum allowable cost price.

Penalty

After determining that an act or practice is prohibited as an unfair practice, the commissioner will issue and serve upon the violating party an order to cease and desist from committing the offending practice. Those who violate a cease and desist order must pay a fine, ranging from $1,000 to $5,000 for each violation. (N.C. Gen. Stat. Ann. §58-63-50).

NORTH DAKOTA

For details on cancellation procedures for the standard policy, refer to the Standard Policy section.

COMMERCIAL LINES
AGRICULTURAL CAPITAL ASSETS; CAPITAL ASSETS; BOP; C. AUTO; CRIME; CGL (GL, EMPLOYMENT, POLLUTION, PRODUCTS); COMMERCIAL PROPERTY; EQUIPMENT BREAKDOWN; FARM; & PROF. LIAB.

North Dakota Century Code §§26.1-30.1-02 through 26.1-30.1-08

Cancellation during the Underwriting Period

Length of Underwriting Period: Ninety days.

Length of Notice: Five days for reasons 10-19 shown below; ten days for any other reason.

Reason for Cancellation: Normally not required by statute. Legal advice suggested if canceling with five days' notice.

Proof Required: Proof of first-class mailing to the first named insured, the contractor and agent, if any, at the last known mailing address.

Cancellation after the Underwriting Period

The policy may be cancelled only for the following reasons:

1. Nonpayment.

2. Misrepresentation or fraud in obtaining the policy or in making a claim.

3. Actions by the insured that have substantially increased or changed the insured-against risk.

4. Refusal of the insured to eliminate known conditions that increase the potential for loss, after notification that the condition must be removed.

5. Substantial change in the risk assumed, except that it should have been reasonably foreseen when writing the policy.

6. Loss of reinsurance by the insurer.

NORTH DAKOTA

7. Determination by the commissioner that continuation of the policy would violate the North Dakota Insurance Code.

8. Nonpayment of dues to an association or organization, where payment of dues is required in order to obtain insurance. This provision does not apply to individuals who are age sixty-two or older and retired or who are disabled according to Social Security standards.

9. Violation of any local fire, health, safety, building or construction regulation, or ordinance with respect to any covered property or its occupancy that substantially increases any insured-against hazard.

10. Buildings with at least 65 percent of the rental units in the building unoccupied.

11. Buildings that have been damaged by a covered cause of loss and the insured has stated or such time has elapsed as clearly indicates that the damage will not be repaired.

12. Buildings to which, following a fire, permanent repairs have not commenced within sixty days following satisfactory adjustment of loss.

13. Buildings that have been unoccupied sixty or more consecutive days, except buildings that have a seasonal occupancy, and buildings actually in the course of construction or repair and reconstruction which are properly secured against unauthorized entry.

14. Buildings that are in danger of collapse because of serious structural conditions or those buildings subject to extremely hazardous conditions not contemplated in filed rating plans such as those buildings that are in a state of disrepair as to be dilapidated.

15. Buildings on which, because of their physical condition, there is an outstanding order to vacate or an outstanding demolition order, or which have been declared unsafe in accordance with applicable law.

16. Buildings from which fixed and salvageable items have been or are being removed and the insured can give no reasonable explanation for the removal.

17. Buildings on which there is reasonable knowledge and belief that the property is endangered and is not reasonably protected from possible arson for the purpose of defrauding an insurer.

18. Buildings with any of the following conditions:

    a. Failure to furnish heat, water, sewer service, or public lighting for thirty consecutive days or more.

NORTH DAKOTA

    b.   Failure to correct conditions dangerous to life, health, or safety.

    c.   Failure to maintain the building in accordance with applicable law.

    d.   Failure to pay property taxes for more than one year.

19. Buildings that have characteristics of ownership condition, occupancy, or maintenance which violate of law or public policy.

Length of Notice: Five days for reasons 10-19 above; ten days for nonpayment; thirty days for reasons 2-9.

Reason for Cancellation: Specific reason is required on the notice.

Proof Required: Proof of first-class mailing to the first named insured, the contractor and agent, if any, at the last known mailing address.

Nonrenewal

Length of Notice: Forty-five days; ninety days if policy provides professional liability coverage for legal and medical services (See NDCC §26.1-39-16).

Reason for Nonrenewal: Required on the notice.

Proof Required: Proof of first class mailing to the first named insured, the contractor and agent, if any, at the last known mailing address. Proof of mailing consists of either a U.S. postal service certificate of mailing to the named insured at the last known address or proof of acknowledgement of U.S. postal service mailing to the named insured at the last known address using IMB tracing or a similar method of first-class mail tracking.

Other Cancellation/Nonrenewal Provisions

On OCP policies (ISO CG 29 21) all notices must also be mailed to the contractor listed on the declarations.

On Railroad Protective policies (ISO CG 00 35) all notices must also be mailed to the contractor, any involved governmental authority or other contracting party listed on the declarations page. Notice of nonrenewal must be mailed or delivered to the first named insured at least thirty days prior to nonrenewal. Proof of mailing is sufficient proof of notice.

On Underground Storage Tank policies a sixty-day notice is required for any reason other than nonpayment or misrepresentation. The sixty-day requirement for UST policies does

NORTH DAKOTA

not appear in the North Dakota Century Code. However, if an insurer has ISO's amendatory endorsement (CG 00 42), it must give a sixty-day notice. Notice of nonrenewal requires a sixty day notice. The UST endorsement also requires certified mailing.

On a BOP, if the insurer is using ISO's BP 01 17, a ninety-day notice of nonrenewal must be given if the policy provides professional liability coverage for legal and medical services.

A ten-day written notice is required if the insurer intends to renew under less favorable terms as to amount of coverage or deductibles, or an increase in rate of more than 15 percent. If the insurer does not notify the policyholder, the policyholder may elect to cancel the renewal policy within the ten-day period after receipt of the notice. Earned premium for the period of coverage, if any, must be calculated on a pro rata basis and the rates must be based on the previous policy term.

A policy may be issued for a term longer than one year or for an indefinite term with a clause providing for cancellation by the insurer at least thirty days prior to any anniversary date.

The notice of cancellation for nonpayment must state the effect of nonpayment by the due date. No cancellation for nonpayment of premium is effective if payment of the amount due is made prior to the effective date set forth in the notice.

COMMERCIAL AUTO

(Applicable when the named insured is an individual and the policy covers six or less private passenger-type autos.)

North Dakota Century Code §§26.1-40-01 through 26.1-40-07

Cancellation during the Underwriting Period

Length of Underwriting Period: Sixty days.

Length of Notice: Ten days for nonpayment; twenty days for any other allowable reason. ISO form PA 02 05 states that the insurer may cancel for any reason with ten-day notice during the underwriting period. Legal advice is recommended.

Reason for notice: Required on the notice for nonpayment. If cancellation is for any other reason, the notice must show the reason or state that the insurer will specify the reasons in writing, upon written request.

Proof Required: A postal service certificate of mailing to the named insured at the address shown in the policy. Proof of mailing of notice must be retained by insurer for at least one year after mailing. Proof of mailing consists of either a U.S. postal service certificate of mailing

NORTH DAKOTA

to the named insured at the last known address or proof of acknowledgement of U.S. postal service mailing to the named insured at the last known address using IMB tracing or a similar method of first-class mail tracking.

Cancellation after the Underwriting Period

The policy may be cancelled **only** for the following reasons:

1. Nonpayment of premium.

2. The named insured or any driver who either lives with the insured or who customarily uses a covered auto has had his or her driver's license suspended or revoked during the policy period or for 180 days preceding the policy period.

   However, the insurer may not cancel for this reason if the operator whose license is suspended or revoked is excluded from coverage under this policy.

3. If the covered auto is:

   a. So mechanically defective that its operation might endanger public safety.

   b. Used in carrying passengers for hire or compensation; provided, however, that the use of an auto for a car pool is not use of an auto for hire or compensation.

   c. Used in the transportation of flammables or explosives or for an illegal purpose.

   d. An authorized emergency vehicle.

   e. Altered by an insured during the policy period so as to substantially increase the risk.

4. The insured moves to a state where the insurer is not licensed to do business.

5. Failure to pay dues or fees where payment of the dues or fees is a prerequisite to obtaining or continuing automobile insurance coverage.

6. A determination by the commissioner that the continuation of the policy would place the insurer in violation of the law or would be hazardous to the interests of policyholders, creditors, or the public.

7. Fraud or material misrepresentation made by or with the knowledge of any insured in obtaining the policy, continuing the policy, or in presenting a claim under the policy.

NORTH DAKOTA

Length of Notice: Ten days nonpayment; twenty days all other allowable reasons. However, insurers using the ISO amendatory endorsement (PA 02 05) must comply with the provisions of that form that require a thirty day notice of cancellation.

Reason for Cancellation: Required on the notice for nonpayment. If cancellation is for any other reason, the notice must show the reason or state that the insurer will specify the reasons in writing, upon written request.

Proof Required: A postal service certificate of mailing to the named insured at the address shown in the policy. Proof of mailing of notice must be retained by insurer for at least one year after mailing. Proof of mailing consists of either a U.S. postal service certificate of mailing to the named insured at the last known address or proof of acknowledgement of U.S. postal service mailing to the named insured at the last known address using IMB tracing or a similar method of first-class mail tracking.

Nonrenewal

Length of Notice: Thirty days.

Reason for Nonrenewal: Must be included in notice or made available upon request within ten days.

Proof Required: A postal service certificate of mailing to the named insured at the address shown in the policy. Proof of mailing of notice must be retained by insurer for at least one year after mailing. Proof of mailing consists of either a U.S. postal service certificate of mailing to the named insured at the last known address or proof of acknowledgement of U.S. postal service mailing to the named insured at the last known address using IMB tracing or a similar method of first-class mail tracking.

Other Cancellation/Nonrenewal Provisions

When a policy is canceled, other than for nonpayment of premium, or in the event of failure to renew a policy, the insured must notify the named insured of the insured's possible eligibility for automobile insurance through the automobile assigned risk plan or automobile insurance plan. The notification must accompany or be included in the notice of cancellation or nonrenewal.

If the policy has been written for a period of more than a year or without a fixed expiration date. The insurer may cancel only at an anniversary of its original effective date.

NORTH DAKOTA

COMMERCIAL UMBRELLA AND FARM EXCESS LIABILITY

North Dakota Century Code §§26.1-39-13 through 26.1-39-16

Length of Underwriting Period: Sixty days.

Length of Notice: Ten days for any reason.

Reason for Cancellation: If the notice does not state the reason, it must include a statement that upon written request, the insurer will specify in writing the reasons for cancellation.

Proof Required: Postal service certificate of mailing.

Cancellation after the Underwriting Period

The policy may be cancelled for the following reasons:

1. Nonpayment.

2. Fraud or material misrepresentation in obtaining the policy or in making a claim.

3. If the insured's willful or reckless actions or omissions substantially increase or change the insured-against risk.

4. A substantial change in the risk which substantially increases the insured-against hazard.

5. A violation of local fire, health, safety, building, or construction regulation or ordinance regarding the insured property or its occupancy which substantially increased the insured-against hazard.

6. If the commissioner determines that continuation of the policy would violate the North Dakota Insurance Code.

7. Conviction of the named insured of a crime, an element of which increases an insured-against hazard.

8. Buildings with at least 65 percent of the rental units in the building unoccupied.

9. Buildings that have been damaged by a peril insured against and the insured has stated or such time has elapsed as clearly indicates that the damage will not be repaired.

NORTH DAKOTA

10. Buildings to which, following a fire, permanent repairs have not commenced within sixty days following satisfactory adjustment of loss.

11. Buildings that have been unoccupied sixty consecutive days, except buildings that have a seasonal occupancy, and buildings actually in the course of construction or repair and reconstruction which are properly secured against unauthorized entry.

12. Buildings that are in danger of collapse because of serious structural conditions or those buildings subject to extremely hazardous conditions not contemplated in filed rating plans such as those buildings that are in a state of disrepair as to be dilapidated.

13. Buildings on which, because of their physical condition, there is an outstanding order to vacate or an outstanding demolition order, or which have been declared unsafe in accordance with applicable law.

14. Buildings from which fixed and salvageable items have been or are being removed and the insured can give no reasonable explanation for the removal.

15. Buildings on which there is reasonable knowledge and belief that the property is endangered and is not reasonably protected from possible arson for the purpose of defrauding an insurer.

16. Buildings with any of the following conditions:

    a. Failure to furnish heat, water, sewer service, or public lighting for thirty consecutive days or more.

    b. Failure to correct conditions dangerous to life, health, or safety.

    c. Failure to maintain the building in accordance with applicable law.

    d. Failure to pay property taxes for more than one year.

17. Buildings that have characteristics of ownership condition, occupancy, or maintenance which are violative of law or public policy.

Length of Notice: Five days' written notice for numbers 8-17; ten days for nonpayment; thirty days for any other allowable reason.

Reason for Cancellation: If the notice does not state the reason, it must include a statement that upon written request, the insurer will specify in writing the reasons for cancellation within ten days after receipt of the written request.

NORTH DAKOTA

Proof Required: A postal service certificate of mailing to the named insured at the address shown in the policy. Proof of mailing consists of either a U.S. postal service certificate of mailing to the named insured at the last known address or proof of acknowledgement of U.S. postal service mailing to the named insured at the last known address using IMB tracing or a similar method of first-class mail tracking.

Nonrenewal

Length of Notice: Forty-five days.

Reason for Nonrenewal: If the notice does not state the reason, it must include a statement that upon written request, the insurer will specify in writing the reasons for cancellation within ten days of receiving a written request.

Proof Required: A postal service certificate of mailing to the named insured at the address shown in the policy. Proof of mailing consists of either a U.S. postal service certificate of mailing to the named insured at the last known address or proof of acknowledgement of U.S. postal service mailing to the named insured at the last known address using IMB tracing or a similar method of first-class mail tracking.

Other Cancellation/Nonrenewal Provisions

ISO Amendatory Endorsement (CX 02 12) permits commercial excess liability coverage cancellation during the ninety day underwriting period to be cancelled with a ten-day notice for any reason.

COMMERCIAL INLAND MARINE

North Dakota Century Code §§26.1-30.1-02, -03, -06, -07, and -08

North Dakota makes no changes from the standard policy.

E-COMMERCE; & MGT. PROT.

North Dakota Century Code §§26.1-30.1-02 through 26.1-30.1 -08

Cancellation during the Underwriting Period

Length of Underwriting Period: Ninety days.

Length of Notice: Ten days for any reason.

Reason for Cancellation: The notice must contain the specific reason as set out below.

NORTH DAKOTA

Proof Required: First-class mail address to the policyholder's last-known address in the policy, also given to the agent of record, if any. Proof of mailing consists of either a U.S. postal service certificate of mailing to the named insured at the last known address or proof of acknowledgement of U.S. postal service mailing to the named insured at the last known address using IMB tracing or a similar method of first-class mail tracking.

Cancellation after the Underwriting Period

The policy may be cancelled **only** for the following reasons:

1. Nonpayment.

2. Material misrepresentation or fraud in obtaining the policy or in making a claim.

3. If the insured's actions have substantially increased or substantially changed the insured-against risk.

4. If the insured refuses to eliminate known conditions that increase the potential for loss, after notification that the condition must be removed.

5. A substantial change in the risk assumed, except that it should have been reasonably foreseen when writing the contract.

6. If the insurer loses its reinsurance on the risk.

7. If the commissioner determines that continuation of the policy would violate the North Dakota Insurance Code.

8. If the named insured does not pay dues to an association or organization, where payment of dues is required in order to obtain insurance.

    This provision does not apply to individuals who are over age sixty-two and retired or who are disabled according to Social Security standards.

9. Violation of any local fire, health, safety, building or construction regulation or ordinance with respect to any covered property or its occupancy that substantially increases any insured-against hazard.

Length of Notice: Ten days for nonpayment; thirty days for any other allowable reason.

Reason for Cancellation: Required on the notice.

NORTH DAKOTA

Proof Required: First-class mail address to the policyholder's last known address in the policy, also given to the agent of record, if any. Proof of mailing consists of either a U.S. postal service certificate of mailing to the named insured at the last known address or proof of acknowledgement of U.S. postal service mailing to the named insured at the last known address using IMB tracing or a similar method of first-class mail tracking.

Nonrenewal

Length of Notice: Sixty days.

Reason for Nonrenewal: Required on the notice.

Proof Required: First-class mail address to the policyholder's last known address in the policy, also given to the agent of record, if any. Proof of mailing consists of either a U.S. postal service certificate of mailing to the named insured at the last known address or proof of acknowledgement of U.S. postal service mailing to the named insured at the last known address using IMB tracing or a similar method of first-class mail tracking.

WORKERS COMPENSATION

North Dakota is a monopolistic workers compensation state.

SURPLUS LINES

North Dakota Century Code §§26.1-30.1-01 to 26.1-30.1-04 and 26.1-44-01 to 26.1-44-11

Surplus lines insurers must follow the cancellation and nonrenewal requirements for admitted companies.

FINANCED PREMIUMS

North Dakota Century Code §§26.1-20.1-08 and 26.1-20.1-09

If the premium finance agreement contains a power of attorney, the finance company may request, in the name of the insured, that the insurer cancel the policy due to nonpayment. The finance company must first give the insured ten days to pay. If the insured fails to make payment within that ten-day period, then the finance company mails the notice of cancellation to both the insurer and the insured and the cancellation is processed as of the finance company's original default date. Return of the policy by the insured is not required.

If statutory, regulatory, or contractual restrictions provide that an insurance policy may not be canceled unless notice is given to a governmental agency, mortgagee, or other third

NORTH DAKOTA

party, the insurer shall give the prescribed notice on behalf of itself or the insured to the governmental agency, mortgagee, or other third party within a reasonable time after the insurer receives the notice of cancellation from the insurance premium finance company. The insurance policy must be continued beyond the date of cancellation requested by the premium finance company until the date specified by the insurance company in the prescribed notice.

PERSONAL LINES
DWELLING FIRE & HOMEOWNERS

North Dakota Century Code §§26.1-25.2-03, 26.1-39-11 to 26.1-39-16

Declinations

In addition to refusal to issue based on an application, a declination also includes:

1. The offering of coverage in a company in the group of insurers that differs from the company requested on the application.

2. The offering of coverage terms that differ from those requested on the application.

The insurer that declines an application must send a written notice advising the applicant of the specific reasons for the declination. If the reason for declination is not sent, the notice must advise the applicant that the reasons will be provided within twenty-one days of his request. The applicant's request must be received within ninety days of the date of the notice.

Cancellation during the Underwriting Period

Length of Underwriting Period: Sixty days unless the policy is a renewal.

Length of Notice: Ten days for nonpayment; thirty days for any other reason.

Reason for Cancellation: If the notice does not state the reason, it must include a statement that upon written request, the insurer will specify in writing the reasons for cancellation.

Proof Required: Postal service certificate of mailing to the named insured at the insured's last known address is conclusive proof of mailing and receipt on the third calendar day after the mailing. Proof of mailing consists of either a U.S. postal service certificate of mailing to the named insured at the last known address or proof of acknowledgement of U.S. postal service mailing to the named insured at the last known address using IMB tracing or a similar method of first-class mail tracking.

NORTH DAKOTA

Cancellation after the Underwriting Period

The policy may be cancelled **only** for the following reasons:

1. Nonpayment.

2. Fraud or material misrepresentation in procuring the insurance or in making a claim.

3. Willful or reckless acts or omissions by the insured which increase any insured-against hazard.

4. A change in the risk which substantially increases the hazard insured against since the policy was issued or renewed.

5. Violation of any local fire, health, safety, building, or construction regulation or ordinance with respect to any covered property or its occupancy that substantially increases any insured-against hazard.

6. Determination by the commissioner that continuing the policy would violate the North Dakota Insurance Code.

7. If the insured is convicted of a crime that involves increasing an insured-against hazard.

8. If at least 65 percent of the rental units in the insured building are unoccupied.

9. If, after a loss, the insured has indicated or such time has elapsed to clearly indicate that the building will not be repaired.

10. If, after a covered loss, the insured has not begun repairs within sixty days after a satisfactory loss settlement.

11. If the building has been unoccupied for sixty consecutive days. This provision does not apply to seasonal unoccupancy, and buildings in the course of construction, renovation, addition or repair which are properly secured against unauthorized entry.

12. If the building is in danger of collapse because of serious structural conditions or subject to extremely hazardous conditions not contemplated in the filed rating plans.

13. If the building is subject to an outstanding order to vacate or demolish or has been declared unsafe in accordance with applicable law.

NORTH DAKOTA

14. If fixed and salvageable items have been or are being removed from the building and the insured can give no reasonable explanation for the removal.

15. If the building is not being protected from possible arson.

16. Buildings with any of the following conditions:

    a. If the insured does not furnish utility service to the building for thirty consecutive days or more.

    b. The insured fails to correct dangerous conditions.

    c. The insured fails to maintain the building in accordance with applicable law.

    d. The insured fails to pay property taxes for more than one year.

17. If the building's characteristics of ownership, condition, occupancy, or maintenance are not in accordance with the law or public policy.

Length of Notice: Ten days for nonpayment; thirty days for reasons 2-7 above; five days for reasons 8-17 above.

Reason for Cancellation: If the notice does not state the reason, it must include a statement that upon written request, the insurer will specify in writing the reasons for cancellation within ten days.

Proof Required: Postal service certificate of mailing to the named insured at the insured's last known address is conclusive proof of mailing and receipt on the third calendar day after the mailing. Proof of mailing consists of either a U.S. postal service certificate of mailing to the named insured at the last known address or proof of acknowledgement of U.S. postal service mailing to the named insured at the last known address using IMB tracing or a similar method of first-class mail tracking.

Nonrenewal

Length of Notice: Forty-five days except that when the policy provides professional liability coverage for legal and medical services, the nonrenewal notice must be mailed or delivered at least ninety days prior to the policy expiration date.

Reason for Nonrenewal: If the notice does not state the reason, it must include a statement that upon written request, the insurer will specify in writing the reasons for nonrenewal.

NORTH DAKOTA

Proof Required: Postal service certificate of mailing to the named insured at the insured's last known address is conclusive proof of mailing and receipt on the third calendar day after the mailing. Proof of mailing consists of either a U.S. postal service certificate of mailing to the named insured at the last known address or proof of acknowledgement of U.S. postal service mailing to the named insured at the last known address using IMB tracing or a similar method of first-class mail tracking.

Other Cancellation/Nonrenewal Provisions

Proof of mailing must be maintained for at least one year after mailing.

An insurer may not consider the following events for purposes of surcharging, declining, nonrenewing, or canceling either personal coverage or a binder for personal coverage. The events include:

1. An insured's inquiry into the type or level of coverage or an inquiry into whether a policy will cover a loss.

2. An insured's inquiry regarding coverage for a loss if the insured files no claim.

3. A claim if the insurer conducts no investigation of a claim or initiates no other claim activity and the claim does not involve deceptive practices on the part of the insured.

4. A claim if the insurer makes no payment to or on behalf of the insured and the claim does not involve deceptive practices on the part of the insured.

5. A first-party property claim resulting from wind or hail if the insured had no previous wind or hail claim on that property within the previous five years regardless of the insurer unless the insurer can provide evidence that the insured unreasonably failed to maintain the property and the failure to maintain the property contributed to the loss.

6. A claim if the claim is over ten years old, unless the insurer can provide evidence that the insured unreasonably failed to maintain the property and the failure to maintain the property contributed to the loss.

PERSONAL AUTO

North Dakota Century Code §§26.1-40-01 through 26.1-40-07

Declinations

In addition to refusal to issue based on an application, a declination also includes:

1. The offering of coverage in a company in the group of insurers that differs from the company requested on the application.

NORTH DAKOTA

2. The offering of coverage terms or rates substantially less favorable than those requested on the application.

Cancellation during the Underwriting Period

Length of Underwriting Period: Sixty days.

Length of Notice: Ten days for nonpayment; twenty days for any other reason.

Reason for Cancellation: Required on the notice for nonpayment. If cancellation is for any other reason, the notice must show the reason or state that the reason will be provided upon written request.

Proof Required: Proof of mailing or delivery. Proof of mailing of notice must be retained by insurer for at least one year after mailing. Proof of mailing consists of either a U.S. postal service certificate of mailing to the named insured at the last known address or proof of acknowledgement of U.S. postal service mailing to the named insured at the last known address using IMB tracing or a similar method of first-class mail tracking.

Cancellation after the Underwriting Period

The policy may be cancelled **only** for the following reasons:

1. Nonpayment.

2. Revocation or suspension of the driver's license of the named insured or any other driver who lives with the named insured or customarily uses the named insured's auto.

    Such revocation or suspension must have occurred during the policy period or 180 days prior to the original effective date. However, the insurer must offer to exclude such a driver.

3. Fraud or material misrepresentation on the application.

The North Dakota Century Code also allows for cancellation for the following additional reasons:

1. If the insured vehicle is so mechanically defective that its operation would be unsafe.

2. If the insured vehicle is used to carry passengers for hire or compensation.

NORTH DAKOTA

3. If the vehicle transports flammables or explosives for an illegal purpose.

4. If the vehicle is an authorized emergency vehicle.

5. If the vehicle is altered so as to increase the risk.

6. If the named insured moves to a state where the insurer is not licensed.

7. If the named insured does not pay any necessary membership dues.

8. If the insurance commissioner determines that continuing the policy would place the insurer in violation of the law or would be hazardous to the interests of policyholders, creditors, or the public.

Since the final eight reasons do not appear on ISO's amendatory endorsement (PP 01 88), they may not be used by an insurer using the ISO personal auto program.

Length of Notice: Ten days for nonpayment; twenty days for any other allowable reason.

Reason for Cancellation: Required on the notice for nonpayment. If cancellation is for any other reason, the notice must show the reason or state that the insurer will specify the reasons in writing, upon written request.

Proof Required: Postal service certificate of mailing. Proof of mailing of notice must be retained by insurer for at least one year after mailing. Proof of mailing consists of either a U.S. postal service certificate of mailing to the named insured at the last known address or proof of acknowledgement of U.S. postal service mailing to the named insured at the last known address using IMB tracing or a similar method of first-class mail tracking.

Nonrenewal

Length of Notice: Thirty days.

Reason for Nonrenewal: Required on the notice or the notice must include a statement that upon written request, the insurer will specify the reasons for nonrenewal in writing.

Proof Required: Postal service certificate of mailing. Proof of mailing of notice must be retained by insurer for at least one year after mailing. Proof of mailing consists of either a U.S. postal service certificate of mailing to the named insured at the last known address or proof

NORTH DAKOTA

of acknowledgement of U.S. postal service mailing to the named insured at the last known address using IMB tracing or a similar method of first-class mail tracking.

Other Cancellation/Nonrenewal Provisions

1. If the policy term is less than six months, the insurer may nonrenew every six months, beginning six months after the original effective date.

2. If the policy term is one year or longer, the insurer may nonrenew the policy at each anniversary of the original effective date.

3. If an insurer cancels a personal auto policy for any reason other than nonpayment—or if it nonrenews—it must notify the insured of the availability of the assigned risk plan.

4. An insurer may not use or rely on the cancellation of a minor's driving privileges as the sole reason to cancel, deny, or not renew the automobile insurance policy of the minor or a parent of the minor unless the points or offenses on the minor's public driving would be a reason to cancel, deny, or not renew the policy.

PERSONAL UMBRELLA

North Dakota Century Code §§26.1-39-11 through 26.1-39-16

Cancellation during the Underwriting Period

Length of Underwriting Period: Sixty days.

Length of Notice: Ten days for nonpayment; thirty days for any other reason.

Reason for Cancellation: If the notice does not state the reason, it must include a statement that upon written request, the insurer will specify, in writing, the reasons for cancellation.

Proof Required: Proof of mailing. Proof of mailing consists of either a U.S. postal service certificate of mailing to the named insured at the last known address or proof of acknowledgement of U.S. postal service mailing to the named insured at the last known address using IMB tracing or a similar method of first-class mail tracking.

Cancellation after the Underwriting Period

A notice of cancellation may only be based on the following reasons:

1. Nonpayment.

2. Fraud or material misrepresentation and the procurement of the insurance or with respect to any claims submitted thereunder.

NORTH DAKOTA

3. Discovery of willful or reckless acts or omissions on the part of the named insured which increase any insured-against hazard.

4. Change in the risk which substantially increases any hazard insured against after insurance coverage has been issued or renewed.

5. Violation of any local fire, health, safety, building, or construction regulation or ordinance with respect to any insured property or the occupancy thereof which substantially increases any insured-against hazard.

6. A determination by the commissioner that continuing the policy would place the insurer in violation of the insurance laws of this state.

7. Conviction of the named insured of a crime having as one of its necessary elements an act increasing any insured-against hazard.

Length of Notice: Ten-day notice for nonpayment; thirty-day notice for any other allowable reason.

Reason for Cancellation: If the notice does not state the reason, it must include a statement that the reason will be provided upon request.

Proof Required: Proof of mailing. Proof of mailing consists of either a U.S. postal service certificate of mailing to the named insured at the last known address or proof of acknowledgement of U.S. postal service mailing to the named insured at the last known address using IMB tracing or a similar method of first-class mail tracking.

Nonrenewal

Length of Notice: Forty-five days.

Reason for Notice: If the notice does not state the reason, it must include a statement that the reason will be provided upon request.

Proof Required: Proof of mailing. Proof of mailing consists of either a U.S. postal service certificate of mailing to the named insured at the last known address or proof of acknowledgement of U.S. postal service mailing to the named insured at the last known address using IMB tracing or a similar method of first-class mail tracking.

NORTH DAKOTA

FRAUD

North Dakota Century Code §§26.1-02.1-01, 26.1-02.1-05, and 26.1-02.1-06

Definition

Under the North Dakota Century Code, a fraudulent insurance act includes the following acts or omissions when they are committed by a person both knowingly and with intent to defraud:

1. Presenting, causing to be presented, or preparing with knowledge or belief that it will be presented to or by an insurer, reinsurer, insurance producer, or any agent thereof, false or misleading information as part of, in support of, or concerning a fact material to one or more of the following:

    a. An application for the issuance or renewal of an insurance policy or reinsurance contract.

    b. Rating of an insurance policy or reinsurance contract.

    c. Claim for payment or benefit pursuant to an insurance policy or reinsurance contract.

    d. Premiums paid on an insurance policy or reinsurance contract.

    e. Payments made in accordance with the terms of an insurance policy or reinsurance contract.

    f. A document filed with the commissioner or the chief insurance regulatory official of another jurisdiction.

    g. The financial condition of an insurer or reinsurer.

    h. The formation, acquisition, merger, reconsolidation, dissolution, or withdrawal from one or more lines of insurance or reinsurance in all or part of this state by an insurer or reinsurer.

    i. The issuance of written evidence of insurance.

    j. The reinstatement of an insurance policy.

    k. The formation of an agency, brokerage, or insurance producer contract.

2. Solicitation or acceptance of new or renewal insurance risks on behalf of an insurer, reinsurer, or other person engaged in the business of insurance by a person who knows or should know that the insurer or other person responsible for the risk is insolvent at the time of the transaction.

3. Removal, concealment, alteration, or destruction of the assets or records of an insurer, reinsurer, or other person engaged in the business of insurance.

4. Theft by deception or otherwise, or embezzlement, abstracting, purloining, or converting of moneys, funds, premiums, credits, or other property of an insurer, reinsurer, or person engaged in the business of insurance.

5. Attempting to commit, aiding or abetting in the commission of, or conspiring to commit the acts or omissions specified in this section.

Reporting Requirements

A person engaged in the business of insurance who knows or has a reasonable belief that a fraudulent insurance act is being, will be, or has been committed shall provide to the commissioner with the information required by, and in a manner prescribed by, the commissioner. Report fraud online at https://eapps.naic.org/ofrs/. If you suspect that a fraudulent insurance act is occurring, or has occurred, please contact the Department at: insurance@nd.gov; or 600 E. Boulevard Ave. Bismarck, ND 58505-0320; or 701.328.2440; or 701.328.4880 fax; or 800.247.0560 toll free; or 800.366.6888 TTY line. Please use the reporting form and instructions available at http://www.nd.gov/ndins/consumers/fraud/.

Any other person having knowledge or a reasonable belief that a fraudulent insurance act is being, will be, or has been committed may provide to the commissioner the information required by, and in a manner prescribed by, the commissioner.

A person who provides nonpublic personal information to the commissioner pursuant to this section does not violate the insurance privacy law under the North Dakota Century Code section 26.1-02-27.

Penalty

Committing a fraudulent insurance act is a felony of varying degrees depending on the pecuniary value of the property or services retained. If a licensed insurance practitioner is found guilty of committing a fraudulent insurance act, the court will notify the relevant licensing authority which will then hold an administrative hearing to consider imposing administrative sanctions against the practitioner. A perpetrator of a fraudulent insurance act must make restitution to the insurer or to any other person who sustained a financial loss from the fraudulent act.

NORTH DAKOTA

Fraud Application Statement
North Dakota Century Code §26.1-33.4-13

Life settlement contracts and applications for life settlement contracts, regardless of the form of transmission, must contain the following statement or a substantially similar statement:

> "Any person that knowingly presents false information in an application for insurance or life settlement contract is guilty of a crime and may be subject to fines and confinement in prison."

FAIR CLAIMS PROCESSING
North Dakota Century Code §26.1-04-03 & 26.1-04-14
Definition

North Dakota law prohibits the following practices if done without just cause and if performed with a frequency indicating a general business practice:

1. Knowingly misrepresenting to claimants pertinent facts or policy provisions relating to coverages at issue.

2. Not acknowledging with reasonable promptness pertinent communications with respect to claims arising under insurance policies.

3. Not adopting and implementing reasonable standards for the prompt investigation of claims arising under insurance policies.

4. Not attempting in good faith to effectuate prompt, fair, and equitable settlements of claims submitted in which liability has become reasonably clear.

5. Compelling insureds to institute suits to recover amounts due under its policies by offering substantially less than the amounts ultimately recovered in suits brought by them when the insureds have made claims for amounts reasonably similar to the amounts ultimately recovered.

6. Making known to insureds or claimants a policy of appealing from arbitration awards in favor of insureds or claimants for the purpose of compelling them to accept settlements or compromises less than the amount awarded in arbitration.

7. Attempting settlement or compromise of claims on the basis of applications which were altered without notice to, or knowledge or consent of, insureds.

NORTH DAKOTA

8. Attempting to settle a claim for less than the amount to which a reasonable person would have believed one was entitled by reference to written or printed advertising material accompanying or made a part of an application.

9. Attempting to delay the investigation or payment of claims by requiring an insured and the insured's physician to submit a preliminary claim report and then requiring the subsequent submission of formal proof of loss forms, both of which submissions contain substantially the same information.

10. Failing to affirm or deny coverage of claims within a reasonable time after proof of loss has been completed.

11. Refusing payment of claims solely on the basis of the insured's request to do so without making an independent evaluation of the insured's liability based upon all available information.

12. Providing coverage under a policy issued under the North Dakota Century Code chapter 26.1-45 or 26.1-36.1 for confinement to a nursing home and refusing to pay a claim when a person is covered by such a policy and the person's physician ordered confinement pursuant to the terms of the policy for care other than custodial care. Custodial care means care which is primarily for the purpose of meeting personal needs without supervision by a registered nurse or a licensed practical nurse.

13. Failure to use the standard health insurance proof of loss and claim form or failure to pay a health insurance claim as required by the North Dakota Century Code section 26.1-36-37.1.

It is not a prohibited practice for a health insurance company with participating provider agreements to require that a subscriber or member using a nonparticipating provider be responsible for providing the insurer a copy of medical records used for claims processing.

Penalty

After a hearing during which the commissioner determines that a person has engaged in one of the unfair practices listed above, the commissioner will issue a cease and desist order to that person. Violating a cease and desist order of this kind exposes an individual to a maximum monetary penalty of $10,000 per violation.

OHIO

For details on cancellation procedures for the standard policy, refer to the Standard Policy section.

COMMERCIAL LINES
AGRICULTURAL CAPITAL ASSETS; BOP; CAPITAL ASSETS; C. AUTO; CRIME; CGL; CIM; C. PROP.; C. UMB.; E-COMMERCE; EQUIPMENT BREAKDOWN; FARM;MGT. PROT.; & PROFESSIONAL LIABILITY
(other than Medical Professional Liability)

Ohio Revised Code §§3937.25 to 3937.27

Cancellation during the Underwriting Period

Length of Underwriting Period: Ninety days.

Length of Notice: Ten days nonpayment; thirty days any other reason.

Note: For allied health care providers, blood banks, diagnostic testing laboratories, hospitals, optometrists, and physicians, surgeons and dentists professional liability, see Medical Professional Liability.

Reason for Cancellation: Required on the notice.

Proof Required: Proof of mailing.

The Ohio Revised Code is unclear as to its requirements for cancellation during the underwriting period. It only specifies that the cancellation restrictions do not apply to a policy that has been in force for ninety days or less.

Cancellation after the Underwriting Period

The policy may be cancelled **only** for the following reasons:

1. Nonpayment of premium.

2. Discovery of fraud or material misrepresentation in the procurement of the insurance or with respect to any claims submitted thereunder.

3. Discovery of moral hazard or willful or reckless acts or omissions on the part of the named insured that increase any hazard insured against.

OHIO

4. The occurrence of a change in the individual risk which substantially increases the hazard insured against after insurance coverage has been issued or renewed, except to the extent the insurer reasonably should have foreseen the change or contemplated the risk in writing the contract.

5. Loss of applicable reinsurance or a substantial decrease in applicable reinsurance, if the superintendent has determined that reasonable efforts have been made to prevent the loss of or substantial decrease in, the applicable reinsurance, or to obtain replacement coverage.

6. Failure of an insured to correct material violations of safety codes or comply with reasonable written loss control recommendations.

7. A determination by the superintendent that the continuation of the policy would create a condition that would be hazardous to the policyholders or the public.

Length of Notice: Ten days for nonpayment; thirty days for all other reasons.

Reason for Cancellation: Required on the notice.

Proof Required: Proof of mailing to the insured's last known address and the insured's agent.

Nonrenewal

Length of Notice: Thirty days.

Reason for Nonrenewal: Not required.

Proof Required: Proof of mailing.

Other Cancellation/Nonrenewal Provisions

All notices must also be sent to the insured's agent.

A thirty-day notice is required (on all the above policies except fidelity/surety bonds and medical professional liability) if the insurer intends to renew under less favorable terms as to dollar amount of coverage or deductibles or a "substantial" increase in rate. Policies written for a term of more than one year or on a continuous basis may be cancelled for any reason at an anniversary date, upon thirty days written notice.

If a renewal is predicated on a "substantial" increase in premium, notification must be sent to both the insured and the insured's agent thirty days prior to renewal date.

OHIO

MEDICAL PROFESSIONAL LIABILITY (MEDICAL MALPRACTICE)
Ohio Revised Code §§3937.28 and 3937.29
Cancellation

There is no underwriting period. The following cancellation requirements apply from policy inception.

The policy may be cancelled **only** for the following reasons:

1. Nonpayment of premium.

2. Discovery of fraud or material misrepresentation in the procurement of the insurance or with respect to any claims submitted thereunder.

3. Discovery of moral hazard or willful or reckless acts or omissions on the part of the named insured that increase any hazard insured against.

4. The occurrence of a change in the individual risk which substantially increases the hazard insured against after insurance coverage has been issued or renewed, except to the extent the insurer reasonably should have foreseen the change or contemplated the risk in writing the contract.

5. Loss of applicable reinsurance or a substantial decrease in applicable reinsurance, if the superintendent has determined that reasonable efforts have been made to prevent the loss of or substantial decrease in, the applicable reinsurance, or to obtain replacement coverage.

6. Failure of an insured to correct material violations of safety codes or comply with reasonable written loss control recommendations.

7. A determination by the superintendent that the continuation of the policy would create a condition that would be hazardous to the policyholders or the public.

Length of Notice: Ten days for nonpayment; sixty days for all other reasons.

Reason for Cancellation: Required on the notice.

Proof Required: Proof of mailing to the insured at the insured's last known address and the insured's agent.

OHIO

Nonrenewal

Length of Notice: Sixty days.

Reason for Nonrenewal: Required on the notice.

Proof Required: Proof of mailing to the agent of record and to the insured at the insured's last known address.

Other Cancellation/Nonrenewal Provisions

A sixty-day notice is required if the insurer intends to renew under less favorable terms as to dollar amount coverage or deductibles or a "substantial" increase in rate.

Policies written for a term of more than one year or on a continuous basis may be cancelled for any reason at an anniversary date, upon sixty days' written notice.

All notices must be sent to the insured's agent.

Blanket cancellation or nonrenewal requires written notice to superintendent in accordance with Ohio Revised Code §3937.29.

WORKERS COMPENSATION

Ohio Revised Code §§3937.25, 3937.26, and 4123.82

Ohio is a monopolistic workers compensation state. Employers Liability and Excess Workers Compensation may be written in compliance with Ohio Revised Code §4123.82. Ohio Revised Code §§3937.25 and 3937.26 apply for cancellation or nonrenewal of the insurance.

SURPLUS LINES

It is recommended that surplus lines insurers follow the cancellation and nonrenewal laws.

FINANCED PREMIUMS

Ohio Revised Code §§1321.80 and 1321.81

When a premium finance agreement contains a power of attorney authorizing the premium finance company to cancel any insurance contract or contracts listed in the agreement, the insurance contract or contracts shall not be cancelled by the premium finance company unless:

1. After expiration of the ten-day period, the premium finance company may cancel, in the name of the insured, such insurance contract or contracts by mailing to the insurer

OHIO

a notice of cancellation, and the insurance contract shall be cancelled as if such notice of cancellation had been submitted by the insured himself, but without requiring the return of the insurance contract or contracts. The premium finance company also shall mail a notice of cancellation to the insured at his last known mailing address, as shown on the records of the premium finance company.

2. Not less than ten days' written notice shall be mailed to the insured at his last known mailing address, as shown on the records of the premium finance company, of the intent of the premium finance company to cancel the insurance contract unless the default is cured within such ten-day period.

3. All statutory, regulatory and contractual restrictions providing that the insurance contract may not be cancelled unless notice is given to a governmental agency, mortgagee, or other third party shall apply. The insurer shall give notice to any governmental agency, mortagee or third party on or before the second business day after the day it receives the notice of cancellation from the premium finance company and shall determine the effective date of cancellation taking into consideration the number of days' notice required to complete the cancellation.

The following provisions apply to finance charges:

1. A delinquency charge of not more than 5 percent of any installment that is in default for a period of more than five days.

2. A cancellation charge of $10 when the default results in the cancellation of any insurance contract described in the agreement.

3. A check collection charge of not more than $10, plus any amount passed on from other financial institutions, for each check, negotiable order of withdrawal, share draft, or other negotiable instrument returned or dishonored for any reason.

PERSONAL LINES
DWELLING FIRE & HOMEOWNERS

Ohio Administrative Code (OAC) 3901-1-18 (C)

Cancellation during the Underwriting Period

Length of Underwriting Period: None specified by law; sixty days if using ISO Amendatory Endorsement DP 01 34 or HO 01 34.

Length of Notice: Ten days for nonpayment, material misrepresentation, or if there is evidence of arson; thirty days for any other reason. The thirty-day notice does not apply to binders of thirty days or less.

OHIO

Reason for Cancellation: Not required.

Proof Required: Proof of mailing.

Cancellation after the Underwriting Period

The policy may be cancelled for reasons including:

1. Nonpayment of premium.

2. Substantial change in the risk.

3. Material misrepresentation of fact related to the insurance.

4. Evidence of arson exists.

Length of Notice: Ten days for nonpayment and reasons 3 and 4 above; thirty days for reason 2 or any other reason. (ISO DP 01 34)

Reason for Cancellation: Not required.

Proof Required: Proof of mailing.

Nonrenewal

Length of Notice: Thirty days.

Reason for Nonrenewal: Not required.

Proof Required: Proof of mailing.

Other Cancellation/Nonrenewal Provisions

When this policy is written for a period of more than one year, the insurer may cancel for any reason at an anniversary by notice of at least thirty days before the date cancellation takes effect.

Cancellation/nonrenewal notice shall explain to the insured the procedures for making application to the Ohio FAIR Plan.

OHIO

PERSONAL AUTO

Ohio Revised Code §§3937.31 to 3937.34 & ISO PP 92 86

Cancellation during the Underwriting Period

The Ohio Revised Code is unclear as to its requirements for cancellation during the underwriting period. It specifies only that the cancellation restrictions do not apply to a policy that has been in force for less than ninety days. However, if an insurer has adopted the ISO Amendatory Endorsement PP 92 86, it must follow the requirements as outlined below.

Length of Underwriting Period: Ninety days.

Length of Notice: Ten days for any reason.

Reason for Cancellation: Required for nonpayment. An explanation of the reason for cancellation and the information upon which it is based, or a statement that such explanation will be furnished to the insured in writing within five days after receipt of a written request.

Proof Required: Proof of mailing to the insured at insured's last known address.

Cancellation after the Underwriting Period

The policy may be cancelled **only** for the following reasons:

1. Nonpayment of premium.

2. Loss of driving privileges through revocation, expiration or suspension of the driver's license of the named insured or any driver who lives with the named insured or customarily uses the named insured's auto.

   The insurer must offer to exclude a driver (other than a named insured or the principal operator) with a revoked or suspended license. Ohio Statute allows cancellation for expiration of driver's license.

3. Material misrepresentation on the application; in renewing the policy; or in filing of a claim. Ohio Statute allows cancellation for fraud and concealment of material fact.

4. Place of residence, registration or license changes to state where insurer is not authorized to write.

Length of Notice: Ten days for nonpayment; thirty days for any other allowable reason.

OHIO

Reason for Cancellation: Required for nonpayment. An explanation of the reason for cancellation and the information upon which it is based, or a statement that such explanation will be furnished to the insured in writing within five days after receipt of a written request.

Proof Required: Proof of mailing to the insured at insured's last known address.

Nonrenewal

Length of Notice: Thirty days.

Reason for Nonrenewal: An explanation of the reason for nonrenewal and the information upon which it is based, or a statement that such explanation will be furnished to the insured in writing within five days after receipt of a written request.

Proof Required: Proof of mailing to the insured at insured's last known address.

Other Cancellation/Nonrenewal Provisions

Nonrenewal may be sent only at each anniversary of the original effective date. Automatic termination is not allowed due to nonpayment of the renewal premium if the insurer issues six month policies.

If the policy period is other than one year, or written without a fixed expiration date, the insurer will have the right not to renew or continue it only at the anniversary of its original effective date.

PERSONAL UMBRELLA

Cancellation during the Underwriting Period

Length of Underwriting Period: None specified.

Notice Requirements: Ten days for any reason. (Recommended, but not required.)

Reason for Cancellation: Not required.

Proof Required: Proof of mailing.

Cancellation after the Underwriting Period

Length of Notice: Ten day notice for nonpayment; thirty day notice for any other reason. (Recommended, but not required.)

Reason for Nonrenewal: Not required.

Proof Required: Proof of mailing.

OHIO

Nonrenewal

Length of Notice: Thirty days. (Recommended, but not required.)

Reason for Nonrenewal: Reason for notice is not required.

Proof Required: Proof of mailing.

FRAUD

Ohio Revised Code §§2913.47 and 3999.42

General Information and Definitions

No person, with purpose to defraud or knowing that the person is facilitating a fraud, shall do either of the following:

1. Present to, or cause to be presented to, an insurer any written or oral statement that is part of, or in support of, an application for insurance, a claim for payment pursuant to a policy, or a claim for any other benefit pursuant to a policy, knowing that the statement, or any part of the statement, is false or deceptive.

2. Assist, aid, abet, solicit, procure, or conspire with another to prepare or make any written or oral statement that is intended to be presented to an insurer as part of, or in support of, an application for insurance, a claim for payment pursuant to a policy, or a claim for any other benefit pursuant to a policy, knowing that the statement, or any part of the statement, is false or deceptive.

Reporting Requirements

If an insurer has a reasonable belief that a person is perpetrating or facilitating an insurance fraud, or has done so, the insurer shall notify the department of insurance. Reporting is not required if the claim for fraud totals less than $1,000. Ohioans aware of insurance fraud can report it to the Ohio Department of Insurance by calling its fraud hotline at 1-800-686-1527 or reporting online at https://gateway.insurance.ohio.gov/UI/ODI.Investigation.Public.UI/FraudComplaintForm.aspx Access a list of red flags at http://www.insurance.ohio.gov/Company/Documents/RedFlagIndicators.pdf

This section applies to insurance fraud perpetrated or facilitated by any person, including, but not limited to, any applicant, policyholder, subscriber, or enrollee, or any officer, director, manager, employee, representative, or agent of the insurer.

Penalties

Whoever violates this section is guilty of insurance fraud. Except as otherwise provided in this division, insurance fraud is a misdemeanor of the first degree. If the amount of the

OHIO

claim that is false or deceptive is $1,000 or more and is less than $7,500, insurance fraud is a felony of the fifth degree. If the amount of the claim that is false or deceptive is $7,500 or more and is less than $150,000, insurance fraud is a felony of the fourth degree. If the amount of the claim that is false or deceptive is $150,000 or more, insurance fraud is a felony of the third degree.

FAIR CLAIMS PROCESSING
Ohio Administrative Code 3901-1-07

It shall be deemed an unfair or deceptive practice to commit or perform with such frequency as to indicate a general business practice any of the following:

1. Knowingly misrepresenting to claimants pertinent facts or policy provisions relating to coverage at issue.

    a. Misrepresenting a pertinent policy provision by making any payment, settlement, or offer of first party benefits, which, without explanation, does not include all amounts which should be included according to the claim filed by the first party claimant and investigated by the insurer.

    b. Denying a claim on the grounds of a specific policy provision, condition, or exclusion without reference to such provision, condition, or exclusion.

2. Failing to acknowledge pertinent communications with respect to claims arising under insurance policies in writing, or by other means so long as an appropriate notation is made in the claim file of the insurer, within fifteen days of receiving notice of a claim in writing or otherwise.

3. Failing to make an appropriate reply within twenty-one days of all other pertinent communications and/or any inquiries of the department of insurance respecting a claim.

4. Failing to adopt and implement reasonable procedures to commence an investigation of any claim filed by either a first party or third party claimant, or by such claimant's authorized representative, within twenty-one days of receipt of notice of claim.

5. Failing to mail or furnish claimant or the claimant's authorized representative, a notification of all items, statements and forms, if any, which the insurer reasonably believes will be required of such claimant, within fifteen days of receiving notice of claim, unless the insurer, based on the information then in its possession does not yet know all such requirements, then such notification shall be sent, within a reasonable time.

OHIO

6. Not offering first party or third party claimants, or their authorized representatives who have made claims which are fair and reasonable and in which liability has become reasonably clear, amounts which are fair and reasonable as shown by the insurer's investigation of the claim, providing the amounts so offered are within policy limits and in accordance with the policy provisions.

7. Compelling insureds to institute suits to recover amounts due under its policies by offering substantially less than the amounts ultimately recovered in suits brought by them when such insureds have made claims for amounts reasonably similar to the amounts ultimately recovered.

8. Making known to insureds or claimants a policy of appealing from arbitration awards in favor of insureds or claimants for the purpose of compelling them to accept settlements or compromises less than the amount awarded in arbitration.

9. Attempting settlement or compromise of claims on the basis of applications which were altered without notice to, or knowledge, or consent of insureds.

10. Attempting to settle or compromise claims for less than the amount which the insureds had been led reasonably to believe they were entitled to, by written or printed advertising material accompanying or made part of an application.

11. Attempting to delay the investigation or payment of claims by requiring an insured and his physician to submit a preliminary claim report and then requiring the subsequent submission of formal proof of loss forms, both of which submissions contain substantially the same information.

12. Failing to advise the first party claimant or the claimant's authorized representative, in writing or by other means so long as an appropriate notation is made in the claim file of the insurer, of the acceptance or rejection of the claim, within twenty-one days after receipt by the insurer of a properly executed proof of loss.

    a. Failing to notify such claimant or the claimant's authorized representative, within twenty-one days after receipt of such proof of loss, that the insurer needs more time to determine whether the claim should be accepted or rejected.
    b. Failing to send a letter to such claimant or, the claimant's authorized representative, stating the need for further time to investigate the claim, if such claim remains unsettled ninety days from the date of the initial letter setting forth the need for further time to investigate.
    c. Failing to send to such claimant or authorized representative every ninety days after the first ninety-day claim investigation period, a letter setting forth the

reasons additional time is needed for investigation, unless the delay is caused by factors beyond the insurer's control.

13. Failing to advise such claimant or claimant's authorized representative, of the amount offered, if such claim is accepted in whole or in part.

14. Refusing payments of claims solely on the basis of the insured's request to do so without making an independent evaluation of the insured's liability based upon all available information.

15. Failing to adopt and implement reasonable standards for the proper handling of written communications, primarily expressing grievances, received by the insurer from insureds or claimants.

16. Failing to pay any amount finally agreed upon in settlement of all or part of any claim or authorized repairs to be made upon final agreement not later than five days from the receipt of such agreement by the insurer at the place from which the payment or authorization is to be made or from the date of the performance by the claimant of any condition set by such agreement, whichever is later.

OKLAHOMA

For details on cancellation procedures for the standard policy, refer to the Standard Policy section.

COMMERCIAL LINES
AGRICULTURAL CAPITAL ASSETS; BOP; CAPITAL ASSETS; C. AUTO; CRIME; CGL (CGL, EMPLOYMENT, LIQUOR, OCP, POLLUTION, PRODS. / COMPLETED OPS.); CIM; C. PROP.; C. UMB., E-COMMERCE; EQUIPMENT BREAKDOWN; FARM; MGT. PROTECTION; & PRO. LIAB.

Okla. Stat. tit. 36, §§1241 and 3639

Cancellation during the Underwriting Period

Length of Underwriting Period: Forty-five business days.

Length of Notice: Ten days for reasons listed in §3639. The Oklahoma code allows for a ten-day notice for any of the reasons listed as allowable after the underwriting period. However, if an insurer has adopted the ISO amendatory endorsements (AG 01 41, BP 01 40, EC 02 09, MP 02 36 and IL 02 36), it must comply with the more restrictive policy language.

Reason for Cancellation: Not required.

Proof Required: Proof of mailing.

Cancellation after the Underwriting Period

The policy may be cancelled **only** for the following reasons:

1. Nonpayment.

2. Fraud or material misrepresentation in obtaining the policy or in pursuing a claim.

3. Willful or reckless acts or omissions by the named insured that increases any insured-against hazard.

4. A change in the risk that substantially increases the insured-against hazard after coverage has been issued or renewed.

5. A violation of any local fire, health, safety, building or construction regulation or ordinance with respect to any insured property or the occupancy thereof that substantially increases any insured-against hazard.

OKLAHOMA

6. A determination by the insurance commissioner that continuation of the policy would place the insurer in violation of the Oklahoma insurance laws.

7. Conviction of the named insured of a crime that increases any insured-against hazard.

8. Loss of or substantial changes in reinsurance on the risk.

Length of Notice: Ten days for nonpayment. The Oklahoma code allows for a ten-day notice for any of these reasons. However, if an insurer has adopted the ISO amendatory endorsements (AG 01 41, BP 01 40, EC 02 09, MP 02 36 and IL 02 36), it must comply with the more restrictive policy language.

Reason for Cancellation: Not required.

Proof Required: Proof of mailing.

Nonrenewal

Length of Notice: Forty-five days.

Reason for Nonrenewal: Not required.

Proof Required: Proof of mailing.

Other Cancellation/Nonrenewal Provisions

A forty-five day written notice is required if the insurer intends to renew under any of the following conditions: increase in premium, change in deductible, or reduction in limits or coverage.

On OCP policies all notices must also be sent to any designated contractor.

When the notice is mailed, it is considered to have been given to the first named insured on the day it is mailed.

COMMERCIAL GENERAL LIABILITY

(Railroad Protective)

Okla. Stat. tit. 36, §3639

Length of Underwriting Period: Forty-five business days.

Length of Notice: Ten days

OKLAHOMA

Reason for Cancellation: N/A.

Proof Required: N/A.

The policy may be cancelled **only** for the following reasons:

1. Nonpayment.

2. Fraud or material misrepresentation in obtaining the policy or in pursuing a claim.

3. Willful or reckless acts by the named insured that increase any insured-against hazard.

4. A violation of any local fire, health, or safety code that substantially increases any insured-against hazard.

5. If the insurance commissioner determines that the continuation of the policy would place the insurer in violation of the Oklahoma insurance laws.

6. Conviction of the named insured of a crime that increases any insured-against hazard.

7. If there is a substantial change in or the insurer loses its reinsurance on the risk.

8. A change in the risk that substantially increases the insured-against hazard.

Length of Notice: Sixty days. Oklahoma statute allows for a ten-day notice for any of these reasons. However, if an insurer has adopted the ISO amendatory endorsement (CG 29 34), it must comply with the more restrictive policy language.

Reason for Cancellation: Not required.

Proof Required: Proof of mailing.

Nonrenewal

Length of Notice: Forty-five days.

Reason for Nonrenewal: Not required.

Proof Required: Proof of mailing.

OKLAHOMA

Other Cancellation/Nonrenewal Provisions

1. All notices must also be sent to any designated contractor and any involved governmental authority.

2. A forty-five day written notice is required if the insurer intends to renew under any of the following conditions: increase in premium, change in deductible, or reduction in limits or coverage.

3. When the notice is mailed, it is considered to have been given to the first named insured on the day it is mailed.

COMMERCIAL GENERAL LIABILITY

(Underground Storage Tanks)

Okla. Stat. tit. 36, §3639

Cancellation during the Underwriting Period

Length of Underwriting Period: Forty-five business days.

Length of Notice: Ten days for nonpayment; thirty days for material misrepresentation or fraud; sixty days for any other reason.

The Oklahoma Code allows ten days' notice for the listed reasons, however, insurers using ISO's CG 30 40 must comply with the more restrictive policy language. Legal advice is suggested.

Reason for Cancellation: Not required.

Proof Required: Certified mail. Oklahoma statutes do not require certified mail. However, insurers using the unmodified ISO amendatory endorsement must comply with the more restrictive requirement.

Cancellation after the Underwriting Period

The policy may be cancelled **only** for the following reasons:

1. Nonpayment.

2. Fraud or material misrepresentation in obtaining the policy or in pursuing a claim.

3. Willful or reckless acts by the named insured that increase any insured-against hazard.

OKLAHOMA

4. A violation of any local fire, health, or safety code with respect to any insured property or the occupancy thereof that substantially increases any insured-against hazard.

5. If the insurance commissioner determines that the continuation of the policy would place the insurer in violation of the Oklahoma insurance laws.

6. Conviction of the named insured of a crime that increases any insured-against hazard.

7. If there is a substantial change in or if the insurer loses its reinsurance on the risk.

8. A change in the risk that substantially increases the insured-against hazard.

Length of Notice: Ten days for nonpayment; thirty days for material misrepresentation or fraud; sixty days for any other reason. The Oklahoma code allows for a ten-day notice for any of these reasons. However, if an insurer has adopted the ISO amendatory endorsement (CG 30 40), it must comply with the more restrictive policy language.

Reason for Cancellation: Not required.

Proof Required: Certified mail. Oklahoma statutes do not require certified mail. However, insurers using the ISO amendatory endorsement (CG 30 40) must comply with the more restrictive requirement.

Nonrenewal

Length of Notice: Forty-five days.

Reason for Nonrenewal: Not required.

Proof Required: Certified mail. Oklahoma statutes do not require certified mail. However, insurers using the ISO amendatory endorsement (CG 30 40) must comply with the more restrictive requirement.

Other Cancellation/Nonrenewal Provisions

A forty-five day written notice is required if the insurer intends to renew under any of the following conditions: increase in premium, change in deductible, or reduction in limits or coverage.

When the notice is mailed, it is considered to have been given to the first-named insured on the day it is mailed.

OKLAHOMA

WORKERS COMPENSATION
Okla. Stat. tit. 36, §3639

Cancellation during the Underwriting Period

Length of Underwriting Period: Forty-five business days.

Length of Notice: Ten days for any of the reasons listed as allowable after the underwriting period.

Reason for Cancellation: Not required.

Proof Required: Proof of mailing.

Cancellation after the Underwriting Period

The policy may be cancelled **only** for the following reasons:

1. Nonpayment.

2. Discovery of fraud or material misrepresentation in obtaining the policy or in pursuing a claim.

3. Discovery of willful or reckless acts or omissions by the named insured that increase any insured-against hazard.

4. The occurrence of a change in the risk that substantially increases any hazard insured against after insurance coverage has been issued or renewed.

5. A violation of any local fire, health, safety, building, or construction regulation or ordinance with respect to any insured property or the occupancy thereof which substantially increases any insured-against hazard.

6. A determination by the insurance commissioner that the continuation of the policy would place the insurer in violation of the Oklahoma insurance laws.

7. Conviction of the named insured of a crime that increases any insured-against hazard.

8. The insurer's loss or substantial changes in applicable reinsurance.

Length of Notice: Ten days.

OKLAHOMA

Reason for Cancellation: Not required on the notice.

Proof Required: Proof of mailing.

Nonrenewal

Length of Notice: Forty-five days.

Reason for Nonrenewal: Not required.

Proof Required: Proof of mailing.

Other Cancellation/Nonrenewal Provisions

Ten days' notice must be filed to office of the Administrator of Workers' Compensation Court or NCCI before cancellation.

A forty-five day written notice is required if the insurer intends to increase in premium, change deductibles, or to reduce limits or coverage. This notice is not required for the following:

1. Changes in a rate or plan filed with or approved by the insurance commissioner applicable to an entire class of business.

2. Changes based upon the altered nature or extent of the risk insured.

3. Changes in policy forms filed with or approved by the insurance commissioner and applicable to an entire class of business.

Coverage under the policy will remain in effect for forty-five days after the written notice. Notice is considered given to the insured on the day it is mailed.

SURPLUS LINES

Okla. Stat. tit. 36, §§3601 and 3639

Surplus lines insurers must follow the cancellation and nonrenewal requirements for admitted companies.

FINANCED PREMIUMS

Okla. Stat. tit. 36, §3639

Oklahoma equates nonpayment of a finance company with nonpayment of an insurer but does not specify procedures to be followed.

OKLAHOMA

PERSONAL LINES
DWELLING FIRE & HOMEOWNERS

Okla. Stat. tit. 36, §§ 3639.1; Okla. Admin. Code 365:15-1-14

Cancellation during the Underwriting Period

Length of Underwriting Period: Forty-five business days.

Length of Notice: Ten days

Reason for Cancellation: Not required.

Proof Required: Proof of mailing.

Cancellation after the Underwriting Period

The policy may be cancelled **only** for the following reasons:

1. Nonpayment.

2. Fraud or material misrepresentation in obtaining the policy or in pursuing a claim.

3. A change in the risk which substantially increases any hazard insured against after insurance coverage has been issued or renewed.

Oklahoma statute also allows for cancellation based on the following. However, insurers who use ISO's dwelling and homeowner policies are restricted to the reasons listed above.

1. Willful or reckless acts by the named insured that increase any hazard insured against.

2. A violation of any local fire, health, safety, building, or construction regulation or ordinance with respect to any insured property or the occupancy thereof which substantially increases any insured-against hazard.

3. If the insurance commissioner determines that the continuation of the policy would place the insurer in violation of the Oklahoma insurance laws.

4. Conviction of the named insured of a crime that increases any insured-against hazard.

Length of Notice: Ten days. Oklahoma requires at least ten days' notice. If an insurer adopted ISO endorsements, it must comply with the more restrictive policy language.

OKLAHOMA

Reason for Cancellation: Not required.

Proof Required: Proof of mailing.

Nonrenewal

Length of Notice: Twenty days. Thirty days for homeowner's policies.

Reason for Nonrenewal: Not required.

Proof Required: Proof of mailing.

Other Cancellation/Nonrenewal Provisions

No insurer shall increase premium rates, cancel a policy, or refuse to issue or renew a policy solely on the basis of a policyholder inquiring about making a claim, if the policyholder does not in fact submit a claim.

The cancellation/nonrenewal requirements do not apply to homeowner policies issued under the voluntary Market Assistance program. (Okla. Stat. tit. 36, §3639.2).

Okla. Stat. tit. 36, §4803 allows for cancellation of fire insurance after five days' within notice. Legal advice suggested.

PERSONAL AUTO

Okla. Stat. tit. 36, §940 through §944; Okla. Admin. Code 365:15-1-14

Oklahoma makes no changes from the standard policy so allowable reasons for cancellation are limited to the following:

1. Nonpayment of premium.

2. If the insured's driver's license or that of any driver who lives with insured; or any driver who customarily uses the insured auto has been suspended or revoked during the policy period; or since the last anniversary of the original effective date if the policy period is other than one year.

3. If the policy was obtained through material misrepresentation.

No insurer shall increase premium rates, cancel a policy, or refuse to issue or renew a policy solely on the basis of a policyholder inquiring about making a claim, if the policyholder does not in fact submit a claim.

OKLAHOMA

PERSONAL UMBRELLA

Okla. Admin. Code 365:15-1-14

Cancellation during the Underwriting Period

Length of Underwriting Period: Forty-five days.

Notice Requirements: Ten days.

Reason for Cancellation: Not required.

Proof Required: Proof of mailing.

Cancellation after the Underwriting Period

Length of Notice: Ten days

Reason for Cancellation: Not required.

Proof Required: Proof of mailing.

Nonrenewal

Length of Notice: Twenty days for any reason other than non-renewal of personal residential insurance coverage which is thirty days.

Reason for Nonrenewal: Reason for notice is not required.

Proof Required: Proof of mailing.

FRAUD

Okla. Stat. tit. 15, §58; tit. 36, §363

Definition

The Oklahoma Statutes do not explicitly define insurance fraud. However, the statutes define fraud generally as the following acts when done with the intent to deceive or induce another to enter a contract:

1. The suggestion, as a fact, of that which is not true, by one who does not believe it to be true.

2. The positive assertion in a manner not warranted by the information of the person making it, of that which is not true, though he believe it to be true.

OKLAHOMA

3. The suppression of that which is true, by one having knowledge or belief of the fact.

4. A promise made without any intention of performing it.

5. Any other act fitted to deceive.

Reporting

Any insurer who has reason to believe that a person or entity has engaged in or is engaging in an act or practice that violates any statute or administrative rule of this state related to insurance fraud shall immediately notify the Anti-Fraud Unit of the Insurance Department.

In the absence of fraud, bad faith, reckless disregard for the truth, or actual malice, no person, insurer, or agent of an insurer shall be liable for damages in a civil action or subject to criminal prosecution for supplying information about suspected insurance fraud to the Anti-Fraud Division of the Insurance Department or any other agency involved in the investigation or prosecution of suspected insurance fraud. The immunity provided in this subsection shall not extend to any person, insurer, or agent of an insurer for communications or publications about suspected insurance fraud to any other person or entity.

Application Fraud Statement
Okla. Stat. tit. 36, §3613.1

Every insurance policy or application and every insurance claim form shall contain a statement that clearly indicates in substance the following:

> "**WARNING:** Any person who knowingly, and with intent to injure, defraud or deceive any insurer, makes any claim for the proceeds of an insurance policy containing any false, incomplete or misleading information is guilty of a felony."

FAIR CLAIMS PROCESSING
Okla. Stat. tit. 36, §§1250.3 through 1250.5

The following practices constitute unfair claims settlement practices and are prohibited under Oklahoma law:

1. Not fully disclosing to first-party claimants, benefits, coverages, or other provisions of any insurance policy or insurance contract when the benefits, coverages or other provisions are pertinent to a claim.

2. Knowingly misrepresenting to claimants pertinent facts or policy provisions relating to coverages at issue.

OKLAHOMA

3. Not adopting and implementing reasonable standards for prompt investigations of claims arising under pertinent insurance policies or contracts.

4. Not making a good faith attempt to promptly, fairly and equitably settle claims submitted in which liability has become reasonably clear.

5. Not complying with Okla. Stat. tit. 36, §1219.

6. Denying a claim for failure to exhibit the property without proof of demand and unfounded refusal by a claimant to do so.

7. Except where a time limit is specified in the policy, making statements, written or otherwise, which require a claimant to give written notice of loss or proof of loss within a specified time limit and which seek to relieve the company of its obligations if the time limit is not complied with unless the failure to comply with the time limit prejudices the rights of an insurer.

8. Requesting a claimant to sign a release that extends beyond the subject matter that gave rise to the claim payment.

9. Issuing checks or drafts in partial settlement of a loss or claim under a specified coverage which contain language releasing an insurer or its insured from its total liability.

10. Denying payment to a claimant on the grounds that services, procedures, or supplies provided by a treating physician or a hospital were not medically necessary unless the health insurer or administrator, as defined in Okla. Stat. tit. 36, §1442, first obtains an opinion from any provider of health care licensed by law and preceded by a medical examination or claim review, to the effect that the services, procedures or supplies for which payment is being denied were not medically necessary. See Okla. Stat. tit. 36, §1250.5 for specifics regarding the reporting of such an opinion to a claimant.

11. Compensating a reviewing physician, as defined in paragraph 10 of this subsection, on the basis of a percentage of the amount by which a claim is reduced for payment.

12. Violating the provisions of the Health Care Fraud Prevention Act (Okla. Stat. tit. 36, §1219.1 *et seq.*).

13. Compelling, without just cause, policyholders to institute suits to recover amounts due under its insurance policies or insurance contracts by offering substantially less than the amounts ultimately recovered in suits brought by them, when the policyholders have made claims for amounts reasonably similar to the amounts ultimately recovered.

OKLAHOMA

14. An insurer failing to maintain a complete record of all complaints received during the preceding three years or since the date of its last financial examination conducted or accepted by the commissioner, whichever time is longer.

15. Requesting a refund of all or a portion of a payment of a claim made to a claimant or health care provider more than twenty-four months after the payment is made, unless:

    a. The payment was made because of fraud committed by the claimant or health care provider.
    b. The claimant or health care provider has otherwise agreed to make a refund to the insurer for overpayment of a claim.

16. Failing to pay, or requesting a refund of a payment, for health care services covered under the policy of a health benefit plan, or its agent, has provided a preauthorization or precertification and verification of eligibility for those health care services. This paragraph shall not apply if:

    a. The claim or payment was made because of fraud committed by the claimant or health care provider.
    b. The subscriber had a preexisting exclusion under the policy related to the service provided.
    c. The subscriber or employer failed to pay the applicable premium and all grace periods and extensions of coverage have expired.

17. Denying or refusing to accept an application for life insurance, or refusing to renew, cancel, restrict or otherwise terminate a policy of life insurance, or charge a different rate based upon the lawful travel destination of an applicant or insured.

OREGON

For details on cancellation procedures for the standard policy, refer to the Standard Policy section.

COMMERCIAL LINES
AGRICULTURAL CAPITAL ASSETS; BOP; CAPITAL ASSETS; C. AUTO; CRIME; CGL (CGL, LIQUOR, PRDS/COMP OPS); CIM; C. PROP.; E-COMMERCE; EQUIPMENT BREAKDOWN; FARM; & PO. LIAB.

Oregon Revised Statutes §§742.224, 742.562, 742.564, 742.566 742.690, 742.702, 742.706, 742.708 and ISO endorsement (IL 02 79)

Cancellation during the Underwriting Period

Length of Underwriting Period: Sixty days.

Length of Notice: Ten working days; for auto. ten days for nonpayment of premium, thirty days any other allowable reason.

Reason for Cancellation: Required on the notice.

Proof Required: Post Office certificate of mailing will be conclusive proof that the first-named insured received the notice on the third calendar day after the date of the certificate of mailing.

Cancellation after the Underwriting Period

The policy may be cancelled **only** for the following reasons:

1. Nonpayment.

2. Fraud or material misrepresentation made in obtaining the policy, in continuing the policy, or in presenting a claim under the policy.

3. Substantial increase in risk. This includes an increase in exposure due to regulation, legislation, or court decision.

4. Failure to comply with reasonable loss control recommendations.

5. Insured commits a substantial breach of contractual duties, conditions, or warranties.

OREGON

6. Determination by the director that the continuation of the policy would place the insurer in violation of any state's insurance laws or would jeopardize the insurer's solvency.

7. Loss of or decrease in the insurer's reinsurance.

8. Any other reason, as approved by the director with regard to the following:

   a. A package policy that includes commercial property and commercial liability insurance.
   b. Commercial Automobile Coverage Part.
   c. Commercial General Liability Coverage Part.
   d. Commercial Property Coverage Part – Legal Liability Coverage Form.
   e. Commercial Property Coverage Part – Mortgageholders Errors and Omissions Coverage Form.
   f. Employment-Related Practices Liability Coverage Part.
   g. Farm Coverage Part – Farm Liability Coverage Form.
   h. Liquor Liability Coverage Part.
   i. Products/Completed Operations Liability Coverage Part.
   j. Medical Professional Liability Coverage Part.

Length of Notice: Other than property only policies (includes mono-line inland marine), generally Oregon Statute requires ten working days' notice. ISO endorsement (IL 02 79) is more restrictive. It requires ten days for nonpayment; thirty days for all other allowable reasons for policies not listed under section 8 above. Property only (includes mono-line marine) Length of notice: thirty days (see OAR 836-085-0010).

Reason for Cancellation: Required on the notice.

Proof Required: Post Office certificate of mailing will be conclusive proof that the first-named insured received the notice on the third calendar day after the date of the certificate of mailing.

Nonrenewal

Length of Notice: Forty-five days. Automobile only policies length of notice thirty days.

Reason for Nonrenewal: Required on the notice.

Proof Required: Post Office certificate of mailing will be conclusive proof that the first-named insured received the notice on the third calendar day after the date of the certificate of mailing.

OREGON

Named Driver Exclusion

A motor vehicle liability insurance policy may exclude from BI and PD coverage, or motor vehicle damage coverage, by naming any person other than the named insured because of the excluded driver's driving record or any other criteria that the director establishes by rule. When an insurer excludes a person, the insurer shall obtain a statement or endorsement, signed by each of the named insureds that the policy will not provide any coverage required by Oregon law when the motor vehicle is driven by any named excluded person. Uninsured Motorist (UM), Underinsured Motorist (UIM), and Automobile Personal Injury Protection (APIP) coverage may not be excluded. (O.R.S. §§742.450, and OAR 836-058-0010).

Other Cancellation/Nonrenewal Provisions

For OCP policies the insurer must notify the named insured and the contractor listed on the declarations.

For Railroad Protective policies, all notices must be sent to the named insured and the contractor and any involved governmental authority designated in the declarations.

A forty-five day written notice must be provided if the insurer plans to renew the policy on less favorable terms or with higher rates.

Oregon statutes specify that cancellation is not effective until after the insured actually receives the notice of cancellation or nonrenewal. If the insurer does not provide such notice, the insured may cancel the renewal policy within forty-five days after receipt. Earned premium for the period of time the renewal policy was in force shall be calculated pro rata at the lower of the current or previous year's rate. If the insured accepts the renewal, any premium increase or changes in terms shall be effective immediately following the prior policy's expiration date. This does not apply to program changes filed with the director.

An insurer offering commercial liability insurance may not cancel or refuse to issue or renew a policy solely on the basis that the policyholder holds a public office or include a provision in the insurance contract limiting coverage under the contract solely on the basis that the policyholder holds a public office.

If a commercial liability policy is issued for a term longer than one year, and a premium is guaranteed for additional consideration, the insurer may not refuse to renew the policy or increase the premium for the term of that policy.

Electronic Notifications: Oregon law allows electronic notifications when all parties agree. However, when special mailing requirements are specified in statute, the insurer must also comply with those provisions. (O.R.S. §84.013).

OREGON

COMMERCIAL GENERAL LIABILITY

(Railroad Protective)

Oregon Revised Statutes §§742.702, 742.706, and 742.710

Cancellation during the Underwriting Period

Length of Underwriting Period: Sixty days.

Length of Notice: Ten working days for any reason.

Reason for Cancellation: Required on the notice.

Proof Required: Post Office certificate of mailing will be conclusive proof that the first-named insured received the notice on the third calendar day after the date of the certificate of mailing. ISO amendatory endorsement (CG 01 90) applies the same standard to all parties.

Cancellation after the Underwriting Period

The policy may be cancelled **only** for the following reasons:

1. Nonpayment.

2. Fraud or material misrepresentation in obtaining the policy, in continuing the policy, or in presenting a claim under the policy.

3. Substantial increase in risk. This includes an increase in exposure due to regulation, legislation, or court decision.

4. Insured commits a substantial breach of contractual duties, conditions, or warranties.

5. Determination by the director that the continuation of the policy would place the insurer in violation of any of the state's insurance laws or would jeopardize the insurer's solvency.

6. Loss of or decrease in the insurer's reinsurance.

7. Failure to comply with reasonable loss control recommendations.

8. Any other reason, as approved by the director.

OREGON

Length of Notice: Ten working days.

Reason for Cancellation: Required on the notice.

Proof Required: Post Office certificate of mailing will be conclusive proof that the first-named insured received the notice on the third calendar day after the date of the certificate of mailing. ISO amendatory endorsement (CG 01 90) applies the same standard to all parties.

Nonrenewal

Length of Notice: Forty-five days.

Reason for Nonrenewal: Required on the notice.

Proof Required: Post Office certificate of mailing will be conclusive proof that the first-named insured received the notice on the third calendar day after the date of the certificate of mailing.

Other Cancellation/Nonrenewal Provisions

All notices must be sent to the named insured and the contractor and any involved governmental authority designated in the declarations.

Cancellation will not be effective until at least ten workings days after the insured, the contractor, and any involved governmental authority receive the insurer's notice.

A forty-five day written notice must be provided if the insurer plans to renew the policy on less favorable terms or with higher rates.

Electronic Notifications: Oregon law allows electronic notifications when all parties agree. However, when special mailing requirements are specified in statute, the insurer must also comply with those provisions. (O.R.S. §84.013).

COMMERCIAL GENERAL LIABILITY

(Underground Storage Tanks)

Oregon Revised Statutes §§742.702, 742.706, and 742.710

Cancellation during the Underwriting Period

Length of Underwriting Period: Sixty days.

Length of Notice: Oregon Statute requires ten working days notice for any reason. ISO amendment endorsement (CG 30 44) requires: ten working days for nonpayment; thirty days for misrepresentation; sixty days for all other reasons.

OREGON

Reason for Cancellation: Required on the notice.

Proof Required: ISO amendment endorsement (CG 30 44) requires certified mail or delivery. Post Office certificate of mailing will be conclusive proof that the first-named insured received the notice on the third calendar day after the date of the certificate of mailing.

Cancellation after the Underwriting Period

The policy may be cancelled **only** for the following reasons:

1. Nonpayment.

2. Fraud or material misrepresentation in obtaining the policy, in continuing the policy, or in presenting a claim under the policy.

3. Substantial increase in risk. This includes an increase in exposure due to regulation, legislation, or court decision.

4. Insured commits a substantial breach of contractual duties, conditions, or warranties.

5. Determination by the director that the continuation of the policy would place the insurer in violation of any state's insurance laws or would jeopardize the insurer's solvency.

6. Loss of or decrease in the insurer's reinsurance.

7. Failure to comply with reasonable loss-control recommendations.

8. Any other reason, as approved by the commissioner.

Length of Notice: Oregon statute requires ten working days notice for any reason. ISO amendment endorsement (CG 30 44) requires: ten working days for nonpayment; thirty days for misrepresentation; sixty days for all other reasons.

Reason for Cancellation: Required on the notice.

Proof Required: ISO amendment endorsement (CG 30 44) requires certified mail or delivery. Oregon statute states: Post Office certificate of mailing will be conclusive proof that the first-named insured received the notice on the third calendar day after the date of the certificate of mailing.

OREGON

Nonrenewal

Length of Notice: Sixty days. The Oregon statute requires only a forty-five-day notice, but if an insurer has adopted the ISO amendatory endorsement (CG 30 44), it must give a sixty-day notice of nonrenewal.

Reason for Nonrenewal: Required on the notice.

Proof Required: Post Office certificate of mailing will be conclusive proof that the first-named insured received the notice on the third calendar day after the date of the certificate of mailing.

Other Cancellation/Nonrenewal Provisions

A forty-five-day written notice must be provided if the insurer plans to renew the policy on less favorable terms or with higher rates.

Electronic Notifications: Oregon law allows electronic notifications when all parties agree. However, when special mailing requirements are specified in statute, the insurer must also comply with those provisions. (O.R.S. §84.013).

COMMERCIAL UMBRELLA

Oregon Revised Statutes §§742.690 through 742.710

There are no changes from the standard policy in Oregon. However, an insurer offering commercial liability insurance may not cancel or refuse to issue or renew a policy solely on the basis that the policyholder holds a public office or include a provision in the insurance contract limiting coverage under the contract solely on the basis that the policyholder holds a public office.

WORKERS COMPENSATION

Oregon Revised Statutes §§656.423 and 656.427

Oregon requires a thirty-day written notice of cancellation and the notice must also be sent to the Department of Consumer and Business Services. If the insurer is cancelling all employers in the same premium category, a ninety day notice is required. If the cancellation of a workers' compensation insurance policy is based on nonpayment of premium, the cancellation is effective not sooner than ten days after the date the notice is mailed to the employer.

The Director of the Department of Consumer and Business Services must receive notice within ten days after the effective date of cancellation provided in the notice given to the employer.

OREGON

Electronic Notifications: Oregon law allows electronic notifications when all parties agree. However, when special mailing requirements are specified in statute, the insurer must also comply with those provisions. (O.R.S. §84.013).

FINANCED PREMIUMS

Oregon Revised Statutes §746.505

If the premium finance agreement contains a power of attorney enabling the premium finance company to cancel any insurance policy listed in the agreement, the finance company may request, in the name of the insured, that the insurer cancel the policy due to nonpayment. The finance company must first give the insured ten days' written notice to pay. A copy of the ten-day written notice must also be sent to the insurance producer. If the insured fails to make payment within that ten-day period, then the finance company mails the notice of cancellation to the insurer, insured, and insurance producer. The insurer shall give the prescribed notice on behalf of itself or the insured to any governmental agency, mortgagee, or other third party on or before the second business day after the day it receives the notice of cancellation from the premium finance company and shall determine the effective date of cancellation taking into consideration the number of days' notice required to complete the cancellation. Return of the policy by the insured is not required.

SURPLUS LINES

Oregon Revised Statutes §742.001

The Oregon cancellation and nonrenewal statutes do not apply to surplus lines.

PERSONAL LINES

DWELLING FIRE

Oregon Revised Statutes §§742.224, 742.226, 742.260, 742.280, 742.690, and 746.663

Cancellation during the Underwriting Period

Length of Underwriting Period: Sixty days.

Length of Notice: Ten days for nonpayment; thirty days for any other reason.

Reason for Cancellation: Required on the notice.

Proof Required: Certificate of mailing will be conclusive proof that the first named insured received the notice on the third calendar day after the date of the certificate of mailing.

OREGON

Cancellation after the Underwriting Period

The policy may be cancelled **only** for the following reasons:

1. Nonpayment.

2. Material misrepresentation of fact which if known, would have caused the insurer to not issue the policy.

3. Substantial change in risk.

Length of Notice: Ten days for nonpayment; Oregon statutes allow insurers to cancel in thirty days for any reason. ISO endorsement (DL 01 36) limits to thirty days for the above reasons.

Reason for Cancellation: Required on the notice.

Proof Required: Certificate of mailing will be conclusive proof that the first named insured received the notice on the third calendar day after the date of the certificate of mailing.

Nonrenewal

A thirty-day advance notice of nonrenewal is required.

Reason for Nonrenewal: Required on the notice.

Proof Required: Certificate of mailing will be conclusive proof that the first-named insured received the notice on the third calendar day after the date of the certificate of mailing.

Other Cancellation/Nonrenewal Provisions

An insurer may not cancel or nonrenew solely because a home daycare business is operated on the residence premises.

An insurer may not cancel or nonrenew based on a consumer's credit history or insurance score.

An insurer may not cancel or nonrenew solely because the policy holder holds public office.

Mortgagees must receive at least ten days' written notice prior to any termination.

OREGON

Electronic Notifications: Oregon law allows electronic notifications when all parties agree. However, when special mailing requirements are specified in statute, the insurer must also comply with those provisions. (O.R.S. §84.013).

PERSONAL LINES

HOMEOWNERS

Oregon Revised Statutes §§742.224; 742.226; 742.260; 742.690; 746.663; 746.687

Cancellation during the Underwriting Period

Length of Underwriting Period: Sixty days.

Length of Notice: Ten days for nonpayment; thirty days for any other reason.

Reason for Cancellation: Required on the notice.

Proof Required: Certificate of mailing or delivery.

Cancellation after the Underwriting Period

The policy may be cancelled **only** for the following reasons:

1. Nonpayment.

2. Fraud or material misrepresentation affecting the policy or in the presentation of a claim under the policy.

3. Substantial increase in the risk of loss. Can include increase in exposure due to rules, legislation or court decisions.

4. Violation of any of the terms and conditions of the policy.

5. Determination by the Director of the Department of Consumer and Business Services that the continuation of a line of insurance or class of business to which the policy belongs will jeopardize an insurer's solvency or place the insurer in violation of the insurance laws of Oregon or any other state, whether because of a loss or decrease in reinsurance covering the risk or other reason determined by the director.

Length of Notice: Ten days for nonpayment, fraud or material misrepresentation; thirty days for reasons 3-5. ISO amendatory endorsement (HO 01 36) only has reasons 1-3.

OREGON

Reason for Cancellation: Required on the notice.

Proof Required: Certificate of mailing will be conclusive proof that the first-named insured received the notice on the third calendar day after the date of the certificate of mailing.

Nonrenewal

Length of Notice: Thirty days.

Reason for Nonrenewal: Required on the notice.

Proof Required: Certificate of mailing.

Other Cancellation/Nonrenewal Provisions

An insurer may not cancel or nonrenew solely because a home daycare business is operated on the residence premises.

An insurer may not cancel or nonrenew based on a consumer's credit history or insurance score.

An insurer may not cancel or nonrenew solely because the policy holder holds public office.

Mortgagees must receive at least ten days' written notice prior to any termination.

Electronic Notifications: Oregon law allows electronic notifications when all parties agree. However, when special mailing requirements are specified in statute, the insurer must also comply with those provisions. (O.R.S. §84.013).

PERSONAL AUTO

Oregon Revised Statutes §§742.450, 742.560, 742.562, 742.564 742.566 and 742.570

Cancellation during the Underwriting Period

Length of Underwriting Period: Sixty days.

Length of Notice: Ten days for nonpayment; thirty days for all other allowable reasons.

Reason for Cancellation: Required on the notice. Although the ISO amendatory endorsement (PP 01 94) is silent on this matter, the Oregon code requires the reason to be shown.

Proof Required: Certificate of mailing.

OREGON

Cancellation after the Underwriting Period

The policy may be cancelled **only** for the following reasons:

1. Nonpayment.

2. Suspension or revocation of the driver's license of:

    a. The named insured.
    b. Any driver who lives with the named insured or who customarily uses the insured auto.

    The suspension or revocation must occur during the policy period or during the 180 days immediately prior to the effective date.

    Does not apply to any license suspended under Oregon Statutes §809.280 or if the suspension was based on a non-driving offense.

3. Fraud or material misrepresentation on the application or in making a claim.

4. Violation of any of the terms and conditions of the policy.

Length of Notice: Ten days for nonpayment; thirty days for all other allowable reasons.

Reason for Cancellation: Required on the notice. Even though the ISO amendatory endorsement (PP 01 94) is silent on this matter, the Oregon code requires the reason for cancellation.

Proof Required: Certificate of mailing.

Nonrenewal

Length of Notice: Thirty days.

Reason for Nonrenewal: Required on the notice. Even though the ISO amendatory endorsement (PP 01 94) is silent on this matter, the Oregon code requires the reason to be shown.

Proof Required: Certificate of mailing.

Named Driver Exclusion

A motor vehicle liability insurance policy may exclude from BI, PD, or automobile physical damage coverage, by name any person other than the named insured because of the excluded

OREGON

driver's driving record or any other criteria that the director establishes by rule. When an insurer excludes a person, the insurer shall obtain a statement or endorsement, signed by each of the named insureds that the policy will not provide any coverage required by Oregon law when the motor vehicle is driven by any named excluded person. Uninsured motorist (UM), underinsured motorist (UIM), and automobile personal injury protection (APIP) coverage may not be excluded (O.R.S. §742.450 and OAR 836-058-0010).

Other Cancellation/Nonrenewal Provisions

If the policy is written for a term of less than six months, the insurer may nonrenew every six months, beginning six months after the original effective date.

If the policy is written for a term of one year or longer, the insurer may nonrenew only at each anniversary of the original effective date.

An insurer may not nonrenew a policy for the reason that the driving privileges of the named insured or any operator either resident in the same household or who customarily operates an automobile insured under the policy were suspended based on a nondriving offense.

These provisions do not apply to policies issued under an automobile assigned risk plan.

Notices of termination, other than for nonpayment must advise the insured of possible eligibility for coverage under an automobile assigned risk plan.

An insurer offering casualty insurance may not cancel or refuse to issue or renew a policy solely on the basis that the policyholder holds a public office or include a provision in the insurance contract limiting coverage under the contract solely on the basis that the policyholder holds a public office.

Electronic Notifications: Oregon law allows electronic notifications when all parties agree. However, when special mailing requirements are specified in statute, the insurer must also comply with those provisions. (O.R.S. §84.013).

PERSONAL UMBRELLA

Oregon Revised Statute §742.690, 742.708

Cancellation during the Underwriting Period

Length of Underwriting Period: Sixty days.

Notice Requirements: Ten days.

OREGON

Reason for Cancellation: Required on the notice.

Proof Required: Certificate of mailing.

Cancellation after the Underwriting Period

Length of Notice: Ten day notice for nonpayment; thirty day notice for any other reason.

Reason for Cancellation: Required on the notice.

Proof Required: Certificate of mailing.

Nonrenewal

Length of Notice: Thirty days.

Reason for Nonrenewal: Required on the notice.

Proof Required: Certificate of mailing.

Other Cancellation/Nonrenewal Provisions

An insurer offering casualty insurance may not cancel or refuse to issue or renew a policy solely on the basis that the policyholder holds a public office or include a provision in the insurance contract limiting coverage under the contract solely on the basis that the policyholder holds a public office.

Electronic Notifications: Oregon law allows electronic notifications when all parties agree. However, when special mailing requirements are specified in statute, the insurer must also comply with those provisions. (O.R.S. §84.013).

FRAUD

Oregon Revised Statutes §§731.592, 731.594, and Oregon Insurance Bulletin INS 2010-3

Definition

The Oregon Revised Statutes do not currently define insurance fraud but instead broadly refer to criminal conduct involving insurance.

Reporting

An insurer must cooperate with any law enforcement agency or other state or federal agency that is investigating or prosecuting suspected criminal conduct involving insurance. The insurer shall provide any information requested by the agency unless the information

OREGON

is subject to a legal privilege that would prohibit disclosure. Furthermore, if an insurer has reason to believe that criminal conduct involving insurance has been, is being, or is about to be committed, the insurer must notify the appropriate agency, but again, the insurer is not required to notify the agency if the information or any part of the information upon which the belief is based is protected from disclosure by legal privilege.

A person who has reason to believe criminal conduct involving insurance has been, is being or is about to be committed, or who collects, reviews or analyzes information concerning suspected criminal conduct involving insurance, may furnish any unprivileged information in the person's possession concerning the suspected criminal conduct to an insurer who requests the information for the purpose of detecting, prosecuting or preventing criminal conduct involving insurance. Failure to report may result in ineligibility for any compensation to which the insurer or agency might otherwise be entitled.

Unless an individual or entity acted with actual malice, a reporting individual or entity that discloses or provides information about criminal conduct involving insurance will be immune from any civil liability that might otherwise be incurred or imposed with respect to the disclosure or provision of the information. A person has the same immunity with respect to participating in any judicial proceeding resulting from the disclosure or provision of information.

Application Fraud Statement

Oregon Revised Statutes §744.374, Oregon Insurance Bulletin INS 2010-3

Life settlements contracts and purchase agreement forms and applications for life settlements, regardless of the form of transmission, must contain the following statement or a substantially similar statement: "Any person who knowingly presents false information in this application is guilty of a crime and may be subject to fines and confinement in prison." All other insurance products are subject to the bulletin.

FAIR CLAIMS PROCESSING

Oregon Revised Statutes §§746.230 and 746.240

Prohibited Practices

The following practices are prohibited under Oregon law as unfair claims settlement practices:

1. Misrepresenting facts or policy provisions in settling claims.

2. Failing to acknowledge and act promptly upon communications relating to claims.

3. Failing to adopt and implement reasonable standards for promptly investigating claims.

OREGON

4. Refusing to pay claims without conducting a reasonable investigation based on all available information.

5. Failing to affirm or deny coverage of claims within a reasonable time after completed proof of loss statements have been submitted.

6. Not making a good-faith attempt to promptly and equitably settle claims in which liability has become reasonably clear.

7. Compelling claimants to litigate to recover amounts due by offering substantially less than amounts ultimately recovered in actions brought by such claimants.

8. Attempting to settle claims for less than the amount to which a reasonable person would believe a reasonable person was entitled after referring to written or printed advertising material accompanying or made part of an application.

9. Attempting to settle claims based on an application that has been altered without notice to or consent of the applicant.

10. Failing, after payment of a claim, to inform insureds or beneficiaries, upon request by them, of the coverage under which payment has been made.

11. Delaying investigation or payment of claims by requiring a claimant or the physician of the claimant to submit a preliminary claim report and then requiring subsequent submission of loss forms when both require essentially the same information.

12. Failing to promptly settle claims under one coverage of a policy where liability has become reasonably clear in order to influence settlements under other coverages of the policy.

13. Failing to promptly provide the proper explanation of the basis relied on in the insurance policy in relation to the facts or applicable law for the denial of a claim.

Under Oregon law, no insurer shall refuse, without just cause, to pay or settle claims arising under coverages provided by its policies with such frequency as to indicate a general business practice in this state, which general business practice is evidenced by:

1. A substantial increase in the number of complaints against the insurer received by the Department of Consumer and Business Services.

OREGON

2. A substantial increase in the number of lawsuits filed against the insurer or its insureds by claimants.

3. Any other relevant evidence.

Oregon law also prohibits any trade practice that, although not expressly defined and prohibited in the Insurance Code, is found by the Director of the Department of Consumer and Business Services to be an unfair or deceptive act or practice in the transaction of insurance that is injurious to the insurance buying public.

PENNSYLVANIA

For details on cancellation procedures for the standard policy, refer to the Standard Policy section.

COMMERCIAL LINES

BOP; CAPITAL ASSETS; C. AUTO; CRIME; CGL (other than UNDERGROUND STORAGE TANKS); C. PROP.; CIM; C.UMB; EQUIPMENT BREAKDOWN; FARM

Pennsylvania Statutes, tit. 40, §§3401, 3402, 3403, 3405, 3407; tit. 75, §1718

Cancellation during the Underwriting Period

Length of Underwriting Period: Sixty days.

Length of Notice: For policies in effect less than sixty days: thirty days provided the notice was issued on or before the sixtieth day.

Reason for Cancellation: Required on the notice.

Proof Required: Proof of mailing via first class or registered mail; proof of delivery.

Cancellation after the Underwriting Period

The policy may be cancelled **only** for the following reasons:

1. Material misrepresentation that affects the insurability of the risk.

2. Nonpayment.

3. The policy was obtained through fraudulent statements, omissions, or concealment of fact.

4. Substantial change in the risk material to insurability that has become known during the policy period.

5. Loss of or a substantial decrease in reinsurance on the risk as certified to the insurance commissioner.

6. Material failure of the named insured to comply with policy terms, conditions, or duties.

7. The insured has requested cancellation.

8. Any other reason approved by the insurance commissioner.

PENNSYLVANIA

Length of Notice: Fifteen days for nonpayment and material misrepresentation; sixty days for all other reasons.

Reason for Cancellation: Required on the notice.

Proof Required: Proof of mailing via first class or registered mail; proof of delivery.

Nonrenewal

Length of Notice: Sixty days not including the day of mailing.

Reason for Nonrenewal: Required on the notice.

Proof Required: Proof of mailing via first class or registered mail; proof of delivery.

Named Driver Exclusion

An insurer or the first named insured may exclude any person or his personal representative from benefits under a policy when the first named insured has requested that the person be excluded from coverage while operating a motor vehicle. However, this only applies if the excluded person is insured on another policy of motor vehicle liability insurance.

Other Cancellation/Nonrenewal Provisions

The policy may be cancelled from its inception if the insurer discovers that "the policy was obtained through fraudulent statements, omissions or concealment of facts material to the acceptance of the risk or to the hazard assumed by [the insurer]" (reason 3 under the preceding section).

On OCP policies all notices must also be sent to the listed contractor.

On railroad protective policies all notices must be sent to the listed contractor and any involved governmental authority.

A thirty-day written notice is required if the insurer intends to renew with an increased premium.

A midterm cancellation or nonrenewal notice shall state that, at the insured's request, the insurer shall provide loss information to the insured for at least three years or the period of time during which the insurer has provided coverage to the insured, whichever is less. The insured's written request must be made within ten days of the insured's receipt of the midterm cancellation or nonrenewal notice. The insurer has thirty days from the date of receipt of the written request to respond.

PENNSYLVANIA

Insurers must provide a sixty-day period, after cancellation or nonrenewal of a claims-made policy is effective, during which time the insured may purchase an extended reporting coverage endorsement, also referred to as tail coverage.

Insurers can cancel from the inception date if both:

1. Information is discovered that could not have been discovered within the first sixty days of the policy.

2. Had the information been known to the insurer, the insurer would not have written the policy.

COMMERCIAL GENERAL LIABILITY

(Underground Storage Tanks)

Pennsylvania Statutes, tit. 40, §§3402, 3403, 3405, and 3407

Cancellation during the Underwriting Period

Length of Underwriting Period: Sixty days.

Length of Notice: Thirty days for nonpayment or material misrepresentation; sixty days for any other reason. Note: the Pennsylvania code makes no mention of the sixty-day requirement. If an insurer has adopted the ISO amendatory endorsement (CG 30 21), it must give a sixty-day notice for cancellation other than nonpayment and material misrepresentation.

Reason for Cancellation: Required on the notice.

Proof Required: Proof of mailing via first class or registered mail; proof of delivery.

Cancellation after the Underwriting Period

The policy may be cancelled **only** for the following reasons:

1. Material misrepresentation which affects the insurability of the risk.

2. Nonpayment.

3. The policy was obtained through fraudulent statements, omissions, or concealment of fact.

4. Substantial change in the risk material to insurability has become known during the policy period.

PENNSYLVANIA

5. Loss of or substantial decrease in reinsurance on the risk as certified to the insurance commissioner.

6. Material failure of the named insured to comply with policy terms, conditions, or duties.

7. The insured has requested cancellation.

8. Any other reason approved by the insurance commissioner.

ISO does not acknowledge reason seven.

Length of Notice: Fifteen days for nonpayment or material misrepresentation; sixty days for any other allowable reasons.

Reason for Cancellation: Required on the notice.

Proof Required: Proof of mailing via first class or registered mail; proof of delivery.

Nonrenewal

Length of Notice: Sixty days.

Reason for Nonrenewal: Required on the notice.

Proof Required: Proof of mailing via first class or registered mail; proof of delivery.

Other Cancellation/Nonrenewal Provisions

The policy may be cancelled from its inception if the insurer discovers that "the policy was obtained through fraudulent statements, omissions or concealment of facts material to the acceptance of the risk or to the hazard assumed by [the insurer]."

A thirty-day written notice is required if the insurer intends to renew with an increased premium.

A midterm cancellation or nonrenewal notice shall state that, at the insured's request, the insurer shall provide loss information to the insured for at least three years or the period of time during which the insurer has provided coverage to the insured, whichever is less.

Insurers must provide a sixty-day period, after cancellation or nonrenewal of a claims-made policy is effective, during which time the insured may purchase an extended reporting coverage endorsement, also referred to as tail coverage.

PENNSYLVANIA

Insurers can cancel from the inception date if both:

1. Information is discovered that could not have been discovered within the first sixty days of the policy.

2. Had the information been known to the insurer, the insurer would not have written the policy.

PROFESSIONAL LIABILITY

Applicable to the following coverage parts (for insureds who are not physicians): allied health care provider; blood banks; diagnostic testing laboratories; optometrists; physicians, surgeons and dentists; and veterinarians.

Pennsylvania Statutes, tit. 40 §1303.747, 3402, 3405

Cancellation during the Underwriting Period

Length of Underwriting Period: Sixty days.

Length of Notice: Thirty days.

Reason for Cancellation: Required on the notice.

Proof Required: Registered or first class mail.

Cancellation after the Underwriting Period

The policy may be cancelled **only** for the following reasons:

1. Material misrepresentation which affects the insurability of the risk.

2. Nonpayment.

3. The policy was obtained through fraudulent statements, omissions, or concealment of fact.

4. Substantial change in the risk, material to insurability becomes known during the policy period.

5. Loss or substantial reduction of reinsurance on the risk as certified to the insurance commissioner.

PENNSYLVANIA

6. Material failure of the named insured to comply with policy terms, conditions, or duties.

7. The insured has requested cancellation.

8. Any other reason approved by the insurance commissioner.

Length of Notice: Fifteen days for nonpayment and material misrepresentation; sixty days for all other reasons.

Reason for Cancellation: Required on the notice.

Proof Required: Proof of mailing via first class or registered mail; proof of delivery.

Nonrenewal

Length of Notice: Sixty days.

Reason for Nonrenewal: Required on the notice.

Proof Required: Registered or first class mail. Proof of mailing will be sufficient proof of notice.

Other Cancellation/Nonrenewal Provisions

The policy may be cancelled from its inception if the insurer discovers that "the policy was obtained through fraudulent statements, omissions or concealment of facts material to the acceptance of the risk or to the hazard assumed by [the insurer]."

A thirty-day written notice is required if the insurer intends to renew with an increased premium.

Insurers can cancel from the inception date if both:

1. Information is discovered that could not have been discovered within the first sixty days of the policy.

2. Had the information been known to the insurer, the insurer would not have written the policy.

PENNSYLVANIA

PROFESSIONAL LIABILITY

(Applicable to the following coverage parts for insureds who are allied health care provider; hospitals; and physicians, surgeons and dentists.)

Pennsylvania Statutes, tit. 40 § 1303.747, 3405

Cancellation during the Underwriting Period

Length of Underwriting Period: Sixty days.

Length of Notice: Thirty days.

Reason for Cancellation: Required on the notice.

Proof Required: Registered or first class mail. Proof of mailing will be sufficient proof of notice.

Cancellation after the Underwriting Period

The policy may be cancelled **only** for:

1. Nonpayment.

2. The named insured's health care license has been suspended or revoked.

Length of Notice: Fifteen days for nonpayment; sixty days for suspension or revocation of license.

Reason for Cancellation: Required on the notice.

Proof Required: Registered or first class mail. Proof of mailing will be sufficient proof of notice.

Nonrenewal

Length of Notice: Sixty days.

Reason for Nonrenewal: Required on the notice.

Proof Required: Registered or first class mail. Proof of mailing will be sufficient proof of notice.

PENNSYLVANIA

Other Cancellation/Nonrenewal Provisions

The policy may be cancelled from its inception if the insurer discovers that "the policy was obtained through fraudulent statements, omissions or concealment of facts material to the acceptance of the risk or to the hazard assumed by [the insurer]."

A thirty-day written notice is required if the insurer intends to renew with an increased premium.

Insurers can cancel from the inception date if both:

1. Information is discovered that could not have been discovered within the first sixty days of the policy.

2. Had the information been known to the insurer, the insurer would not have written the policy.

WORKERS COMPENSATION

Pennsylvania Statutes, tit. 40 §§813, 3401 and 3404

Pennsylvania allows cancellation **only** for nonpayment of premium.

Nonrenewal

Length of Notice: Sixty days.

Reason for Nonrenewal: Reason for notice is required.

Proof Required: Proof of mailing.

Other Provisions

The insured must be given at least thirty days' advance notification of increase in premium. This requirement is satisfied if the renewal policy is issued at least thirty days prior to its effective date; this provision does not apply to policies rated under a retrospective rating plan.

If the company cancels the policy, unearned premium must be returned to the insured within ten business days. If the insured requests cancellation, unearned premium must be returned to the insured within thirty days after the effective date of cancellation. These provisions do not apply to policies rated under a retrospective rating plan.

PENNSYLVANIA

SURPLUS LINES

Pennsylvania Statutes, tit. 40 §3407

Surplus lines insurers must follow the cancellation and nonrenewal requirements for admitted companies.

FINANCED PREMIUMS

Pennsylvania Statutes, tit. 40 §3310

If the premium finance agreement contains a power of attorney, the finance company may request, in the name of the insured, that the insurer cancel the policy due to nonpayment. The finance company must first give the insured fifteen days to pay. If the insured fails to make payment within that fifteen day period, then the finance company mails the notice of cancellation to the insurer and the insured. The cancellation is processed as of the finance company's original default date. Return of the policy by the insured is not required.

PERSONAL LINES

DWELLING FIRE

(Applicable to one to four family dwellings, not occupied in whole or in part by the named insured.)

Pennsylvania Statutes, tit. 40, §§3402, 3405. See ISO - DP 02 04

Cancellation during the Underwriting Period

Length of Underwriting Period: Sixty days.

Length of Notice: Thirty days for any reason.

Reason for Cancellation: Reason must be on notice and not prohibited by statute.

Proof Required: Proof of mailing.

Cancellation after the Underwriting Period

The policy may be cancelled **only** for the following reasons:

1. Material misrepresentation which affects the insurability of the risk.

2. Nonpayment.

3. The policy was obtained through fraudulent statements, omissions, or concealment of fact.

PENNSYLVANIA

4. Substantial change in the risk, material to insurability becomes known during the policy period.

5. Loss or substantial reduction of reinsurance on the risk as certified to the insurance commissioner.

6. Material failure of the named insured to comply with policy terms, conditions, or duties.

7. The insured has requested cancellation.

8. Any other reason approved by the insurance commissioner.

ISO does not acknowledge reason seven.

Length of Notice: Fifteen days for nonpayment and material misrepresentation; sixty days for all other reasons.

Reason for Cancellation: Must be on the notice.

Proof Required: Proof of mailing.

Nonrenewal

Length of Notice: Sixty days.

Reason for Nonrenewal: Must be on the notice.

Proof Required: Proof of mailing.

Other Cancellation/Nonrenewal Provisions

The policy may be cancelled from its inception if the insurer discovers that "the policy was obtained through fraudulent statements, omissions or concealment of facts material to the acceptance of the risk or to the hazard assumed by [the insurer]" that cannot be discovered during the sixty-day underwriting period.

A thirty-day written notice is required if the insurer intends to renew with an increased premium.

Insurers can cancel from the inception date if both:

1. Information is discovered that could not have been discovered within the first sixty days of the policy.

2. Had the information been known to the insurer, the insurer would not have written the policy.

PENNSYLVANIA

The standard policy listed in 40 P.S. §636 allows for cancellation after five days notice. Variation to the standard policy must be approved by the commissioner. Legal advice suggested.

HOMEOWNERS

Pennsylvania Statutes, tit. 40 §1171.5; 31 PA Code 59.1 through 59.13

Cancellation during the Underwriting Period

Length of Underwriting Period: Sixty days.

Length of Notice: Thirty days.

Reason for Cancellation: Must be on the notice.

Proof Required: Proof of mailing.

Cancellation after the Underwriting Period

The policy may be cancelled **only** for the following reasons:

1. The policy was obtained through material misrepresentation, fraudulent statements, omissions or concealment of fact material to the acceptance of the risk.

2. Substantial change or increase in the risk since the policy was issued.

3. Substantial change in hazard due to willful or negligent acts or omissions by the insured.

4. Nonpayment.

5. Any other reason approved by the insurance commissioner.

Length of Notice: Thirty days.

Reason for Cancellation: Required on the notice.

Nonrenewal

Length of Notice: Thirty days.

Reason for Nonrenewal: Required on the notice.

Proof Required: Proof of mailing.

PENNSYLVANIA

Other Cancellation/Nonrenewal Provisions

The allowable reasons for nonrenewal are the same as those permitted for cancellation.

In the ISO homeowners forms, the cancellation and nonrenewal provisions are incorporated into the forms themselves, and do not appear as amendatory endorsements.

Insurers can cancel from the inception date if both:

1. Information is discovered that could not have been discovered within the first sixty days of the policy.

2. Had the information been known to the insurer, the insurer would not have written the policy.

PERSONAL AUTO

Pennsylvania Statutes, tit. 40, §§991.2002, .2004, and .2006; tit. 75, §1718; 31 PA Code 61.1 through 61.14.

Cancellation during the Underwriting Period

Length of Underwriting Period: Sixty days.

Length of Notice: Sixty days.

Reason for Cancellation: Required on the notice.

Proof Required: Proof of delivery or proof of mailing.

Cancellation after the Underwriting Period

The policy may be cancelled **only** for the following reasons:

1. Nonpayment.

2. Suspension or revocation of the driver's license of the named insured.

    Statutes do not permit cancellation of the policy due to suspension or revocation of another driver's license. Under those circumstances, the other driver may be excluded. This is not mentioned in ISO's amendatory endorsement (PP 01 51), however it does specify that it is subject to any limitations contained in applicable Pennsylvania statutes.

PENNSYLVANIA

The suspension or revocation must occur during the policy period; or since the last anniversary date.

3. Material misrepresentation on the application.

Length of Notice: Fifteen days for nonpayment and license suspension; sixty days for material misrepresentation.

Reason for Cancellation: Required on the notice. Even though the Pennsylvania amendatory endorsement does not mention the notice requirement the reason must be shown.

Proof Required: Proof of delivery or proof of mailing.

Nonrenewal

Length of Notice: Fifteen days for nonpayment and suspension or revocation of the driver's license of the named insured; thirty days in all other cases. The number of days notice in all cases does not include the date of mailing.

Reason for Nonrenewal: Required on the notice. Even though the Pennsylvania amendatory endorsement (PP 01 51) does not mention the notice requirement, the reason must be shown.

Proof Required: Proof of mailing.

Named Driver Exclusion

An insurer or the first named insured may exclude any person or his personal representative from benefits under a policy when the first named insured has requested that the person be excluded from coverage while operating a motor vehicle. However, this only applies if the excluded person is insured on another policy of motor vehicle liability insurance.

Other Cancellation/Nonrenewal Provisions

If the insured fails to pay a renewal premium, the policy automatically terminates.

If the driver's license of a household resident or one who customarily operates the car is under suspension or revocation during the policy period, the driver can be excluded from coverage, but the policy cannot be cancelled. The insured must be advised of his possible eligibility for insurance through the assigned risk plan. The insured must be advised of his right to request in writing, within thirty days of the receipt of notice of cancellation or nonrenewal, that the insurance commissioner reviews the action of the insurer. If coverage

PENNSYLVANIA

is to be terminated because the suspension results from failure to respond to a citation, the coverage cannot terminate if the insured provides proof that the citation has been responded to and all fines and penalties paid.

Insurers can cancel from the inception date if both:

1. Information is discovered that could not have been discovered within the first sixty days of the policy.

2. Had the information been known to the insurer, the insurer would not have written the policy.

PERSONAL UMBRELLA
ISO DL 98 01

Cancellation during the Underwriting Period

Length of Underwriting Period: Sixty days.

Length of Notice: Ten days.

Reason for Cancellation: Required.

Proof Required: Proof of mailing.

Cancellation after the Underwriting Period

Length of Notice: Ten-day notice for nonpayment; thirty-day notice for any other reason.

Reason for Cancellation: Reason for notice required.

Proof Required: Proof of mailing.

Nonrenewal

Length of Notice: Thirty days.

Reason for Nonrenewal: Required.

Proof Required: Proof of mailing.

PENNSYLVANIA

FRAUD

Pennsylvania Consolidated Statutes 18 Pa. Cons. Stat. Ann. §4117, 75 Pa.C.S. §§1795, 1817, 1818

Definition

Pennsylvania's statutes classify the following activities as insurance fraud:

1. Knowingly and with the intent to defraud a state or local government agency filing, presenting, or causing to be filed with or presented to the government agency a document that contains false, incomplete, or misleading information concerning any fact or thing material to the agency's determination in approving or disapproving a motor vehicle insurance rate filing, a motor vehicle insurance transaction or other motor vehicle insurance action which is required or filed in response to an agency's request.

2. Knowingly and with the intent to defraud any insurer or self-insured, presenting or causing to be presented to any insurer or self-insured any statement forming a part of, or in support of, a claim that containing false, incomplete or misleading information concerning any fact or thing material to the claim.

3. Knowingly and with the intent to defraud any insurer or self-insured, assisting, abetting, soliciting or conspiring with another to prepare or make any statement that is intended to be presented to any insurer or self-insured in connection with, or in support of, a claim that contains any false, incomplete or misleading information concerning any fact or thing material to the claim, including information which documents or supports an amount claimed in excess of the actual loss sustained by the claimant.

4. Engaging in unlicensed agent, broker, or unauthorized insurer activity as defined by The Insurance Department Act of 1921, knowingly and with the intent to defraud an insurer, a self-insured, or the public.

5. Knowingly benefiting, directly or indirectly, from the proceeds of a violation of 18 P.S. §4117 due to the assistance, conspiracy, or urging of any person.

6. Owning, administering or being an employee of any health care facility and knowingly allowing the use of such facility by any person in furtherance of a scheme or conspiracy to violate 18 P.S. §4117.

7. Borrowing or using another person's financial responsibility or other insurance identification card or permitting his or her financial responsibility or other insurance identification card to be used by another, knowingly and with intent to present a fraudulent claim to an insurer.

8. For pecuniary gain, directly or indirectly soliciting any person to engage, employ or retain either oneself or any other person to manage, adjust or prosecute any claim or cause of action against any person for damages for negligence or for pecuniary gain for oneself or another, directly or indirectly soliciting other persons to bring causes of action to recover damages for personal injuries or death, provided, however, that this paragraph shall not apply to any conduct otherwise permitted by law or by rule of the Supreme Court.

Penalties

Victims of insurance fraud may sue to recover compensatory damages, including reasonable investigation expenses, costs of suit, and, attorney fees from the perpetrator of the fraud. If the perpetrator engaged in a pattern of insurance fraud, the victim may also sue to recover treble damages. Violators also face civil penalties of not more than $5,000 for the first violation, $10,000 for the second violation, and $15,000 for each subsequent violation.

Reporting Requirements

Every insurer licensed to do business in Pennsylvania, and its employees, agents, brokers, motor vehicle physical damage appraisers and public adjusters, or public adjuster solicitors, who has a reasonable basis to believe insurance fraud has occurred shall be required to report the incidence of suspected insurance fraud to Federal, State or local criminal law enforcement authorities. Licensed insurance agents and physical damage appraisers may elect to report suspected fraud through the affected insurer with which they have a contractual relationship. All reports of insurance fraud to law enforcement authorities shall be made in writing. Where insurance fraud involves agents, brokers, motor vehicle physical damage appraisers, public adjusters or public adjuster solicitors, a copy of the report shall also be sent to the department.

Generally, an insurance company, and any of its agents, servants, or employees acting in the course and scope of their employment, shall be immune from civil or criminal liability arising from the supply or release of information to any duly authorized Federal or State law enforcement agency, including the insurance department, upon compliance when:

1. The information is supplied to the agency in connection with an allegation of fraudulent conduct on the part of any person relating to the filing or maintenance of a motor vehicle insurance claim for bodily injury or property damage.

2. The insurance company, agent, servant or employee has probable cause to believe that the information supplied is reasonably related to the allegation of fraud.

An insurance company must send written notice to the policyholder or policyholders about whom the information pertains unless the insurance company receives notice that

PENNSYLVANIA

the authorized agency finds, based on specific facts, that there is reason to believe that the information will result in: danger to the life or physical safety of any person; flight from prosecution; destruction or tampering with evidence; intimidation of any potential witnesses; or obstruction of serious jeopardy to an investigation.

An insurance company shall send written notice not sooner than forty-five days nor more than sixty days from the time the information is furnished to an authorized agency except when the authorized agency specifies that a notice should not be sent in accordance with the exceptions enumerated in 75 P.S. §1795 in which event the insurance company shall send written notice to the policyholder not sooner than 180 days nor more than 190 days following the date the information is furnished.

Those who comply with or attempt in good faith to comply with subsection the aforementioned policyholder notice requirements shall be immune from civil liability arising out of any acts or omissions in so doing. Also, no person shall be subject to civil liability for libel, violation of privacy, or otherwise by virtue of the filing of reports or furnishing of other information, in good faith and without malice, required by Pennsylvania's anti-insurance fraud laws.

Application Fraud Statement
18 Pa.C.S. §4117

All applications for insurance and all claim forms shall contain or have attached thereto the following notice: "Any person who knowingly and with intent to defraud any insurance company or other person files an application for insurance or statement of claim containing any materially false information or conceals for the purpose of misleading, information concerning any fact material thereto commits a fraudulent insurance act, which is a crime and subjects such person to criminal and civil penalties."

Note: Cases which have ruled portions of §4117 unconstitutional do not apply to any of the sections mentioned above. Those are still valid.

FAIR CLAIMS PROCESSING
Pennsylvania Statutes, tit. 40 §1171.5

The following practices are prohibited by the Pennsylvania Statutes when they are committed and performed so frequently as to indicate a business practice:

1. Misrepresenting pertinent facts or policy or contract provisions relating to coverages at issue.

2. Failing to acknowledge and act promptly upon written or oral communications with respect to claims arising under insurance policies.

PENNSYLVANIA

3. Failing to adopt and implement reasonable standards for the prompt investigation of claims arising under insurance policies.

4. Refusing to pay claims without conducting a reasonable investigation based upon all available information.

5. Failing to affirm or deny coverage of claims within a reasonable time after proof of loss statements have been completed and communicated to the company or its representative.

6. Not making a good-faith attempt to effectuate prompt, fair, and equitable settlements of claims in which the company's liability under the policy has become reasonably clear.

7. Compelling persons to litigate to recover amounts due under an insurance policy by offering substantially less than the amounts due and ultimately recovered in actions brought by such persons.

8. Attempting to settle a claim for less than the amount to which a reasonable person would have believed he or she was entitled by reference to written or printed advertising material accompanying or made part of an application.

9. Attempting to settle or compromise claims on the basis of an application which was altered without notice to or knowledge or consent of the insured of such alteration at the time of the alteration.

10. Making claims payments to insureds or beneficiaries not accompanied by a statement setting forth the coverage under which payments are being made.

11. Making known to insureds or claimants a policy of appealing from arbitration awards in favor of insureds or claimants to induce or compel them to accept settlements or compromises less than the amount awarded in arbitration.

12. Delaying the investigation or payment of claims by requiring the insured, claimant, or the physician of either to submit a preliminary claim report and then requiring the subsequent submission of formal proof of loss forms, both of which submissions contain substantially the same information.

13. Failing to promptly settle claims, where liability has become reasonably clear, under one portion of the insurance policy coverage in order to influence settlements under other portions of the insurance policy coverage or under other policies of insurance.

PENNSYLVANIA

14. Failing to promptly provide a reasonable explanation of the basis in the insurance policy in relation to the facts or applicable law for denial of a claim or for the offer of a compromise settlement.

15. Refusing payment of a claim solely based on an insured's request to do so unless:

    a. The insured claims sovereign, eleemosynary, diplomatic, military service, or other immunity from suit or liability with respect to such claim.

    b. The insured is granted the right under the policy of insurance to consent to settlement of claims.

    c. The refusal of payment is based upon the insurer's independent evaluation of the insured's liability based upon all available information.

PUERTO RICO

For details on cancellation procedures for the standard policy, refer to the Standard Policy section. Every policy must be offered in Spanish and the insured has the option of requesting the policy in English. Endorsement IL 01 36 requires the insurer to cancel the policy within twenty days of nonpayment.

COMMERCIAL PACKAGE POLICIES; EXCESS OR UMBRELLA POLICIES; COMMERCIAL INLAND MARINE; BOILER AND MACHINERY; COMMERCIAL AUTO; WORKERS COMPENSATION AND EMPLOYERS LIABILITY; BUILDERS RISK; MORTGAGE GUARANTY INSURANCE; AIRCRAFT; COMMERCIAL GENERAL LIABILITY; PROFESSIONAL LIABILITY; CRIME; FARM; CREDIT INSURANCE; TITLE INSURANCE; SURETY (Except as Provided under Rule XXIV-A of the Regulations of the Insurance Code).

26 L.P.R.A. §1126, 1127, and 2716; ISO EC 02 22

Cancellation

Length of Underwriting Period: Sixty days

Length of Notice: Ten days for nonpayment; not less than thirty days for any other reason.

Reason for Cancellation: Not required on the notice but must be provided upon request.

Proof Required: Proof of mailing or certified mail.

Nonrenewal

Length of Notice: N/A.

Reason for Nonrenewal: N/A.

Proof Required: N/A.

Other Cancellation/Nonrenewal Provisions

Any insurance policy terminating by its terms at a specified expiration date and not otherwise renewable, may be renewed or extended at the option of the insurer, upon a currently authorized policy form and at the premium rate then required therefor, for a specific additional period or periods by a certificate or by endorsement of the policy, and without requiring the issuance of a new policy.

Any sum collected as premium or charge for insurance in excess of the amount actually expended for insurance or for medical examination in the case of life insurance, applicable

PUERTO RICO

to the subject on account of which the premium or charge was collected shall be returned to the person entitled thereto within thirty days from the date in which it is requested, and if not requested, within the term of ninety days.

Any person who fails to return said sums within the term set forth in this subsection shall be bound to pay legal interest on the amount to be returned.

COMMERCIAL AUTO
26 L.P.R.A. §§1127, 1128 and 8051

SURPLUS LINES

Surplus lines insurers are not required to follow the cancellation and nonrenewal requirements for admitted companies.

PERSONAL LINES
DWELLING FIRE & HOMEOWNERS
26 L.P.R.A. §1127

Cancellation during the Underwriting Period

Length of Underwriting Period: Sixty days.

Length of Notice: Ten days for any reason during this period.

Reason for Cancellation: Not required but must be provided upon request.

Proof Required: Proof of mailing.

Cancellation after the Underwriting Period

Length of Notice: Ten days for nonpayment; thirty days* for any reason stated above (reasons permitted by law).

Reason for Cancellation: Not required but must be provided upon request.

Proof Required: Proof of mailing.

Nonrenewal

Length of Notice: Thirty days.*

Reason for Nonrenewal: Required on the notice.

PUERTO RICO

Proof Required: Proof of mailing.

*These are the terms stated in the standard policies, the term stated by law is not less than twenty days (refer to Rule LV of the Regulations of the Insurance Code).

Other Cancellation/Nonrenewal Provisions

When written for a term of more than one year, the policy may be cancelled at the anniversary date with a thirty-day notice.

Refunds of premium must be made within thirty days of the request for refund or within ninety days after date of cancellation if not requested.

PERSONAL AUTO

26 L.P.R.A. §1127, 8051 and 8053

Cancellation during the Underwriting Period

Length of Underwriting Period: Sixty days.

Length of Notice: Ten days for any reason during this period.

Reason for Cancellation: Not required but must be provided upon request.

Proof Required: Proof of mailing.

Cancellation after the Underwriting Period

The policy may be cancelled **only** for the following reasons:

1. Nonpayment of premium.

2. If your driver's license or that of:

    a. Any driver who lives with you.
    b. Any driver who customarily uses "your covered auto" has been suspended or revoked. This must have occurred:

    (1) During the policy period.
    (2) Since the last anniversary of the original effective date if the policy period is other than one year.

3. If the policy was obtained through fraudulent misrepresentation.

PUERTO RICO

Length of Notice: Ten days for nonpayment of premium; not less than twenty days for any reason stated above (reasons permitted by law).

Reason for Cancellation: Not required but must be provided upon request.

Proof Required: Proof of mailing.

Nonrenewal

Length of Notice: Not less than twenty days.

Reason for Nonrenewal: Not required but must be provided upon request.

Proof Required: Proof of mailing.

Other Cancellation/Nonrenewal Provisions

If the named insured shown in the Declarations cancels or does not accept an offer to renew or continue this policy the compulsory property damage liability coverage required by the Puerto Rico "Motor Vehicle Compulsory Liability Insurance Act" must be continued until the date of expiration of each covered auto. In this event the provisions of the Personal Auto Policy will no longer apply; and the provisions of the Compulsory Liability Insurance Policy attached to this policy will become effective. The insurer will provide compulsory property damage liability coverage until the insured obtains similar or broader property damage liability coverage or the auto is declared a total loss.

Refunds of premium must be made within thirty days of the request for cancellation or within ninety days after date of cancellation if not requested.

Subject to the notice requirement, if the policy period is:

1. Less than six months, the insurance company may exercise the right not to renew or continue this policy every six months, beginning six months after its original effective date.

2. Six months or longer, but less than one year, the insurance company may exercise the right not to renew or continue this policy at the end of the policy period.

3. One year or longer, the insurance company may exercise the right not to renew or continue this policy at each anniversary of its original effective date.

PUERTO RICO

PERSONAL WATERCRAFT

26 L.P.R.A. §1127

Cancellation during the Underwriting Period

Length of Underwriting Period: Sixty days.

Length of Notice: Ten days for any reason during this policy period.

Reason for Cancellation: Not required but must be provided upon request.

Proof Required: Proof of mailing.

Cancellation after the Underwriting Period

The policy may be cancelled **only** for the following reasons:

1. Nonpayment of premium.

2. Reasons listed in policy.

Length of Notice: Ten days for nonpayment of premium; not less than twenty days for any reason stated above or permitted by law.

Reason for Cancellation: Not required but must be provided upon request.

Proof Required: Proof of mailing.

Nonrenewal

Length of Notice: Not less than twenty days.

Reason for Nonrenewal: Not required but must be provided upon request.

Proof Required: Proof of mailing.

FRAUD

26 L.P.R.A. §2720

Definition

Any person that knowingly and intentionally engages in any of the following shall be deemed to have committed fraud.

PUERTO RICO

1. Present a false or fraudulent claim, or alter or omit information or any evidence in support thereof, for the payment of a loss, in reference to an insurance policy.

2. Help or participate in the filing of a fraudulent claim, or alter or omit information or any evidence in support thereof, for the payment of a loss, pursuant to an insurance contract.

3. Prepare, make, or sign or alter or omit, or help or participate in preparing, making or signing, or altering or omitting any account, certificate, sworn statement, proof of loss or any other false document or writ, with the intention that the same be presented or used in support of said claim.

4. File a claim that affects the subrogation right held by an insurer to recover amounts paid under an insurance contract. A subrogation right shall be deemed to be the right that the insurer has to recover the damages that it has had to pay to an insured person under his/her policy. Said right arises by function of law when the insurer makes a payment to the insured.

5. File more than one claim for the same damage, loss or service on the same insured property, except in the case of life insurance.

Penalties
26 L.P.R.A. §2736

Any person who has committed fraud, as defined in §§2706, 2719, 2720, 2720a, 2730 of this title, shall incur a felony, and if convicted, shall be sanctioned for each violation by a penalty of a fine of not less than $5,000, nor more than $10,000, or a penalty of imprisonment for a fixed term of three years, or both penalties. If there were aggravating circumstances, the fixed penalty may be increased up to a maximum of five years. If there were extenuating circumstances, the fixed penalty may be reduced to a minimum of two years. In addition, any person who, as a result of the fraud committed is benefited in any way to obtain insurance, or in the payment of a loss pursuant to an insurance contract, must be imposed the payment of restitution of the amount of money resulting from the fraud.

Reporting Requirements
26 L.P.R.A. §2726

Any insurer, health services organization, general agent, producer, authorized representative, solicitor or adjuster who has a well-grounded knowledge that an act described in §§2706, 2719, 2720, and 2720a of this title has been committed, is being committed or shall be committed, will be bound to submit to the commissioner the information he has available on such act, to conduct an investigation, and otherwise facilitate it. Any insurer, health service organization,

PUERTO RICO

general agent, producer, authorized representative, solicitor or adjuster who fails to comply with this provision shall be punished by an administrative fine pursuant to the provisions of §2735 of this title.

Office of the Commissioner of Insurance web site and contact information is available:

In English at http://www.ocs.gobierno.pr/enocspr/ and

In Spanish at http://www.ocs.gobierno.pr/ocspr/.

In addition, the NAIC has a fraud reporting form available at: https://eapps.naic.org/ofrs/.

Fraud Application Statement
26 L.P.R.A. §2732

Insurers and health service organizations are bound to include in every insurance application form and in every insurance claim form, a conspicuous and legible notice with the following information:

> "Any person who knowingly and with the intention of defrauding presents false information in an insurance application, or presents, helps, or causes the presentation of a fraudulent claim for the payment of a loss or any other benefit, or presents more than one claim for the same damage or loss, shall incur a felony and, upon conviction, shall be sanctioned for each violation by a fine of not less than $5,000 and not more $10,000, or a fixed term of imprisonment for three years, or both penalties. Should aggravating circumstances be present, the penalty thus established may be increased to a maximum of five years, if extenuating circumstances are present, it may be reduced to a minimum of two years."

FAIR CLAIMS PROCESSING
26 L.P.R.A. §2716a

Definition

In the adjustment of claims no person shall incur or carry out any of the following unfair actions or practices:

1. Misrepresent the facts or the terms of a policy relative to a coverage in dispute.

2. Fail to acknowledge receipt and act reasonably prompt within ninety days after a claim has been filed and notified under the terms of a policy.

PUERTO RICO

3. Fail to adopt and implement reasonable methods for the expeditious investigation of claims, which may arise from the terms of a policy.

4. Refuse to pay a claim without carrying out a reasonable investigation based on the information available.

5. Refuse to confirm or deny coverage of a claim within a reasonable term after the loss statement is completed.

6. Not to attempt in good faith to make a rapid, fair and equitable adjustment of a claim when responsibility is clearly present.

7. Compel insureds or claimants to institute litigation to recover amounts due under the terms of a policy, by offering the insured claimant substantially less than the amount ultimately recovered in actions brought or by wrongfully denying coverage under the terms of the policy.

8. Attempt to settle a claim for less than the amount to which the claimant or insured is reasonably entitled to by reference to the written or printed material sent to him/her or that was made part of the application.

9. Attempt to settle a claim based on an altered application without the consent or knowledge of the insured.

10. Make payments of claim to the insured or beneficiaries that are not accompanied by a statement showing the coverage under which payment is made.

11. Make the policyholder or claimants believe in the practice of appealing from an arbitration award in favor of the claimant or policyholder with the intention of forcing them to accept a transaction or adjustment for less than the amount awarded by the arbitrator.

12. Refuse to settle rapidly a claim when the responsibility is clearly and reasonably established under a part of the coverage for the purpose of inducing him to a transaction under another part of the coverage of the policy.

13. Refuse to offer a reasonable explanation of the terms of a policy with regard to the facts and the law applicable so as to refuse a claim or an offer of transaction.

14. Delay an investigation or the payment of a claim by requiring from the insured, claimant or his physician to submit a preliminary report of the claim and then require

a formal statement of loss, which substantially contains the same information of the preliminary report.

15. Deny the existence of the policy coverage when the insured turned down the payment offer of a claim for such coverage.

16. Deny the payment for a valid claim solely due to a mere suspicion of fraud or misrepresentation of the facts.

17. Deny the payment for a claim on the pretext of insufficient information when the same could have been acquired through regular investigation methods.

18. Compel the insured or claimant to sign a waiver which may be construed as releasing the insurer of such contractual obligations that were not the object of the transaction.

19. Require unreasonable conditions to the insured or claimant in order to conduct or delay the claim adjustment.

The commissioner shall adopt the necessary regulations to make effective the provisions of this section.

RHODE ISLAND

For details on cancellation procedures for the standard policy, refer to the Standard Policy section.

COMMERCIAL LINES
CAPITAL ASSETS; CGL (CGL, EMPLOYMENT-RELATED PRACTICES, LIQUOR, OCP, POLLUTION, PRODS. /COMPLETED OPS.); CIM; C. PROP.; FARM; & PROF. LIAB

R.I. Gen. Laws Ann. §§27-8-11, 27-29-17.1 through 27-29-17.4; 230 RICR 020-20-1

Cancellation during the Underwriting Period

Length of Underwriting Period: Sixty days.

Length of Notice: Ten days for nonpayment; thirty days for any other reason.

Reason for Cancellation: Must be provided by insurer if requested.

Proof Required: Proof of U.S. Postal Service certificate of mailing or delivery.

Cancellation after the Underwriting Period

The policy may be cancelled **only** for the following reasons:

1. Nonpayment.

2. Fraud or material misrepresentation in obtaining the policy, in continuing the policy, or in pursuit of a claim.

3. Activities or omissions of the insured which increases the risk of loss, including failure to comply with loss control recommendations.

4. A change in the risk increases the hazard. This includes an increase in exposure due to regulation, legislation, or court decision.

5. The insurer loses, or suffers a decrease in, its reinsurance covering all or part of the risk or exposure covered by the policy.

6. The commissioner determines that continuing the policy would jeopardize the insurer's solvency or place it in violation of the law.

RHODE ISLAND

7. Arson by the owner or the occupant.

8. The insured violates any of the terms and conditions of the policy.

9. The property is a constructive or actual total loss.

10. Any other reasons that are approved by the commissioner of insurance.

Length of Notice: Ten days for nonpayment; thirty days for all other reasons.

Reason for Cancellation: Must be provided by insurer if requested in writing.

Proof Required: Proof of U.S. Postal Service certificate of mailing or delivery.

Nonrenewal

Length of Notice: Sixty days.

Reason for Nonrenewal: Not required on the notice, but must be provided upon written request.

Proof Required: Proof of U.S. Postal Service certificate of mailing or delivery. Notice may alternatively be given electronically if the insured consents and if the insurer has complied with the Electronic Transaction Act R.I. Gen. Laws §42-127.1-1 *et seq*. RI Insurance Regulation 38(7A).

Other Cancellation/Nonrenewal Provisions

On OCP policies all notices must be sent to the named insured and to any designated contractor.

Sixty days notice is required for changes to premiums or coverage. (R.I. Gen Laws Ann. §27-29-17.3).

BUSINESSOWNERS

R.I. Gen. Laws Ann. §§27-8-11, 27-29-17.1 through 27-29-17.4; 230 RICR 020-20-1

Cancellation during the Underwriting Period

Length of Underwriting Period: Sixty days.

Length of Notice: Ten days for nonpayment; thirty days for any other reason.

RHODE ISLAND

Reason for Cancellation: Must be provided by insurer if requested.

Proof Required: Proof of U.S. Postal Service certificate of mailing or delivery.

Cancellation after the Underwriting Period

The policy may be cancelled **only** for the following reasons:

1. Nonpayment.

2. Fraud or material misrepresentation in obtaining the policy, in continuing the policy, or in pursuit of a claim.

3. Activities or omissions of the insured which increase the risk of loss, including failure to comply with loss control recommendations.

4. A change in the risk increases the hazard. This includes an increase in exposure due to regulation, legislation, or court decision.

5. The insurer loses, or suffers a decrease in, its reinsurance covering all or part of the risk or exposure covered by the policy.

6. The commissioner determines that continuation of the policy would jeopardize the insurer's solvency or place it in violation of the law.

7. Arson by the owner or the occupant.

8. The insured violates any of the terms and conditions of the policy.

9. The property is a constructive or actual total loss.

10. Any other reasons that are approved by the commissioner.

Length of Notice: Ten days for nonpayment; thirty days for all other reasons.

Reason for Cancellation: Must be provided by insurer if requested.

Proof Required: Proof of U.S. Postal Service certificate of mailing or delivery.

Nonrenewal

Length of Notice: Sixty days.

Reason for Nonrenewal: Not required on the notice, but must be provided upon request.

RHODE ISLAND

Proof Required: Proof of U.S. Postal Service certificate of mailing or delivery. Notice may alternatively be given electronically if the insured consents and if the insurer has complied with the Electronic Transaction Act R.I. Gen. Laws §42-127.1-1 *et seq*. RI Insurance Regulation 38(7A).

Sixty days notice is required for changes to premiums or coverage. (R.I. Gen Laws Ann. §27-29-17.3).

COMMERCIAL AUTO

R.I. Gen. Laws Ann. §§27-8-11, 27-29-17.1 through 27-29-17.4; 230 RICR 020-20-1

Length of Underwriting Period: Sixty days.

Length of Notice: Ten days for nonpayment; thirty days for any other reason.

Reason for Cancellation: Must be provided by insurer if requested.

Proof Required: Proof of U.S. Postal Service certificate of mailing or delivery.

Cancellation after the Underwriting Period

The policy may be cancelled **only** for the following reasons:

1. Nonpayment.
2. Fraud or material misrepresentation in obtaining the policy, in continuing the policy, or in pursuit of a claim.
3. Activities or omissions of the insured which increase the risk of loss, including failure to comply with loss control recommendations.
4. A change in the risk increases the hazard. This includes an increase in exposure due to regulation, legislation, or court decision.
5. The insurer loses, or suffers a decrease in, its reinsurance covering all or part of the risk or exposure covered by the policy.
6. The commissioner determines that continuation of the policy would jeopardize the insurer's solvency or place it in violation of the law.
7. Arson by the owner or the occupant.
8. The insured violates any of the terms and conditions of the policy.

RHODE ISLAND

9. The property is a constructive or actual total loss.

10. Any other reasons that are approved by the commissioner.

Length of Notice: Ten days for nonpayment; thirty days for all other reasons.

Reason for Cancellation: Must be provided by insurer if requested.

Proof Required: Proof of U.S. Postal Service certificate of mailing or delivery.

Nonrenewal

Length of Notice: Sixty days.

Reason for Nonrenewal: Not required on the notice, but must be provided upon request.

Proof Required: Proof of mailing. Notice may alternatively be given electronically if the insured consents and if the insurer has complied with the Electronic Transaction Act R.I. Gen. Laws §42-127.1-1 *et seq*. RI Insurance Regulation 38(7A).

Sixty days notice is required for changes to premiums or coverage. (R.I. Gen Laws Ann. §27-29-17.3).

COMMERCIAL GENERAL LIABILITY
(Railroad Protective)

R.I. Gen. Laws Ann. §§27-8-11, 27-29-17.1 through 27-29-17.4; 230 RICR 020-20-1

Cancellation during the Underwriting Period

Length of Underwriting Period: Sixty days.

Length of Notice: Sixty days if using ISO Amendatory Endorsement CG 29 17 01 10. Regulations require ten days for nonpayment and thirty days for all other reasons.

Reason for Cancellation: Must be provided by insurer if requested.

Proof Required: Proof of U.S. Postal Service certificate of mailing or delivery.

Cancellation after the Underwriting Period

The policy may be cancelled **only** for any of the following reasons:

1. Nonpayment.

RHODE ISLAND

2. Fraud or material misrepresentation in obtaining the policy, in continuing the policy, or in pursuit of a claim.

3. Activities or omissions of the insured which increase the risk of loss, including failure to comply with loss control recommendations.

4. A change in the risk increases the hazard. This includes an increase in exposure due to regulation, legislation, or court decision.

5. The insurer loses, or suffers a decrease in, its reinsurance covering all or part of the risk or exposure covered by the policy.

6. The commissioner determines that continuation of the policy would jeopardize the insurer's solvency or place it in violation of the law.

7. Arson by the owner or the occupant.

8. The insured violates any of the terms and conditions of the policy.

9. The property is a constructive or actual total loss.

10. Any other reasons that are approved by the commissioner.

Length of Notice: Ten days for nonpayment; thirty days for all other reasons.

Reason for Cancellation: Must be provided by insurer if requested.

Proof Required: Proof of U.S. Postal Service certificate of mailing or delivery.

Nonrenewal

Length of Notice: Sixty days.

Reason for Nonrenewal: Not required on the notice.

Proof Required: Proof of U.S. Postal Service certificate of mailing or delivery. Notice may alternatively be given electronically if the insured consents and if the insurer has complied with the Electronic Transaction Act R.I. Gen. Laws §42-127.1-1 *et seq*. RI Insurance Regulation 38(7A).

Other Cancellation/Nonrenewal Provisions

All notices must be sent to the named insured, any governmental authority, and to any contractor shown in the declarations.

RHODE ISLAND

Sixty days notice is required for changes to premiums or coverage. (R.I. Gen Laws Ann. §27-29-17.3).

COMMERCIAL GENERAL LIABILITY

(Underground Storage Tanks)

R.I. Gen. Laws Ann. §§27-8-11, 27-29-17.1 through 27-29-17.4; 230 RICR 020-20-1

Cancellation during the Underwriting Period

Length of Underwriting Period: Sixty days.

Length of Notice: If using ISO Amendatory Endorsement CG 30 12 01 10, ten days for nonpayment; thirty days for fraud or material misrepresentation; sixty days for any other reason. Regulations require ten days for nonpayment and thirty days for all other reasons.

Reason for Cancellation: Must be provided by insurer if requested.

Proof Required: Proof of U.S. Postal Service certificate of mailing or delivery.

Cancellation after the Underwriting Period

The policy may be cancelled **only** for the following reasons:

1. Nonpayment.

2. Fraud or material misrepresentation on the application, in continuing the policy, or in pursuit of a claim.

3. Activities or omissions of the insured which increase any insured-against hazard, including failure to comply with loss control recommendations.

4. A change in the risk that increases the hazard. This includes an increase in exposure due to regulation, legislation, or court decision.

5. The insurer loses, or suffers a decrease in, its reinsurance covering all or part of the risk or exposure covered by the policy.

6. The commissioner determines that continuing the policy would jeopardize the insurer's solvency or place it in violation of the law.

7. Arson by the owner or the occupant.

RHODE ISLAND

8. The insured violates any of the terms and conditions of the policy.

9. The property is a constructive or actual total loss.

10. Any other reasons that are approved by the commissioner.

Length of Notice: If using ISO Amendatory Endorsement CG 30 12 01 10, ten days for nonpayment; thirty days for fraud or misrepresentation; sixty days for any other permissible reason. Regulations require ten days for nonpayment and thirty days for all other allowable reasons.

Reason for Cancellation: Must be provided upon request.

Proof Required: Proof of U.S. Postal Service certificate of mailing or delivery.

Nonrenewal

Length of Notice: Sixty days.

Reason for Nonrenewal: Not required on the notice, but must be provided upon request.

Proof Required: Proof of U.S. Postal Service certificate of mailing or delivery. Notice may alternatively be given electronically if the insured consents and if the insurer has complied with the Electronic Transaction Act R.I. Gen. Laws §42-127.1-1 *et seq*. RI Insurance Regulation 38(7A).

Sixty days notice is required for changes to premiums or coverage. (R.I. Gen Laws Ann. §27-29-17.3).

COMMERCIAL UMBRELLA

R.I. Gen. Laws Ann. §§27-8-11, 27-29-17.1 through 27-29-17.4

Cancellation during the Underwriting Period

Length of Underwriting Period: Sixty days.

Length of Notice: Ten days for nonpayment; thirty days for any other reason.

Reason for Cancellation: Must be provided by insurer if requested.

Proof Required: Proof of U.S. Postal Service certificate of mailing or delivery.

RHODE ISLAND

Cancellation after the Underwriting Period

The policy may be cancelled **only** for the following reasons:

1. Nonpayment.

2. Fraud or material misrepresentation in obtaining the policy, in continuing the policy, or in pursuit of a claim.

3. Activities or omissions by the insured which increase any hazard, including failure to comply with loss control recommendations.

4. A change in the risk that increases the insured-against hazard. This includes an increase in exposure due to regulation, legislation, or court decision.

5. The insurer loses, or suffers a decrease in, its reinsurance covering all or part of the risk or exposure covered by the policy.

6. The commissioner determines that continuing the policy would jeopardize the insurer's solvency or place it in violation of the law.

7. Arson by the owner or the occupant.

8. The insured violates any of the terms and conditions of the policy.

9. The property is a constructive or actual total loss.

10. Any other reasons that are approved by the commissioner.

Length of Notice: Ten days for nonpayment; thirty days for any other permissible reason.

Reason for Cancellation: Must be provided upon written request.

Proof Required: Proof of U.S. Postal Service certificate of mailing or delivery.

Nonrenewal

Length of Notice: Sixty days.

Reason for Nonrenewal: Not required on the notice, but must be provided upon request. Notice may alternatively be given electronically if the insured consents and if the insurer has complied with the Electronic Transaction Act R.I. Gen. Laws §42-127.1-1 *et seq*. RI Insurance Regulation 38(7A).

RHODE ISLAND

Proof Required: Proof of U.S. Postal Service certificate of mailing or delivery.

Sixty days notice is required for changes to premiums or coverage. (R.I. Gen Laws Ann. §27-29-17.3).

WORKERS COMPENSATION
R.I. Gen. Laws Ann. §27-7.1-19

A workers compensation policy may be cancelled midterm **only** for the following reasons:

1. Nonpayment.

2. Fraud or material misrepresentation.

3. A substantial increase in the hazard insured against.

SURPLUS LINES
02 RICR 030-011

The Rhode Island cancellation and nonrenewal requirements do not apply to surplus lines commercial policies.

FINANCED PREMIUMS
R.I. Gen. Laws Ann. §19-14.6-4

If the premium finance agreement contains a power of attorney, the finance company may request, in the name of the insured, that the insurer cancel the policy due to nonpayment. The finance company must first give the insured ten days to pay. If the insured fails to make payment within that ten day period, then the finance company mails the notice of cancellation to the insurer and the cancellation is processed as of the finance company's original default date. Return of the policy by the insured is not required.

PERSONAL LINES

DWELLING FIRE
R.I. Gen. Laws Ann. §§27-5-1 to 27-5-3.4, 27-29-4.1, 27-29-4.3, 27-8-11 and http://www.dbr.state.ri.us/documents/rules/insurance/InsuranceRegulation15.pdf

Cancellation during the Underwriting Period

Length of Underwriting Period: Sixty days. Rhode Island statutes are silent about underwriting periods for dwelling and homeowners insurance.

RHODE ISLAND

Length of Notice: Ten days for nonpayment; thirty days for all other reasons.

Reason for Cancellation: Not required on the notice.

Proof Required: Proof of U.S. Postal Service certificate of mailing or delivery.

Cancellation after the Underwriting Period

The policy may be cancelled **only** for the following reasons:

1. Nonpayment.

2. Material misrepresentation on the application.

3. Substantial change in the risk since the policy was issued.

4. The building has been vacant or unoccupied for sixty consecutive days. This provision does not apply to:

    a. Seasonal unoccupancy.
    b. Buildings in the course of construction, renovation, or addition.

    A building fits this provision if 65 percent of its rental units are unoccupied or 65 percent of its floor space is vacant.

5. After a covered loss, the insured has not begun (or contracted for) repairs within sixty days after the insurer's initial payment.

6. The building has been ordered vacated, demolished, or declared unsafe by a governmental authority.

7. Fixed and salvageable items are being removed from the building and not being replaced. This doesn't apply during remodeling or renovation.

8. The insured does not furnish utility service to the building for thirty consecutive days (other than during seasonal occupancy).

9. The insured is more than one year behind in payment of property taxes on the building.

RHODE ISLAND

Length of Notice: Ten days for nonpayment; thirty days for all other reasons.

Reason for Cancellation: Not required on the notice.

Proof Required: Proof of U.S. Postal Service certificate of mailing or delivery.

Nonrenewal

Length of Notice: Thirty days.

Reason for Nonrenewal: Not required on the notice.

Proof Required: Proof of U.S. Postal Service certificate of mailing or delivery.

Other Cancellation/Nonrenewal Provisions

An insurer may not decline or cancel coverage on an owner occupied dwelling because of the area in which the property is situated.

Notice is also sent to any mortgagee to whom the policy is made payable.

An insurer may not refuse to issue or charge an increased premium for a standard fire insurance policy for an occupied dwelling solely because of the fact that the building has formerly been unoccupied or vacant.

All renewal offers must include notice of any material changes in policy deductibles, limits, coverages, conditions or definitions. The notice must be prominent, in clear and unambiguous language and fully disclose all material changes.

The commissioner of insurance may promulgate rules and regulations which insurers are responsible for following. Those rules may include a thirty day notice of changes to policies being renewed marked by the words "NOTICE OF REDUCTION IN COVERAGE." These changes must be approved by the insurance division. (R.I Gen. Laws Ann §27-8-11).

HOMEOWNERS

R.I. Gen. Laws Ann. §§27-5-3.4, 27-29-4.1, 27-29-4.3, 27-8-11 and
http://www.dbr.state.ri.us/documents/rules/insurance/InsuranceRegulation15.pdf.

Cancellation during the Underwriting Period

Length of Underwriting Period: Sixty days. Rhode Island statutes are silent about underwriting periods for dwelling and homeowners insurance.

Length of Notice: Ten days.

RHODE ISLAND

Reason for Cancellation: Not required on the notice.

Proof Required: Proof of U.S. Postal Service certificate of mailing or delivery.

Cancellation after the Underwriting Period

The policy may be cancelled **only** for any of the following reasons:

1. Nonpayment.

2. Material misrepresentation on the application.

3. Substantial change in the risk since the policy was issued.

4. The building has been vacant or unoccupied for sixty consecutive days. This provision does not apply to:

   a. Seasonal unoccupancy.
   b. Buildings in the course of construction, renovation, or addition.

   A building fits this provision if 65 percent of its rental units are unoccupied or 65 percent of its floor space is vacant.

5. After a covered loss, the insured has not begun (or contracted for) repairs within sixty days after the insurer's initial payment.

6. The building has been ordered vacated, demolished, or declared unsafe by a governmental authority.

7. Fixed and salvageable items are being removed from the building and not being replaced. Again, this doesn't apply during remodeling or renovation.

8. The insured does not furnish utility service to the building for thirty consecutive days (other than during seasonal occupancy).

9. The insured is more than one year behind in payment of property taxes on the building.

Length of Notice: Ten days for nonpayment; thirty days for all other reasons.

Reason for Cancellation: Not required on the notice.

Proof Required: Proof of U.S. Postal Service certificate of mailing or delivery.

RHODE ISLAND

Nonrenewal

Length of Notice: Thirty days.

Reason for Nonrenewal: Not required on the notice.

Proof Required: Proof of U.S. Postal Service certificate of mailing or delivery.

Other Cancellation/Nonrenewal Provisions

An insurer may not decline or cancel coverage on an owner-occupied dwelling because of the area in which the property is situated.

An insurer may not refuse to issue or charge an increased premium for a standard fire insurance policy for an occupied dwelling solely because of the fact that the building has formerly been unoccupied or vacant.

All renewal offers must include notice of any material changes in policy deductibles, limits, coverages, conditions or definitions. The notice must be prominent, in clear and unambiguous language and fully disclose all material changes.

The commissioner of insurance may promulgate rules and regulations which insurers are responsible for following. Those rules may include a thirty day notice of changes to policies being renewed marked by the words "NOTICE OF REDUCTION IN COVERAGE." These changes must be approved by the insurance division. (R.I Gen. Laws Ann §27-8-11 and Insurance Regulation 38).

PERSONAL AUTO

230 RICR 020-05-2; R.I Gen. Laws Ann §27-8-11

Cancellation during the Underwriting Period

Length of Underwriting Period: Sixty days.

Length of Notice: Ten days for nonpayment; thirty days for any other reason.

Reason for Cancellation: Required on the notice. ISO's PP 01 89 does not specify that the reason must be shown; however, 230 RICR 020-05-2 requires it. (R.I. Insurance Regulation 16 (5)(A)).

Proof Required: Proof of mailing. Insurance Regulation 16(5)(B).

RHODE ISLAND

Cancellation after the Underwriting Period

The policy may be cancelled for the following reasons:

1. Nonpayment.

2. Suspension or revocation of the driver's license of the named insured or any driver who lives with the named insured or who customarily operates the insured auto. The suspension or revocation must occur during the policy period or since the last anniversary date if the policy period is other than one year.

3. If the policy was obtained through fraudulent misrepresentation.

4. There has been a violation of any of the terms or conditions of the policy.

5. The named insured or any other operator of the automobile either resident in the same household or who customarily operates the automobile is subject to epilepsy or heart attacks, provided such individual cannot produce a certificate from a physician testifying to unqualified ability to operate a motor vehicle.

6. The named insured or any other operator of the automobile either resident in the same household or who customarily operates the automobile has been convicted of or forfeits bail for three or more violations, committed within a period of eighteen months, of any ordinance or regulation limiting the speed of motor vehicles or any provision constituted a misdemeanor by the motor vehicle laws of any state.

7. The named insured or any other operator of the automobile either resident in the same household or who customarily operates the automobile has been convicted of or forfeits bail during the thirty months immediately preceding the effective date of the policy, or during the policy term, for any felony; homicide or assault arising out of the operation of a motor vehicle, or criminal negligence in the operation of a motor vehicle resulting in death; operating a motor vehicle while in an intoxicated condition or, while under the influence of drugs; leaving the scene of an accident without stopping to report; theft of a motor vehicle; or making false statements in an application for a driver's license.

Length of Notice: Ten days for nonpayment; thirty days for all other reasons.

Reason for Cancellation: Required on the notice. ISO's PP 01 89 does not specify that the reason must be shown; however, 230 RICR 020-05-2 requires it.

Proof Required: Proof of mailing. Insurance Regulation 16(5)(B).

RHODE ISLAND

Nonrenewal

Length of Notice: Thirty days.

Reason for Nonrenewal: Required on the notice. ISO's PP 01 89 does not specify that the reason must be shown; however, 02 RICR 030-016 does.

Proof Required: Proof of delivery or proof of mailing.

Other Cancellation/Nonrenewal Provisions

No insurance company shall fail to renew a private passenger automobile policy because of a loss occurrence only, unless a Chargeable Loss Occurrence or more than two (2) Non-Chargeable Loss Occurrences, involving insureds, have taken place within the annual policy year. All renewal offers must include notice of any material changes in policy deductibles, limits, coverages, conditions or definitions. The notice must be prominent, in clear and unambiguous language and fully disclose all material changes.

The commissioner of insurance may promulgate rules and regulations which insurers are responsible for following. Those rules may include a thirty day notice of changes to policies being renewed marked by the words "NOTICE OF REDUCTION IN COVERAGE." These changes must be approved by the insurance division. (R.I Gen. Laws Ann §27-8-11 and Insurance Regulation 97).

PERSONAL UMBRELLA

R.I. Gen. Laws Ann. §§27-5-3.4, 27-29-4.1, 27-29-4.3, and §27-8-11

Cancellation during the Underwriting Period

Length of Underwriting Period: Sixty days. Rhode Island statutes are silent about underwriting periods for umbrella policies.

Length of Notice: Ten days.

Reason for Cancellation: Not required.

Proof Required: Proof of U.S. Postal Service certificate of mailing or delivery.

Cancellation after the Underwriting Period

Length of Notice: Ten-day notice for nonpayment; thirty-day notice for any other reason.

Reason for Cancellation: Not required.

Proof Required: Proof of U.S. Postal Service certificate of mailing or delivery.

RHODE ISLAND

Nonrenewal

Length of Notice: Thirty days.

Reason for Nonrenewal: Not required.

Proof Required: Proof of U.S. Postal Service certificate of mailing or delivery.

The commissioner of insurance may promulgate rules and regulations which insurers are responsible for following. Those rules may include a thirty day notice of changes to policies being renewed marked by the words "NOTICE OF REDUCTION IN COVERAGE." These changes must be approved by the insurance division. (R.I Gen. Laws Ann §27-8-11).

FRAUD

R.I. Gen. Laws Ann. §§11-41-29, 27-49-1 to -6, 27-63-1, 27-72-14; RI Insurance Bulletin 2010-3

Definition

The following activities are prohibited under Rhode Island's insurance fraud statute:

1. Intentionally deceiving by preparing or assisting, abetting, or soliciting another to prepare or make any written statement that is intended to be presented to any insurer in connection with, or in support of, any application for the issuance of an insurance policy, knowing that the statement contains any false information material to the application.

2. Intentionally deceiving by preparing or assisting, abetting, or soliciting another to prepare or make any written statement, including computer-generated documents, that is intended to be presented to any insurer in connection with, or in support of, any claim for payment or other benefit pursuant to an insurance policy, knowing that the statement contains any false information material to the claim.

3. Intentionally deceiving by presenting or causing to be presented to any insurer any written statement, including computer-generated documents, as part of or in support of a claim for payment or other benefit pursuant to an insurance policy, knowing that the statement contains false information material to the claim.

4. Intentionally deceiving by presenting or causing to be presented to any claimant any written statement, including computer-generated documents, as part of or in support of its contest of any claim for payment or other benefit pursuant to an insurance policy, knowing that the statement contains any false information material to the claim.

RHODE ISLAND

Reporting Requirements
R.I. Gen. Laws §27-49-1

Insurers must generally report to governmental agencies acts of insurance fraud when they have knowledge or a reasonable belief that insurance fraud is being, will be, or has been committed. Insurers enjoy immunity from civil liability stemming from their report of suspected insurance fraud as long as they acted in good faith and without actual malice.

Application Fraud Statement
R.I. Gen. Laws Ann. §27-72-14 and 27-29-13.3

Every claim form and application for insurance, regardless of the form of transmission, shall contain the following statement or a substantially similar statement:

> "Any person who knowingly presents a false or fraudulent claim for payment of a loss or benefit or knowingly presents false information in an application for insurance is guilty of a crime and may be subject to fines and confinement in prison."

FAIR CLAIMS PROCESSING
R.I. Gen. Laws Ann. §§27-9.1-3 through 27-9.1-7

Definition

The following acts are prohibited under Rhode Island law if they are committed flagrantly and in conscious disregard of the law or have been committed so frequently as to indicate a general business practice of engaging in such conduct:

1. Misrepresenting to claimants and insured relevant facts or policy provisions relating to coverage at issue.

2. Not acknowledging and acting with reasonable promptness upon pertinent communications with respect to claims.

3. Not adopting and implementing reasonable standards for the prompt investigation and settlement of claims.

4. Not making a good-faith attempt to effectuate prompt, fair, and equitable settlement of claims submitted in which liability has become reasonably clear.

5. Compelling insured, beneficiaries, or claimants to litigate to recover amounts due by offering substantially less than the amounts ultimately recovered in suits brought by claimants.

RHODE ISLAND

6. Refusing to pay claims without conducting a reasonable investigation.

7. Not affirming or denying coverage of claims within a reasonable time after having completed an investigation related to the claim or claims.

8. Attempting to settle or settling claims for less than the amount that a reasonable person would believe the insured or beneficiary was entitled by reference to written or printed advertising material accompanying or made part of an application.

9. Attempting to settle or settling claims on the basis of an application that was materially altered without notice to, or knowledge or consent of, the insured.

10. Making claims payments to an insured or beneficiary without indicating the coverage under which each payment is being made.

11. Unreasonably delaying the investigation or payment of claims by requiring both a formal proof of loss form and subsequent verification that would result in duplication of information and verification appearing in the formal proof of loss form.

12. Failing in the case of claims denials or offers of compromise settlement to promptly provide a reasonable and accurate explanation of the basis of those actions.

13. Not providing forms necessary to present claims within ten calendar days of a request with reasonable explanations regarding their use.

14. Not adopting and implementing reasonable standards to assure that the repairs of a repairer owned by or required to be used by the insurer are performed in a workmanlike manner.

15. Misleading a claimant as to the applicable statute of limitations.

16. Not responding to a claim within thirty days, unless the insured shall agree to a longer period.

17. Engaging in any act or practice of intimidation, coercion, threat or misrepresentation of consumers rights, for or against any insured person, claimant, or entity to use a particular rental car company for motor vehicle replacement services or products; provided, however, nothing shall prohibit any insurance company, agent or adjuster from providing to such insured person, claimant or entity the names of a rental car company with which arrangements have been made with respect to motor vehicle replacement services; provided, that the rental car company is licensed pursuant to R.I. Gen. Laws Ann. §31-5-33.

RHODE ISLAND

18. Refusing to honor a "direction to pay" executed by an insured, claimant, indicating that the insured or claimant, wishes to have the insurance company directly pay his or her motor vehicle replacement vehicle rental benefit to the rental car company of the consumer's choice; provided, that the rental car company is licensed pursuant to R.I. Gen. Laws Ann. §31-5-33. Nothing in this section shall be construed to prevent the insurance company's ability to question or challenge the amount charged, in accordance with its policy provisions, and the requirements of the department of business regulation.

19. Modifying any published manual relating to auto body repair without prior agreement between the parties.

20. Not using a manual or system in its entirety in the appraisal of a motor vehicle.

21. Refusing to compensate an auto body shop for documented charges as identified through industry recognized software programs or systems for paint and refinishing materials in auto body repair claims.

22. Failing to comply with the requirements of R.I. Gen. Laws Ann. §31-47-12.1.

23. Not having an appraisal performed by a licensed appraiser where the motor vehicle has sustained damage estimated to exceed $2,500.

24. Not performing a supplemental appraisal inspection of a vehicle within four business days after a request is received from an auto body repair shop.

25. Designating a motor vehicle a total loss if the cost to rebuild or reconstruct the motor vehicle to its pre-accident condition is less than 75 percent of fair market value.

Penalties

If after a hearing, the director determines that an insurer engaged in an unfair claims practice, the director will issue an order directing the insurer to cease and desist the offending act or practice. The director may punish those who violate the statute by imposing a $25,000 penalty for each and every act or violation not to exceed a $250,000 maximum; suspending or revoking the insurer's license; or imposing both the penalty and a suspension/revocation of the insurer's license. (R.I. Gen. Laws § 27-9.1-6).

SOUTH CAROLINA

For details on cancellation procedures for the standard policy, refer to the Standard Policy section.

COMMERCIAL LINES
AGRICULTURAL CAPITAL ASSETS; CAPITAL ASSETS; BOP; CRIME; CGL (CGL, EMPLOYMENT, LIQUOR, OCP, POLLUTION, PRODS. /COMPLETED OPS.; RR); CIM; C. PROP.; C. UMB.; E. COMMERCE; EQUIPMENT BREAKDOWN; FARM; MGT. PROT.; PRO. LIAB; & WORK. COMP.

Code of Laws of South Carolina §§38-75-730, 38-75-740, 38-75-750, 38-75-760, 38-75-1160, and 38-75-1200

Cancellation during the Underwriting Period

Length of Underwriting Period: One hundred twenty days.

Length of Notice: Ten days for nonpayment; thirty days for any other reason.

Reason for Cancellation: Not required on the notice.

Proof Required: Proof of mailing.

Cancellation after the Underwriting Period

The policy may be cancelled **only** for the following reasons:

1. Nonpayment.

2. Material misrepresentation on the application that, if known, would have caused the company not to issue the policy.

3. Substantial change in the risk assumed, except to the extent the insurer should have foreseen the change or contemplated the risk in writing the policy.

4. Substantial breach of contractual duties, conditions, or warranties.

5. If the insurer loses its reinsurance for the risk or continuation of the policy would jeopardize the insurer's solvency or place it in violation of the law.

SOUTH CAROLINA

For reason 5, the insurer must give the commissioner a sixty-day notice. The commissioner will rule on the request within thirty days.

Length of Notice: Ten days for nonpayment; thirty days for all other allowable reasons.

Reason for Cancellation: The precise reason is required on the notice.

Proof Required: Proof of mailing.

Nonrenewal

Length of Notice: For policies written for a term of one year or less, sixty days prior to the expiration date for nonrenewals effective between November 1 and May 31; ninety days for nonrenewals effective between June 1 and October 30. For policies written for more than one year, sixty days prior to the anniversary date for nonrenewals effective between November 1 and May 31; ninety days for nonrenewals effective between June 1 and October 30.

Reason for Nonrenewal: The precise reason is required on the notice.

Proof Required: Proof of mailing.

Other Cancellation/Nonrenewal Provisions

On OCP policies all notices must also be sent to any designated contractor.

On RR policies all notices must also be sent to any designated contractor and any governmental authority shown in the declarations.

All notices of cancellation or refusal to renew must be sent to the insured and the agent of record.

All notices of cancellation or refusal to renew must inform the insured of the right to have the action reviewed by the director of insurance. Such a disclaimer must contain in bold print the following:

> **"IMPORTANT NOTICE:** Within thirty days of receiving this notice, you or your attorney may request in writing that the director review this action to determine whether the insurer has complied with South Carolina laws in canceling or nonrenewing your policy. If this insurer has failed to comply with the cancellation or nonrenewal laws, the director may require that your policy be reinstated. However, the director is prohibited from making underwriting judgments. If this insurer has complied with the cancellation or nonrenewal laws, the director does not have the authority to overturn this action."

SOUTH CAROLINA

All applications must advise the insured of the insurer's right to cancel a new policy with the first ninety days without cause with the following disclaimer in bold:

> **THE INSURER CAN CANCEL THIS POLICY FOR WHICH YOU ARE APPLYING WITHOUT CAUSE DURING THE FIRST NINETY DAYS. THAT IS THE INSURER'S CHOICE. AFTER THE FIRST NINETY DAYS, THE INSURER CAN ONLY CANCEL THIS POLICY FOR REASONS STATED IN THE POLICY.**

If the insurer fails to furnish the renewal terms and statement of premium or estimated premium due within thirty days of the anniversary date, the insured may elect to cancel the renewal policy within the thirty-day period following receipt of the renewal terms and statement of premium or estimated premium due. Earned premium for any period of coverage must be calculated pro rata based upon the premium applicable to the original policy and not the premium applicable to the renewal policy.

If a policy has been issued for a term longer than one year and for additional premium consideration renewal of the policy or an annual premium has been guaranteed, it is unlawful for the insurer to refuse to renew the policy or to increase the annual premium during the term of that policy.

Cancellation or nonrenewals based on changes in climatic conditions must be based on statistical data relative to South Carolina that have been approved by the director.

COMMERCIAL AUTO

Code of Laws of South Carolina §§38-77-120, 38-77-121, 38-77-123, and 38-75-1160

Cancellation during the Underwriting Period

Length of Underwriting Period: Ninety days.

Length of Notice: Fifteen days for nonpayment; thirty days for any other reason. Any notice sent during the underwriting period may not be effective until the sixty-first day of the policy. If the policy is canceled for nonpayment of premium, the cancellation will become effective only on or after the thirty-first day of the policy period.

Reason for Cancellation: Required on the notice.

Proof Required: Proof of mailing.

Cancellation after the Underwriting Period

The policy may be cancelled **only** for the following reasons:

1. Nonpayment.

SOUTH CAROLINA

2. If named insured or any other operator residing in the same household or who customarily operates a motor vehicle insured by the policy had driver's license suspended or revoked.

Length of Notice: Ten days for nonpayment; thirty days for any other reason. South Carolina laws concerning automobiles specify the notice of cancellation must be at least fifteen days for any allowable reason. Insurers using the ISO form (CA 02 30) must comply with the thirty-day requirement.

Reason for Cancellation: The specific reason is required on the notice.

Proof Required: Proof of mailing.

Nonrenewal

Length of Notice: Insurers using the ISO amendatory endorsement (CA 02 30) must comply with a thirty-day notice requirement; however, South Carolina law only requires a notice of not less than fifteen days for automobiles.

Reason for Nonrenewal: The specific reason is required on the notice. Nonrenewal for the specific reasons listed under §38-77-123 are strictly prohibited.

Proof Required: Proof of mailing.

Other Cancellation/Nonrenewal Provisions

All notices of cancellation or refusal to renew must inform the insured of the right to have the action reviewed by the director of insurance. Such a notice must state:

> **"IMPORTANT NOTICE:** Within fifteen days of receiving this notice, you or your attorney may request in writing that the director review this action to determine whether the insurer has complied with South Carolina laws in canceling or nonrenewing your policy. If this insurer has failed to comply with the cancellation or nonrenewal laws, the director may require that your policy be reinstated. However, the director is prohibited from making underwriting judgments. If this insurer has complied with the cancellation or nonrenewal laws, the director does not have the authority to overturn this action."

The insured must also be advised of the possibility of obtaining other insurance from his agent, another insurer, or the Associated Auto Insurers Plan.

All applications must advise the insured of the insurer's right to cancel a new policy within the first ninety days without cause (see commercial lines, above, for the exact wording required).

SOUTH CAROLINA

COMMERCIAL GENERAL LIABILITY
(Underground Storage Tanks)

Code of Laws of South Carolina §§38-75-730 and 38-75-740

Cancellation during the Underwriting Period

Length of Underwriting Period: One hundred twenty days.

Length of Notice: Ten days for nonpayment; thirty days for misrepresentation; sixty days for any other reason. The laws of South Carolina do not support a thirty-day notice for misrepresentation nor do they require a sixty-day notice in other cases. However, insurers using the ISO form (CG 30 35) must comply with these requirements. Legal advice is suggested.

Reason for Cancellation: The precise reason is required on the notice.

Proof Required: Certified mail. South Carolina law specifies proof of mailing is sufficient. However, insurers using the ISO form (CG 30 35) must comply with this requirement.

Cancellation after the Underwriting Period

The policy may be cancelled **only** for the following reasons:

1. Nonpayment.

2. Material misrepresentation on the application that, if known, would have caused the company not to issue the policy.

3. Substantial change in the risk assumed, except to the extent the insurer should have foreseen the change or contemplated the risk in writing the policy.

4. Substantial breach of contractual duties, warranties, or conditions.

5. If the insurer loses its reinsurance for the risk or continuing on the policy would jeopardize the insurer's solvency or place it in violation of the law.

For reason 5, the insurer must give the commissioner a sixty-day notice. The commissioner will rule on the request within thirty days.

Length of Notice: Ten days for nonpayment; thirty days misrepresentation; sixty days for all other reasons. The laws of South Carolina do not require a thirty-day notice for misrepresentation nor do they require a sixty-day notice in other cases. Legal advice is suggested prior to cancellation.

Reason for Cancellation: The precise reason is required on the notice.

SOUTH CAROLINA

Proof Required: Certified mail. South Carolina law specifies proof of mailing is sufficient. However, insurers using the ISO form (CG 30 35) must comply with this requirement.

Nonrenewal

Length of Notice: For policies written for a term of one year or less, sixty days prior to the expiration date for nonrenewals effective between November 1 and May 31; ninety days for nonrenewals effective between June 1 and October 30. For policies written for more than one year, sixty days prior to the anniversary date for nonrenewals effective between November 1 and May 31; ninety days for nonrenewals effective between June 1 and October 30.

Reason for Nonrenewal: The precise reason is required on the notice.

Proof Required: Certified mail. South Carolina law specifies proof of mailing is sufficient. However, insurers using the ISO form (CG 30 35) must comply with this requirement.

Other Cancellation/Nonrenewal Provisions

All notices of cancellation or refusal to renew must inform the insured of the right to have the action reviewed by the director of insurance (see commercial lines, above, for the exact wording required).

All notices of cancellation or refusal to renew must be sent to the insured and the agent of record.

All applications must advise the insured of the insurer's right to cancel a new policy with the first ninety days without cause (see commercial lines, above, for the exact wording required).

Cancellation or nonrenewals based on changes in climatic conditions must be based on statistical data relative to South Carolina that have been approved by the director.

SURPLUS LINES

Code of Laws of South Carolina §§38-1-20; 38-75-710; 38-75-770

The South Carolina cancellation and nonrenewal laws apply to surplus lines. The timely giving of all notices required by this article to the licensed broker who placed the insurance and represents the insured is considered notice to the insured.

FINANCED PREMIUMS

Code of Laws of South Carolina §38-39-90

If the premium finance agreement contains a power of attorney, the finance company may request, in the name of the insured, that the insurer cancel the policy due to nonpayment.

SOUTH CAROLINA

The finance company must first give the insured ten days written notice to pay. If the insured fails to make payment within that ten-day period, then the finance company may request cancellation from the insurer beginning five days after the expiration of the notice. The insurer shall give the prescribed notice on behalf of itself or the insured to any governmental agency, mortgagee, or holders of certificates of insurance by the second business day after the day it receives the notice of cancellation from the premium service company and shall determine the effective date of cancellation taking into consideration the number of days' notice required to complete the cancellation. The cancellation is processed as of the finance company's original default date. Return of the policy by the insured is not required.

PERSONAL LINES
DWELLING FIRE & HOMEOWNERS

Code of Laws of South Carolina §§38-75-730, 38-75-740; 38-75-790, 38-75-1160; 38-75-1200; and 38-75-1220

Cancellation during the Underwriting Period

Length of Underwriting Period: One hundred twenty days.

Length of Notice: Ten days for nonpayment; thirty days for any other reason.

Reason for Cancellation: Required on the notice.

Proof Required: Proof of mailing.

Cancellation after the Underwriting Period

The policy may be cancelled **only** for the following reasons:

1. Nonpayment.

2. Material misrepresentation on the application that, if known, would have caused the company not to issue the policy.

3. Substantial change in the risk assumed, except to the extent the insurer should have foreseen the change or contemplated the risk in writing the policy.

4. Substantial breach of contractual duties, conditions, or warranties.

5. If the insurer loses its reinsurance for the risk or continuation of the policy would threaten the insurer's solvency or place it in violation of the law.

For reason 5, the insurer must give the commissioner a sixty-day notice. The commissioner will rule on the request within thirty days.

SOUTH CAROLINA

Length of Notice: Ten days for nonpayment; thirty days for all other reasons.

Reason for Cancellation: Required on the notice.

Proof Required: Proof of mailing.

Nonrenewal

Length of Notice: For policies written for a term of one year or less, sixty days prior to the expiration date for nonrenewals effective between November 1 and May 31; ninety days for nonrenewals effective between June 1 and October 30. For policies written for more than one year, sixty days prior to the anniversary date for nonrenewals effective between November 1 and May 31; ninety days for nonrenewals effective between June 1 and October 30.

Reason for Nonrenewal: The precise reason is required on the notice.

Proof Required: Proof of mailing.

Other Cancellation/Nonrenewal Provisions

A homeowner policy may not be nonrenewed due to the insured's filing a claim for "damages resulting from an act of God."

All notices of cancellation or refusal to renew must be sent to the insured and the agent of record.

If the policy is written for a period of more than one year or for an indefinite term, the insurer may cancel on the anniversary date with a written notice sixty days prior to the expiration date for nonrenewals effective between November 1 and May 31; ninety days for nonrenewals effective between June 1 and October 30. For policies written for more than one year, sixty days' notice is required prior to the anniversary date for nonrenewals effective between November 1 and May 31; ninety days for nonrenewals effective between June 1 and October 30.

All notices of cancellation or refusal to renew must inform the insured of the right to have the action reviewed by the director of insurance (see commercial lines, above, for the exact wording required). The insured must also be advised of the possibility of obtaining other insurance from his agent or another insurer and the Department of Insurance has available a buyer's guide regarding property insurance shopping and availability.

All applications must advise the insured of the insurer's right to cancel a new policy with the first ninety days without cause (see commercial lines, above, for the exact wording required).

SOUTH CAROLINA

Cancellation or nonrenewals based on changes in climatic conditions must be based on statistical data relative to South Carolina that have been approved by the director.

Cancellation and nonrenewal for all reasons listed under §38-75-1220 is strictly prohibited. Insurers must keep all records of cancellation and nonrenewal for at least three years.

All applications must advise the insured of the insurer's right to cancel a new policy with the first ninety days without cause with the following disclaimer in bold:

> "THE INSURER CAN CANCEL THIS POLICY FOR WHICH YOU ARE APPLYING WITHOUT CAUSE DURING THE FIRST NINETY DAYS. THAT IS THE INSURER'S CHOICE. AFTER THE FIRST NINETY DAYS, THE INSURER CAN ONLY CANCEL THIS POLICY FOR REASONS STATED IN THE POLICY." (§38-75-1200).

PERSONAL AUTO

Code of Laws of South Carolina §§38-77-120 through 38-77-123, and 38-77-390

Cancellation during the Underwriting Period

Length of Underwriting Period: Ninety days.

Length of Notice: Fifteen days. If using ISO form (PP 01 89), if cancelled within the first sixty days, the cancellation is effective only on or after the sixty-first day. If the cancellation is for nonpayment, the cancellation is effective only on or after the thirty-first day.

Reason for Cancellation: Not required on the notice. If the reason for cancellation is not given, notice must specify that specific reasons will be provided upon written request.

Proof Required: Proof of mailing.

Cancellation after the Underwriting Period

The policy may be cancelled **only** for the following reasons:

1. Nonpayment.

2. Suspension or revocation of the driver's license of the named insured, any driver living with the named insured, or any driver who customarily uses the insured's covered auto. The suspension or revocation must occur during the policy period or within ninety days immediately preceding the original effective date.

Length of Notice: Fifteen days.

SOUTH CAROLINA

Reason for Cancellation: Must state the specific reason.

Proof Required: Proof of mailing.

Nonrenewal

Length of Notice: Fifteen days.

Reason for Nonrenewal: Must state the specific reason.

Proof Required: Proof of mailing.

Other Cancellation/Nonrenewal Provisions

All notices of cancellation or refusal to renew must inform the insured of the right to have the action reviewed by the director of insurance (see commercial auto, above, for the exact wording required). The insured must also be advised of the possibility of obtaining other insurance from his agent, another insurer, or the Associated Auto Insurers Plan.

All applications must advise the insured of the insurer's right to cancel a new policy within the first ninety days without cause (see commercial lines, above, for the exact wording required).

Each insurer shall maintain for at least three years, records of cancellation and refusal to renew and copies of every notice or statement referred to in Section 38-77-120 that it sends to any of its insureds. (S.C. Code §38-77-123).

South Carolina law prohibits an insurer from refusing to renew based on any of the following factors:

1. Age, sex, location of residence in the state, race, color, creed, national origin, ancestry, marital status and income level.

2. Lawful occupation, including the military service.

3. Lack of driving experience, or number of years of driving experience.

4. Lack of supporting business or lack of the potential for acquiring such business.

5. One or more accidents or violations that occurred more than thirty-six months immediately preceding the upcoming anniversary date.

6. One or more claims submitted under the uninsured motorists coverage of the policy where the uninsured motorist is known or there is physical evidence of contact.

SOUTH CAROLINA

7. Single claim by a single insured submitted under the medical payments coverage or medical expense coverage due to an accident for which the insured was neither wholly nor partially at fault.

8. One or more claims submitted under the comprehensive or towing coverages. However, nothing in this section prohibits an insurer from modifying or refusing to renew the comprehensive or towing coverages at the time of renewal of the policy on the basis of one or more claims submitted by an insured under those coverages, provided that the insurer mails or delivers to the insured at the address shown in the policy written, notice of the change in coverage at least thirty days before the renewal.

9. Two or fewer motor vehicle accidents within a three-year period unless the accident was caused either wholly or partially by the named insured, or a resident of the same household, or other customary operator.

10. An insured who uses his personal automobile for volunteer emergency services and who provides a copy of the policy promulgated by the chief of his department to his insurer on request.

No insurer or agent shall refuse to issue or fail to renew a policy of motor vehicle liability insurance solely because of the age of the motor vehicle to be insured, provided the motor vehicle is licensed.

PERSONAL UMBRELLA

Code of Laws of South Carolina §§38-75-730, 38-75-740, 38-75-790, 38-75-1160, 38-75-1200, and 38-75-1220

Cancellation during the Underwriting Period

Length of Underwriting Period: One hundred twenty days.

Length of Notice: Ten day notice for nonpayment; thirty-day notice for any other reason.

Reason for Cancellation: Reason is required.

Proof Required: Proof of mailing.

Cancellation after the Underwriting Period

Length of Notice: Ten day notice for nonpayment; thirty-day notice for any other reason.

Reason for Cancellation: The precise reason is required.

Proof Required: Proof of mailing.

SOUTH CAROLINA

Nonrenewal

Length of Notice: For policies written for a term of one year or less, sixty days prior to the expiration date for nonrenewals effective between November 1 and May 31; ninety days for nonrenewals effective between June 1 and October 30. For policies written for more than one year, sixty days prior to the anniversary date for nonrenewals effective between November 1 and May 31; ninety days for nonrenewals effective between June 1 and October 30.

Reason for Nonrenewal: Precise reason for notice is required.

Proof Required: Proof of mailing.

Other Cancellation/Nonrenewal Provisions

All notices of cancellation or refusal to renew must inform the insured of the right to have the action reviewed by the director of insurance (see commercial lines, above, for the exact wording required).

All applications must advise the insured of the insurer's right to cancel a new policy within the first ninety days without cause (see commercial lines, above, for the exact wording required).

All applications must advise the insured of the insurer's right to cancel a new policy with the first ninety days without cause with the following disclaimer in bold:

> "THE INSURER CAN CANCEL THIS POLICY FOR WHICH YOU ARE APPLYING WITHOUT CAUSE DURING THE FIRST NINETY DAYS. THAT IS THE INSURER'S CHOICE. AFTER THE FIRST NINETY DAYS, THE INSURER CAN ONLY CANCEL THIS POLICY FOR REASONS STATED IN THE POLICY." (§38-75-1200).

FRAUD

Code of Laws of South Carolina §38-55-540

A person who knowingly makes a false statement or misrepresentation, and any other person knowingly, with an intent to injure, defraud, or deceive, or who assists, abets, solicits, or conspires with a person to make a false statement or misrepresentation, is guilty of a:

1. Misdemeanor, for a first offense violation, if the amount of the economic advantage or benefit received is less than one thousand dollars. Upon conviction, the person must be fined not less than $100 or more than $500 or imprisoned not more than thirty days.

2. Misdemeanor, for a first offense violation, if the amount of the economic advantage or benefit received is $1,000 or more but less than $10,000. Upon conviction, the

SOUTH CAROLINA

    person must be fined not less than $2,000 or more than $10,000 or imprisoned not more than three years, or both.

3. Felony, for a first offense violation, if the amount of the economic advantage or benefit received is $10,000 or more but less than $50,000. Upon conviction, the person must be fined not less than $10,000 or more than $50,000 or imprisoned not more than five years, or both.

4. Felony, for a first offense violation, if the amount of the economic advantage or benefit received is $50,000 or more. Upon conviction, the person must be fined not less than $20,000 or more than $100,000 or imprisoned not more than ten years, or both.

5. Felony, for a second or subsequent violation, regardless of the amount of the economic advantage or benefit received. Upon conviction, the person must be fined not less than $20,000 nor more than $100,000 or imprisoned not more than ten years, or both.

In addition to the criminal penalties set forth above, a person convicted pursuant to the provisions of this section must be ordered by the court to make full restitution to a victim for any economic advantage or benefit which has been obtained by the person as a result of that violation, and to pay the difference between any taxes owed and any taxes the person paid, if applicable.

Reporting
Code of Laws of South Carolina §§38-55-560 and 38-55-570

Any person, insurer, or authorized agency having reason to believe that another has made a false statement or misrepresentation or has knowledge of a suspected false statement or misrepresentation shall notify the Insurance Fraud Division. Upon request by the fraud division, any person shall relate any and all information relating to false statements or misrepresentations to the division including but not limited to insurance policy information, policy premium payment records, claims history, or other information.

Application Fraud Statement
Code of Laws of South Carolina §38-55-170

South Carolina does not require a fraud warning statement on applications or claims. However, a person who knowingly causes to be presented a false claim for payment to an insurer transacting business in this state, to a health maintenance organization transacting business in this state, or to any person, including the state of South Carolina, providing benefits for health care in this state, whether these benefits are administered directly or through a third person, or who knowingly assists, solicits, or conspires with another to present a false claim for payment as described above, is guilty of a:

1. Felony if the amount of the claim is $10,000 or more. Upon conviction, the person must be imprisoned not more than ten years or fined not more than $5,000, or both.

2. Felony if the amount of the claim is more than $2,000 but less than $10,000. Upon conviction, the person must be fined in the discretion of the court or imprisoned not more than five years, or both.

3. Misdemeanor triable in magistrates court or municipal court, if the amount of the claim is $2,000 or less. Upon conviction, the person must be fined not more than $1,000, or imprisoned not more than thirty days, or both.

FAIR CLAIMS PROCESSING

Code of Laws of South Carolina §38-59-20

Any of the following acts by an insurer doing accident and health insurance, property insurance, casualty insurance, surety insurance, marine insurance, or title insurance business, if committed without just cause and performed with such frequency as to indicate a general business practice, constitutes improper claim practices:

1. Knowingly misrepresenting to insureds or third-party claimants pertinent facts or policy provisions relating to coverages at issue or providing deceptive or misleading information with respect to coverages.

2. Failing to acknowledge with reasonable promptness pertinent communications with respect to claims arising under its policies, including third-party claims arising under liability insurance policies.

3. Failing to adopt and implement reasonable standards for the prompt investigation and settlement of claims, including third-party liability claims, arising under its policies.

4. Not attempting in good faith to effect prompt, fair, and equitable settlement of claims, including third-party liability claims, submitted to it in which liability has become reasonably clear.

5. Compelling policyholders or claimants, including third-party claimants under liability policies, to institute suits to recover amounts reasonably due or payable with respect to claims arising under its policies by offering substantially less than the amounts

SOUTH CAROLINA

ultimately recovered through suits brought by the claimants or through settlements with their attorneys employed as the result of the inability of the claimants to effect reasonable settlements with the insurers.

6. Offering to settle claims, including third-party liability claims, for an amount less than the amount otherwise reasonably due or payable based upon the possibility or probability that the policyholder or claimant would be required to incur attorneys' fees to recover the amount reasonably due or payable.

7. Invoking or threatening to invoke policy defenses or to rescind the policy as of its inception, not in good faith and with a reasonable expectation of prevailing with respect to the policy defense or attempted rescission, but for the primary purpose of discouraging or reducing a claim, including a third-party liability claim.

8. Any other practice which constitutes an unreasonable delay in paying or an unreasonable failure to pay or settle in full claims, including third-party liability claims, arising under coverages provided by its policies.

SOUTH DAKOTA

For details on cancellation procedures for the standard policy, refer to the Standard Policy section.

COMMERCIAL LINES

BUSINESSOWNERS; C. AUTO; CGL (OTHER THAN UNDERGROUND STORAGE TANKS); CRIME; CIM; C. PROP.; C. UMB.; EQUIPMENT BREAKDOWN; FARM; PRO. LIAB.

South Dakota Codified Laws §§58-1-14, 58-33-60, 58-33-61

Cancellation during the Underwriting Period

Length of Underwriting Period: Sixty days.

Length of Notice: Twenty days.

Reason for Cancellation: Required on the notice. Even though the South Dakota amendatory endorsements (BM 02 06, CP 01 19, CG 28 22, CG 28 63, CR 02 08, and IL 02 32) are silent on the matter, South Dakota law requires a written explanation for cancellation to accompany all notices.

Proof Required: Proof of mailing.

Cancellation after the Underwriting Period

The policy may be cancelled **only** for the following reasons:

1. Nonpayment of premium.

2. Fraud or material misrepresentation in obtaining the policy, continuing the policy, or in pursuit of a claim.

3. Acts or omissions of the named insured which increase any hazard insured against.

4. Substantial increase in any hazard insured against.

5. Violation of any local fire, health, safety, building, or construction regulation or ordinance with respect to any covered property or its occupancy that substantially increases any hazard insured against.

6. A determination by the director of the division of insurance that the continuation of the policy coverage would jeopardize a company's solvency or place the insurer in violation of South Dakota law.

SOUTH DAKOTA

7. Violation or breach by the insured of any policy terms or conditions.

8. Any other reasons that are approved by the director of the division of insurance.

Length of Notice: Twenty days.

Reason for Cancellation: Required on the notice. Even though the South Dakota amendatory endorsements (BM 02 06, CP 01 19, CG 28 22, CG 28 63, CR 02 08, and IL 02 32) are silent on the matter, South Dakota law requires a written explanation for cancellation to accompany all notices.

Proof Required: Proof of mailing.

Nonrenewal

Length of Notice: Sixty days.

Reason for Nonrenewal: Not required on the notice.

Proof Required: Proof of mailing.

Other Cancellation/Nonrenewal Provisions

On OCP policies all notices must be sent to the named insured and to any designated contractor.

On Railroad Protective policies all notices must be sent to the named insured, any governmental authority involved, and to any other contracting party shown in the declarations.

Department of Revenue and Regulation Bulletin 07-03 clarifies that NSF checks are treated like nonpayment and have the same notice requirements.

COMMERCIAL GENERAL LIABILITY

(Underground Storage Tanks)

South Dakota Codified Laws §§58-1-14, 58-33-60, 58-33-61

Cancellation during the Underwriting Period

Length of Underwriting Period: Sixty days.

Length of Notice: Twenty days for nonpayment, fraud, or material misrepresentation; sixty days for any other reason. South Dakota law does not require a sixty-day notice for any other

SOUTH DAKOTA

reason. This policy provision is more favorable to the insured than the law is; therefore an insurer must follow the provision if it has adopted the ISO amendatory endorsement (CG 30 31).

Reason for Cancellation: Required on the notice. Even though the South Dakota amendatory endorsement is silent on the matter, South Dakota law requires a written explanation for cancellation to accompany all notices.

Proof Required: Certified mail.

Cancellation after the Underwriting Period

The policy may be cancelled **only** for the following reasons:

1. Nonpayment of premium.

2. Fraud or material misrepresentation in obtaining the policy, continuing the policy, or in pursuit of a claim.

3. Acts or omissions of the named insured which increase any hazard insured against.

4. Substantial increase in any hazard insured against.

5. Violation of any local fire, health, safety, building, or construction regulation or ordinance with respect to any insured property or occupancy thereof that substantially increases any hazard insured against.

6. A determination by the director of the division of insurance that the continuation of the policy coverage would jeopardize a company's solvency or place the insurer in violation of South Dakota law.

7. Violation or breach by the insured of any policy terms or conditions.

8. Any other reasons that are approved by the director of the division of insurance.

Length of Notice: Twenty days for nonpayment, fraud, or material misrepresentation; sixty days for any other reason. South Dakota law does not require a sixty-day notice for any other reason. However, because this policy provision is more favorable to the insured than the law is, an insurer must follow the provision if it has adopted the ISO amendatory endorsement.

Reason for Cancellation: Required on the notice. Even though the South Dakota amendatory endorsement (CG 30 31) is silent on the matter—implying that the reason for cancellation

SOUTH DAKOTA

is not required—South Dakota law clearly requires the reason to be shown on all notices of cancellation.

Proof Required: Proof of mailing (Certified mail if adopting CG 30 31).

Nonrenewal

Length of Notice: Sixty days.

Reason for Nonrenewal: Not required on the notice.

Proof Required: Certified mail.

Other Cancellation/Nonrenewal Provisions

Department of Revenue and Regulation Bulletin 07-03 clarifies that NSF checks are treated like nonpayment and have the same notice requirements.

WORKERS COMPENSATION

South Dakota Codified Laws §§58-1-14, 58-20-14,

Cancellation during the Underwriting Period

Length of Underwriting Period: Sixty days.

Length of Notice: Ten days for nonpayment; twenty days for any other reason.

Reason for Cancellation: Required on the notice.

Proof Required: Registered or certified mail.

Cancellation after the Underwriting Period

The policy may be cancelled **only** for the following reasons:

1. Nonpayment of premium.

2. Fraud or material misrepresentation in obtaining the policy, continuing the policy, or in pursuit of a claim.

3. Acts or omissions of the named insured which increase any hazard insured against.

4. Substantial increase in any hazard insured against.

SOUTH DAKOTA

5. Violation of any local fire, health, safety, building, or construction regulation or ordinance with respect to any insured property or the occupancy thereof that substantially increases any hazard insured against.

6. A determination by the director of the Division of Insurance that the continuation of the policy would jeopardize a company's solvency or would place the insurer in violation of the insurance laws of this state.

7. Violation or breach by the insured of any policy terms or conditions.

8. Such other reasons as are approved by the director of the Division of Insurance.

Length of Notice: Ten days for nonpayment; twenty days for any other reason.

Reason for Cancellation: Required.

Proof Required: Registered or certified mail.

Nonrenewal

Length of Notice: Sixty days.

Reason for Nonrenewal: Not required.

Proof Required: Proof of mailing.

Other Cancellation/Nonrenewal Provisions

The South Dakota code requires that cancellation notices be sent to the employer and to the State Department of Labor and Regulation.

If the insured is a partnership, notice may be given to any one of the partners.

SURPLUS LINES

South Dakota Codified Laws §58-32

The South Dakota cancellation and nonrenewal laws are not addressed in section 58-32.

PERSONAL LINES
DWELLING FIRE & HOMEOWNERS

South Dakota Codified Laws §§58-1-14, 58-33-60, 58-33-61

Cancellation during the Underwriting Period

Length of Underwriting Period: Sixty days.

Length of Notice: Twenty days.

SOUTH DAKOTA

Reason for Cancellation: Required on the notice.

Proof Required: Proof of mailing.

Cancellation after the Underwriting Period

The policy may be cancelled **only** for the following reasons:

1. Nonpayment of premium.

2. Fraud or material misrepresentation in obtaining the policy, continuing the policy, or in pursuit of a claim.

3. Acts or omissions of the insured which increase any hazard insured against.

4. Substantial increase in any hazard insured against.

5. If the named insured breaches any policy term or condition.

6. Violation of any local fire, health, safety, building, or construction regulation or ordinance with respect to any insured property or the occupancy thereof that substantially increases any hazard insured against.

Length of Notice: Twenty days unless ISO amendatory endorsements (DP 01 40 and HO 01 40) have been adopted, then twenty days for nonpayment; thirty days for any other reason.

Reason for Cancellation: Required on the notice.

Proof Required: Proof of mailing.

Nonrenewal

Length of Notice: Thirty days.

Reason for Nonrenewal: Not required on the notice.

Proof Required: Proof of mailing.

Other Cancellation/Nonrenewal Provisions

Department of Revenue and Regulation Bulletin 07-03 clarifies that NSF checks are treated like nonpayment and have the same notice requirements.

SOUTH DAKOTA

PERSONAL AUTO

South Dakota Codified Laws §§58-11-46, 58-11-47, 58-11-49, 58-11-50, 58-11-51, and 58-11-53

Cancellation during the Underwriting Period

Length of Underwriting Period: Sixty days.

Length of Notice: Twenty days. South Dakota law states that notice must be given prior to the expiration of sixty days from the policy effective date.

Reason for Cancellation: Except for nonpayment, reason not required on the notice. Reason must be provided upon request.

Proof Required: Proof of mailing.

Cancellation after the Underwriting Period

The policy may be cancelled **only** for the following reasons:

1. Nonpayment.

2. The driver's license or motor vehicle registration of the name insured or of any other operator who either resides in the same household or customarily operates an automobile insured under the policy has been under suspension or revocation during the policy period or, if the policy is a renewal, during its policy period or the one hundred eighty days immediately preceding its effective date.

3. For any person insured based upon participation in the 24/7 sobriety program and who is no longer a participant in the 24/7 sobriety program due to noncompliance with the program.

Length of Notice: Twenty days.

Reason for Cancellation: Except for nonpayment, the reason is not required on the notice. The reason must be provided upon request.

Proof Required: Proof of mailing.

Nonrenewal

Length of Notice: Sixty days.

Reason for Nonrenewal: Not required on the notice.

Proof Required: Proof of mailing.

SOUTH DAKOTA

Other Cancellation/Nonrenewal Provisions

Where the reason for cancellation does not accompany or is not included in the notice of cancellation, the insurer shall upon written request of the named insured, mailed or delivered to the insurer not less than fifteen days prior to the effective date of cancellation, specify in writing the reason for such cancellation. Such reason shall be mailed or delivered to the named insured within five days after receipt of such request. When an auto policy is cancelled or not renewed for reasons other than nonpayment of premium, or in the event of failure to renew a policy of automobile liability insurance, the insurer shall notify the named insured of his possible eligibility for automobile liability insurance through the automobile liability assigned risk plan. Such notice shall accompany or be included in the notice of cancellation or the notice of intent not to renew. Department of Revenue and Regulation Bulletin 07-03 clarifies that NSF checks are treated like nonpayment and have the same notice requirements.

PERSONAL UMBRELLA

South Dakota Codified Laws §§58-1-14, 58-33-60, and 58-33-61

Cancellation during the Underwriting Period

Length of Underwriting Period: Sixty days.

Length of Notice: Twenty days.

Reason for Cancellation: Required.

Proof Required: Proof of mailing.

Cancellation after the Underwriting Period

The policy may be cancelled **only** for the following reasons:

1. Nonpayment of premium.

2. Fraud or material misrepresentation in obtaining the policy, continuing the policy, or in pursuit of a claim.

3. Substantial increase in any hazard insured against.

4. Acts or omissions of the named insured which increase any hazard insured against.

5. Violation or breach by the insured of any policy term or condition.

SOUTH DAKOTA

6. Violation of any local fire, health, safety, building, or construction regulation or ordinance with respect to any insured property or the occupancy thereof that substantially increases any hazard insured against.

7. A determination by the director of the Division of Insurance that the continuation of the policy would jeopardize a company's solvency or would place the insurer in violation of the insurance laws of this state.

8. Such other reasons as are approved by the director of the Division of Insurance.

Length of Notice: Twenty days unless ISO amendatory endorsement DL 01 40 has been adopted, then a twenty-day notice for nonpayment; a thirty-day notice for any other reason. Also, reasons 7 and 8 are not applicable where DL 01 40 has been adopted.

Reason for Cancellation: Reason for notice is required.

Proof Required: Proof of mailing.

Nonrenewal

Length of Notice: Thirty days.

Reason for Nonrenewal: Reason for notice is not required.

Proof Required: Proof of mailing.

Other Cancellation/Nonrenewal Provisions

Department of Revenue and Regulation Bulletin 07-03 clarifies that NSF checks are treated like nonpayment and have the same notice requirements.

FRAUD

South Dakota Codified Laws §58-4A-2

Definition

A person commits a fraudulent insurance act if the person:

(1) Knowingly and with intent to defraud or deceive issues or possesses fake or counterfeit insurance policies, identification cards, binders, certificates of insurance;

(2) Is engaged in the business of insurance, whether authorized or unauthorized, receives money for the purpose of purchasing insurance and converts the money to

SOUTH DAKOTA

the person's own benefit or for a purpose not intended or authorized by an insured or prospective insured;

(3) Willfully embezzles, abstracts, steals, or misappropriates, or convert money, funds, premiums, credits or other property of an insurer or person engaged in the business or insurance or of an insured or prospective insured;

(4) Knowingly and with intent to defraud or deceive makes false entry of a material fact in pertaining to any document or statement filed with or required by the Division of Insurance;

(5) Knowingly and with intent to defraud or deceive removes, conceals, alters, diverts, or destroys records or assets of an insurer or other person engaged in the business of insurance;

(6) Knowingly and with intent to defraud or deceive presents or causes to be presented or prepares with knowledge or belief that it will be presented to or by an insurer, or any insurance producer of an insurer any statement as part of a claim, in support of a claim, or in denial of a claim for payment or other benefit pursuant to an insurance policy knowing that the statement contains any false, misleading or incorrect statements concerning any fact or thing material to a claim;

(7) Assists, abets, solicits, or conspires with another to prepare or make any statement that is intended to be presented to or by an insurer or person in connection with or in support of any claim for payment or other benefit, or denial, pursuant to an insurance policy knowing that the statement contains any false, incomplete, or misleading information concerning any fact or thing material to the claim; or

(8) Makes false representations as to death or disability of a policy or certificate holder in any statement or certificate for the purpose of fraudulently obtaining money or benefit from an insurer.

Penalties

Any violation of this section for an amount of $400 or less is a Class 2 misdemeanor. Any violation of this section for an amount in excess of $400 and less than $1,000 is a Class 1 misdemeanor. Any violation of this section for an amount of $1,000 and greater is a Class 4 felony. Any other violation of this section is a Class 1 misdemeanor.

Application Fraud Statement

South Dakota Codified Laws §58-33-37

South Dakota law does not require a fraud warning statement. However, any person who knowingly makes any false or fraudulent statement or representation with reference to any application for insurance is guilty of a Class 1 misdemeanor. Any person who knowingly presents or causes to be presented a false or fraudulent claim for the purpose of obtaining any money or benefit, or who submits any proof in support of such a claim for the payment of a loss upon a contract of insurance, or who prepares, makes, or subscribes a false or fraudulent account, certificate, affidavit or proof of loss, or other document or writing, with intent that the same may be presented or used in support of such a claim, is guilty of a Class 2 misdemeanor if such claim is for an amount of $400 or less; a Class 1 misdemeanor if such claims is for an amount greater than $400 and less than $1,000; and a Class 4 felony if such claim is $1,000 or greater.

FAIR CLAIMS PROCESSING

South Dakota Codified Laws §§58-12-19; 58-12-20; 58-33-67

General Information

A clean claim is considered to be a claim for which there is no need for additional information to determine eligibility or adjudicate the claim. The term does not include a claim for payment of expenses incurred during a period of time for which premiums are delinquent, except to the extent otherwise required by law or a claim for which fraud is suspected. Clean claims are to be paid to the person entitled thereto, denied, or settled within thirty calendar days after receipt if submitted electronically and within forty-five calendar days after receipt and if the claim is payable. If more information in needed in order to determine eligibility or adjudicate the claim, the carrier will request said information within thirty days of receipt of the claim.

Nothing in §§ 58-12-19 to 58-12-21, inclusive, apply to disability income policies or certificates, accident only, credit health, workers' compensation, long-term care, Medicare supplement, automobile medical payment, or other types of health insurance that are not medical expense policies or certificates. Nothing in §§ 58-12-19 to 58-12-21, inclusive, grants a private right of action.

Unfair or Deceptive Practices

In dealing with the insured or representative of the insured, unfair or deceptive acts or practices in the business of insurance include, but are not limited to, the following:

1. Failing to acknowledge and act within thirty days upon communications with respect to claims arising under insurance policies and to adopt and adhere to reasonable standards for the prompt investigation of such claims.

2. Making claims payments to any claimant, insured, or beneficiary not accompanied by a statement setting forth the coverage under which the payments are being made.

SOUTH DAKOTA

3. Failing to promptly provide a reasonable explanation of the basis in the insurance policy in relation to the facts or applicable law for denial of a claim or for the offer of a compromise settlement.

4. Failing to promptly settle claims, where liability has become reasonably clear under one portion of the insurance policy coverage to influence settlements under other portions of the insurance policy coverage.

5. Requiring as a condition of payment of a claim that repairs to any damaged vehicle shall be made by a particular contractor or repair shop.

6. Failing to make a good faith assignment of the degree of contributory negligence in ascertaining the issue of liability.

7. Unless permitted by law and the insurance policy, refusing to settle a claim of an insured or claimant on the basis that the responsibility should be assumed by others.

TENNESSEE

For details on cancellation procedures for the standard policy, refer to the Standard Policy section.

COMMERCIAL LINES

BOP; CAPITAL ASSETS; C. AUTO.; CRIME; CGL; C. PROP; CIM; C. UMB; EQUIPMENT BREAKDOWN; PROF. LIAB; & WORKERS COMPENSATION

Tennessee Code §§56-7-1803 through 56-7-1805

Cancellation during the Underwriting Period

Length of Underwriting Period: Sixty days.

Length of Notice: Ten days.

Reason for Cancellation: Required on the notice.

Proof Required: Proof of mailing or delivery.

Cancellation after the Underwriting Period

The policy may be cancelled **only** for the following reasons:

1. Nonpayment (including additional premiums justified by a physical change in the insured property or its occupancy or use).

2. If the named insured is convicted of a crime that involves an act that increases an insured-against hazard.

3. Fraud or material misrepresentation in obtaining the policy or in the pursuit of a claim.

4. The named insured's failure to comply with written loss-control recommendations.

5. A material increase in the risk of loss.

6. Determination by the commissioner that for the insurer to continue the policy would jeopardize its solvency or would violate any state's insurance code.

7. The insured violates any policy conditions or terms.

8. Other reasons, as approved by the commissioner.

TENNESSEE

Length of Notice: Ten days.

Reason for Cancellation: Required on the notice.

Proof Required: Proof of mailing or delivery.

Nonrenewal

Length of Notice: Sixty days.

Reason for Nonrenewal: Not required on the notice.

Proof Required: Proof of delivery or proof of mailing.

Other Cancellation/Nonrenewal Provisions

On OCP policies notice of cancellation or nonrenewal must also be sent to the listed contractor.

On Railroad Protective policies notice of cancellation or nonrenewal must also be sent to the listed contractor, any involved governmental authority, or any other contracting party. (See ISO Amendment CG 28 85).

A sixty-day written notice is required if the insurer intends to renew the policy under any of the following conditions: reduction of limits, elimination of coverages, or a rate increase of more than 25 percent. (See T.C.A. §56-7-1806).

Notice of nonrenewal is not required if:

1. The insurer has offered to issue a renewal policy.

2. Where the named insured has obtained replacement coverage or has agreed in writing to obtain replacement coverage.

COMMERCIAL GENERAL LIABILITY

(Underground Storage Tanks)

Tennessee Code §§56-7-1803 through 56-7-1805

Cancellation during the Underwriting Period

Length of Underwriting Period: Sixty days.

Length of Notice: Ten days.

TENNESSEE

Reason for Cancellation: Required on the notice.

Proof Required: Proof of mailing or delivery.

Cancellation after the Underwriting Period

The policy may be cancelled **only** for the following reasons:

1. Nonpayment (including additional premiums justified by a physical change in the insured property or its occupancy or use).

2. If the insured is convicted of a crime that involves an act increasing an insured-against hazard.

3. Fraud or material misrepresentation in obtaining the policy or in the pursuit of a claim.

4. The named insured's failure to comply with the written loss-control recommendations.

5. A material increase in the risk of loss.

6. If the commissioner determines that for the insurer to continue the policy would jeopardize its solvency or would violate the state's insurance code.

7. The named insured violates any policy condition.

8. Other reasons, as approved by the commissioner.

Length of Notice: Ten days.

Reason for Cancellation: Required on the notice.

Proof Required: Proof of mailing or delivery.

Nonrenewal

Length of Notice: Sixty days.

Reason for Nonrenewal: Not required on the notice.

Proof Required: Proof of delivery or proof of mailing.

TENNESSEE

If ISO Amendatory Endorsement CG 30 28 has been adopted, notice of ten days is required for nonpayment and sixty days for any other reason for either cancellation or nonrenewal. Additionally, proof of certified mail is required.

FARM

Tennessee makes no changes from the standard policy.

SURPLUS LINES

Tennessee Code §56-7-1802

The Tennessee cancellation and nonrenewal laws do not apply to surplus lines.

FINANCED PREMIUMS

Tennessee Code §56-37-110

If the premium finance agreement contains a power of attorney, the finance company may request, in the name of the insured, that the insurer cancel the policy due to nonpayment. The finance company must first give the insured ten days to pay. If the insured fails to make payment within that ten day period, then the finance company mails the notice of cancellation to the insurer and the cancellation is processed as of the finance company's original default date. Return of the policy by the insured is not required.

PERSONAL LINES

DWELLING FIRE

Tennessee Code §§56-7-804, 56-7-1901 and 56-7-1902

Cancellation during the Underwriting Period

Length of Underwriting Period: Sixty days.

Length of Notice: Ten days.

Reason for Cancellation: Required on the notice.

Proof Required: Proof of mailing.

Cancellation after the Underwriting Period

The policy may be cancelled **only** for the following reasons:

1. Nonpayment.

2. Material misrepresentation in obtaining the policy.

TENNESSEE

3. Substantial change in the risk.

4. The building has been vacant or unoccupied for sixty consecutive days. This provision does not apply to seasonal unoccupancy; buildings in the course of construction, renovation, or addition; or buildings to which the Vacancy Permit endorsement applies. A building fits this provision if 65 percent of its rental units are unoccupied or 65 percent of its floor space is vacant.

5. If, after a covered loss, the insured has not begun (or contracted for) repairs within thirty days after the insurer's initial payment.

6. If the building has been ordered vacated, demolished, or declared unsafe by a governmental authority.

7. If fixed and salvageable items are being removed from the building and not being replaced. Again, this doesn't apply during remodeling or renovation.

8. If the insured does not furnish utility service to the building for thirty consecutive days (other than during seasonal unoccupancy).

9. If the insured is more than one year behind in payment of property taxes on the building.

Length of Notice: Ten days for nonpayment; thirty days for reasons 2 and 3; five days for reasons 4-9.

Reason for Cancellation: Not required on the notice.

Proof Required: Proof of mailing.

Nonrenewal

Length of Notice: Thirty days.

Reason for Nonrenewal: Not required on the notice but must be furnished upon request.

Proof Required: Proof of mailing.

Other Cancellation/Nonrenewal Provisions

If the policy is written for a period of more than one year, the insurer may cancel on the anniversary date with a thirty day written notice. Note: the only cancellation/nonrenewal issue addressed by the Tennessee code is the length of notice required for nonrenewal. If an insurer

TENNESSEE

has adopted the ISO amendatory endorsement (DP 01 41), it must follow those provisions. Legal advice is suggested.

HOMEOWNERS

Tennessee Code §§56-7-1901 and 56-7-1902

Cancellation during the Underwriting Period

Length of Underwriting Period: Sixty days.

Length of Notice: Ten days.

Reason for Cancellation: Required on the notice.

Proof Required: Proof of mailing or delivery.

Cancellation after the Underwriting Period

The policy may be cancelled **only** for the following reasons:

1. Nonpayment.

2. Material misrepresentation on the application.

3. Substantial change in the risk.

Length of Notice: Ten days for nonpayment; thirty days for all other reasons.

Reason for Cancellation: Not required on the notice.

Proof Required: Proof of mailing or delivery.

Nonrenewal

Length of Notice: Thirty days.

Reason for Nonrenewal: Not required on the notice but must be furnished upon request.

Proof Required: Proof of delivery or proof of mailing.

Other Cancellation/Nonrenewal Provisions

If the policy is written for a period of more than one year, the insurer may cancel on the anniversary date with a thirty day written notice. Note: the only cancellation/nonrenewal

TENNESSEE

issue addressed by the Tennessee Code is the length of notice required for nonrenewal. If an insurer has adopted the ISO policy HO 00 08, it must follow those provisions. Legal advice is suggested.

PERSONAL AUTO

Tennessee Code §§56-7-1302 through 56-7-1304

Cancellation during the Underwriting Period

Length of Underwriting Period: Sixty days.

Length of Notice: Ten days.

Reason for Cancellation: Not required on the notice.

Proof Required: Proof of delivery or proof of mailing.

Cancellation after the Underwriting Period

The policy may be cancelled **only** for the following reasons:

1. Nonpayment.

2. Material misrepresentation on the application.

3. The named insured failed to disclose fully the insured's motor vehicle accidents and moving traffic violations for the preceding thirty-six months if called for in the application.

4. The named insured failed to disclose in the written application or in response to inquiry by the insured's broker or by the insurer or its agent information necessary for the acceptance or proper rating of the risk.

5. Violation of any terms or conditions of the policy by any insured.

6. Any insured made a false or fraudulent claim or knowingly aided or abetted another in the presentation of such a claim.

7. If, after the effective date of the insurance, the policy is extended, with or without charge, to provide coverage for the operation of an automobile by a person or persons not listed on the original application, or a supplement thereto, the company shall be allowed sixty days, after written request to the company for insurance on such driver or drivers, to accept or reject the additional risk and, if the additional risk is

TENNESSEE

not acceptable to the company, the policy may be cancelled; provided, that notice shall be mailed within sixty days from the date of such request.

8. The named insured or any other operator, either resident in the same household, or one who customarily operates an automobile insured under the policy:

   a. Has had a driver's license or motor vehicle registration suspended or revoked within the thirty-six months prior to notice of cancellation.
   b. Is or becomes subject to epilepsy or heart attacks and cannot produce a certificate from a physician testifying to such person's unqualified ability to operate a motor vehicle.
   c. Is or has been convicted of or forfeits bail, during the thirty-six months immediately preceding the effective date of the policy or during the policy period, for:

      (1) Any felony.
      (2) Criminal negligence resulting in death, homicide, or assault, arising out of the operation of a motor vehicle.
      (3) Operating a motor vehicle while in an intoxicated condition or while under the influence of drugs.
      (4) Leaving the scene of an accident without stopping to report.
      (5) Theft of a motor vehicle.
      (6) Making false statements in an application for a driver's license.
      (7) A third violation, committed within a period of thirty-six months, of:

         (a) Any ordinance, law, or regulation limiting the speed of motor vehicles.
         (b) Any motor vehicle laws of any state, the violation of which constitutes a misdemeanor, whether or not the violations were repetitions of the same offense or were different offenses.

9. The insured automobile is:

   a. Altered so as to increase the risk substantially.
   b. Used as an authorized emergency vehicle.
   c. Subject to an inspection law and has not been inspected or, if inspected, has failed to qualify.

No automobile liability insurance policy may be cancelled solely because the driver was involved in a collision not adjudicated the driver's fault.

Length of Notice: Ten days for nonpayment; twenty days for all other reasons.

Reason for Cancellation: Not required on the notice, but must be provided upon request.

Proof Required: Proof of delivery or proof of mailing.

TENNESSEE

Nonrenewal

Length of Notice: Thirty days.

Reason for Nonrenewal: Not required on the notice but must be provided upon request.

Proof Required: Proof of mailing.

Other Cancellation/Nonrenewal Provisions

If ISO Amendatory Endorsement PP 92 92 has been adopted, then if the policy term is less than six months, the insurer may nonrenew every six months, beginning six months after the original effective date. If the policy term is one year or longer, the insurer may nonrenew the policy at each anniversary of the original effective date.

Notices of cancellation or nonrenewal must advise the insured of the right to request the reasons for the notice.

In all cases except nonpayment, the insurer must notify the insured of possible eligibility for the assigned risk plan. (See T.C.A. §56-7-1305).

PERSONAL UMBRELLA

Tennessee Code §§56-7-1901 and 56-7-1902

Cancellation during the Underwriting Period

Length of Underwriting Period: Sixty days.

Length of Notice: Ten days.

Reason for Cancellation: Required on the notice.

Proof Required: Proof of mailing.

Cancellation after the Underwriting Period

Length of Notice: Ten day notice for nonpayment; thirty day notice for any other reason.

Reason for Cancellation: Not required.

Proof Required: Proof of mailing.

TENNESSEE

Nonrenewal

Length of Notice: Thirty days.

Reason for Nonrenewal: Not required.

Proof Required: Proof of delivery or proof of mailing.

Note: The only cancellation/nonrenewal issue addressed by the Tennessee Code is the length of notice required for nonrenewal. If an insurer has adopted the ISO policy DL 98 01, it must follow those provisions. Legal advice is suggested.

FRAUD

Tennessee Code §§39-14-133, 56-47-110, 56-53-102, 56-53-103, 56-53-105, and 56-53-107

Definition

Any person who, knowingly and with intent to defraud, and for the purpose of depriving another of property or for pecuniary gain, commits, participates in or aids, abets, or conspires to commit or solicits another person to commit, or intentionally permits its employees or its agents to commit any of the following acts, has committed a fraudulent insurance act:

1. Presents, causes to be presented, or prepares with knowledge or belief that it will be presented, by or on behalf of an insured, claimant or applicant to an insurer, insurance professional or premium finance company in connection with an insurance transaction or premium finance transaction, any information that contains false representations as to any material fact, or that withholds or conceals a material fact concerning any of the following:

    a. The application for, rating of, or renewal of, any insurance policy.
    b. A claim for payment or benefit pursuant to any insurance policy.
    c. Payments made in accordance with the terms of any insurance policy.
    d. The application used in any premium finance transaction.

2. Presents, causes to be presented, or prepares with knowledge or belief that it will be presented, to or by an insurer, insurance professional or a premium finance company in connection with an insurance transaction or premium finance transaction, any information that contains false representations as to any material fact, or that withholds or conceals a material fact, concerning any of the following:

    a. The solicitation for sale of any insurance policy or purported insurance policy.
    b. An application for certificate of authority.

TENNESSEE

    c. The financial condition of any insurer.
    d. The acquisition, formation, merger, affiliation or dissolution of any insurer.

3. Solicits or accepts new or renewal insurance risks by or for an insolvent insurer.

4. Removes the assets or records of assets, transactions and, affairs or a material part of the assets or records, from the home office or other place of business of the insurer, or from the place of safekeeping of the insurer, or destroys or sequesters the same from the department.

5. Diverts, misappropriates, converts or embezzles funds of an insurer, an insured, claimant or applicant for insurance in connection with:

    a. An insurance transaction.
    b. The conduct of business activities by an insurer or insurance professional.
    c. The acquisition, formation, merger, affiliation or dissolution of any insurer.

It is illegal for any person to commit, or to attempt to commit, or aid, assist, abet or solicit another to commit, or to conspire to commit a fraudulent insurance act.

NOTE

The civil insurance fraud statutes only include 1-3. Legal advice is suggested.

Penalty

Under Tennessee law, criminal insurance fraud is punishable as the crime of theft. Also, those injured by another's commission of insurance fraud may recover any profit, benefit, compensation, or payment received by the perpetrator of the fraud in addition to reasonable attorney's fees, reasonable legal expenses, court costs, reasonable investigative fees, and all other economic damages directly resulting from the insurance fraud. Additionally, perpetrators of insurance fraud face a fee ranging from $100 to $10,000.

These damages are exacerbated when the insurance fraud was habitual. Any person injured in the person's business or property by a person violating Tennessee's criminal insurance fraud statute, upon a showing of clear and convincing evidence that the violation was part of a pattern or practice of such violations, shall be entitled to recover threefold the injured person's economic damages. Treble (threefold) damages must be sought within three years of the violation.

A person convicted of a violation of Tennessee's criminal insurance fraud statute shall be ordered to make monetary restitution for any financial loss or damages sustained by any other person as a result of the violation. Financial loss or damage shall include, but is not necessarily

TENNESSEE

limited to, loss of earnings, out-of-pocket and other expenses, paid deductible amounts under an insurance policy, insurer claim payments, costs reasonably attributed to investigations and recovery efforts by owners, insurers, insurance professionals, law enforcement, and other public authorities, and cost of prosecution.

Reporting Requirements

When any law enforcement official or authority, any insurance department, state division of insurance fraud, or state or federal regulatory or licensing authority requests information from an insurer or insurance professional for the purpose of detecting, prosecuting or preventing insurance fraud, the insurer or insurance professional shall take all reasonable actions to provide the information requested, subject to any legal privilege protecting the information.

Any insurer or insurance professional who has reasonable belief that an act violating Tennessee's insurance fraud laws will be, is being, or has been committed shall furnish and disclose any information in the insurance professional's possession concerning the act to the appropriate law enforcement official or authority, insurance department, state division of insurance fraud, or state or federal regulatory or licensing authority, subject to any legal privilege protecting the information.

Any person who has a reasonable belief that a violation of Tennessee's insurance laws, is being, or has been committed, or any person who collects, reviews or analyzes information concerning insurance fraud may furnish and disclose any information in the person's possession concerning the act to an authorized representative of an insurer who requests the information for the purpose of detecting, prosecuting or preventing insurance fraud.

Failure to cooperate with a request for information from an appropriate local, state or federal governmental authority shall bar a person's eligibility for restitution from any proceeds resulting from the governmental investigation and prosecution.

Application Fraud Statement
Tennessee Code §56-53-111

All applications for insurance, and all claim forms regardless of the form of transmission provided and required by an insurer or required by law as a condition of payment of a claim, shall contain a statement, permanently affixed to the application or claim form, which clearly states in substance the following, or words to that effect:

> "It is a crime to knowingly provide false, incomplete or misleading information to an insurance company for the purpose of defrauding the company. Penalties include imprisonment, fines and denial of insurance benefits."

TENNESSEE

FAIR CLAIMS PROCESSING

Tennessee Code §§56-8-103, 56-8-104, 56-8-105, and 56-8-108

Unfair Claims Practices Defined

Any of the following acts by an insurer or person constitutes an unfair claims practice:

1. Knowingly misrepresenting relevant facts or policy provisions relating to coverages at issue.

2. Failing to acknowledge with reasonable promptness pertinent communications with respect to claims arising under its policies.

3. Failing to adopt and implement reasonable standards for the prompt investigation and settlement of claims arising under its policies.

4. Except when the prompt and good-faith payment of claims is governed by more specific standards, not attempting in good faith to effectuate prompt, fair and equitable settlement of claims submitted in which liability has become reasonably clear.

5. Compelling insureds or beneficiaries to a life insurance contract to institute suits to recover amounts due under its policies by offering substantially less than the amounts ultimately recovered in suits brought by them; provided, that equal consideration is given to the relationship between the amount claimed and the amounts ultimately recovered through litigation or other valid legal arguments.

6. Refusing to pay claims without conducting a reasonable investigation except when denied because of an electronic submission error by the claimant.

7. Not affirming or denying coverage of claims within a reasonable time after proof of loss statements have been completed.

8. Attempting to settle or settling claims for less than the amount that a reasonable person would believe the insured or beneficiary was entitled by reference to written or printed advertising material accompanying or made part of an application.

9. Attempting to settle or settling claims on the basis of an application that was materially altered without notice to, or knowledge or consent of, the insured.

10. Making claims payments to an insured or beneficiary without indicating the coverage under which each payment is being made.

TENNESSEE

11. Unreasonably delaying the investigation or payment of claims by requiring both a formal proof of loss form and subsequent verification that would result in duplication of information and verification appearing in the formal proof of loss form.

12. Failing, in the case of claims denials or offers of compromise settlement, to promptly provide a reasonable and accurate explanation of the basis for such actions.

13. In response to a request for claims forms, failing to provide forms necessary to present claims within fifteen calendar days of such a request with reasonable explanations regarding their use.

14. If the insurer owns a repairer or requires a repairer to be used, the insurer's failure to adopt and implement reasonable standards to assure that the repairs are performed in a workmanlike manner.

15. Failing to make payment of workers' compensation benefits as such payment is required by the commissioner of labor and workforce development or by title 50, chapter 6 of the Tennessee Code.

In addition to the practices listed above, the commissioner may declare by rule certain acts to be unfair trade practices that are not specifically defined.

TEXAS

For details on cancellation procedures for the standard policy, refer to the Standard Policy section.

COMMERCIAL LINES

AGRICULTURAL CAPITAL ASSETS; CAPITAL ASSETS; C. PROP. & CRIME

ISO makes two changes in these policies to comply with Texas statutory requirements:

1. Mortgage holders and each unit owner of a condominium association must be given a thirty day notice of cancellation for any reason.

2. The policy may not be cancelled or nonrenewed solely because the insured is an elected official.

BOP; C. AUTO; CGL (CGL, LIQUOR, OCP, POLLUTION, PRODS./COMP. OPS.); E-COMMERCE; & MGT. PROT.

Texas Insurance Code §§551.001 to 551.152; 28 Texas Administrative Code §5.7013

Cancellation during the Underwriting Period

Length of Underwriting Period: Sixty days.

Length of Notice: Ten days.

Reason for Cancellation: Required on the notice.

Proof Required: Proof of delivery or proof of mailing.

Cancellation after the Underwriting Period

The policy may be cancelled only for the following reasons:

1. Nonpayment.

2. Fraud in obtaining coverage.

3. Increase in hazard within the insured's control that produces a rate increase.

4. Loss of reinsurance.

TEXAS

5. If the insurer is placed in supervision, conservatorship, or receivership and the cancellation is approved or directed by the supervisor, conservator, or receiver.

Length of Notice: Ten days for any allowable reason. Texas insurance regulation would seem to require a forty-five-day notice for allowable reasons other than nonpayment or substantial change in exposure. Legal advice is suggested.

Reason for Cancellation: Required on the notice.

Proof Required: Proof of delivery or proof of mailing.

Nonrenewal

Length of Notice: Sixty days. Texas insurance regulation would seem to allow a forty-five-day notice. Legal advice is suggested.

Reason for Nonrenewal: Required on the notice.

Proof Required: Proof of delivery or proof of mailing.

Other Cancellation/Nonrenewal Provisions

Mortgageholders and each unit owner of a condominium association must be given a thirty-day notice of cancellation for any reason. (Tex. Prop. Code Ann. §82.111).

The insurer may not cancel or nonrenew solely because the insured is an elected official.

Under the OCP coverage part, notice of cancellation or nonrenewal must also be sent to the listed contractor.

If notice of nonrenewal is mailed less than sixty days prior to the effective date, coverage will remain in effect until after the sixty-first day after the date notice was mailed.

Insurer shall renew a personal automobile insurance policy that was written for a term of less than one year, except that the insurer may refuse to renew the policy on any twelve-month anniversary of the original effective date of the policy. (Tex. Ins. Code Ann. §551.106).

COMMERCIAL INLAND MARINE

The policy may not be cancelled or nonrenewed solely because the insured is an elected official. (Tex. Ins. Code §551.152)

TEXAS

COMMERCIAL UMBRELLA

ISO makes no changes from the standard policy in Texas.

COMMERCIAL GENERAL LIABILITY

(Railroad Protective)

Texas Insurance Code §§551.001-.055 and 28 Texas Administrative Code §5.7013

Cancellation during the Underwriting Period

Length of Underwriting Period: Sixty days.

Length of Notice: Ten days for nonpayment; sixty days for any other reason. The Texas statute does not contain the sixty-day requirement. However, if an insurer has adopted the ISO form (CG 28 56), it must comply with the sixty-day notice requirement.

Reason for Cancellation: Required on the notice.

Proof Required: Proof of delivery or proof of mailing.

Cancellation after the Underwriting Period

The policy may be cancelled **only** for the following reasons:

1. Nonpayment.

2. Fraud in obtaining coverage.

3. Increase in hazard, within the insured's control, that produces a rate increase.

4. Loss of reinsurance.

5. If the insurer is placed in supervision, conservatorship, or receivership and the cancellation is approved or directed by the supervisor, conservator, or receiver.

Length of Notice: Ten days for nonpayment; sixty days for all other allowable reasons. The Texas Statute does not contain the sixty-day requirement. However, if an insurer has adopted the ISO form (CG 28 56), it must comply with the sixty-day notice requirement.

Reason for Cancellation: Required on the notice.

Proof Required: Proof of delivery or proof of mailing.

TEXAS

Nonrenewal

Length of Notice: Sixty days.

Reason for Nonrenewal: Required on the notice.

Proof Required: Proof of delivery or proof of mailing.

Other Cancellation/Nonrenewal Provisions

The insurer may not cancel or nonrenew solely because the insured is an elected official.

Notice of cancellation or nonrenewal must also be sent to the listed contractor and any involved governmental authority.

If notice of nonrenewal is mailed less than sixty days prior to the effective date, coverage will remain in effect until after the sixty-first day after the date notice was mailed.

EQUIPMENT BREAKDOWN

ISO makes no changes from the standard policy in Texas.

FARM

Texas Insurance Code §§551.002, 551.102, 551.104, 551.105, and 551.152

Cancellation during the Underwriting Period

Length of Underwriting Period: Ninety days.

Length of Notice: Ten days.

Reason for Cancellation: Required upon request.

Proof Required: Proof of delivery or proof of mailing.

Cancellation after the Underwriting Period

The policy may be cancelled **only** for the following reasons:

1. Nonpayment.

2. The insured submits a fraudulent claim.

TEXAS

3. Increase in hazard within the insured's control that produces a rate increase.

4. The department determines that continuation of the policy would result in a violation of this code or any other law governing the business of insurance in Texas.

Length of Notice: Ten days for any allowable reason.

Reason for Cancellation: Required upon request.

Proof Required: Proof of delivery or proof of mailing.

Nonrenewal

Length of Notice: Thirty days.

Reason for Nonrenewal: Required on the notice.

Proof Required: Proof of delivery or proof of mailing.

Other Cancellation/Nonrenewal Provisions

The insurer may not cancel or nonrenew solely because the insured is an elected official.

If notice of nonrenewal is mailed less than thirty days prior to the expiration of the policy, an insurer must renew an insurance policy at the request of the insured on the expiration of the policy.

PROFESSIONAL LIABILITY

(Physicians and Health Care Professional Liability)

Texas Insurance Code §1901.253

Cancellation during the Underwriting Period

Length of Underwriting Period: Ninety days.

Length of Notice: Ten days for nonpayment or if insured is no longer licensed; ninety days for any other reasons. This notice must be sent within the first ninety days from the effective date of the policy.

Reason for Cancellation: Required on the notice.

Proof Required: Proof of mailing.

TEXAS

Cancellation after the Underwriting Period

The policy may be cancelled **only** for the following reasons:

1. Nonpayment.

2. The insured is no longer licensed.

Length of Notice: Ten days for any allowable reason.

Reason for Cancellation: Required on the notice.

Proof Required: Proof of mailing.

Nonrenewal

Length of Notice: Ninety days.

Reason for Nonrenewal: Required on the notice.

Proof Required: Proof of mailing.

Other Cancellation/Nonrenewal Provisions

The insurer may not cancel or nonrenew solely because the insured is an elected official.

A ninety day notice is required if premiums are increased. The notice must state the amount of the increase.

WORKERS COMPENSATION

Texas Labor Code §406.008 and 28 Tex. Admin Code §43.10

Length of Notice: Ten days for nonpayment or specific reasons listed below; thirty days for any other reasons.

Reason for the Notice: Not required on the notice.

Proof Required: Certified mail.

Policy may be cancelled or nonrenewed with a ten-day notice for any of the following reasons:

1. Fraud in obtaining coverage.

2. Misrepresentation of the amount of payroll for purposes of premium calculation.

3. Failure to pay a premium when payment was due.

4. Increase in hazard that results from an action or omission and that could produce an increase in the rate, including an increase because of a failure to comply with reasonable loss control recommendations or to comply within a reasonable period with recommendations designed to reduce a hazard within the insured's control.

5. If the commissioner determines that to continue the policy would place the company in violation of the law or would be hazardous to the interests of subscribers, creditors, or the general public.

Nonrenewal

Length of Notice: Thirty days.

Reason for Nonrenewal: Not required on the notice.

Proof Required: Certified mail.

Other Cancellation/Nonrenewal Provisions

Copies of all notices must also be filed with the Industrial Accident Board on or before the effective date of termination.

SURPLUS LINES

The Texas cancellation and nonrenewal statutes do not apply to surplus lines.

FINANCED PREMIUMS

Texas Insurance Code §651.161

The premium finance agreement must be in writing and contain the finance charge, and number and amount of installments. This agreement may contain a power of attorney enabling the finance company to cancel the policy due to nonpayment. The finance company must first mail the insured a ten-day notice to pay with a copy of the notice to the insurance agent or broker. If the insured fails to make payment within that ten-day period, then the finance company mails the notice of cancellation to the insurer and the cancellation is processed as of the finance company's original default date. Return of the policy by the insured is not required. When determining its effective date for cancellation, the insurance company must provide statutory or contractual notifications to governmental agencies, loss payees, or other parties.

TEXAS

PERSONAL LINES

DWELLING FIRE

Texas Insurance Code §§551.101, 551.102, 551.104, 551.105, 551.107, and 551.152

Cancellation during the Underwriting Period

Length of Underwriting Period: Sixty days provided that the insurer identifies a condition that creates an increased risk or hazard; was not disclosed in the application for insurance coverage, and is not the subject of a prior claim. An insurer may also cancel within sixty days if before the effective date of the policy, the insurer does not accept a copy of a required inspection report that was completed by an inspector who is licensed by the Texas Real Estate Commission or who is otherwise authorized to perform inspections and is dated not earlier than the ninetieth day before the policy's effective date.

Length of Notice: Ten days for nonpayment; thirty days for any other reason.

Reason for Cancellation: Required upon request.

Proof Required: Proof of delivery or proof of mailing.

Cancellation after the Underwriting Period

The policy may be cancelled **only** for the following reasons:

1. Nonpayment.

2. If the Texas Department of Insurance determines that continuation of the policy would result in a violation of the Texas Insurance Code or any other laws governing the business of insurance.

3. If the insured submits a fraudulent claim.

4. Increase in hazard within the insured's control that would produce an increase in the premium rate.

Length of Notice: Ten days for any allowable reason.

Reason for Cancellation: Required upon request.

Proof Required: Proof of delivery or proof of mailing.

TEXAS

Nonrenewal

Length of Notice: Thirty days.

Reason for Nonrenewal: Required upon request.

Proof Required: Proof of delivery or proof of mailing.

Other Cancellation/Nonrenewal Provisions

The insurer may not cancel or nonrenew solely because the insured is an elected official or because of claims for losses resulting from natural causes.

The insurer may refuse to renew a policy if the insured has filed three or more claims under the policy in any three year period that do not result from natural causes.

When deciding to issue or to decline a policy, an insurer may not consider a customer inquiry concerning the process for filing a claim, and whether a policy will cover a loss, unless the question concerns specific damage that has occurred and results in an investigation or claim as a basis for declination. (See Tex. Ins. Code §551.113).

Insurer's using ISO's DP 01 42 are required to notify an insured after the second non-weather related claim that a third claim within three years of the first one will result in nonrenewal. Failure to provide this notice prohibits the insurer from issuing a nonrenewal due to losses. Claims do not include claims filed but not paid.

HOMEOWNERS

Texas Insurance Code §§551.002, 551.101 to 551.107, and 551.152

Cancellation during the Underwriting Period

Length of Underwriting Period: Sixty days provided that certain criteria are met.

Length of Notice: Ten days for nonpayment and reasons 4 through 6; thirty days for reasons 1 or 2.

Reason for Cancellation: Required upon request.

Proof Required: Proof of delivery or proof of mailing.

An insurer may cancel a homeowner's insurance policy if the policy has been in effect less than sixty days and one of the following applies:

TEXAS

1. The insurer identifies a condition that creates an increased risk of hazard that was not disclosed in the application for insurance coverage; and is not the subject of a prior claim.

2. Before the effective date of the policy, the insurer does not accept a copy of a required inspection report that was completed by an inspector licensed by the Texas Real Estate Commission or who is otherwise authorized to perform inspections and is dated not earlier than the ninetieth day before the effective date of the policy.

3. Nonpayment.

4. The Texas Department of Insurance determines that continuation of the policy would place the insurer in violation of the Texas Insurance Code.

5. The insured submits a fraudulent claim.

6. There is an increase in the hazard covered by this policy that is within the insured's control and that would produce an increase in the premium rate of this policy.

Cancellation after the Underwriting Period

The policy may be cancelled **only** for the following reasons:

1. Nonpayment.

2. If the Texas Department of Insurance determines that continuation of the policy would result in a violation of the Texas Insurance Code or any other laws governing the business of insurance.

3. If the insured submits a fraudulent claim.

4. Increase in hazard that is within the insured's control that would produce an increase in the policy's premium rate.

Length of Notice: Ten days for any allowable reason.

Reason for Cancellation: Required on the notice.

Proof Required: Proof of delivery or proof of mailing.

Nonrenewal

Length of Notice: Thirty days.

TEXAS

Reason for Nonrenewal: Not required on the notice but must be provided upon request.

Proof Required: Proof of delivery or proof of mailing.

Other Cancellation/Nonrenewal Provisions

The insurer may not cancel or nonrenew solely because the insured is an elected official.

A notice of nonrenewal will also be sent to any mortgagee named on the declarations page or because of claims for losses resulting from natural causes.

The insurer may refuse to renew a policy if the insured has filed three or more claims under the policy in any three year period that do not result from natural causes.

Claims that are filed but not paid may not be used as a basis for cancellation or nonrenewal.

Insurer's using ISO's HO 01 42 are required to notify an insured after the second non-weather related claim that a third claim within three years of the first one will result in nonrenewal. Failure to provide this notice prohibits the insurer from issuing a nonrenewal because of losses. Claims do not include claims that are filed but not paid.

Insurers who fail to notify policyholders that submission of a third claim during any three year period are prohibited from using claims as a reason for termination. Notification must use the following language: "The filing by you of another claim, except for a claim resulting from a loss caused by natural causes, a claim filed but not paid or payable under the policy under which it was filed, or an appliance-related claim that we are prohibited from using could cause us to refuse to renew your policy."

PERSONAL AUTO

Texas Insurance Code §§551.101 to 551.106, 551.109, 551.152;

28 Tex. Administrative Code. §§5.7002, 5.7005

Cancellation during the Underwriting Period

Length of Underwriting Period: Sixty days.

Length of Notice: Ten days for any reason.

Reason for Cancellation: Not required on the notice but must be provided upon request.

Proof Required: Proof of mailing.

TEXAS

Cancellation after the Underwriting Period

The policy may be cancelled **only** for the following reasons:

1. Nonpayment.

2. Suspension or revocation of the driver's license of or vehicle registration of the named insured or any driver who lives with the named insured or who customarily uses the insured auto. The suspension or revocation must occur during the policy period or since the last anniversary of the original effective date. The insured may exclude the driver with the suspension or revocation. The insurer may not cancel for this reason if the named insured agrees to exclude the person with the suspended or revoked license.

3. If the board determines that continuation of the policy would result in a violation of state code or any other law governing the business of insurance in this state.

In addition to the items listed above, Texas insurance law allows cancellation if the insured submits a fraudulent claim. Additionally, a company may cancel personal automobile policies irrespective of the reasons that prompt it to do so if the purpose is to terminate coverage concurrently with the expiration of any annual period, beginning with the original effective date of the policy and thirty days' notice is given. However, since these reasons do not appear on ISO's PP 01 50, insurers using this form may not use them. Legal counsel is suggested.

Length of Notice: Ten days. If using ISO PP 01 50 then ten days for nonpayment, twenty days for any other reason.

Reason for Cancellation: Not required on the notice but must be provided upon request.

Proof Required: Proof of mailing.

Nonrenewal

Length of Notice: Thirty days.

Reason for Nonrenewal: Not required on the notice but must be provided upon request.

Proof Required: Proof of mailing.

Other Cancellation/Nonrenewal Provisions

The insurer may not cancel or nonrenew solely because the insured is an elected official or based on the age of the insured or any family member.

TEXAS

Insurer shall renew a personal automobile insurance policy that was written for a term of less than one year, except that the insurer may refuse to renew the policy on any twelve-month anniversary of the original effective date of the policy. (Texas Ins. Code Ann. Insurance Code §551.106).

PERSONAL UMBRELLA

Texas Insurance Code §§551.002, 551.101, 551.107, 551.152;

28 Texas Administrative Code §5.1201

Cancellation during the Underwriting Period

Length of Underwriting Period: Sixty days. Texas statutes allow an underwriting period of ninety days. ISO's amendatory endorsement DL 98 38 restricts this period to sixty days.

Length of Notice: Ten days for any reason.

Reason for Cancellation: Not required but must be provided upon request.

Proof Required: Proof of delivery or proof of mailing.

Cancellation after the Underwriting Period

The policy may be cancelled **only** for the following reasons:

1. Nonpayment of premium.

2. Fraud in obtaining coverage.

3. An increase in hazard within the insured's control which would produce an increase in rate.

4. Loss of the insurer's reinsurance covering all or part of the risk covered by the policy.

5. If the insurer has been placed in supervision, conservatorship, or receivership and the cancellation is approved or directed by the supervisor, conservator, or receiver.

Length of Notice: Ten day notice for nonpayment; thirty day notice for any other reason.

Reason for Cancellation: Required upon request.

Proof Required: Proof of delivery or proof of mailing.

TEXAS

Nonrenewal

Length of Notice: Sixty days. Texas statutes allow for nonrenewal with a thirty-day notice. However, insurers using ISO's amendatory endorsement DL 98 38 must comply with the sixty-day requirement.

Reason for Nonrenewal: Not required, but must be provided upon request.

Proof Required: Proof of delivery or proof of mailing.

Other Cancellation/Nonrenewal Provisions

Policy may not be terminated solely because the named insured is an elected official.

If the insurer does not provide at least sixty days' notice before the expiration date of the policy, the policy shall remain in effect until sixty-one days after delivery of notice to the insured. Premium for the extended period of coverage after the policy expiration date will be computed pro rata based on the previous year's premium.

FRAUD

Texas Penal Code §35.02, Texas Insurance Code §§701.051, 701.052

Definition

A person commits insurance fraud if, with the intent to defraud or deceive an insurer, the person, in support of a claim for payment under an insurance policy prepares (or causes to be prepared) and presents a statement that the person knows to contain false or misleading material information to an insurer. It is also insurance fraud for a person, with the same intent, to present or cause to be presented to an insurer a statement that the person knows contains false or misleading material information.

It is also insurance fraud for a person, with the intent to defraud or deceive an insurer and in support of an application for an insurance policy to prepare (or cause to be prepared) and present a statement that the person knows contains false or misleading material information to an insurer. Likewise, one commits insurance fraud when, with the intent to defraud or deceive, one presents or causes to be presented to an insurer a statement that the person knows contains false or misleading material information.

Finally, a person commits insurance fraud when, with the intent to defraud or deceive an insurer, the person solicits, offers, pays, or receives a benefit in connection with the furnishing of goods or services for which a claim for payment is submitted under an insurance policy.

TEXAS

Penalty

In Texas, the penalty for insurance fraud varies depending on the pecuniary value of the fraudulent claim.

Reporting Requirements

Not later than the thirtieth day after the date that the person determines or reasonably suspects that a fraudulent insurance act has been or is about to be committed in this state, the person must report the information in writing to the Insurance Fraud Unit of the Texas Department of Insurance, in the format prescribed by the fraud unit or by the National Association of Insurance Commissioners. Someone with such a reasonable suspicion may also report the information to another authorized governmental agency.

Reporters generally enjoy immunity from liability stemming from their report of insurance fraud or suspected insurance fraud. (Tex. Ins. Code §701.051).

Application Fraud Statement
Texas Insurance Code §704.002

A plan issuer who provides a form for a person to make a claim against or to give notice of the person's intent to make a claim against a policy, certificate, contract, or evidence of coverage issued by the issuer must include on the form, in comparative prominence with the other content on the form, a statement that is substantially similar to the following: "Any person who knowingly presents a false or fraudulent claim for the payment of a loss is guilty of a crime and may be subject to fines and confinement in state prison."

FAIR CLAIMS PROCESSING

Texas Insurance Code §§542.003 and 542.010

The following unfair claims settlement practices are prohibited under Texas law:

1. Knowingly misrepresenting to a claimant pertinent facts or policy provisions relating to coverage at issue.

2. Not acknowledging with reasonable promptness pertinent communications relating to a claim arising under the insurer's policy.

3. Not adopting and implementing reasonable standards for the prompt investigation of claims arising under the insurer's policies.

4. Not making a good-faith attempt to effectuate a prompt, fair, and equitable settlement of a claim submitted in which liability has become reasonably clear.

TEXAS

5. Compelling a policyholder to institute a suit to recover an amount due under a policy by offering substantially less than the amount ultimately recovered in a suit brought by the policyholder.

6. Not maintaining the information required by Tex. Ins. Code §542.005.

7. Committing another act the commissioner determines by rule constitutes an unfair claim settlement practice.

Penalties

If the Texas Department of Insurance determines that an insurer has violated this subchapter, the department will issue a cease and desist order to the insurer directing the insurer to stop the unlawful practice. If the insurer fails to comply with the cease and desist order, the department may revoke or suspend the insurer's certificate of authority or limit, regulate, and control the insurer's line of business, the insurer's writing of policy forms or other particular forms, and the volume of both the insurer's line of business or writing of policy forms or other particular forms.

UTAH

For details on cancellation procedures for the standard policy, refer to the Standard Policy section.

COMMERCIAL LINES
AGRICULTURAL CAPITAL ASSETS; BOP; CAPITAL ASSETS; C. AUTO; CRIME; CGL; CIM; C. PROP.; C. UMB.; EQUIPMENT BREAKDOWN; FARM; & PROF. LIAB.

Utah Code §31A-21-303

Cancellation during the Underwriting Period

Length of Underwriting Period: Sixty days.

Length of Notice: Ten days.

Reason for Cancellation: Required on the notice for nonpayment; otherwise if reason is not shown on the notice, it must be provided upon request.

Proof Required: Proof of first-class mailing.

Cancellation after the Underwriting Period

The policy may be cancelled **only** for the following reasons:

1. Nonpayment.

2. Material misrepresentation.

3. Substantial change in the risk assumed if such change should not have been foreseen by the insurer or contemplated in the rate.

4. Substantial breach of contractual duties or conditions or warranties.

5. Attainment of the specified terminal age by the insured.

6. For commercial auto, if the license of the named insured or any customary operator of the car is revoked or suspended.

UTAH

Length of Notice: Ten days for nonpayment; thirty days for all other reasons.

Reason for Cancellation: Required on the notice for nonpayment; otherwise, if reason is not shown on the notice, it must be provided upon request.

Proof Required: Proof of first-class mailing.

Nonrenewal

Length of Notice: Thirty days.

Reason for Nonrenewal: Not required on the notice. If reason is not shown on the notice, it must be provided upon request.

Proof Required: Proof of first-class mailing.

Other Cancellation/Nonrenewal Provisions

Statutes require notices to be sent by first-class mail.

A thirty-day written notice is required if the insurer intends to renew on less favorable terms or at higher rates. On the OCP coverage part, notice must also be sent to any named contractor.

On the railroad protective coverage part notice must also be sent to any named contractor and any involved governmental authority.

Notices of cancellation and nonrenewal must include information about the policyholder's right to request the facts on which the insurer's decision was based.

An insurer may nonrenew when one of the following criteria is satisfied:

1. The insurer provides a thirty-day nonrenewal notice.

2. The insurer provides a notice not more than forty-five days nor less than fourteen days, stating the renewal premium, how the renewal premium may be paid, and failure to pay by the due date extinguishes the insured's right to renewal.

3. The insured has accepted replacement coverage.

4. The insured has requested or agreed to nonrenewal.

5. The policy is expressly designated as nonrenewable.

UTAH

COMMERCIAL GENERAL LIABILITY

(Underground Storage Tanks)

Utah Code §31A-21-303

Cancellation during the Underwriting Period

Length of Underwriting Period: Sixty days.

Length of Notice: Ten days for nonpayment; sixty days for any other reason. The sixty-day requirement does not appear in the Utah Code. However, if an insurer has adopted the ISO amendatory endorsement (CG 30 27), it must give a sixty-day notice of cancellation.

Reason for Cancellation: Required on the notice for nonpayment. If reason is not shown on the notice, it must be provided upon request.

Proof Required: Proof of first-class mailing; certified mail if using ISO Amendatory Endorsement CG 30 27.

Cancellation after the Underwriting Period

The policy may be cancelled **only** for the following reasons:

1. Nonpayment.

2. Material misrepresentation.

3. Substantial change in the risk assumed if such change should not have been foreseen by the insurer or contemplated in the rate.

4. Substantial breach of contractual duties or conditions or warranties.

5. Attainment of the specified terminal age by the insured.

6. For commercial auto, if the license of the named insured or any customary operator of the car is revoked or suspended.

Length of Notice: Ten days for nonpayment; thirty days for all other reasons. If the insurer has adopted ISO amendatory endorsement CG 30 27 then it must provide ten days for nonpayment; thirty days for material misrepresentation; and sixty days for all other reasons.

Reason for Cancellation: Required on the notice for nonpayment. If reason is not shown on the notice, it must be provided upon request.

UTAH

Proof Required: Proof of first-class mailing, certified mail if using ISO Amendatory Endorsement CG 30 27.

Nonrenewal

Length of Notice: Thirty days according to the Utah code. If an insurer has adopted ISO amendatory endorsement CG 30 27 it must provide a sixty-day notice of cancellation.

Reason for Nonrenewal: Not required on the notice. If the reason is not shown on the notice, it must be provided upon request.

Proof Required: Proof of first-class mailing, certified mail if using ISO Amendatory Endorsement CG 30 27.

Other Cancellation/Nonrenewal Provisions

Notices of cancellation and nonrenewal must include information about the policyholder's right to request the facts on which the insurer's decision was based.

WORKERS COMPENSATION

Utah Code §§31A-21-303 and 31A-22-1002

Cancellation during the Underwriting Period

Length of Underwriting Period: Sixty days.

Length of Notice: Ten days.

Reason for Cancellation: Required on the notice when cancellation is for nonpayment; otherwise if reason is not shown on the notice, it must be provided upon request.

Proof Required: Proof of first-class mailing.

Cancellation after the Underwriting Period

The policy may be cancelled **only** for the following reasons:

1. Nonpayment.

2. Material misrepresentation.

3. Substantial change in the risk assumed if such change should not have been foreseen by the insurer or contemplated in the rate.

UTAH

4. Substantial breach of contractual duties or conditions or warranties.

5. Attainment of the specified terminal age by the insured.

6. For commercial auto, if the license of the named insured or any customary operator of the car is revoked or suspended.

Length of Notice: Ten days for nonpayment; thirty days for all other reasons.

Reason for Cancellation: Required on the notice when cancellation is for nonpayment; otherwise, if reason is not shown on the notice, it must be provided upon request.

Proof Required: Proof of first-class mailing.

Nonrenewal

Length of Notice: Thirty days.

Reason for Nonrenewal: Not required on the notice. If reason is not shown on the notice, it must be provided upon request.

Proof Required: Proof of first-class mailing.

Other Cancellation/Nonrenewal Provisions

Renewal on less favorable terms requires a thirty-day notice. Notices of cancellation and nonrenewal must include information about the policyholder's right to request the facts on which the insurer's decision was based. This provision does not apply if the only change is a rate increase generally applicable to the insured's class of business, a rate increase resulting from a classification change, or a policy form change made to make the form consistent with Utah law. Proof of first-class mailing is required for these notices.

Failure to notify the division will result in the continued liability of the carrier until the date that notice of cancellation is received by the division or its designee.

Filings shall be made within thirty days of (1) the reinstatement of a policy; (2) the changing or addition of a name or address of the insured; or (3) the merger of an insured with another entity.

SURPLUS LINES

Utah Code §31A-21-101

The Utah cancellation and nonrenewal statutes do not apply to surplus lines.

UTAH

FINANCED PREMIUMS

Utah Code §31A-21-305

If the premium finance agreement contains a power of attorney or other authority to cancel, the finance company may order, on behalf of the insured, that the insurer cancel the policy due to nonpayment. The finance company must first give the insured ten days to pay. The insurance producer is entitled to the same notice. If the insured fails to make payment within that ten-day period, then the finance company mails the notice of cancellation to the insurer and the cancellation is processed as of the finance company's original default date. Return of the policy by the insured is not required.

PERSONAL LINES

DWELLING FIRE & HOMEOWNERS

Utah Code §31A-21-303

Cancellation during the Underwriting Period

Length of Underwriting Period: Sixty days.

Length of Notice: Ten days.

Reason for Cancellation: Required on the notice for nonpayment. Even though the requirement for a reason to be shown due to nonpayment does not appear on the ISO amendatory endorsements (DP 01 43 and HO 01 43), the Utah Code requires a reason to be shown when canceling for nonpayment. If reason is not shown on the notice, it must be provided upon request.

Proof Required: Proof of first-class mailing.

Cancellation after the Underwriting Period

The policy may be cancelled **only** for the following reasons:

1. Nonpayment.

2. Material misrepresentation.

3. Substantial change in the risk assumed if such change should not have been foreseen by the insurer or contemplated in the rate.

4. Substantial breach of contractual duties or conditions or warranties.

UTAH

5. Attainment of the specified terminal age by the insured.

6. For commercial auto, if the license of the named insured or any customary operator of the car is revoked or suspended.

Length of Notice: Ten days for nonpayment; thirty days for all other reasons.

Reason for Cancellation: Required on the notice for nonpayment. Even though the requirement for a reason to be shown due to nonpayment does not appear on ISO's amendatory endorsement (DP 01 43 or HO 01 43), a reason must be shown when cancelling for nonpayment. If reason is not shown on the notice, it must be provided upon request.

Proof Required: Proof of first-class mailing.

Nonrenewal

Length of Notice: Thirty days.

Reason for Nonrenewal: Not required on the notice. If reason is not shown on the notice, it must be provided upon request.

Proof Required: Proof of first-class mailing.

Other Cancellation/Nonrenewal Provisions

If the policy is written for a period of more than one year, the insurer may cancel on the anniversary date with a thirty-day written notice. Notices of cancellation and nonrenewal must include information about the policyholder's right to request the facts on which the insurer's decision was based.

PERSONAL AUTO

Utah Code §§31A-22-302.5 and 31A-21-303

Cancellation during the Underwriting Period

Length of Underwriting Period: Sixty days.

Length of Notice: Ten days.

Reason for Cancellation: Required on the notice for nonpayment. Even though the requirement for a reason to be shown due to nonpayment does not appear on the ISO amendatory endorsement PP 01 93, the Utah Code requires a reason to be shown when canceling for nonpayment. If reason is not shown on the notice it must be provided upon request.

UTAH

Proof Required: Proof of first-class mailing.

Cancellation after the Underwriting Period

The policy may be cancelled **only** for the following reasons:

1. Nonpayment.

2. Material misrepresentation.

3. Substantial change in the risk assumed if such change should not have been foreseen by the insurer or contemplated in the rate.

4. Substantial breach of contractual duties or conditions or warranties.

5. Attainment of the specified terminal age by the insured.

6. For commercial auto, if the license of the named insured or any customary operator of the car is revoked or suspended.

The Utah Code also allows for cancellation due to the reasons listed under the homeowners section, above. However, if an insurer has adopted the ISO amendatory endorsement PP 01 93, it may only use the reasons as outlined under Personal Auto.

Length of Notice: Ten days for nonpayment; thirty days for all other reasons.

Reason for Cancellation: Required on the notice for nonpayment. Even though the requirement for a reason to be shown due to nonpayment does not appear on the ISO amendatory endorsement PP 01 93, a reason must be shown when cancelling for nonpayment. If reason is not shown on the notice, it must be provided upon request.

Proof Required: Proof of first-class mailing.

Nonrenewal

Length of Notice: Thirty days.

Reason for Nonrenewal: Not required on the notice; otherwise if reason is not shown on the notice, it must be provided upon request.

Proof Required: Proof of first-class mailing.

UTAH

Other Cancellation/Nonrenewal Provisions

If the policy term is less than six months, the insurer may nonrenew every six months, beginning six months after the original effective date. If the policy term is one year or longer, the insurer may nonrenew the policy at each anniversary of the original effective date.

Notices of cancellation and nonrenewal must include information about the policyholder's right to request the facts on which the insurer's decision was based.

Named Driver Exclusion

The named driver exclusion is effective only if:

1. At the time of the proposed exclusion, each person excluded satisfies the owner's or operator's security requirement under Utah Code Section §41-12a-301, independently of the named insured's proof of owner's or operator's security.

2. Any named insured and the person excluded from coverage each provide written consent to the exclusion.

3. The insurer includes the name of each person excluded from coverage in the evidence of insurance provided to an additional insured or loss payee.

PERSONAL UMBRELLA

Utah Code §31A-21-303

Cancellation during the Underwriting Period

Length of Underwriting Period: Sixty days.

Length of Notice: Ten days.

Reason for Cancellation: Required on the notice for nonpayment, otherwise if reason is not shown, it must be provided upon request.

Proof Required: Proof of first-class mailing.

Cancellation after the Underwriting Period

The policy may be cancelled **only** for the following reasons:

1. Nonpayment.

UTAH

2. Material misrepresentation.

3. Substantial change in the risk assumed if such change should not have been foreseen by the insurer or contemplated in the rate.

4. Substantial breach of contractual duties or conditions or warranties.

5. Attainment of the specified terminal age by the insured.

6. For commercial auto, if the license of the named insured or any customary operator of the car is revoked or suspended.

Length of Notice: Ten days for nonpayment; thirty days for any other reason.

Reason for Cancellation: Required on the notice for nonpayment, otherwise if reason is not shown, it must be provided upon request.

Proof Required: Proof of first-class mailing.

Nonrenewal

Length of Notice: Thirty days.

Reason for Nonrenewal: Required on the notice for nonpayment, otherwise if reason is not shown, it must be provided upon request.

Proof Required: Proof of first-class mailing.

INSURANCE FRAUD
Utah Code §§31A-31-103

Definition

1. A person commits a fraudulent insurance act if that person with intent to deceive or defraud:

    a. Knowingly presents or causes to be presented to an insurer any oral or written statement or representation knowing that the statement or representation contains false, incomplete, or misleading information concerning any fact material to an application for the issuance or renewal of an insurance policy, certificate, or contract.

    b. Knowingly presents or causes to be presented to an insurer any oral or written statement or representation; as part of, or in support of, a claim for payment

or other benefit pursuant to an insurance policy, certificate, or contract; or in connection with any civil claim asserted for recovery of damages for personal or bodily injuries or property damage; and knowing that the statement or representation contains false, incomplete, or misleading information concerning any fact or thing material to the claim.
  c. Knowingly accepts a benefit from the proceeds derived from a fraudulent insurance act.
  d. Assists, abets, solicits, or conspires with another to commit a fraudulent insurance act.
  e. Knowingly supplies false or fraudulent material information in any document or statement required by the department.
  f. Knowingly fails to forward a premium to an insurer in violation of Utah Code §31A-23a-411.1.
  g. Knowingly employs, uses, or acts as a runner for the purpose of committing a fraudulent insurance act.

2. A service provider commits a fraudulent insurance act if that service provider with intent to deceive or defraud:

  a. Knowingly submits or causes to be submitted a bill or request for payment:

     (1) Containing charges or costs for an item or service that are substantially in excess of customary charges or costs for the item or service.
     (2) Containing itemized or delineated fees for what would customarily be considered a single procedure or service.

  b. Knowingly furnishes or causes to be furnished an item or service to a person:

     (1) Substantially in excess of the needs of the person.
     (2) Of a quality that fails to meet professionally recognized standards.

  c. Knowingly accepts a benefit from the proceeds derived from a fraudulent insurance act.

  d. Assists, abets, solicits, or conspires with another to commit a fraudulent insurance act.

3. An insurer commits a fraudulent insurance act if that insurer with intent to deceive or defraud:

  a. Knowingly withholds information or provides false or misleading information with respect to an application, coverage, benefits, or claims under a policy or certificate.

UTAH

    b. Assists, abets, solicits, or conspires with another to commit a fraudulent insurance act.
    c. Knowingly accepts a benefit from the proceeds derived from a fraudulent insurance act.
    d. Knowingly supplies false or fraudulent material information in any document or statement required by the department.

4. An insurer or service provider is not liable for any fraudulent insurance act committed by an employee without the authority of the insurer or service provider unless the insurer or service provider knew or should have known of the fraudulent insurance act.

Civil Penalties

Utah Code §31A-31-109

In addition to other penalties provided by law, a perpetrator of insurance fraud must make full restitution and pay the costs of enforcing Utah's insurance laws for the case in which the person is found to have violated those laws including costs of investigators, attorneys, and other public employees; and in the discretion of the court, may be required to pay to the state a civil penalty not to exceed three times that amount of value improperly sought or received from the fraudulent insurance act.

Reporting Requirements

Utah Code §31A-31-110

Insurers and persons who are related to or an auditor in the field of title insurance must report a fraudulent insurance act to the department if the person has a good-faith belief on the basis of a preponderance of the evidence that a fraudulent insurance act is being, will be, or has been committed by a person other than the person making the report. This report must be in writing and provide detailed information relating to: The fraudulent insurance act; the perpetrator of the fraudulent act; and state whether the reporter also reported the fraudulent insurance act to the attorney general, a state law enforcement agency, a criminal investigative department of the United States, a district attorney, or the prosecuting attorney of a municipality or county. The report must disclose the specific entity to which the reporter revealed the suspected insurance fraud. A person required to submit such a written report shall submit the written report to the department by no later than ninety days from the day on which the person required to report the fraudulent insurance act has a good-faith belief on the basis of a preponderance of the evidence that the fraudulent insurance act is being, will be, or has been committed.

Contact information for reporting insurance fraud is available at: https://insurance.utah.gov/agent/fraud/report.php or call (801) 531-5380.

UTAH

Application Fraud Statement
Utah Code §31A-36-113

An application or contract for a life settlement, however transmitted, shall contain the following or a substantially similar statement: "A person that knowingly presents false information in an application for insurance or a life settlement is guilty of a crime and may be subject to fines and confinement in prison."

FAIR CLAIMS PROCESSING
Utah Code §§31A-26-303; Utah Administrative Code R590-190

The Utah Code prohibits the following unfair claims settlement practices:

1. The following are always considered to be an unfair claims settlement practice:

    a. Knowingly misrepresenting material facts or the contents of insurance policy provisions at issue in connection with a claim under an insurance contract; however, this provision does not include the failure to disclose information.
    b. Attempting to use a policy application which was altered by the insurer without notice to, or knowledge, or consent of, the insured as the basis for settling or refusing to settle a claim.
    c. Failing to settle a claim promptly under one portion of the insurance policy coverage, where liability and the amount of loss are reasonably clear, in order to influence settlements under other portions of the insurance policy coverage, but this applies only to claims made by persons in direct privity of contract with the insurer.

2. The following are considered to be unfair claim settlement practices if they are committed or performed with such frequency as to indicate a general business practice by an insurer or persons representing an insurer:

    a. Not acknowledging and acting promptly upon communications about claims under insurance policies.
    b. Not adopting and implementing reasonable standards for the prompt investigation and processing of claims under insurance policies.
    c. Compelling insureds to institute litigation to recover amounts due under an insurance policy by offering substantially less than the amounts ultimately recovered in actions brought by those insureds when the amounts claimed were reasonably near to the amounts recovered.
    d. Failing, after payment of a claim, to inform insureds or beneficiaries, upon request by them, of the coverage under which payment was made.

UTAH

  e. Not promptly providing to the insured a reasonable explanation of the basis for denial of a claim or for the offer of a compromise settlement.
  f. Appealing from substantially all arbitration awards in favor of insureds for the purpose of compelling them to accept settlements or compromises for less than the amount awarded in arbitration.
  g. Delaying the investigation or payment of claims by requiring an insured, claimant, or the physician of either to submit a preliminary claim report and then requiring the subsequent submission of formal proof of loss forms which contain substantially the same information.
  h. Not making a good-faith attempt to effectuate a prompt, fair, and equitable settlement of claims in which liability is reasonably clear.

The Utah Administrative Code enumerates additional prohibited unfair trade practices by the type of insurance claim involved in R590-190 through R590-192.

VERMONT

For details on cancellation procedures for the standard policy, refer to the Standard Policy section.

COMMERCIAL LINES

AGRICULTURAL CAPITAL ASSETS; BOP; CAPITAL ASSETS; C. AUTO.; CRIME; CGL (CGL, EMPLOYMENT PRACTICES, LIQUOR, OCP, POLLUTION, PRODUCTS/COMPLETED OPERATIONS, UNDERGROUND STORAGE TANKS); CIM; C. PROP; C. UMB.; EQUIPMENT BREAKDOWN; FARM; & PRO. LIAB.

8 V.S.A. §§3879 to 3885 – Fire & Casualty

8 V.S.A. §§4711 to 4714 – Commercial Risk

Cancellation during the Underwriting Period

Length of Underwriting Period: Sixty days.

Length of Notice: Fifteen days for nonpayment (or substantial increase in hazard if fire & casualty insurance); forty-five days for any other reason.

Reason for Cancellation: Required on the notice.

Proof Required: Certified mail or certificate of mailing for nonpayment; certified mail for all other reasons. Proof of delivery is also acceptable for any cancellation.

Cancellation after the Underwriting Period

The policy may be cancelled **only** for the following reasons:

1. Nonpayment.

2. Fraud or material misrepresentation affecting the policy or in the pursuit of a claim.

3. If the insured violates any policy provision.

4. Substantial increase in hazard. This reason requires prior approval of the commissioner.

Length of Notice: Fifteen days for nonpayment or substantial increase in hazard; forty-five days for all other reasons.

Reason for Cancellation: Required on the notice.

VERMONT

Proof Required: Certified mail or certificate of mailing for nonpayment; certified mail for all other reasons. Proof of delivery is acceptable for any cancellation.

Nonrenewal

Length of Notice: Forty-five days.

Reason for Nonrenewal: Not required.

Proof Required: Certificate of mailing for nonpayment; certified mail for all other reasons. Proof of delivery is also acceptable for all nonrenewals.

Other Cancellation/Nonrenewal Provisions

On OCP policies notices of cancellation or nonrenewal must also be sent to the listed contractor.

Even though there is no amendatory endorsement for underground storage tanks, insurers must follow the cancellation and nonrenewal requirements as outlined for other Commercial General Liability lines.

COMMERCIAL GENERAL LIABILITY
(Railroad Protective)

8 V.S.A. §§3879 to 3882

Cancellation during the Underwriting Period

Length of Underwriting Period: Sixty days.

Length of Notice: Fifteen days for nonpayment; forty-five days for any other reason. If using ISO policy (CG 00 35 or CG 28 69) the insurer must give a sixty-day notice for any reason.

Reason for Cancellation: Required on the notice. The ISO amendatory endorsement (CG 28 69) is silent on this matter, but statute requires that the reasons for cancellation must be given.

Proof Required: Certified mail or certificate of mailing for nonpayment; certified mail for all other reasons. Proof of delivery is also acceptable for all cancellations.

Cancellation after the Underwriting Period

The policy may be cancelled **only** for the following reasons:

1. Nonpayment.

2. Fraud or material misrepresentation on the application or in the pursuit of a claim.

VERMONT

3. If the insured violates any policy provision.

4. Substantial increase in hazard. This requires approval of the commissioner.

Length of Notice: Fifteen days for nonpayment or substantial increase in hazard; forty-five days for all other reasons. The Vermont statute requires only the same notice of cancellation for railroad protective as for other lines. However, if an insurer has adopted the ISO policy (CG 00 35) and amendatory endorsement (CG 28 69), it must give a sixty-day notice for midterm cancellation for any reason.

Reason for Cancellation: Required on the notice. Even though the Vermont amendatory endorsement is silent on the matter, implying that the reason does not need to be shown, statute requires that the reason must be shown.

Proof Required: Certified mail or certificate of mailing for nonpayment; certified mail for all other reasons. Proof of delivery is also acceptable for all cancellations.

Nonrenewal

Length of Notice: Forty-five days.

Reason for Nonrenewal: Not required.

Proof Required: Certified mail or certificate of mailing for nonpayment; certified mail for all other reasons. Proof of delivery is also acceptable for all nonrenewals.

Other Cancellation/Nonrenewal Provisions

Notices of cancellation or nonrenewal must also be sent to the listed contractor and any involved governmental authority.

WORKERS COMPENSATION

21 V.S.A. §§696 and 697

Length of Notice: Forty-five days for cancellation or nonrenewal.

Reason for Nonrenewal: Not required.

Proof Required: Certified mail or certificate of mailing. Copies of all notices must also be sent to the Commissioner of Labor and Industry.

SURPLUS LINES

8 V.S.A. §5029

Surplus lines insurers must follow the cancellation and nonrenewal requirements for admitted companies.

VERMONT

FINANCED PREMIUMS
8 V.S.A. §7009

If the premium finance agreement contains a power of attorney, the finance company may cancel the policy due to nonpayment. The finance company must mail the insured a ten day notice to pay. If the insured fails to make payment within that ten day period, then the finance company mails the notice of cancellation to the insurer and the cancellation is effective not less than ten days after the notice of cancellation is mailed to the insurer. The insurer shall give the prescribed notice on behalf of itself or the insured to any governmental agency, mortgagee, or other third party on or before the second business day after the day it receives the notice of cancellation from the premium finance company and shall determine the effective date of cancellation taking into consideration the number of days' notice required to complete the cancellation. Return of the policy by the insured is not required.

PERSONAL LINES
DWELLING FIRE & HOMEOWNERS
8 V.S.A. §§3879 to 3884

Cancellation during the Underwriting Period

Length of Underwriting Period: Sixty days.

Length of Notice: Fifteen days for nonpayment or substantial increase in hazard; forty-five days for all other reasons.

Reason for Cancellation: Required on the notice. The ISO amendatory endorsements (DP 01 44 and HO 01 44) are silent on this matter, but statute requires that the reasons for cancellation must be given.

Proof Required: Certificate of mailing for nonpayment; certified mail for all other reasons. Proof of delivery is also acceptable for all cancellations.

Cancellation after the Underwriting Period

The policy may be cancelled **only** for the following reasons:

1. Nonpayment.

2. Fraud or material misrepresentation on the application or in the pursuit of a claim or violation of any provisions of the policy.

VERMONT

3. If the insured violates any policy provision.

4. Substantial increase in hazard. This requires approval of the commissioner.

Length of Notice: Fifteen days for nonpayment or substantial increase in hazard; forty-five days for all other reasons.

Reason for Cancellation: Required on the notice. The ISO amendatory endorsements (DP 01 44 and HO 01 44) are silent on this matter, but statute requires that the reasons for cancellation must be given.

Proof Required: Certificate of mailing for nonpayment; certified mail for all other reasons. Proof of delivery is also acceptable for all cancellations.

Nonrenewal

Length of Notice: Forty-five days.

Reason for Nonrenewal: Not required.

Proof Required: Certificate of mailing for nonpayment; certified mail for all other reasons. Proof of delivery is also acceptable for all nonrenewals.

Other Cancellation/Nonrenewal Provisions

If the policy is written for a period of more than one year, the insurer may cancel on the anniversary date with a forty-five-day written notice for any reason.

PERSONAL AUTO

8 V.S.A. §§4223 to 4227

Cancellation during the Underwriting Period

Length of Underwriting Period: Sixty days.

Length of Notice: Fifteen days for nonpayment; forty-five days for any other reason.

Reason for Cancellation: Required on the notice. The ISO amendatory endorsement (PP 01 72) is silent on this matter, but statute requires that the reasons for cancellation must be given.

Proof Required: Certified mail or certificate of mailing for nonpayment; proof of certified mailing for all other reasons. Proof of delivery is also acceptable for all cancellations.

VERMONT

Cancellation after the Underwriting Period

The policy may be cancelled **only** for the following reasons:

1. Nonpayment.

2. Suspension or revocation of the driver's license of the named insured or any driver who lives with the named insured or who customarily uses the insured auto. The suspension or revocation must occur during the policy period, or if the policy is a renewal, during its policy period or the 180 days immediately prior to the effective date.

3. Fraud or material misrepresentation on the application.

Length of Notice: Fifteen days for nonpayment; forty-five days for any other reason.

Reason for Cancellation: Required on the notice. The ISO amendatory endorsement (PP 01 72) is silent on this matter, but statute requires that the reasons for cancellation must be given.

Proof Required: Certificate of mailing for nonpayment; proof of certified mailing for all other reasons. Proof of delivery is also acceptable for all cancellations.

Nonrenewal

Length of Notice: Forty-five days.

Reason for Nonrenewal: Not required.

Proof Required: Certificate of mailing for nonpayment; proof of certified mailing for all other reasons. Proof of cancellation is also acceptable for all nonrenewals.

Other Cancellation/Nonrenewal Provisions

If the policy term is less than six months, the insurer may nonrenew every six months, beginning six months after the original effective date. If the policy term is one year or longer, the insurer may nonrenew the policy at each anniversary of the original effective date.

The insurer must notify the insured of possible eligibility in the Vermont Automobile Insurance Plan with any termination other than for nonpayment.

If policy is filed as proof of financial responsibility for a person convicted of drunk driving, a fifteen-day notice must be given to the Department of Motor Vehicles regardless of whether termination is cancellation or nonrenewal. (http://www.dfr.vermont.gov/sites/default/files/BUL-I-122.pdf)

VERMONT

PERSONAL UMBRELLA
8 V.S.A. §§3879 to 3883

Cancellation during the Underwriting Period

Length of Underwriting Period: Sixty days.

Length of Notice: Fifteen days for nonpayment or substantial increase in hazard; forty-five days for all other reasons.

Reason for Cancellation: Reason for notice must be stated. The ISO amendatory endorsement (DL 98 93) is silent on this matter, but statute requires that the reasons for cancellation must be given.

Proof Required: Certified mail or certificate of mailing for nonpayment; certified mail for all other reasons. Proof of delivery is also acceptable for all cancellations.

Cancellation after the Underwriting Period

The policy may be cancelled **only** for the following reasons:

1. Nonpayment of premium.

2. Substantial increase in hazard provided that in the case of substantial increase in hazard, the insurer has secured approval for the cancellation from the commissioner of insurance. This can be done by letting insured know fifteen days before the date cancellation takes effect.

3. Fraud or material misrepresentation affecting the policy or in the presentation of a claim, or violation of any provisions of the policy.

Length of Notice: Fifteen days for nonpayment and substantial increase in hazard; forty-five days for any other allowable reason.

Reason for Cancellation: Reason for notice must be stated. The ISO amendatory endorsement (DL 98 93) is silent on this matter, but statute requires that the reasons for cancellation must be given.

Proof Required: Certified mail or certificate of mailing for nonpayment; certified mail for all other reasons. Proof of delivery is also acceptable for all cancellations.

VERMONT

Nonrenewal

Length of Notice: Forty-five days.

Reason for Nonrenewal: Not required.

Proof Required: Certified mail. The ISO amendatory endorsement (DL 98 93) only requires proof of mailing for nonrenewal, however Vermont law requires certified mail for nonrenewal.

FRAUD
13 V.S.A. §§2031

Definition

Under Vermont law, a person commits a fraudulent insurance act when, with the intent to defraud, a person presents or causes to be presented a claim for payment or benefit, pursuant to any insurance policy, that contains false representations as to any material fact or which conceals a material fact. It is also a fraudulent insurance act for a person, who has the intent to defraud, to present or cause to be presented any information which contains false representations as to any material fact or which conceals a material fact concerning the solicitation for sale of any insurance policy or purported insurance policy, an application for certificate of authority, or the financial condition of any insurer.

The falsity of a statement in the application for a policy covered by such provisions shall not bar the right to recovery thereunder unless such false statement was made with actual intent to deceive or unless it materially affected either the acceptance of the risk or the hazard assumed by insurer. (8 V.S.A. §4205).

How do I report a suspected incident of insurance fraud?

If you believe that you have been a victim of insurance fraud, or if you are aware of an instance of insurance fraud, it is important to: Contact the Vermont Insurance Division's consumer services section to file a complaint against the insurance company. Call toll free: 1-800-964-1784, or go to Filing a Complaint on this web site. You can also visit http://www.naic.org/ and complete the form provided by the Online Fraud Reporting System (OFRS). Through the OFRS, the NAIC and state regulators are encouraging consumers to take a proactive role in identifying and reporting insurance fraud.(https://www.naic.org/documents/committees_d_antifraud_form_instructions.pdf, http://www.dfr.vermont.gov/).

Penalties

The fines and prison sentences imposed by the Vermont statutes on perpetrators of insurance fraud vary depending on the pecuniary value of the benefit wrongfully obtained or

VERMONT

the loss that any person has suffered as a result of a fraudulent insurance act. When an insurance practitioner is convicted of committing a fraudulent insurance act, the prosecutor in the case will inform the appropriate licensing authorities.

Immunity

No insurer or insurance professional acting in good faith and furnishing or disclosing information to the appropriate law enforcement official shall be subject to civil liability for libel, slander, or any other cause of action arising from the furnishing or disclosing information regarding alleged insurance fraud, except if the information is furnished solely to obtain an advantage in connection with a claim that will be, is being, or has been filed.

Application Fraud Statement
8 V.S.A. §3847

Life settlement contracts and applications for life settlements, regardless of the form of transmission, shall contain the following statement or a substantially similar statement:

> "Any person who knowingly presents false information in an application for insurance or life settlement contract may be guilty of a crime and may be subject to fines and confinement in prison."

FAIR CLAIMS PROCESSING
8 V.S.A. §§4723 and 4724

Vermont law prohibits anyone from engaging in the following practices when they are committed or performed with such frequency as to indicate a business practice:

1. Misrepresenting pertinent facts or insurance policy provisions relating to coverage at issue.

2. Not acknowledging and acting reasonably promptly upon communications with respect to claims arising under insurance policies.

3. Not adopting and implementing reasonable standards for the prompt investigation of claims arising under insurance policies.

4. Refusing to pay claims without conducting a reasonable investigation based upon all available information.

5. Not affirming or denying coverage of claims within a reasonable time after proof of loss statements have been completed.

VERMONT

6. Not making a good-faith attempt to effectuate prompt, fair and equitable settlements of claims in which liability has become reasonably clear.

7. Attempting to settle a claim for less than the amount to which a reasonable person would have believed he or she was entitled by reference to written or printed advertising material accompanying or made a part of the application.

8. Attempting to settle claims on the basis of an application which was altered without notice to, or knowledge or consent of the insured.

9. Making claim payments to insureds or beneficiaries not accompanied by a statement setting forth the coverage under which the payments are made.

10. Making known to insureds or claimants a policy of appealing from arbitration awards in favor of insureds or claimants for the purpose of compelling them to accept settlements or compromises less than the amount awarded in arbitration.

11. Delaying the investigation or payment of claims by requiring an insured, claimant, or the physician of either to submit a preliminary claim report and then requiring the subsequent submission of formal proof of loss forms, both of which submissions contain substantially the same information.

12. Failing to promptly settle claims where liability has become reasonably clear under one portion of the insurance policy coverage in order to influence settlements under other portions of the insurance policy coverage.

13. Failing to promptly provide a reasonable explanation on the basis in the insurance policy in relation to the facts or applicable law for denial of a claim or for the offer of a compromise settlement.

VIRGIN ISLANDS

For details on cancellation procedures for the standard policy, refer to the Standard Policy section.

COMMERCIAL LINES
22 V.I.C. §826; 827

Cancellation

Length of Underwriting Period: N/A.

Length of Notice: Fifteen days for nonpayment or discovery of fraud or misrepresentation in obtaining the policy or in presenting a claim; thirty days for any other reason.

Reason for Cancellation: Not required.

Proof Required: Actual delivery or certified mail.

Nonrenewal

Length of Notice: Thirty days.

Reason for Nonrenewal: Not required.

Proof Required: *Actual delivery or certified mail*

AGRICULTURAL CAPITAL ASSETS; BOP; & CRIME
22 V.I.C. §§809; 826; 827

Cancellation

Length of Underwriting Period: N/A.

Length of Notice: Fifteen days for nonpayment or discovery of fraud or misrepresentation in obtaining the policy or in presenting a claim; thirty days for any other reason.

Reason for Cancellation: Not required.

Proof Required: Actual delivery or certified mail.

Nonrenewal

Length of Notice: Thirty days.

VIRGIN ISLANDS

Reason for Nonrenewal: Not required.

Proof Required: Actual delivery or certified mail.

Other Cancellation/Nonrenewal Provisions

The policy may be voided at any time in any case of fraud by the named insured or if the named insured conceals or misrepresents material facts or circumstance concerning the policy, covered property, the insured's interest in the policy, or a claim under the policy. Concealment or misrepresentation is not considered material unless it is done with intent to deceive.

Unearned premium must be returned within thirty days.

CAPITAL ASSETS; CIM; C. PROP; E-COM.; CGL (All lines except UST); EQUIPMENT BREAKDOWN; & MGT. PROT.

22 V.I.C. §§826; 827

Cancellation

Length of Underwriting Period: N/A.

Length of Notice: Fifteen days for nonpayment or discovery of fraud or misrepresentation in obtaining the policy or in presenting a claim; thirty days for any other reason.

Reason for Cancellation: Not required.

Proof Required: Actual delivery or certified mail.

Nonrenewal

Length of Notice: Thirty days.

Reason for Nonrenewal: Not required.

Proof Required: Actual delivery or certified mail.

Other Cancellation/Nonrenewal Provisions

Notice must be given to each mortgagee or any other person shown in the policy to have an interest in loss under the policy.

For OCP policies, notice must be given to the contractor, involved governmental authority and to each mortgagee shown in the policy.

Unearned premium must be returned within thirty days.

VIRGIN ISLANDS

C. AUTO. & C. UMB.

22 V.I.C. §827

Cancellation

The policy may be cancelled for any reason.

Length of Notice: Fifteen days for nonpayment, or discovery of fraud or misrepresentation in obtaining the policy or in presenting a claim, or the suspension or revocation of the driver's license of the named insured or any other person who customarily operates the automobile insured under the policy; thirty days for any other reason.

Reason for Cancellation: Not required.

Proof Required: Actual delivery or certified mail.

Nonrenewal

Length of Notice: Thirty days.

Reason for Nonrenewal: Not required.

Proof Required: Actual delivery or certified mail.

Other Cancellation/Nonrenewal Provisions

Notice must be given to any loss payee or other person shown by the policy to have an interest.

Unearned premium must be returned within thirty days.

COMMERCIAL GENERAL LIABILITY

(Underground Storage Tanks)

22 V.I.C. §827

Cancellation

The policy may be cancelled for any reason.

Length of Notice: Fifteen days for nonpayment or discovery of fraud or misrepresentation in obtaining the policy or in presenting a claim; sixty days for any other reason. Nothing in the Virgin Island statutes requires a sixty-day notice for other cancellations. However, if an insurer has adopted the ISO CG 00 42, it must give ten days notice for nonpayment or misrepresentation, sixty days' notice for any other reason.

VIRGIN ISLANDS

Reason for Cancellation: Not required.

Proof Required: Actual delivery or certified mail.

Nonrenewal

Length of Notice: Sixty days. Nothing in the Virgin Island Statutes requires a sixty-day notice for other cancellations. However, if an insurer has adopted the ISO CG 00 42, it must give sixty days' notice.

Reason for Nonrenewal: Not required.

Proof Required: Actual delivery or certified mail.

Other Cancellation/Nonrenewal Provisions

Unearned premium must be returned within thirty days.

WORKERS COMPENSATION
22 V.I.C. §875

The Virgin Islands Statutes change the ten-day notice from the standard NCCI policy provision to at least a five-day notice.

SURPLUS LINES
22 V.I.C. §203

Surplus lines must follow the cancellation requirements.

FINANCED PREMIUMS
22 V.I.C. §1642

When a premium finance agreement contains a power of attorney enabling the premium finance company to cancel the policy, the insurance contract shall not be cancelled unless at least fifteen days written notice is mailed to each insured shown on the premium finance agreement of the intent of the premium finance company to cancel the insurance contract unless the installment payment is received within fifteen days. The premium finance company may then mail to the insurer, with a copy to the insured, at his last known address as shown on the premium finance agreement, a request for cancellation of the policy. Upon a receipt of this notice, the insurance contract shall be cancelled with the same force and effect as if the notice of cancellation has been submitted by the insured, without requiring any further notice to the insured or the return of the policy. The insurer must give notice to such governmental

VIRGIN ISLANDS

agency, person, mortgagee, or individual; and determine the effective date of cancellation from the premium finance company. The insurer shall promptly return the unpaid balance due under the finance contract, up to the gross amount available upon the cancellation of the policy, to the premium finance company and any remaining unearned premium to the agent or the insured.

PERSONAL LINES
DWELLING FIRE & HOMEOWNERS
22 V.I.C. §827

Length of Underwriting Period: N/A. Virgin Island Statutes **do not** utilize an underwriting period.

Length of Notice: Fifteen days for nonpayment or discovery of fraud or misrepresentation in obtaining the policy or in presenting a claim; thirty days for any other reason.

Virgin Island statutes do not limit the reasons for cancellation. However, Virgin Island statutes require the policy to be cancellable by its own terms and all policies must be filed and approved prior to use.

Reason for Cancellation: Not required.

Proof Required: Actual delivery or certified mail.

Nonrenewal

Length of Notice: Thirty days.

Reason for Nonrenewal: Not required.

Proof Required: Actual delivery or certified mail.

Other Cancellation/Nonrenewal Provisions

The policy may be voided at any time in any case of fraud by the named insured, or if the named insured conceals or misrepresents material facts or circumstance concerning the policy, covered property, the insured's interest in the policy, or a claim under the policy. Concealment or misrepresentation is not considered material unless it is done with intent to deceive.

Notice must be given to each mortgagee and to any other person shown by the policy to have an interest.

Unearned premium must be returned within thirty days.

VIRGIN ISLANDS

Policies written for a period of more than one year may be cancelled on the anniversary date with a thirty day notice sent certified mail.

PERSONAL AUTO
22 V.I.C. §827

Length of Underwriting Period: N/A. Virgin Island Statutes **do not** utilize an underwriting period.

Length of Notice: Fifteen days for nonpayment, or discovery of fraud or misrepresentation in obtaining the policy or in presenting a claim, or the suspension or revocation of the driver's license of the named insured or any other person who customarily operates the automobile insured under the policy; thirty days for any other reason.

Virgin Island Statutes do not limit the reasons for cancellation. However, Virgin Island Statutes require the policy to be cancellable by its own terms and all policies must be filed and approved prior to use.

Reason for Cancellation: Not required.

Proof Required: Actual delivery or certified mail.

Nonrenewal

Length of Notice: Thirty days.

Reason for Nonrenewal: Not required.

Proof Required: Actual delivery or certified mail.

Other Cancellation/Nonrenewal Provisions

Unearned premium must be returned within thirty days.

PERSONAL UMBRELLA
22 V.I.C. §827

Length of Underwriting Period: N/A. Virgin Island Statutes **do not** utilize an underwriting period.

Length of Notice: Fifteen days for nonpayment, or discovery of fraud or misrepresentation in obtaining the policy or in presenting a claim, or the suspension or revocation of the driver's

VIRGIN ISLANDS

license of the named insured or any other person who customarily operates the automobile insured under the policy; thirty days for any other reason.

Virgin Island Statutes do not limit the reasons for cancellation. However, Virgin Island Statutes require the policy to be cancellable by its own terms and all policies must be filed and approved prior to use.

Reason for Cancellation: Not required.

Proof Required: Actual delivery or certified mail.

Nonrenewal

Length of Notice: Thirty days.

Reason for Cancellation: Not required.

Proof Required: Actual delivery or certified mail.

Other Cancellation/Nonrenewal Provisions

Unearned premium must be returned within thirty days.

FAIR CLAIM PRACTICES
22 V.I.C. §1201

1. No person engaged in the business of insurance shall engage in unfair methods of competition or in unfair or deceptive acts or practices in the conduct of such business as such methods, acts, or practices are defined pursuant to subsection 2 of this section.

2. In addition to such unfair methods and unfair or deceptive acts or practices as are expressly defined and prohibited by this title, the commissioner may from time to time by regulations promulgated only after a hearing thereon, define other methods of competition and other acts and practices in the conduct of such business reasonably found by him to be unfair or deceptive.

3. No such regulation shall be made effective prior to the expiration of thirty days after the date of the order on hearing by which it is promulgated.

4. If the commissioner has cause to believe that any person is violating any such regulation he shall order such person to cease and desist therefrom. The commissioner shall deliver such order to such person direct or mail it to the person by registered mail with

VIRGIN ISLANDS

return receipt requested. If the person fails to comply therewith before expiration of ten days after the cease and desist order has been received by him, he shall forfeit to the people of this territory a sum not to exceed $250 for each violation committed thereafter, such penalty to be recovered by an action prosecuted by the commissioner.

FRAUD
22 V.I.C. §§1223-1224

While not defining fraud directly, the statute states that any person, who, with intent to defraud or prejudice the insurer thereof, willfully burns or in any manner injures or destroys property which is insured at the time against loss or damage by fire or by any other casualty, under such circumstances not making the offense arson, is guilty of a felony.

Likewise, any person who presents, or causes to be presented, a false or fraudulent claim, or any proof in support of such claim, for the payment of a loss under a contract of insurance; or prepares, makes or subscribes to any false or fraudulent account, certificate, affidavit, or proof of loss, or other document or writing, with intent that it be presented or used in support of such a claim, is guilty of a gross misdemeanor.

Application Fraud Statement
14 V.I.C. §842

The Virgin Islands statutes do not require an application fraud statement. However, whoever:

1. Presents any false or fraudulent claim, or any proof in support of such claim, upon any contract of insurance for the payment of any loss.

2. Prepares, makes, or subscribes any account, certificate of survey, affidavit, or proof of loss, or other book, paper, or writing, with intent to present or use the same, or to allow it to be presented or used in support of any such claim shall be fined not more than $1,000 or imprisoned not more than five years, or both.

VIRGINIA

For details on cancellation procedures for the standard policy, refer to the Standard Policy section.

COMMERCIAL PROPERTY

The policy may be cancelled for any reason.

Length of Underwriting Period: N/A.

Length of Notice: Per policy terms and conditions.

Reason for Cancellation: Per policy terms and conditions.

Proof Required: Per policy terms and conditions.

Nonrenewal

Length of Notice: Per policy terms and conditions.

Reason for Nonrenewal: Per policy terms and conditions.

Proof Required: Per policy terms and conditions.

BUSINESSOWNERS; CGL; E-COMMERCE; FARM & MGT. PROT.

Va. Code Ann. §38.2-231

The policy may be cancelled for any reason.

Length of Underwriting Period: N/A.

Length of Notice: Fifteen days for nonpayment; forty-five days for all other reasons.

Reason for Cancellation: Required on the notice.

Proof Required: Certified mail, registered mail, Intelligent Mail barcode tracing (IMb), electronically with evidence of transmittal, or regular mail with postal receipt. A certificate of bulk mailing does not count.

Nonrenewal

Length of Notice: Forty-five days.

Reason for Nonrenewal: Required on the notice.

VIRGINIA

Proof Required: Certified mail, registered mail, Intelligent Mail barcode tracing (IMb), or ordinary mail with postal receipt. Notices may also be delivered electronically. The insurer must retain a record of the electronic transmittal or receipt of notification for at least one year from the date of transmittal. A certificate of bulk mailing does not count.

Other Cancellation/Nonrenewal Provisions

A forty-five-day notice is required if the insurer intends to renew with a reduction in coverage or a rate increase of more than 25 percent. This notice must give the reason for the increase or advice that such information may be obtained from the agent or the insurer. The old rates or more favorable policy terms remain in effect until this notice is given.

The notice must advise the insured of his right to request in writing, within fifteen days of the receipt of the notice, that the Commissioner of Insurance reviews the action of the insurer.

Cancellation and nonrenewal notices must be written in at least eight-point type.

If the terms of the policy require the notice of cancellation, refusal to renew, reduction in coverage, or increase in premium to be given to any lienholder, the insurer and lienholder may agree by separate agreement that such notices may be transmitted electronically, provided that the insurer and lienholder agree upon the specifics for transmittal and acknowledgement of notification. Evidence of transmittal or receipt of the required notification shall be retained by the insurer for at least one year from the date of termination.

The insurer is required to maintain records of all cancellations, nonrenewals, reductions in coverage, and notifications of premium increase of 25 percent or more for at least one year from the date of termination.

COMMERCIAL AUTO; COMMERCIAL UMBRELLA

Va. Code Ann. §38.2-231

The policy may be cancelled for any reason.

Length of Underwriting Period: N/A.

Length of Notice: Fifteen days for nonpayment; forty-five days for all other reasons.

Reason for Cancellation: Required on the notice.

Proof Required: Certified mail, registered mail, Intelligent Mail barcode tracing (IMb), or regular mail with postal receipt. A certificate of bulk mailing does not count.

VIRGINIA

Nonrenewal

Length of Notice: Forty-five days.

Reason for Nonrenewal: Required on the notice.

Proof Required: Certified mail, registered mail, Intelligent Mail barcode tracing (IMb), or ordinary mail with postal receipt. Notices may also be delivered electronically. The insurer must retain a record of the electronic transmittal or receipt of notification for at least one year from the date of transmittal. A certificate of bulk mailing does not count.

Other Cancellation/Nonrenewal Provisions

A forty-five-day notice is required if the insurer intends to renew with a reduction in coverage or a rate increase of more than 25 percent. This notice must give the reason for the increase or advice that such information may be obtained from the agent or the insurer. The old rates or more favorable policy terms remain in effect until this notice is given.

The notice must advise the insured of his right to request in writing, within fifteen days of the receipt of the notice, that the Commissioner of Insurance reviews the action of the insurer.

Cancellation and nonrenewal notices must be written in at least eight-point type.

If the terms of the policy require the notice of cancellation, refusal to renew, reduction in coverage, or increase in premium to be given to any lienholder, the insurer and lienholder may agree by separate agreement that such notices may be transmitted electronically, provided that the insurer and lienholder agree upon the specifics for transmittal and acknowledgement of notification. Evidence of transmittal or receipt of the required notification shall be retained by the insurer for at least one year from the date of termination.

The insurer is required to maintain records of all cancellations, nonrenewals, reductions in coverage, and notifications of premium increase of 25 percent or more for at least one year from the date of termination.

NAMED EXCLUDED DRIVER

Va. Code Ann. §38.2-2204

An insurer may exclude any person from coverage under a personal umbrella or excess policy, if the exclusion is requested in writing by the first-named insured and is acknowledged in writing by the excluded driver.

VIRGINIA

CRIME

Length of Notice: Per policy terms and conditions.

Reason for Cancellation: Per policy terms and conditions.

Proof Required: Per policy terms and conditions.

Nonrenewal

Length of Notice: Per policy terms and conditions.

Reason for Nonrenewal: Per policy terms and conditions.

Proof Required: Per policy terms and conditions.

COMMERCIAL GENERAL LIABILITY
(incl. Railroad Protective)
Va. Code Ann. §38.2-231

The policy may be cancelled for any reason.

Length of Notice: Fifteen days for nonpayment and forty-five days for any other reason. An insurer must give sixty days' notice if it has adopted the ISO amendatory endorsement (CG 28 59, Virginia Changes that modify the Railroad Protective Liability Coverage Part).

Reason for Cancellation: Required on the notice.

Proof Required: Registered mail, certified mail, Intelligent Mail barcode tracing (IMb), or regular mail with postal receipt. A certificate of bulk mailing does not count.

Nonrenewal

Length of Notice: Forty-five days. An insurer must give fifteen days' notice for nonpayment of premium if it has adopted ISO amendatory endorsement (CG 28 59, Virginia Changes that modify the Railroad Protective Liability Coverage Part).

Reason for Nonrenewal: Required on the notice.

Proof Required: Registered mail, certified mail, Intelligent Mail barcode tracing (IMb), or regular mail with postal receipt. Notice may also be delivered electronically. The insurer must retain a record of the electronic transmittal or receipt of notification for at least one year from the date of transmittal. A certificate of bulk mailing does not count.

VIRGINIA

Other Cancellation/Nonrenewal Provisions

All notices must also be sent to the designated contractor and to any involved governmental authority.

A forty-five-day notice is required if the insurer intends to renew with a reduction in coverage or a rate increase of more than 25 percent. Even though this requirement does not appear on the amendatory endorsement for this line of business, the forty-five-day notice for changed renewal must be sent.

If the terms of the policy require the notice of cancellation, refusal to renew, reduction in coverage, or increase in premium to be given to any lienholder, the insurer and lienholder may agree by separate agreement that such notices may be transmitted electronically provided that the insurer and lienholder agree upon the specifics for transmittal and acknowledgement of notification. Evidence of transmittal or receipt of the required notification shall be retained by the insurer for at least one year from the date of termination.

WORKERS COMPENSATION
Va. Code Ann. §65.2-804

A ten-day notice of cancellation is required for nonpayment of premium. A thirty-day notice is required for any other cancellation and for nonrenewal. Copies of all notices must also be sent to the Virginia Workers Compensation Commission.

SURPLUS LINES
Va. Code Ann. §38.2-318

Surplus lines policies must follow the cancellation and nonrenewal laws of Virginia.

FINANCED PREMIUMS
14 Va. Admin. Code §5-390-40

No notice of intent to cancel may be given prior to default in the insurance premium finance contract. Prior to any cancellation, the licensee shall advise the insured and the agent in writing of its intent to cancel insurance policies unless all payments in default are received within ten days of the date the notice is mailed or delivered. After providing the appropriate notice of intent to cancel, the licensee may exercise its right to cancel if the default has not been cured or if the additional premium has not been financed or otherwise paid. A copy of the notice of cancellation shall be mailed or delivered to the insured and insurance agent with an effective date of cancellation no earlier than five days after its mailing or delivery. No later than the effective date of cancellation, the licensee shall send the notice of cancellation to the

VIRGINIA

insurer, provided the default remains uncured. The insurer must give statutory notices to any governmental agencies, loss payees, or other third parties.

PERSONAL LINES
DWELLING FIRE; HOMEOWNERS & FARM

(For policies covering a 1, 2, 3, and 4-family dwelling)

Va. Code Ann. §§38.2-610 to 38.2-612; 38.2-2113 and 38.2-2114

Cancellation during the Underwriting Period

Length of Underwriting Period: Ninety days.

Length of Notice: Ten days for any reason.

Reason for Cancellation: Required on the notice.

Proof Required: Registered mail, certified mail, Intelligent Mail barcode tracing (IMb), or regular mail with a postal receipt. A certificate of bulk mailing does not count.

Cancellation after the Underwriting Period

The policy may be cancelled **only** for the following reasons:

1. Nonpayment.

2. Conviction arising out of acts increasing the probability that a peril insured against will occur.

3. Discovery of fraud or material misrepresentation.

4. Willful or reckless acts or omissions that increase the probability that a peril insured against will occur as determined from a physical inspection of the property.

5. Physical changes in the property make it uninsurable as determined from a physical inspection of the property.

6. Foreclosure efforts by the secured party against the subject property covered by the policy that have resulted in the sale of the property by a trustee under a deed of trust as duly recorded in the land title records of the jurisdiction in which the property is located.

Length of Notice: Ten days for nonpayment; thirty days for all other reasons.

VIRGINIA

When HO 23 42 VA, Permitted Incidental Occupancies-Residence Premises; HO 24 43, Permitted Incidental Occupancies-Other Residence; HO 24 71, Business Pursuits; HO 23 39 VA, Home Day Care Coverage, or DP 04 20 Permitted Incidental Occupancies are added, a fifteen-day notice is required for nonpayment and a forty-five-day notice for all other cancellations.

Reason for Cancellation: Required on the notice.

Proof Required: Registered mail, certified mail, Intelligent Mail barcode tracing (IMb), or regular mail with postal receipt. A certificate of bulk mailing does not count.

Nonrenewal

Length of Notice: Thirty days.

When HO 23 42 VA, Permitted Incidental Occupancies–Residence Premises; HO 24 43, Permitted Incidental Occupancies–Other Residence; HO 24 71, Business Pursuits; HO 23 39 VA, Home Day Care Coverage, or DP 04 20 Permitted Incidental Occupancies are added, a fifteen day notice is required for nonpayment and a forty-five day notice for nonrenewal.

Reason for Nonrenewal: Required on the notice.

Proof Required: Registered mail, certified mail, Intelligent Mail barcode tracing (IMb), or regular mail with a postal receipt. Notices may also be delivered electronically. The insurer must retain a record of the electronic transmittal or receipt of notification for at least one year from the date of transmittal. A certificate of bulk mailing does not count.

Other Cancellation/Nonrenewal Provisions

At the time of termination, for reasons other than nonpayment, the insurer must advise the insured that within ten days of receipt of the notice of termination he may request in writing that the commissioner review the action of the insurer in terminating the policy or contract and advise the insured of his possible eligibility for fire insurance coverage through the Virginia Property Insurance Association.

If the terms of the policy require the notice of cancellation, refusal to renew, reduction in coverage, or increase in premium to be given to any lienholder, the insurer and lienholder may agree by separate agreement that such notices may be transmitted electronically provided that the insurer and lienholder agree upon the specifics for transmittal and acknowledgement of notification. Evidence of transmittal or receipt of the required notification shall be retained by the insurer for at least one year from the date of termination.

VIRGINIA

No insurance institution or agent may base an adverse underwriting decision in whole or in part on the fact that an individual previously obtained insurance coverage through a residual market mechanism or on the fact that an individual previously obtained insurance coverage from a particular insurance institution or agent.

In the event of an adverse underwriting decision, the insurance institution or agent responsible for the decision shall give a written notice in a form approved by the commission that:

1. Either provides the applicant, policyholder, or individual proposed for coverage with the specific reason or reasons for the adverse underwriting decision in writing, or advises such person that upon written request he may receive the specific reason or reasons in writing.

2. Provide the applicant, policyholder, or individual proposed for coverage with a summary of rights.

Upon receipt of a written request within ninety business days from the date of the mailing of notice or other communication of an adverse underwriting decision to an applicant, policyholder, or individual proposed for coverage, the insurance institution or agent shall furnish to such person within twenty-one business days from the date of receipt of the written request:

1. The specific reason or reasons for the adverse underwriting decision, in writing, if that information was not initially furnished in writing pursuant to state law.

2. The specific items of personal and privileged information that support those reasons.

PERSONAL AUTO

Va. Code Ann. §§38.2-2208 and 38.2-2212

Cancellation during the Underwriting Period

Length of Underwriting Period: Sixty days.

Length of Notice: Ten days for any reason.

Reason for Cancellation: Required on the notice. (Not on amendatory endorsement.)

Proof Required: Certified mail, registered mail, Intelligent Mail barcode tracing (IMb), or regular mail with postal receipt, with a written receipt from the Post Office. A certificate of bulk mailing does not count.

VIRGINIA

Cancellation after the Underwriting Period

The policy may be cancelled **only** for the following reasons:

1. Nonpayment.

2. Suspension or revocation of the driver's license of the named insured or any driver who lives with the named insured or who customarily uses the insured auto. The suspension or revocation must occur during the policy period or within the previous ninety days.

3. If the covered auto is garaged in another state and the driver has changed to a legal resident of a state other than Virginia.

Length of Notice: Fifteen days for nonpayment; forty-five days for any other allowable reason.

Reason for Cancellation: Required on the notice. This requirement is not on ISO's amendatory endorsement (PP 01 99) but is required by statute.

Proof Required: Certified mail, registered mail, Intelligent Mail barcode tracing (IMb), or regular mail with postal receipt. A certificate of bulk mailing does not count.

Nonrenewal

Length of Notice: Forty-five days.

Reason for Nonrenewal: Required on the notice. This requirement is not on ISO's amendatory endorsement (PP 01 99) but is required by statute.

Proof Required: Certified mail, registered mail, Intelligent Mail barcode tracing (IMb), or regular mail with a postal receipt. Notices may also be delivered electronically. The insurer must retain a record of the electronic transmittal or receipt of notification for at least one year from the date of transmittal. A certificate of bulk mailing does not count.

NAMED EXCLUDED DRIVERS

Va. Code Ann. §§38.2-2204, 38.2-2212

An insurer may exclude any person from coverage under a personal umbrella or excess policy, if the exclusion is requested in writing by the first-named insured and is acknowledged in writing by the excluded driver.

Other Cancellation/Nonrenewal Provisions

The application for coverage must include a warning that the policy, if issued, is subject to cancellation without cause during the first sixty days. The wording required can be found at Va. Code Ann. §38.2-2210.

VIRGINIA

Any notice must advise the insured of its right to request in writing that the Commissioner of Insurance review the action of the insurer. This notice must be sent to the insurer within fifteen days of the receipt of the notice.

If the terms of the policy require the notice of cancellation, refusal to renew, reduction in coverage, or increase in premium to be given to any lienholder, the insurer and lienholder may agree by separate agreement that such notices may be transmitted electronically provided that the insurer and lienholder agree upon the specifics for transmittal and acknowledgement of notification. Evidence of transmittal or receipt of the required notification shall be retained by the insurer for at least one year from the date of termination.

Insurer must notify the insured of the following:

1. The right to request, in writing, that the insurance commissioner review the action of the insurer.

2. The possible availability of other insurance which may be obtained through his agent, through another insurer, or through the Virginia Automobile Insurance Plan. (Va. Code Ann. §38.2-231)

An insurer may not nonrenew for any of the following reasons:

1. Age, sex, residence, race, color, creed, national origin, ancestry, marital status, lawful occupation (including military), lack of driving experience or number of years of experience.

2. Lack of supporting business.

3. One or more accidents or tickets that occurred more than forty-eight months previously.

4. UM claims where there is evidence of contact or where the uninsured motorist is known.

5. A single medical claim for a not-at-fault accident.

6. Comprehensive or towing claims. Renewal may be issued with changes with a forty-five-day notice.

7. Two or fewer not-at-fault accidents within a three-year period.

8. Credit information contained in a consumer report.

9. Refusal to provide access to recorded data from a recording device.

VIRGINIA

From Va. Code §38.2-2217.1: If an insurer issues or renews a policy of motor vehicle liability insurance to an insured who intends to use a vehicle for vanpooling which was not so used at the time the policy was issued or last renewed has received written notice by certified mail that the insured intends to use the vehicle for vanpooling, the insurer shall not cancel or refuse to renew a policy of liability insurance coverage for such motor vehicle used in vanpooling, except for one or both of the following specified reasons:

1. The named insured fails to discharge when due any payment of the premium for the policy or any installment thereof.

2. The driving record of the named insured or any regular driver is such that it substantially increases the risk.

PERSONAL UMBRELLA

Per policy provisions.

FRAUD

Va. Code Ann. §§52-36, 52-40, and 18.2-178

Definition

"Insurance fraud" means any commission or attempted commission of the criminal acts and practices prohibited under Virginia's larceny statute. Under that statute it is illegal for any person to obtain, by any false pretense or token, from any person, with the intent to defraud, money, a gift certificate or other property that may be the subject of larceny. Likewise, if a person obtains, by any false pretense or token, with the intent to defraud, the signature of any person to a writing, the false making of which would be forgery, he commits a felony.

Penalty

Since the Code of Virginia classifies insurance fraud as larceny, it is punishable as a felony.

Reporting Requirements

If any insurer, any employee thereof, or any insurance professional has knowledge of, or has reason to believe that insurance fraud will be, is being, or has been committed, that person shall furnish and disclose any information in his possession concerning the fraudulent act to the department, subject to any legal privilege protecting such information.

View reporting instructions at http://www.stampoutfraud.com/default.aspx.

Application Fraud Statement

All applications for insurance and all claim forms provided and required by an insurer or required by law as a condition of payment of a claim shall contain a statement, permanently

VIRGINIA

affixed to, or included as a part of the application or claim form, that clearly states in substance the following:

> "It is a crime to knowingly provide false, incomplete or misleading information to an insurance company for the purpose of defrauding the company. Penalties include imprisonment, fines and denial of insurance benefits."

FAIR CLAIMS PROCESSING
Va. Code Ann. §38.2-510

Virginia law prohibits the following activities as unfair claim settlement practices when they are committed with such frequency as to indicate a general business practice:

1. Misrepresenting pertinent facts or insurance policy provisions relating to coverages at issue.

2. Failing to acknowledge and act reasonably promptly upon communications with respect to claims arising under insurance policies.

3. Failing to adopt and implement reasonable standards for the prompt investigation of claims arising under insurance policies.

4. Refusing arbitrarily and unreasonably to pay claims.

5. Failing to affirm or deny coverage of claims within a reasonable time after proof of loss statements have been completed.

6. Not making a good-faith attempt to promptly, fairly, and equitably settle claims in which liability has become reasonably clear.

7. Compelling insureds to institute litigation to recover amounts due under an insurance policy by offering substantially less than the amounts ultimately recovered in actions brought by such insureds.

8. Attempting to settle claims for less than the amount to which a reasonable person would have believed he was entitled by reference to written or printed advertising material accompanying or made part of an application.

9. Attempting to settle claims on the basis of an application that was altered without notice to, or knowledge or consent of, the insured.

10. Making claims payments to insureds or beneficiaries not accompanied by a statement setting forth the coverage under which payments are being made.

VIRGINIA

11. Making known to insureds or claimants a policy of appealing from arbitration awards in favor of insureds or claimants for the purpose of compelling them to accept settlements or compromises less than the amount awarded in arbitration.

12. Delaying the investigation or payment of claims by requiring an insured, a claimant, or the physician of either to submit a preliminary claim report and then requiring the subsequent submission of formal proof of loss forms, when both contain substantially the same information.

13. Not promptly settling claims where liability has become reasonably clear, under one portion of the insurance policy coverage in order to influence settlements under other portions of the insurance policy coverage.

14. Not promptly providing a reasonable explanation of the basis in the insurance policy in relation to the facts or applicable law for denial of a claim or for the offer of a compromise settlement.

15. Not complying with Va. Code Ann. §38.2-3407.15, or to perform any provider contract provision required by that section.

16. Payment to an insurer or its representative by a repair facility, or acceptance by an insurer or its representative from a repair facility, directly or indirectly, of any kickback, rebate, commission, thing of value, or other consideration in connection with such person's appraisal service.

17. Appraising the cost of repairing an automobile that has been damaged as a result of a collision unless such appraisal is based upon a personal inspection by a representative of the repair facility or the insurer who is making the appraisal. Insurers may use photos and videos submitted by the insured in addition to personal inspection, however, no insurer may require an owner of a motor vehicle to submit photographs, videos, or electronically transmitted digital imagery as a condition of an appraisal.

Furthermore, no insurer may prepare an estimate or use an estimate of the cost of automobile repairs based on the use of an after-market part unless the insurer discloses to the client the written disclaimer in Va. Code Ann. §38.2-510(C)(1).

WASHINGTON

For details on cancellation procedures for the standard policy, refer to the Standard Policy section.

COMMERCIAL LINES

AGRICULTURAL CAPITAL ASSETS; BOP; C. PROP.; FARM; C. ASSETS; CRIME; CIM; C. UMB.; EQUIPMENT BREAKDOWN; & PRO. LIAB.

Rev. Code Wash. §§48.18.289, 48.18.290, 48.18.2901, 48.53.030, and 48.53.040

Cancellation

Length of Notice: Ten days for nonpayment; forty-five days for all other reasons except as noted. Like notice must also be sent to mortgage holder, pledge, or other person shown in the policy to have an interest in any loss under the policy. If the insurer is using ISO Common Policy Condition Forms, then twenty days' notice to mortgage holder, pledge, or other person of interest.

Reason for Cancellation: Required on the notice.

Proof Required: Proof of delivery or proof of mailing. An affidavit is prima facie evidence of mailing of a cancellation notice.

The policy may be cancelled for any reason.

The following applies to Commercial Property, Agricultural Capital Assets, and Capital Assets (Output Policy) Coverage Parts:

The policy may be cancelled with a five-day notice when two or more of the following conditions exist:

1. Without reasonable explanation, the building is unoccupied for more than sixty consecutive days, or at least 65 percent of the rental units are unoccupied for more than 120 consecutive days, unless the building is maintained for seasonal occupancy or is under construction or repair.

2. Without reasonable explanation, progress toward completion of permanent repairs to the building has not occurred within sixty days after receipt of funds following satisfactory adjustment or adjudication of loss resulting from a fire.

3. Because of its physical condition, the building is in danger of collapse.

WASHINGTON

4. Because of its physical condition, a vacation or demolition order has been issued for the building, or it has been declared unsafe in accordance with applicable law.

5. Fixed and salvageable items have been removed from the building, indicating an intent to vacate the building.

6. Without reasonable explanation, heat, water, sewer, and electricity are not furnished for the building for sixty consecutive days.

7. The building is not maintained in substantial compliance with fire, safety, and building codes.

Nonrenewal

Length of Notice: Forty-five days. Like notice must also be sent to mortgage holder, pledge, or other person shown in the policy to have an interest in any loss under the policy. If the insurer is using ISO Common Policy Condition Forms, then twenty days' notice to mortgage holder, pledge, or other person of interest.

Reason for Nonrenewal: Required on the notice and must describe the significant risk factors that led to the insurer's underwriting action.

Proof Required: Proof of delivery or proof of mailing. An affidavit is prima facie evidence of mailing of a cancellation notice.

Other Cancellation/Nonrenewal Provisions

Insurers are required to renew a policy unless the contract clearly states that it is nonrenewable.

A copy of any notice of cancellation or nonrenewal must also be sent to each mortgagee, pledgee, or other person shown by the policy to have an interest. Electronic transmittal is permitted.

Whenever a notice of cancellation or nonrenewal or an offer to renew is furnished to an insured, a copy of such notice or offer shall be provided within five working days to the producer. When possible, the copy to the agent or broker may be provided electronically.

When a five-day notice of cancellation is allowed, the notice must provide a copy of Chapter 48.53 of the Code of Washington, regarding Fire Insurance-Arson Fraud Reduction. Such a notice must also be sent be either certified mail or first class mail.

WASHINGTON

C. AUTO; E-COMMERCE; CGL (All lines except UST); & MGT. PROT.

Wash. Rev. Code Ann. §§48.18.290, 48.18.2901, and 48.53.030
(Not applicable to individually-owned private passenger type vehicles)

Cancellation

Length of Notice: Ten days for nonpayment; forty-five days for all other reasons; like notice to mortgage holder, pledge, or other person shown in the policy to have an interest in any loss under the policy. If the insurer is using ISO Common Policy Condition Forms, then twenty days' notice to mortgage holder, pledge, or other person of interest.

Reason for Cancellation: Required on the notice.

Proof Required: Proof of delivery or proof of mailing. An affidavit is prima facie evidence of mailing of a cancellation notice.

Nonrenewal

Length of Notice: Forty-five days.

Reason for Nonrenewal: Required on the notice. Like notice to mortgage holder, pledge, or other person shown in the policy to have an interest in any loss under the policy. If the insurer is using ISO Common Policy Condition Forms, then twenty days' notice to mortgage holder, pledge, or other person of interest.

Proof Required: Proof of delivery or proof of mailing. An affidavit is prima facie evidence of mailing of a cancellation notice.

Other Cancellation/Nonrenewal Provisions

Under the OCP coverage part, notice of cancellation or nonrenewal must also be sent to the listed contractor.

Under the Railroad Protective coverage part, notice of cancellation or nonrenewal must also be sent to the listed contractor and any involved governmental authority.

Insurers are required to renew a policy unless the contract clearly states that it is nonrenewable.

The following applies to the Commercial Auto Coverage Part, when the policy covers a named individual who owns a private passenger type vehicle, and the policy does not cover

WASHINGTON

garages, automobile sales agencies, repair shops, service stations, or public parking place operations:

> After the policy is in effect for sixty days or more, the policy may be cancelled with a twenty-day notice due to suspension, revocation, or cancellation of the driver's license of the named insured or of the driver's license of any driver who lives with the named insured or who customarily uses the insured auto. The suspension or revocation must occur during the policy period or within the previous 180 days.

COMMERCIAL GENERAL LIABILITY

(Underground Storage Tank Policy)

Wash. Rev. Code Ann. §§48.18.290 and 48.18.2901

Cancellation

Length of Notice: Ten days for nonpayment; forty-five days for material misrepresentation, sixty days for all other reasons if using ISO Amendatory Endorsement CG 30 17. Washington statutes require forty-five days' notice for all reasons except nonpayment, which only requires ten days' notice.

Reason for Cancellation: Required on the notice.

Proof Required: Proof of delivery or proof of mailing. Certified mail if using ISO Amendatory Endorsement CG 30 17. An affidavit is prima facie evidence of mailing of a cancellation notice.

Nonrenewal

Length of Notice: Sixty days if the insurer is using ISO amendatory endorsement CG 30 17. Forty-five days according to Washington statute.

Reason for Nonrenewal: Required on the notice.

Proof Required: Proof of delivery or proof of mailing. Certified mail if using ISO Amendatory Endorsement CG 30 17. An affidavit is prima facie evidence of mailing of a cancellation notice.

PROFESSIONAL LIABILITY

Wash. Rev. Code Ann. §§48.18.290 and 48.18.2901

Cancellation

Length of Notice: Ten days for nonpayment; forty-five days for all other reasons. For medical malpractice liability insurance, ten days for nonpayment, ninety days for any other reason.

WASHINGTON

For any permitted reason other than nonpayment, the length of notice may be extended by using ISO form PR 02 00.

Reason for Cancellation: Required on the notice. Medical malpractice cancellation must also describe the significant risk factors that led to the insurer's underwriting action.

Proof Required: Proof of delivery or proof of mailing. An affidavit is prima facie evidence of mailing of a cancellation notice.

Nonrenewal

Length of Notice: Ninety days.

Reason for Nonrenewal: Required on the notice.

Proof Required: Proof of delivery or proof of mailing. An affidavit is prima facie evidence of mailing of a cancellation notice.

Other Cancellation/Nonrenewal Provisions

Insurers are required to renew a policy unless the contract clearly states that it is nonrenewable.

WORKERS COMPENSATION

Washington is a monopolistic workers compensation state.

SURPLUS LINES

Wash. Admin. Code §284-30-590

Surplus lines insurers may not issue policies that may be cancelled by fewer than ten days for nonpayment or by fewer than twenty days for any other reason.

FINANCED PREMIUMS

Wash. Rev. Code Ann. §§48.56.100 through 48.56.120

If the premium finance agreement contains a power of attorney, the finance company may cancel the policy due to nonpayment. The finance company must first give the insured ten days to pay. If the insured fails to make payment within that ten-day period, then the finance company mails the notice of cancellation to the insurer and insured and the cancellation is processed as of the finance company's original default date. Return of the policy by the insured is not required.

WASHINGTON

All statutory, regulatory, and contractual restrictions providing that the insurance contract may not be cancelled unless notice is given to a governmental agency, mortgagee, or other third party shall apply where cancellation is effected under the provisions of this section. The insurer shall give the prescribed notice on behalf of itself or the insured to any governmental agency, mortgagee, or other third party on or before the second business day after the day it receives the notice of cancellation from the premium finance company and must determine the effective date of cancellation taking into consideration the number of days' notice required to complete the cancellation.

PERSONAL LINES

DWELLING FIRE & HOMEOWNERS

Wash. Rev. Code Ann. §§48.18.290, 48.18.2901, 48.53.030, and 48.53.040

Cancellation during the Underwriting Period

Length of Notice: Ten days for nonpayment; forty-five days for any other reason. The policy may be cancelled with a five-day notice when two or more of the following conditions exist:

1. Without reasonable explanation, the building is unoccupied for more than sixty consecutive days, or at least 65 percent of the rental units are unoccupied for more than 120 consecutive days unless the building is maintained for seasonal occupancy or is under construction or repair.

2. Without reasonable explanation, progress toward completion of permanent repairs to the building has not occurred within sixty days after receipt of funds following satisfactory adjustment or adjudication of loss resulting from a fire.

3. Because of its physical condition, the building is in danger of collapse.

4. Because of its physical condition, a vacation or demolition order has been issued for the building, or it has been declared unsafe in accordance with applicable law.

5. Fixed and salvageable items have been removed from the building, indicating an intent to vacate the building.

6. Without reasonable explanation, heat, water, sewer, and electricity are not furnished for the building for sixty consecutive days.

7. The building is not maintained in substantial compliance with fire, safety, and building codes.

Reason for Cancellation: Required on the notice.

WASHINGTON

Proof Required: Proof of delivery or proof of mailing. An affidavit is prima facie evidence of mailing of a cancellation notice.

Cancellation after the Underwriting Period

In addition to the reasons previously listed, the policy may be cancelled **only** for the following reasons:

1. Nonpayment.
2. Material misrepresentation on the application.
3. Substantial change in the risk since the policy was issued.

There is no statutory requirement for an underwriting period with regard to personal property policies.

The only state-imposed restriction to cancellation is that the policy may not be more restrictive than the standard fire policy.

Length of Notice: Ten days for nonpayment; forty-five days for reasons 2 and 3; five days if any of the reasons for the five-day cancellation during the underwriting period exist. Any mortgagees must be given at least twenty days' notice.

Reason for Cancellation: Required on the notice.

Proof Required: Proof of delivery or proof of mailing.

Nonrenewal

Length of Notice: Forty-five days.

Reason for Nonrenewal: Required on the notice.

Proof Required: Proof of delivery or proof of mailing. An affidavit is prima facie evidence of mailing of a cancellation notice.

Other Cancellation/Nonrenewal Provisions

Insurers are required to renew a policy unless the contract clearly states that it is nonrenewable.

A five-day notice must also be sent be either certified mail or first class mail.

WASHINGTON

PERSONAL AUTO

(Also applicable to COMMERCIAL AUTO policies covering individually-owned private passenger type vehicles not used in business)

Wash. Rev. Code Ann. §§48.18.291, 48.18.292, and 48.30.310

Cancellation during the Underwriting Period

Length of Underwriting Period: Sixty days.

Length of Notice: Ten days for nonpayment or during the first thirty days after the insurance is in effect; twenty days for any other reason.

Reason for Cancellation: Required on the notice.

Proof Required: Proof of mailing.

Cancellation after the Underwriting Period

A notice of cancellation sent more than sixty days after the contract has been in effect is not valid unless one of the following reasons applies:

1. Nonpayment.

2. Suspension, revocation, or cancellation of the driver's license of the named insured or of the driver's license of any driver who lives with the named insured or who customarily uses the insured auto. The suspension or revocation must occur during the policy period or within the previous 180 days.

Length of Notice: Ten days for nonpayment; twenty days for all other reasons.

Reason for Cancellation: Required on the notice.

Proof Required: Proof of mailing.

Nonrenewal

Length of Notice: Twenty days.

Reason for Nonrenewal: Required on the notice.

Proof Required: Proof of mailing.

WASHINGTON

Other Cancellation/Nonrenewal Provisions

An insurer may not nonrenew based on comprehensive, road service, or towing claims. If the policy term is less than six months, the insurer may nonrenew every six months, beginning six months after the original effective date. If the policy term is one year or longer, the insurer may nonrenew the policy at each anniversary of the original effective date. Insurers are required to renew a policy unless the contract clearly states that it is nonrenewable.

Modification by the insurer of automobile physical damage coverage by the inclusion of a deductible not exceeding one hundred dollars is not a cancellation of the coverage or of the policy.

An insurer cannot cancel a personal auto policy or discriminate to terms or conditions of the policy based upon the applicant's commercial motor vehicle employment driving record.

A termination is not valid if the reason for the action is not provided.

PERSONAL UMBRELLA

Wash. Rev. Code Ann. §§48.18.290, 48.18.2901, 48.53.030, and 48.53.040

Cancellation

Length of Notice: Ten days for nonpayment; forty-five days for any other reason. Like notice to mortgage holder, pledge, or other person shown in the policy to have an interest in any loss under the policy.

Reason for Cancellation: Required on the notice.

Proof Required: Proof of delivery or proof of mailing. An affidavit is prima facie evidence of mailing of a cancellation notice.

Nonrenewal

Length of Notice: Forty-five days.

Reason for Nonrenewal: Required on the notice.

Proof Required: Proof of delivery or proof of mailing.

WASHINGTON

FRAUD

Wash. Rev. Code Ann. §§48.135.010, 48.135.050, and 48.01.190

Definition

"Insurance fraud" means an act or omission committed by a person who, knowingly, and with intent to defraud, commits, or conceals any material information concerning, one or more of the following:

1. Presenting, causing to be presented, or preparing with knowledge or belief that it will be presented to or by an insurer, insurance producer, or surplus line broker, false information as part of, in support of, or concerning a fact material to one or more of the following:

    a. An application for the issuance or renewal of an insurance policy.
    b. The rating of an insurance policy or contract.
    c. A claim for payment or benefit pursuant to an insurance policy.
    d. Premiums paid on an insurance policy.
    e. Payments made in accordance with the terms of an insurance policy.
    f. The reinstatement of an insurance policy.

2. Willful embezzlement, abstracting, purloining, or conversion of moneys, funds, premiums, credits, or other property of an insurer or person engaged in the business of insurance.

3. Attempting to commit, aiding or abetting in the commission of, or conspiracy to commit the acts or omissions specified in this subsection.

Washington's definition of insurance fraud is **illustrative** only.

Penalties

Perpetrators of insurance fraud may have to make restitution to the defrauded insurance company and may face additional criminal penalties.

Reporting Requirements

Any insurer or licensee of the commissioner that has reasonable belief that an act of insurance fraud which is or may be a crime under Washington law has been, is being, or is about to be committed shall furnish and disclose the knowledge and information to the commissioner or the National Insurance Crime Bureau, The National Association of Insurance Commissioners, or similar organization, who shall disclose the information to the commissioner, and cooperate fully with any investigation conducted by the commissioner.

WASHINGTON

Any person that has a reasonable belief that an act of insurance fraud which is or may be a crime under Washington law has been, is being, or is about to be committed; or any person who collects, reviews, or analyzes information concerning insurance fraud which is or may be a crime under Washington law may furnish and disclose any information in its possession concerning such an act to the commissioner or to an authorized representative of an insurer that requests the information for the purpose of detecting, prosecuting, or preventing insurance fraud.

Report insurance fraud at https://www.insurance.wa.gov/insurance-fraud or call 360-586-2566.

Any person who files reports, or furnishes other information, required under the insurance title of the Washington revised code (Title 48), required by the commissioner under authority granted by that title, useful to the commissioner in its administration, or furnished to the National Association of Insurance Commissioners at the request of the commissioner or pursuant to that title, shall be immune from liability in any civil action or suit arising from the filing of any such report or furnishing such information to the commissioner or the National Association of Insurance Commissioners, unless actual malice, fraud, or bad faith is shown.

Application Fraud Statement
Wash. Rev. Code Ann. §48.102.140

Life settlement contracts and applications for life settlement contracts, regardless of the form of transmission, shall contain the following statement or a substantially similar statement:

> "Any person who knowingly presents false information in an application for insurance or life settlement contract is guilty of a crime and may be subject to fines and confinement in prison."

FAIR CLAIMS PROCESSING

Wash. Rev. Code Ann. §48.30.010; Wash. Admin. Code §§284-30-330 and 284-30-390

The following are prohibited claims settlement practices:

1. Misrepresenting pertinent facts or insurance policy provisions.

2. Not acknowledging and acting reasonably promptly upon communications with respect to claims arising under insurance policies.

3. Not adopting and implementing reasonable standards for the prompt investigation of claims arising under insurance policies.

WASHINGTON

4. Refusing to pay claims without conducting a reasonable investigation.

5. Not affirming or denying coverage of claims within a reasonable time after fully completed proof of loss documentation has been submitted.

6. Not making a good-faith attempt to effectuate prompt, fair and equitable settlements of claims in which liability has become reasonably clear.

7. Compelling a first-party claimant to initiate or submit to litigation, arbitration, or appraisal to recover amounts due under an insurance policy by offering substantially less than the amounts ultimately recovered in such actions or proceedings.

8. Attempting to settle a claim for less than the amount to which a reasonable person would have believed he or she was entitled by reference to written or printed advertising material accompanying or made part of an application.

9. Making a claim payment to a first-party claimant or beneficiary not accompanied by a statement setting forth the coverage under which the payment is made.

10. Asserting to a first-party claimant a policy of appealing arbitration awards in favor of insureds or first-party claimants for the purpose of compelling them to accept settlements or compromises less than the amount awarded in arbitration.

11. Delaying the investigation or payment of claims by requiring a first-party claimant or his or her physician to submit a preliminary claim report and then requiring subsequent submissions which contain substantially the same information.

12. Not promptly settling claims, where liability has become reasonably clear, under one portion of the insurance policy coverage in order to influence settlements under other portions of the insurance policy coverage.

13. Not promptly providing a reasonable explanation of the basis in the insurance policy in relation to the facts or applicable law for denial of a claim or for the offer of a compromise settlement.

14. Unfairly discriminating against claimants because they are represented by a public adjuster.

15. Not expeditiously honoring drafts given in settlement of claims.

16. Not adopting and implementing reasonable standards for the processing and payment of claims after the obligation to pay has been established. The current regulation

WASHINGTON

specifies check or draft payment. Amendment 2016 WA REG TEXT 426764 (NS) would expand this to allow for electronic payment as well, if passed.

17. Delaying appraisals or adding to their cost under insurance policy appraisal provisions through the use of appraisers from outside of the loss area.

18. Failing to make a good-faith effort to settle a claim before exercising a contract right to an appraisal.

19. Negotiating or settling a claim directly with any claimant known to be represented by an attorney without the attorney's knowledge and consent.

In addition to the unfair claims settlement practices specified in this regulation, the following acts or practices of the insurer are hereby defined as unfair methods of competition and unfair or deceptive acts or practices in the business of insurance, specifically applicable to the settlement of motor vehicle claims:

1. Not making a good-faith effort to communicate with the repair facility chosen by the claimant.

2. Arbitrarily denying a claimant's estimate for repairs.

    a. A denial of the claimant's estimate for repairs to be completed at the chosen repair facility based solely on the repair facility's hourly rate is considered arbitrary if the rate does not result in a higher overall cost of repairs.
    b. If the insurer pays less than the amount of the estimate from the claimant's chosen repair facility, the insurer must fully disclose the reason or reasons it paid less than the claimant's estimate, and must thoroughly document the circumstances in its claim file.

3. Requiring the claimant to travel unreasonably to:

    a. Obtain a repair estimate.
    b. Have the loss vehicle repaired at a specific repair facility.
    c. Obtain a temporary rental or loaner vehicle.

4. Not preparing or accepting an estimate provided by the claimant that will restore the loss vehicle to its condition prior to the loss.

    a. If the insurer prepares the estimate, it must provide a copy of the estimate to the claimant.

WASHINGTON

    b. If a claimant provides the estimate and the insurer, after evaluation of the claimant's estimate, determines it owes an amount that differs from the estimate the claimant provided, the insurer must fully disclose the reason or reasons for the difference to the claimant, and must thoroughly document the circumstances in the claim file.

    c. If the claimant chooses to take the loss vehicle to a repair facility where the overall cost to restore the loss vehicle to its condition prior to the loss exceeds the insurer's estimate, the claimant must be advised that he or she may be responsible for any additional amount above the insurer's estimate.

5. If requested by the claimant and if the insurer prepares the estimate, failing to provide a list of repair facilities within a reasonable distance of the claimant's principally garaged area that will complete the vehicle repairs for the estimated cost of the insurer prepared estimate.

6. Failing to consider any additional loss related damage the repair facility discovers during the repairs to the loss vehicle.

7. Not limiting deductions for betterment and depreciation to parts normally subject to repair and replacement during the useful life of the loss vehicle. Deductions for betterment and depreciation are limited to the lesser of:

    a. An increase in the actual cash value of the loss vehicle caused by the replacement of the part.

    b. An amount equal to the value of the expired life of the part to be repaired or replaced when compared to the normal useful life of that part.

8. If provided for by the terms of the applicable insurance policy, and if the insurer elects to exercise its right to repair the loss vehicle at a specific repair facility, failing to prepare or accept an estimate that will restore the loss vehicle to its condition prior to the loss at no additional cost to the first party claimant other than as stated in the applicable policy of insurance.

9. If liability and damages are reasonably clear, recommending that claimants make a claim under their own collision coverage solely to avoid paying claims under the liability insurance policy.

WEST VIRGINIA

For details on cancellation procedures for the standard policy, refer to the Standard Policy section. With respect to commercial policies issued in West Virginia, the policy language would control.

COMMERCIAL LINES

AGRICULTURAL CAPITAL ASSETS; CAPITAL ASSETS; CGL; CIM & EQUIPMENT BREAKDOWN;

West Virginia makes no changes from the standard policies.

BOP; CRIME; E-COMMERCE & MGT. PROT.

The only change from the standard policies is that West Virginia removes the proof of mailing requirement.

COMMERCIAL AUTO

(This section applies when the policy does not cover individually owned private passenger type vehicles.)

The policy language would control.

COMMERCIAL AUTO; COMMERCIAL UMBRELLA; FARM UMBRELLA

(This section applies when the policy covers individually owned private passenger type vehicles.)

Declination

The policy language would control.

COMMERCIAL PROPERTY & FARM

These sections are not applicable to commercial lines.

The policy language would control.

COMMERCIAL PROPERTY AND FARM

(Policies other than those previously listed.)

W. Va. Code §§ 33-22-14 and 33-22-15

The only change in these policies is to remove the proof of mailing requirement and to include an alternative nonrenewal provision that allows an insurer to nonrenew for any reason consistent with its underwriting standards.

WEST VIRGINIA

For Farmers' Mutual Fire Insurance Companies in specific, cancellation notices are valid if mailed in a sealed envelope or personally hand delivered, and the company may cancel any policy with at least five days written notice. These companies may also write into their policies, provisions suspending liability from the date when an unpaid assessment becomes due, if notice is given five days before suspension takes effect.

PROFESSIONAL LIABILITY

W. Va. Code §§33-20C-1 through 33-20C-5, and 33-1-10

Cancellation during the Underwriting Period

Length of Underwriting Period: Sixty days.

Length of Notice: Thirty days.

Reason for Cancellation: Required on the notice.

Proof Required: Certified mail, return receipt requested.

Cancellation after the Underwriting Period

The policy may be cancelled **only** for the following reasons:

1. Nonpayment.

2. Fraud or material misrepresentation in obtaining the policy.

3. Violation of a material provision of the policy.

4. The unavailability of reinsurance. This must be approved by the commissioner.

5. Any purported cancellation of a policy providing malpractice insurance attempted in contravention of this section is void.

Length of Notice: Thirty days.

Reason for Cancellation: Required on the notice.

Proof Required: Certified mail, return receipt requested.

Nonrenewal

Length of Notice: Ninety days.

WEST VIRGINIA

Reason for Nonrenewal: Not required on the notice.

Proof Required: Certified mail, return receipt requested.

WORKERS COMPENSATION
W. Va. CSR §85-8-9
Cancellation after the Underwriting Period

Length of Notice: Ten days for nonpayment of initial premium; thirty days for all other reasons.

Reason for Cancellation: Required on the notice.

Proof Required: Proof of mailing.

Nonrenewal

Length of Notice: Sixty days.

Reason for Nonrenewal: Required on the notice.

Proof Required: Proof of mailing.

The rating organization must be notified of cancellations ten days in advance of the cancellation.

SURPLUS LINES

Surplus lines must follow the cancellation and nonrenewal laws of the insurer's domiciliary laws regarding cancellation/nonrenewal.

FINANCED PREMIUMS
W. Va. Code §33-17A-3

West Virginia equates nonpayment of a finance company with nonpayment of an insurer but does not specify procedures to be followed.

PERSONAL LINES
W. Va. Code §33-6B-4
Declination

Declination is the refusal to issue based on an application. The insurer must provide a written notice of declination within thirty days.

WEST VIRGINIA

DWELLING FIRE, HOMEOWNERS

W. Va. Code §§33-6-37, 33-17A-4, 33-17A-4a, and 33-17A-5

Cancellation during the Underwriting Period

Length of Underwriting Period: Sixty days.

Length of Notice: Ten days.

Reason for Cancellation: Required on the notice.

Proof Required: Proof of first-class mailing.

Cancellation after the Underwriting Period

The policy may be cancelled **only** for the following reasons:

1. Nonpayment.

2. The insured is convicted of a crime having as one of its necessary elements an act that increases the insured-against hazard.

3. Fraud or material misrepresentation in obtaining the policy, in continuing the policy, or in pursuit of a claim.

4. Any willful or reckless acts or omissions that increase the insured-against hazard.

5. Changes in risk which substantially increase the insured-against hazard since the policy was issued.

6. A violation of any local fire, health, or safety code that substantially increases any hazard insured against which substantially increases the hazard.

7. A determination by the insurance commissioner that the continuation of the policy would place the insurer in violation of the West Virginia insurance laws.

8. The insured is two or more years behind in payment of real property taxes and continues to be delinquent at the time notice of cancellation is issued.

9. The insurer stops writing this line or ceases to do business in West Virginia.

10. Substantial breach of policy provisions.

WEST VIRGINIA

Length of Notice: Ten days for nonpayment of initial premium; thirty days for all other reasons.

Reason for Cancellation: Required on the notice.

Proof Required: Proof of mailing.

Nonrenewal

Length of Notice: Thirty days.

Reason for Nonrenewal: Required on the notice.

Proof Required: Proof of first-class mailing.

Other Cancellation/Nonrenewal Provisions

If the policy has been in effect four or more years, the insurer may nonrenew only for the reasons allowed for midterm cancellation or when the insurer has paid two or more claims within thirty-six months, each of which occurred after July 1, 2005. Alternatively, an insurer may nonrenew for any reason consistent with its underwriting standards.

An alternative method of nonrenewal is available which allows the insurer to nonrenew up to 1 percent of its policies in a county each year, subject to approval of a plan which must be filed with the commissioner. If the alternative method of nonrenewal is selected, it must be followed for five years.

An insurer may cancel or nonrenew a combination automobile and homeowners policy of insurance if either the automobile or homeowners insurance in such policy may be cancelled or nonrenewed pursuant to the cancellation or nonrenewal provisions of chapter 33 pertaining to such insurance. However, the insurer must offer to issue a policy, effective as of the date of cancellation of the combination policy, to the insured for the insurance that was not cancelled or nonrenewed and issue such policy if the offer is accepted by the insured. For the purposes of cancellation, nonrenewal and termination of policies, the inception date of a reissued policy is the inception date of the combination policy.

PERSONAL AUTO

W. Va. Code §§33-6-37; 33-6A-1 through 33-6A-4b

Cancellation during the Underwriting Period

Length of Underwriting Period: Sixty days.

Length of Notice: Ten days for nonpayment of initial premium; thirty days for any other reason.

WEST VIRGINIA

Reason for Cancellation: Not required on the notice but must be provided within thirty days of the request.

Proof Required: Proof of first-class mailing.

Cancellation after the Underwriting Period

The policy may be cancelled **only** for the following reasons:

1. Nonpayment.

2. Material misrepresentation in obtaining the policy.

3. Violation of the material terms and conditions of the policy.

4. If the named insured or any other driver who lives with the insured or customarily uses the insured vehicle:

    a. Has his driver's license suspended or revoked. The suspension must occur during the policy period. This provision does not apply to operators under twenty-one who lose their license for a blood alcohol content between .02 and .08.
    b. Is or becomes subject to epilepsy or heart attacks and cannot produce a certificate from a physician testifying to his or her ability to operate a motor vehicle.

5. If the named insured or any regular user of the covered auto is or has been convicted of any of the following during the policy period:

    a. Any felony or assault involving the use of a motor vehicle.
    b. Negligent homicide arising out of the operation of a motor vehicle.
    c. Operating a motor vehicle while intoxicated or under the influence of liquor or drugs.
    d. Leaving the scene of the accident.
    e. Theft of a motor vehicle.
    f. Making false statements in an application for a driver's license.
    g. Three or more moving violation in twelve months, each of which results in three or more points.

Length of Notice: Ten days for nonpayment of initial premium; thirty days for any other reason.

Reason for Cancellation: Not required on the notice but must be provided upon request.

Proof Required: Proof of first-class mailing.

WEST VIRGINIA

Nonrenewal

Length of Notice: Forty-five days.

Reason for Nonrenewal: Not required on the notice.

Proof Required: Proof of first-class mailing.

Other Cancellation/Nonrenewal Provisions

If the policy term is less than six months, the insurer may nonrenew every six months, beginning six months after the original effective date. If the policy term is one year or longer, the insurer may nonrenew the policy at each anniversary of the original effective date.

An insurer may not fail to renew an outstanding automobile liability or physical damage insurance policy which has been in existence for two consecutive years or longer except for the following reasons:

1. Nonpayment.

2. The policy is obtained through material misrepresentation.

3. Violation of any of the material terms and conditions of the policy.

4. The named insured or any other operator, either residing in the same household or who customarily operates an automobile insured under the policy:

    a. Has had her driver's license suspended or revoked during the policy period.
    b. Is or becomes subject to a physical or mental condition that prevents the insured from operating a motor vehicle, and the individual cannot produce a certificate from a physician testifying to his ability to operate a motor vehicle.

5. The named insured or any other operator, either residing in the same household or who customarily operates an automobile insured under the policy, is convicted of or forfeits bail during the policy period for any of the following reasons:

    a. Any felony or assault involving the use of a motor vehicle.
    b. Negligent homicide arising out of the operation of a motor vehicle.
    c. Operating a motor vehicle while under the influence of alcohol or drugs.
    d. Leaving the scene of an accident.
    e. Theft of a motor vehicle or the unlawful taking of a motor vehicle.
    f. Making false statements in an application for a driver's license.

WEST VIRGINIA

6. The named insured or any other operator, either residing in the same household or who customarily operates an automobile insured under the policy, is convicted of or forfeits bail during the policy period for two or more moving traffic violations committed within a period of twelve months, each of which results in three or more points being assessed on the driver's record by the division of motor vehicles, whether or not the insurer renewed the policy without knowledge of all of the violations.

7. The named insured or any other operator either residing in the same household or who customarily operates an automobile insured under the policy has had a second at-fault motor vehicle accident within a period of twelve months, whether or not the insurer renewed the policy without knowledge of all of the accidents.

8. The insurer ceases writing automobile liability or physical damage insurance policies in West Virginia.

The insurer must provide a written notice of declination within thirty days.

An alternative method of nonrenewal is available which allows the insurer to nonrenew up to 1 percent of its policies in a county each year. The reason for nonrenewal must be specifically stated. The insurer must notify the insurance commissioner of its choice of options. The selection must be followed for five years.

An insurer may cancel or nonrenew a combination automobile and homeowners policy if either the automobile or homeowners insurance in such policy may be cancelled or nonrenewed. However, the insurer must offer to issue a policy, effective as of the date of cancellation of the combination policy, to the insured for the insurance that was not cancelled or nonrenewed and issue such policy if the offer is accepted by the insured. For the purposes of cancellation, nonrenewal and termination of policies, the inception date of a reissued policy is the inception date of the combination policy.

PERSONAL UMBRELLA

W. Va. Code §§33-6-37 and 33-17A-4

Cancellation during the Underwriting Period

Length of Underwriting Period: Sixty days.

Length of Notice: Ten days.

Reason for Cancellation: Not required.

Proof Required: Proof of mailing.

WEST VIRGINIA

Cancellation after the Underwriting Period

Length of Notice: Ten-day notice for nonpayment of initial premium; thirty-day notice for any other reason.

Reason for Cancellation: Not required.

Proof Required: Proof of mailing.

Nonrenewal

Length of Notice: Thirty days.

Reason for Nonrenewal: Not required.

Proof Required: Proof of mailing.

FRAUD

W. Va. Code §§33-41-1 through 33-41-12

Definition

The West Virginia Code defines insurance fraud to include instances where any person who knowingly and willfully and with intent to defraud submits a materially false statement in support of a claim for insurance benefits or payment pursuant to a policy of insurance or who conspires to do so. The statute no longer lists specific fraud actions.

Penalty

Perpetrators of insurance fraud face several consequences, including suspension or revocation of a license or certificate of authority, a civil penalty of up to ten thousand dollars per violation, or both a revocation or suspension and civil penalties. Perpetrators may also be required to make reasonable restitution to persons aggrieved by their violations. Finally, perpetrators of insurance fraud may have to reimburse the West Virginia Insurance Fraud Unit for the cost of investigating the perpetrator's fraud.

Those who submit fraudulent claims to insurance companies face a range of penalties that correspond to the pecuniary value of their fraud.

Reporting Requirement

A person engaged in the business of insurance having knowledge or a reasonable belief that fraud or another crime related to the business of insurance is being, will be or has been committed shall provide to the commissioner the information required by, and in a manner prescribed by, the commissioner.

WEST VIRGINIA

Contact information and instructions for reporting fraud are available at http://www.wvinsurance.gov/OIGFraudUnit(ReportFraud)/tabid/204/ItemId/1881/Default.aspx

Application Fraud Statement
W. Va. Code §33-41-3

Claims forms and applications for insurance, regardless of the form of transmission, may contain the following warning or a substantially similar caveat:

> "Any person who knowingly presents a false or fraudulent claim for payment of a loss or benefit or knowingly presents false information in an application for insurance is guilty of a crime and may be subject to fines and confinement in prison."

FAIR CLAIMS PROCESSING
W. Va. Code §§33-11-3 and 33-11-4

The West Virginia Code prohibits the following practices when performed with such frequency as to indicate a general business practice:

1. Misrepresenting pertinent facts or insurance policy provisions relating to coverages at issue.

2. Not acknowledging and acting reasonably promptly upon communications with respect to claims arising under insurance policies.

3. Not adopting and implementing reasonable standards for the prompt investigation of claims arising under insurance policies.

4. Refusing to pay claims without conducting a reasonable investigation based upon all available information.

5. Not affirming or denying coverage of claims within a reasonable time after proof of loss statements have been completed.

6. Not attempting in good faith to effectuate prompt, fair, and equitable settlements of claims in which liability has become reasonably clear.

7. Compelling insureds to institute litigation to recover amounts due under an insurance policy by offering substantially less than the amounts ultimately recovered in actions brought by the insureds, when the insureds have made claims for amounts reasonably similar to the amounts ultimately recovered.

WEST VIRGINIA

8. Attempting to settle a claim for less than the amount to which a reasonable person would have believed he was entitled by reference to written or printed advertising material accompanying or made part of an application.

9. Attempting to settle claims based on an application which was altered without notice to, or knowledge or consent of, the insured.

10. Making claims payments to insureds or beneficiaries not accompanied by a statement setting forth the coverage under which payments are being made.

11. Making known to insureds or claimants a policy of appealing from arbitration awards in favor of insureds or claimants for the purpose of compelling them to accept settlements or compromises less than the amount awarded in arbitration.

12. Delaying the investigation or payment of claims by requiring an insured, claimant, or the physician of either to submit a preliminary claim report and then requiring the subsequent submission of formal proof of loss forms, both of which submissions contain substantially the same information.

13. Not promptly settling claims, where liability has become reasonably clear, under one portion of the insurance policy coverage in order to influence settlements under other portions of the insurance policy coverage.

14. Not promptly providing a reasonable explanation of the basis in the insurance policy in relation to the facts or applicable law for denial of a claim or for the offer of a compromise settlement.

15. Failing to notify the first-party claimant and the provider(s) of services covered under accident and sickness insurance and hospital and medical service corporation insurance policies whether the claim has been accepted or denied and if denied, the reasons therefor, within fifteen calendar days from the filing of the proof of loss.

WISCONSIN

For details on cancellation procedures for the standard policy, refer to the Standard Policy section.

COMMERCIAL LINES
AGRICULTURAL CAPITAL ASSETS; BOP; CAPITAL ASSETS; C. AUTO; CRIME; CGL (OTHER THAN UNDERGROUND STORAGE TANKS); CIM; C. PROP.; C. UMB.; E-COMMERCE; EQUIPMENT BREAKDOWN; FARM; & MGT. PROT.

Wisconsin Statutes §§631.11 and 631.36

Cancellation during the Underwriting Period

Length of Underwriting Period: Sixty days.

Length of Notice: Ten days for any reason.

Reason for Cancellation: Not required on the notice.

Proof Required: Proof of first-class mailing or proof of delivery.

Cancellation after the Underwriting Period

The policy may be cancelled **only** for the following reasons:

1. Nonpayment.

2. Material misrepresentation.

3. Substantial change in the risk assumed if such change should not have been foreseen by the insurer or contemplated in the risk in writing the contract.

4. Substantial breach of contractual duties, conditions, or warranties.

Wisconsin statutes also allow cancellation due to attainment of the age specified as the terminal age for coverage, in which case the insurer may cancel by notice accompanied by a tender of a proportional return of premium. However, this is not permitted under the ISO program.

If ISO amendatory endorsement IL 02 83 is adopted, in addition to cancellation, Capital Assets Program, Crime and Fidelity, Commercial Inland Marine, Commercial Property, Equipment Breakdown, and Farm polices may be rescinded for the following reasons:

1. Misrepresentation, if the person knew or should have known that the representation was false.

WISCONSIN

2. If the insured breaches an affirmative warranty he made in the negotiations for the procurement of the policy.

3. Failure of a condition before a loss if such failure exists at the time of loss.

4. Breach of a promissory warranty.

The insurer may not use reasons 3 or 4 unless such failure or breach increases the risk at the time of loss; or contributes to the loss.

Length of Notice: Ten days for any allowable reason; notice of rescission must be sent within sixty days of the time the insurer acquires the necessary knowledge of sufficient facts to constitute grounds for rescission.

Reason for Cancellation: Required on the notice.

Proof Required: Proof of first-class mailing or proof of delivery.

Nonrenewal

Length of Notice: Sixty days.

Reason for Nonrenewal: Required on the notice.

Proof Required: Proof of mailing or proof of delivery.

Other Cancellation/Nonrenewal Provisions

Renewal may be offered with amended terms under the same provisions as nonrenewal.

An insurer may not cancel or nonrenew the liability coverage of a commercial auto policy based on the age, sex, residence, race, color, creed, religion, national origin, ancestry, marital status, or occupation of any insured.

On OCP policies all notices must also be sent to any designated contractor.

On Railroad Protective polices the listed contractor and any involved governmental authority must also be notified.

Notice of cancellation or nonrenewal not based on nonpayment must include adequate instructions for applying to a risk sharing plan under ch. 619, if a risk sharing plan exists for the kind of coverage being canceled or nonrenewed, except if the notice is issued by the

WISCONSIN

mandatory health care liability risk sharing plan. Adequate instructions include the correct address of the applicable risk sharing plan.

An additional notice of cancellation is not needed for nonpayment of renewal premium if notice was sent not more than seventy-five days prior to the renewal date or not less than ten days prior to the premium due date and the notice clearly stated the effect of nonpayment by the due date.

COMMERCIAL GENERAL LIABILITY

(Underground Storage Tanks)

Wisconsin Statutes §631.36

Cancellation during the Underwriting Period

Length of Underwriting Period: Sixty days.

Length of Notice: Ten days for nonpayment or material misrepresentation; sixty days for any other reason. Nothing in the Wisconsin Statutes requires a sixty-day notice by certified mail for other cancellations. However, if an insurer has adopted the ISO amendatory endorsement CG 00 42, it must give sixty days' notice.

Reason for Cancellation: Not required.

Proof Required: Proof of first-class mailing or proof of delivery.

Cancellation after the Underwriting Period

The policy may be cancelled **only** for the following reasons:

1. Nonpayment.

2. Material misrepresentation.

3. Substantial change in the risk assumed if such change should not have been foreseen by the insurer or contemplated in the rate.

4. Substantial breach of contractual duties, warranties, or conditions.

Length of Notice: Ten days for nonpayment or material misrepresentation; sixty days for any other reasons. Nothing in the Wisconsin Statutes requires a sixty-day notice for other cancellations. However, if an insurer has adopted the ISO amendatory endorsement CG 00 42, it must give sixty days' notice by certified mail.

WISCONSIN

Reason for Cancellation: Required on the notice.

Proof Required: Proof of first-class mailing or proof of delivery.

Nonrenewal

Length of Notice: Sixty days.

Reason for Nonrenewal: Required on the notice.

Proof Required: Proof of first-class mailing or proof of delivery.

Other Cancellation/Nonrenewal Provisions

Renewal may be offered with amended terms under the same provisions as nonrenewal.

The use of certified mail for cancellation and nonrenewal notices is an ISO program requirement rather than statutory compliance, if not using ISO amendatory endorsement CG 00 42 then proof of first class mailing is sufficient.

PROFESSIONAL LIABILITY

Wisconsin Statute §631.36

Cancellation during the Underwriting Period

Length of Underwriting Period: Sixty days.

Length of Notice: Ten days for any reason.

Reason for Cancellation: Not required on the notice.

Proof Required: Proof of first-class mailing or proof of delivery.

Cancellation after the Underwriting Period

The policy may be cancelled **only** for the following reasons:

1. Nonpayment.

2. Material misrepresentation.

3. Substantial change in the risk assumed if such change should not have been foreseen by the insurer or contemplated in the rate.

WISCONSIN

4. Substantial breach of contractual duties, warranties, or conditions.

Wisconsin statutes also allow cancellation due to attainment of the age specified as the terminal age for coverage, in which case the insurer may cancel by notice accompanied by a tender of a proportional return of premium. However, this is not permitted under the ISO program.

Length of Notice: Ten days for nonpayment; sixty days for any other allowable reason. Nothing in the Wisconsin code requires a sixty-day notice for other cancellations. However, if an insurer has adopted ISO's amendatory endorsement (PR 01 30), it must give sixty days' notice.

Reason for Cancellation: Required on the notice.

Proof Required: Proof of first-class mailing or proof of delivery.

Nonrenewal

Length of Notice: Sixty days.

Reason for Nonrenewal: Required on the notice.

Proof Required: Proof of mailing or proof of delivery.

Other Cancellation/Nonrenewal Provisions

Renewal may be offered with amended terms under the same provisions as nonrenewal.

Cancellation or nonrenewal will not be effective with respect to any claim made or suit brought against the insured unless written notice, providing the effective date of cancellation, has been received by the insured at least:

a. Ten days before the effective date of cancellation for nonpayment of premium or loss of license or certificate of registration.

b. Sixty days before the effective date of cancellation for any other reason. The insurer will notify the commissioner of insurance of the cancellation.

WORKERS COMPENSATION

Wisconsin Statutes §§ 102.31, 631.36; Wis. Admin. Code Ins 21.01

Cancellation during the Underwriting Period

Length of Underwriting Period: Sixty days.

WISCONSIN

Length of Notice: Thirty days.

Reason for Cancellation: Not required.

Proof Required: Proof of first-class mailing or proof of delivery.

Cancellation after the Underwriting Period

The policy may be cancelled **only** for the following reasons:

1. Nonpayment.

2. Material misrepresentation.

3. Substantial breach of the obligations, conditions, or warranties under the policy.

4. Substantial change in the risk assumed unless such change should have been foreseen by the insurer or contemplated in the rate when the policy was issued.

Length of Notice: Thirty days.

Reason for Cancellation: Required on the notice.

Proof Required: Proof of first-class mailing or proof of delivery.

Nonrenewal

Length of Notice: Sixty days.

Reason for Nonrenewal: Required on the notice.

Proof Required: Proof of mailing or proof of delivery.

Other Provisions

An insurer may refuse to renew or may cancel a worker's compensation policy solely because of the termination of an insurance marketing intermediary's contract with the insurer only if the notice of nonrenewal or cancellation contains an offer to continue or renew the policy with the insurer if the insurer receives a written request from the policyholder prior to the cancellation or renewal date. The insurer shall continue or renew the policy if a timely request is received unless the policyholder does not meet normal underwriting criteria. However, the cancellation or nonrenewal is effective whether the notice contains an offer to continue or renew the policy upon the effective date of replacement insurance coverage obtained by the

WISCONSIN

employer or of an order exempting the employer from carrying insurance, or the effective date of an election by an employer to self-insure its liability for the payment of compensation under Wis. Stat. § 102.28 (2).

If the insured purchases replacement insurance, the cancellation becomes effective on the date the new coverage becomes effective. If no replacement coverage is purchased, the cancellation will be effective thirty days after the receipt of written notice by the Wisconsin Compensation Rating Bureau.

If the insurer offers to renew the policy on less favorable terms, notice of the new terms must be sent by first-class mail at least sixty days prior to the renewal date. The definition of "terms" does not include manual rates, experience modification factors, or classification of risks.

If the insurer provides such notice within sixty days prior to the renewal date, the new terms will not take effect until sixty days after the notice is mailed or delivered, in which case the policyholder may elect to cancel the renewal policy at any time during the sixty-day period. The notice will include a statement of the insured's right to cancel. If the insured elects to cancel the renewal policy during the sixty-day period, the return premium or additional premium charges shall be calculated on the basis of the old premiums.

This requirement does not apply to a premium increase that:

a. Is less than 25 percent.
b. Results from a change based on the insured's action that alters the nature and extent of the risk insured against, including, but not limited to, a change in the classifications for the business.

SURPLUS LINES
Wisconsin Statutes §§618.40 & 618.41

The Wisconsin cancellation and nonrenewal laws do not apply to surplus lines.

FINANCED PREMIUMS
Wisconsin Statutes §138.12(12)

If the agreement contains a power of attorney or other authority that allows the insurance premium finance company to cancel the insurance contract listed in the agreement, the finance company must first mail the insured ten days' written notice. Notice should also be sent to the insurance agent or broker indicated on the premium finance agreement. After the required ten-day notice period, the premium finance company may cancel on behalf of the insured by mailing notice of cancellation to the insurer and the insured. Return of the insurance contract is not required.

WISCONSIN

Where statutory, regulatory or contractual restrictions provide that the insurance contract may not be canceled unless notice is given to a governmental agency, mortgagee, or other third party, the insurer shall give the prescribed notice on behalf of itself or the insured to such governmental agency, mortgagee, or other third party within a reasonable time after the day it receives the notice of cancellation from the premium finance company.

PERSONAL LINES
DWELLING FIRE & HOMEOWNERS

Wisconsin Statute §631.36

Cancellation during the Underwriting Period

Length of Underwriting Period: Sixty days.

Length of Notice: Ten days for any reason.

Reason for Cancellation: Not required.

Proof Required: Proof of first-class mailing or proof of delivery.

Cancellation after the Underwriting Period

The policy may be cancelled **only** for the following reasons:

1. Nonpayment.

2. Material misrepresentation.

3. Substantial change in the risk assumed if such change should not have been foreseen by the insurer or contemplated in the rate.

4. Substantial breach of contractual duties, conditions, or warranties.

Length of Notice: Ten days for any allowable reason.

Reason for Cancellation: Required on the notice. Even though the ISO amendatory endorsements DP 01 48 and HO 01 48 are silent on the matter, the Wisconsin code requires the reason to be shown.

Proof Required: Proof of first-class mailing or proof of delivery.

Nonrenewal

Length of Notice: Sixty days.

WISCONSIN

Reason for Nonrenewal: Required on the notice.

Proof Required: Proof of mailing or proof of delivery.

PERSONAL AUTO

Wisconsin Statutes §§344.34 and 631.36

Cancellation during the Underwriting Period

Length of Underwriting Period: Sixty days.

Length of Notice: Ten days for any reason.

Reason for Cancellation: Not required on the notice.

Proof Required: Proof of first-class mailing or proof of delivery.

Cancellation after the Underwriting Period

The policy may be cancelled **only** for the following reasons:

1. Nonpayment.

2. Material misrepresentation.

3. Substantial change in the risk assumed if such change should not have been foreseen by the insurer or contemplated in the rate.

4. Substantial breach of contractual duties, conditions, or warranties.

    The Wisconsin Statutes also allow cancellation due to attainment of the age specified as the terminal age for coverage, in which case the insurer may cancel by notice accompanied by a tender of a proportional return of premium. However, this is not permitted under the ISO program.

Length of Notice: Ten days for any allowable reason.

Reason for Cancellation: Required on the notice. Although not mentioned in ISO's amendatory endorsement PP 01 55, except for cancellation during the first sixty days, all notices of termination must include the reason.

Proof Required: Proof of first-class mailing or proof of delivery.

WISCONSIN

Nonrenewal

Length of Notice: Sixty days.

Reason for Nonrenewal: Required on the notice.

Proof Required: Proof of mailing or proof of delivery.

Other Cancellation/Nonrenewal Provisions

If the policy term is less than six months, the insurer may nonrenew every six months, beginning six months after the original effective date. If the policy term is one year or longer, the insurer may nonrenew the policy at each anniversary of the original effective date. If the renewal policy is mailed no more than seventy-five and no less than ten days prior to renewal date, then the automatic termination provision is operable.

Any termination of a policy which certifies financial responsibility must be filed with the Department of Motor Vehicles.

If the insurer has certified a motor vehicle liability policy as proof of financial responsibility, the insurer must file notice of cancellation in the office of the secretary at least ten days prior to terminating the policy. The certified policy may not be cancelled during the initial ninety days from the effective date if the reason is for nonpayment or premium.

PERSONAL UMBRELLA

Wisconsin Statute §631.36 and Wis. Admin. Code Ins 6.77

Cancellation during the Underwriting Period

Length of Underwriting Period: Sixty days.

Length of Notice: Ten days for any reason.

Reason for Cancellation: Not required.

Proof Required: Proof of first-class mailing or proof of delivery.

Cancellation after the Underwriting Period

Length of Notice: Ten days for any reason. If using ISO amendatory endorsement DL 98 01, a ten-day notice for nonpayment and a thirty-day notice for all other reasons must be provided prior to cancellation.

Reason for Cancellation: Required on the notice.

WISCONSIN

Proof Required: Proof of first-class mailing or delivery.

Nonrenewal

Length of Notice: Sixty days. If using ISO amendatory endorsement DL 98 01, a thirty-day notice must be provided prior to nonrenewal.

Reason for Nonrenewal: Required on the notice.

Proof Required: Proof of mailing or proof of delivery.

FRAUD

Wisconsin Statutes §§ 102.125, 895.486, and 943.395

Definition

Whoever, knowing it to be false or fraudulent, does any of the following commits insurance fraud:

1. Presenting or causing to be presented a false or fraudulent claim, or any proof in support of such claim, to be paid under any contract or certificate of insurance.

2. Preparing, making, or subscribing to a false or fraudulent account, certificate, affidavit, proof of loss, or other document or writing, with knowledge that the same may be presented or used in support of a claim for payment under a policy of insurance.

3. Presenting or causing to be presented a false or fraudulent claim or benefit application, or any false or fraudulent proof in support of such a claim or benefit application, or false or fraudulent information which would affect a future claim or benefit application, to be paid under any employee benefit program created by chapter 40 of the Wisconsin Statutes.

4. Makes any misrepresentation in or with reference to any application for membership or documentary or other proof for the purpose of obtaining membership in or noninsurance benefit from any fraternal subject to chapters 600 to 646 of the Wisconsin Statutes, for himself or herself or any other person.

Penalty

Wisconsin's punishment for committing insurance fraud directly corresponds to the pecuniary value of the fraud. Insurance fraud relating to a claim or benefit of $2,500 or less is a class A misdemeanor. Insurance fraud relating to a claim or benefit exceeding $2,500 is a Class I felony.

WISCONSIN

Reporting Requirements

Wisconsin law only requires the reporting of insurance fraud related to worker's compensation insurance.

If an insurer or self-insured employer has evidence that a worker's compensation claim is false or fraudulent and if the insurer or self-insured employer is satisfied that reporting the claim to the Department of Workforce Development will not impede its ability to defend the claim, the insurer or self-insured employer shall report the claim to the department. The department may require an insurer or self-insured employer to investigate an allegedly false or fraudulent claim and may provide the insurer or self-insured employer with any records of the department relating to that claim. An insurer or self-insured employer that investigates a claim under this section shall report on the results of that investigation to the department. If based on the investigation, the department has a reasonable basis to believe that insurance fraud has occurred; the department shall refer the results of the investigation to the district attorney of the county in which the alleged violation occurred for prosecution, or to the Department of Justice.

Any person who, absent malice, files a report with or furnishes information concerning suspected, anticipated, or completed insurance fraud is immune from civil liability for his or her acts or omissions in filing the report or furnishing the information to any of the following or to their agents, employees or designees:

1. The office of the commissioner of insurance.

2. A law enforcement officer.

3. The National Association of Insurance Commissioners.

4. Any governmental agency established to detect and prevent insurance fraud.

5. Any nonprofit organization established to detect and prevent insurance fraud.

6. Any insurer or authorized representative of an insurer.

Application Fraud Statement

Wisconsin Statute §632.69

Life settlement contracts, purchase agreements, and applications for life settlements, regardless of the form of transmission, shall contain the following statement or a substantially similar statement:

> "Any person who knowingly presents false information in an application for insurance, a life settlement, or a purchase agreement may be subject to civil and criminal penalties."

WISCONSIN

FAIR CLAIMS PROCESSING
Wis. Admin. Code Ins 6.11

Any of the following acts, if committed by any person without just cause and performed with such frequency as to indicate a general business practice, shall constitute unfair methods and practices in the business of insurance:

1. Not promptly acknowledging pertinent communications with respect to claims arising under insurance policies.

2. Not initiating and concluding a claims investigation with all reasonable dispatch.

3. Not promptly providing necessary claims forms, instructions and reasonable assistance to insureds and claimants under its insurance policies.

4. Not making a good-faith attempt to effectuate fair and equitable settlement of claims submitted in which liability has become reasonably clear.

5. Failure upon request of a claimant, to promptly provide a reasonable explanation of the basis in the policy contract or applicable law for denial of a claim or for the offer of a compromise settlement.

6. Knowingly misrepresenting to claimants pertinent facts or policy provisions relating to coverages involved.

7. Not affirming or denying coverage of claims within a reasonable time after proof of loss has been completed.

8. Not settling a claim under one portion of the policy coverage in order to influence a settlement under another portion of the policy coverage.

9. Except as may be otherwise provided in the policy contract, not offering settlement under applicable first-party coverage on the basis that responsibility for payment should be assumed by other persons or insurers.

10. Compelling insureds and claimants to institute suits to recover amounts due under its policies by offering substantially less than the amounts ultimately recovered in suits brought by them.

11. Refusing payment of claims solely on the basis of the insured's request to do so without making an independent evaluation of the insured's liability based upon all available information.

WISCONSIN

12. Failure, where appropriate, to make use of arbitration procedures authorized or permitted under any insurance policy.

13. Adopting or making known to insureds or claimants a policy of appealing from arbitration awards in favor of insureds or claimants for the purpose of compelling them to accept settlements or compromises less than the amount awarded in arbitration.

Any of the following acts shall constitute unfair methods and practices in the business of insurance:

1. Knowingly misrepresenting to claimants pertinent facts or policy provisions relating to coverages involved.

2. Not making provision for adequate claims handling personnel, systems and procedures to effectively service claims in this state incurred under insurance coverage issued or delivered in this state.

3. Failure to adopt reasonable standards for investigation of claims arising under its insurance policies.

4. Violating the requirements established in section §632.85 of the Wisconsin Statutes.

WYOMING

For details on cancellation procedures for the standard policy, refer to the Standard Policy section.

COMMERCIAL LINES

AGRICULTURAL CAPITAL ASSETS; CAPITAL ASSETS; BOP; C. AUTO; CRIME; CGL (CGL, LIQUOR, OCP, POLLUTION, PRODS. /COMPLETED OPS.); CIM; C. PROP.; C. UMB.; E-COMMERCE; EQUIPMENT BREAKDOWN; FARM; & MGT. PROT.

Wyoming Statutes §§26-35-101; 26-35-202 through 26-35-204

Cancellation during the Underwriting Period

Length of Underwriting Period: Sixty days.

Length of Notice: Not required. If using IL 02 52, ten days for nonpayment; thirty days for any other reason.

Reason for Cancellation: Not required.

Proof Required: Proof of delivery or proof of mailing to the insured and their agent at their addresses of last record with the insured.

Cancellation after the Underwriting Period

The policy may be cancelled **only** for the following reasons:

1. Nonpayment.

2. Material misrepresentation on the application.

3. Substantial change in the risk assumed if such change should not have been foreseen by the insurer or contemplated in the rate.

4. Substantial breach of contractual duties, conditions or warranties.

Length of Notice: Ten days for nonpayment; forty-five days for all other allowable reasons except material misrepresentation.

Reason for Cancellation: Required on the notice.

WYOMING

Proof Required: Proof of delivery or proof of mailing to the insured and their agent at their addresses of last record with the insured.

Nonrenewal

Length of Notice: Forty-five days.

Reason for Nonrenewal: Required on the notice.

Proof Required: Proof of delivery or proof of mailing to the insured and their agent at their addresses of last record with the insured.

Other Cancellation/Nonrenewal Provisions

A forty-five day written notice is required if the insurer intends to renew on less favorable terms or at a higher rate. On OCP policies all notices must be sent to the named insured and to the contractor shown in the declarations.

All of the coverage parts referenced above omit the cancellation notice time for material misrepresentation. Legal advice is suggested.

Prior to cancellation an insurer must refund any unearned premium to the policyholder. (Wyo. Stat. §26-35-102).

COMMERCIAL GENERAL LIABILITY

(Railroad Protective)

Wyoming Statutes §§26-35-101; 26-35-202 through 26-35-204

Cancellation during the Underwriting Period

Length of Underwriting Period: Sixty days.

Length of Notice: Not required. If using IL 02 52, ten days for nonpayment; thirty days for any other reason.

Reason for Cancellation: Not required.

Proof Required: Proof of delivery or proof of mailing to the insured and their agent at their addresses of last record with the insured.

Cancellation after the Underwriting Period

The policy may be cancelled **only** for the following reasons:

WYOMING

1. Nonpayment.

2. Material misrepresentation on the application.

3. Substantial change in the risk assumed if such change should not have been foreseen by the insurer or contemplated in the rate.

4. Substantial breach of contractual duties, conditions, or warranties.

Length of Notice: Ten days for nonpayment; forty-five days for all other allowable reasons except material misrepresentation.

Reason for Cancellation: Required on the notice.

Proof Required: Proof of delivery or proof of mailing to the insured and their agent at their addresses of last record with the insured.

Nonrenewal

Length of Notice: Forty-five days.

Reason for Nonrenewal: Required on the notice.

Proof Required: Proof of delivery or proof of mailing to the insured and their agent at their addresses of last record with the insured.

Other Cancellation/Nonrenewal Provisions

A forty-five-day written notice is required if the insurer intends to renew on less favorable terms or at a higher rate.

All notices must be delivered or mailed to the named insured, the contractor, and any involved governmental authority, or any other contracting party designated in the declarations.

All of the coverage parts referenced above omit the cancellation notice time for material misrepresentation. Legal advice is suggested.

Prior to cancellation an insurer must refund any unearned premium to the policyholder. (Wyo. Stat. §26-35-102).

WYOMING

COMMERCIAL GENERAL LIABILITY

(Underground Storage Tanks)

Wyoming Statutes §§26-35-101; 26-35-202 through 26-35-204

Cancellation during the Underwriting Period

Length of Underwriting Period: Sixty days.

Length of Notice: Not required. If using IL 02 52, ten days for nonpayment; thirty days for any other reason.

Reason for Cancellation: Not required.

Proof Required: Proof of delivery or proof of mailing to the insured and their agent at their addresses of last record with the insured. Certified mail if using ISO.

Cancellation after the Underwriting Period

The policy may be cancelled **only** for the following reasons:

1. Nonpayment.

2. Material misrepresentation on the application.

3. Substantial change in the risk assumed if such change should not have been foreseen by the insurer or contemplated in the rate.

4. Substantial breach of contractual duties, conditions, or warranties.

Length of Notice: Ten days for nonpayment; forty-five days for all other allowable reasons except material misrepresentation.

Reason for Cancellation: Required on the notice.

Proof Required: Proof of delivery or proof of mailing to the insured and their agent at their addresses of last record with the insured. Certified mail if using ISO.

Nonrenewal

Length of Notice: Forty-five days.

Reason for Nonrenewal: Required on the notice.

WYOMING

Proof Required: Proof of delivery or proof of mailing to the insured and their agent at their addresses of last record with the insured. Certified mail if using ISO.

Other Cancellation/Nonrenewal Provisions

The use of certified mail and the sixty-day notice requirement for cancellation and nonrenewal notices are ISO program requirements rather than statutory compliance.

A forty-five-day written notice is required if the insurer intends to renew on less favorable terms or at a higher rate.

All notices must be sent to the named insured, the contractor, any involved governmental authority, or other contracting party shown in the declarations.

Prior to cancellation an insurer must refund any unearned premium to the policyholder. (Wyo. Stat. §26-35-102).

MEDICAL PROFESSIONAL LIABILITY

Wyoming Statutes §§26-35-101; 26-35-202 through 26-35-204

The policy may be cancelled **only** for the following reasons:

1. Nonpayment.

2. Material misrepresentation on the application.

3. Substantial change in the risk assumed if such change should not have been foreseen by the insurer or contemplated in the rate.

4. Substantial breach of contractual duties, conditions, or warranties.

Length of Notice: Ten days for nonpayment; forty-five days for all other allowable reasons except material misrepresentation.

Reason for Cancellation: Required on the notice.

Proof Required: Proof of delivery or proof of mailing to the insured and their agent at their addresses of last record with the insured.

Nonrenewal

Length of Notice: Forty-five days.

WYOMING

Reason for Nonrenewal: Required on the notice.

Proof Required: Proof of delivery or proof of mailing to the insured and their agent at their addresses of last record with the insured.

WORKERS COMPENSATION

Wyoming Statutes §§26-35-101; 26-35-202 through 26-35-204

(Not applicable to policies written in the compulsory state fund for certain industries.)

Wyoming is a monopolistic workers compensation state.

SURPLUS LINES

Wyoming Statutes §26-11-109

The Wyoming cancellation and nonrenewal laws do not apply to surplus lines.

FINANCED PREMIUMS

Not addressed.

PERSONAL LINES

DWELLING FIRE & HOMEOWNERS

Wyoming Statutes §§26-35-101; 26-23-107, 26-23-108, 26-35-202, and 26-35-203

Cancellation during the Underwriting Period

Length of Underwriting Period: Sixty days.

Length of Notice: Not required.

Reason for Cancellation: Not required on the notice.

Proof Required: Proof of delivery or proof of mailing to the insured and their agent at their addresses of last record with the insured.

Cancellation after the Underwriting Period

The policy may be cancelled **only** for the following reasons:

1. Nonpayment.

2. Material misrepresentation of fact on the application.

WYOMING

3. Substantial violation of policy conditions or breach of contractual duties.

4. Substantial change in the risk assumed if such change should not have been foreseen by the insurer or contemplated in the rate.

Length of Notice: Ten days for nonpayment; thirty days for material misrepresentation; forty-five days for all other allowable reasons. The notification periods listed are as included in ISO's amendatory endorsements (DP 01 49 and HO 01 49); however, Wyoming Statute §26-35-202 indicates ten days for nonpayment; forty-five days for all other allowable reasons except material misrepresentation.

Reason for Cancellation: Required on the notice.

Proof Required: Proof of delivery or proof of mailing to the insured and their agent at their addresses of last record with the insured.

Nonrenewal

Length of Notice: Forty-five days.

Reason for Nonrenewal: Required on the notice. Although not mentioned in ISO's amendatory endorsements (DP 01 49 and HO 01 49), Wyoming Statute §26-35-203 requires the reason to be given.

Proof Required: Proof of delivery or proof of mailing to the insured and their agent at their addresses of last record with the insured.

Other Cancellation/Nonrenewal Provisions

No homeowner's insurance policy shall be denied renewal as a result of a single claim within a three-year period arising from natural causes.

No homeowner's insurance policy shall be cancelled during its term as a result of any claim arising from natural causes.

No insurer shall cancel, refuse to renew or offer to renew at a higher premium a homeowner's insurance policy based in any manner upon the claims history of a named insured unless the claims history excludes customer inquiries. Customer inquiries are defined as telephone calls or other requests for information made by the named insured or a person who would be a named insured under the policy, that reference the terms, conditions or coverage afforded under an insurance contract and do not result in claims being filed or paid.

WYOMING

The following provisions apply only to binders on homeowner coverage:

1. Failure of the insurer, within forty-five calendar days of issuing a binder, to act upon the information precludes the insurer from declining insurance coverage or terminating a binder of insurance coverage based on the information.

2. An insurer may decline or terminate insurance coverage based on the condition of the premises as determined through a physical inspection of the premises. This section applies only to homeowner's insurance and does not apply to a policy renewal.

3. Prior to cancellation an insurer must refund any unearned premium to the policyholder. (Wyo. Stat. §26-35-102).

PERSONAL AUTO

Wyoming Statutes §26-35-105; WCWR 044-0002-14 (section 2 through 7)

Cancellation during the Underwriting Period

Length of Underwriting Period: Sixty days.

Length of Notice: Ten days for any reason.

Reason for Cancellation: Not required on the notice.

Proof Required: Proof of mailing by affidavit to the policyholder at the last known address shown in the policy.

Cancellation after the Underwriting Period

The policy may be cancelled **only** for the following reasons:

1. Nonpayment.

2. Driver's license or motor vehicle registration of the named insured, any resident operator or any customary operator is suspended or revoked. This must have occurred during the policy period or since the last anniversary or the original effective date if the policy period is other than one year. The insurer must offer to exclude the unacceptable driver before cancelling. Refusal of that exclusion is grounds for cancellation.

3. Fraud on the application.

4. For any reason determined appropriate by the commissioner after a hearing thereon.

WYOMING

Length of Notice: Ten days for nonpayment; twenty days for all other allowable reasons.

Reason for Cancellation: Not required on the notice.

Proof Required: Proof of mailing by affidavit of the person mailing to the last known address of the policyholder for reasons 1 and 3; affidavit of delivery by the person making the delivery or U.S. mails "return receipt requested" for reasons 2 and 4. If return receipt is requested but is returned to the sender marked "refused" or words with similar character, the sender is deemed as having complied.

Nonrenewal

Length of Notice: Thirty days.

Reason for Nonrenewal: Not required on the notice.

Proof Required: Proof of mailing by affidavit of the person so mailing to the last known address of the policyholder.

Other Cancellation/Nonrenewal Provisions

If the policy term is less than six months, the insurer may nonrenew every six months, beginning six months after the original effective date. If the policy term is one year or longer, the insurer may cancel the policy at each anniversary of the original effective date.

An insurer may in lieu of nonissuance, cancellation, nonrenewal or premium increase offer to issue, continue or renew a motor vehicle insurance policy but to exclude from coverage, by name, the person whose claim experience or driving record would have justified the nonissuance, premium increase, cancellation or nonrenewal.

When automobile liability coverage is either canceled or nonrenewed by an insurer, except for nonpayment of premium, the insurer shall notify the policyholder of his possible eligibility for automobile insurance through the Wyoming automobile insurance plan.

Prior to cancellation an insurer must refund any unearned premium to the policyholder. (Wyo. Stat. §26-35-102).

PERSONAL UMBRELLA

Wyoming Statutes §§26-35-101; 26-35-202 through 26-35-204

Cancellation during the Underwriting Period

Length of Underwriting Period: Sixty days.

WYOMING

Length of Notice: Not required.

Reason for Cancellation: Not required on the notice.

Proof Required: Proof of delivery or proof of mailing to the insured and their agent at their addresses of last record with the insured.

Cancellation after the Underwriting Period

Length of Notice: Ten-day notice for nonpayment; forty-five days for all other reasons except material misrepresentation.

Reason for Cancellation: Reason for notice not required.

Proof Required: Proof of delivery or proof of mailing to the insured and their agent at their addresses of last record with the insured.

Nonrenewal

Length of Notice: Forty-five days.

Reason for Nonrenewal: Required.

Proof Required: Proof of delivery or proof of mailing to the insured and their agent at their addresses of last record with the insured.

All of the coverage parts referenced above omit the cancellation notice time for material misrepresentation. Legal advice is suggested.

FRAUD

Wyoming Statutes §§26-13-101 through 26-13-124

Wyoming does not define insurance fraud but generally prohibits fraudulent acts in the insurance industry.

Report Insurance fraud in Wyoming at: https://eapps.naic.org/ofrs/.

Application Fraud Statement

Wyoming Statute §26-13-201

Wyoming does not require a fraud warning statement; however, no person shall knowingly or willfully:

WYOMING

1. Make any false or fraudulent statement or representation in or with reference to any application for insurance or for the purpose of obtaining any money or benefit.

2. Present or cause to be presented a false or fraudulent claim or any proof in support of a claim for the payment of the loss upon a contract of insurance.

3. Prepare, make or subscribe a false or fraudulent certificate, or other document with intent that the certificate or other document may be presented or used in support of the claim.

FAIR CLAIMS PROCESSING

Wyoming Statutes §§26-13-124 and 26-1-107 (amended by 2015 Wyoming Laws Ch. 13 (H.B. 3)).

Definition

The following unfair claim settlement practices are prohibited under Wyoming law when they are committed or performed with such frequency as to indicate a general business practice:

1. Misrepresenting pertinent facts or insurance policy provisions relating to coverages at issue.

2. Failing to acknowledge and act reasonably promptly upon communications regarding claims arising under insurance policies.

3. Not adopting and implementing reasonable standards for the prompt investigation of claims arising under insurance policies.

4. Refusing to pay claims without conducting a reasonable investigation based upon all available information.

5. Not affirming or denying coverage of claims within a reasonable time after proof of loss statements has been completed.

6. Not making a good-faith attempts to effectuate prompt, fair and equitable settlements of claims in which liability has become reasonably clear.

7. Compelling insureds to institute litigation to recover amounts due under an insurance policy by offering substantially less than the amounts ultimately recovered in actions brought by such insureds.

8. Attempting to settle a claim for less than the amount to which a reasonable person would have believed he or she was entitled by reference to written or printed advertising material accompanying or made part of an application.

WYOMING

9. Attempting to settle claims on the basis of an application which was altered without notice to, or knowledge or consent of, the insured.

10. Making claims payments to insureds or beneficiaries not accompanied by a statement setting forth the coverage under which the payments are being made.

11. Making known to insureds or claimants a policy of appealing from arbitration awards in favor of insureds or claimants for the purpose of compelling them to accept settlements or compromises less than the amount awarded in arbitration.

12. Delaying the investigation or payment of claims by requiring an insured, claimant or the physician of either to submit a preliminary claim report and then requiring the subsequent submission of formal proof of loss forms, both of which submissions contain substantially the same information.

13. Not promptly settling claims, where liability has become reasonably clear, under one portion of the insurance policy coverage in order to influence settlements under other portions of the insurance policy coverage.

14. Not promptly providing a reasonable explanation of the basis in the insurance policy in relation to the facts or applicable law for denial of a claim or for the offer of a compromise settlement.

15. Denying or failing to timely pay disability insurance claims for medically necessary services, procedures or supplies as required by Wyo. Stat. §26-40-201.

16. Not complying with the external review procedures required by Wyo. Stat. §26-40-201.

17. Not paying a claim after an external review organization has declared such claim to be a benefit covered under the terms of the insurance policy.

Penalty

Once the commissioner determines that one of the aforementioned acts has occurred, the commissioner will order the offending party to cease and desist. Any person who violates any final order of the commissioner, any provision of this code, or any lawful rule, or instructs an adjuster or agent to do so, shall pay a civil penalty in an amount the commissioner determines of not more than $5,000 for each offense, or $50,000 in the aggregate for all such offenses within any one year period. In the case of individual agents or adjusters, the civil penalty shall be not more than $1,000 for each offense or $10,000 in the aggregate for all such offenses within any one year period. (Wyo. Stat. §26-1-107).